PEOPLE OF PARADOX

PEOPLE OF PARADOX

A History of Mormon Culture

TERRYL L. GIVENS

OXFORD

UNIVERSITY PRESS

2007

OXFORD
UNIVERSITY PRESS

Oxford University Press, Inc., publishes works that further
Oxford University's objective of excellence
in research, scholarship, and education.

Oxford   New York
Auckland   Cape Town   Dar es Salaam   Hong Kong   Karachi
Kuala Lumpur   Madrid   Melbourne   Mexico City   Nairobi
New Delhi   Shanghai   Taipei   Toronto

With offices in
Argentina   Austria   Brazil   Chile   Czech Republic   France   Greece
Guatemala   Hungary   Italy   Japan   Poland   Portugal   Singapore
South Korea   Switzerland   Thailand   Turkey   Ukraine   Vietnam

Published by Oxford University Press, Inc.
198 Madison Avenue, New York, New York 10016

www.oup.com

Oxford is a registered trademark of Oxford University Press

Library of Congress Cataloging-in-Publication Data
Givens, Terryl.
People of paradox : a history of Mormon culture / Terryl L. Givens.
p. cm.
Includes bibliographical references and index.
ISBN 978-0-19-516711-5
1. Mormon arts.   2. Arts and religion.   I. Title.
NX663.U6G58 2007
700.88'2893—dc22   2007007587

1 3 5 7 9 8 6 4 2

Printed in the United States of America
on acid-free paper

To
Larry H. Peer and
the memory of Eugene H. Falk,
my teachers

PREFACE

This work has benefited enormously from the expertise and tender mercies of a host of readers and critics. Vern Swanson is a gold mine of knowledge about Utah art; the LDS art historian Richard Oman provided valuable criticism and suggestions. Daniel Fairbanks is an accomplished artist from a line of superb artists, and his guidance and friendship alike were invaluable. Also a published geneticist, Daniel made important contributions to my sections on science as well as those on art. Steve Harper, Reid Neilson, David Whittaker, and Richard Bushman represent the acme of new and experienced Mormon scholarship, and I count them all as friends and mentors. Gideon Burton was helpful with matters of literature and film. Michael Hicks made pertinent critiques that extended beyond my music sections. Grant and Heather Hardy are exacting critics and scholars and made extensive, helpful criticisms. Larry Peer read a draft, and Armand Mauss continued his role as friend and guide in much that appears here. Lavina Fielding Anderson provided astute comments as well as encouragement, and Paul Anderson shared his expertise in Mormon architecture. As always, my friend Anthony Russell shared valuable perspectives from outside the traditions here discussed. I also thank Bill Slaughter, the master of LDS photo archives; my son, Nathaniel, for his insights and productive leads; my research assistant, Colin Tate, for help in tracking down arcane sources; and Josh Probert for his suggestions with matters artistic and architectural. As always, the first and last reader and critic was Fiona Givens, my North Star.

All were helpful, and I must emphasize that virtually all championed additions and perspectives which lost out to limitations of space—or of my own abilities. I alone bear responsibility for the idiosyncrasies and omissions in the examples covered. "There is no arguing about taste," said the critic Horace. In fact, few things are the subject of more dispute than taste. For we are all critics after our own fashion, and a study claiming to address the sweeping subject of a religious culture is bound to offend almost everyone by dint of something left out, something overpraised, or something undervalued. I can only insist that I made no attempt at comprehensiveness. My purpose is to plumb in tentative fashion the range of Mormonism's intellectual and artistic productions, to see if one can find there the contours of consistent themes and preoccupations, a unity between theological foundations and history, on the one hand, and cultural production, on the other. My ambition is not to define definitively Mormon culture, but to delineate some key components of that cultural identity as it appears through artistic and intellectual activity, from Mormonism's origins up to the new millennium.

It will immediately be obvious to readers that my study excludes vast swaths of material and popular culture, including folk expressions in art and music and media from furniture to quilts. They deserve—and will doubtless receive—thorough treatments of their own. I recognize as well that in a church and culture increasingly dominated by a Southern rather than Western hemispheric membership, some of the conceptual categories and distinctions implicit in my treatment—like "high culture" or "serious art"—are already in the process of losing their authority. Finally, I hope the historical compression necessary to a study of this nature does not obscure the richness, variety, and subtleties of those individuals and their contributions that will always transcend facile categories, makeshift periods, and the efforts of scholars striving imperfectly to honor them.

CONTENTS

INTRODUCTION

The circle is perfect and infinite in its nature; but it is
fixed forever in size; it can never be larger or smaller.
But the cross, though it has at its heart a collision and a
contradiction, can extend its four arms forever without
altering its shape. . . . It has a paradox in its center.

~ G. K. Chesterton

By proving contraries, truth is made manifest.
~ Joseph Smith

On August 8, 1844, the restive crowd began assembling in the heat well before
10:00 in the morning. William Marks, president of the Nauvoo Stake, called the
meeting to choose a successor to Joseph Smith, who had been murdered in a
Carthage jail together with his brother Hyrum six weeks earlier. For ninety
minutes, Sidney Rigdon, one-time counselor and confidant of the Prophet, ha-
rangued the Saints, urging that he be sustained as the "guardian" of the church.
After a break for lunch, Brigham Young addressed the reconvened assembly,
expressing his concern that because of their great number, all might not be able to
hear. "Heretofore you have had a Prophet as the mouth of the Lord to speak to
you," he said, "but he has sealed his testimony with his blood, and now, for the first
time, are you called to walk by faith, and not by sight." Then he asked, "Do you, as
individuals, at this time, want to choose a Prophet or a guardian to lead you?"

No one raised a hand. "Elder Rigdon claims to be spokesman to the Prophet,"
he continued:

Very well, he was; but . . . if he wants now to be a spokesman for the Prophet,
he must go to the other side of the veil, for the Prophet is there. . . . If 10,000
men rise up and say they have the Prophet Joseph's shoes, I know they are
imposters. . . . [N]o man can put another between the Twelve [Apostles] and
the Prophet Joseph.[1]

The assembly was persuaded. By the end of the afternoon, there was a virtually unanimous vote to reject any individual's attempt to inherit Joseph's title or status. Three weeks later, the Prophet's brother William would concur that Joseph's role was irreplaceable. He petitioned Brigham to be named Hyrum's successor as patriarch, but said he did not wish to be "prophet in Joseph's place for no man on Earth can fill his place[.] [H]e is our prophet seer revelator Priest & King in time & in Eternity."[2]

So, on August 8, the Quorum of the Twelve, as a body, was sustained "to stand as the head." Brigham Young, as president of the Twelve, would be the chief executive. But it would take three long years, the unprecedented orchestration of a 2,000-mile exodus, and the successful resettlement in Utah of thousands of refugees and convert immigrants before Brigham Young, the American Moses, would presume to take the title that had graced the name of Joseph. Even then, he continued to be known throughout his long tenure as President Young, not "the Prophet Brigham." Now, more than a century and a half later, Mormon custom only reaffirms the truth first evident in that Nauvoo meeting: there could be only one Joseph. When Latter-day Saints refer to "the Prophet" in the past tense, there can be no mistake. It is the Prophet Joseph, matchless in his stature and role within Mormonism, who is the once and forever Mormon prophet.

Joseph's unique place in Mormonism is in this regard rather like George Washington's. There can only be one first Mormon prophet, as there can be only one first American president and father of his people. But in both cases, more is at work than mere chronological primacy. No successor to Joseph even begins to approach the scope of his creative energy as a thinker, a system builder, a revelator. The Book of Mormon he produced is revered as a scripture more correct than the Bible, and it is longer than the Quran or the New Testament. The Doctrine and Covenants (D&C), another compilation of Mormon scripture, has 138 sections. All but 4 were produced by Joseph Smith.[3] The Pearl of Great Price, the final volume of Mormon scripture, is entirely a product of his writings, translations, and revelations. It is for the sheer volume of his scriptural production, the comprehensive scope of his religion-making imagination, and the audacity of his theological innovations that Joseph deserves the title of "authentic religious genius."[4]

As a leader of his people, Brigham Young's thirty-three-year tenure is more than double Joseph's scant fourteen. Young colonized over 300 towns and cities, compared to Joseph's handful; he governed a territory larger than Texas and a church that comprised 130,000 Saints at his death. Young was also a man of profound intellect and imagination. Under his theocratic leadership, Mormon life was more thoroughly pervaded by his temporal and spiritual dictates than was that of any comparable group of individuals in American history. Joseph Smith laid the foundations, and for the balance of Mormonism's first half-century, Brigham Young shaped the Mormon experience. It is on those twin pillars that the Mormon intellectual and cultural heritage rests.

This book is an exploration of the Mormon cultural identity that Smith and, to a lesser extent, Young founded. What such a study might entail is by no means self-evident. "[N]othing is more indeterminate," wrote the great German philosopher Herder, "than this word [culture]." At the same time, short of identifying culture with all dimensions of human life in a given society, three meanings are commonly invoked by the term: a general habit of mind, the intellectual development of a society, and its general body of arts.[5] I have taken these three emphases, and their interrelationships, as my particular focus: the seminal ideas that constitute a Mormon "habit of mind," their development and elaboration over time, and their manifestations and permutations across a spectrum of artistic media.

Speaking of the development of early Christian cultural identity, Graydon Snyder has written that "it took over a century for the new community of faith to develop a distinctive mode of self-expression."[6] Mormonism has been around for nearly two centuries. While it is still a new religious community compared to the great world faiths and even to Protestant denominations, many factors have conspired to foster its development as a community with a distinctive world view, powerful cultural cohesion, and its own forms of artistic and intellectual expression. A radical theology, emphasizing chosenness and exclusive stewardship over divine truth and authority, a history of persecution and alienation from the American mainstream, together with enormous institutional demands of religious commitment, personal sacrifice, and distinctive religious practices have welded the adherents of Mormonism into a people who so powerfully identify with one another that one writer did not hesitate to call them the only instance in American history of a people who became almost an ethnic community.[7] That striking fact, together with the increasingly real possibility that Mormonism may, indeed, become the first new world faith since Islam, provides ample justification for a study of this nature.

A chronological survey of the varieties of artistic and intellectual expression would miss the point of cultural formation. For some of the most productive stimulants to such expression are the unresolved tensions inherent in a culture—tensions with the dominant society in the context of which a new cultural group emerges, or internal tensions that never manage to find full and satisfactory resolution. Frederick Barnard points to Herder's observation that a people "may have the most sublime virtues in some respect and blemishes in others . . . and reveal the most astonishing contradictions and incongruities." Therefore, Barnard writes, "a cultural whole is not necessarily a way of referring to a state of blissful harmony; it may just as conceivably refer to a field of tension."[8]

A field of tension seems a particularly apt way to characterize Mormon thought. It may be that all systems of belief rooted in the notion of a God who dies have, as Chesterton suggests, "a collision and a contradiction" at their heart.[9] Yet Mormonism, a system in which Joseph Smith collapsed sacred distance to bring a whole series of opposites into radical juxtaposition, seems especially rife with paradox—or tensions that only appear to be logical contradictions.

Such dynamic tensions give cultural expression much of its vitality, but are hardly productive of a cultural tradition that is systematic or linear. For that reason, I have chosen to organize this study around what I take to be four especially rich and fertile tensions, or thematic pairings, in Mormon thought, which have inspired recurrent and sustained engagement on the part of writers, artists, and thinkers in the Mormon community. Obviously, these four do not pretend to comprise all the paradoxes one could locate in Mormonism's intellectual or artistic or cultural heritage. And they are hardly manifest in every instance of Mormon cultural expression. But they provide an effective framework for an exploration of at least a substantial sampling of the several chapters in the history of Latter-day Saints' efforts to make sense of their place in the world and to orient themselves to new concepts of the human and the divine.

The first chapter of the book deals with the polarity of authoritarianism and individualism. It is in the context of those two competing values that Mormon artists and intellectuals have had to negotiate their place in their culture. One paradox of Mormon cultural history is its rootedness in a rigidly hierarchical, authoritarian church—and yet this church was established in the context of two fanatically individualistic phenomena that converged in antebellum America: Western Romanticism and Jacksonian democracy. Smith's version of human freedom was as radical as Rousseau's, even as the model of spiritual authority he enacted earned Mormonism the name "American popery." Mormonism is, after all, a religion in which the authority of the one living prophet at the head of the church is every bit as literal and all-encompassing as that of Moses over the children of Israel. But it is also a religion in which the priesthood authority is also given to virtually every active Mormon male, and all members are vouchsafed the right to personal, literal, dialogic revelation with God. Chapter 1 explores the impact of those dynamic tensions on the cultural foundations of a Mormon intellectual and artistic tradition.

The second chapter explores a second fundamental paradox in Joseph Smith's religion making. The Prophet emphasized in his religious thinking the possibility of epistemological certainty even as he elaborated a theology of audacious scope and a program of eternal learning. Smith made intellectual pursuit a quest of holiness, founding the School of Prophets, establishing a fledgling university, and devoting himself to the study of ancient languages and lore even as he claimed to bypass the learned systems of men with his powers of seership and translation. So it is that Mormons today inherit a tradition rooted relatively recently in concrete artifacts like gold plates verified by eleven witnesses, in accounts of resurrected beings laying physical hands on founding prophets, and in Joseph's testimony of the audible words and visible appearing of Deity itself. And Mormons inhabit a rhetorical world where members give not assertions of fervent belief, but public testimony that they have spiritual knowledge of those events as historical realities. At the same time, such credentials do not attest to personal salvation or blessedness, but only betoken the commencement of an eternal quest for saving knowledge and the burden of an endlessly sought perfection. The mix of intellectual certitude and intellectual insatiability Joseph exuded has left a mixed heritage with which aspiring LDS artists and intellectuals must reckon. While his relentless eclecticism, syncretism, and system building could provoke and inspire, great works of the mind and heart have seldom emerged in the context of the spiritual complacency and sense of plenitude that his theology could also encourage. Chapter 2 assesses the impact of those tensions—searching and certitude—on Mormon understanding of intellectual and artistic endeavor.

The third chapter examines one of the most culturally—and theologically—potent innovations of the Mormon world view, one that appears more as a collapse of polarities than as a tension between them: the disintegration of sacred distance. With God an exalted man, man a God in embryo, the family a prototype for heavenly sociality, and Zion a city with dimensions and blueprints, Joseph rewrote conventional dualisms as thoroughgoing monism. The resulting paradox is manifest in the recurrent invasion of the banal into the realm of the holy and the infusion of the sacred into the realm of the quotidian. The consequent reconceptualization of grace, of humanity's relationship to the divine, and a pervasive suspicion of transcendence and mystery—all follow in turn from the radical paradigm shift instituted by Joseph Smith. Such a reconfigured view of the sacred demands new artistic approaches to the sublime.

Finally, chapter 4 looks at two related tensions in Mormonism: exile and integration, and a gospel viewed as both American and universal. The quest for Zion was for the Saints a search for Eden—but it was always an Eden in exile. The cost of their chosen status appears recurrently in the Mormon psyche as both nostalgia and alienation; and the opposing movement toward integration into the larger world they had fled was fueled by both a longing for inclusion and an imperative to redeem the world. From its earliest days, Mormon converts embraced a sense of themselves as people of the covenant, peculiar, chosen. Casting all others as "gentiles," and fellow Christians as inheritors of a great apostasy, this rhetoric of difference, together with a history of persecution and geographical remoteness, compounded their isolation into a virtue and a sign of blessedness. But their art and literature reveal a recurrent unease with such difference. Isolation is often felt as a burden of exclusion and is frequently transformed into a quest for connections and universals. Mormons insist on the need for a gospel restoration, but then feel the sting of being excluded from the fold of Christendom they have just dismissed as irredeemably apostate. Or, in a parallel way, Mormons have long identified their faith with America's providential role in history. Mormon origins, the Book of Mormon as artifact and as history, church headquarters, the garden of Eden, and the New Jerusalem—all are identified with a specifically American locale. But in an age of internationalization and global growth, Mormons are necessarily rethinking the limitations and obstacles created by a presentation of the church as an American institution and raising the possibility of a church surreptitiously engrafted with at least some expendable and merely accidental local baggage. In their thoughtful and provocative exploration of these distinctions, Mormon artists and intellectuals may be an effective prod in facilitating the transition of Mormonism into a truly international faith.

The chapters that follow are organized by genre, but also grouped into two major chronological epochs. I make here the usual caveats about periodization: all demarcations are artificial, and others could well be argued for. I have chosen to consider the period from the founding until roughly 1890 as one epoch, because in that year Wilford Woodruff called for the end of polygamy—the practice which served as the most publicly recognizable sign of Mormon difference. Three other contemporaneous developments symbolically if not actually reversed the trend of Mormon cultural self-sufficiency and alienation from the larger society: the fading of the call to Mormons to gather into one geographically bounded cultural community; Orson Whitney's call for the self-conscious production of a Mormon literature; and the sending of art missionaries from the remote Utah desert to the academies of Paris.

The second era I trace from 1890 until the present. This era of LDS history has been almost entirely dominated by first a Utah, and then an American, orientation and has only in recent years seen the beginnings of an international church. The period has seen important changes in Mormon self-conceiving before the world. Mormon intellectual life has been transformed as the church has addressed the challenges of racial controversies, feminism, and the politics of dissent. Adding to the ferment, Mormon historians began to integrate their studies into secular models, and vice versa, resulting in dramatic tensions between conventional and revisionist modes of understanding the Mormon past and, by extension, Mormon identity itself. Also, under LDS president Spencer W. Kimball's administration, leaders, painters, and writers renewed the emphasis on the project of a Mormon artistic tradition. Equally significant for Mormon culture, Kimball's ambitious vision for an invigorated missionary program and a worldwide church have instigated a still-continuing redefinition of Mormonism as an international, rather than American, institution.

Today, only 14 percent of Mormons live in Utah, and while it is true that Mormonism has at the beginning of the twenty-first century achieved a balance of members that is weighted more heavily with non-Americans than Americans, the fact remains that for the first century and more of its history, Mormon culture was largely a Utah construction. That, and the impossibility of giving fair representation to the forms which the Mormon faith is acquiring in over 100 countries where it is currently practiced, have led me to focus on Mormonism as the essentially American religion it was until the current generation. I express the sincere hope that scholars better qualified will produce examinations of Mormon culture in the truly international complexion being ushered in by the new millennium.

Part I

Foundations and Paradoxes in Mormon Cultural Origins

~ 1 ~

THE IRON ROD AND
THE LIAHONA
Authority and Radical Freedom

Wherefore, meaning the church, thou shalt give heed
unto all his words and commandments which he shall
give unto you, . . . for his word ye shall receive as if from
mine own mouth.

~ Doctrine and Covenants 21:4–5[1]

It is love of liberty which inspires my soul—civil and
religious liberty to the whole of the human race. Love of
liberty was diffused into my soul by my grandfathers
while they dandled me on their knees.

~ Joseph Smith

If any myth can make a claim to near-universality among the cultures and
religions of the world, it is probably the primeval conflict between good and evil.
Christianity has long contended with scattered, cryptic biblical allusions to a
conflict in the celestial realms that antedated even the creation of the earth. "And
there was war in heaven," says the writer of Revelation in the most prominent
example. "Michael and his angels fought against the dragon; and the dragon
fought and his angels, and prevailed not, neither was their place found any more
in heaven" (12:7–8).

Biblical commentators have long relegated those passages to "rabbinic traditions" or "Jewish apocalyptic literature," with only symbolic relevance for Christians. Thus Adam Clarke, in the early nineteenth century, for instance, calls
John's images "peculiarly rabbinical," and J. R. Dummelow suggests the meaning
that, in Christ's death, resurrection, and ascension, "Satan was already essentially
conquered."[2] John Milton, however, like many Christians of an earlier age, took
the passage as a quite literal allusion to warfare in high places in eons long past,

finding therein the historical origins of Satan. In the process of recreating epic warfare on high, Milton, in book VI of *Paradise Lost*, transforms the rebel angel Lucifer into the world's first Romantic hero, warring defiantly against God's omnipotent tyranny. In 1835, Joseph Smith produced a text purporting to contain lost writings of Abraham, in which the nature and origins of this crisis in the harmony of heaven are described. Abraham presents readers with an account of a celestial assemblage of unborn spirits, "intelligences organized before the world was."[3] Joseph preferred the word "organize" to "create," since the latter connoted fabrication ex nihilo, which he discounted. It is not clear, therefore, whether this "organization" of "intelligences" has reference to the process by which God worked with primeval human substance, or intelligence, and fashioned or begat it into individual spirits, or whether this phrase has reference to a kind of mustering or ordering of preexistent spirit entities into some assemblage.[4] In any case, the motif of the grand heavenly council, alluded to in Psalm 82, where "God presides in the divine council, [and] in the midst of the gods adjudicates" (Anchor Bible translation), has extensive representation in Middle Eastern traditions and in apocryphal literature.[5] In Joseph's version, God stands in the midst of many "noble and great" spirits, and declares his intentions with regard to these future inhabitants of the earth. "We will go down, . . . and we will make an earth whereon these may dwell; and we will prove them herewith, to see if they will do all things whatsoever the Lord their God shall command them." In response, "one among them that was like unto God" offers himself as executor and instrument of the Father's plan, apparently indicating a willingness to expiate the sins that will inevitably accrue to all mankind in the wake of such a probationary scheme (Abraham 3, PGP).

It is at this point, according to a revelation Joseph had published five years earlier, that a second figure steps forward with a competing proposal. Referring to Satan, God tells the prophet Moses:

> . . . [He] came before me, saying—Behold here am I, send me, I will be thy Son, and I will redeem all mankind, that one soul shall not be lost, and surely I will do it; wherefore, give me thine honor. But, behold, my Beloved Son, which was my Beloved and Chosen from the beginning, said unto me—Father, thy will be done, and the glory be thine forever. Wherefore, because that Satan rebelled against me, and sought to destroy the agency of man, which I, the Lord God, had given him; and also, that I should give unto him mine own power; by the power of mine Only Begotten, I caused that he should be cast down; and he became Satan, yea, even the devil, the father of all lies, to deceive, and to blind men, and to lead them captive at his will. (Moses 4:1–4, PGP)

According to this scenario, then, the first cosmic conflict on record is between the principle of agency and the threat of compulsion. Whether we see that attempt at coercion as the first form that evil took, as an evil secondary to a dissent from God's proffered plan, or, more radically, as preceding revolt and rebellion—and thus the primal evil itself—it is clear that Joseph Smith is making moral agency the locus and origin of the moral dualism of the universe. To leave no doubt as to this precedence accorded to the will, Joseph would reveal that moral agency is in fact the indispensable foundation of the soul's very existence. In 1833, he made the astonishing claim that "man was also in the beginning with God. Intelligence, or the light of truth, was not created or made, neither indeed can be," adding, "All truth is independent in that sphere in which God has placed it, to act for itself, as all intelligence also; otherwise there is no existence. Behold, here is the agency of man" (D&C 93:29–30).

It is no coincidence that Joseph here links a pronouncement on the supreme importance of moral agency with a claim that human intelligence is uncreated. The formulation cuts through a Gordian knot that had confounded religious philosophy in America since before its founding, and had earlier echoes going back to debates between Erasmus and Luther and, before that, Pelagius and Augustine: the conflict over freedom and determinism. The most famous American philosophical text through the nineteenth century, writes one scholar, was Jonathan Edwards's *Freedom of the Will*. In that treatise, Edwards had struggled to reconcile God's omnipotence with individual accountability. Calvinism, with its doctrine of total depravity and determinism, was interpreted by non-Calvinists to deny freedom of the will. But Edwards insisted that "freedom was having a will. Having a will meant possessing overriding habits, inclinations, desires, motives, and so on. God could not create free beings unless he created them in such a way that their actions would be morally determined."[6] In this way, Edwards tried to argue that men are both free *and* morally determined.

According to this position, the opposite of moral determinism is not freedom, but irrationality, unpredictability, and random spontaneity. If people did not act in predictable, rational accord with their proclivities, motives, and character, then we would be thrown into a world in which cause and effect break down. We would not inhabit a realm of freedom but of behavioral anarchy and arbitrariness. In the later eighteenth century, philosopher William Godwin put the case simply: "If voluntary conduct, as well as material impulse, were not subjected to general laws, and a legitimate topic of prediction and foresight," the social world would disintegrate, and "there could be no such thing as character or as a ground of inference enabling us to predict what men would be from what they have been."[7]

Even Edwards's adroit reasoning and Godwin's logic, however, could not stem the growing tide of hostility to anything that denigrated the independent self. In Edwards's day, for example, it was still possible to arrest dissenters like Robert Breck of Massachusetts for atheism and blasphemy. Even though a confirmed Calvinist (he affirmed the Westminster Confession), Breck had dared to assert that God "would hold people responsible only for that which was in their power to do."[8] Increasingly, the influence of Jacob Arminius (1560–1609) was gaining sway. A Dutch Reformed theologian, he argued for the compatibility of freedom of the will and God's sovereignty, finding avid followers and a lasting place in the history of theology. In America, popular preachers John Wesley (1703–1791), Alexander Campbell (1788–1866), and Charles Finney (1792–1875) all were associated with the Arminian strain, which emphasized individual responsibility and a self-determining will. As one scholar writes, "the liberal Christianity of the new republic would be built around such moral principles."[9]

In the era of Joseph Smith's religious culture, as in Jacksonian America generally, any theory that privileged individual responsibility over deterministic models was bound to be popular—even if Arminianism itself was far from endorsing limitless human freedom. Jacob Arminius had written of the human condition:

> [I]n this state, the Free Will of man towards the True Good is not only wounded, maimed, infirm, bent, and weakened; but it is also imprisoned, destroyed, and lost: And its powers are not only debilitated and useless unless they be assisted by grace, but it has no powers whatever except such as are excited by Divine grace.[10]

Still, it provided the best alternative to the irresistible grace of the Calvinists.

Indeed, the phenomenal growth of both Methodism and the Campbellite movement, as well as of Finney's exuberant brand of revivalism, attest to the great attraction that individualistic religion had for Americans. This elevation of the individual, this "new importance given to the single person" was, in Emerson's 1837 words, a veritable "sign of our times."[11] The heritage of American independence, the infusions of Romantic sensibility from abroad, the vastness and rapidity of territorial expansion, and the volatile populism of Jackson—all conspired to create an ambience of unfettered ambition. As Richard Bushman remarks, by Joseph's day, "it is hard to imagine another time in the world's history when a culture of boundlessness prevailed so widely."[12] Theologies that constrained human will, like those that limited human potential, could hardly hope to compete with doctrines of limitlessness and a fully liberated human agency. In Joseph's radical rewriting of Genesis, which we saw above, even the elemental particles of the universe cooperate actively in their own material creation. The Gods organize the two great lights, for instance, to rule the day and the night, and then, "the Gods watched those things which they had ordered until they obeyed" (Abraham 4:18, PGP). As Hugh Nibley comments, "'They obeyed' is the active voice, introducing a teaching that . . . is by far the most significant and distinct aspect of Mormonism. It is the principle of maximum participation, of the active cooperation of all of God's creatures in the working out of his plans, which, in fact, are devised for their benefit."[13]

Out of this context, however, Joseph's contributions went far beyond quibbling about the compatibility of absolute sovereignty and free will, or merely privileging the latter. Edwards, for example, thought he had reconciled the two principles by asserting that human beings were free in the only way that mattered, i.e., "their choices were thoroughly their own, not bound except by their *own* moral natures and inclinations."[14] That formulation, of course, only revealed—rather than solved—the most fundamental challenge to free will, which neither Calvinists nor Arminians could easily dodge. For in addition to the problems of behavioral irrationality, or a disordered and unpredictable world, proponents of human free will cannot escape the problem posed by the principle of causality itself. If every action presupposes a cause, then all human action is traceable to prior causes, eventuating in a first one, which is God. If this first cause determines every subsequent action, then responsibility—and freedom—can reside only in the realm of that first cause. It is therefore hard, in the final analysis, to avoid an even more inflexible determinism than the Calvinists': as creator of the human soul, God is ultimately responsible for the human soul's nature—its proclivities, tendencies, and appetites. Edwards acknowledged this problem, responding that "every version of Christianity had the same problem. All Christians taught that there *is* sin in the world and that God created the world."[15] Aquinas had addressed this issue in his *Summa Theologica*, recognizing the logical difficulty presented by his own acknowledgment, on the one hand, of God as "First Cause," and on the other, of Aristotle's dictum that *only* that which is "cause of itself" is free.[16] God can be free, therefore, but nothing that derives from, exists outside, or follows upon that first cause can be. In other words, belief in God as the source of all being would seem to be fundamentally incompatible with human moral agency if human beings are his creatures.[17] And that God is the source of all things in existence, no orthodox Christian disputed ("He is the alone fountain of all being," as the Westminster Confession puts it). Or as one philosopher has put the case more simply: "an omnipotent God could have prevented all sin by creating us with better natures and in more favorable surroundings.... Hence we should not be responsible for our sins to God."[18] The entire problem of a first cause could be obviated, of course, only by a radical rejection of God as absolutely sovereign, which would in turn pave the way for eliminating a temporal point of origin for the human soul. But as Edwards noted, no such Christian conception existed in his day.

"We say that God Himself is a self-existent God," said Joseph:

> Who told you that man did not exist in like manner upon the same principle? . . . The mind of man—the intelligent part—is as immortal as, and is coequal [co-eternal][19] with, God Himself.... I might with boldness proclaim from the housetop that God never had the power to create the spirit of man at all.... Intelligence is eternal and exists upon a self-existent principle. It is a spirit from age to age and there is no creation about it. The first principles of man are self-existent with God.[20]

Joseph's formulation is nothing less than a reconceptualization of the most fundamental division in Christian metaphysics: we move from a binary opposition between a unique Creator and infinite creatures/creations, into a universe divided, as the Book of Mormon states the case, between "things to act, and things to be acted upon" (2 Nephi 2:14). We will further explore in chapter 3 the shattering implications of situating man on God's side of the most essential divide in the universe. For now, it is sufficient to point out that being coeternal with God, man is free like God. Along with Satan, Joseph taught, God and man constitute the "independent principles" of the universe.[21] Or, as Brigham Young was fond of saying, "Men are organized to be just as independent as any being in eternity."[22]

Certainly individual, moral agency occupies a remarkably privileged place, according to Joseph and Brigham, in cosmological history and in Mormon theology. Given these positions on freedom of the will and man's ontological autonomy, one might expect to find in Mormonism an uncommon hostility to dogma, hierarchy, and church authority. Indeed, Joseph affirmed the sanctity of conscience when he insisted that he only taught his people "correct principles, and they govern themselves," elsewhere adding that "we are not disposed, had we the power, to deprive any one of exercising that free independence of mind which heaven has so graciously bestowed upon the human family as one of its choicest gifts."[23] So it is all the more ironic that the church Joseph founded is one of the most centralized, hierarchical, authoritarian churches in America to come out of the era famous for the "democratization of religion."[24]

To understand this paradox, it is essential to know that Joseph Smith considered two ingredients essential to true Christianity, both of which he declared lost in the "great apostasy," and both of which he claimed to restore. First was the fullness of gospel truth. Primary in this regard was what Joseph called "a correct idea of [God's] character, perfections and attributes" ("necessary in order that any rational and intelligent being may exercise faith in God unto life and salvation," he believed).[25] Among other things, this correct idea would entail a radically unorthodox rendering of the godhead as three distinct individuals (God and Christ both having corporeal form). Added to the equation were man's pre-existent state and the possibility of eternal family units presided over by exalted men and women. But wedded to his focus on a restoration of gospel truth was Joseph's particular construction of and emphasis on priesthood authority. Combining the restricted sacerdotalism of Roman Catholicism with the quasi universalism of Protestantism, Joseph forged a new version altogether.

Like Catholicism, Joseph held that Christ dispensed specific authorization to particular individuals to preach the gospel and administer the ordinances of salvation and that, subsequent to his death, control over this authority and over its various areas of efficacy (called "keys") were centered in Peter. This priesthood, Joseph taught, was an actual power, as well as a principle of authority, that is coexistent with God himself and connected to his own sovereignty. In defining salvation, Joseph said it was "nothing more nor less than to triumph over all our enemies and put them under our feet . . . and the last enemy was death. . . . [U]ntil a man can triumph over death, he is not saved. A knowledge of the priesthood alone will do this."[26]

The power of resurrection, in other words, is one priesthood key.[27] But an additional way in which Joseph considered that priesthood provided an indispensable power over death was in its capacity to cement human relationships eternally:

> All covenants, contracts, bonds, obligations, oaths, vows, performances, connections, associations, or expectations, that are not made and entered into and sealed by the Holy Spirit of promise, of him . . . whom I have appointed on the earth to hold this power (and I have appointed unto my servant Joseph to hold this power in the last days, and there is never but one on the earth at a time on whom this power and the keys of this priesthood are conferred), are of no efficacy, virtue, or force in and after the resurrection from the dead; for all contracts that are not made unto this end have an end when men are dead. (D&C 132:7)

This priesthood, according to Joseph, is an eternal power, physically transmitted (by the laying on of hands) from agent to agent in a chain extending back to its primeval origin. In this world, he wrote, "The priesthood was first given to Adam; he obtained the First Presidency, and held the keys of it from generation to generation. He obtained it in the Creation, before the world was formed." In fact, he continued, "the priesthood is an everlasting principle, and existed with God from eternity, and will to eternity, without beginning of days or end of years."[28] Adam bequeathed the priesthood to his descendants, and so on through the years of human history. In Joseph's version of dispensationalism, however, the chain is not an unbroken one. Sporadic interruptions have occurred across the millennia, necessitating the ordination of new prophets by heaven-sent messengers. Preceding Christ's ministry, for example, John the Baptist was ordained by an angel at the age of eight days (D&C 84:28). Following the dispersal and death of Christ's personally ordained apostles, a hiatus of 1,800 years occurred before John the Baptist and later Peter, James, and John appeared to Joseph Smith in resurrected form and manually conferred upon him their respective priesthood keys and authority. Other messengers would follow, including Moses and Elijah. Believing himself the recipient of literal priesthood authorization by resurrected beings, Joseph thus avoided the problem of self-doubt about authority that had plagued second-wave reformer Roger Williams or, later, Charles Wesley. Motivated to forge a dissenting movement, Williams nevertheless agonized over his own lack of manifest authority. Soon after his rupture with the Puritans, he withdrew from his own fledgling church because of such doubts, and resigned himself to waiting until "God should stir up himself or some other new Apostles."[29]

Williams's predicament revealed a drawback of the Protestant appeal to biblical authority alone: it lacked the certainty and singularity of a visible conduit and unambiguous line of transmission, and hence the assurance that it was divinely approved rather than of human initiation. Joseph embraced the advantages of the Catholic model, even as he shunned its elitism. So while the priesthood he claimed to restore was not a "priesthood of all believers," he did expand the spiritual franchise to virtually all worthy LDS males.[30] Initially, such ecclesiastical egalitarianism proved appealing and effective. Especially since, from the perspective of administering church sacraments and ordinances, no apparent reason existed to restrict priesthood access. But from the standpoint of church governance, Joseph learned quickly, a church full of prophets was a holy bedlam. Hiram Page was one of the eight men who saw and handled the gold plates, and his name is appended to an affidavit so testifying. Some five months after the Mormon church's organization, he began to make use of a seer stone, through which he claimed to receive revelations for that church. Many members, including Joseph's own scribe, Oliver Cowdery, were persuaded by them, prompting Joseph to produce a revelation that established for all time the principle of the supreme spiritual authority in the church. The revelation, by declaring that "no one shall be appointed to receive revelations and commandments [for] this church excepting my servant Joseph Smith, . . . until I shall appoint . . . another in his stead" (D&C 28:2, 7), effectively transformed the role of a prophet into the office of Prophet. (The principle was reaffirmed in similar language a few months later [D&C 43:3–5].)

It wasn't Joseph's assumption of the prophetic title that marked a distinctive turn in Mormonism's cultural evolution. It was the construction of that calling into an office, which had no precedent in American religious history. His 1820 visitation from God he had interpreted as a personal response to a personal spiritual quest. From 1823 to 1827, his communications with the angel Moroni (who delivered to him the Book of Mormon) he had seen as personal, heavenly tutorials, preparing him for the work of translating the Book of Mormon. Then, even before the church's organization in 1830, he had begun to pronounce God's will for several other individuals: his father (D&C 4 in February 1829); Martin Harris (D&C 5 in March of the same year); Oliver Cowdery (D&C 6–9 in April); his brother Hyrum (D&C 11 in May); friend and supporter Joseph Knight, Sr. (D&C 12 also in May), and the three Whitmer brothers (D&C 14–16 in June). In fact, all fourteen revelations Joseph received that year addressed or mentioned some individual known to the Prophet. Mostly, these pronouncements offered encouragement or general admonitions to "keep my commandments" or "declare repentance" or "establish the cause of Zion." As such, they could easily be construed to be generic counsel of general applicability.

As the organization of the church approached and then passed, revelations became increasingly diverse in their domain of influence—and increasingly focused and individual-specific in their content. A revelation in March 1830 commanded Martin Harris to "not covet [his] own property, but impart it freely to the printing of the Book of Mormon" (D&C 19:26). In another telling development, persons were rebuked for personal failings in divine pronouncements that were publicly promulgated. David Whitmer was too attuned to "the things of the earth" (D&C 30:2); James Covill had succumbed to "pride and the cares of the world" (D&C 39:9); Frederick Williams, Sidney Rigdon, and Newel K. Whitney were censured as negligent fathers (D&C 93:41–50). Though Joseph did not exempt himself from public reproof (D&C 3:4–9; 5:21; 93:47), he was never called "a wicked man," as was the erratic Martin Harris (D&C 3, 10), nor rebuked for murmuring and courting adultery as was the hapless William McLellin. (D&C 66:10; 75:7).

After relocating the church center from upstate New York to Kirtland, Ohio, and in the midst of growing numbers and internal dissensions there, Joseph announced a new place of gathering that would be the Zion of prophecy, a "New Jerusalem," a city of God built from the ground up as a theocratic community with ownership of all things in common. On the borders of the civilized world, erecting their wilderness utopia, the group's spiritual leader became its de facto city planner, school administrator, and law giver. Continuing to exercise his authority as prophet and revelator, Joseph told followers what businesses to pursue and where, as part of the movement's communal endeavor: Newel K. Whitney was instructed to "retain his store . . . [in Ohio] yet for a little season" (D&C 63:42), while in the same revelation Joseph announced that God had given him the power "to discern by the Spirit those who shall go up unto the land of Zion [Missouri], and those of my disciples who shall tarry [in Ohio]" (D&C 41). Sidney Gilbert was one of the former. He was ordered to "plant himself in [Jackson County, Missouri], and establish a store" in July 1831 (D&C 57:8). His colleague W. W. Phelps was called by the voice of God—through Joseph—to "be established as a printer" (D&C 57:11); he had earlier been commanded to do the work "of selecting and writing books for schools in this church" (D&C 55:4). Other assignments were similarly ordained.

In the days before disestablishment, American Puritans had found no difficulty in wedding the political, the civic, and the spiritual. As one religious historian has remarked, "Puritanism and its Reformed-pietist successors" frequently engaged in the project of "rebuilding Christendom by making towns and eventually nations into virtually Christian societies." One consequence, especially under the school of thought associated with the influential grandfather of Jonathan Edwards, Solomon Stoddard, "was that church and town were more or less coextensive."[31] After the Revolution, however, church authoritarianism that blurred the lines between spiritual guidance and secular control, and intruded into the economic in particular, was bound to meet resistance. And it did.

In early 1838, the man who had transcribed almost the entirety of the Book of Mormon, Oliver Cowdery, left the church over just this issue. Cowdery had sold some of his land holdings in Missouri, in defiance of a revelation by Joseph. Charged by a church council in Far West, Missouri, with "virtually denying the faith by declaring that he would not be governed by any ecclesiastical authority or revelations whatever in his temporal affairs," Cowdery readily admitted the offense: "I will not be influenced, governed, or controlled, in my temporal interests by any ecclesiastical authority or pretended revelation whatever, contrary to my own judgment."[32] In the newfound spirit of American republicanism, Cowdery invoked his "constitutional privileges," the rights adumbrated by Locke, and his Plymouth ancestors. That the high council rejected the charge against Cowdery suggests the extent to which Joseph's authority to dictate in temporal matters was still a matter of controversy, uncertainty, and discontent.[33]

Throughout those formative years, however, the majority of Latter-day Saints clearly *were* willing to sacrifice economic self-interest, family ties, and self-determination in answering the call to abandon homes and flocks and families and to gather to new locales and to serve missions without purse or script. Why were the majority of Latter-day Saints willing to cede those English/American liberties in deference to a homespun prophet and visionary? Part of the explanation lies in Joseph's reformulation of traditional categories. "All things to me are spiritual," said Joseph's God, "and not at any time have I given unto you a law which was temporal; . . . for my commandments are spiritual; they are not natural nor temporal, neither carnal nor sensual" (D&C 29:34–35). Literalizing the gathering of Israel as a physical congregating of the righteous and literalizing the building of Zion as a process using plats as well as prophetic pronouncements made it impossible for his followers to metaphorize such biblically ordained imperatives or divorce them from the central pursuits of personal and community life. Suddenly, being a Latter-day Saint meant full engagement in a life of re-settlement, community building, temple construction, economic communalism, and millennial preparation. That left precious little room for a private domain of entirely personal prerogatives.[34]

At least three other factors reinforced the scope and authority of the prophetic office in Mormonism. First was the geography of the Mormon experience. The gathering in western Missouri was at the fringes of civilization, where persecution and relocation heightened dependence on the group and its charismatic leader. The next location, Nauvoo, Illinois, was a virtual city-state, with a prophet who also assumed the roles of lieutenant general of a numerous militia and mayor of the city, making him the political, military, and spiritual leader of his people. Death added martyr to his titles. With the exodus to Utah, Brigham Young consolidated and expanded several of those roles. Joseph was mayor of Nauvoo, a city of 12,000. Young presided as governor (with short-lived official sanction, but permanent de facto authority), prophet, and church president over an enormous—and remote—territory that, by his death, encompassed over 100,000 followers. Critics blasted what they considered his despotic control over all affairs in Utah, both ecclesiastical and temporal. Even admirers have not always disputed such characterizations. As Hugh Nibley writes of Young's followers:

[W]hat else *could* they think of any man who rolled over all opposition, amassed substance and power, and commanded the absolute obedience that Brigham

Young did? To do that in terms of our world, a man must needs be a combination of Tamerlaine, Caesar Borgia, and Boss Tweed, and as such even the Latter-day Saints have pictured Brigham Young.[35]

Mormons do not understand the prophetic office in terms familiar to the world at large. This brings us to the second factor reinforcing its powerful purchase on Mormon faithfulness: an idiosyncratic understanding of inspiration. In an essay revealingly titled "The Scandal of Revelation," critic George Steiner writes, "personally, I find scriptural literalism or any peremptory attribution to God of 'speech acts' such as we know and use them, to be unacceptable. . . . Such attribution only offends reason and historical evidence."[36] Steiner's is not the only example. Referring to theological developments in particular, one religious historian has written:

> To claim that God reveals Himself to man but to reject the [belief that] he reveals Himself by speaking to man is to so whittle away the analogy on which the concept of divine revelation is built that it must be seriously asked whether the concept of divine revelation has enough content to license its continued use. Revelation in the fully personal sense characteristic of personal agents has been abandoned.[37]

In the face of such widespread rejection of Old Testament literalism regarding God's interaction with human beings, Mormonism is emphatically regressive. Joseph was inflexible in his insistence that his encounters with Deity involved literal speech acts between divine persons and himself. The Book of Mormon he produced emphasizes as one of its cardinal teachings the urgency of embracing dialogic revelation as the birthright of righteous seekers in all ages. From Brigham Young onward, LDS prophets have muted their claims to divine epiphanies. The last visitation acknowledged by a modern Mormon prophet was Christ's appearing to the fifth president, Lorenzo Snow, in the Salt Lake Temple in 1898, and that experience was shared privately.[38] But what is important is that the heritage of encounters with a physically embodied Deity who speaks his will to a prophet continues to inform Mormon understanding of the prophetic role. So when President Kimball announced in 1978 that "a revelation and assurance [extending the priesthood to black members] came to me so clearly that there was no question about it,"[39] his words carried the same weight with—and claimed the same assent from—members as when Joseph Smith decreed yet another place of gathering. Mormons by and large believe that God's revealing of himself to his prophets is just as literal as it ever was. Such manifestations may be less dramatic, or they may only be less publicly discussed, but members are confident that, as a recent president, Ezra Taft Benson, declared, "today in Christ's restored church, The Church of Jesus Christ of Latter-day Saints, [Christ] is revealing Himself and His will—from the first prophet of the Restoration, even Joseph Smith, to the present."[40]

Finally, Mormon scriptures make it clear that acceptance of LDS church presidents as inspired spokesmen for God is a religious imperative. An early revelation commanded members to "give heed unto all [Joseph Smith's] words and commandments which he shall give unto you as he receiveth them.... For his word ye shall receive, as if from mine own mouth.... For by doing these things, the gates of hell shall not prevail against you" (D&C 21:4–6). A subsequent revelation enjoined the faithful to "uphold him before me by the prayer of faith" (D&C 43:12). Today, members celebrate the office with rousing anthems ("We Thank Thee, O God, for a Prophet"); publicly avow their support of the living tenant of that office as "prophet, seer, and revelator" in ward, stake, and general conferences of the church; and must confirm to the bishop their assent to the prophet's unique authority over the church as a condition of temple admission.

The consequence of these two traditions of emphasis on freedom and authority is an ever-present tension in Mormon culture between submission to an ecclesiastical authoritarianism without parallel in modern Christianity and an emphasis on and veneration for the principle of individual moral agency so pronounced that it leads even careful observers into major misperceptions (Mormons "earn their way to godhood by the proper exercise of free will, rather than through the grace of Jesus Christ," reports one news magazine).[41] Without moral independence, says the LDS scripture, "there is no existence." "When our leaders speak, the thinking has been done," says the (officially disavowed but widely accepted) LDS saw.[42]

Certainly when the LDS leaders speak, they do so with an unusually high rate of responsiveness from church members, even compared to another authoritarian institution, Roman Catholicism. Theologian Richard P. McBrien, a passionate admirer of the most popular pope of modernity, John Paul II, for example, acknowledged that notwithstanding his having "more prestige than any pope in history," the pope had "very little influence on the lives of Catholic lay people. They see him and cheer for him. But there's not much substance" in his influence over them.[43] To cite one example, the Catholic church maintains an official opposition to abortion even more emphatic than Mormonism's. Yet statistics reveal no discernible influence of that position on the numbers of American Catholics having abortions; they obtain them at a rate even higher than their

Protestant counterparts. Mormons, on the other hand, undergo abortions at a rate dramatically lower than the national average.[44] The category of mothers who work outside the home is another area where "the influence of prophetic instruction . . . is substantial."[45] Mormon youth as well, a comprehensive study finds, "showed a greater willingness to adhere to the requirement of their faith" than youth of any other religious group in America.[46] Certainly, LDS conformity to church teachings is a mixed bag, but one sociologist notes with surprise that "even the readers of *Dialogue*, presumably an independent-minded lot, in a 1984 survey, expressed a willingness by a margin of two to one to go along with Church policies that displeased them—perhaps with some question but with no 'dissent,' even privately."[47]

Some critics—even in the church—find such patterns prima facie evidence of mindless conformity to authority. For example, in February 1981, 53 percent of respondents in southwestern Utah opposed the proposed MX missile system. After the First Presidency in May publicly criticized the proposal, the opposition increased to 76 percent. "It seems clear," wrote one disgruntled Mormon critic, "that Mormons in that poll had simply allowed the Church leaders to do their political thinking for them."[48] Other Mormons could, with equal plausibility, applaud the promptness of their peers to fall in line with God's directives as revealed through his mouthpiece the prophet.

For intellectuals and artists, the tension is especially stark. Intellectual inquiry and artistic exploration should thrive in a culture like the Mormon one, which opposes as evil any attempt "to deprive us of the slightest respect for free agency."[49] At the same time, LDS artists and intellectuals find themselves constrained by the church's insistence that all inspiration is not equal, and they discover that the same prophetic prerogatives that impeded Cowdery's exercise of autonomy may cramp the style of maverick intellectuals and artists today. "The mantle [of holy office] is far, far greater than the intellect," warned Boyd K. Packer. "[T]he priesthood is the guiding power."[50]

The resulting collision of views and valuations is inevitable. No consensus is ever likely to emerge in the Mormon community about the proper reconciliation of authority and independence, faithfulness and freedom. On the contrary, Richard Poll once found it convenient to improvise categories that respond to the growing sense of a fundamental dichotomy in Mormon culture between "Iron Rod Mormons" and "Liahona Mormons." According to this dichotomy, Iron Rod Mormons find comfort and safety in reliance upon the institutions and authoritative oracles God has put in place. "In the pronouncements of the General Authorities, living and dead," he writes, "the Iron Rod finds many answers. . . . This reliance extends to every facet of life." For the Liahona Mormon, the central concept of the gospel is freedom; "my range of freedom is left large, and arbitrary divine interference with that freedom is kept minimal, in order that I may grow."[51]

This cultural divide is not always so neat and precise, but more important, the divide Poll describes is one that, at some level, operates *within* thoughtful Mormons as much as *among* them. That is why both institutional conflict and personal anguish will continue to characterize artists and intellectuals who struggle to find their comfortable place in a culture where proponents of opposing views each cite scripture and prophetic precedent for support. And indeed, in Joseph's vision, the quest for salvation poses challenges of both an intellectual and imaginative nature. "Thy mind O Man, if thou wilt lead a soul unto salvation must stretch as high as the utmost Heavens, and search into and contemplate the lowest considerations of the darkest abyss, and Expand upon the broad considerations of Eternal Expanse."[52]

Young, perhaps the most authoritarian Mormon prophet in history, himself protested the perils of conformity. "I am not a stereotyped Latter-day Saint," he said, "and do not believe in the doctrine. . . . Away with stereotyped 'Mormons'!"[53] Neither did he wish for slavish obedience and fawning submission: "I do not wish any Latter-day Saint in this world, nor in heaven, to be satisfied with anything I do, unless the Spirit of the Lord Jesus Christ, the spirit of revelation, makes them satisfied. I wish them to know for themselves and understand for themselves."[54] Elsewhere, he reaffirmed:

> I am more afraid that this people have so much confidence in their leaders that they will not inquire for themselves of God whether they are led by him. I am fearful that they settle down in a state of blind self-security, trusting their eternal destiny in the hands of their leaders with a reckless confidence that in itself would thwa[r]t the purposes of God.[55]

What this means is that, as in Joseph's claim that his followers govern themselves, priesthood authority directs man in the use of his agency, it does not coerce or preempt it. At the same time, personal agency is preserved by personal knowledge. Coercion and ignorance alike are antithetical to human autonomy.

His beloved younger colleague, the colorful J. Golden Kimball, reminded his audience:

> There are not enough Apostles in the Church to prevent us from thinking, and they are not disposed to do so; but some people fancy that because we have the Presidency and Apostles of the Church that they will do the thinking for us.

There are men and women so mentally lazy that they hardly think for themselves. To think calls for effort, which makes some men tired and wearies their souls. No man or woman can remain in this Church on borrowed light.[56]

In 1945, when a church magazine urged, "When our leaders speak, the thinking has been done," an indignant President George Albert Smith repudiated the statement. "Even to imply that members of the Church are not to do their own thinking," he wrote, "is grossly to misrepresent the true ideal of the Church."[57]

On the other side of the equation, the same Joseph who reveled in freedom of the mind also produced a powerful instance of supremely docile obedience. In a retelling of the aftermath of Adam's expulsion from the garden, an angel asks Adam why he performs sacrifice. He answers, "I know not, save the Lord commanded me" (Moses 5:6, PGP), which one LDS leader called "a glorious example . . . of compliance to counsel without knowledge of the reason."[58] And the same Brigham Young who decried conformity could also insist that loyalty to a prophet trumped personal judgment. Finding fault in his heart with Joseph's financial dealings, Young quickly felt it needful to repent: "The spirit of revelation manifested to me that if I was to harbor a thought in my heart that Joseph could be wrong in anything, I would begin to lose confidence in him" to the point that he could not believe anything that Joseph said. Young concluded, "Though I [knew] that Joseph was a human being and subject to err, still it was none of my business to look after his faults. . . . It was not my prerogative to call him in question with regard to any act of his life. He was God's servant, and not mine."[59]

No wonder the whole tension provokes a kind of cultural cognitive dissonance. And the tensions are only exacerbated by a burgeoning population, across continents and cultures, that leaders work to keep in check with increasingly centralized administration and correlation. Since the early 1960s, a priesthood correlation program has served to centralize and coordinate all church organizational structures, planning, programs, and teaching curricula and manuals. This has been an extremely efficient factor in maintaining strict control over how the Latter-day Saints' version of the gospel is taught and administered. There is an important historical dimension to George Q. Cannon's proud claim that "the people who have embraced this Gospel have had to think for themselves. It is no light matter to become a 'Mormon.' "[60] But what was true in 1881, when to be LDS meant to willingly affiliate with the small, besieged, and most reviled religious group in America, is not true in the twenty-first century, with Mormonism a prosperous, respected church, touted as a burgeoning world religion.

Clearly, control and regimentation will increasingly contend with size and global dispersion, perhaps eliciting growing signs in the LDS community of independence and resistance to the ongoing stages of institutionalization. And history is a factor as well in the shifting value of rhetorical terms. Concepts like personal freedom have much greater modern resonance than respect for authority, and diversity is a vastly more alluring value than conformity. Apostle Dallin H. Oaks is clearly attempting to counter the declining cultural currency of those unfashionable terms. In one sermon, he urges that "diversity for its own sake is meaningless. . . . What unites us is far more important than what differentiates us. Consequently, our members are asked to concentrate their efforts to strengthen our unity—not to glorify our diversity."[61] And at the same time, he argues that the primacy of agency over coercion does not translate into choice without accountability.

Still, a segment of Mormon society will always be disposed to see unquestioning obedience to priesthood counsel as weakness and abdication of moral autonomy, while others will see independent-mindedness as a euphemism for the fetishizing of difference and pride. And the tensions will doubtless be fiercest among those whose life work calls them to worship God through creative expression and intellectual pursuits.

~ 2 ~

THE ENDLESS QUEST AND
PERFECT KNOWLEDGE
Searching and Certainty

And now, behold, because ye have tried the experiment,
and planted the seed, and it swelleth and sprouteth, and
beginneth to grow, ye must needs know that the seed is
good. And now, behold, is your knowledge perfect?
Yea, your knowledge is perfect in that thing, and your
faith is dormant.

~ Alma 32:33–34

You must begin with the first and go on until you learn
all the principles of exaltation. But it will be a great
while after you have passed through the veil before you
will have learned them.

~ Joseph Smith

Joseph Smith taught that "there is no pain so awful as that of suspense; this is the
punishment of the wicked; their doubt, anxiety and suspense cause weeping,
wailing and gnashing of teeth."[1] In a religious context, faith is generally seen as
the antidote to uncertainty about the state of the soul, or its eventual fate. And
religious faith, presumably, is a willful decision to believe, to choose conviction in
the absence of empirical proof or epistemological certainty. The case of Joseph
Smith presents us with several anomalies in this regard. First of all, a man in-
ducted into his religious vocation with a literal visit by an embodied God and
Christ is not likely to view his religious convictions in the same terms as a typical
Christian believer. Translating scripture out of tangible metal plates weighing
forty or fifty pounds is not of the same order of prophetic utterance as expressing
mere spiritual intimations. Feeling the weight of angelic hands belonging to

resurrected apostles on his head, conferring upon him the priesthood of God, produced a crystalline certainty about his authority. Joseph Smith, in other words, did not simply believe he was a prophet inspired to act in God's name. In his mind, he was as certain as any man could be on any subject, sacred or secular. "I knew it, and I knew that God knew it," he said of his initial encounter with Deity (Joseph Smith—History 1:25, PGP). Joseph claimed his formative experiences, both as a fourteen-year-old seeker, and as a prophet and religion maker, were saturated in the physical, the tangible, the material, and the visible.

Certainty is a term that frequently appears in the ministry of Joseph Smith, often in a doctrinally prominent position. In the *Lectures on Faith*, which he employed in teaching the elders in Kirtland, it is affirmed that from earliest times, faith has been a prelude to sure knowledge:

> [T]he inquiry and diligent search of the ancient saints to seek after and obtain a knowledge of the glory of God . . . [were rooted in] the credence they gave to the testimony of their fathers. . . . The inquiry frequently terminated, indeed always terminated when rightly pursued, in the most glorious discoveries and eternal certainty.[2]

Two religious awakenings on American soil as well as European history had been replete with accounts of visions and heavenly voices. Joseph was as skeptical as any that all such experiences were valid, but he believed self-examination could free the individual from the pitfalls of self-delusion:

> [W]e may look for Angels & receive their ministering but we are to try the spirits & prove them for it is often the case that men make a mistake in regard to these things. God has so ordained that when he has communicated by vision no vision [is] to be taken but what you see by the seeing of the eye or what you hear by the hearing of the ear. . . . There must be certainty in this matter.[3]

In his own case, Joseph never admitted a particle of possible self-deception. As he wrote to his wife, "Forasmuch as I know for a certainty of eternal things, if the heavens linger, it is nothing to me."[4] Such certainty, he believed, may be temporally late in coming, but is logically the starting point of true religion. "It is the first principle of the gospel," he wrote, "to know for a certainty the character of God, and to know that we may converse with him as one man converses with another."[5] It is easy to see why his personal encounter with a conversing Deity would ground his own sense of epistemological certainty. But he clearly saw his own experience as a prototype to which others could—and should—aspire. An

1833 revelation had the Lord declaring that "every soul who forsaketh his sins and cometh unto me, and calleth on my name, and obeyeth my voice, and keepeth my commandments, shall see my face, and know that I am" (D&C 93:1). This possibility Joseph related to the doctrine of the second comforter, spoken of by Christ when he addressed his disciples before his crucifixion. On that occasion, he promised that the Father would send them "another Comforter, that he may abide with you for ever" (John 14:16). Joseph gave his gloss of this passage years later:

> Now what is this other Comforter? It is no more nor less than the Lord Jesus Christ Himself; and this is the sum and substance of the whole matter; that when any man obtains this last Comforter, he will have the personage of Jesus Christ to attend him or appear unto him from time to time, and even He will manifest the Father unto him, and they will take up their abode with him, and the visions of the heavens will be opened unto him, and the Lord will teach him face to face, and he may have a perfect knowledge of the mysteries of the Kingdom of God.[6]

Joseph apparently believed that the personal epiphany he experienced in his visitation by the Father and the Son, heralding full immersion in the divine light, with all its epistemological fullness and certainty, betokened an order of knowledge that was the right and destiny of all faithful Saints. A principal tool in shaping Mormon aspirations to such perfect knowledge was the Book of Mormon. It was not just that as a material artifact it so visibly and insistently trumpeted the claim that angels were again visiting the earth. The thematic thread that pervaded the text from first to last was the timeless accessibility to all persons of revelatory experience. Visions, visitations, and dialogic encounters with a God, a Christ, and a Holy Spirit that communicate in discernible human language fill the narrative. Initiating the model that Joseph would expand, Nephi, first author of the Book of Mormon record, discovers in dramatic fashion that human beings are eligible not merely to feel or intuit divine truths, but to literally "see, and hear, and know of these things, by the power of the Holy Ghost, which is the gift of God unto all those who diligently seek him" (1 Nephi 10:17). In contradistinction to Old Testament patterns, the Book of Mormon chronicles an array of divinely communicated speech that extends not to prophets alone, but to wayward sons, anxious fathers, military leaders, and questing individuals. And the content of those communications can be as portentous as word of a coming messiah, or as quotidian as the location of game sought by a hungry family. Then, at the conclusion of the Book of Mormon, in a gesture the echoes of which still shape the central thrust of modern Mormon missionary work, the scripture's ancient final editor, Moroni, challenges his future readers to secure their own spiritual knowledge of the record's truthfulness. Imploring an audience remote in time to "ask God, the Eternal Father, in the name of Christ, if these things are not true," he promises them that "he will manifest the truth of it [and "the truth of all things"]...by the power of the Holy Ghost" (Moroni 10:4–5).

In America's colonial years, Anne Hutchinson would be censured and banished from Massachusetts for taking such doctrine literally. Interrogated about her purported revelations, she was asked, "'How do you know that was the Spirit[?]' She replied[,] 'How did Abraham know that it was God that bid him offer his son...?' 'By an immediate voice,' Thomas Dudley replied, meaning the direct voice of God, unmediated by Scripture or a minister. 'So to me,' Anne Hutchinson said."[7]

"The ground work of her revelations," Governor John Winthrop pronounced at her trial, "is the *immediate* revelation of the spirit and not *by* the ministry of the word" (emphases in original). Unfortunately for Hutchinson, as her biographer notes and the verdict revealed, "professed direct revelation from God...[was] an ecclesiastical crime."[8] Even a committed restorationist and anticipator of "new revelation" like Joseph's contemporary Alexander Campbell thought Mormonism was pushing the envelope of spiritual ways of knowing too far. He asked:

> Do not the experiences of all the religions—the observations of the intelligent— the practical result of all creeds, reformations, and improvements—and the expectations and longings of society—warrant the conclusion that either some new revelation, or some new development of the revelation of God must be made...?[9]

But he responded to Moroni's guarantee of the confirmation of new revelations with scorn:

> If there was anything plausible about Smith, I would say to those who believe him to be a prophet, hear the question which Moses put into the mouth of the Jews, and his answer to it—"And if thou say in thine heart, How shall we know the word which the Lord hath not spoken?"—Does he answer, "Ask the Lord and he will tell you?"...Nay, indeed.[10]

The Methodists were as open to spiritual gifts as any Christians, but a few generations earlier, John Wesley had declared that "a man had no other way of knowing God's will but by consulting his own reason and his friends, and by observing the order of God's providence." (At one time of urgent decision making, he had himself relied upon drawing lots to make a determination.[11]) In response to reports of extensive spiritual outpourings in Joseph Smith's day, Gilbert Wardlaw, an Edinburgh minister, admonished his American audience against believing in the possibility of spiritual manifestations that were "actually miraculous, something altogether new to the church in the present day, conferred independently of the word, and in a manner almost perceptible to the senses."[12]

Doubtless, the promise of revelatory experience that could bring spiritual certainty appealed to many of Mormonism's first converts. In a remarkable sermon on faith, Book of Mormon prophet Alma the Younger describes faith as merely a prelude to a spiritual knowledge that is radically based in the language of empiricism. By planting the true word in one's heart, Alma says, one may observe that it "beginneth to enlarge [the] soul; yea it beginneth to enlighten [the] understanding." The "swelling motions" in the breast can be *"felt,"* he writes. Having "tried the *experiment,"* one can discern an effect that "is *real* . . . because it is light; and whatsoever is light, is good, because it is *discernible."* As a consequence of this process, he asks, "is your knowledge perfect? Yea, your knowledge is perfect in that thing, and your faith is dormant" (Alma 32:28–34; emphases mine).

"A man is saved no faster than he gains knowledge," wrote Joseph, virtually codifying Mormonism's gnostic bent. Initiated into a routine of heavenly dialogue as a young boy, Joseph would outline the soaring heights of heavenly knowledge attainable to human beings a dozen years later in a preface to the most extensive revelation he ever received, referred to by early Mormons as simply *"the* vision." Joseph records the Lord as promising that, to the righteous,

> will I reveal all mysteries, yea all the hidden mysteries of my kingdom from days of old, and for ages to come. . . . Yea, even the wonders of eternity shall they know, and things to come will I show them, even the things of many generations. And their wisdom shall be great, and their understanding reach to heaven. . . . For by my Spirit will I enlighten them, and by my power will I make known to them the secrets of my will—yea, even those things which eye has not seen, nor ear heard, nor yet entered into the heart of man. (D&C 76:7–10)

Within a few years of publishing the Book of Mormon, Joseph further exploded the Christian canon by claiming to recuperate lost writings of Enoch and Moses missing from the text of Genesis, and Abrahamic material recounting a great premortal council in heaven. He had already added recovered writings of

John the Beloved in 1829 (D&C 7) and added more writings of John in 1833 (D&C 93). The cumulative weight of these experiences seems to have created in Joseph's mind a major paradigm shift, a wholesale inversion of the traditional model of biblical fullness and prisca theologia (the idea that one can find scattered cryptic suggestions and fragments of gospel truth in ancient myth and religion). Rather than finding in the pagan and other ancient religions foreshadowings and tantalizing hints of God's revelation which will culminate in the Christian scriptures, Joseph worked, with growing momentum, backward and outward, as if he gradually conceived of his objective as nothing less than a totalizing recuperation of gospel fullness that transcended and preceded and encompassed all particular incarnations, the Bible included.

With one exception, no new revelation has been added to the Mormon canon in generations.[13] Today, few Mormons talk of having experienced visions or visitations. But the rhetoric of certainty and fullness are still distinguishing features of Mormon religious culture. This is most evident in the church's "fast and testimony meetings," usually held the first Sunday of each month. In this worship service, members rise spontaneously to "bear testimony" to gospel truths as they feel moved upon by the Spirit, in a manner vaguely similar to the conduct of Quaker services. The details and degree of eloquence vary tremendously, but the template seldom does: variations of "I *know* Christ lives," "I *know* Joseph Smith was a prophet of God," and "I *know* the church is true" constitute the core of the message. So central to Mormonism is this affirmation of absolute certainty about saving truths that it indelibly alters the very nature of religious conversion.[14]

In a significant twist on the witnessing of evangelicals, the moment of conversion for Mormons is not generally seen as the recognition of one's sinful nature and transformation to a state of grace, but the moment of one's coming into possession of the truths that pertain to external realities. Theologically, the atonement of Christ is primary; and knowing Christ and experiencing his redeeming love is the heart of LDS soteriology. But in the lexicon of Mormon religious culture, to be converted is to experience a moment of recognition, or receive through the Spirit a confirmation, of certain truths that one can henceforth confidently affirm as part of a publicly transmissible "testimony." When Mormons speak of their conversion, they almost universally have in mind the moment when they came to know through the Spirit that Joseph Smith was a prophet, that the Book of Mormon is true, and that the church he founded is "the only true and living church upon the face of the whole earth" (D&C 1:30).

This sense of certainty and spiritual self-confidence may certainly parallel the experience that being "born again" provides to evangelical Christians, but it is a certainty that pertains to claims beyond the personal—and that is to cross a crucial threshold in the decorum of religious discourse. It is one thing to insist on one's own status before God. It is quite another to universalize convictions about institutions and historical persons, and to lay claim to certain, divinely revealed knowledge of those things. This distinctive Mormon rhetoric of "knowing" creates both an impression of arrogance and smugness to outsiders, and immense cultural pressure on adherents to know for themselves rather than to merely believe.

Joseph's own experience was the prototype for this language of conversion: when he returned from the grove where he had experienced his First Vision of God and Christ, his first words proclaimed his personal acquisition of knowledge—"I have learned for myself that Presbyterianism is not true"—not an experience of grace or conversion.[15] True enough, in his first recorded version of the episode (1832), he noted that Christ "spake unto me saying Joseph my son thy sins are forgiven thee."[16] But that detail was dropped from the official account of the First Vision, canonized as scripture. That 1838 version, which remains the basis of convert catechism, emphasizes Joseph's prayer as an informational as much as a spiritual quest: "I asked the personages who stood above me in the light, which of all the sects was right," and the reply was informational: "I was answered that I must join none of them, for they were all wrong."[17] The monthly intonations of "I know the church is true," heard in thousands of Mormon chapels around the world, are palpable if attenuated echoes of Joseph Smith's first verbal testimony and define the most fundamental commonality in Mormon culture, both by their content and by their expression, as an experiential certainty. His associates apparently shared this sense of a knowledge distinct from and moving beyond mere religious faith. Lorenzo Snow, for example, Joseph's younger contemporary and eventually the fifth prophet of Mormonism, was converted to the new faith and baptized in 1836. Yet two weeks later, he recorded, "while engaged in my studies, I began to reflect upon the fact that I had not obtained a *knowledge* of the truth of the work" (emphasis in original). Retiring to a grove, as had his more famous predecessor, he engaged in private prayer and experienced an "almost instantaneous transition . . . into a refulgence of light and knowledge, as it was at that time imparted to my understanding. I then received a perfect knowledge that God lives, that Jesus Christ is the Son of God, and of the restoration of the holy Priesthood, and the fulness of the Gospel."[18]

Powerful conversion experiences and epiphanies that provide spiritual insight and knowledge are part of all religious traditions. But there seems in Mormonism an emphasis on certainty, rather than faith, that is theologically, rhetorically, and culturally pervasive. Certainty—even the ritualistic expression of certainty—easily blurs into a sentiment of plenitude and completeness in Mormon discourse. For many observers, the supreme confidence and amplitude of Mormons' pronouncements upon their own faith smack of spiritual arrogance and self-complacency. But these tendencies operate in tandem with a powerful countercurrent: salvation is for Mormons an endless project, not an event, and is therefore never complete, never fully attained, never a realized state or object of secure possession. It is, in a word, agonistic—that is, predicated on a process of ceaseless struggle. "The Mormon emphasis is upon action," notes Thomas O'Dea, upon "the vigorous exercise of the will," and even "God's supreme position is understood not in terms of his being a First Necessary Being but rather as a result of a 'conquest.' "[19]

This aspect is as central in Joseph's life and thought as his self-assurance. Every great thinker of the nineteenth century situated struggle at the center of the age's paradigm shift. "Without contraries is no progression," wrote William Blake.[20] Hegel made this principle, of dialectical progression, the heart of his philosophy of history. Marx picked up the theme, as did Darwin in biology and Nietzsche in philosophy. They all saw a world characterized not by the heavenly harmony of the spheres, but by struggle, opposition, dynamic processes and encounters that are generative of all that is good. Joseph did not only apply this paradigm to an ambitious doctrine of personal probation and growth that could culminate in theosis (as we will see in the next chapter), but insisted that struggle, opposition, contestation also describe an intellectual dynamic that moves us ahead in our quest for understanding. "I am like a huge, rough stone rolling down from a high mountain," Joseph said, "and the only polishing I get is when some corner gets rubbed off by coming in contact with something else, striking with accelerated force against religious bigotry, priestcraft, ... the authority of perjured executives ... and corrupt men and women."[21] This is not just a description of his character development, but of his intellectual modus operandi: exploring the limits, challenging conventional categories, and dynamic engagement with the boundaries—all in the interest of productive provocation. Or, as he said more simply, shortly before his death, "by proving contraries, truth is made manifest."[22]

If his revealed doctrines had a common theme, it was their dramatic juxtaposition—audacious or brash or blasphemous opposition, some would say— to the status quo. Joseph knew that it was this collapse of sacred distance, the enunciation of the forbidden, the articulation of the ineffable, the concretization of the abstract, and the invasion of sacred space that characterized both the bane and boon of his calling. "In reply to Mr. Butterfield," he wrote:

I stated that the most prominent difference in sentiment between the Latter-day Saints and sectarians was, that the latter were all circumscribed by some peculiar creed, which deprived its members [of] the privilege of believing anything not contained therein, whereas the Latter-day Saints have no creed, but are ready to believe all true principles that exist, as they are made manifest from time to time.[23]

This resistance to formal creeds, to a closed canon, and to conventional opinion, are all so many versions of resistance to finality, to fixity, or to what he called "circumscription"—being bound and hemmed in by orthodoxy. Elsewhere, he called it "the first and fundamental principle of our holy religion" to be free "to embrace all, and every item of truth, without limitation or without being circumscribed or prohibited by the creeds or superstitious notions of men, or by the dominations of one another."[24]

To one of his friends, he lamented:

[H]e did not enjoy the right vouchsafed to every American citizen—that of free speech. He said that when he ventured to give his private opinion on any subject of importance, his words were often garbled and their meaning twisted, and then given out as the word of the Lord because they came from him.[25]

His insistence that his pronouncements did not always carry prophetic weight was not just a safety net or a convenient means of prudent retreat if things didn't work out. It meant that the process, the ongoing, dynamic engagement, the exploring, questing, provoking dialectical encounter with tradition, with boundaries, and with normative thinking should not be trammeled by or impeded with clerks, scribes, and disciples looking for a final word, interrupting a productive process of reflection, contestation, and creation. Sometimes, it would appear, he just wanted the privilege of thinking out loud, but that is hard to do when one is surrounded by court stenographers with their sharpened pencils. In this regard, he would have seconded the memorable protest of Virginia Woolf: "I should never be able to fulfill what is, I understand, the first duty of a lecturer—to hand you after an hour's discourse a nugget of pure truth to wrap up between the pages of your notebooks and keep on the mantel-piece for ever."[26]

In other words, Joseph's concept of revelatory process paralleled his concept of salvation itself, both being construed as products of ceaseless struggle through which we must engage the universe—and define ourselves morally. It is perhaps a more extreme version of the attitude some of the English Protestants shared, which evoked criticism from the Moravian Peter Böhler. "Our mode of believing is so easy to the Englishmen," he complained to a superior, "that they cannot reconcile themselves to it."[27] Like Faust in his dispute with Mephistopheles, who insisted "once come to rest, I am enslaved," Joseph saw dynamic transformation, not static bliss, as the existential ideal.[28]

It is not just lifelong fidelity to the faith that can be fearfully demanding; Mormonism holds out the promise of a salvation in which any rest is purely metaphorical. Joseph's crowned Saints are no angelic choirs passively basking in the glory of their God, but Faustian strivers endlessly seeking to shape themselves into progressively better beings, fashioning worlds and creating endless posterity, eternally working to impose order and form on an infinitely malleable cosmos. "This is a wide field for the operation of man," said Brigham Young, "that reaches into eternity."[29] "When you climb up a ladder," Joseph explained:

> you must begin at the bottom, and ascend step by step, until you arrive at the top; and so it is with the principles of the Gospel—you must begin with the first and go on until you learn all the principles of exaltation. But it will be a great while after you have passed through the veil before you will have learned them. It is not all to be comprehended in this world; it will be a great work to learn our salvation and exaltation even beyond the grave.[30]

"Learning" salvation, and "beyond the grave" at that? Once again, we see here the emphasis on the acquisition of spiritual knowledge as a determinative factor in spiritual progress, which is ongoing. Salvation becomes a project and a process, not an event. This is again affirmed by Joseph in an 1843 revelation asserting, "Whatever principle of intelligence we attain unto in this life, it will rise with us in the resurrection. And if a person gains more knowledge and intelligence in this life through his diligence and obedience than another, he will have so much the advantage in the world to come" (D&C 130:19). In a remarkable sermon he delivered on the nature of man and human happiness, Brigham Young made the unceasing pursuit of knowledge not just an ingredient in salvation, but the essence of the only joy man will find fulfilling:

> All men should study to learn the nature of mankind, and to discern that divinity inherent in them. A spirit and power of research is planted within, yet they remain undeveloped.... What will satisfy us? If we understood all principles and powers that are, that have been, and that are to come, and had wisdom sufficient to control powers and elements with which we are associated,

perhaps we would then be satisfied. If this will not satisfy the human mind, there is nothing that will. . . . If we could so understand true philosophy as to understand our own creation, and what it is for . . . and could understand that matter can be organized and brought forth into intelligence, and to possess more intelligence, and to continue to increase in that intelligence; and could learn those principles that organized matter into animals, vegetables, and into intelligent beings; and could discern the Divinity acting, operating, and diffusing principles into matter to produce intelligent beings, and to exalt them— to what? Happiness. Will nothing short of that fully satisfy the spirits implanted within us? No.[31]

Salvation as process has other implications. In the eighteenth century, John and Charles Wesley had contended, as many fellow Christians have, over the timing of salvation: "We sang and fell into dispute," Charles recorded in his journal, "whether conversion was gradual or instantaneous. My brother was very positive for the latter and very shocking. . . . I insisted a man need not know when he first had faith."[32] Joseph effectively sidestepped one of the primary theological controversies of his age by reframing the issue. Situating salvation in a distant future, and defining it as an eternal process of transformation rather than an earthly state of justification or sanctification, he took the question of its identifiability out of debate entirely. Brigham Young was emphatic in this same view, and urged patience with those converts new to the Mormon perspective:

It is true that we are continually gathering in new materials—men and women with no experience; these are mixed with those who have been with us for years, and many of them have, apparently, little or no capacity for improvement or advancement; they seem incapable of understanding things as they are; they are as they were, and I fear will remain so. They are first-rate Methodists, and you know they are always the biggest when they are first born. In all their after experience they refer to the time of their religious birth as the happiest moment they ever saw, and are constantly afterwards, as long as they live, praying for and seeking with groans and tears their first love. Instead of this, if they were truly born of God, their path would shine brighter and brighter unto the perfect day.[33]

The consequence of all this for Mormonism is that the certainty of such "conversion" and the lack of closure, of finality about salvation or sanctification, coexist in sometimes uneasy tension.[34] Mormonism invites its adherents to a dauntingly eternal process of self-transformation rather than giving them comforting assurance of blessedness. The prospect of a perfection that must be gradually achieved rather than definitely bestowed (although made possible by Christ's atonement) can be more conducive of feelings of inadequacy than of comfort or complacency. Brigham Young acknowledged as much, when he characterized the gospel as a source of provocation rather than consolation, agonistic struggle with inner failings rather than acquiescence to grace:

> The gospel . . . causes men and women to reveal that which would have slept in their dispositions until they dropped into their graves. The plan by which the Lord leads this people makes them reveal their thoughts and intents, and brings out every trait of disposition lurking in their [beings]. . . . Every fault that a person has will be made manifest, that it may be corrected by the Gospel of salvation, by the laws of the Holy Priesthood.[35]

Perpetual, painful self-revelation and inadequacies ameliorated only through eons of schooling, standing in stark tension with confidently expressed certainties about theological truths and spiritual realities, certainly result in one of Mormonism's most dynamic paradoxes. Latter-day Saints presume to know positively where they came from, why they are here, and where they are headed. But such confidence is paired with the sometimes disheartening personal recognition that salvation itself must wait upon complete personal transformation into a godly individual, the laborious acquisition of an unfathomable scope of knowledge. That which Mormons know, they are sure they know, and personally and institutionally it is beyond compromise or negotiation. But that which they don't know will occupy them in the schoolrooms of the life beyond, says Joseph, for "a great while after passing through the veil." The problem is, in a church almost entirely lacking creeds or formal theology, the two realms—the settled and orthodox, and the unfixed and unfathomed—are not clearly demarcated.

A related tension not always fully visible to outsiders is one in which Mormons publicly express absolute certitude about the great issues of faith and existence, but may privately harbor doubts for which Mormon culture has few avenues of sanctioned expression. All faiths may have their closet doubters. But Mormonism's lay ministry, congregational participation in sermons, public testimony meetings, and highly social, closely knit communities make personal belief fairly transparent, and it is difficult if not impossible to sidestep expressions of conviction in a culture so saturated in the language of religious certainty. Even devout believers are not always comfortable with a discourse so out of tune with the spirit of modernity. "The spirit of liberty is the spirit which is not too sure that it is right," said the jurist Learned Hand.[36] In a world that increasingly associates absolute conviction with religious fundamentalism, extremism, and cultural imperialism, Hand's epistemological humility is the safer theological tone. But Mormon culture today—at least its public face—persists stubbornly in its personal and public expressions of religious certainty, even as its members pursue an educational agenda with an anticipated span of eons. Like the contest between authoritarianism and independence, the uneasy coexistence of certainty and searching spurs vigorous debates in the Mormon intellectual community and provides fodder for artists who both explore and depict the cultural tensions that result.

Doubtless, the certainty side of the paradox presents both intellectual and artistic culture with special challenges. Two examples may suggest the aesthetic loss that prophetic plenitude entails. Malachi, Mormons well know, promised to send Elijah before the great and dreadful day of the Lord, to turn the heart of the fathers to the children and the heart of the children to their fathers (Malachi 4:6). No clear consensus, among Jews or Christians, has emerged as to the meaning of this cryptic prophecy. Mormons are certain that, as Joseph declared, the prediction refers to the literal return of Elijah to the Kirtland Temple, on April 3, 1836, when he transmitted to the Latter-day Prophet priesthood authority to seal families together, beyond death's parting power. On the other hand, Jewish tradition, full of anticipation and yearning, weaves this story:

> At the coming of the great judgment day, the children of the wicked who had to die in infancy will be found among the just, while their fathers will be ranged on the other side. The babes will implore their fathers to come to them, but God will not permit it. Then Elijah will go to the little ones, and teach them how to plead in behalf of their fathers. They will stand before God and say, "Is not the measure of good, the mercy of God, larger than the measure of chastisements? . . . [May they] be permitted to join us in Paradise?" God will give assent to their pleadings, and Elijah will have fulfilled the word of the prophet Malachi; he will have brought back the fathers to the children.[37]

Or one could turn to the dilemma in which medieval Christianity found itself, inheriting both a belief in the necessity for universal baptism and the Augustinian view of children's inherent sinfulness. Following the lead of Thomas Aquinas, the great poet Dante finds the specter of infant damnation intolerable, and fashions in his *Inferno* a medial ground called limbo. It is not the best solution, but it is a memorable one and, ensconced in the supreme artistic effort of medieval Europe, displays such aesthetic and theological appeal that, though never countenanced officially by the Holy See, the doctrine found approbation and acceptance among more than a billion believers.[38]

These illustrations suggest that at least *one* catalyst for high cultural production is relatively lacking in Mormonism: a revelatory vacuum in which artistic imagination responds to the great moral dilemmas of life and ambiguities of doctrine. Latter-day Saints don't claim to have all the answers. But they certainly find themselves in a dispensation whose very rhetoric suggests satiety. Latter-day Saints call this age "the dispensation of the *fulness* of times," allude to Joseph's *restoration* and Peter's prediction of "the restitution of *all things*" (Acts 3:21), refer to truth "flooding the earth," find in the Book of Mormon "the *fulness* of the gospel," and believe its characterization of these latter days, when "*all things* shall be revealed . . . which ever have been among the children of men, and which ever will be" (2 Nephi 27:11). So the Saints may not look to art, as others have done, with the same desperate hope of finding consolation for a heaven that has failed us. Or to flesh out the details of a sketchy and antique revelation. After all, it may seem presumptuous—or at least redundant—to turn to poets when God sends prophets.

It is against this backdrop that Mormonism's obsession with certainty, with plenitude and prophets and gospel fullness, can be intensely sterile ground for the artistic endeavor. So much of the world's great art is produced in the face of loss, of suffering, and of struggle—physical as well as metaphysical. The Latter-day Saints have endured physical hardship. But they do not wrestle much with metaphysical anguish. In spite of the possibilities suggested by both the unfathomable darkness of Gethsemane and the weeping God of Enoch, Mormonism has no patience with a tragic vision, not having learned from the compelling insight of Hegel. Tragedy, the philosopher argued, is not the triumph of evil over good. That is a monstrosity, a perversion, and in mankind's particular history as in the universal conflict, only a temporary chapter now and then. Hegel recognized that in the eternal narrative, tragedy is what happens when good is overcome by another good. And that may well be considered an enduring condition of the universe. "Other things, other blessings, other glories," writes C. S. Lewis, in Milton's shadow and the shadow of Eden. "But never that. Never in all the worlds, that. God can make use of all that happens. But the loss is real."[39]

But if Mormonism is possessed of a relentlessly optimistic theology, it is also characterized by a vision of salvational fullness that is frustratingly, endlessly deferred. Just as is the Zion that Saints hoped (and still hope) to build in Missouri, personal perfection, salvation, even spiritual rest are relegated to a future that seems infinitely remote. Even death does not bring repose or closure to the valiant themselves. Fourth president of the church Wilford Woodruff recorded how, years after the martyrdom of Joseph:

[B]y and by I saw the Prophet again, and I got the privilege to ask him a question. "Now," said I, "I want to know why you are in a hurry. I have been in a hurry all through my life but I expected my hurry would be over when I got into the kingdom of heaven, if I ever did." Joseph said, "I will tell you, Brother Woodruff, . . . so much work has to be done and we need to be in a hurry in order to accomplish it."[40]

Tellingly, Mormons measure their commitment to their church not in terms like "devout," "lapsed," or "believing," but as "active" or "inactive."

Eternal engagement in an eternal process, alongside authoritative restoration and gospel fullness. A theology of endless searching and a rhetoric of stolid certainty. The sobering injunction of Joseph to "search into and contemplate the darkest abyss, and the broad expanse of eternity," given to the same Saints who are reminded that they "are not sent forth to be taught, but to teach the children of men" the truths of the gospel definitively known (D&C 43:15). Joseph may have found his own model for this paradoxical stance in his recovery of a Mosaic text, received as a revelation only months after the Book of Mormon came off the press. In this account, we read of a stupendous vision given to the ancient prophet: "And it came to pass that Moses looked, and beheld the world upon which he was created; and Moses beheld the world and the ends thereof, and all the children of men which are, and which were created; of the same he greatly marveled and wondered." Moses's response to a vision of such plenitude and authority is undoubtedly a newfound certainty and self-assurance. Relative to the vastness of eternity, he acknowledges moments later, "I know that man is nothing, which thing I never had supposed." Thus humbled but armed with knowledge, he fends off a subsequent assault of Satan by affirming resiliently, "behold, I am a son of God, in the similitude of his Only Begotten" (Moses 1:12, PGP).

But the more salient point is that, following his experience of both plenitude and certitude, Moses's appetite is whetted, not sated. "And again Moses said: I will not cease to call upon God, I have other things to inquire of him." And so he does, initiating theophanies of even greater amplitude. It is no wonder that Mormon culture expresses itself in inconsistent bursts of the pat and the provocative, the clichéd and the astonished, the complacent and the yearning. "Art is born of humiliation," said the poet Auden, and it may be in that very space between security born of possessing precious certainties and abject smallness before the magnitude of an almost unquenchable ignorance that Mormonism finds a tension productive of a genuinely religious art and intellectual expression.

~ 3 ~

EVERLASTING BURNINGS
AND CINDER BLOCKS
The Sacred and the Banal

When I saw Joseph Smith, he took heaven, figuratively
speaking, and brought it down to earth; and he took the
earth, brought it up, and opened up, in plainness and
simplicity, the things of God; and that is the beauty of
his mission.

~ Brigham Young

They are busy all the time establishing factories to make
saints and crockery ware, also prophets and white paint.

~ *New York Herald*'s James Gordon Bennett

Human beings do not seem designed for happiness. Generations of divines long
taught that as creatures of God, our primary obligation is obedience and humble
resignation to our subordinate place in the great chain of being. But as rational
creatures with intimations of the eternal, we aspire, Icarus-like, to transcend
earthly constraints and human limitations. The two imperatives inevitably collide. As Jonathan Edwards put the case, we mortals are weighed down with "a
heavy moulded body, a lump of flesh and blood which is not fitted to be an organ
for a soul inflamed with high exercises of divine love.... Fain would they fly, but
they are held down, as with a dead weight at their feet."[1] In the Romantic era of
Joseph's lifetime, this lament became the theme of almost every poet. Byron's
Lucifer taunts the man Cain, because he is a creature of "high thought ... linked
to a servile mass of matter."[2] "Man is of the dust," muses the great Wordsworth,
but "ethereal hopes are his." Nevertheless, "too, too contracted are these walls of
flesh ... for any passion of the soul that leads to ecstasy."[3] "Certain it is that the
soul is eternally craving," writes Chateaubriand, "and the whole universe cannot
satisfy it. Infinity is the only field adapted to its nature."[4] The poet Robert

Browning described the quintessentially tragic human plight more simply as the intersection of "infinite passion, and the pain / Of finite hearts that yearn."[5]

Desperate efforts to break free of the constraints of a rigid moral system can thus be seen as noble struggle or as Satanic rebellion—or as both at the same time. The wonderful tension in Christopher Marlowe's *Dr. Faustus* (1604), the first English-language treatment of the pact-with-the-devil theme, is the result of just such a collision between conventional religious imperatives and a humanistic sensibility coming into its glorious prime. A German treatment had earlier appeared in translation with the instructive title, *The History of the Damnable Life and Deserved Death of Dr. Faustus* (1588). No tension there. Since Eve's first dealings with the serpent, any consorter with demons or devils—however noble the motive—was consigned by universal ecclesiastical opinion to a fiery fate. Marlowe's protagonist, however, elicits a mixed sympathy. His Faust, a professor recently awarded his diploma, has mastered the disciplines of his day—from logic to theology—and now stands like a forlorn Alexander, with no more intellectual worlds to conquer. Possessed of a ravenous soul, he is utterly insatiable—mentally, sensually, and spiritually. Finding no food adequate to his titanic appetite in the paltry morsels of scholastic theology and the college curricula of the medieval world, he accepts the offer of Lucifer's servant Mephistopheles. The demon promises to enlarge Faust's horizons, free him of the constraints of space and time, and "resolve [him] of all ambiguities."

The doctor's eventual fate is just as inevitable and horrid as his German counterpart's. But Marlowe has made us more aware of the painful dilemma we humans face, caught as we are between the demands of faith and the pursuit of knowledge, infinite aspirations and finite limitations, resignation in the face of providence and responsiveness to a felt, unbounded potential. Morality play Marlowe's *Faustus* may be, but it nonetheless hints that the fallen protagonist is really a tragic hero—a victim of the need to choose between two competing goods: faithful submission to God and impassioned embrace of the human.

If the plight of Faustus is tinged with ambiguity, Joseph Smith's ambitious designs for mankind were not. It would be hard to conceive an idea more calculated to offend, more outrageous to Christian dogma, and more hostile to the very cosmology underlying a conventionally theistic universe than the pronouncement of Joseph Smith in a conference address referred to as the King Follett discourse: "You have got to learn how to make yourselves Gods . . . and be kings and priests to God, the same as all Gods have done by going from a small capacity to a great capacity, from a small degree to another, from grace to grace . . . from exaltation to exaltation."[6] The idea that man is a God in embryo was not new with Joseph Smith, of course. The psalmist had written, "ye are gods, and all of you are children of the most High," and Jesus had quoted that verse in John (10:34). Christian writers from Justin Martyr and St. Clement, to Athanasius and Augustine, as well as the modern C. S. Lewis, have articulated some version of the same idea.[7] Most modern theologians take exception to the literal reading Mormons impose upon these parallel pronouncements. They are doubtless correct that Joseph Smith went further than any of his predecessors in the specificity with which he described human potential to acquire a divine nature.

First of all, Joseph does not portray the quest for godlike status as a human ambition that God merely condones. Joseph ascribes to God the intention to shepherd man through the process of theosis, an intention that precedes the very creation of the earth. "God Himself found Himself in the midst of spirits and glory. Because He was greater He saw proper to institute laws whereby the rest, who were less in intelligence, could have a privilege to advance like Himself *and be exalted with Him*," he said.[8]

Second, Joseph explains with startling novelty in just what this exaltation consists:

> Ye shall come forth in the first resurrection . . . and shall inherit thrones, kingdoms, principalities, and powers, dominions, all heights and depths. . . . And they shall pass by the angels, and the gods, which are set there, to their exaltation and glory in all things, . . . which glory shall be a fullness and a continuation of the seeds forever. (D&C 132:19)

Continuation of the seeds, eternal increase, posterity as numerous as the sands of the shore—the essence of exaltation, according to Joseph, is the power to create life endlessly within the context of an eternal family. As one Mormon philosopher has summarized the doctrine, "divine families encircled by his fire and light are the very essence of life and eternal life; without them this earth—indeed this cosmos—will have missed the measure of its creation."[9]

And third, a distinctive feature of Joseph's conception of the divine potential is its intense existentialism, almost naturalism. In other words, salvation cannot be bequeathed through God's grace, if that implies a conception of salvation as something that may be externally bestowed as a gift or reward. Sanctification is strictly connected to self-conformity with laws that are intrinsically transformative. That is emphatically declared by Joseph: "That which is governed by law is also . . . perfected and sanctified by the same. That which breaketh a law, and abideth not by law, . . . cannot be sanctified by law, *neither by mercy, justice, nor judgment*" (D&C 88:3–35; emphasis added). In Mormon thought, as LDS leader Bruce Hafen writes:

> [T]he doctrines of grace and repentance are rehabilitative in nature. The great Mediator asks for our repentance *not* because we must "repay" him in exchange for his paying our debt to justice, but because repentance initiates a developmental process that, with the Savior's help, leads us along the path to a saintly character.[10]

Joseph taught, "If you wish to go where God is, you must be like God, or possess the principles which God possesses."[11]

In another version of this principle, Joseph's Book of Mormon declares that those who exist in a state "contrary to the nature of God . . . are in a state contrary to the nature of happiness" (Alma 41:11). Conformity to immutable laws of holiness, then, is not an arbitrary condition imposed by a sovereign Deity as the price of admission to heaven, but neither is it in any sense a measure of personal merit that earns salvation. It is simply the condition of God himself. Grace is the necessary condition that, in God's primeval design of enabling weak and fallible souls "to advance like himself," makes the entire enterprise possible. Christ's atonement is an unearned gift and indispensable power that makes possible man's repentance and transformation. In this light, commandments result from the fact that "God has given certain laws to the human family, which, if observed, are sufficient to prepare them to inherit this rest."[12] But ultimately, man can achieve conformity to divine law only as a consequence of a fully engaged human will that at no point cedes sovereignty over the self to a higher force.

In the medieval calculus of crime and punishment, only an infinite expiation by a perfect being could counterbalance the infinite hubris of such pretensions to divine stature. Human acceptance of the serpent's invitation to "be as gods" (Genesis 3:5) was the primal instance of human sinfulness. Plato found it unproblematic to assert why the Creator made this world: "He was good, and in him that is good no envy ariseth ever concerning anything; and being devoid of envy He desired that all should be, so far as possible, like unto Himself."[13] But Augustine's astonishment at such aspirations was typical of the general Christian response. "What could be worse pride," he asked, "than the incredible folly in which I asserted that I was by nature what You are?"[14] This audacity was likewise the most heinous of all human evils in Dante's catalog of evil. So profoundly wrong was it, his angelic guide explained, that "Man, in his limits, could not recompense: / for no obedience, no humility, / he offered later could have been so deep / that it could match the heights he meant to reach / through disobedience."[15] As one of Dante's editors paraphrases, "only the act of infinite humility whereby Christ became incarnate and suffered the Passion, could compensate for the infinite presumptuousness of man."[16] True enough, disobedience compounded the crime, but it was this sheer "presumptuousness," the audacity of challenging an unbreachable divide, that motivates a whole tradition of indignation. Jonathan Edwards echoed Dante's horror at human rebellion against a "holiness that was infinitely beyond human standards." This infinite disparity between the human and the divine, he wrote, made the attempt "infinitely evil."[17] Seemingly, only Lucifer's attempted emulation of Deity can equal, as it foreshadowed, such insolence. "I will exalt my throne above the stars of God," Isaiah has the archangel saying (the context refers more immediately to Nebuchadnezzar). "I will sit also upon the mount of the congregation, in the sides of the north: I will ascend above the heights of the clouds; I will be like the most High." As a consequence of this Satanic arrogance, the prophet declares, "thou shalt be brought down to hell, to the sides of the pit" (Isaiah 14:13–15).

Milton and countless other poets and commentators saw those Isaiah passages as a veiled reference to Satan's pre-earthly designs upon the throne of God himself. "I disdained subjection, and thought one step higher Would set me highest," says the bitter fallen angel in *Paradise Lost* (book IV), only to learn that "Who aspires must down as low / As high he soared" (book IX). Christ may have been the second Adam, but Adam was himself a second Lucifer, according to conventional wisdom, in his reenactment of a fall defined as overreaching turned catastrophic. The builders of Babel worked to the same tune. And classical traditions from Icarus to Ariadne to Bellerophon record the recurrent allure of godlike ambitions that precipitate tragedy and divine retribution. Later secular imitators from Faust to the Byronic hero have followed the same pattern—and suffered similar punishment. And so mankind, caught in this impossible bind between an irrepressible hunger for the infinite and orthodox constraints, is forever consigned to a Faustian dilemma that finally erupts in a surge of nineteenth-century rebellion. But Faust, like the Romantic heroes that followed his example, only reinforces through tragic reenactment the entrenched Western sensibility that holds the Creator-creature distinction to be sacrosanct, and any breach—or attempted breach—of that divide to be deserving of the most energetic denunciation and definitive sanctions.

In Joseph Smith's vision, however, a godly destiny is precisely what humans are called to pursue. In theory, the distance they must close is, as Joseph intimated, almost unfathomably immense—the stuff of eternal effort and aspiration. But in practice, the real, actual, and vivid possibility is an occasion for a rhetoric fraught with dangers. In conventional Christian cosmology, God is the origin and source of mankind, but certainly not his future image. In Mormonism, the formula is reversed. God is not the maker of man's soul, he is an eternally coexisting superior being. And man sees in him something very like his own inherent potential. In this new universe where, as Joseph said, God and man are arrayed together on the same side of the equation as "independent principles," the sacred distance at the heart of Western religious experience comes near to collapsing. God is no longer outside human categories of understanding, but the very template for human striving. As LDS prophet Lorenzo Snow so starkly simplified Joseph's radical theology: "As man now is, God once was. As God now is, man may become."[18] Parley P. Pratt elaborated the principle in more sweeping, panoramic fashion:

> Gods, angels, and men are all of one species, one race, one great family, widely diffused among the planetary systems. . . . All these are so many colonies of our race, multiplied, extended, transplanted, and existing for ever and ever, . . . that do now exist or that will roll into order and be peopled. . . . These king-doms present every variety and degree in the progress of the great science of life, from the lowest degradations amid the realms of death, or the rudimental [*sic*] stages of elementary existence, upward through all the ascending scale or all the degrees of progress in the science of eternal life and light.[19]

In so literally embracing the divine potential in man, Mormons ennoble human nature to such a degree that even the most exuberant Renaissance humanists would blanch.

The principal danger here is that the sacred as a category threatens to dis-appear altogether (and with it, perhaps, worshipful reverence). That is because in this model, transcendence is virtually annihilated as a possibility. As the poet Samuel Coleridge put the case, "The very ground of all Miracle is the hetero-geneity of Spirit and Matter."[20] But even this ontological distinction is van-quished by Joseph's unrelenting metaphysical monism: "there is no such thing as immaterial matter. All spirit is matter, but it is more fine or pure, and can only be discerned by purer eyes; We cannot see it; but when our bodies are purified we shall see that it is all matter" (D&C 131:7–8).

The paradox that results from these contrary tendencies is a culture that sacralizes and exalts the mundane even as it naturalizes and domesticates the sacred. That men and women may become Gods is taken literally enough by Mormons to affront the orthodox. And the reality of divine intrusions into the human sphere—of actual heavenly ministrants, celestial epiphanies, miraculous artifacts, is not explained away as myth or metaphor, but brazenly celebrated:

> And again, what do we hear? Glad tidings from Cumorah! Moroni, an angel from heaven, declaring the fulfilment of the prophets—the book to be revealed.
> A voice of the Lord in the wilderness of Fayette, Seneca County, declaring the

three witnesses to bear record of the book! The voice of Michael on the banks of the Susquehanna, detecting the devil when he appeared as an angel of light! The voice of Peter, James, and John in the wilderness between Harmony, Susquehanna County, and Colesville, Broome County, on the Susquehanna river, declaring themselves as possessing the keys of the kingdom, and of the dispensation of the fulness of times! And again, the voice of God in the chamber of old Father Whitmer, in Fayette, Seneca County, and at sundry times, and in divers places through all the travels and tribulations of this Church of Jesus Christ of Latter-day Saints! And the voice of Michael, the archangel; the voice of Gabriel, and of Raphael, and of divers angels, from Michael or Adam down to the present time, all declaring their dispensation, their rights, their keys, their honors, their majesty and glory. (D&C 128:21–23)

Providing access to the miraculous, write two sociologists of religion, is a key component of flourishing religious movements in the modern era.[21] John Greenleaf Whittier noted this same dimension of Mormonism a century and a half ago. The religion spoke, he wrote, "a language of hope and promise to weak, weary hearts, tossed and troubled, who have wandered from sect to sect, seeking in vain for the primal manifestations of the divine power."[22] The Hebrews had an ark with sacred relics to commemorate the reality of a moment when God spoke from a burning bush and made a rod break out in buds. New Testament Christianity was founded on the miracle of the empty tomb. Mormonism had its gold plates and seer stones. Jews and Christians have had millennia to accommodate themselves to the passing of the dispensation of old-fashioned miracles. Mormonism is still young enough for the angel Moroni to seem a near-contemporary. And Mormonism's stolid unwillingness to cede ground on the question of the Book of Mormon's historicity, belief in a living prophet who receives revelation, patriarchal blessings (prayerful pronouncements of the recipient's Israelite lineage and a prophetic statement of his or her life mission), priesthood healings, and magnificent, otherworldly temples reminiscent of Solomon's, where sacred rituals are performed and the mysteries of godliness are unfolded—all of these contribute to an abiding suffusion of the miraculous in LDS religious culture.

On the other hand, this collapse of sacred distance is not without its cost and dilemmas. The most extreme example, of course, would be the obverse of Joseph's claim that man can become like God: "What kind of a being was God in the beginning, before the world was?" he asks, and replies, "God Himself who sits enthroned in yonder heavens [was] a Man like unto one of yourselves—that is the great secret!"[23] If envisioning the theosis of man is presumption, then asserting the human origins of Deity would seem blatant sacrilege. At a minimum, it intrudes terrestrial contexts and aspects into the very definition of Deity.

The pattern persists in a second way that is theologically unusual. Any religion that preaches the impossibility of man's being saved alone could hardly be expected to shy away from the intermingling of the sexes in this sphere. And of course, with the possible exception of Swedenborgianism, Mormonism was perhaps alone among Christian faiths in exalting the marriage relation to a status reserved in the eternities for the inhabitants of heaven. (Perhaps more striking yet, the church may also be alone in its countenancing of the possibility of a married Christ.)[24] In endowing marital love with the highest spiritual as well as eternal value, Joseph Smith followed in a line that stretches at least from Milton, through Swedenborg, and to the eighteenth-century poet/mystic William Blake. "Love not the Heavenly Spirits," asks Milton's Adam of the angel Raphael, "and how their love express they?" To which the angel replies,

> Whatever pure thou in the body enjoy'st
> (And pure thou wert created) we enjoy
> In eminence, and obstacle find none
> Of membrane, joynt, or limb, exclusive barrs:
> Easier than Air with Air, if Spirits embrace,
> Total they mix, Union of Pure with Pure.[25]

Emanuel Swedenborg, the Swedish mystic, posed the question of whether married couples "will be parted after death or live together," and insisted by way of reply that "marital love persists. Two partners usually meet after death, recognize each other, associate again, and for a time live together. . . . If they can live together, they remain partners. . . . Partners enjoy an intercourse like that in the world, but pleasanter and more blessed; but without prolification [offspring]."[26] And for Blake, as the critic Alfred Kazin wrote, sexuality "meant enjoyment framed in wonder";[27] in his inversion of the conventional Christian view, sexuality is not a consequence of fallenness; the shame associated with it is. His dictum that "Shame is Pride's cloak" is not the scandalous provocation of a libertine, but the earnest attempt of a devout Christian mystic to turn back the clock on the Platonization of Christianity, to combat the prudish disdain for God's crowning creation—the human body. "Born between urine and feces" (*Intra feces et urinas nominem natus est*), Augustine reportedly said, with illuminating self-contempt.[28] "The nakedness of woman is the work of God," replied Blake stubbornly.[29]

In its explicit rejection of a triune God "without body, parts or passions," in its embrace of a corporeal Deity, in its conviction that only when spirit is combined with element and "inseparably connected" can humans find "a fulness of joy" (D&C 91:33), and by its association of sexuality with eternal states and relationships, Mormonism embraced the earthly as a sacred sphere and rejected the dichotomies and biases that necessitated a guarded response to worldly pleasures. It is thus a synthesis that Mormonism effects, and not, as O'Dea believed, "a repudiation of spirituality in favor of materiality."[30] "Our organism makes us capable of exquisite enjoyment," remarked Young.[31] But that condition is more than a threatening distraction; it is very much to the divine purpose: "We are to learn how to enjoy the things of life," he would later expand,

> how to pass our mortal existence here. There is no enjoyment, no comfort, no pleasure, nothing that the human heart can imagine . . . that tends to beautify, happify, make comfortable and peaceful, and exalt the feelings of mortals, but what the Lord has in store for his people. He never objected to their taking comfort. He never revealed any doctrine, that I have any knowledge of, but what in its nature is calculated to fill with peace and glory, and lift every sentiment and impulse of the heart above every low, sad, deathly, false and groveling feeling. The Lord wishes us to . . . bid farewell to all that gloomy, dark, deathly feeling that is spread over the inhabitants of the earth.[32]

As one scholar concludes, "the Mormons have spiritualized recreation."[33]

As they spiritualized the physical, so did they eternalize the intellectual. As radical as Joseph's notion that eternal education constitutes the basis of human salvation and fulfillment is his insistence that spiritual and earthly spheres of knowledge are not distinct categories, nor are physical laws and spiritual laws distinct realms. Brigham Young self-consciously emphasized the eradication of such distinctions, believing this cosmic eclecticism was a hallmark of Joseph's approach to learning:

> We are not at all under the necessity of falling into the mistake that the Christian world falls into. They think, when they are handling or dealing in the things of this world, that those things have nothing to do with their religion. Our religion takes within its wide embrace not only things of heaven, but also things of earth. It circumscribes all art, science, and literature pertaining to heaven, earth, and hell.[34]

The consequent imagery could at times be disconcerting in its literalism. "When the elements melt with fervent heat, the Lord Almighty will send forth his angels, who are well instructed in chemistry, and they will separate the elements and make new combinations thereof."[35] Orson Pratt would elaborate this view a few years later:

> The study of science is the study of something eternal. If we study astronomy, we study the works of God. If we study chemistry, geology, optics, or any other branch of science, every new truth we come to the understanding of is eternal; it is a part of the great system of universal truth. It is truth that exists throughout universal nature; and God is the dispenser of all truth—scientific, religious, and political.[36]

Man and God, building bridges and creating worlds, practicing chemistry and endowing the earth with its celestial glory—the mundane and the miraculous are but different degrees on an eternal scale of knowledge acquisition.

This theme runs consistently through Brigham Young:

> How gladly would we understand every principle pertaining to science and art, and become thoroughly acquainted with every intricate operation of nature, and with all the chemical changes that are constantly going on around us! How delightful this would be, and what a boundless field of truth and power is open for us to explore! We are only just approaching the shores of the vast ocean of information that pertains to this physical world, to say nothing of that which pertains to the heavens, to angels and celestial beings, to the place of their habitation, to the manner of their life, and their progress to still higher degrees of perfection.[37]

But there are other palpable, culturally pervasive indications of Mormonism's tendency to thoroughly infuse sacred space with seemingly pedestrian elements, or to conflate heaven and earth. It is everywhere true of Mormons, as it was of their founder, according to Josiah Quincy, that "no association with the sacred phrases of Scripture could keep the inspirations of this man from getting down upon the hard pan of practical affairs."[38] The same prophetic voice of Joseph could one minute dictate revelations of sublime poetry: "The earth rolls upon her wings, and the sun giveth his light by day, and the moon giveth her light by night, and the stars also give their light, as they roll upon their wings in their glory, in the midst of the power of God" (D&C 88:45); and the next, invoke the same revelatory power and authority to declare in the voice of God, "let my servant Oliver Cowdery have the lot which is set off joining the house, which is to be for the printing office, which is lot number one, and also the lot upon which his father resides" (D&C 104:28). Indeed, one researcher found that of 112 revelations announced by Joseph Smith, "eighty-eight dealt partly or entirely with matters that were economic in nature."[39] Jan Shipps was not exaggerating when she described the visible manifestations of Mormonism's assimilation of the banal into sacred projects. The Saints, she wrote, saw their religious imperative as "building up the kingdom and inhabiting it," and the most "expressive worship signs were irrigation canals, or neatly built and nicely decorated houses, or good crops of sugar beets."[40]

Sociologist Armand Mauss has referred to a kindred, perennial tension in Mormonism as "an unending struggle between the angel and the beehive," where the angel, perched atop the Salt Lake and other temples, represents "Mormonism's other-worldly heritage, the spiritual and prophetic elements, eternal ideals, and remarkable doctrines revealed through Joseph Smith." The beehive, by contrast, atop the nearby Joseph Smith Memorial Building, "has since come to be considered primarily as a symbol of worldly enterprise throughout the Mormon heartland," representing Mormon industriousness and economic activity.[41]

Much of the early ridicule and persecution directed against Mormonism was clearly provoked by this unseemly blending and blurring of sacred and secular categories. As the editor James Gordon Bennett noted wryly, Joseph's doctrine— like Brigham Young's subsequent Utah kingdom—made little distinction between the production of saints and crockery. "A spirit or soul that has been conceived and comprehended no longer prompts to 'shuddering' . . . [and] thereby ceases to be of interest for the psychology of religion," wrote Rudolf Otto.[42] But Joseph's claims to dialogic revelation conducted with resurrected beings and with a God of flesh and bones annihilated the sacred distance that lay at the heart of most religious sensibilities. Mockery of his name (" 'Smith!' said Miss Priscilla, with a snort. 'That's a fine name for a prophet, isn't it?' "), of his undignified deportment ("habitual proneness to jesting and joking," fumed one defector), of the concrete, historical details of his alleged scripture ("it furnishes us with the names and biograph[ies] of the principal men . . . , with many of the particulars of their wars for several centuries. But seriously," mocked one reviewer), and of his introducing Pentecost into his modern planned communities ("visions in an age of railways?" laughed Dickens)[43]—these and other complaints pounded home the fact that Americans were not ready to disregard the boundaries that kept heaven and earth apart.

An embodied God must certainly be one of the Mormon doctrines with greatest relevance to a Mormon aesthetics. For it is hard to fall into conventional cultural dichotomies inherited from Plato, which oppose the divine ineffability of spirit to the degraded physicality of flesh, when God himself is seen as a glorified being of flesh and bones. From its theological core, then, Mormonism is ill disposed to maintain a simple hierarchy that privileges spiritual activity over physical, or the contemplative over the active.

But at the same time, the problem this confusion of categories creates in Mormon culture can be challenging for the worshiper. Coleridge thought the miraculous possible only in a dualistic universe. "No mystery, no God," convention and theology alike implied. Or as Friedrich Nietzsche put it more harshly, "votaries of the unknown and mysterious as such, they now worship the *question mark itself* as God" (emphasis in original).[44] If God is shorn of ineffability and transcendence, or is construed in human terms, how does one find the reverential awe that moves one to true worshipfulness? If Jesus is our "big brother," how can he be our Lord and God? Reverence before the Almighty must be freshly conceptualized in such a reconfigured heaven and earth. But the dilemmas for the artist are especially vexing: in a universe devoid of transcendence and sacred distance (at least as conventionally constructed), how can wonder flourish?

To allege that sublime mystery has itself become an idol may be disputable. But no religious historian can contest the trappings of a trend too conspicuous to challenge seriously. From Nicaea to negative theology to the great mystics of Spain and Germany and beyond, religious experience is increasingly tied to unfathomable mystery, and it is our utter intellectual capitulation in the presence of the ineffable that renders such terms as holiness, worshipfulness, and reverence the very essence of religion. Such distance comes close to being the sine qua non of all Western religious faith and practice. Rudolf Otto is emphatic on this point. In *The Idea of the Holy*, he insists that this category of experience, this *mysterium tremendum*, is not merely an attribute of divinity, but "the deepest and most fundamental element in all . . . religious devotion." It is something "beyond conception or understanding, extraordinary and unfamiliar, . . . before which we therefore recoil in a wonder that strikes us chill and numb." In sum, the mysterious is "that which lies altogether outside what can be thought, and is, alike in form, quality, and essence, the utterly and 'wholly other.' "[45]

Such mystery has not traditionally been characterized as merely incidental to God's nature or to our fallen condition. In Emil Brunner's words, "God's revelation of Himself always occurs in such a way as to manifest more deeply his inaccessibility to our thought and imagination. All that we can know is the world. God is not the world. . . . He is Mystery."[46] As Elizabeth Johnson writes:

> The history of theology is replete with this truth: recall Augustine's insight
> that if we have understood, then what we have understood is not God;

Anselm's argument that God is that than which nothing greater can be conceived; Hildegard's vision of God's glory as Living Light that blinded her sight; Aquinas's working rule that we can know that God is and what God is not, but not what God is; Luther's stress on the hiddenness of God's glory in the shame of the cross; Simone Weil's conviction that there is nothing that resembles what she can conceive of when she says the word God; Sallie McFague's insistence on imaginative leaps into metaphor since no language about God is adequate and all of it is improper.[47]

So it is that from the early Middle Ages, the sacred has come to be largely grounded in any number of discontinuities. The sacred is beyond the rational, as in the case of Tertullian's reputed *credo quia absurdum est* (I believe because it is absurd);[48] beyond history, as in the more subtle form of fundamentalism's antihistoricism (the Bible, God's word, is considered outside the normal processes of historical development); or beyond language, as George Steiner explains: "the motif of semantic inadequacy is an ancient one. However artful, however inspired, the words of the poet, of the philosopher, will fall short of the numinous intensities of certain phenomena and states of felt being."[49]

These discontinuities are so many forms by which distance guarantees the sacred's status as sacred. But in one of the great intellectual confluences in Western history, such mystification becomes central to aesthetic sensibility as well. On the eve of the revolutionary intellectual ferment known as Romanticism, Edmund Burke published an essay that took mystery, obfuscation, and darkness out of the limited realm of religious discourse, the only place where (until then) they had extensive legitimacy, and assigned those attributes to what he called "the sublime," launching that redefined category into a central place in the aesthetic and intellectual universe of the eighteenth century. In his 1757 treatise, *A Philosophical Enquiry into the Origin of Our Ideas of the Sublime and Beautiful*, Burke summarized the new sensibility:

> Hardly any thing can strike the mind with its greatness, which does not make some sort of approach towards infinity; which nothing can do whilst we are able to perceive its bounds; but to see an object distinctly, and to perceive its bounds, is one and the same thing. A clear idea is therefore another name for a little idea. . . . It is our ignorance of things that causes all our admiration and chiefly excites our passions.

His reference to a "clear idea" was a blatant dig at thinkers like René Descartes and John Locke, who had considered "clear and distinct ideas" the hallmark and legitimate goal of true philosophizing. Now we leave those ideals behind, and instead enter a world in which Milton is the exemplar, because in his work, "all is dark, uncertain, confused, terrible and sublime to the last degree,"[50] and René Chateaubriand can write rapturously in 1800 that "there is nothing beautiful, pleasing, or grand in life, but that which is more or less mysterious. The most wonderful sentiments are those which produce impressions difficult to be explained"; "Mystery is of a nature so divine."[51]

The stunning success of Romanticism as an intellectual watershed, as a genuine paradigm shift, as a movement of huge cultural appeal and success, is in large part a result of, and an indication of, the near-universal allure of this secularization of religious impulses. The psychologist William James could have predicted all of this. As he wrote in his monumental *Varieties of Religious Experience*, for many humans "richness is the supreme imaginative requirement. The inner need is [for] something . . . complex, majestic in the hierarchic interrelatedness of its parts, with authority descending from stage to stage, and at every stage objects for adjectives of mystery and splendor."[52] In other words, it doesn't much matter if we call it religion, or art, or something else. What we really crave is a source of mystery and splendor.

C. S. Lewis has suggested the enormous psychological investment we have in maintaining as fundamental a distinction as that separating the human and the divine, and hints at the crisis their conflation would occasion. When "the distinction between natural and supernatural [breaks] down," he writes:

> one realize[s] how great a comfort it had been—how it had eased the burden of intolerable strangeness which this universe imposes on us by dividing it into two halves and encouraging the mind never to think of both in the same context. What price we may have paid for this comfort in the way of false security and accepted confusion of thought is another matter.[53]

A few years before Joseph Smith's First Vision, Mary Shelley wrote an allegory about the loss of mystery in the world and a universe suddenly turned monochromatic. The aspiring creator, the young Viktor Frankenstein, grows weary with life in a world of pedestrian science, limited to "realities of little worth." Immersing himself in the occult learning of alchemists and magicians, he yearns, Faust-like, to reach heavenward, to explore and master "chimeras of boundless grandeur." He revels in the abstract contemplation of what he calls the "partially unveiled . . . face of Nature," whose "immortal lineaments were still a wonder and a mystery."[54] The crucial truth he does not yet recognize is that his wonder is inseparable *from* the mystery, his sense of grandeur is dependent *upon* the fact that nature is still partially veiled. In Shelley's version of the story, as Viktor plumbs the hidden secrets of life and constructs his artificial human, it is significant that she describes the creature as having limbs all "in proportion," with features entirely "beautiful."[55] Only when the abstraction, the dream of new life, finds complete incarnation, when the veil of mystery is stripped away and his vision is actualized, embodied, then, Viktor records, "the beauty of the dream vanished."[56] The famous consequence is a creature both unsightly and destructive. To some extent, Shelley's is a novel about the seduction of, and our infatuation with, mystery. It explores the romance of wonder, our trembling before the hidden springs of life and majestic power almost, but not quite, laid bare. And it is a novel about the cataclysmic consequences of eradicating sacred distances, by bringing the fire of the gods down to earth, and elevating man to the status of Creator. It is not for nothing that Shelley subtitled her work, "The Modern Prometheus."

Joseph could also be seen as such a Prometheus, and his collapse of heaven into earth as a work of religious hubris. Where is there room for sacred mystery, awe, and reverence before the ineffably divine in all of this? "The font of genuine thinking is astonishment. Astonishment at and before being," wrote Martin Heidegger.[57] "The mysterious . . . stands at the cradle of true art and true science," Einstein agreed.[58] What, one might ask, will be the effects on cultural expression of a world view shorn of transcendence, ineffability, mystery, and the sublime?

It is possible, of course, to see Joseph Smith as expanding rather than contracting the sphere of the sacred. The emphasis on eternal origins and godlike potential could be said to substitute divine immanence for abstract transcendence. Coming from an infinite premortal past, "trailing clouds of glory," in Wordsworth's expression, humans possess a sublime history rich in wondrous possibilities, occluded by the veil of birth. To assert anthropomorphic deities of flesh and bone is to endow human physicality with unprecedented sanctity. Temples where sacred rituals and ordinances are enacted make the powers of godliness evident in this fallen realm, and create a microcosm of heaven in architectural space. And dialogic revelation, priesthood power, and restoration of charismatic gifts—all immerse believers in a sea of spiritual forces, powers, and manifestations. All that is certain is that, by collapsing heaven into earth, as Young described Joseph's essential mission, the young Mormon Prophet effected a paradigm shift that undermined traditional theological constructs predicated on their opposition. Those inhabiting the theological universe he created find themselves in a place where the sacred, the human, and the divine find new meanings and require new orientations.

~ 4 ~

PECULIAR PEOPLE AND
LONELINESS AT THE TOP
Election and Exile

The Personage who addressed me said that all their
creeds were an abomination in his sight.

~ Joseph Smith

Behold O Lord, the desire of this thy people to go forth
from among the Gentiles, who have sorely persecuted
them all the day long.

~ Orson Pratt

How often have you heard the question, "Are Mormons
Christians?" ... One wonders why there should be the
question.

~ President Spencer W. Kimball

"When the Puritans arrived in America in the early seventeenth century," writes
one historian of philosophy, "they brought not only their strong theological orientation but also tenacious communal impulses, utopian hopes, a sense of being
chosen, and a belief in social and religious exclusivity and uniformity."[1] This
description sounds uncannily prophetic of the Mormon experiment of 200 years
later. The Latter-day Saints also gathered to a physical place of refuge (several
times in succession), initiated a communal society, captured utopian moments and
millennialist glimpses in Kirtland and Nauvoo, heard themselves declared a chosen
people, and differentiated themselves with unique beliefs, practices, and covenants.
But the Mormons reenacted these Puritan aspirations to spiritual exclusivity with a
monumental difference: they did it in the context of a hostile culture consisting of
fellow citizens rather than in the relative isolation of a wilderness refuge. The
Babylon the Puritans left behind was so geographically remote as to be little more

than a rhetorical trope. Their principal adversary in spiritual warfare was a devil whose menace preachers had to assert through harrowing sermons (or who would occasionally reveal his hand through troublesome witches or marauding Indians). Mormon religious difference, on the other hand, was emphatically demonstrated by perennial conflict with neighbors and militia that frequently amounted to bloodshed, and fellow Christians who threatened a very literal extermination. Even once removed to the remote Utah desert, Mormons found themselves besieged by a federal army, federal judges, and punitive federal laws.

The Mormon emphasis on exceptionalism is traceable to the first recorded spiritual experience of the young Joseph Smith. Long before he ever heard the word Mormon, or had an inkling of what his life or ministry would stand *for*, he learned what he was to be set *against*. Having knelt in a wooded grove on his family's farm and inquired of God what church he should join to find salvation, he found that he was not be a fellow traveler with any Christian then alive: "I was answered that I must join none of them, for they were all wrong; and the Personage who addressed me said that all their creeds were an abomination in his sight; that those professors were all corrupt" (JS—History 1:19, PGP). Like many religious revolutionaries, Joseph early saw his relationship to the world in thoroughly adversarial terms: "I was destined to prove a disturber and an annoyer of his kingdom; else why should the powers of darkness combine against me? Why the opposition and persecution that arose against me, almost in my infancy?" From the time he was "an obscure boy, only between fourteen and fifteen years of age," he would later record, "all the sects . . . united to persecute me" (JS—History 1:22, PGP). Less than two years before his death, he would boast that "deep water is what I am wont to swim in. It all has become a second nature to me; and I feel, like Paul, to glory in tribulation" (D&C 127:2). Jonathan Edwards similarly gloried, "I am born to be a man of strife,"[2] and Luther's self-conception was famously an embattled one.

What was different about Joseph's posture was how effectively he imbued an entire people with this same sense of hostile separation from the world. It didn't hurt that he had the weight of scripture to reinforce Latter-day Saint exceptionalism. A revelation received a year after the church's founding declared that Mormonism was "the only true and living church upon the face of the whole earth, with which I, the Lord, am well pleased" (D&C 1:30)—a designation "too low to scorn" in the view of one Baptist preacher writing in 1843.[3] Reformation churches of the era contended vociferously over doctrine and converts, but made virtually no comparably sweeping institutional claims. Such rhetoric was until then largely associated with a church that contemporaries would liken to Mormonism: Roman Catholicism.[4]

But Mormons went far beyond mere allusions to their church as "the only true" one. Early on, Joseph introduced a geographical gathering based on reference to a chosen lineage. Mormons were not unique in this regard; Christians had long seen themselves as spiritual Israel, and religious figures would occasionally insist on going beyond metaphor. (Most famous in this regard, perhaps, was Joanna South-cott and her Christian Israelite movement, but an array of other, smaller movements erupted in the eighteenth and nineteenth centuries.)[5] But as Armand Mauss traces in great detail, "Smith's teachings went beyond those which were generally accepted, among them the importance of literal Israelite lineage, especially from Ephraim."[6] Reading themselves into the biblical promises to a chosen lineage, and buttressed by Joseph's own pronouncements that the Holy Ghost was "more powerful in expanding the mind, enlightening the understanding, and storing the intellect with present knowledge [in] a man who is of the literal seed of Abraham," Mormonism's self-construction into a distinct and chosen group "began a process of expansion," writes Mauss, "that lasted well into the twentieth century."[7] That expansion would come to merge with doctrines of premortal existence to posit a chosen status and assignment to a particular lineage that preceded birth itself. These doctrinal emphases faded by the latter half of the twentieth century, but the cultural vocabulary born of earlier years continues to reinforce difference. Following Book of Mormon cues, Mormons have long employed the word "gentile" to refer to nonmembers, and even though the term is today used with gentle irony by Mormons among themselves, the world is still effectively polarized in Mormon discourse between members and nonmembers.

The Mormon emphasis on covenant making is a powerful tool for articulating and ritually enacting, and therefore reifying, categories of difference. Baptism is common to most Christian groups. However, Mormons undertake additional covenants, embracing higher laws and grand promises, in the temple, where sacred secrecy and the additional selectivity of participants pushes yet further the sense of a people apart. To this day, the Mormon temple concretizes Mormon exceptionalism by the practice, perhaps unique in modern Christendom, of physically isolating a kind of spiritual elect in their own domain, while holding the rest of the world at bay, through strictly enforced admission procedures involving worthiness tests. Mormons are certainly justified in emphasizing that temple practices are sacred rather than secret, but that does not diminish the effect on participants: the knowledge that they are privy to "higher" obligations and truths, which must not be publicly shared, cannot but heighten self-awareness of their difference from the Christian (and even other Mormon) masses. The effect on everyone else is the obverse. The alienating secrecy and exclusivity of the temple ceremonies become the fodder of speculation, ridicule, or resentment.

In Mormonism's early years, differences could also be the product of diverse cultural backgrounds as much as a language of religious elitism. As the Missouri settlers complained in their explanation of regional tensions in the 1830s:

> They are eastern men, whose manners, habits, customs, and even dialect, are essentially different from our own.... The religious tenets of this people are so different from the present churches of the age, that they always have, and always will, excite deep prejudices against them in any populous country where they may locate.[8]

For Mormon leaders, as for religious zealots in any age, the friction of difference could be a positive sign of the blessedly persecuted. "I am satisfied that it will not do for the Lord to make this people popular," said the ever-pugnacious Brigham Young. "Why? Because all hell would want to be in the church. The people must be kept where the finger of scorn can be pointed at them."[9] The stark difference between the chosen and the excluded is more than a sign—it is a shaping influence on those who come to inhabit Zion; therefore, the difference is a measure of the church's spiritual health and the individual's spiritual prospects. As Joseph's brother Hyrum proudly pronounced, "Men's souls conform to the society in which they live, with very few exceptions, and when men come to live with the Mormons, their souls swell as if they were going to stride the planets."[10]

Hostile outsiders were happy to cooperate in the construction of Mormon difference; two physicians delivered a paper at the meeting of the New Orleans Academy of Sciences in 1861, in which they described (in most unflattering terms) the components of the new Mormon "racial type."[11] Today, Mormons have their own entry in the *Harvard Encyclopedia of Ethnic Groups*. That is a sign of both success and loss in Mormonism. Success, because any covenant people without the actions or fruits or special character that betoken their status as a "peculiar people" may be said to have failed in those covenantal practices that are the mark of their distinction from a fallen world. Mormons have certainly succeeded in becoming recognizably distinct. Loss, because an evolved cultural identity may be taken to suggest elitism, a gaze and culture more attuned to the self than the other, an impetus toward what is insular and exceptional rather than what is universal and fraternal.

In a historical context, for example, persecution may be a marker of blessedness, but the time may come when opposition can threaten to undermine the very possibility of the whole program of Christian regeneration and Zion building. The individual may lay down his life in the comfort that his sacrifice has purchased eternal life. But if the institution or movement is itself eradicated, then a selfish martyrdom has little redemptive value in the larger context. In the 1880s, crippled by the antipolygamy crusade, Mormonism teetered on the brink of just such total disintegration. Leaders were in prison or in hiding, the political franchise had been revoked, church assets had been confiscated, and worse measures loomed ahead. If the temples were appropriated or desecrated, a major purpose of the restoration would fail: the ordinances considered to be absolutely necessary for salvation of the living and the dead would cease entirely, and earth would again fall into spiritual blight.

At least, that was the rationale of God's decision to revoke the law of polygamy, according to church president Wilford Woodruff.[12] At the same time, the long-running campaign for statehood required that Mormons prove themselves to be true-blue Americans, in spite of pervasive journalistic, fictional, and political depictions of the Mormons as ethnically distinct. Lumped variously with Chinese or Irish immigrants, vaguely "oriental" people, or a "new race" bred of polygamy, Mormons faced decades of derision as an alien viper on the American family hearth.[13] Establishing affinities with the dominant culture was suddenly necessary to guarantee the church's survival and ability to serve as a force for good.

Theologically, other reasons had always existed to emphasize universalism over particularism.[14] Not only God's figurative Fatherhood, but his literal role as the Father of all human spirits made the universal brotherhood of man a truth that extended for Mormons into an infinite past in which the entire human family jointly inhabited the same primeval world. And when he revealed that "the same sociality that exists here, will exist in the eternal world" (D&C 130:2), Joseph was affirming the fact that heaven is constructed out of a web of human relationships that extends infinitely in every direction. By the time his work was done, he had laid the groundwork for men to be sealed to their wives across the eternities. For parents to be sealed to their children, and their children's children, and to their parents, and their parents' parents, across infinite generations. And for friends to be bound to friends in a great assembly and church of the firstborn. This was not just incidental to the restoration, it was its primary purpose. "It was my endeavor," Joseph wrote, "to so organize the Church, that the brethren might eventually be independent of every encumbrance beneath the celestial kingdom, by bonds and covenants of mutual friendship, and mutual love."[15] Today, a vigorous program of family history research aspires to link all descendants of Adam in a vast family tree. And finally, for a church that fields the largest number of missionaries in the Christian world, common bonds with peoples and races throughout the world are to some degree an ideological precondition and an idealized aspiration.

The Mormon sense of uniqueness and exile is thus counterbalanced with a theology, rituals, and research programs that aspire to universal integration. This conflict between exclusivity, on the one hand, and, on the other, a moral imperative (not to say primal longing) for universal community and acceptance in a larger fellowship is manifest at many levels of Mormon culture. Most ironic, perhaps, is the dilemma in which Mormons find themselves with regard to the community of Christian churches. After predicating their very existence on the corruption of all other Christian faiths ("I was answered that I must join none of them, for they were all wrong"), and asserting their unique claim to be its "only true" embodiment, Latter-day Saints are chagrined when they are excluded from the very community of believers they have just excoriated. In May 2000, the United Methodist Church passed a resolution insisting that the Church of Jesus Christ of Latter-day Saints "does not fit within the bounds of the historic, apostolic tradition of Christian faith," citing "radically differing doctrine on such matters of belief as the nature and being of God; the nature, origin, and purpose of Jesus Christ; and the nature and way of salvation." The Presbyterian Church U.S.A. and the Southern Baptist Convention have passed similar resolutions. The Vatican declared Mormon baptisms to be invalid in 2001.[16] Latter-day Saints react to such announcements with hurt and shock. Mormon apologists write books in which they respond with an emphatic yes to the rhetorical question, "are Mormons Christian?" or make the case so strongly that they can ask with no small irony, "are Christians Mormon?"[17] This is in some ways curious, since Mormons tend to endorse the view of Jan Shipps, who has written that Mormons have the same relationship to Christianity that early Christians had to Judaism.[18] And this without seeming to realize that, at some point, early Christians stopped being offended when they were no longer considered Jewish.[19]

The physical congregating in Utah ceased as the official program of the LDS church a century ago, but leaders still inculcate in young and old alike the imperative to maintain discernible difference. President Spencer W. Kimball encouraged (female) members to be "seen as distinct and different—in happy ways—from the [people] of the world."[20] Gordon B. Hinckley, current prophet and president of the church, has shown a fondness for the words of Peter, believing they serve as both characterization of and challenge to the Latter-day Saints: "Ye are a chosen generation, a royal priesthood, an holy nation, a peculiar people" (1 Peter 2:9). He can also use less apostolic language on the subject. "We're not a weird people," he said to interviewer Mike Wallace.[21] Such peculiarity is reinforcing as a boundary marker but, as the latter comment reveals, it can be a hindrance to bridge building, to missionary work, and perhaps most poignantly, to Mormons who must engage the world as participants in a human community that increasingly transcends Utah's boundaries.

In the case of proselytizing, even the LDS missionary program has alternated between periods where the emphasis is on Christian commonalities, and missionaries begin the catechism of students of Mormonism (investigators) with a lesson on the role of Christ, and periods where the emphasis is on Mormon distinctness from the Christian tradition, at which times the First Vision of Joseph Smith is the introductory lesson. The church has scolded members and the media alike for avoiding the official designation Church of Jesus Christ of Latter-day Saints in preference for the simpler "Mormonism," but the overwhelming persistence of the term by Mormons themselves may indicate not just verbal economy, but pride in a label that emphasizes cultural identity over Christian commonality.

Artists and intellectuals are notorious for participating in a kind of cultural cosmopolitanism that undermines the solidarity of nationalist, provincial, or tribalist agendas (hence their summary dispatch in so many revolutionary upheavals). Nazi science and Maoist art are but two extreme examples of the grotesque consequences of self-imposed isolation from the larger currents of intellectual and cultural life that transcend national boundaries. In the case of early Mormonism, persecution, isolation, survival, and the absence of prior models all helped to dictate the terms of cultural borrowing. However, as the twentieth century neared, Mormonism's relationship to the wider culture grew less inhibited, more complex, and more subject to negotiation. The Saints were still called to be a chosen people, but the physical gathering was at an end. Integration into the wider society meant Mormon identity was both more indistinct and more vulnerable to contamination.[22] The larger world was still a corrupt Babylon, but Joseph's open eclecticism ("we will claim truth as ours wherever we find it") meant some borrowings were not only allowed, but mandated. Individually and institutionally, Mormons continue to work through the paradox of an existence that is both Eden and exile, that embraces difference even as it yearns for integration.

The tension between Mormon clannishness and Christian brotherhood is echoed in a parallel tension that exists between American provincialism and Mormon internationalization. Observers from Leo Tolstoy to Harold Bloom have seen Mormonism as the quintessentially American religion.[23] The intensely American flavor of Mormonism is rooted in a plethora of circumstances. Joseph revealed that Spring Hill, in Daviess County, Missouri, was the abode of Adam and the place of his future return (D&C 116; 117:8). The Book of Mormon related how "the Spirit of God . . . came down and wrought upon [a] man; and he went forth upon the many waters, even unto the seed of my brethren, who were in the promised land"

(1 Nephi 13:12). Columbus, according to the LDS gloss of this passage, was thus divinely inspired to discover the land of America. Later, Joseph taught, God would establish "the Constitution of this land by the hand of wise men whom [he] raised up unto this very purpose" (D&C 101:80).

David Whitmer related to a *Chicago Times* reporter in the late nineteenth century that "three times has he been at the hill Cumorah and seen the casket that [at one time] contained the tablets, and the seer-stone. Eventually the casket had been washed down to the foot of the hill, but it was to be seen when he last visited the historic place."[24] Mormonism, in other words, literally emerged from American soil, even leaving behind physical traces of the process. And as Joseph taught on the expedition known as Zion's camp, the plains were littered with the remains of Nephite and Lamanite warriors. America was thus read by early members as a physical map on which the sacred history of the Book of Mormon unfolded.

Perhaps the most quoted passage from the Book of Mormon in early church publications was Ether 13:4–8: "Behold, Ether saw the days of Christ, and he spake concerning a New Jerusalem upon *this* land.... Wherefore, the remnant of the house of Joseph shall be built upon this land; and it shall be a land of their inheritance; and they shall build up a holy city unto the Lord, like unto the Jerusalem of old."[25] Not just the Latter-day church, but, as the Tenth Article of Faith affirms, "Zion will be built upon this [the American] continent." So from Eden to Columbus to Book of Mormon history to founding fathers to the church's founding to the establishment of a future Zion, America is the stage on which God unfolds the central acts in his divine drama of world history.

Certainly, identification of Mormonism with "the American religion" finds ample validation in the intensely American complexion of its scripture and Joseph's prophetic pronouncements. So it is not just a historical rootedness, but Mormonism's theologies of place that make the internationalization of Mormonism particularly daunting. But by the new millennium, LDS church growth had already turned English into a minority language, and Americans into a minority population within an increasingly Latin American church. At the same time, leaders have long been insisting, as President Harold B. Lee did in 1971, that "it's not just an American church—this is the Church of Jesus Christ in all the world."[26] Founding history, demographics, and doctrinal content conspired to give the church an intensely American complexion. Negative impressions of America abroad, growth of the international membership, proselytizing aspirations in new missionary markets, and enthusiastic dreams of becoming a world religion now conspire to forge a rhetoric of Mormonism as a universal church.

Prepared or not to make the transformation from an American into a truly multinational church, in other words, Mormonism is de facto becoming one. The complication that inheres in this polarity, however, is the difficulty of sorting out exactly which aspects of Mormonism are essential constituents of the faith and which are expendable features deriving from American culture. Because America *does* have a doctrinally rooted role in Mormon theology, and because the church was nurtured for a century and a half in a predominantly American setting, the two cultures have become imperceptibly fused.

Mormon leaders have addressed the other side of the equation, as when Apostle Dallin H. Oaks preached that "the traditions or culture or way of life of a people inevitably include some practices that must be changed by those who wish to qualify for God's choicest blessings."[27] Cultural particularism, in other words, must make way for gospel universals. But the more vexing question may be, what aspects of Mormonism are themselves culturally particular rather than theologically essential? This is a question that pertains not just to matters of faith and practice, but to matters of cultural expression. Because art and intellect, like worship, can suffer from both embracing too much and embracing too little. In balancing covenantal obligations with life in Babylon, dangers lurk in both directions. Exclusivity can produce pride, self-righteousness, and spiritual sterility. But at the same time, to accept and esteem everything is to value nothing. (Only an auctioneer can equally appreciate all art, said Oscar Wilde.)

The ancient Israelites, millennia earlier, were faced with a similar challenge. They too were imbued with a belief that they were "an holy people unto the Lord thy God . . . chosen . . . to be a special people unto himself, above all people that are upon the face of the earth" (Deuteronomy 7:6). Yet exclusivity and self-sufficiency are hard to maintain through a history of bondage, occupation, and the realpolitik of international affairs. Israelites found a powerful solution and set a precedent for resolving the tension as they prepared to depart Egypt. At God's urging, the fleeing Hebrews availed themselves of their captors' "jewels of silver, and jewels of gold, and raiment," and thus accrued the heathen materials that they would mold and fashion into the accoutrements, wealth, and resources of their civilization-in-exile (Exodus 3:22). Centuries later, artists and intellectuals of Europe would justify their emulation of pagan models by reference to this archetypal "spoiling of the Egyptians."

In the dispensation heralded by Joseph Smith, the Saints were, like the Hebrews before them, commanded to "stand independent above all other creatures beneath the celestial world" (D&C 78:14). At the same time, as Young declared, "we believe in all good. If you can find a truth in heaven, earth or hell, it belongs to our doctrine. We believe it; it is ours; we claim it."[28] So, like their exiled predecessors, without the benefits of social stability, abundant resources, or a prosperous prehistory, Mormons were surrounded by the cultural riches of a host society that offered both temptation and promise. Once again, the challenge would be to exploit the accoutrements of that host culture without suffering contamination or loss of mission and identity in the process. The difficulty in "spoiling the Egyptians" has ever been the same: to turn the plundered riches into temple adornments rather than golden calves.

PART II

THE VARIETIES OF MORMON CULTURAL EXPRESSION

Beginnings (1830–1890):
The Dancing Puritans

There is some of the smartest and best men and women
here there is in the world, They dress superior to your
New Salem people [even] if they have had to winter in
log cabins.

> ~ Ursulia B. Hascall to Colonel Wilson Andrews,
> from Camp of Israiel [*sic*], Winter Quarters,
> Indian Territory, April 1847

The pioneers are commonly the off-scourings of civilized society.

> ~ Ralph Waldo Emerson

Even as he endeavored in 1836 to "expose . . . these palpable impositions of the
apostles of Mormonism," the Reverend Truman Coe confessed that "candor
obliges me to say" of the Kirtland Saints that "some are enterprising and intelligent, conversant with the bible, and fond of reading: and here, I apprehend,
many who have heard of them only by common report, are mistaken; supposing
them all to be ignorant and degraded, and beneath the notice of all respectable
people."[1] These "common reports" had dogged the Smith family in New York,
and followed the Saints as they moved west from Ohio into the Missouri frontier.
There, in 1833, the paradox unfolded of these same religious refugees who, even

as they expressed dismay at finding border society to be primitive and uncouth, found themselves demeaned to the governor by old locals as "the very dregs" of society, "lazy, idle and vicious."[2] In the initial stages of the Mormon conflicts, the Saints would lose the public relations campaign. And to the sting of widespread, slanderous characterizations would be added the humiliation of enforced destitution, exile, and isolation from the trappings of civilized society. It was difficult to insist on one's cultural pedigree and state of refinement while living in log huts and subsisting on corn meal and wild roots. Hascall's defiant boast to her comfortable, well-fed New England relatives therefore has as much pathos and hurt pride as bravado.

This contested cultural status of the displaced Saints is just one context that adds an important dimension to understanding what was at stake in the Mormon cultural production of those early decades. Self-vindication was not the primary motive and objective for Mormon art and intellectual activity—but it was an important factor, as is clear from the "so there!" attitude that trumpeted accomplishments ranging from an incipient university in Nauvoo to an opulent theater in early Salt Lake City. Defensiveness was still apparent forty years after Utah's settlement, when a church editor admitted:

> The education and training of the young men, owing to the unfavorable circumstances of a new country, had not been such as to cultivate intellectuality among them, or to clothe their manners with too much grace. They ... found their amusements in other than intellectual pursuits, causing some of the older inhabitants to have grave fears for the future.[3]

In addition to affirming intellectual and cultural identity in those formative generations, brass bands, singing schools, amateur drama, and the ever-present dancing were also healthy distractions from hardship and persecution, as well as powerful affirmations of both Joseph Smith's and Brigham Young's gospel paradigm, which embraced vibrant physicality along with spiritual discipline.

"THE GLORY OF GOD
IS INTELLIGENCE"

Mormons and the Life of the Mind

What is the Divine Spirit? Is the Holy Ghost any other
than an Intellectual fountain? . . . To Labour in Knowledge is to Build up Jerusalem.

~ William Blake (to the Christians)

The glory of God is intelligence.

~ D&C 93:36

In these respects we differ from the Christian world, for
our religion will not clash with or contradict the facts of
science in any particular.

~ Brigham Young

"It sounds strange to hear of a church having a 'location,'" remarked Charles
Dickens of the Mormon gathering, "but a 'location' was the term they applied
to their place of settlement."[1] The physical congregating of nineteenth-century
Mormons served many purposes: literal enactment of a prophesied gathering of
the righteous; the mustering of persons and resources sufficient to construct holy
temples in which sacred ordinances could be performed; creation of a Zion people
separated from the world by distinctive practices and united by shared values and
beliefs, all pertaining to a higher, or celestial order; and the establishment of a
communitarian system replicating the communalism of first-century Christians.
But Joseph Smith proposed yet another purpose, little commented upon by scholars or observers. "Intelligence is the great object of our holy religion," he declared.
And intelligence, he continued, "is the result of education, and education can only
be obtained by living in compact society. . . . One of the principal objects, then, of

our coming together, is to obtain the advantages of education; and in order to do this, compact society is absolutely necessary."[2]

The state of American education in Joseph Smith's era was lamentable. As one historian of education remarks, "there were few public schools in 1825, and those that did exist were of low esteem and generally hard beset."[3] The great era of America's "educational awakening," as this historian calls it, began in the same years that Mormonism appeared on the scene. In a country and era where 93 percent of the people lived on farms, Joseph's youthful experience was typical.[4] His family history refers to sporadic schooling; though his older brother Hyrum was fortunate enough to board for a time at an academy in Hanover, New Hampshire, Joseph and the younger children were lucky to have occasional attendance at a common school. The academy was generally a private or semi-private school where tuition-paying boys boarded; by 1800, it had largely come to replace the old Puritan-favored, tax-supported, and classically oriented grammar schools that catered to more privileged or ambitious adolescents. Common schools at the time were highly uneven attempts to offer young children universal access to free education; they would become increasingly standardized and professionalized in the great common school reform of the 1830s and 1840s, largely under the national leadership of Horace Mann.

As a rural farm boy in upstate New York, Joseph was not unusual in putting family obligations and financial imperatives ahead of formal schooling. Even while in his early adolescence, he would later remember, he was "under the necessity of obtaining a scanty maintenance by his daily labor."[5] By his later teens, he and his brothers habitually hired themselves out at times and for stretches that rendered school attendance altogether impossible. One might expect such origins to foster an indifference if not disdain for book learning and the life of the mind. But Joseph's heritage revealed eruptions of intellectual aspirations in spite of penury and lives of manual labor. His grandfather Solomon Mack had published as a chapbook his own "highly readable" spiritual autobiography,[6] and his hardscrabble-farming father had once been a schoolteacher. This family background typifies if it does not explain Joseph's—and Mormonism's—comfortable accommodation of the pragmatic and the contemplative. "He seemed much less inclined to the perusal of books than any of the rest of our children," remembered his mother, "but far more given to meditation and deep study."[7] The statement is curious, initially hinting as it does of an indifference toward books, but actually suggesting that it was the casual or cursory he shunned. Deep study rather than perusal characterized his mind.

From America's beginnings, education was deeply intertwined with religion. "Puritans stressed the importance of reading and writing," writes one historian, "because they believed that each person should be able to encounter God's word through Bible reading, advised the reading of printed sermons and religious treatises, encouraged the taking and review of sermon notes, and valued keeping a spiritual diary."[8] In addition to the importance of general literacy and access to the word of God, Puritans stressed the necessity for shepherds of the people to have the intellectual qualifications and academic credentials necessary to "rightly divide the word of truth," to effectively teach and preach to a literate congregation. Most of the first religious immigrants to America were literate; in fact 130 alumni of Oxford, Cambridge, and Dublin universities emigrated to New England before 1646.[9] By the next year, 1647, Massachusetts laws mandating local teachers for small towns and grammar schools for larger ones ensured that education would continue as the handmaiden of religion in the new colony.[10]

In the next century, as religious diversity grew throughout the new republic, debates about the value of education in American life continued to focus on the academic training deemed necessary for clerics. The implications of these debates were profound, since whatever value clergy placed on academic training and the varieties of secular knowledge translated into more pervasive attitudes about the worth of education generally.

The Presbyterians, true to their Puritan roots, were maintaining their allegiance to high educational standards for ministers. In 1827, for example, one western presbytery examined a candidate over a two-day period as follows:

[P]roceeded to examine Mr Holeman on the Greek & Latin languages, which was unanimously sustained. . . . Further proceeded to the examination of Mr Holeman as to his knowledge of Rhetoric, Logic, Natural Philosophy, Philosophy of Mind, Geography & Astronomy, all which were sustained unanimously as parts of trial. . . . Then assigned Mr Holeman as further subject of trial a Latin exegesis on the following words. *An sit Christus vere Deus* & a critical exercise on Heb. VI. 4–8, inclusive.[11]

As the numbers of Baptists and Methodists outstripped those of the Presbyterians and Congregationalists, the elitism and intellectualism of Puritanism increasingly found its counterweight in a frontier ethos that paid much less attention to scholarly attainments in the ministry. In part, this shift was a consequence of a postrevolutionary distrust of or outright hostility to professional clergy—"priests" and "priestcraft"—but other factors were operative as well. In the Methodist case, church growth far outstripped the availability of trained clergy. (By 1840, the Methodist Episcopal church was the largest in America, with over a million members.) Though he was personally concerned about the Christian education of children, Wesley acknowledged that the dearth of qualified teachers could not easily be remedied by the new class of Methodist preachers, since compared to their better-trained Anglican peers and bishops, "they have not weight or light enough." Still, he insisted, in the words of his biographer, "what they lacked in learning they more than made up in piety."[12] Consequently, in 1755, Wesley declared the requirement for episcopal ordination "an entire mistake" and commissioned preachers by putting his hand on their head, handing them a New Testament, and saying, "Take this authority to preach the gospel."[13] His colleague Francis Asbury (eventually the first Methodist bishop in America) was even more determined to avoid the "evils" of "human learning" in the ministry, though the denomination's position had softened by Joseph Smith's day. In fact, in 1816, the American Methodist Episcopalians broke with their English counterparts, in part over this very issue. On that occasion, American delegates at a Baltimore conference officially voiced their insistence that "although a collegiate education" was not "deemed essential" by the Wesleyan Methodists, "every one . . . who would be useful as a minister in the Church, should, to a sincere piety and laudable zeal for the salvation of souls, add an ardent desire for useful knowledge." Consequently, to counteract the "manifest indifference of some who remain with us to this important branch of ministerial duty," they were recommending that "it be the duty of the bishop or bishops, or a committee which they may appoint in each annual conference, to point out a course of reading and study proper to be pursued by candidates for the ministry."[14]

As for the Baptists, as early as 1746 the Philadelphia Association officially responded to a "Query from the church of Philadelphia: Whether it be lawful or regular for any person to preach the gospel publicly without ordination? Answer: that which we have both rule and precedent for in the word of God, is, and must be, both lawful and regular."[15] Their skepticism about the merits or appropriateness of education for the ministry is apparent in the fact that, by 1823, only 100 of 2,000 of their ministers were beneficiaries of liberal education.[16] The early Campbellites, contemporary with Joseph, similarly rejected ordination as necessary for the ministry. Suspicion rather than simple pragmatism was the reason. Alexander Campbell himself would write:

[T]he scheme of a learned priesthood chiefly composed of beneficiaries, has long since proved itself to be a grand device to keep men in ignorance and bondage; a scheme by means of which the people have been shrewdly taught to put out their own eyes, to fetter their own feet, and to bind the yoke upon their own necks.[17]

Most of the primitivist movements spawned across the country as protests against mainline Christianity were of a similar mind. As one historian writes, "usually each group was led by a layman or a man with limited clerical training who was influenced by a strong, anticlerical bias."[18]

So nineteenth-century America had become a checkerboard of educational as well as religious diversity, exhibiting the entire spectrum of clerical credentials. As an Illinois gazetteer stated the case in 1834:

> [T]he qualifications of the clergymen are various. A number of them are men of talents, learning, influence, and unblemished piety. Others have but few advantages in acquiring either literary or theological information, and yet are good speakers and useful men. Some are very illiterate, and make utter confusion of the word of God.[19]

In this environment, Joseph was not unusual in presuming to inaugurate a new religious movement with no training and little formal education. And as a prophet, of course, his authority was manifest to followers in his spiritual gifts and in the tangible fruit of those gifts, namely, the Book of Mormon, not in his scholarly revision of Christian theology. The prophetic tradition has never paid allegiance to the fountains of earthly knowledge; seminaries are not prone to produce seers. Lack of schooling is not generally a handicap to one such as Joseph who belongs to a restorationist rather than reformationist tradition. "I can take my Bible," he told his mother while still a youth, "and go into the woods and learn more in two hours, than you can learn at meeting in two years."[20]

What is surprising in the case of Joseph Smith, then, has nothing to do with his lack of educational or professional credentials. The pervasive currents of anticlericalism; the popular appeal of frontier religions, with their greater orientation toward the charismatic and emotional rather than the rational or intellectual; Joseph's particular claims of authority rooted in the miraculous rather than in human institutions or even *sola scriptura*—all of these conditions made his intellectual or academic background almost entirely uncontroversial.

What is surprising, rather, is how quickly Joseph would nonetheless turn to incorporate the intellectual with the mystical, ancient learning with modern revelation, formal schooling with heavenly authority, making of the new faith an amalgam that Harold Bloom has called "a purely American gnosis."[21] The label can be misleading in the case of Mormonism since, unlike the ancient Gnostics, Mormons do not believe that knowledge—a secret knowledge bestowed upon an elite, privileged few—displaces Christ as the means of salvation. But Mormons are profoundly gnostic in a related sense. Thomas O'Dea astutely discerned the logic of Mormonism's emphasis on intellectual growth a half-century ago: "the Mormon definition of life makes the earthly sojourn basically an educative process. Knowledge is necessary to mastery, and the way to deification is through mastery, for not only does education aid man in fulfilling the present tasks, it advances him in his eternal progress."[22] The theological foundations of this view Joseph would not fully elaborate until his famous 1844 King Follett discourse, in which the Mormon God emerged fully fashioned as a being who was not the source of all knowledge and truth, but was an exalted, perfected man possessing all knowledge and truth. Therefore, Joseph explained to his probably stunned audience, "You have got to learn how to make yourselves Gods" by following the same process of incremental development, "till you are able to sit in everlasting burnings and everlasting power and glory as those who have gone before, sit enthroned."[23]

This pronouncement hints at why emphasis on Mormonism's more esoteric roots is a misdirection. In late 1983, a letter purportedly written by Joseph's associate Martin Harris surfaced that connected Mormonism's beginnings to a tradition of folk magic and superstition. The document proved to be a forgery, but it added fuel to the search for ancient, arcane roots of Joseph Smith's thought, which continues unabated.[24] D. Michael Quinn fleshed out the culture of folk magic in early America and Joseph Smith's background in particular in his 1986 study.[25] John L. Brooke explored more hermetic antecedents to Mormonism in his 1994 work, noting the "striking parallels between the Mormon concepts of coequality of matter and spirit, of the covenant of celestial marriage, and of an ultimate goal of human godhood and the philosophical traditions of alchemy and Hermeticism, drawn from the ancient world and fused with Christianity in the Italian Renaissance."[26] Literary critic Harold Bloom has remarked on the striking parallels between the writings of Joseph and ancient Jewish mystical texts (Kabbalistic writings), saying, "I can only attribute to his genius or daemon his uncanny recovery of elements in ancient Jewish theurgy."[27] "What is clear," he continues:

> is that Smith and his apostles restated what Moshe Idel, our great living scholar of Kabbalah, persuades me was the archaic or original Jewish religion.... My observation certainly does find enormous validity in Smith's imaginative recapture of crucial elements, elements evaded by normative Judaism and by the Church after it. The God of Joseph Smith is a daring revival of the God of some of the Kabalists [*sic*] and Gnostics, prophetic sages who, like Smith himself, asserted that they had returned to the true religion.... Either there was a more direct Kabalistic influence upon Smith than we know, or, far more likely, his genius reinvented Kabala in the effort necessary to restore archaic Judaism.[28]

Few if any of the parallels noted by scholars in this field have been advanced to the category of influences, since Joseph's access to or familiarity with such ancient sources is difficult to prove and doubtful at best. ("It is not entirely clear how hermeticism might have been conveyed from late-sixteenth-century Europe to the New York countryside in the early nineteenth century," Brooke himself acknowledges.)[29] And while they may provide fascinating parallels and tantalizing suggestions of source material for elements of Joseph's scriptural production and temple rituals, such antecedents register little to no lasting significance for Joseph's intellectual development or for the intellectual trajectory of Mormon culture. The role and content of the knowledge that Joseph makes central to Mormon theology is neither mysterious nor cryptic. Knowledge is primarily to be painstakingly acquired the old-fashioned way: slogging through textbooks, learning languages, attending lectures, and culling the best of modern science.[30]

This conflation of divine and secular categories is essential in the development of a Mormon intellectual tradition. Religious institutions may choose to dictate the proper sphere and limitations of worldly learning, as they did in the days of Galileo (and perhaps among biblical fundamentalists today). Or they may choose to emphasize the incommensurate scope of those domains. Religion and science ask different questions, and thus cannot be in contradiction, seems to be the modern consensus, especially among the more liberal-minded theologians and believers of many persuasions. Such facile dichotomies trouble prominent biologist Richard Dawkins, who dismisses as specious

> the argument that religion and science operate on separate dimensions and are concerned with quite separate sorts of questions. Religions have historically always attempted to answer the questions that properly belong to science. Thus religions should not be allowed now to retreat away from the ground upon which they have traditionally attempted to fight.[31]

Mormonism similarly rejects the distinction, but for rather different reasons. Mormonism's insistence that "all things unto [God] are spiritual," that spirit is simply "more fine or pure matter" (D&C 29:34; 131:7), and that God is an exalted man effectively eradicates such binary thinking and predicates not just a compatibility, but a thoroughgoing interpenetration of sacred and secular truth. In this last regard in particular, and simply extrapolating from Joseph's King Follett remarks, Brigham Young asserted that Mormonism "embraces all truth and every fact in existence . . . and the sciences are facts as far as men have proved them. . . . The Lord is one of the most scientific men who ever lived; you have no idea of the knowledge he has with regard to the sciences."[32] Young's successor would similarly assert this model of eternal, intellectual eclecticism: "it embraces every principle of truth and intelligence pertaining to us as moral, intellectual, mortal and immortal beings, pertaining to this world and the world that is to come. We are open to truth of every kind, no matter whence it comes, where it originates, or who believes in it."[33]

Resurrection from the dead, and justification—or absolution from the damning effects of our own sins—are made possible only by the atonement of Jesus Christ, Mormons believe. But essential to fully acquiring the "divine nature" and a life like that of God is the patient, steadfast, laborious acquisition of all knowledge. And this particular brand of perfectionism, which incorporates the sacred and the worldly and which reconciles certainty with ceaseless searching, is the pattern that Joseph initiated and emulated almost from the foundations of Mormonism.

The King Follett discourse and temple rituals were a long way in the future when Joseph organized the church in April 1830. But his first concrete steps toward inculcating intellectual values were not. In June 1831, a little more than a year after the church's organization in Fayette, New York, Joseph received a revelation instructing him that the city of Zion was to be built in the land of Missouri. Joseph arrived there in mid-July, and on the twentieth the Lord revealed to him that the sacred site of Independence was "the land of promise, and the place for the city of Zion," with "a spot for the temple . . . lying westward" (D&C 57:2–3). On August 3, 1831, Joseph dedicated the parcel of land for what was planned as the first temple of the restoration, a type of building that in its subsequent incarnations would be the most holy edifice in the new faith, a locus of spiritual manifestations, covenant making, and the most sacred rituals. But on the day before this temple site was consecrated by prayer, the foundations of another building were laid. Twelve men, in honor of the twelve tribes of Israel, carried the first log for a schoolhouse, "as a foundation of Zion."[34] It was following that ceremony, not the one establishing a site for the temple, that Joseph's associate Sidney Rigdon consecrated the land of Zion. A school, not a temple, launched the millennial enterprise.

Joseph then returned to Kirtland, Ohio, where he resumed work on a project he had begun almost immediately after publishing the Book of Mormon: a "new translation" of the Bible. It was during this process that Joseph took another decisive step in his synthesis of the prophetic and the intellectual. In the course of his revisions, which he made on an inspired rather than scholarly basis (he worked with no original manuscripts), he produced revelations which purported to reproduce entire stretches of ancient writing. In June 1830, he had revealed one such account of "the words of God, which he spake unto Moses at a time when Moses was caught up into an exceedingly high mountain" (Moses 1:1,

PGP). Over the next eighteen months, he added to his expanding canon almost fifty other revelations on topics of contemporary relevance, and began to organize them for a publication planned for November 1831. Meanwhile, he continued to devote the bulk of his efforts to the work on the Bible—which undertaking he considered so important he called it "a branch of his calling."[35] Significantly, he had produced the 500-page Book of Mormon in about three months of spontaneous, unrevised dictation. And yet he would labor intermittently on biblical interpolations and edits from June 1830 until July 1833, and come to only a provisional termination then.[36] By that date, Joseph had made a momentous shift in his approach to biblical study.

Just at the moment when Joseph was finishing his work on the New Testament, and before he returned to reconsider his Old Testament "translation," he pronounced his 1832 "olive leaf" revelation, in which he announced the inauguration of a "school of the prophets" to be held in a temple built for that (and other) purposes (D&C 88). The name School of the Prophets had been used for a college formed in Wales (at Trevecka) in 1768 for the training of Methodist clergy. It is doubtful that Joseph knew of the precedent, but his modest program did share some of the ambitious breadth of a college curriculum. In January 1833, on the second floor of the Newel K. Whitney store, the school commenced operation. In those cold, drafty chambers, fourteen elders and high priests undertook to study

> things both in heaven and in the earth, and under the earth; things which have been, things which are, things which must shortly come to pass; things which are at home, things which are abroad; the wars and perplexities of the nations, and the judgments which are on the land; and a knowledge also of the countries and of kingdoms.

To this course of study was shortly added the injunction to "become acquainted with all good books, and with languages, tongues, and people" (D&C 88:79; 90:16). So in the School of the Prophets, Joseph and other men studied the scriptures and theology—but also German and eventually Hebrew. (Parley P. Pratt led a Missouri version of the school that summer.)

The significance of this development was not that it suggested an effort to breed a class of Mormon intellectuals. But neither was it a simple effort to catechize Mormon men in the principles of Joseph's new gospel, in preparation for their missionary labors. True, initially the focus was on scripture and doctrine, and each daily session included ritual foot washing and a ritual salutation. But secular subjects like government, geography, and current issues were included in the day-long curriculum led by Orson Hyde, and the school would go on to become in some ways a fairly conventional effort to provide adult education along the model pioneered only a few years earlier in Millbury, Massachusetts, when Josiah Holbrook's program of adult education courses inaugurated the lyceum movement in America. That development gave impetus to a virtual mania across America for programs of self-improvement. In the second quarter of the nineteenth century especially, one historian writes:

> [T]he [educational] ferment wrought so actively as to generate a numerous, heterogeneous brood of systems, plans, and institutions, ... [including] school systems, ... mechanics' institutions, lyceums, societies for the diffusion of knowledge, mercantile associations, library associations, book clubs, reading associations.[37]

The Saints in Kirtland, as later in Nauvoo and Utah, were thus participating in a mass movement through their adult school, which would eventually flower into myriad intellectual initiatives.

The real meaning of Joseph's School of the Prophets, however, is to be fathomed from its timing and growing direction in the context of his own prophetic career: *after* the youthful leader had established his credentials as Prophet and translator, *after* he had personally manifested his power to reveal the fullness of saving truth directly from heaven, and *after* he claimed receipt of the authority to perform all saving ordinances in the new church. At that moment when he had powerfully demonstrated to his followers the irrelevance of priestly training, clerical degrees, and scholarly credentials, he changed modus operandi in midstream. For while he had in the past translated "reformed Egyptian" and the New Testament by dint of his unaided spiritual gifts, he would in the future "translate" much of the Old Testament and, beginning in 1835 when he acquired some Egyptian mummies and accompanying papyri, "translate" Abraham's Egyptian writings even as he studied the Hebrew language and labored to fashion his own Egyptian grammar. It is to this two-pronged approach that we may trace the Mormon paradox of a culture of spiritual certainty—a group embrace of a rhetoric of absolute self-assurance about spiritual truths—coexisting with a conception of education as the endless and eternal acquisition of the knowledge that leads to godhood.

The School of the Prophets' first session lasted only a few months, and it then reopened in November 1834 with two divisions. The School of Elders focused on theological training for missionary work—with a focus on seven Lectures on Faith, which were given canonical status by their inclusion in the Doctrine and Covenants the next year. In the other division, which became Kirtland High School, nearly 100 students studied Burdick's *Arithmetic*, Kirkham's *Grammar*, and Olney's *Geography*.[38] In January, classes moved to the temple, befitting the sacral status that study was being given by Joseph. The session lasted until March 1835 with another winter session the following year, adhering to the pattern of dismissing school for spring plantings and convening when the cold winter months precluded farm labor and most missionary service. In an expanding curriculum, philosophy, literature, and history were added to the course of study. In the second session, Joseph turned his interests toward the Hebrew language.

In early November, Joseph contracted as an instructor Dr. Daniel Peixotto—a Jewish physician from nearby Willoughby College—and sent Oliver Cowdery to New York for relevant materials. Cowdery returned on the twentieth, recorded Joseph, "bringing with him a quantity of Hebrew books, for the benefit of the school. He presented me with a Hebrew Bible, Lexicon, and Grammar, also a Greek Lexicon, and Webster's English Dictionary." The next day, Joseph "spent the day at home, in examining my books, and studying the Hebrew alphabet." Fired with enthusiasm for the subject, but deeming their present teacher to be inadequate to the task, Joseph recorded that he attended Hebrew class the next night and made arrangements to replace Peixotto with a better-qualified scholar named Joshua Seixas.[39]

Under the tutelage of this one-time Hebrew instructor at Oberlin College and the Western Reserve College, what Joseph referred to as the Hebrew school got seriously under way in late January 1836. Seixas contracted to teach forty students, but the number quickly grew to eighty and beyond, organized into four classes that met six days a week. "Spent the day reading," "spent the day studying German," and "spent the day studying Hebrew" became common entries in Joseph's journal over the ensuing weeks. "O may God give me learning, even language; and endue [*sic*] me with qualifications to magnify His name," he prayed.[40] But while he prayed he also labored. In February, he would record with marked enthusiasm:

> [I] attend[ed] the school and read and translated with my class as usual, and my soul delights in reading the word of the Lord in the original, and I am determined to pursue the study of languages until I shall become master of them, if I am permitted to live long enough, at any rate so long as I do live I am determined to make this my object.[41]

His zeal was contagious. Heber C. Kimball recollected:

> [S]chools were initiated for the use of the Elders and others. Some studied grammar and other branches. We also employed the celebrated Hebrew

teacher Mr Seixas, who gave us much insight in a short time into that language. The first presidency, the twelve, the bishops, high councilors and Elders and church had been previously commanded to seek learning and study the best books, and get a knowledge of countries, kingdoms, languages &c, which inspired us with an untiring thirst after knowledge.[42]

John Hess observed, "at that time Joseph was studying Greek and Latin. When he got tired studying, he would go and play with the children in their games about the house, to give himself exercise. Then he would go back to his studies."[43] As a visiting elder from Missouri enthused, Joseph inspired the Saints with "an extravagant thirst after knowledge."[44] Although the course was relatively short in duration, a number of the students achieved a high degree of proficiency. Orson Pratt, for instance, received a certificate from Professor Seixas certifying his qualifications to teach the language.[45]

Even enemies and otherwise critical outsiders were impressed with the success of Joseph's intellectual agenda. In spite of the impoverished condition of converts and immigrating New York Saints, noted one such observer:

[T]he Mormons appear to be very eager to acquire education. Men, women and children lately attended school, and they are now employing Mr. Seixas, the Hebrew teacher, to instruct them in Hebrew; and about seventy men in middle life, from twenty to forty years of age, are most eagerly engaged in the study. They pursue their studies alone until twelve o'clock at night, and attend to nothing else. Of course many make rapid progress. I noticed some fine looking and intelligent men among them.... They are by no means, as a class, men of weak minds.[46]

Indeed, Joseph managed to gather to his inner circle a modestly impressive group of men, with a concentration of educational backgrounds unusual in a frontier setting. In addition to his own father, his close associates Oliver Cowdery, Sidney Rigdon, William E. McLellin, and Orson Hyde had all taught school prior to the church's organization. Of the first eighty converts to the fledgling faith identified by profession, eleven were schoolteachers and fifteen were doctors or lawyers.[47] One such gifted early convert was Orson Hyde, whom Joseph chose as a teacher for his School of Prophets and also to be one of the Twelve Apostles in the new church. He was born in 1805, the same year as Joseph. Orphaned young, he determined upon a rigorous course of self-improvement as a young man. His description of that process is a window into a special type—the self-educated man of the frontier:

[F]eeling my great deficiency in learning, I resolved to go to school. Accordingly, I took up my abode in Mentor, [Ohio,] in the house of Elder Sidney Rigdon, and began the study of English grammar under his tuition. Elder Rigdon took unwearied pains and care to instruct me in this elementary science. . . . After spending several months in this way, studying day and night, I went two quarters to the Burton Academy and placed myself under the tuition of the preceptor, Reuben Hitchcock, Esq. (since judge of the court). Here I reviewed grammar, geography, arithmetic and rhetoric; then returned to Mentor and spent one season with a young man by the name of Matthew J. Clapp, at his father's house, where the public library was kept. Here I read history and various other works, scientific and literary.[48]

One year later, Hyde was himself a schoolteacher in nearby Florence. He joined the church in 1831. Even more renowned as an early intellectual light of Mormonism was Orson Pratt (1811–1881). Also one of the church's original apostles, he acquired his early education through common schools and a boarding academy, and was teaching school in Kirtland the year of his call to the Twelve. Lacking any advanced formal training, he nonetheless became proficient as a published scientist and mathematician. Although his contributions were not spectacularly original, his achievements are the more impressive for his autodidacticism. (Though clearly hyperbolic, non-Mormon scientist Richard Anthony Proctor's reference to Pratt as one of the four real mathematicians in the world is striking.)[49] He was without a doubt the leading intellectual of Mormonism's first generation.

Orson Pratt was baptized by his brother Parley P., who had secured a copy of the Book of Mormon and joined the church in the fall of 1830. With even less formal education than his brother, Parley would prove to be an equally dynamic popularizer and systematizer of LDS doctrine. A fourth associate who would be pivotal in establishing Mormonism as a system was William W. Phelps (1792–1872). An experienced newspaperman, he had edited the *Western Courier* in New York, the *Lake Light* in Trumansburg, and the anti-Masonic *Ontario Phoenix* in Canandaigua, before joining the church a year after its founding.

One of the most highly educated first-generation Mormons was Wilford Woodruff, who after finishing common school attended an academy for four years, where he studied classical languages along with chemistry, mathematics, and other advanced subjects.[50] Converted to Mormonism in 1833, he left on a mission a year later. In the midst of preaching throughout the Tennessee Valley, he still found time, his journal records, to study Hebrew, English grammar, and a book on deism. Returning to Kirtland after his mission, he resumed his study of Greek and Latin in 1836.[51]

Even more advanced in his training was Lorenzo Snow, who joined in that same year, 1836. His sister Eliza remembered him as

> ever a student, at home as well as in school, (most of his schooling after his twelfth year was during the winter terms,) his book was his constant companion when disengaged from filial duties; and when sought by his associates, "hid up with his book" became proverbial. With the exception of one term in a High School in Ravenna, Ohio, also a special term of tuition under a Hebrew professor, he completed his scholastic training in Oberlin College.[52]

It wasn't just leaders and missionaries whom Joseph wanted to benefit from education. The Latter-day Saints were unusually progressive on the subject of female education as well. Through both informal and formal channels, female Mormons found access to educational opportunities. Sarah Kimball, for example, who would go on to become a well-known intellectual, suffrage crusader, and women's leader, attended the School of the Prophets alongside the men while still a teenager. Although women didn't participate in the Hebrew school, they seem in some cases to have benefited at one remove. Caroline Crosby, for instance, was instructed daily by her husband upon his returning from the Hebrew school—and she eventually acquired reading proficiency.[53] And girls were admitted to the Kirtland High School, even though Eliza R. Snow ran her own "select school" for young women as well. A few years later, a Judge Thorp of Clay County, Missouri, witness to the migration of Mormons into Illinois, would observe that the LDS women were "generally well educated and as a rule were quite intelligent."[54] In 1842, this general issue was explicitly broached when a Nauvoo lyceum was held on the question, "Should Females be educated to the same extent of Males?" The verdict is not known, but is implicit in county records showing that over half the students enrolled in Nauvoo's schools were female. It has even been suggested that the Mormons' liberal views on the equality of the sexes were in part responsible for hostility to the church in Illinois.[55] High schools accepting girls in this decade were still not the rule; in Cleveland, Ohio, for instance, girls were admitted in 1847, but "against the protest of the principal."[56]

To ensure intellectual development and literacy among the rising generations, the Saints undertook in Kirtland the establishment of a public school system. Other denominations were coming to recognize their responsibility—and opportunities—in this regard. An 1816 General Conference of Methodists, for example, issued a resolution for each annual conference to establish a school, but as one historian remarks, "hostility to educational projects was still strong enough to paralyze all efforts to put the resolution into effect."[57] The western

Baptists, the same source reports, were so hostile to education that "most Baptist meetings there did not dare to have even Sunday schools," and faith and secular culture would be seen as incompatible for some time to come.[58] Efforts were more successful in the next generation, as public education gained momentum.

The Latter-day Saints, initially at least, seem to have been united in their appreciation for the benefits of secular education. In June 1831, Oliver Cowdery and William McLellin were commanded in a revelation to "do the work of printing, and of selecting and writing books for schools in this church, that little children may also receive instruction" (D&C 55:4). Initially, the few established schools in the Kirtland area were adequate, but as the gathering drew hundreds of converts to the area, the Saints needed to establish their own.

The first such institution, as we saw, broke off from the School of the Prophets and was called the Kirtland School (later, the Kirtland High School), opening in late 1834. The first modern high school had opened a bare thirteen years earlier in Boston, offering a general, nonclassical curriculum to sons of "the mercantile and mechanic classes" twelve years and older.[59] New York followed in 1825, and by 1827, Massachusetts attempted to legislate free high school education throughout the state, but succeeded only three decades later. Kirtland's high school shared a curriculum similar to those public schools, and was opened to such enthusiastic response that more children of all ages enrolled than could be accommodated. In February 1835, a reduced class of 100 began instruction under William McLellin. Penmanship, arithmetic, English grammar, and geography were taught initially. History, Latin, and the classics were later added. By the winter of 1836–1837, classes were meeting in the attic story of the temple, and the 140 or so students were divided into three divisions: juveniles were taught by Elias Smith, the advanced students by Marcellus F. Cowdery, and Greek and Latin were taught to adults by Professor H. M. Haws. The latter especially attracted a number of LDS leaders. "I then attended the Kirtland high school and commenced the study of the Latin language. I continued this employment until May [1837]," recorded Erastus Snow.[60] George A. Smith remembered studying *Jacob's Latin Grammar* in the same era, and Wilford Woodruff noted in his journal, "Feb 1st I again commenced School confining myself to the Latin language mostly."[61]

Journals of the era make reference to a number of other opportunities for education. In addition to such evening classes as those in geography and writing, one pastime of the Saints brought together the intellectual and the pragmatic in entertaining fashion—and this was the art of debate. It is hard to say exactly when the art of public oratory began its rapid cultural decline in America, but it was in full bloom in the mid-nineteenth century. Joseph himself apparently engaged in the art from his youth, according to the recollection of a (generally unsympathetic) contemporary, who grudgingly paid tribute to both Lucy Mack and Joseph. "The mother's intellect occasionally shone out in him feebly," Orsamus Turner recalled, "especially when he used to help us solve some portentous questions of moral or political ethics, in our juvenile debating club, which we moved down to the old red school house on Durfee street, to get rid of the annoyance of critics that used to drop in upon us in the village."[62] In Kirtland, Joseph mentioned several occasions on which he attended debates—which often became marathon sessions. In November 1835, he found

> some of the young Elders were about engaging in a debate on the subject of miracles. The question—"Was it, or was it not, the design of Christ to establish His Gospel by miracles?" After an interesting debate of three hours or more, during which time much talent was displayed, it was decided, by the President of the debate, in the negative, which was a righteous decision.[63]

A few weeks later, he was again attending such an event, this time as a participant in what he referred to as his brother William's debating school, usually held at his father's home. The topic this time addressed the question, "Was it necessary for God to reveal Himself to mankind in order for their happiness?" Joseph took the affirmative position, but was called away "while listening with interest to the ingenuity displayed on both sides."[64]

Joseph noted after one of these oratorical encounters that there was too "much warmth displayed, too much zeal for mastery, too much of that enthusiasm that characterizes a lawyer at the bar, who is determined to defend his cause, right or wrong."[65] His concerns were more than vindicated a few days later, when he returned to his brother's house for a continuation of the debate earlier interrupted. William Smith, apparently a supporter of the losing side, was insistent upon a rematch that same evening. Consequently,

> some altercation took place upon the propriety of continuing the school [debate] fearing that it would not result in good. Brother William Smith opposed these measures, and insisted on having another question proposed, and at length became much enraged, particularly at me, and used violence upon my person, and also upon Elder Jared Carter, and some others, for which I am grieved beyond measure, and can only pray God to forgive him, inasmuch as he repents of his wickedness, and humbles himself before the Lord.[66]

In Nauvoo, debates became a standard feature of social and intellectual life. Joseph recorded, in February 1842, that he spent the evening attending a debate, then added that "at this time debates were held weekly, and entered into by men of the first talents in the city, young and old, for the purpose of eliciting truth, acquiring knowledge, and improving in public speaking."[67]

Clearly, debates afforded an excellent exercise in logical thinking and expression. Joseph valued the practice, that his followers "might improve their minds and cultivate their powers of intellect in a proper manner."[68] But it was also, of course, a powerful proselytizing tool, in an age when religious controversies were routinely subjected to the judgment of public spectators to these contests between oratorical gladiators. In 1837, for instance, the Catholic archbishop John Baptist Purcell faced off against the popular preacher Alexander Campbell in Cincinnati, in a match that came to be known as "The Battle of the Giants." Mormons prided themselves on their ability to best any and all sectarian comers. While doing missionary work in the Isle of Man in 1840, John Taylor's success was such that a "Staunch Wesleyan" wrote to an editor to lament "such a wholesale conversion to Mormonism [as] was never before witnessed in any town or country," apparently resulting from a public debate between Taylor and Methodist representatives. The outcome was apparently lopsided. "What will become of poor Mr. Hays, that nice and humble man, who so nobly stood forward to expose the errors of the Mormon system," wondered the stupefied Wesleyan. As for the defeated Reverend Thomas Hamilton, we have only Taylor's words, written in either honesty or modesty: the victory, he wrote, was "No great honor, however, as he was a very ignorant man."[69]

Another typical instance was recorded of Orson Hyde, who reluctantly accepted a challenge with a clergyman to a public debate in front of "an acre" of people. After several hours, the cleric withdrew in exasperation. Hyde remarked of his undignified exit:

> The priest did not appear to think half so much of his scurrilous books, pamphlets and newspapers, when he was gathering them up to take away, as when he brought them upon the stand. Their virtue fled like chaff before the wind. About forty persons were baptized into the church in that place (Scarborough [Canada]) immediately after the debate.[70]

There may be instances of Mormon failure in these forums, but as a rule their skills seem to have been formidable. One Bostonian asked:

> Where is the priest that dare meet the elders of the Mormons on any of these questions? I have heard Elder Page, time and again, publicly challenge the whole clergy of Boston to meet him on any of these questions, using their own

hall free of expense, the Bible being the rule of evidence, and where is there one that dare do it?[71]

With the removal of the church to Nauvoo in 1839, the educational agenda became even more ambitious. At the time of Mormon settlement there, only one in six children in the upper Mississippi Valley had access to public education; in Illinois, as few as one in fourteen actually attended school.[72] The availability of free schools, the costs of private ones, and the requirements of farm work—all factored into the equation. In Hancock County, where Nauvoo was located, a number of schools quickly sprang up to accommodate the influx of converts and refugees, supported by a mix of private, county, and city funds. Public records and private journals reveal an extremely fluid educational scene, with as many as eighty teachers initiating subscription schools, seminaries, institutes, and other educational forums.[73] Warren Foote, a sometime coach driver and furniture maker, found twelve students and set up a school a short distance east of Quincy.[74] Eliza R. Snow initiated a three-month curriculum above Nauvoo's Masonic Lodge.[75] Joseph and Adelia Cole advertised tuition rates for twelve-week quarters in their Nauvoo Seminary, held in a room above Joseph Smith's store: reading, writing, and spelling were a packaged bargain at $2, but the course in astronomy cost twice that. Harold and Martha Coray were so successful with their school that they rented the 150-seat capacity Music Hall, and nearly filled it.[76] Some standardization of the common schools was introduced in early 1841, when the city council transferred their supervision from itself to the chancellor and regents of the University of Nauvoo.

The university had been organized shortly before. A state-issued charter of 1840 granted the city the right to "establish and organize an institution of learning . . . for the teaching of the Arts, Sciences, and Learned Professions, to be called the 'University of the City of Nauvoo.'"[77] Church sponsorship of higher education was becoming common at this time. After Dartmouth College defended itself against state takeover in 1816, private colleges proliferated—adding 100 new institutions to the nation's numbers by midcentury.[78] Most of these were one-building affairs, run by churches largely for the training of clerics—but not all of them. The Illinois Conference of Methodists had formed McKendree College in 1834. Methodists had also inaugurated Wesleyan in 1831, Allegheny in 1834, and Indiana Asbury in 1837. (Of course, creating their own universities was a virtual necessity for the Methodists. In Indiana, for instance, they petitioned the legislature for representation on the Presbyterian-controlled board of Indiana University. Legislators dismissed the petition, feeling "there was not a Methodist in America with sufficient learning to fill a professor's chair.")[79]

The University of Nauvoo was founded in an era when, as Richard Hofstadter writes, most colleges were "precarious little institutions, denomination-ridden, poverty-stricken . . . in fact not colleges at all, but glorified high schools or academies that presumed to offer degrees."[80] Like the Methodists, the Mormon example demonstrated that some churches could sponsor education entirely apart from ministerial interests. Nauvoo University had no campus, but it was still a university in more than aspiration. Joseph himself described his ambitions for the project in January 1841:

> "The University of the City of Nauvoo" will enable us to teach our children wisdom, to instruct them in all the knowledge and learning, in the arts, science and learned professions. We hope to make this institution one of the great lights of the world, and by it and through it to diffuse that kind of knowledge which will be of practicable utility, and for the public good, and also for private and individual happiness.[81]

A few weeks later, the city council organized the university with the appointment of a board of trustees, "to-wit—John C. Bennett, chancellor; William Law, registrar; and Joseph Smith, Sidney Rigdon, Hyrum Smith, . . . [and twenty others], Regents of the 'University of the City of Nauvoo.' "[82] The university also had a president (James Kelley) and a building committee. Though several men served as professors, Orson Pratt was the most accomplished and soon emerged as the primary force behind the university. W. W. Phelps called Pratt the "gauge of philosophy,"[83] and he probably had no intellectual equal in Mormonism's first century. He was an astronomer as well as a mathematician, and later conducted observations from an adobe observatory that he built in the shadow of the rising Salt Lake Temple in 1869. Other teachers included Sidney Rigdon and Orson Spencer, who was a college and seminary graduate.

The building committee served more to organize the campus than to build it; most monies of the impoverished Saints went to the temple, and in any case, educational purposes appear to have been part of the design of many of Nauvoo's major structures. "We hope to accomplish much by a combination of effort, and a concentration of action," Joseph recorded, "and erect the Temple and other public buildings, which we so much need for our mutual instruction and the education of our children."[84] As it turned out, many edifices lent themselves readily to an effectual campus: the Masonic Hall, the Concert Hall, the Seventies Hall,[85] the red brick store, and the unfinished temple, as well as private homes. The ambitious curriculum included courses in chemistry, geology, several areas of mathematics, literature, philosophy, history, religion, music, and foreign languages (German, French, Latin, Greek, and Hebrew). Solidifying the sense of a genuine milestone in Mormon intellectual aspirations, Mormon poet Eliza R. Snow even dedicated a poem to the students of the new university called "The Gem and the Tool," which concluded:

> That tool requires a skilful hand—
> That gem, no charm should bind;
> That tool is Education, and
> That gem, the Human Mind.[86]

Three honorary degrees were given to two prominent editors and a lawyer. The editors were John Wentworth of the *Chicago Democrat* and James Gordon Bennett of the *New York Herald*, who wrote with mock enthusiasm: "Wonders never cease. Hereafter I am James Gordon Bennett, Freeman of the Holy City of Nauvoo, LL.D. of the University of Nauvoo . . . with the fair prospect of being a prophet soon, and a saint in Heaven hereafter."[87] The honor was also extended to James Arlington Bennett, a New York attorney and friend to the church.

Although classes were held for at least three years, and one scholar indicates that regular degrees were conferred as well, it is likely that growing harassment, expanding missionary activity, and the 1844 death of the Prophet would have made classes irregular and graduation infrequent.[88] Nonetheless, the effort under such circumstances was audacious, and the presence on the Illinois frontier of a city of religious refugees with such educational zeal impressed at least one outsider. An artillery officer observed with alarm the growing presence around Nauvoo of thousands of "warlike fanatics." Even so, he enthused:

> [E]cclesiastical history presents no parallel to this people, inasmuch as they are establishing their religion on a learned footing. All the sciences are taught, and to be taught in their colleges, with Latin, Greek, Hebrew, French, Italian, Spanish, &c., &c. The mathematical sciences, pure and mixed, are now in successful operation, under an extremely able professor of the name of Pratt, and [James Kelley,] a graduate of Trinity College, Dublin, is president of their University.[89]

In addition to a theology linking intelligence to spiritual growth, Joseph was motivated in his zeal for learning by his belief in the service that antiquities especially could render to the cause of Zion. The church had paid a Pennsylvania entrepreneur a hefty $2,400 for four Egyptian mummies and various scrolls of papyri in 1835. Out of Joseph's study of those documents emerged the Book of Abraham. Then in late 1841, Joseph first learned of John Lloyd Stephens's explorations of the Yucatan, and his discovery there of magnificent ancient ruins. Joseph was quickly convinced that the find "corresponds with & supports the testimony of the Book of Mormon."[90] Clearly, Joseph must have thought, the study of antiquities was both productive and supportive of new scripture and saving gospel truths. Confidence in this particular link between secular and spiritual knowledge found expression in a city newspaper announcement in mid-1843:

> According to a Revelation, received not long since, it appears to be the duty of the members of the Church of Jesus Christ of Latter Day Saints to bring to Nauvoo their precious things, such as antiquities, . . . as well as inscriptions and hieroglyphics, for the purpose of establishing a Museum of the great things of God, and the inventions of men, at Nauvoo.

The collection of "ancient records, manuscripts, paintings and hieroglyphics," like the city library, was to be housed in the Seventies Hall.[91] Designs for the library's museum were ambitious:

> Among the improvements going forward in this city, none merit higher praise, than the Seventies' Library. The concern has been commenced on a footing and scale, broad enough to embrace the arts and sciences, every where: so that the Seventies' while traveling over the face of the globe, as the Lord's "Regular Soldiers," can gather all the curious things, both natural and artificial, with all the knowledge, inventions, and wonderful specimens of genius that have been gracing the world for almost six thousand years. Ten years ago but one seventy, and now "fourteen seventies" and the foundation for the best library in the world! It looks like old times when they had "Kirjath Sapher [sic]," the city of books.[92]

As for books in the lives of Nauvoo residents, minutes of the Nauvoo Library and Literary Institute suggest that Mormon tastes in reading at this time tended more to the intellectual than the frivolous; patrons shunned novels and inclined to history and philosophy. John Locke's *Essay Concerning Human Understanding*, biographies of Napoleon, and English, French, and American histories circulated frequently. Among the books Joseph donated to the library were Thomas Dick's *Philosophy of a Future State*, Mosheim's *Church History*, and the *Histoire de Charles*.[93]

A successful movement requires more than visionary men or women with powerful ideas, missionaries who preach on street corners, and orators who address crowds of hundreds. It requires a press. Though he had received his first heavenly visitations in 1820 and claimed receipt of priesthood keys and authority from a variety of sources over the next nine years, Joseph would not take the step of organizing the church until the Book of Mormon appeared in print. Once the first run of 5,000 copies was available to the public, Joseph waited mere days for formal incorporation of the Church of Christ.

From the first fires of the Reformation, it was printing that had made religious pluralism and innovation feasible. The Puritan revolt, the Great Awakening of the 1740s, and the Second Great Awakening of the early nineteenth century were religious movements largely fueled and sustained by vigorous conversation made possible by abundant presses. By 1783, writes one authority, "not one important inland town [in America] lacked its own press."[94] And many of these were producing a veritable flood of religious propaganda. By the time of Joseph's first visit from the angel Moroni, in 1823, the New England Tract Society had "printed and distributed nearly eight hundred thousand tracts and was publishing a bimonthly magazine, a Christian almanac, and a series of children's books."[95]

Once settled in Cambridge, Massachusetts, the Puritans had taken nine years to establish their press. The Latter-day Saints acted much more quickly. The imperative to have their own press was driven home to Joseph by their difficulties in securing a printer for the Book of Mormon. When initially approached, the Palmyra bookseller and printer Egbert B. Grandin was reluctant to take on the controversial project, and he agreed at last only because Joseph threatened to take the work to Rochester; even then, Grandin acquiesced only after he received a hefty security deposit. And then, midway through the process, Grandin temporarily suspended work because of a threatened boycott by the community.

A month after the June 1831 baptism of W. W. Phelps, the same revelation that designated Independence, Missouri, as the location of Zion designated Phelps "printer unto the church" (D&C 57:11). At the next conference, Phelps was directed to purchase a press and type in Cincinnati and to establish a newspaper in Independence. In June 1832, the Mormon firm of W. W. Phelps and Company produced the first issue of the *Evening and the Morning Star*, a monthly newspaper of the Saints. Phelps was given enough editorial authority to impress his own brand of the restorationist message upon his paper—and that message was "militantly millennialist."[96] Phelps's editing and printing of the paper, then, along with the revelations of Joseph he included, were the primary ingredients in shaping the first public perception of Mormonism as a new religious system.

Responsibility for printing and distributing the Prophet's revelations had originally been assigned in 1831 to a group of men designated as "the Literary Firm," comprising Joseph Smith, Martin Harris, Oliver Cowdery, John Whitmer, Sidney Rigdon, and W. W. Phelps. Their work on the first edition of Joseph's collected revelations was nearly complete when a Missouri mob destroyed Phelps's press in July 1833. Printing operations moved to Kirtland, where Mormon publications were coming off the press months later. The *Evening and the Morning Star*, as its first issue had stated, was produced "not only . . . to bring the Revelations and Comons and Commandments of God which have been, but to publish those that God gives Now."[97] The church press, and the newspaper in particular, made it possible not just to disseminate Joseph's revelations, but to comment, editorialize, and expand upon his thought. As missionaries fanned out across the country, they preached the gospel, left copies of the Book of Mormon, and also sold subscriptions to church periodicals to members and nonmembers alike, in order to disseminate the new gospel. Wilford Woodruff, for example, traveled as a missionary through Tennessee and Kentucky in 1835–1836, and compiled a subscription list of fifty-eight names. More than half were nonmembers. In addition to promulgating Joseph's revelations and church teachings, those periodicals were effective in rebutting disinformation about the church. Woodruff records one occasion, for example, when he read "the 7th No of the M[essenger] & Ad[vocate]" and thereby pacified a crowd grown agitated over the church's alleged abolitionist stance.[98]

Though Joseph was the only person authorized "to receive revelations and commandments [for] this church" (D&C 28:2), he was not a systematic thinker or writer. In 1835, he penned a statement of doctrine for the benefit of the traveling elders of the church. In it, he rehearsed the doctrine of the gathering, repentance, and baptism; addressed the duties of elders; and refuted anti-Mormon charges.[99] In 1842, Joseph formulated the Thirteen Articles of Faith as a synopsis of Mormon belief for a Chicago editor.[100] But except for passing mention of the Book of Mormon, both of these documents emphasized those doctrines that the Latter-day Saints shared with fellow Christians. And (except for Article Nine's reference to limitless, literal revelation) neither one begins to encompass the breadth or novelty of Joseph's religious thinking.

The church having its own press and a cadre of educated, articulate leaders, individuals soon emerged who assumed the task of ordering and packaging Joseph's teachings and revelations into something approaching a theology or doctrinal system. Orson Hyde and the Pratt brothers spearheaded this work. The first extended foray in this regard was the *Voice of Warning* (1837) of Parley Pratt, called the "Father of Mormon Pamphleteering." "In both quality and quantity," writes David Whittaker, "he was the most important writer that early

Mormonism produced," and his *Voice* was "the first systematic statement and defense of the fundamentals of Mormonism."[101] Pratt's book-length argument builds carefully from a foundation resting on prophecy as a principle with a demonstrable record of vindication. After rehearsing those biblical prophecies yet unfulfilled of the gathering of Israel, he moves to the predicted inauguration of a new covenant. Having first to prove the breaking of the old one, Pratt describes the church in the days of the apostles, with its "offices, authorities, powers, and blessings," and asks "the world of Christendom, or either of its sects or parties, if they have apostles, prophets, evangelists, pastors, and teachers . . . together with the gifts and blessings of the Holy Spirit? . . . Having settled this question," he continues, "the reader will see the need of a new covenant."[102]

Parley Pratt's first rendering of Joseph's prophetic work did little more than hint at its ambitious scope. Like his fellow Saints, Pratt saw Joseph's principal work to be a gathering of scattered Israel out of an apostate world, the restoration of a broken covenant. As for the Book of Mormon, Pratt suggested its principal importance was its revelation of the true origin of the American Indians. Its role in the greater unfolding drama was that, as conspicuous fulfillment of Isaiah's prophecy of "a marvelous work and a wonder" (Isaiah 29:14), it heralded "the restoration of Israel in the last days."[103] After affirming belief in the imminence of a New Jerusalem and the millennial era, Pratt concluded this first elaboration of the Mormon gospel by enumerating the "Doctrine of Christ" as restored by Joseph. The sixty-odd verses he then cites—all New Testament passages—emphasize charismatic gifts, the ministry of angels, ethics, authority, and offices as outlined in the New Testament, along with repentance, baptism, and gifts of the Holy Ghost.

Given this public face of Mormonism, early critics were justified in seeing the church as a knockoff of other restoration movements (with the added twist of an impertinent new scripture), and understandably failed to assess the cumulative significance of Joseph's intellectual ambitions and revelatory production. Alexander Campbell, for instance, accused Joseph of simply stealing his own theology (with the complicity of ex-Campbellite Sidney Rigdon). And indeed, many parallels were clear. As a "reforming" Baptist, for instance, the early shaper of the Disciples of Christ movement Walter Scott emphasized five cardinal doctrines of the "Gospel Restored," which would also be the core doctrines of Joseph's "Restored Gospel": "faith, repentance, and baptism for the remission of sins." To this, he added the gift of the Holy Spirit and the granting of eternal life.[104] Joseph dropped the fifth as a principle, and preferred to call the fourth the gift of the Holy Ghost.

It was in the Nauvoo period, of course, commencing a few years after Pratt's synthesis, that Joseph revealed the full range of his radical theology in a barrage of novelty. In the fall of 1840, Joseph taught the doctrine of salvation for the dead and soon the first baptisms on behalf of the deceased were being performed in the Mississippi. In 1841, he shared the principles of plural marriage with members of the Quorum of the Twelve, and two years later committed the doctrine to writing (D&C 132). The Book of Abraham was published in two installments in March and May 1842, introducing its doctrine of premortal existence and a heavenly council. That same May, Joseph first introduced the temple endowment ceremony to a small group of initiates, conveying to them the covenants and teachings necessary to achieve exaltation in the celestial kingdom of God. Couples were sealed together in marriage relationships of eternal duration. A month earlier, Joseph had publicly declared, "The Father has a body of flesh and bones as tangible as man's; the Son also; but the Holy Ghost has not a body of flesh and bones, but is a personage of Spirit" (D&C 130:22). Finally, only months before his death, Joseph delivered in April 1844 his King Follett discourse, in which he laid the foundation for believing, as Lorenzo Snow put it, that "as man now is, God once was; as God now is, man may become."

The martyrdom that followed in June cut short the Prophet's most prolific phase, and ended the LDS era of major doctrinal innovation and scriptural production. The Book of Mormon that Joseph translated was complete and already circulating abroad in the original and three subsequent editions. The revisions of the Old and New Testaments would not be resumed by subsequent prophets. *The Pearl of Great Price*, first published in 1851, now contains exclusively the writings of Joseph Smith (the Books of Moses and Abraham, a revision of Matthew 24, excerpts from the Prophet's personal history, and the Articles of Faith). And the Doctrine and Covenants contains 138 sections—134 of which came through the mind of Joseph Smith.

But the martyrdom did not extinguish Mormon aspirations to pursue the legacy Joseph left. Writing in the aftermath of his death, an editorialist insisted, "the day is not far distant when all nations will marvel at the knowledge and wisdom of the church of Jesus Christ of Latter Day Saints. What has been done can be done again. When they find a place of 'rest'—a Library, a Museum, and a place of Antiquities, will be among the first works of wisdom."[105]

The date December 23, 1847, found Brigham Young at "Winter Quarters, Omaha Nation, west bank of Missouri River, near Council Bluffs, North America," performing one of his last tasks as president of the Quorum of the Twelve Apostles (he would be sustained as Joseph's successor and president of the church four days later). On that occasion, he and the other eleven apostles issued a "General Epistle" to "the Church of Jesus Christ of Latter-day Saints abroad." Young began by reminding his followers that "at no period since the organization of the Church on the 6th of April, 1830, have the Saints been so extensively scattered, and their means of receiving information from the proper source, so limited, as since their expulsion from Illinois." He rehearsed "all the horrors of war" that had befallen them, and described the new land of promise discovered by the pioneer company of Saints earlier that July ("a beautiful valley of some twenty by thirty miles in extent, with a lofty range of mountains on the east, capped with perpetual snow, and a beautiful line of mountains on the west, watered with daily showers"). As he directed them in the best routes by which to assemble in the West, giving counsel for preparations and execution of the arduous trek, he included this exhortation as "made manifest by [God's] Spirit":

> It is very desirable that all the Saints should improve every opportunity of securing at least a copy of every valuable treatise on education—every book, map, chart, or diagram that may contain interesting, useful, and attractive matter, to gain the attention of children, and cause them to love to learn to read; and, also every historical, mathematical, philosophical, geographical, geological, astronomical, scientific, practical, and all other variety of useful and interesting writings, maps, &c., to present to the General Church Recorder, when they shall arrive at their destination, from which important and inter-esting matter may be gleaned to compile the most valuable works, on every science and subject, for the benefit of the rising generation.
>
> We have a printing press, and any who can take good printing or writing paper to the valley will be blessing themselves and the Church. We also want all kinds of mathematical and philosophical instruments, together with all rare specimens of natural curiosities and works of art that can be gathered and brought to the valley, where, and from which, the rising generation can receive instruction; and if the Saints will be diligent in these matters, we will soon have the best, the most useful and attractive museum on the earth.[106]

As the Saints traded residence in the city of Joseph for life in the territory of Deseret, Brigham Young's passion for the practical, and his blurring of spiritual and temporal kingdoms, eclipsed even Joseph Smith's. Scratching out an exis-tence in the Utah wilderness, the Saints had respite—for a few years—from hostile neighbors, but not from the Herculean task of making a desert yield a scanty sustenance, let alone "blossom like a rose" (Isaiah 35:1). In such a climate, devotion was measured by the establishment of material steps toward an earthly Zion, not by psalms and canticles or saintly study. As one historian of Mor-monism notes, the religious imperative "was building up the kingdom and inhabiting it," and the most "expressive worship signs were irrigation canals, or neatly built and nicely decorated houses, or good crops of sugar beets."[107] In such a light, writes one scholar, the lack of a stronger pioneer intellectual subculture "seems less a cause for wonder than that there *was* a strong intellectual thrust" in spite of "the exigencies of pioneer necessity" and other factors.[108]

From their way station in Winter Quarters, the Illinois exiles had established a press and produced what may have been the first printing west of the Mississippi (the epistle to the scattered Saints). Then, in 1850, only three years after settlement in the valley, the Mormons opened the University of Deseret (later, the University of Utah), the first university west of the Missouri. It was a false start, not getting seriously under way for two decades, but the will was there if not yet the means. Perhaps surprisingly, the legislature repeated the Nauvoo strategy of establishing the school as a secular institution (Nauvoo University's first president does not even appear to have been LDS). True, in both cases, LDS faculty and students occupied all—or virtually all—of the spots. And the lack of official LDS sponsorship might be thought to make little difference in a virtual theocracy (as both Nauvoo and Utah Territory were). But the decision could also be seen, in the latter case especially, as a forward-looking embrace of public education and an educational system free of religious control. As an explicit gesture of liberal thinking, it was no more than consistent with the Nauvoo Ordinance, which had guaranteed that "the Catholics, Presbyterians, Methodists, Baptists, Latter-Day Saints, Quakers, Episcopalians, Universalists, Unitarians, Mohammedans, and all other religious sects and denominations whatever, shall have free toleration and equal privileges in the city."[109] The next year, Young sent John Bernhisel to New York to spend $5,000 which the Saints had secured from Congress to stock a territorial library. It opened in 1852 with 1,900 volumes, about the same time that Boston's first public library opened, and before Chicago had one of its own.[110]

It is remarkable that less than a decade after entering the barren valley, some LDS leaders believed they were now in an optimum position to advance their educational agenda. The church, said Orson Hyde in 1855:

> when she was in her infancy, . . . did not attract the attention and gaze of the world. She had little use for scientific knowledge, and little or no time to acquire it; but having become stronger in her intellectual and physical organization . . . she begins to have greater use for science, and is more eligibly situated to acquire it in these peaceful valleys than when buffeted in the States upon the waves of political strife and religious intolerance.[111]

The intellectual culture of a people cannot of course be mandated from above or measured entirely by institutional support. In the case of the Utah Mormons, a number of independent initiatives revealed great interest at the popular level in the life of the mind, consistent with Anglo-American passion in this era for educational forums and societies. In 1854, the Saints had been in the valley less than seven years. That winter, at Lorenzo Snow's large and spacious house, several men and women met to participate in the newly organized Polysophical Society. They played instruments (from the piano to bagpipes), sang, recited original poetry, and discoursed extemporaneously. The small group swelled with members anxious to enrich their minds and souls with a healthy dose of refinement in the midst of a cultural and agricultural desert. Outgrowing the private home of Snow, the society soon occupied the public Seventies Hall and occasionally the capacious Social Hall. Of course, motives were not always passionate intellectualism. David Whittaker has noted that "leaders since Brigham Young's time had struggled with what to do with the young boys who did not always adhere to the values and teachings of the Church as they grew up." The young men's auxiliary was one solution, but another was to create "literary societies for reading and debate."[112] Not all church leaders approved of such measures. Just two years after its formation, for example, the Polysophical Society was dissolved in response to ecclesiastical pressures (from Jedediah Grant and Heber C. Kimball especially), and replaced by the Deseret Theological Class.[113]

A number of factors colluded to undermine Mormon ardor for cultural and intellectual pursuits, at this time especially. Obviously, the exigencies of the westward trek, settlement, and survival took the upper hand in Mormon consciousness. But that is far from sufficient as an explanation; Kirtland, Ohio; settlements in Missouri; and Nauvoo, Illinois, had all been loci of violent opposition and city building, but schools, a university, and doctrinal exposition flourished nonetheless in those near-impossible conditions. But Young was of a more pragmatic bent than Joseph. At times, he could be downright hostile to what he feared might become intellectualism unmoored from spiritual foundations. "We should seek substantial information," he advised, "and trust little to that so-called learning that is based upon theory."[114] In addition, the years 1856–1857 saw the spread of a "Mormon reformation," a period of puritanical retrenchment in which Mormon fire-breathers barnstormed Utah, railing against complacency and backsliding. In the absence of extermination orders and pogroms, LDS leaders seemed to think, Mormons were losing their spiritual focus; bluestocking diversions suggested too much longing for the refinements of a Babylon they had fled. Finally, the invasion and quartering of a federal army in the winter of 1857–1858 created fear and a sense of looming crisis that distracted from relatively idle pursuits.

Even so, cultural societies continued to flourish. In February 1855, sixty men had met in the Salt Lake City Council House and formed the Universal Scientific Society with Wilford Woodruff as president. Woodruff expressed the society's goals in a presidential address: "We are desirous of learning and possessing every truth which will exact and benefit mankind. . . . We wish to be made acquainted . . . with art, science, or any other subject which has ever proved of benefit to God, angels or men." The society went on to establish its own library, reading room, and museum.[115]

The rising generation would form its own organizations, in at least one instance in a lighter vein. Notes of the Wasatch Literary Association (founded in 1874) capture the flavor of cultural diversions that mixed sobriety of purpose with recreational humor. Organized by Salt Lake young adults to promote "the social advancement and the improvement of its members in general literature, music and drama," the meetings originally featured readings of Wordsworth, Byron, Goldsmith, Gray, Longfellow, Pope, Scott, and Shakespeare. Later, more lively activities included spelling matches, musical numbers, brief theatricals, and poetic parodies, like Bud Whitney's surprisingly accomplished take on Oliver Goldsmith's "Deserted Village," a portion of which survived in oral lore:

> Removed from Brigham Street a league or two,
> The estate stands whereon our hero grew.
> Not large the lands, nor spacious are the halls,
> No costly chattels hang the simple walls.
> No shimmering font the sportive eye delights,
> No grassy lawn the travelers toil invites.
> Far from these, the vain display of wealth
> Is here exchanged for free and rugged health.
> . . . .
> Each Sunday morn to visit Mrs. Sears,
> The lovely form of little Em appears.
> Unconscious, half of all her blooming charms,
> Yet well inured to love and loves alarms.
> White gauzy skirts pinned backward hard and tight,
> Still other charms afford the eager sight.[116]

In this same decade, B. H. Roberts reminisced, he had belonged to the Young Men's Club of Centerville, Utah. This remarkable, independent group of boys paid the then hefty initiation fee of $2.50 (and $.50 monthly) "all of which was turned into books." The group existed expressly "to encourage reading and meet . . . at stated periods—usually once a week—and to retell the stories of their reading." They amassed "a rather considerable library" and even raised enough funds to build their own public hall.[117]

The demise of the Polysophical Society and its resurrection as the Deseret Theological Class was both symbol and portent of tensions in Mormon culture between authority and individualism, dogmatism and unimpaired inquiry, Faustian questing and acquiescence to truth and structure, which continue to characterize Mormon culture today. In 1838, Oliver Cowdery's church trial had signaled the difficulty of subjecting independent-minded Mormons to theocratic principles. Now, as Young exercised his authority without impediment, rebellion arose again.

What began as resentment of Young's economic isolationism and anti-mining views blossomed among a group of liberals and intellectually inclined individuals who were also increasingly impatient with the church's ultraconservatism. Led by William S. Godbe and Elias L. T. Harrison, the "Godbeites" established not only a sect with a spiritualist orientation, but the Liberal Institute as well. The reform-minded group attracted to the institute's 1871 dedication not only Susan B. Anthony, but Elizabeth Cady Stanton, who lectured on "The True Republic." Initially steeped in a rhetoric of free-thinking liberalism, the institute aspired to be a public forum for genuine intellectual diversity and progressivism. This would not be the last time that dissent from within was spurred by a sense that Mormonism was becoming inhospitable to true intellectuals. For a number of years, the institute served a variety of functions, from the venting of anti-Mormonism to providing genuine alternatives to the church's theological and intellectual agenda. But increasingly, religious offerings concentrated on spiritualist lecturers and mediums, and the cultural offerings grew unremarkable and indistinguishable from city offerings, including theatricals and Salt Lake's first boxing exhibition.

The institute's initial success suggested a hunger for more cultural diversity and openness, and its demise in a little more than a decade, because it occurred simultaneously with the erection of the magnificent Walker Opera House, suggested that enough infiltration of "gentile" values and entertainments was occurring to weaken Brigham Young's monopoly on cultural and artistic expression—even if theological expression remained firmly under Young's control.[118] As for intellectual life, much of it at the highest levels now centered on defense of the front-burner issue of polygamy. Orson Pratt had produced two important series of articles on Mormon theology, published as *The Kingdom of God* in 1848–1849 and *Divine Authenticity of the Book of Mormon* in 1850–1851. But with the public acknowledgment of plural marriage in 1852, the burden of Mormon theology was divided between efforts to synthesize, order, and occasionally elaborate

Joseph's corpus, and the need to defend the contentious doctrine now arousing the indignation of America.

One version that this mixed imperative took was Orson Pratt's *The Seer*, named in commemoration of the Prophet Joseph. The publication—which would run from February 1853 until mid-1854—promised to "illucidate" three of Joseph's distinctive doctrines in particular: "the ancient Patriarchal Order of Matrimony, or Plurality of Wives, . . . The Celestial origin and pre-existence of the spirits of men . . . and their final redemption and exaltation, as Gods." Pratt's real ambition was to present the totality of Joseph Smith's thought as a coherent system, together with "all the principal features, characterizing this great and last 'dispensation of the fulness of times.'"[119] For the first several months, Pratt's obligatory essays on plural marriage alternated with a long series on "The Pre-Existence of Man." In his first foray into this subject, Pratt goes beyond the mere assertion of a novel tenet to elaborate an entirely new cosmology by integrating disparate elements of Joseph's teachings. Christ was in the beginning with God, but so too was man. Human coexistence with God throws in doubt conventional Christian dualisms. "The heterogeneity of Spirit and matter," affirmed Samuel T. Coleridge in this era, "is the very ground of all Miracle."[120] But not for Pratt, who insisted that "the difference between our world and a Heavenly one, consists, not in the diversity of the elements, for they are the same, but in the difference of the organization of these elements." And man and God, sharing the same elements and eternal nature, have a common heritage: "The Gods who dwell in the Heaven from which our spirits came, are beings who have been redeemed from the grave in a world which existed before the foundations of the earth were laid." And common heritage may produce common destiny. "Heaven, then, is a redeemed glorified world, inhabited by the Gods, and by their sons and daughters, who are the fruit of their own loins. . . . These Gods, being redeemed from the grave with their wives, are immortal and eternal, and will die no more."[121]

The celestial order of marriage is thus the principle that underlies the familial nature of heavenly existence; it is the relational structure that links God to his posterity, and the mechanism by which both earthly existence and the possibility of eternal life are perpetuated throughout the generations of eternity. For one full year, digressing only once to discourse on priesthood, Pratt used these twin concepts of celestial marriage and preexistence to encompass in their logical interconnectedness and implications Joseph Smith's entire scheme of salvational history and doctrine. As T. Edgar Lyon wrote in 1932:

> Orson Pratt did more to formulate the Mormon idea of God, the religious
> basis of polygamy (polygyny), the pre-existence of spirits, the doctrine of the

gathering, the resurrection, and eternal salvation than any other person in the Church, with the exception of Joseph Smith. . . . Due to his efforts . . . the odds and ends of Joseph Smith's utterances were constructed and expanded into a philosophic system.[122]

It was at this time that Orson's brother Parley made his most influential contribution to Mormon theology with his *Key to the Science of Theology* (1855). It went beyond the scope of his earlier treatise and was broader in compass than Orson's work as well. Peter Crawley describes this book as "Mormonism's earliest comprehensive synthetical work."[123] It was "synthetical" not just in its organization, but in its philosophical thrust. Going beyond the first principles of the gospel, Pratt wove Joseph Smith's teachings into a coherent cosmology and ontology that further collapsed Christian dualities. When he claimed that "Gods, angels, and men are all of one species, one race, one great family," he was but elaborating Joseph's doctrine of human potential, describing man as "a candidate for a series of progressive changes" that take him along a continuum to divinity. Christendom's error, he argued, was in compartmentalizing the human and the divine "as if God and man were two distinct species."[124] It would follow, he reasoned, that the scientific laws of nature and the laws of God are one. As the current dispensation mirrors the apostolic, so does the world of spirits reflect the world of mortality. The spirit world is "here on the very planet where we were born," and in it, as in the earthly church, one finds "apostles, prophets[,] elders and members of the church . . . holding keys of priesthood and power to teach, comfort, instruct, and proclaim the gospel to their fellow spirits."[125] And he envisioned a distant time when the "science of geography will then be extended to millions of worlds" and the "science of history will embrace the vast univercoelum of the past and present . . . and include all nations, all ages, and all generations, all the planetary systems in all their varied progress and changes."[126] Seen in their proper relations, all things heavenly and all things earthly, the sacred and the profane, the holy and the secular, are blended in a synthesis reminiscent of the Swedish mystic Emanuel Swedenborg.

Unlike Parley, Orson Pratt was more primed to debate than to systematize, to dialogue than to monologue. This was evident not only in the energy with which he directed his writings at the opponents of polygamy and Mormonism in general, but in his relations within the Mormon hierarchy as well. This side of Orson Pratt reveals as much about the evolving intellectual culture of the LDS church as about Joseph's teachings. Young was at this time making public statements about the origin of man, postulating that Adam and Eve were resurrected beings, and that "Mankind are here because they are the offspring of parents who were first brought here from another planet."[127] It was, in its own way, no more daring or astounding a claim than Joseph's statements at the funeral of King Follett—but the teaching elicited no enthusiasm among members and rejection on the part of some in the Quorum of the Twelve, most vocally by Orson Pratt, who was then a senior apostle. Soon, Pratt was using the *Seer* to promulgate his own view of Adam's creation along a model of biblical literalism. In addition, he interpreted Joseph's teachings on the plurality of gods, the omniscience and progression of the Father and Son, and the nature of the Holy Ghost in ways that diverged from Young's public teachings and personal interpretations. As a consequence, in early 1855, Young prohibited the republication of articles from the *Seer*, citing "erroneous doctrine" as the reason.[128] Pratt acquiesced with apologies, but continued his maverick streak in public gatherings.

The resulting clash of personalities brought into sharp relief the irreconcilability at the heart of Mormonism's central paradox: personal autonomy and intellectual freedom contending against prophetic authority and institutional power. As Young insisted on his right to establish church doctrine, future president Wilford Woodruff gave voice to the majority perspective when he said:

> It is our privilege so to live as to have the spirit of God to bear record of the Truth of any revelation that comes from God through the mouth of his Prophet who leads his people and it has ever been a key with me that when the Prophet who leads presents a doctrine or principle or says thus saith the Lord I make it a policy to receive it even if it comes in [conflict] with my tradition or views being well satisfied that the Lord would reveal the truth unto his Prophet whom he has called to lead his Church before he would unto me, and the word of the Lord through the Prophet is the End of the Law unto me.[129]

Orson Pratt, on the other hand, could be adamant that prophetic authority not preempt reason or judgment. "I must have something more than a declaration of President Young to convince me. I must have evidence." Like Job defending his integrity before an irresistible power presiding over a universe suddenly incoherent, Pratt repeatedly insisted on his own sincerity, and the impossibility of relinquishing beliefs he could not in conscience abandon. Finally, he found a formula that came close to appeasing his personal integrity and the demands of institutional loyalty, which recognized the sanctity of conscience and the principle of priesthood leadership: "If I cannot fully understand his views, it is my duty at least to be silent in regard to my own," he said, while publicly expressing contrition and fealty to Brother Brigham.[130] From this point on, the controversy would diminish, though Pratt learned, as had Thomas More before him, that powerful leaders require more than tacit acquiescence from influential public figures.

Considered as a whole, Orson Pratt's was an ambitious and intellectually earnest effort to go beyond mere synthesis to actual exploration of a Mormon theology. Though some of his views were publicly censured by Young and his independence tamed, it is still significant that Young continued to tolerate his presence in the Quorum, apparently believing his brilliance and faithfulness more than compensated for his heresies. A telling footnote to the Pratt-Young episode concerns a favor the repentant apostle asked of the president. The day before his public confession, Pratt entered Young's office and asked if the prophet could give his son a position as a clerk. The prophet replied by indicating his intention to appoint the elder Pratt to be a teacher, "as [Young] meant to promote education as much as possible."[131]

And indeed, Young vigorously continued in Utah the educational agenda initiated in the East. Scant months after arrival in the valley, Mary Dilworth began teaching school in the Salt Lake Fort. Attention to classical languages continued, as did the teaching of languages useful for expanding missionary work abroad (Tahitian, French, and German were taught in "a large number of schools" during the winter of 1848–1849).[132] At this point, while given encouragement by Young and other leaders, most schools were private. Young encouraged the legislature in 1851 to foster "the advancement and encouragement of primary schools," and urged their public funding in 1855, but the legislature declined to do so, leaving their operation largely a private affair.[133]

The tolerance and progressivism evident in the decision to make the University of Deseret a secular institution were also propitious for female accomplishments in Mormon culture. This may seem ironic in an era of plural marriage. Nevertheless, when the University of Deseret reopened in 1868 after a hiatus of some years, women comprised almost 50 percent of the class.[134] (At this time, American women received less than 15 percent of bachelor's degrees awarded; all told, only 0.7 percent of American women eighteen to twenty-one years of age were attending college in 1870.)[135]

Brigham Young was on record as saying, "We believe that women . . . should . . . study law or physics or become good bookkeepers and be able to do the business in any counting house."[136] He also advised women to attend medical schools; consequently, the women's relief society supported a number of sisters who went east to obtain training. Romania B. Pratt Penrose, Ellis Shipp, and Margaret Shipp Roberts (sister wives), together with Martha Hughes Cannon and many others returned with degrees in hand to establish practices and teach classes. Eliza Snow even attempted to establish a female medical college so Utah could train its own women doctors.[137] By the turn of the century, more female American medical students hailed from Utah than from any other state in the union.[138]

Bookkeeping and medicine are, of course, practical pursuits. There is no denying that Young's emphasis was on the pragmatic benefits of education. His influence was still evident in the closing years of the century in a church editorial titled "True Knowledge." In the ongoing struggle in Mormon thought between Young's heavily pragmatic bent and the speculative inquiries of Joseph, between the acquisition of knowledge as means and the pursuit of knowledge as ends, Young's vision had come out on top. "The best thing ever said concerning knowledge," wrote the LDS editor:

> is that it is a *power*—the power of taking it in through the senses, and working it over so as to serve the best uses of life.... There are thousands who can repeat nearly all they ever read, but are practical failures. Now, the fact is, the ordinary man gets along with very little knowledge of what books teach.[139]

But thanks to Young and his successors' support of education, most Saints had ready access to "what books teach." In 1870, Utah children attended school at a higher rate than those in New York, Pennsylvania, or Massachusetts, the birthplace of public education. Even so, Brigham Young in that year ratcheted up the level of institutional support by establishing a series of LDS academies (tuition-supported high schools) throughout the Mormon West. In large part spurred by Catholic and Protestant success in establishing Utah academies, three years after Young's death, there were some two dozen Mormon academies from Canada to Mexico. That year, according to the 1880 census, Utah's literacy rate (ages ten and above) was 95 percent, when in the country as a whole it was 87 percent, placing it ahead of thirty-four states and territories.[140] To manage the church's growing educational system, a board of education was organized in 1888.

The first generation of Mormon leaders, of widely disparate dispositions, were generally united in their confidence that the life of the mind and the life of the spirit were not just compatible, but mutually reinforcing. Joseph's enthusiasm for the value of classical languages and Young's embrace of the practical benefits of useful education had alike conspired to affirm the value of learning and its seamless integration into a gospel that sought within its ample jurisdiction to produce both "saints and crockery ware." But as the century closed, the rumbles set in motion by the rise of geology, the Darwinian revolution, and higher criticism would force a reexamination of the role of the intellect—and the intellectual—in Mormon culture.

~ 6 ~

"ZION SHALL BE BUILT"
Architecture and City Planning

John Wesley had no wish to change the way in which
society was organized.... When he spoke of needing
new men to build a new world, it was Christ's kingdom, inhabited by his saints, which he was offering to
his followers. John Wesley believed that virtue must be
built within the established order.

~ Roy Hattersley, *Life of John Wesley*[1]

Now, what has religion to do with building a house?
Much.

~ Brigham Young

A literal congregating of people does not make of them a distinct culture. But it
does make visually manifest certain concrete dimensions of their beliefs, and
provide the occasion for erecting tangible monuments to their values. In no other
aspect of their religious or cultural lives would the Saints so conspicuously
reveal—and work through—some of the paradoxes and tensions of their faith.

Mormons were not alone in believing that God designed to erect on this continent an American Zion. Seventeenth-century New England Puritans saw this
country as a city on a hill, destined to be a nation of the righteous. Indeed, Joseph
Smith was certainly right in asserting that "the building up of Zion is a cause that
has interested the people of God in every age; it is a theme upon which prophets,
priests and kings have dwelt with peculiar delight." More debatable was his claim
that while these latter "died without the sight; we are the favored people that God
has made choice of to bring about the Latter-day glory; it is left for us to see,
participate in and help to roll forward the Latter-day glory."[2] Many of his words
on this topic elaborated the millennial dreams common to his age and to many of
his contemporaries, who might well have shared in his rhapsodic description:

[There will come a time when] the Saints of God will be gathered in one from every nation, and kindred, and people, and tongue, when the Jews will be gathered together into one, the wicked will also be gathered together to be destroyed, as spoken of by the prophets; the Spirit of God will also dwell with His people, and be withdrawn from the rest of the nations, and all things whether in heaven or on earth will be in one, even in Christ. . . . The Spirit of God will be showered down from above, and it will dwell in our midst. . . . A work [will go forth] that is destined to bring about the destruction of the powers of darkness, the renovation of the earth, the glory of God, and the salvation of the human family.[3]

But in 1830, few people—observers or followers—were prepared for the literalism of the project envisioned by Joseph Smith. In articulating their peculiar version of Zion, as we saw, Joseph and the early Mormons turned to the vision of Book of Mormon prophet Ether, who "spake concerning a New Jerusalem upon this land," prophesying that "the house of Joseph shall be built upon this land; and it shall be a land of their inheritance; and they shall build up a holy city unto the Lord, like unto the Jerusalem of old" (Ether 13:4–8).

Joseph's contemporary Disciple of Christ founder Alexander Campbell was a fervent millennialist who, like Smith, believed that the American Revolution was a precursor to a new gospel dispensation. Speaking in the same year that Joseph organized the LDS church, Campbell preached a coming new social and religious order that would crown a national process of spiritual regeneration. But in response to Joseph's version of a literal New World Zion, Campbell called him an "ignorant and impudent liar."[4] Robert Owen, meanwhile, had established New Harmony, a secular utopia, in Indiana in 1825. But as Owen was abandoning Indiana and looking elsewhere for fertile soil, and as Campbell continued to await society-wide renewal, Joseph started laying bricks.

The first hint that the Saints' gathering was to be more than metaphor came only months after the church was organized. "No man knoweth where the city Zion shall be built, but it shall be given hereafter," said a September 1830 revelation (D&C 28:9). A month later, the Saints were told that they were "called to bring to pass the gathering of mine elect," in biblical language understood by generations of preachers and missionaries to refer to the process of conversion to the body of believers in Christ.[5] But the revelation in this case clarified "that they shall be gathered in unto one place upon the face of this land . . . to be prepared in all things" (D&C 29:7–8). The first directive specifying the place of gathering for the LDS faithful came in December, instructing the Saints to "assemble together at the Ohio" (D&C 37:3), a gathering that soon turned out to be provisional. A few months later, it became clear that the long-term effort was more than a casual convocation of like-minded believers seeking an Ohio refuge and strength in numbers. The design for the literal Zion of biblical prophecy quickly took shape. A few years after the fact, Joseph recounted the pivotal moments:

> I received, by a heavenly vision, a commandment in June [1831], to take my journey to the western boundaries of the State of Missouri, and there designate the very spot which was to be the central place for the commencement of the gathering together of those who embrace the fulness of the everlasting Gospel. Accordingly I undertook the journey, with certain ones of my brethren, and after a long and tedious journey, suffering many privations and hardships, arrived in Jackson County, Missouri, and after viewing the country, seeking diligently at the hand of God, he manifested himself unto us, and designated, to me and others, the very spot upon which he designed to commence the work of the gathering, and the upbuilding of an "holy city," which should be called Zion.... And thus the sound of the gathering, and of the doctrine, went abroad into the world.[6]

Latter-day Saints were aware that their literal reading of Old Testament prophecies on the subject put them at odds with Christian understanding of the principle. But if God told Israel through Isaiah, "For a small moment have I forsaken thee; but with great mercies will I gather thee" (Isaiah 54:7), the Mormons stood ready to cooperate in the scripture's physical fulfillment, and their leaders admonished members to ignore "evil minded men, [who] ridicule the idea of the gathering of Israel."[7] But their establishment of Zion became an increasingly meticulous exercise in executing every aspect of their plan to transform a heavenly ideal into an earthly reality. And that meant beginning with a plat for the city. Joseph first produced a city plan in 1833, two years after the first Saints began arriving in Jackson County, Missouri. The plat encompasses one mile square, a common practice with city planning of the era. But additional features included the reservation of central blocks for church buildings and of other special blocks for public buildings, and the inclusion of farmers' and ranchers' domiciles within the city boundaries. Barns, corrals, and agricultural zones were relegated to the outskirts or beyond.

With the modern cessation of physical gathering, Latter-day Saints have increasingly turned to a metaphorical definition of Zion given in the Doctrine and Covenants: "this is Zion—the pure in heart" (97:21). Nevertheless, the repercussions of first-generation literalism linger on in the current practice of organizing LDS congregations—wards—according to strict geographical boundaries. In the logic of Zion building, Saints must build heaven where they find themselves gathered; they do not go in search of the heavenly city—or a more heavenly congregation. Thus, Zion building continues to have precisely determined geographical referents.

It would be hard to overestimate the impact this physical boundedness has had on the shaping of Mormon culture. Like the family into which one is born, wards become the inescapable condition of a Mormon's social and spiritual life. Just as, ironically, siblings forge fiercer bonds of loyalty and love to those with whom they never freely chose to associate, so does the arbitrariness of ward boundaries create an inevitability about the LDS ward's cohesion. Congregations and their bishops do not audition for the adherent's willful association. They are instantaneously designated a new congregant's adoptive family, without the member's right of dissent or appeal. While not all family relations are idyllic, most are remarkably strong and a primary source for the individual's identity.

And like Crusoe on his island, Mormons implicitly recognize that any resources they need to employ for the erection of Zion must be found within themselves or their immediate environs, not among more congenial fellow Saints or under the tutelage of more inspiring leaders the next block over. The seeking out of more satisfying spiritual nourishment has long been a heritage of the Protestant Reformation. So much so that in 1559, the Act of Uniformity required all English people to attend their own parish church.[8] Mormon practice has fully achieved what the English Parliament could not. On the one hand, the ward system is an unparalleled instance of authoritarian preemption of a decision that all other Christians take for granted. On the other hand, since those wards have no professional clergy or permanent leadership, individual ward members are themselves empowered and self-directing to a significant degree.

Another, more palpable legacy of Joseph's plan for the city of Zion are the more than 500 communities founded by the Saints in the western United States, Canada, and Mexico, which followed roughly the same design established in Joseph Smith's plat for the city of Zion.[9] Communities large and small throughout the intermountain West bear the influence of those blueprints for Zion. Those cloned communities were anticipated in marginal notations on the first plat: "When this square is thus laid off and supplied, lay off another in the same way, and so fill up the world in these last days; and let every man live in the city for this is the city of Zion."[10] Those words, which bespeak Joseph's easy transition from local to global planning, also conceal the enduring ambivalence between Mormonism's sequestered exclusivity and optimistic universalism.

~

Like virtually all emergent faiths, Mormonism began with families and associates meeting together in private homes. Joseph naturally shared his first visions and experiences with his immediate family. His mother, Lucy, recorded how Joseph gave "recitals . . . in the course of our evening conversations" on what the angel Moroni had revealed to him, covering everything from the warfare of America's ancient inhabitants to their religious worship.[11] As the circle of his friends and supporters grew, his family home continued to be the locus of discussion about the gold plates. In December 1827, a few months after he claimed to have retrieved them from the hillside, hostility and harassment led him to seek the seclusion and refuge of Harmony, Pennsylvania. Work on the translation never picked up steam until the arrival in Harmony of Oliver Cowdery in the spring of 1829. With translation proceeding apace, the old opposition was renewed, and Joseph relocated to the home of Cowdery's friend David Whitmer in Fayette, New York, in early June.

By the time the completed manuscript went to the printer in Palmyra, the centers of the fledgling movement had shifted to the Whitmer home and the Smith family home near Palmyra. In April 1830, the formal meeting to organize the church took place in the Whitmers' log home. So too did the first conference of the church, a few months later. At the second conference, held in September, the venue switched back to the Palmyra area. Parley P. Pratt recalled that, on that occasion, he "saw for the first time Joseph Smith, the Prophet, at his father's house in Manchester, heard him preach, and preached in his house, at the close of which meeting we baptized seven persons."[12]

Until the Saints migrated to the far West, they probably constructed no chapels at all.[13] (Ironically, the first LDS chapel may have been in England, not the United States. On a mission in 1840, Wilford Woodruff baptized hundreds of United Brethren in the area of Gadfield Elm. Two of the converts, John Benbow and Thomas Knighton, turned their chapel over to the ownership of the church they had just joined.) Nevertheless, while worship services and conferences were largely confined to private residences, and chapel construction would come much later, the Saints did erect a house of worship in the first place of their true gathering: Kirtland, Ohio. Prompted by the successful conversion of over 100 Campbellites in that area at the hand of Oliver Cowdery and three companion missionaries in the fall of 1830, on their way to preach to Native Americans on the frontier, Joseph in December directed his followers "to assemble together at the Ohio" (D&C 37:3). Then and there began the literal enactment of prophecies delivered by Isaiah and other Old Testament writers that the Lord in the latter days would "assemble the outcasts of Israel, and gather together the dispersed of Judah from the four corners of the earth" (Isaiah 11:12). Months later, a second place of gathering was indicated in Missouri, slowing the influx of LDS converts to Ohio. The congregation there would grow very slowly in the next few years, while converts flooded into Missouri by the hundreds—over 1,000 by mid-1833.

When the Saints began to filter into Kirtland, Congregationalists and Methodists were worshiping in their own meetinghouses. Two Baptist groups, like the Latter-day Saints, were meeting in members' homes.[14] With only 100 or so members scattered in the area, and gathering now centered elsewhere, it would have been logical for the Saints to continue their practice of home meetings, or perhaps to build a modest chapel. So it was at first unclear what was intended when Joseph announced a revelation at the end of 1832 declaring the Lord's will that his people "establish a house, even a house of prayer, a house of fasting, a house of faith, a house of learning, a house of glory, a house of order, a house of God" (D&C 88:119). Exactly when Joseph recognized in this wording an injunction to build a temple, a special structure of ambitious scale to be used for enacting sacred ordinances, is not clear. The word had appeared earlier in a July revelation, indicating a site for the building of a temple in Missouri (D&C 57:3), but persecution and expulsion from Jackson County would forestall that assignment. And in any case, Webster's *Dictionary* of 1828 indicates some of the ambiguity inhering in that term: Webster defined *temple* as simply "a church; an edifice erected among Christians as a place of public worship."

Having in the vicinity only a small, impoverished band of disciples, with a grave crisis brewing in the West (conflicts in Missouri with old settlers would lead to a public ultimatum demanding the Saints' ouster just a month later), and lacking details of the Lord's house to be built, Joseph could be excused for procrastination in fulfilling the directive. But in June, according to a new revelation, the Lord rebuked the Saints for their delay, provided some specifics for the building's construction, and hinted at its purpose. Most significantly for the future direction of church architecture, the revelation directed Joseph Smith to "appoint and ordain" two other men, to whom the Lord would show the design for the holy house (D&C 95:14). Days later, according to Frederick G. Williams, who had been selected for the privilege along with Sidney Rigdon, "we went upon our knees, called on the Lord, and the building appeared within viewing distance, I being the first to discover it. Then we all viewed it together. After we had taken a good look at the exterior, the building seemed to come right over us."[15] Apparently, they must have concluded, aesthetics—or at least architectural form—was a matter of sufficient import to God to warrant a divine manifestation. And though Joseph and subsequent prophets would later call upon the most skilled architects and craftsmen to work on temples, the best of secular training would have to accommodate guidelines revealed by or through the Prophet.

A people's religious structures are visible manifestations of religious values—or more specifically, a way of ordering those values—and this is especially true of LDS temples. The cruciform shape of English churches, for example, physically evokes the cross. Puritan starkness not only conveyed the principle of an unadorned, unmediated, and demystified approach to godliness, it also amounted to a denial of the very idea of the church as sacred space. But it was a religious statement nonetheless, insofar as it repudiated the compartmentalizing of religious activity. Mormonism, of course, moved in the opposite direction with temple building. By consciously invoking the precedent of Solomon's Temple, Joseph Smith was emphasizing continuity with ancient times and practice wherein common worship by the masses coexisted with sacred priestly rites performed in the house of God. Even the Aaronic priesthood he restored in 1830 foreshadowed such a dualism ("Aaron and his sons shall order [the Tabernacle] from evening to morning before the Lord: it shall be a statute for ever unto their generations," declared the Lord in Exodus 27:21). But this Mormon concept of sacred space would be a generation and more in working out.

The architectural precedent that this process established also asserted a distinct and prominent role for divine inspiration, even as it incorporated traditional elements and styles. In the Book of Mormon, when Nephi, a young man in a wilderness far from home, is commanded to build a ship, he records, "I did not work the timbers after the manner which was learned by men, neither did I build the ship after the manner of men; but I did build it after the manner which the Lord had shown unto me" (1 Nephi 18:2). Similarly, Joseph was commanded by the Lord to build the temple "not after the manner of the world, . . . [but] after the manner" which he was to show him (D&C 95:13–14).

Even though the general arrangement of the temple was given by revelation, its final shape owed more to American architectural forms than to Solomon's edifice. The designers of the Kirtland Temple (and of the virtually identical proposed Independence, Missouri, Temple) had no architectural training. They were a farmer, an ex-preacher, and a physician. The resulting design was an eclectic mix of Georgian, Federal, Greek Revival, and Gothic elements. Classical influences are dominant in the first three of these styles. Georgian architecture, an English style of the preceding century, emphasizes symmetrical, heavy details, with classical columns and oversized doors crowned by semicircular windows. The Federal style is essentially a lighter, more delicate adaptation of that English style. Greek Revivalism, on the other hand, evokes the temples of Athens, with shallow pitched roofs, prominent pediments, and columns. Lacking the columns typical of most neoclassicism, the Kirtland Temple is essentially a Greek Revival building, with the taller proportions of the Federal and details that are Georgian and Gothic. The pointed, arched windows are a fairly conventional Gothic feature common in period churches. Taken as a whole, the Kirtland Temple was an elegant blend of styles, eclectic in a way that many meetinghouses of the period were. If the Mormons failed at this time to develop a distinctive architectural style, they were in good company. As one historian remarks, "from Bulfinch and Jefferson to Latrobe and the Greek Revival, American architects strove for an American style, never quite finding it. . . . The architecture of the United States, even by 1850, would not yet really be called American."[16]

The principal distinction of the Kirtland sacred edifice from contemporary religious buildings was in its function, wherein it gestured toward Hebraic tradition. The connection was at first tenuous—evoked in the very name, house of God, which was used anciently of both the Tabernacle and later the Temple of Solomon. The revelation's reference to the main chambers of the temple as the "lower court" and "upper court" further established a connection with Solomon's great Temple with its two courts (2 Kings 21, 23). While the Kirtland Temple had neither the ornateness nor the ritual functions that later Mormon temples would acquire, it did embody the sacral principle of sacrifice. Heber C. Kimball recalled the Herculean task of constructing a major building in the midst of poverty, persecution, and scant manpower (the Saints' relief expedition to Missouri—Zion's camp—virtually halted progress):

> At this time the brethren were laboring night and day building the house of
> the Lord. Women were engaged in spinning and knitting in order to clothe
> those who were laboring at the building, and the Lord only knows the scenes
> of poverty, tribulation, and distress which we passed through in order to
> accomplish this thing.

Sidney Rigdon, he continued, "Looking at the sufferings and poverty of the church, . . . frequently used to go upon the walls of the building both by night and day and frequently wetting the walls with his tears, crying aloud to the Almighty to send means whereby we might accomplish the building."[17]

Visible from some distance, the imposing structure was especially striking on account of its sparkling stucco exterior, which glistened and shimmered in the sun. Even if the Mormon myth of housewives donating their cherished china for the glaze is not factual, the spirit of sacrifice those tales convey is, as Kimball's journal attests. Another telling dimension of that stucco façade is the recipe's origin. The mix of cement, ground crockery, and pulverized glass, said Artemus Millet, was given to him by revelation.[18] Visionary blueprints incorporating conventional styles, discarded crockery going into divinely revealed recipes—from such sacred and profane sources did Mormonism's first temple emerge.

With internal dissension cleaving the church and threatening the Prophet's personal safety, Joseph fled Kirtland in early 1838, most of the Saints following in the next few months. Temples were planned for gathering sites in Missouri, but violent conflict there prevented even preliminary execution. The church would not embark on another major architectural project until it was safely ensconced in the malarial swampland of Commerce, Illinois, which was renamed Nauvoo. There, in April 1841, cornerstones were laid for an imposing edifice 60 percent larger than its Kirtland predecessor.

As in Kirtland, the Nauvoo Temple had its origins in a revelation, wherein Joseph was commanded as to its purpose and location (D&C 124:40–43). Also as before, he asserted that he had been given the design as well. "I have seen in vision the splendid appearance of the building illuminated," Joseph would explain when some details flew in the face of prevailing practice, "and will have it built according to the pattern shown me."[19] Joseph may have seen in vision the general appearance, but he appealed to architects to submit detailed drawings. The pool of talent to draw upon was considerably larger than in Kirtland. Instead of the 100 or so members who populated the Ohio town when that temple was announced in 1832, Nauvoo in 1841 was the center of a burgeoning Illinois Mormon population in excess of some 12,000. By the end of the project, this meant that "two hundred builders were working on the Temple, requiring six hundred support workers to supply them with lumber and stone."[20] By then, one touring lecturer was calling it the largest building west of Cincinnati and north of St. Louis, and John Greenleaf Whittier predicted that, at its completion, it would be "the most splendid and imposing architectural monument in the New World . . . a temple unique and wonderful as the faith of its builders."[21]

William Weeks was a trained architect and builder who migrated to Nauvoo with the exiled Missouri Saints. According to family tradition, Joseph "advertised for plans for a temple. [Weeks] said several architects presented their plans, but none seemed to suit the prophet. So when he went in and showed his plans, Joseph grabbed him, hugged him and said 'you are the man I want.'"[22] Weeks worked in a purer style of Greek Revival, which is one reason the Nauvoo structure was similar in design to the Kirtland Temple, but architecturally more unified. Some features broke with tradition because they were part of the revealed configuration (as in the round rather than semicircular windows, for instance). Others were of more pragmatic origin. Joseph had the classical pediment of Weeks's original design replaced by an attic story to provide space for offices and added a baptismal font in the basement. The result was a more complex edifice; as in Kirtland, it was an eclectic blend of styles, influences, and innovation, a synthesis of revelation and conventional designs, but with more subtlety and sophistication in the overall result.

As the Nauvoo Temple was taking shape, Joseph preached to his flock "on the keys of the kingdom," telling them, "the keys are certain signs and words by which false spirits and personages may be detected from true, which cannot be revealed to the elders till the temple is completed."[23] Soon, he indicated other sacred purposes associated with the Nauvoo Temple. "As soon as the temple and baptismal font are prepared," he said, "we calculate to give the Elders of Israel their washings and anointings, and attend to those last and more impressive ordinances, without which we cannot obtain celestial thrones. But there must be a holy place prepared for that purpose."[24] By the temple's completion, Joseph had moved beyond the simple washings and anointings to conduct an ordinance he called the *endowment*, reserved at first for an elite inner circle and then extended to faithful members generally.

At the time of Joseph's murder, the walls of the temple were only to the first-story windows. The exodus of Nauvoo had been under way for almost three months when, in a show of prodigious fidelity to the temple and the ordinances performed therein, workers finally completed its construction at the end of April 1846. The building was privately dedicated by Joseph Young on April 30, and publicly dedicated the next day by Orson Hyde. But the crowning architectural glory of early Mormonism was abandoned even as it was completed, and it succumbed a few years later to the fires of an arsonist and a tornado's coup de grâce. For a century and a half, scant rubble remained to bear mute testimony to the desecration and pillaging of eastern Mormonism's greatest work of sacrifice. Like the martyrs' blood on the floor of Carthage jail, the ruins were a somber and iconic reminder to Mormon pilgrims and curious tourists of the passions that divided Mormons from their fellow citizens, and the heritage that bound the faithful to each other. But in the 1970s, President Spencer W. Kimball had the stains removed from the jail in a gesture of conciliation ("it is time to forgive," he reportedly said).[25] And in 1999, Gordon B. Hinckley announced plans to rebuild the Nauvoo Temple, turning a monument to persecution into a symbol of return, renewal, and restoration. Thus, when commemoration of the past threatens to memorialize exile, the recent Mormon leadership moves in the direction of integration.

Flight to the Salt Lake Valley and settlement there had great repercussions for architecture and city planning alike. A permanent settlement allowed the much more protracted development and elaboration of individual productions, spanning an entire sweep of country. The single most-conspicuous architectural element of Mormonism would undoubtedly be the Salt Lake Temple, initiated in 1853 and entirely unlike either the Kirtland or the Nauvoo edifices in exterior appearance. A number of factors conspired to effect a dramatically different architectural form than that practiced earlier. First, in the last years of his life, Joseph's temple theology developed to the point of necessitating a structure different in appearance and function from the meetinghouse design seen in Kirtland and, to a lesser degree, in Nauvoo. Second, the antagonistic relationship to the America that had forced the Saints' exodus likely provoked a desire to employ emerging Gothic and Romanesque influences, radically unlike the forms typical of the republic that had exiled them, which were dominated by Federal and Greek Revival styles. Although those styles were incorporated into some Utah buildings, they would not characterize the holiest and most exclusively Mormon edifices. Finally, a feisty Brigham Young chose a style that self-consciously evoked defiance and physical permanence. The neo-Gothic Salt Lake Temple, battlement-clad and fortresslike, together with its three Utah variants (in St. George, Manti, and Logan), fit the bill perfectly. The Gothic Revival had penetrated American church architecture the previous decade, but Brigham Young and church architect Truman Angel modified it, employed Mormon iconography first used in Nauvoo, and produced what architectural historians call "a new architecture," one that was "unique and isolated in history."[26] It certainly succeeded in conveying the twin inclinations toward militant solidity and otherworldly intimations; a collective "here we stand" echoes from the massively thick walls even as the soaring towers bespeak lofty, spiritual aspirations.

The project dwarfed the Nauvoo Temple. It had taken five years of enormous effort and sacrifice to build the commanding 50,000-square-foot structure in Illinois, and it was one of the most impressive buildings on the frontier. This temple would be several times that size, take four decades, and soar to 210 feet. (The towers of Notre Dame Cathedral rise to 267.) As Heber J. Grant described the process:

> [I]t took an ox team several days to go to the mountains and bring one solitary stone for the structure. It took several weeks of work by hand to cut that stone. The footings of the building are sixteen feet; the walls are eight feet thick; and it was built, as Brigham Young advised everybody to build, "to last a thousand years."[27]

Given the urgency of their temple-building projects in Ohio and Illinois, the Saints were unlikely to wait the four decades this mammoth construction project took, in order to have a place to perform temple ordinances.[28] So Young launched a Nauvoo-sized temple in St. George in 1871. He lived just long enough to dedicate it in April 1877 and to break ground a few weeks later for the larger temple in Manti (1877–1888). His counselor John Young would break ground in May for the similarly sized Logan Temple (1877–1884). All move decisively beyond the New England meetinghouse influences of the two eastern temples, and all three mimic the Gothic style of the Salt Lake Temple, with massive walls and towers. The St. George Temple, of whitewashed sandstone, has a vestigial pediment at either end, castellations and buttresses, and a single tower that clearly evokes its Nauvoo predecessor. The Manti and Logan temples, near-twins, add two pairs of castellated, octagonal side towers (one pair of towers is squared in Logan's case), further enhancing the fortress motif.

William Harrison Folsom was put in charge of the Manti Temple, and he has been called "without question, the most sophisticated architect working for the Mormons."[29] Under Folsom's supervision, and in spite of its blatantly Gothic fundamentals, Manti became the first Mormon temple to turn eclecticism into a completely successful and original style, as Laurel Andrew argues:

> Folsom . . . truly understood the aims of architecture for the kingdom of God, for there is no element of the Manti temple which can in any way be associated with an ecclesiastical building. The towers no longer refer to the spire of a church and the proportions are not those of a conventional religious structure. The Masonic influences contributing to the appearance of the Salt Lake Temple have been completely absorbed and diffused. Even the style suggests the uniqueness of the temple, for the Second Empire was used elsewhere in the country exclusively for civic or domestic buildings, not for churches. . . . A thoroughly eclectic edifice, the temple borrows and recombines historical motifs in a resultant nonrevival building which can only be called Mormon in style.[30]

The Mormons of the early Utah period were, like the first generation of Latter-day Saints, steeped in millennialist expectations and believed, as the Tenth LDS Article of Faith still affirms, that "Christ will reign personally upon the earth." And perhaps Andrew is right in believing that anticipation of a kingdom that Christ would personally administer from Utah explains in part the building of four temples that exude political and administrative rather than—or as well as—religious purposes. But Joseph never saw the church he restored as a church among churches; nor did Brigham Young ever see his role or the domain he administered as a strictly spiritual one. Expectations of an imminent Second Coming are not necessary to explain an architecture that reflects the sacred-temporal polarity that Mormonism has always collapsed.

But if Utah Mormons were prepared to lavish decades of their lives and vast resources on spectacular temples, to whatever purposes, they continued to show little predilection for ornate houses of common worship. Referring to the Nauvoo Temple, a revelation to Joseph Smith had commanded the Saints to come with "all your gold, and your silver, and your precious stones, . . . and build a house to my name, for the Most High to dwell therein" (D&C 124:26–27); at the same time, the Book of Mormon had rebuked those who took pride in the "adorning of your churches" (Mormon 8:37), and Young and his people took both admonitions to heart. A week after the Saints' arrival in the valley, members of the Mormon Battalion spent one day erecting a bower of poles and brush. Its successive incarnations were only slightly more refined. It could hold 8,000 auditors in semi-sweltering shade or frigid winter weather, with no danger of anyone falling asleep in upholstered comfort.

The first religious building erected with any hope of permanence in the valley was the Old Tabernacle, a large adobe structure accommodating 2,500, which was finished in 1852. Intermediate between the massive, lavishly executed temples of exalted purpose, and the meetinghouses of more practical, quotidian employment, was this third category of building, which generally served for stake assemblies. Impressive but neither ornate nor grand, these were executed in midcentury in the popular styles of Federal and Greek Revival, then later in the century in more elaborate classical and Gothic Revival styles. Unlike the famous Tabernacle on Temple Square, an utterly unique execution of an idea by Brigham Young himself, subsequent tabernacles were generally fairly conventional, sometimes vaguely cruciform in plan. In fact, the residents of Provo initially opposed Young's directive to build a tabernacle, complaining that it was "so much like a Presbyterian meetinghouse."[31] In the last decades of the nineteenth century, however, several tabernacles of magnificent design were built in Paris, Idaho; and Lehi, Richfield, Provo, and Brigham City, Utah. This intermediate form, combining the demands of large congregational meetings with elegant, at times lavish designs and individual character, eventually died out altogether. Perhaps this occurred, as one historian has argued, because the Mormon paradox between the sublime and the functional cannot be bridged: "Tabernacles did not serve as art and symbol in the same way the temples did, and yet they were certainly more than simple shelter. The ambivalence about which category these buildings fitted may, in fact, be a major reason why tabernacles became an extinct Mormon building form."[32]

Other more-pragmatic considerations were at work as well. Simpler, cheaper, more-functional stake centers would take the place of tabernacles for stake gatherings, and the focus of church life was increasingly centered in the local units called wards. The original political entities had been transformed into ecclesiastical units in Nauvoo, principally as a way of managing more efficiently the needs of the poor. Two years after arriving in the valley, Brigham Young organized Salt Lake City into nineteen wards. Congregational services for these units were initially held in log or adobe meetinghouses, which were soon supplanted by one-room adobe structures. Those buildings acquired classically styled cornices or other architectural adornments to provide minimal marks of distinction from secular structures.[33] As both human and monetary resources increased, so did the quality of meetinghouses throughout Utah. Most were of one-story rectangular design, but a more elaborate two-story design, called podium base or split level, also appeared.[34]

It is in the omnipresent meetinghouses that soon dotted the Salt Lake Valley that Mormon architecture of the sacred embodied the most visible evidence of an unresolved tension between the polarities of the sublime and the banal. There has always been evident in most Mormon meetinghouses a stark minimalism. To start with, Mormons shun virtually all representations of the cross and, by extension, the passion, in both art and sculpture. "Members of The Church of Jesus Christ of Latter-day Saints . . . emphasize the resurrected and living Jesus Christ; the symbol of the cross or of the crucifix, which depicts the dead or dying Christ, is therefore not part of our worship," reads one typical explanation.[35] That would explain a relative nonchalance or lack of enthusiasm for those emblems. They have, however, always been scrupulously and positively shunned in LDS culture. The Puritans despised the cross as "an idle apishe toye," "a part of deuill worship" for its evocation of Catholicism, and condemned "the idolatrie of the Crosse, the Superstition of the Crosse, the Hipocrisie of the Crosse, the impietie of the Crosse, the injustice of the Crosse and the soule murther of the Crosse."[36]

Mormons doubtless imbibed much of the anti-Catholicism pervasive on the (largely Protestant) frontier. The luridly anti-Catholic *Book of Martyrs* was a standard fixture in personal homes and village libraries (including the Manchester Library of Joseph's youth).[37] A vividly illustrated American edition of 1833 offered itself as "an antidote to the insidious poison [of the] professors of popery."[38]

Early Latter-day Saints, like the Puritans, could at times resort to a rhetoric of harsh difference, one that emphasized the apostate condition of orthodox Christian practice. As the dominant religion devolving from primitive, pristine Christianity, the Catholic church especially embodied for Latter-day Saints an essentially corrupt tradition. Since the late twentieth century, as liberal Protestantism has come to diverge from Mormon teachings more and more emphatically, Latter-day Saints have, ironically, found that Catholicism's unyielding conservatism on moral issues (like abortion, premarital sex, homosexuality, feminism) make it a welcome political ally and congenial fellow traveler. Still, the age-old association of the crucifix with the Catholicism of the "great apostasy" established negative connotations that will most likely never change.[39] So Mormon sanctuaries have historically been and will most likely continue to be lacking in those visible emblems most typical of Christian worship.

This minimalism, traceable to the New England Puritanism of Joseph's and Brigham Young's ancestors, however, and most evident in the Kirtland Temple's white interiors, might have been tempered in the Utah period by European and British influences. "In pioneer Utah," Josh Probert has noted, "different liturgical cultures meet." British and Scandinavian converts in particular were more comfortable with iconography and painted interiors, like the large secco of Joseph Smith that Young commissioned for the Bountiful Tabernacle (1863) and the ornate ceiling of the later Salt Lake Assembly Hall (1880). The consequence was a middle ground between Puritan austerity and Catholic ornateness.[40]

Utah's cultural isolation broke down as its geographic isolation did; the railroads brought "gentiles" in, and an expanding missionary program sent Mormon elders abroad. Both brought contemporary American cultural influences into the valley. The Gothic style already registering on the Utah temples extended to Mormon chapels. In a pattern that mirrored LDS efforts to find statehood and wider acceptance, LDS chapel architecture reached a golden age manifest in wonderfully diverse and aesthetically indulgent examples in the years after the manifesto. The Salt Lake Nineteenth Ward Meetinghouse was capped by an extravagant onion dome, lending at least localized support to popular depictions of Utah as "Orientalism in the extreme Occident."[41] Riverton Ward's building (1898–1900), done in the Beaux Arts style, featured a magnificent dome atop a massive, squarish base. Other chapels featured exoticism and eclecticism, employing Romanesque, Norman, Gothic, Victorian, and other styles. It was as if the four similarly themed Utah temples, all completed by 1893, assumed the burden of epitomizing Mormonism, leaving local wards free to reflect both individualism and creative expression.

In the last years of the nineteenth century, converted Saints were being enjoined to stay in their home nations and to build Zion there. The era of gathering, like the era of colonization, was at an end. In the future, Mormons would have to limit their physical imprint to their sacred edifices, rather than entire communities. As the new century approached, Mormonism was unquestionably about to be launched into a new era of respectability and assimilation, with their attendant blessings and curses. It was no coincidence that the passage would be marked with the completion of a project which had lasted longer than even the presidential career of Brigham Young. Forty years had been the length of Israel's sojourn in the wilderness, culminating in the Israelites' arrival in the promised land. For the Mormons, the end of forty years of temple construction marked something like the last phase of their exile as well. It was as if once fully come to fruition, the Salt Lake Temple, majestic monument to pioneer sacrifice, craftsmanship, and distinctive cultural expression, established an unequivocal Mormon identity. Like this icon of permanence and self-sufficiency, with foundations as deep as the church's sense of self, Latter-day Saints could now, and only now, venture into a new world of compromise, openness, and cultural integration. "A short time ago," wrote a church editor in 1890, "a friend of ours, walking down North Temple Street, glanced at the Temple of the Lord, and made these significant remarks: 'Mormonism can never die out. It has an architecture and a literature.' "[42] He was at least half right.

~ 7 ~

"No Music in Hell"
Music and Dance

After all was settled the ship did plow its way over the
briny deep and what did we the Swiss hear and see.
Hand organ, violin music and then dancing. We did
not like that and asked one another what kind of people is this? One of our elders, . . . [who] could . . . speak
English fluently, told us they were all Mormons. We
were horror stricken in hearing this. We never expected
that Latter-day Saints would indulge in such worldly
pleasures. We were disgusted.

~ Johann Lebrecht Baer, Mormon immigrant

There is no music in hell.

~ Brigham Young

In 1883, a Lutheran pastor inquired of the president of the Missouri Synod if it
was acceptable to introduce the singing of Methodist hymns into a Lutheran
Sunday school. C. F. W. Walther replied with a stinging rebuke that must have
startled the unknown inquirer: "No, this is not advisable, rather very incorrect
and pernicious," wrote the aged Lutheran. Part of the president's refusal could
be dismissed as so much sectarian pride. "The singing of such hymns would
make the rich Lutheran Church into a beggar which is forced to beg from a
miserable sect . . . of Methodist fanatics," he wrote. But Walther also recognized
that hymns are invested with doctrinal messages and that they serve as powerful
barometers of the authenticity and self-sufficiency of a religious culture. Many
Methodist hymns, especially those dealing with the sacraments, he judged to be
"completely in error" and so "false" as to constitute "spiritual poison" and even
"soul-murder." Equally important, only Lutheran hymns could adequately capture "the true Lutheran spirit." To go elsewhere for musical edification or

worship, he argued, would be to deny that "our church itself has everything it needs," or to imply that "one religion is as good as another."[1]

Of course, Walther acknowledged, a generation earlier, American Lutherans could be forgiven for borrowing elsewhere when they were newcomers to American soil. After all, he might have pointed out, Christ's disciples sang Jewish psalms, not Christian hymns, on the eve of their Savior's death. And so, too, it was only natural that at the first conference of the Church of Jesus Christ of Latter-day Saints, held in June 1830, Mormons would have opened their meeting "by singing and prayer,"[2] singing, that in all likelihood, would have included those Methodist hymns so familiar to the Smith family and their neighbors. But it was equally natural that the Saints would soon strike out to forge their own musical forms of worship. More surprising, perhaps, was the promptness with which such an initiative began. Only days after that June conference, Joseph produced a revelation in which his wife, Emma, was directed "to make a selection of sacred hymns, as it shall be given thee, which is pleasing unto me, to be had in my church" (D&C 25:11). Of all artistic endeavors, then, music may justly be named as the first to claim divine support and prophetic direction for its development in the fledgling LDS church.

MUSIC IN AMERICAN RELIGION

In 1640, the *Bay Psalm Book* became the first book printed in North America. The author of its polemical preface (either Richard Mather or John Cotton) indicates that some questions regarding hymnody have proved a "matter of discord" in the church, and he aims to clearly settle the correct theology of singing in Puritan worship. First in this regard, he writes, is the question of "what psalms are to be sung in churches? Whether David's and other scripture psalms, or the psalms invented by the gifts of godly men in every age of the church." His unambiguous answer is that singing hymns composed in modern times is utterly without scriptural "warrant or precedent in any ordinary officers of the Church." As for those early Christians who produced "spiritual songs by the extraordinary gifts of the Spirit (common in those days)," he can only reply, "if they [gifts of the Spirit] were still in the Churches, we should allow them the like liberty now." In sum, concludes the preface writer on the subject of modern hymns, "there is not the least foot-step of example, or precept, or ... reason for such bold practice."[3]

In Europe, the Lutherans, under the Great Reformer's own example, were more open to devotional songs of their own composing. Even earlier, the Hussites had published the first Protestant hymnal in 1501. But it was their descendants the Moravians, resurgent under the leadership of Count Nicholas Zinzendorf (1700–1760), who made the singing of hymns a defining feature of their faith. (His biographer records a 1732 service in which "perhaps as many as a hundred hymns were sung.")[4] It was not long before the new mode of worship began to infiltrate other movements.

A pivotal encounter in this regard was the young John Wesley's (1703–1791) flirtation with the Moravian faith. They won him over to the power of vernacular hymns as a more passionate expression of devotion. The fervent, sincere music, with its contemporary expression and familiar forms, made it more efficacious in consolation and vastly more appealing to religious affections. Wesley was quick to recognize the power of the new music and to adopt the practice for a burgeoning Methodist movement. By 1766, the American Baptists also were ready to embrace the changing form of worship. In that year, they published *Hymns and Spiritual Songs*, borrowing largely from the hymns of Isaac Watts (1674–1748). An English dissenter, Watts was a phenomenally productive writer of hymns, composing some 600 over his life and earning the title of "Founder of English Hymnody."

Though Watts had a few, relatively obscure predecessors, it was his contributions that produced a sea change. One of his biographers summarizes his contribution this way: "The poetry of Watts took the religious world of dissent by storm. It gave an utterance till then unheard in England, to the spiritual emotions, in their contemplation of God's glory in nature and his revelation in Christ, and made hymn-singing a fervid devotional force."[5] From the publication of his first compilation in 1707, *Hymns*, the newer, flourishing varieties of Protestantism had an abundant source of those heartfelt hymns that nourished their members and magnified the appeal of popular religion.

EMMA'S HYMNS

By the time of Emma's charge to select hymns for the new faith, there were well over 2 million Methodists in America and a comparable number of Baptists, outnumbering descendants of both the Puritans and the Anglicans.[6] The Smiths, and most of their prospective converts, were therefore steeped in a religious culture in which worship was virtually unthinkable apart from the congregational singing of popular hymns. Emma Smith spent almost two years compiling hymns according to the directive she had received. The Methodists had by this time published eight editions of hymns, some hopefully intended, as one subtitle indicated, "for the pious of all denominations." Emma relied upon her own copy of one such hymnal for many of her selections.[7] In July 1832, the lyrics to those first selections were printed in the second number of the church's official periodical, the *Evening and the Morning Star*. "The Celestial Home" and "The Pilgrim's Hymn" were strictly conventional in the former's evocation of "those blissful regions" on high, and the latter in its millennial anticipation of Christ's appearing and a thousand years of peace. A selected hymn or two became a feature of several subsequent monthly editions of the church paper, with the same theme of Zion a prominent thread. "Zion" had, in fact, been the name of a popular hymn by John Newman:

> Glorious things of thee are spoken
> Zion, city of our God!
> He whose word can ne'er be broken
> Forms thee for his own abode.

Unsurprisingly, Newman's was the first hymn known by name to have been sung in the new LDS faith, being referred to by the first three sets of conference minutes to name the music on the program.[8] Clearly, the Saints were quick to become attached to the theme that they were transforming from abstraction into architecturally incarnate reality.

By February 1833, the first hymns of Mormon authorship were appearing in the *Evening and the Morning Star*, preaching a version of the gospel not likely to be found in any collection of Wesley. "An angel came down from the mansions of glory," began the anonymous selection for that month. "And told that a record was hid in Cumorah, Containing the fulness of Jesus's gospel; And also the cov'nant to gather his people." With this "new hymn's" tale of a "heavenly treasure; a book full of merit," the church was on its way to an authentically Mormon musical tradition.[9]

Other distinctively Mormon themes soon appeared. Joseph had revealed new scripture on the ministry of the biblical figure Enoch in late 1830, including a poignant epiphany where he marvels at a God who weeps over his creation, beholds the human evil and suffering behind such heavenly grief, and comes to fully participate in a costly compassion: "wherefore Enoch knew, and looked upon their wickedness and misery, and wept and stretched forth his arms, and his heart swelled wide as eternity; and his bowels yearned; and all eternity shook" (Moses 7:41, PGP). A hymnist wove this material into a sacred ballad that combines a traditional Christian rhetoric of God's love and heavenly throngs, with the particularism of Mormonism's expanding canon, a weeping God, and an Imitatio Christi that foreshadows the radicalism of Joseph's King Follett discourse:

His soul o'erwhelm'd with boundless love,
He sang a song in heav'nly lays,
While angels' tongues join'd him in praise.
With finger end God touch'd his eyes
That he might gaze within the skies;
His voice he rais'd to God on high,
Who heard his groans and drew him nigh.
With joy and wonder, all amaz'd,
Amid the heav'nly throng, he gaz'd!
While heav'nly music charm'd his ear,
And angels' notes, remov'd all fear.[10]

When Emma's selections were published in 1835 as *A Collection of Sacred Hymns, for the Church of the Latter Day Saints*, well over a third of its ninety were of LDS authorship. The preface left some doubt as to whether borrowing from Protestant tradition was a temporary expedient or a perennial possibility, but hinted at the former: "It is necessary that the church of the Latter Day Saints should have a collection of 'SACRED HYMNS,' adapted to their faith and belief." The church being still in its infancy, the preface continued, "it is sincerely hoped that the following collection . . . may answer every purpose till more are composed, or till we are blessed with a copious variety of the songs of Zion."[11]

External borrowings and original compositions reflected the duality of the new Mormon faith itself, in the process of defining both its commonalities with, and differences from, American varieties of Christianity. For example, "The Freedom of the Will" was an unabashed paean to individual agency:

Know this that ev'ry soul is free,
To choose his life and what he'll be
For this eternal truth is given,
That God will force no man to heaven.

While the hymn (with its strident Arminianism) was taken from an 1805 camp-meeting collection,[12] its honored place as the opening hymn in Emma's collection suggested the special emphasis the new faith would place on individualism and free will. As another example, Mormons were not alone in believing that the American Indians were somehow connected with Israel; but the Book of Mormon was unique in arguing their descent from Ephraim and Manasseh in particular. William W. Phelps's "Red Man" thus proposes to solve the enigma of Indian origins:

O stop and tell me, Red Man,
Who are you, why you roam,
And how you get your living;
Have you no God, no home?
With stature straight and portly,
And decked in native pride,
With feathers, paints and brooches,
He willingly replied:
"I once was pleasant Ephraim,
When Jacob for me prayed;
But oh, how blessings vanish,
When man from God has strayed!
Before your nation knew us,
Some thousand moons ago,
Our fathers fell in darkness,
And wandered to and fro."[13]

In the church's early years, congregational singing of hymns was not the only form that music took in worship services. Charismatic manifestations abounded—especially speaking in tongues and even singing in tongues. (Joseph had even blessed one sister, Elizabeth Ann Whitney, with that particular gift.)[14] Interpretations were generally provided, and one recorded example conveys a further glimpse into an emergent religious culture that was drawing upon its own unique mythology to create distinctive forms of religious expression. Lucy Smith rendered one such tongue singing as "Moroni's Lament," based on the Book of Mormon's prophet's grief at his people's apocalyptic destruction:

I have no home, where shall I go?
While here I'm left to weep below
My heart is pained, my friends are gone,
And here I'm left on earth to mourn.
I see my people lying around,
All lifeless here upon the ground;
Young men and maidens in their gore,
Which does increase my sorrows more.
My father looked upon this scene
And in his writings has made plain
How every Nephite's heart did fear,
When he beheld his foes draw near.

With ax and bow they fell upon
Our men and women, sparing none;
And left them prostrate on the ground—
Lo here they now are bleeding round. . . .
Well might my father in despair,
Cry, O ye fair ones! once how fair
How is it that you've fallen! Oh!
My soul is fill'd with pain for you.
My life is sought! where shall I flee?
Lord take me home to dwell with thee,
Where all my sorrow will be o'er,
And I shall sigh and weep no more
Thus sung the son of Mormon, when
He gazed upon his Nephite men;
And women, too, which had been slain,
And left to moulder on the plain.[15]

Though the church was too young to have an extensive history upon which to draw, the Book of Mormon's miraculous appearance, more than the characters, themes, and tragic conflicts that filled its pages, provided an instant source of material that Saints could weave into the first chapters of a new cultural tradition. It was as if, for the Mormons, who lacked a past of their own, the Book of Mormon became a surrogate history, a repository of vicarious cultural memory and experience. From its earliest days to the present, that record forms the basis of a cultural vocabulary that is more a sign of denominational difference than it is a source of real theological distinctness. That is apparent in the relatively superficial ways in which hymnody drew upon the Book of Mormon. Apart from the miracle of its appearing and translation, and its connection to American Indians, the scripture was largely untapped as a source of distinctively Mormon material.

It would appear, at least in regard to cultural production, that the first generations of Mormons, steeped as they were in a biblical culture, were much more prone to resort to familiar sources for song and poetry than to their prized—but not yet culturally assimilated—new scripture. This fact was still evident at the time of the great exodus west. True enough, Utah would eventually include the towns of Lehi and Bountiful, but it is the Jordan River, not the Sidon, that waters the valley, and it was the camp of Israel, not the caravans of Lehi, that moved across the plains. Old Testament names and places occur almost twenty times on Utah maps. Book of Mormon sources are confined to three prophets, one city, and a honeybee.[16] Long before assimilation and political and cultural accommodation became imperatives, at a time when Mormon cultural pride and autonomy were most pronounced, it didn't seem to occur to the Mormons to fashion their own cultural selfhood in light of the master narrative of their defining scriptural work, when it would have suited the task so perfectly. Perhaps the security of a shared Judeo-Christian template trumped the temptation to self-identify with such a radically distinct scriptural epic. Sometimes, self-imposed cultural exile is more daunting than the embrace of elect status is alluring.

In Mormonism's first generation, LDS hymnody was limited to the writing of lyrics; it would be more than a half-century before Mormons added their own musical compositions. In the early nineteenth century, it was still standard practice to print only lyrics, to be sung by congregations to any of a number of well-known tunes. Emma's hymnal was therefore typical for the period in offering only words. And even though a number of her selections were borrowed hymns, as the Saints dedicated their first temple in Kirtland, Ohio, on March 27, 1836, it was apparent that their own voice was becoming more dominant. On this occasion, a choir sang as an opening hymn "Ere Long the Veil Will Rend in Twain," with words by Parley P. Pratt. Sidney Rigdon's two-and-a-half-hour sermon was preceded by "O Happy Souls, Who Pray" and followed by "Now Let Us Rejoice in the Day of Salvation," both written by William W. Phelps. After an intermission, the service continued with the congregation singing a third Phelps hymn, "Adam-ondi-Ahman," before Joseph Smith addressed the throng. Isaac Watts was at last represented by his hymn "How Pleased and Blessed Was I." After Joseph's dedicatory prayer, an LDS tradition was inaugurated with the singing of Phelps's rousing "The Spirit of God Like a Fire Is Burning." Written for the Kirtland services, the hymn is now a standard feature of all temple dedications. Of those numbers sung on that 1836 day, two of them, "Now Let Us Rejoice" and "The Spirit of God," survive in the current (1985) edition of the LDS hymnal, along with two dozen others of Emma's original selections.

Even when Mormon hymnists resorted to themes popular with contemporary Christians, such as millennialism, they frequently reshaped and particularized them in distinctive ways. It was common sentiment, as expressed in "Now Let Us Rejoice," that "shortly the hour of redemption [would] come" and that soon "the earth [would] appear as the Garden of Eden." But the Saints' allusion to biblical forecasts of "Israel [coming] home" was, in their eyes, being literally fulfilled in Kirtland and Missouri, and their sung hope for a day when "none [would] molest them from morn until ev'n" was both poignant and prescient, coming as it did after their expulsion from Jackson County, but before Haun's Mill, the martyrdom, and the flight to Utah.

Similarly, Phelps's "Spirit of God" described an outpouring of divine manifestations consistent with the visionary subculture in which many Christians were participating. But there is a marked exuberance in this hymn, born of a concreteness and recognized specificity behind the formulaic phrases. "The visions and blessings of old are returning, and angels are coming to visit the earth" conjures for Mormons the First Vision in the sacred grove, the restoration of priesthood through Peter, James, and John, and visits by Moroni and others. But even more important for the place of this anthem in Mormon culture was the prophetic aptness of its claim "the veil o'er the earth is beginning to burst" to the Pentecostal events surrounding its first public performance. In January 1835, there began a season of visions, angelic visitations, speaking and singing in tongues, pillars of fire and mighty winds—all witnessed by hundreds of worshipers and observers. The reported phenomena peaked at the dedicatory service and in the days immediately afterward. To this day, singing the stirring anthem in LDS settings, including temple dedications, powerfully evokes the most sacred moments in the Mormon collective memory.

The choir that sang most of the hymns at the dedication was no casual affair. Some years after their arrival in Kirtland, the Saints manifested an interest in musical education that was general throughout much of early America. Since the 1700s, most communities had hosted short courses in singing, usually offered by itinerant singing masters during the agriculturally slack winter months. They taught a simplified system for both sight-reading and choral performance. It had long been recognized that assigning syllables to degrees of the scale helped a singer's memory of pitch. In England, a four-note system was developed in Elizabethan times, with the assigned syllables fa-sol-la-mi (hence the name, Fa-Sol-La singing). Printers sometimes placed the first letters of the syllables under the notes as an aid, then began to print them in the place of the note heads. By the early 1800s, many were following the lead of William Smith and William Little's *Easy Instructor*, which assigned one of four shapes to each note (a diamond, oval, square, and triangle), and printed those shapes in place of the note heads. A prime advantage of this method was its suitability for large groups and for those without musical training or special gifts. One typical manual, *The Psalmody Reformer* published in Halifax in 1853, promised success even for those "with the weakest capacity for music (idiots excepted)."[17]

Singing schools also served the purpose of imposing order and system on congregational singing, which was often chaotic—given widespread musical illiteracy, the frequent lack of standardized texts, and the singing style employed previous to (or contemporarily with) Fa-Sol-La singing. "Old way" singing was deemed an authentic and spontaneous expression of worship by some, and the sound of bedlam by others. Thomas Walter remarked in 1721 that "the Tunes that are already in use in our Churches . . . are now miserably tortured, and twisted, and quavered . . . into an horrid Medley of confused and disorderly Noises. This must necessarily create a most disagreeable Jar in the Ears of all that can judge better of singing than these Men." The culprit, he declared, was not hard to find. "Our tunes are, for Want of a Standard to appeal to in all our Singing, left to the Mercy of every unskilful Throat to chop and alter, twist and change, according to their infinitely divers and no less odd Humours and Fancies." As a consequence, "one man is upon this note while another is on the note before him, which produces something so hideous and disorderly as is beyond expression bad."[18]

As one might expect, denominations that departed from high church ritual and establishment orthodoxy were suspicious of singing that needed to be taught and rehearsed. The Campbellites, for example, shunned the singing schools. In the case of Mormonism, however, emphasis on individual freedom and personal spiritual experience gave way to other considerations. The singing schools provided benefits in addition to musical quality and conformity that must have appealed mightily to Joseph Smith. They were powerful community-building activities that provided a healthy environment for socializing. As such, they were the period's most important musical institutions and a communal activity perhaps second in importance only to public worship. By the early nineteenth century, these forums of instruction were immensely popular, and several competing systems emerged, each with its own methods and tune books.

On January 4, 1836, the Mormons held a meeting in the unfinished temple to make plans for their own singing school in Kirtland. A committee of six was appointed and began sessions soon after. Presumably, this was the same group meeting a year later in the completed temple. On appointed evenings, Joseph recorded, "the singers met [there] under the direction of Elders Luman Carter and Jonathan Crosby, Jun., who gave instruction in the principles of vocal music."[19] We hear little more about musical diversions in Kirtland over the next two years. With the dawn of 1838, the animosity of dissenters forced Joseph to move his headquarters to Missouri, and circumstances there were not hospitable to cultural concerns, musical or otherwise.

Joseph had first ventured to Missouri to scout a location for the city of the New Jerusalem. His initial reaction to frontier society revealed fearful forebodings about the new cultural wasteland facing the Saints. The beautiful temple, singing school, and choir may have represented modest efforts at cultural refinement, but humble as they were, the aspirations they represented stood in painful contrast to the coarseness of the frontier. "Our reflections were many," he mused with understatement:

> coming as we had from a highly cultivated state of society in the east, and standing now upon the confines or western limits of the United States, and looking into the vast wilderness of those that sat in darkness; how natural it was to observe the degradation, leanness of intellect, ferocity and jealousy of a people that were nearly a century behind the times, and to feel for those who roamed about without the benefit of civilization, refinement, or religion.[20]

When Joseph removed to Missouri in early 1838, the Saints were in a virtual state of siege, having twice fled counties to the south. Forced out of Jackson County in 1834, they found temporary refuge principally in Clay County. After two years, they had aroused the ire of fellow citizens there and retreated northeast to Caldwell County, which was specially carved out as a refuge for the embattled Saints. By the fall of 1838, mere months after Joseph's arrival, a Missouri war had resulted in the total capitulation of the Mormons and their forced exodus from the state.

Established in their new home of Nauvoo, Illinois, the Saints were at last in a position of sufficient stability and political autonomy to move forward with cultural endeavors. Empowered in December 1840 by a liberal charter to establish a university, the Saints did so; included in the university's divisions was a Department of Music. One apparent function of the university was to provide teacher education for the community. Accordingly, in late 1841, the Music Department's professor and warden formally organized the Musical Lyceum of the University of Nauvoo, making provision for "instruction in the art of sacred singing in the schools of this city."[21] About the same time, a group calling itself the "Choir of the Stake of Zion in the City of Nauvoo" successfully petitioned the Music Department to organize a board "for the regulation of music in this city."[22] Over the next generation, lyricists and poets would build upon the foundations of a sacred music tradition laid by W. W. Phelps and others. However, it was during this Nauvoo era that music would increasingly be associated in Mormon culture with recreation and entertainment. This is no mere historical happenstance; the blurring would be emblematic of one of Mormonism's most distinctive developments. In the sphere of music, as in most every other realm, Mormonism's absence of an ecclesiastical line of demarcation between the sacred and the secular would prove to be as typical of the new faith as it was idiosyncratic in American religious culture.

THE NAUVOO MUSIC SCENE

Most of the early Kirtland converts had come from the Campbellite religious tradition, which opposed choirs and musical training. Having overcome those inherited inhibitions, Mormon advocates of a musical culture were reinforced as British converts poured into Nauvoo, many with strong backgrounds in singing, composing, and performing. In Nauvoo, both the origins and the abiding nucleus of the music scene would not be choral, but martial. The same charter that authorized the city to found a university also granted permission to organize a militia, which would be called the Nauvoo Legion. And like most large military units, the thousands-strong Nauvoo Legion wasted little time in creating its own fife and drum corps. It had some dozen members, presided over by E. P. Dusette, chief of music in the legion, with Levi W. Hancock as fife major and Dimick B. Huntington as drum major. Dusette was also their "beat drummer" and apparently something of a sensation. Of his performance on the drum, one admirer would recollect years later that she "never saw [it] equaled."[23]

While this martial band, as it was called, proved adequate for parade and drill functions, the ranks of the legion were populated with more—and more diverse—talent than was found among the fifers and drummers. Learning that many men among the legion's ranks were skilled on other instruments, Joseph Smith, as the legion's lieutenant general, convened a meeting in January 1842 to organize a larger musical ensemble. Some eighteen musicians, representing trombones, clarinets, French horns, bass drum, piccolos, and cavalry cornet, were accordingly organized as the Nauvoo Brass Band under the leadership of William Pitt, trumpet. Other players joined over time.[24] According to an oft-quoted popular tradition, most of the original group had been converted in England and migrated together to Nauvoo.[25] The truth, a band historian recorded, was that "the few that commenced to learn under [William Pitt] were ignorant of the principles of music, and new beginners upon their instruments; it therefore required great patience and exertion in our captain to fit us and bring us forth as a band of music for the Nauvoo Legion."[26] One researcher notes that an entire band was converted to the church in England and immigrated to Nauvoo. But they refused to play with the Nauvoo Legion band, "thinking it beneath their caliber."[27]

Occasionally, the band played in the Masonic Hall, but the Nauvoo Legion frequently mustered, drilled, and paraded, and it was on these outdoor occasions that the band normally regaled audiences with its brassy music. Soon, the group aspired to be more than open-air musicians, so the brass band began to raise funds for a concert hall, performing benefit concerts and, on one occasion, offering a musical trip on the steamboat *Maid of Iowa*. On April 19, 1843, Joseph himself selected the location for the future Music Hall on the corner of Woodruff and Young streets. Even his tragic death did not halt work on the project. On October 23, 1844, the *Nauvoo Neighbor* announced the "music and concert hall in process of construction [which] will house the Nauvoo Choir, numbering over 100 members, and band."[28] On January 24, 1845, workers were finishing plastering the hall, which was described as a building "thirty feet by fifty and eleven feet high. The ceiling is arched and has sounding jars. It has been built amidst difficulty and discouragement in consequence of poverty, and has cost nearly one thousand dollars."[29] In March 1845, the Concert Hall was dedicated, and audiences of up to 1,000, though the hall was designed for 700, enjoyed marathon (five-hour) performances until the time of the forced exodus approached.[30]

Choirs were also organized both in Nauvoo and in the outlying settlements. Until the Nauvoo Music Hall was completed, they too gave many open-air concerts—some rather informal affairs, as a member reminisced:

> The first New Year's Eve after the Prophet moved into the Mansion, our choir, under the leadership of Stephen Goddard, to which I became a member some time previous, gave them a serenade. We met at our usual place of practice, on the hill near the temple, and although the night was unfavorable, being dark and rainy, we, nothing daunted, started out between twelve and one o'clock, we struck up and sang the New Year's hymn. The inmates were highly gratified, and the Prophet came out and invited us to come in; but being late we declined. After singing one or two anthems he pronounced his blessing upon the orchestra and choir, which repaid the brethren and sisters for all their trouble.[31]

Related to the brass band, a smaller group was created called the quadrille band, consisting of string and reed instruments. It apparently debuted at Joseph Smith's mansion house, where he sponsored the first of many all-night dancing parties. Reference is also made to a small orchestra that played on occasion at dances and also in the temple.

The records of the brass band portray a church that relied upon secular music to allay sorrow as well as to celebrate and entertain. In the fall of the year subsequent to Joseph's death, the band was reorganized, even as preparations carried on apace for the Saints' departure. One evening, a visitor pleased the members with his display of solidarity and virtuosity alike:

> Joseph Herring, an Indian, . . . requested permission to talk to us. He . . . told of his sympathy for the Mormons, that the Indians would defend them on their

journey west, of his hatred for Mormon persecutors and the American government, his determination to have full vengeance upon them, etc. The Indian then called for "Fisher's Hornpipe," and danced off admirably, to the pleasure and satisfaction of us all.[32]

Over the next weeks, the band played in small settings where Brigham Young and other leaders were reported to have enjoyed the music and an opportunity to dance. Rather remarkably, considering the circumstances of destitution and imminent exile (planned for the spring), the band at this time purchased new instruments in St. Louis, going into debt to do so. As it had done so often before, the band scheduled a benefit concert to retire the debt. In January 1846, it played the following program at the Concert Hall three times to full houses: "1. Introduction, Brass Band; 2. Song, Duet; 3. 'No. 1, Salisbury,' Quadrille Band; 4. Song, 'Satan, Spare the Saints,' Trio; 5. Comic Song, 'Bogus,' Solo and Chorus; 6. Song, 'The Wolf,' Solo; 7. Finale, Brass Band." As would be expected of a faith that was constantly collapsing the sacred into the mundane and vice versa, Nauvoo music struck some reviewers as an odd mix of sensibilities, such as the one who noted a program blending "the sacred, sentimental, and comic, and done up to the very best sense of the heart."[33]

As the time for the exodus neared, the group's minutes record the pressures of displacement intruding upon the members' musical vocations. Again manifesting the tenacious hold of music in their persecuted lives, the members now organized—as band members—to construct their wagons for the band's departure with the Saints. Then the poignant entry: "February 7, 1846. A few of the band met at the usual place, but there was nothing done with the exception of talking about what to do with the timber we should leave when we went west." And then, almost as a postscript:

> February 9. By request of Brother B. Young, the band met in the upper room
> of the Temple; played a few tunes, after which Brother Young arose and said
> that, as we were about to leave Nauvoo, we had come together, to pass off the
> evening, and that he thought it no harm to have a little recreation in singing,
> etc., as long as it is done in righteousness. He then called on the Lord to take
> charge of the meeting; the brethren and sisters then joined in and danced;
> during the evening they handed round some of our Nauvoo grape wine, which
> was excellent. About 3 o'clock they dismissed and all went home.[34]

Two days later, reported the *Warsaw Signal*, 1,000 Saints were wending their way across the Mississippi River.

In the days ahead, the role of music shifted in a dramatic way. What had seemed a pleasant pastime or form of Sunday devotion now became a defining and unifying dimension of the pioneer identity, a spiritually and emotionally indispensable asset in the largest and most successful organized migration in American history. Colonel Thomas Kane, friend of the Saints, described the scene when he visited the Saints encamped on the prairie along the Missouri, several months after their Nauvoo exodus and a full year before they would find refuge in the West:

> [T]heir orchestra in service on this occasion astonished me by its numbers and fine drill. . . . When the [Mormon] battalion was enlisted, some of the performers were to accompany it; but they all refused. Their fortunes went with the Camp of the Tabernacle. They had led the Farewell Service in the Nauvoo Temple. Their office now was to guide the monster choruses and Sunday hymns; . . . and to knoll the people into church. Some of their wind instruments, indeed, were uncommonly full and pure-toned, and in that clear dry air could be heard to a great distance. It had the strangest effect in the world, to listen to their sweet music winding over the uninhabited country. Something in the style of a Moravian death-tune blown at day-break, but altogether unique. . . . The wind rising would bring you the first faint thought of a melody; and as you listened, borne down upon the gust that swept past you a cloud of the dry sifted sands, you recognised it—perhaps a home-loved theme of Henry Proch or Mendelssohn. Mendelssohn-Bartholdy, away out there in the Indian Marshes![35]

THE DANCING PURITANS

Hymns were worshipful, moral tracts could edify, and even drama had a genre denominated the "morality play." So music, literature, and drama were not unambiguously devices of devils. But dancing was more difficult to reconcile with American religious mores of the nineteenth century. Associated as it so often was with decadent theater, devil music, and frivolity in general, it was almost universally condemned. "In practically all communities predominantly Protestant," writes one scholar, "dancing was . . . taboo. The fiddle was the 'instrument of the devil,' and all who danced to its strains were unfit for membership in the community church." Strictly regulated "play-games" permitted a highly regulated form of dance under controlled circumstances. That exception aside, "Quakers, Disciples, Methodists, Baptists, [and] Presbyterians . . . were one in opposing the dance as a wicked sport."[36]

The story is told of the famous Bishop Asbury, who visited an old Methodist family only to find their daughter employed playing the piano. Noting the three righteous generations that preceded the girl's own, the bishop remarked bitingly that "at this rate of progress, the *fifth* generation of Methodists will be sent to dancing school."[37] As another moralist of the age opined, "more devils lurked in catgut and horsehair than Lucifer ever dreamed of."[38]

Dance is the most emphatically sensual of the arts, and it is likely the form's pure physicality that offends a religious sensibility that, in the West at least, has tended to equate the spirit with godliness, while lumping together "the world, the flesh, the devil" in John Donne's memorable triad.[39] At least one visionary preceded Joseph in finding a more congenial alliance of soul and body, the sacred and the profane. In 1790, the poet/prophet William Blake published an attack on what he saw as the evils of a puritanical Christian culture. In this anti-Bible, provocatively titled *The Marriage of Heaven and Hell*, he blamed "all sacred codes" for causing the following "Errors":

1. That Man has two real existing principles Viz: a Body & a Soul.
2. That Energy, call'd Evil, is alone from the Body, & that Reason, call'd Good, is alone from the Soul.
3. That God will torment Man in Eternity for following his Energies.

In opposition to what he considered to be insidious doctrines, he articulated what he called "True Contraries":

1. Man has no Body distinct from his Soul for that call'd Body is a portion of Soul discern'd by the five Senses, the chief inlets of Soul in this age.
2. Energy is the only life and is from the Body and Reason is the bound or outward circumference of Energy.
3. Energy is Eternal Delight.[40]

Blake, like many of his fellow Romantics of the age, was protesting a contemporary religious morality that equated the natural with the depraved, and the repressed with the spiritually exalted. In large measure, his was a protest against the omnipresent influence of the Platonic heritage and its Christian counterpart, a deep-seated distrust of the body and its pleasures. Linking "the world, the flesh, and the devil" was nowhere more extensively and more lastingly practiced than among the Puritans of New England. The Methodists, for example, could allow themselves exuberant participation in rousing hymns and emotional outbursts in their worship, but Wesley himself had expressed in no uncertain terms his contempt for energy directed to less than pious purposes. And his dour strictures were not confined to the mature. "He that plays when he is a child," he said, "will play when he is a man."[41] As a consequence, the Methodist Episcopal church in America ruled in 1792, "We prohibit play in the strongest terms."[42] One American historian notes that Mormonism early developed what he called "an 'ideology' of play at a time when most other American clerics still thought of play as the devil's invention."[43]

The net cast by this condemnation was a large one. The tremendously influential eighteenth-century religious thinker and mystic William Law had written in his *Serious Call to a Devout and Holy Life* that rejecting worldly pleasures meant avoiding "reading and hearing plays and romances . . . operas, assemblies, balls and diversions."[44] That the music intended by God for his holy adoration could so easily be perverted into mere recreation was a cause for special vigilance. As one tract written by an eighteenth-century cleric put it, "Music is not an amusement for the careless or idle vulgar; the musician is somewhat more than a Mountebank or Rope-Dancer; he should preserve his dignity, he must not trifle and play tricks, he must not be gay, he must be serious."[45]

With such Puritanism, Mormonism found little common ground. In part, this was, as we have seen, rooted in Mormonism's collapse of sacred and mundane spheres and its refusal to disparage the flesh as inherently carnal and devilish. Indeed, on this point Young sounds like an echo of Blake himself: "Our eyes are delighted in seeing, our ears in hearing. . . . Our senses, if properly educated are channels of endless felicity to us."[46] Mormonism's decidedly un-Puritan dimensions were also largely a consequence of Mormonism's intense emphasis on sociability. "Friendship is one of the grand fundamental principles of 'Mormonism,'" said Joseph, and in his view, a lively conviviality covered a multitude of sins:

> I see no faults in the Church, and therefore let me be resurrected with the Saints, whether I ascend to heaven or descend to hell, or go to any other place. And if we go to hell, we will turn the devils out of doors and make a heaven of it. Where this people are, there is good society. What do we care where we are, if the society be good.[47]

Young agreed, teaching that "social enjoyment [was] ordained of God for his glory and our benefit."[48] This sociability was not a distraction from a higher order of things, but a preview of higher things. "The same sociability which exists among us here will exist among us there," Joseph proclaimed, "only it will be coupled with eternal glory, which glory we do not now enjoy" (D&C 130:2).

Of course, sociability can all too often verge on improper congress of the sexes. This possibility would seem to be a major source of Puritan suspicion of the social pleasures. But Mormonism can hardly even envision a solitary spirituality. The extremely sociable dimension of Mormonism—and of Joseph Smith—could lead to tensions and inconsistencies in their position regarding this morally ambiguous aspect of musical culture. Joseph himself had allowed his mansion house to be used for dances, but was reputed to retire alone to his room as a sign of quiet disapproval. After his death, in a reformist spirit, Heber C. Kimball associated dancing with "grog-shops and bad houses, drunkenness, and such things," claiming that "when the prophet had a dance at his house he said everything against it he could, and now men go and practise the same things."[49] It was true that initially, at least, dancing could even be a cause for loss of membership. On October 22, 1837, the Kirtland church disfellowshiped twenty-two brethren and sisters "until they make satisfaction for uniting with the world in a dance the Thursday previous."[50] It is not clear if the dancing itself was the error, or the company. At this period in Kirtland, the leaders had declared a time of retrenchment and reform in response to rampant apostasy, internal dissension, and external opposition. Fraternizing with the enemy in a time of crisis, rather than the form of entertainment, may have been the problem.

On other occasions, however, Kimball had himself been at the center of action. After a long day of labor building the temple, for instance:

> [I]t was thought proper to have a little season of recreation. Accordingly, Brother Hans C. Hanson was invited to produce his violin, which he did, and played several lively airs, accompanied by Elisha Averett on his flute, among others, some very good lively dancing tunes. This was too much for the gravity of Brother Joseph Young, who indulged in dancing a hornpipe, and was soon joined by several others, and before the dance was over, several French fours were indulged in. The first was opened by President Brigham Young and Sister Whitney and Elder Heber C. Kimball and partner. The spirit of dancing increased until the whole floor was covered with dancers.[51]

The hornpipe was a lively sailor's dance, performed solo. The French four was a type of quadrille, probably of Scottish origin (in spite of the title), in which only two couples engaged (quadrilles usually required four or more). What they had in common was the emphasis on technique, virtuosity, and enjoyable spectatorship. Other popular dances, like reels and polkas, also required a healthy dose of skill.

It could be that Joseph's attitude softened in his last years, when he authorized the creation of a quadrille band, formed with brass band members, for use at all of the dance parties of the Saints. About this time, William Cahoon remembered what he said was the first such party approved by the Prophet. It was especially memorable, apparently, for the "hornpipe executed by James Standing, who, being called upon by Joseph Smith for that exercise, astonished the Prophet and every one else with his marvellous dexterity in dancing."[52] In the relative seclusion of Nauvoo, gloomy feelings were for a time at least quite done away with. Like Kirtland, Nauvoo would have its choirs and sacred music, but its inhabitants were more prone to recollect the distinctive sounds of the Nauvoo Brass Band and the fiddle music that accompanied many an all-night dance.

The mixed signals coming from the Prophet on the subject were great enough that "a father and elder in Israel" pleaded with the editor of the church newspaper in early 1844 for official guidance—preferably from Joseph himself "if the prophet could spare the time." The answer was the closest to an official declaration on the subject the church would have: muted condemnation of contemporary practice that had little in common with the biblically sanctioned variety. Lacking scriptural justification, the writer reasoned, dance was perfectly fine in the abstract but problematic as practiced, because it "leads people into bad company and causes them to keep untimely hours, [and] has a tendency to enervate and weaken the system, and lead to profligate and intemperate habits. And so far as it does this, so far it is injurious to society, and corrupting to the morals of youth." As for the biblical, God-glorifying type, the anonymous editor (probably John Taylor) wrote, "when we can see such a dance, we shall join in it heartily."[53]

Nevertheless, it would appear that then, as now, dancing was an activity whose social benefits outweighed its dubious inherent moral implications. Mormonism could have gone the route of more-fundamentalist faiths, banning an activity with clear tendencies toward worldliness. Instead, the church opted to embrace dancing, institutionalize it, and thereby turn it into an instrument of socialization and harmless amusement. So while Heber Kimball protested the impropriety of dancing in a mansion house still marked with blood from the Prophet's bleeding corpse, others had already determined that dancing would be both a diversion from grief and a gesture that their spirits, like their faith, would not be subdued.[54] Definitive approval for the latter came at a time when thousands of Saints would need the emotional refreshment such diversion could lend to the brutal trek westward. From Winter Quarters in January 14, 1847, Brigham Young pronounced it the will of the Lord that "If thou art merry, praise the Lord with singing, with music, [and] with dancing" (D&C 136:28).

And so they did, to the astonishment of critics and the admiration of friends like Thomas L. Kane. Shortly before Young had added divine sanction to his own, Kane witnessed a celebration in which defiant celebration overshadowed hardship and large-scale family separation. Captain James Allen had arrived at the Saints' Iowa camp to enlist soldiers for the U.S. Army, to be engaged in the war just declared against Mexico. Young recognized that the effort served the self-interest of both parties, since the destitute Mormons sorely needed the funds offered to each volunteer, and President Polk could use a hardy corps, already assembled at the frontier's edge, ready to march nearly 2,000 miles to join the Army of the West in California. Over 500 men were mustered into the service on July 16, most of them leaving behind a $42 clothing allowance and, in some cases, wives and children to face the ordeal of their trek to Salt Lake alone.

The same Colonel Kane who described the plaintive tones of their orchestra piercing the prairie stillness, mentioned above, also described the more festive side of Mormon music:

> The afternoon before was appropriated to a farewell ball; and a more merry dancing rout I have never seen. . . . It was the custom, whenever the large camps rested for a few days together to make great arbors, or boweries, as they called them, of poles and brush. . . . In one of these where the ground had been trodden firm and hard . . . was gathered now the mirth and beauty of the Mormon Israel. . . . With the rest, attended the Elders of the Church within call, including nearly all the chiefs of the High Council, with their wives and children. They, the gravest and most troubleworn, seemed the most anxious of any to be the first to throw off the burden of heavy thoughts. Their leading off the dancing in a great double cotillion, was the signal bade the festivity commence. To the canto of debonair violins, the cheer of horns, the jingle of sleigh-bells, and the jovial snoring of the tambourine, they did dance! . . . French fours, Copenhagen jigs, Virginia reels, and the like; forgotten figures executed with the spirit of people too happy to be slow, or bashful, or con-strained. Light hearts, lithe figures, and light feet had it their own way from an early hour till after the sun dipped behind the sharp skyline of the Omaha hills. . . . Well as I knew the peculiar fondness of the Mormons for music, their orchestra in service on the occasion astonished me by its numbers and fine drill. . . . When the refugees from Nauvoo were hastening to part with their table ware, jewelry, and almost every other fragment of metal wealth which they possessed that was not iron, they had never thought of giving up the instruments of this favorite band.[55]

They did not in every case give up even their pianos. One visitor noted in 1855 the presence of five pianos in the territory. Violins, he added, were heard everywhere.[56] Not just their greater portability, but their indispensability to the dance would seem to be a reason. Writing at the same time as that visitor, a fierce critic of the Saints complained:

> [T]he Mormons love dancing. Almost every third man is a fiddler, and every one must learn to dance. . . . School-houses occupied by the classes during the day, are turned into dancing academies in the evening. There are many who can afford only to pay one tutor. Their children *ought* to learn to read, but they *must* learn to dance. . . . In the winter of 1854–5, there were dancing-schools in almost every one of the nineteen school-houses.[57]

The forms of dance most commonly countenanced in this era were square and line dances, which included cotillions or quadrilles and popular forms like the Virginia reel. As the waltz and other forms of round dancing gained favor in midcentury, however, Brigham Young drew a line, associating them with "brothel-house dances." Even the stodgy Young, however, soon succumbed to the tides of the new. Heber J. Grant recalled how, as a youth leader in charge of a dance to benefit the St. George Temple, he argued the necessity of including the popular waltz. He won his point with his bishop, and daringly invited the prophet to attend. The musical program ended with a "waltz quadrille":

> President Young said: "They are waltzing."
> I said, "No, they are not waltzing; when they waltz they waltz all around the room; this is a quadrille."
> He turned to me and laughed and said: "Oh, you boys, you boys."

Within weeks of Young's death, the church's newspaper was opining that even the waltz might be permissible among small circles of friends.[58] Dancing in the Nauvoo Temple and waltzing in support of the St. George Temple—compromise with this dubious mode of entertainment was fast becoming something nearer to unalloyed embrace.

UTAH HYMNODY

The seminal experiences of early Mormonism and the migration west provided rich materials for a hymnody that is the most distinctively Mormon element of their musical heritage. If "The Spirit of God" is the LDS anthem from the Kirtland years, commemorating seminal moments and experiences of the restoration, "Come, Come, Ye Saints" is the anthem of the exodus, a poignant ballad of subdued triumph. Composed by William Clayton on the Iowa prairie, between flight from Nauvoo and refuge in the West, the hymn borrowed an old tune, but employed words that more than any other lyrics capture the essence of pioneer perseverance in the face of trial. Several features contribute to the enduring popularity of the hymn, while some other period pieces have not worn as well. The hymn is devoid of rancor or militarism or defiance in the face of persecution; rather, the words invoke a joyful embrace of the lot that has befallen the Saints, and enjoin courage in the face of a pilgrimage which is both spiritual metaphor and all-too-real ordeal: "though hard to you, this journey may appear, grace shall be as your day." It holds out the promise of a refuge in Zion, which again reverberates with both timeless appeal and a moment of real historical sanctuary: "we'll find the place, which God for us prepared, . . . where none shall come to hurt or make afraid." And the stirring final chorus sings joyously that "should we die, before our journey's through, Happy day! All is well!" The knowledge that thousands of Saints lie buried along the trail and at journey's end makes the hymn a reverential paean to the faithful dead. But the closing words celebrate life, not martyrdom, and congregations and choirs always finish with a stirring crescendo, as they affirm:

> If our lives are spared again
> To see the Saints their rest obtain,
> O how we'll make this chorus swell,
> All is well! All is well!

The hymn appeared in the new hymnal published in 1851, and is near enough to canonical status to assure immortality in the Mormon tradition. At one time, it was even published in two public school music series and called one of the ten best American hymns.[59]

Hymns like "Come, Come, Ye Saints" could be immensely inspiring and comforting. Other music could, in the aftermath of bitter persecution and exile, be more therapeutic and cathartic—sometimes dangerously so. Charles Penrose at least waited for Utah refuge before publishing the lyrics to "Up Awake Ye Defenders of Zion" (1857), with its references to the "plundering wretches" who persecuted the Saints. (The 1985 version has slightly more muted language, but still urges the hearer to "remember the wrongs of Missouri" and to "forget not the fate of Nauvoo.") But Warren Foote records a tragic-comic moment when a fellow Mormon lacked such prudence. Foote spent a nervous night with one Jim

Lemmons who, fleeing Nauvoo for Iowa, found himself alone in a hostile crowd. They required a song, and the intellectually challenged saint

> was foolish enough to sing the "Mobbers of Missouri," a song composed by someone when we were driven out of that state. This made some of them angry, and although they all dispersed before night, Jim was afraid to stay there alone, thinking that we would not be back.[60]

In the years after Emma's first hymnal, Mormon writers continued to elaborate, commemorate, and celebrate uniquely Latter-day Saint doctrines and events through their hymnody, and Mormon composers began to provide music of their own creation. One of the early products was Parley Pratt's "The Morning Breaks," with music by George Careless (written more than a decade before its first publication in 1876). Like Clayton's hymn, Pratt borrowed the key phrase from a familiar source (the hymn "All Is Well" in the former case; a Charles Wesley poem, "Wrestling Jacob," in the latter) and adapted even the signature phrases to a Mormon context. All art is adaptive; incorporation and assimilation are largely how artistic history unfolds. But in the LDS case, the borrowings and recontextualizations are often a sign of something different: a sense that in Mormonism, prior types and shadows are at last finding their literal fulfillment. Often it appears as if prior scriptures, poetic fragments, and melodic refrains are not merely transmitted and reiterated in LDS music, but are celebrated there as at last transpiring in fact. Thus, for instance, the morning breaking, which was only poetic imagery in the Wesley poem, becomes for Pratt a reference to the inauguration of the new dispensation of gospel fullness:

> The clouds of error disappear
> Before the rays of truth divine;
> The glory bursting from afar,
> The glory bursting from afar
> Wide o'er the nations soon will shine.
> The Gentile fulness now comes in,
> And Israel's blessings are at hand.

Similarly, the angel of indefinite provenance or identity mentioned in Revelation 14:6 ("I saw another angel fly in the midst of heaven") becomes in LDS culture and hymnody a concrete reference to a very particular angel named Moroni, sung of in Pratt's "An Angel from on High," which appeared in the

1840 hymnal. John Tullidge provided its present tune in 1857, along with settings for thirty-six other hymns, with the publication of his *Latter Day Saints' Psalmody*. Another prolific hymnist, George Careless, studied music at the Royal Academy of Music at London before joining the church in 1850 and migrating to Utah. His sixty-plus hymn melodies are marked by a gentle, reverential quiet, as in the almost mournful "Though Deep'ning Trials Throng Your Way." Most productive of all Mormon composers, however, was Evan Stephens, who contributed almost 100 hymns to the Mormon repertoire.

Once settled in Utah, Brigham Young and the Saints engaged in a program of musical culture far more ambitious than anything seen in their earlier history. The Nauvoo Legion Band was reorganized in 1850, and Young himself contributed funds for a band carriage, parades, and immigrant escorts. Domenico Ballo (1805–1861), a Milan-trained ex-bandmaster of West Point, entered the city two years later, reformed the wind band into a twenty-player ensemble, and soon won Young's esteem for their broad repertoire and skilled musicianship. They played everything from popular songs to classical music by Rossini and Mozart. Within a decade, the talented clarinetist had become "almost a household name." By the time of Ballo's death in 1861, there were over forty bands in Utah Territory, and double that by 1875. Long after his passing, residents would reportedly lament, "we have never had any music out here since Ballo died."[61]

THE MORMON TABERNACLE CHOIR

It was of course the Tabernacle Choir that would become the most visible and powerful instance of Mormon cultural achievement and recognition. "Someone would strike up a song, and the valley would ring with the sound of many voices—for singing is in my people as sight is in the eye," says Huw in reminiscing about the Welsh village of his youth.[62] Hundreds of Welsh converts migrated to Utah after the pioneers arrived, and many of them found a comfortable home in the newly constituted Nauvoo choir. The group soon acquired the name of the Tabernacle Choir, not from singing in the great domed building they have since made famous, but from performing in its crude, adobe 1852 predecessor. Initially, the Tabernacle Choir was a modest assemblage, dwarfed by larger groups like the singing school choir organized by David Calder, which sang with some 260 members at an 1863 conference.[63] Calder's singing school became the Deseret Musical Association, a much-loved ensemble that had Young's enthusiastic support. Young even dictated many of its musical selections, and directed Calder on one occasion to order pieces by Haydn, Mozart, and Mendelssohn, as well as Handel's *Messiah*.[64]

Fortuitously for music lovers, the same year of Ballo's death, Charles John Thomas arrived in Salt Lake, and he soon took over Ballo's band, as well as the fledgling Tabernacle Choir and the Salt Lake Theatre Orchestra. He worked to both refine and encourage Mormon appreciation of great music, and produced his own. He wrote music ranging from anthems ("God Bless Brigham Young") to marches like the one played at the Salt Lake Temple capstone ceremony. Young was clearly devoted to musical culture before he was honored with personal anthems, but his enthusiasm for the role of music in Mormon culture was such that in 1865, he sent Thomas on a mission to southern Utah, for the purpose of founding singing schools and to teach and direct music.

Musical developments took another drastic turn in these decades, consistent with the theology of Joseph Smith. It was his intention, Joseph had indicated, "to so organize the Church, that the brethren might eventually be independent of every encumbrance beneath the celestial kingdom."[65] In the 1860s and 1870s, Young grew ever more concerned about consolidating LDS economic self-sufficiency, as one means of establishing and safeguarding their overall religious and cultural autonomy in Utah. So imperative did Young deem economic self-reliance that he advocated growing for local use products prohibited by the church's health code rather than see them imported, since the "community has not yet concluded to entirely dispense with the[ir] use."[66] Building up Zion in ways consistent with the program of self-sufficiency, in other words, trumped at that time faithfulness to particular dietary proscriptions.[67]

It was only logical that leaders and artists alike would transpose those same ideals of economic autonomy to areas of devotional and artistic expression. Tullidge had extended Emma Smith's original project of Mormon hymnody when he published, in 1857, his *Psalmody*. But a more expansive vision of Mormon musical culture appeared when, in 1877, David Calder and George Careless insisted that "a home-made music" was as essential to cultural self-sufficiency as "home-made cloth."[68] They even published a musical journal to educate and elevate musical tastes and to create a more fertile ground for local musical accomplishment.

Mormonism was a lay church, and music frequently a lay pastime. But great art is seldom produced by part-time dilettantes, and professional musicians in the Utah valley early recognized this, even if their leaders and peers, at first, did not. This generation of European-trained musicians had aided Young in his aspirations for a more culturally refined people. But tensions inevitably flared between uncritical appreciation of local music and aspirations toward technical excellence.

One British import at this time was the previously mentioned John Tullidge, who had made his mark as a tenor and music teacher in York, England. Coming to Salt Lake, he perhaps tried to ratchet the level of musical appreciation a notch too high by publishing in 1863 exacting reviews of musical performances that were more critical than most contemporary audiences.

Tullidge's high standards were a bit premature for a struggling musical culture. In the next generation, however, Mormon hopes to establish their identity through music would shift dramatically to performance rather than composition to accomplish that feat. The locus of growing hopes of a Mormon musical culture would come to center in the still-undistinguished Mormon Tabernacle Choir. Growing to eighty-five voices in the 1870s, and then reaching a hundred in the early 1880s, it as yet had done nothing to suggest the potential that was soon to manifest itself triumphantly on the national stage, with repercussions extending well beyond the realm of Mormon musical appreciation.

~ 8 ~

"ON A CANNIBAL ISLAND"

Theater

A dancing school among the Tuscaroras is not a greater absurdity than a masquerade in America. A theatre under the best regulations is not essential to our public and private happiness.

~ Noah Webster

Pizarro

Cast of Players

The High Priest......................Brigham Young

~ playbill for Nauvoo production

From its inception in ancient Greece, Western drama has oscillated between the spheres of the sacred and the profane. In the earliest theaters, the performance was centered—physically as well as dramatically—on the altar. Drama began as a form of religious ritual—a meditation on the relation of the human to the divine, an exploration of the violence and irrationality of the universe, and an inoculation against or purification of the pity and fear we experience in the human condition. And such religious intent has never been far removed from the wellsprings of the dramatic tradition. At the same time, ribald sexual humor, enacted in the satyr play, became standard as welcome comic relief after the relentless pathos of a tragic trilogy.

The medieval Christian church found in drama an apt vehicle for public edification. Mystery plays and miracle plays, performed with pomp and spectacle in churches, on cathedral steps, and in marketplaces, enacted the drama of the passion and vignettes of the Virgin and myriad saints. But with the allegories known as morality plays, drama again veered toward the secular. In the era of the Reformation, Protestant decision makers associated the theater with both

Catholic didacticism and worldly impulses. And even the non-Christian Plato had warned of the moral dangers attendant upon artistic forms with deception and illusion at their heart, and vice and folly as their subject. So, with the triumph of English Puritanism in 1642, the theaters of England were shuttered. In the English-speaking world, the dramatic arts would long carry the stigma of an entertainment at odds with virtue and true religion.

When the Puritans closed the English theaters, they initiated a tradition of suspicion and hostility toward the dramatic arts that would resurface persistently in the American religious tradition through the nineteenth century (and beyond). Even a man of letters like Joseph Smith's contemporary Ralph Waldo Emerson, as a Harvard undergraduate, held the theater in contempt. "Theatre," he said, "is the sewer in which the rebellious vices exhaust themselves."[1]

But suspicion of the theater was not confined to Puritans and prudes. "The social and psychological sources of this intense and persistent hostility to the stage," writes Joseph Ellis, "were deeply embedded in Western history. As a result, the theater was undoubtedly the most hated of all the fine arts in eighteenth-century America."[2] The dramatist, impresario, and historian William Dunlap worked assiduously to give the arts—and theater especially—greater respectability in the new republic, asking, "what engine is more powerful than the theatre? No arts can be made more effectual for the promotion of good than the dramatic and the histrionic. . . . The engine is powerful for good or ill—it is for society to choose."[3] High culture in the European tradition had largely been created and patronized by aristocrats. The future of arts in America, which was largely lacking such a class, was long in dispute. Would the virtuous soil of republicanism be found incompatible with the self-indulgence, effetism, and decadence of high art, or would the new democracy, as Dunlap and others believed, "become the cultural center of the world, because all its people, not just a privileged aristocracy, were potential consumers and creators of culture?"[4]

Dunlap's personal experiment failed: the oldest theater company in America, which he owned and directed, closed its doors in 1805, the year of Joseph Smith's birth. Two decades later, theater was still not faring well for the most part. The jaded observer Fanny Trollope recorded:

[T]he theatre was closed when we were in Baltimore, but we were told that it was very far from being a popular or fashionable amusement. We were, indeed, told this every where throughout the country, and the information was generally accompanied by the observation, that the opposition of the clergy was the cause of it.[5]

She added her personal belief that a dour American character as much as clerical hostility was to blame.

Indeed, many clergymen were active in opposing theatrical institutions. The Presbyterian minister Joshua Wilson led community efforts against theater in Cincinnati in the early nineteenth century, and Methodists were also opposed. Bishop Asbury's colleague James Finley considered even Shakespearean theater "a school of vice" to be shunned, and as late as 1927, one writer noted with contempt that he knew of "more cases than one, where men have passed for Methodists at home, and when they have gone to Indianapolis, they have attended a low, vile thing, called a theater."[6] One scholar has noted that into the first half of the nineteenth century, "many—perhaps most—other Christian ministers viewed fiction suspiciously [and] identified the theater with the brothel."[7]

It was against this tide of moralism that Brigham Young protested:

Now understand it—when parents whip their children for reading novels, and never let them go to the theater, or to any place of recreation and amusement, but bind them to the moral law, until duty becomes loathsome to them; when they are freed by age from the rigorous training of their parents, they are more fit for companions to devils, than to be the children of such religious parents.[8]

Elsewhere, he recognized that Mormon embrace of the profane arts, like modern staged dramas, was against the grain of most American religious traditions:

"My son," says the Christian father, "you should not attend a theatre, for there the wicked assemble; nor a ball-room, for there the wicked assemble; you should not be found playing ball, for the sinner does that." Hundreds of like admonitions are thus given, for so we have been thus traditioned. . . . [But] it is our privilege and our duty to search all things upon the face of the earth, and learn what there is for man to enjoy.[9]

Joseph as well was famously intolerant of sanctimoniousness, and apparently found nothing to condemn in theatrical entertainments per se. Once church life in Nauvoo—the first place of lasting peaceful refuge for the Saints—assumed a semblance of normalcy, a variety of cultural amusements was quick to spring up. Young members especially were drawn to stage their own informal productions. During the cold winter months of 1841, Warren Foote recorded that "a few of the young folks met at the schoolhouse and organized an exhibition [a kind of theater]. I was elected secretary."[10] At least twice in the next few weeks he noted resultant performances. Some time later, Joseph himself organized the Nauvoo Dramatic Company, aided by Thomas A. Lyne, a tragic actor from Philadelphia who had played supporting roles to Edwin Forrest, the elder Booth, and other famous actors.[11] Lyne's performances (he was both producer and star) reportedly drew large crowds to the Masonic Hall, later also called the Cultural Hall, which served as the Nauvoo theater. It was Lyne, apparently, who steered Brigham Young toward his lasting affection for the theater, by casting him in the role of the Peruvian high priest in a Nauvoo production of *Pizarro*. Lyne forever after expressed mock regret for the decision. When asked why, he replied, "Why don't you see . . . , [Young's] been playing the character with great success ever since."[12]

It was no surprise, after the Nauvoo experience, that Brigham Young became in the early Utah era a true patron of the dramatic arts. "If I were placed on a cannibal island," he famously said, "and given a task of civilizing its people, I should straightway build a theatre."[13] The Salt Lake Valley wasn't a cannibal island, but when Young and the Saints arrived, it was similarly isolated, hostile to newcomers, and uncongenial to frivolous pastimes. Still, Young was not long in building his theater. On July 28, 1847, days after arriving in the valley, Young paced out the lot for the temple, which would be forty years in the building. The very next day, he put crews to work building a bower on the temple block, where public meetings could be held. This building would be a hundred feet long by sixty wide, built on 104 posts, and covered at first with tree boughs and eventually with boards. So the very same year that Chicago opened its first permanent theater, Saints in the Utah desert were building their first crudely constructed public building where, less than three years after their arrival in the valley, the play *Robert Macaire* was performed before a pioneer audience. The sponsoring organization was the Musical and Dramatic Association; the old Nauvoo Brass Band supplied both orchestra members and many of the actors.

There was nothing incongruous, in the Mormon mind, with alternating theatrical performances and religious services in the same space (in a typical layout, Mormons today blithely extend overflow seating at stake conferences from the pulpit to an elevated stage at the opposite end of a "cultural hall," complete with basketball hoops and free-throw lines). Nevertheless, Young had built in 1852 the Social Hall, which was more particularly designed for theatricals and social functions. A two-level adobe structure, it measured seventy-three by thirty-three feet. One local actor who performed there, Phil Margetts, joined with Henry Bowring to form the Mechanics Dramatic Association, which gave performances in Bowring's unfinished home, dubbed the "Bowring Theater." In the winter of

1860, hoping to secure Young's support for their endeavors, Margetts invited the church president and his counselor Heber C. Kimball to attend a performance together with their families. The evening produced historic results. As one of Young's daughters would write:

> They accepted the invitation, although "bringing their families" meant that a crowd of slightly less than a hundred must be accommodated in the tiny building. Father was very much pleased with the project and at the end of the play announced that the time was ripe for the building of a big theatre and made his statement which has since become famous, "The people must have amusement as well as religion."[14]

The construction project was a bold one in many ways. The size of the proposed theater was economically ambitious, given the Saints' scarce resources. It was culturally ambitious, given the relative dearth of trained talent to sustain a public theater. And the church's unabashed endorsement of a building dedicated to "theater" was striking in an age when, as one historian remarks, it was generally necessary to employ words like " 'museum' and 'lecture hall' [as] euphemisms for theater that allowed those opposed to entertainment to attend 'educational' plays."[15]

Construction began that summer, and during the winter of 1861, according to popular memory, "the center of interest with Salt Lake's population alternated between two points—(1) the wall in front of the *Deseret News*, whereon were posted bulletins of the great Civil War then raging and (2) the great building two blocks away, the mammoth 'New Theatre.' "[16] The project proceeded rapidly, benefiting immensely from materials left at nearby Camp Floyd when it was abandoned by federal soldiers. With no railroad, all other materials were necessarily native stone, timber, and adobe.

The theater was designed and its construction supervised by church architect William H. Folsom. Elias L. T. Harrison, a recently converted architect from London, assisted Folsom and helped to create a building conspicuously inspired by Drury Lane Theatre. Dimensions and appointments were ambitious, considering Salt Lake's population at that time numbered perhaps 20,000: 80 by 144 feet and four stories high. The building housed three balconies and was graced by two imposing Doric columns on the exterior. The interior was equally dramatic, as Young's daughter Clarissa recalled:

> Lighting of the building was accomplished during the first few years with oil lamps, nearly four hundred of them being required for the purpose. On either

side of the stage were posts holding kerosene lamps placed one above another, which served to light the stage well, if not brilliantly. The footlights presented rather a difficult problem but were controlled to some degree by a small shaft which ran from lamp to lamp and was turned to right or left as the lighting required. When the first plays were presented the lights were blown out if the stage needed to be darkened and relighted as the scene demanded.[17]

An orchestra of twenty provided music, and for choral effects (as in *Macbeth*) the entire Tabernacle Choir was employed. According to the well-traveled Lyne, "nowhere outside of the houses of the great populous cities, and in but few of them, was there such completeness of stage appointments, scenery and accessories as were found in Brigham Young's theatre, in the heart of the Rockies, in 1862."[18] A Massachusetts editor apparently agreed, calling the theater

> a rare triumph of art and enterprise. No eastern city of one hundred thousand inhabitants—remember Salt Lake City has less than twenty thousand—possesses so fine a theatrical structure. It ranks, alike in capacity, and elegance of structure and finish, along with the opera houses and academies of music of Boston, New York, Philadelphia, Chicago and Cincinnati.[19]

Upon its completion, the Salt Lake Theatre, dubbed the "cathedral in the desert," emerged as a dominant institution—architecturally, culturally, and visually. One contemporary recalled how "the building...dominated its locality. How calmly imposing, how grandly massive it then appeared! For many blocks one could then see the theatre, dark in the twilight, or its walls white in the sun and moonlight."[20]

The dedication took place in March 1862. After the prayer, Young took occasion to inveigh

> somewhat extravagantly against tragedy and declared he wouldn't have any tragedies or blood-curdling dramas played in this theater. This people had seen tragedy enough in real life and there was no telling the far-reaching and evil effects tragedies on the stage might have. He strongly opposed, too, the idea of having any Gentile actors play in this theatre. We had plenty of home talent and did not need them.[21]

The appetite for violent melodramas was at this moment becoming a national passion. The New York Bowery Theatre (largest in the country at its 1826 opening) came to stage such gory performances that it was nicknamed "the slaughter house."[22] Reliance on home-grown talent would also be bucking a national trend. In the first years of the early republic, most theaters had depended upon resident acting troupes. In 1810, the English actor George Frederick Cooke toured America, whetting a public taste for famous acting stars. Edmund Kean, perhaps the most renowned actor in English or American theater, visited the country a decade later, and this time the enthusiasm of American audiences was sufficient to firmly establish a trend. By the 1830s and 1840s, venues as far west as New Orleans were part of highly publicized theatrical tours by greats like Charles Mathews, Charles Kean, William Charles Macready, and Charles and Fanny Kemble.

For Brigham Young to build the most expensive structure to date in the Utah territory, a temple devoted to drama, and expect the managers to avoid both the most popular theatrical genre and the billing of gentile celebrities to fill the seats must have appeared, even to Young himself, as wishful thinking. The policies were not long in crumbling. Thomas Lyne, who had left the church almost two decades earlier in Nauvoo, reappeared now in Salt Lake, drawn by the new theater. He quickly accepted a position as the "tutor" to the theater, and opened in the lead role on January 14, 1863, in the Elizabethan tragic-comedy *Damon* to a full and appreciative house. He followed up this role with lead parts in both James Sheridan Knowles's *Virginius* and *Othello*. The staging of the former was a more dire threat to Young's policy than the latter. For *Othello* was a dark tragedy indeed, but in the former case, the murderous knife was thrust into the bosom of the fair Virginia, who was played by none other than Young's favored daughter Alice Clawson. Thus with one blow, the tragic heroine and Young's prohibition met their simultaneous and definitive ends.

Not that local talent didn't try their hand at authoring works of more edifying content. Edward W. Tullidge wrote a few historical dramas, and other Mormons made sporadic offerings. But the public appetite, now whetted by exposure to secular drama and the professional talents of Lyne, the eagerness of prominent actors attracted by the quality of the Salt Lake Theatre, and the ever-present profit motive all conspired to open the theater's floodgates to a torrent of premier actors from the national lineup who headlined in Salt Lake, playing parts in the best dramas that the world, rather than the church, had to offer. Succeeding Lyne as a popular draw were Mr. and Mrs. Selden Irwin in 1863. The next year brought George Pauncefort, an accomplished actor with London theatrical experience "who probably exerted the strongest influence for refinement in art and modern methods of any other artist of those days." Then came an actress whom the same critic considered "the most brilliant star that ever illuminated the western theatrical horizon, Julia Dean Hayne, who played in 1865 and 1866."[23] The actress stayed for a ten-month engagement, long enough to win the very public esteem of Young himself. He had a large, six-horse sleigh built, which he named the *Julia Dean Hayne*. Other notables included C. W. Couldock, Sara Alexander, E. L. Davenport, John McCullough, and James A. Herne with his wife, Lucille Western.

The timing of Young's theatrical foray was propitious, for the theater in America was at last entering into a period of respectability. One Mormon critic, fifty years later, would opine that the church's

> historic temple of the drama . . . was erected in the middle of the three decades which [were] the really golden period in the history of the American drama, the fifties, sixties, and seventies, a period that saw the advent of our Forrests, Booths, McCulloughs, Barretts, Keenes, Adamses, Jeffersons, Cushmans, Neilsons, Haynes, Andersons, and of our never-to-be-forgotten New York, Boston and San Francisco stock companies.[24]

An old Salt Lake actor recalled the era in similar terms, noting an audience more taken by personalities than by playwrights:

> That was the strong time of the legitimate drama. Even the people of the west became connoisseurs. People would go not to see a new play, but to see a new actor in an old part. How many actors did I see in the play of Hamlet? Pauncefort, Lyne, Adams, Kean, McCullough, Davenport, Miss Evans, Chaplin, Barrett, Booth—that is not half.[25]

With the coming of the railroad in 1869, Salt Lake's position on the national theater circuit was even more firmly entrenched. But by then, Young's failure to foster a dramatic tradition different in any notable way from popular, secular drama was complete. In 1873, the theater was sold to H. B. Clawson and some associates. The church's official role as sponsor of the valley's theatrical entertainments was over.

The construction of a theater in the wilderness—not just a makeshift affair for amateur theatricals, but a stunning edifice with the opulence and splendor of Drury Lane—was more than just a diversion to entertain weary pioneers. The initiative was a defiant affirmation of a harrowed people's most humane yearnings, and of their refusal to acquiesce to the role of benighted outcasts. The symbolic role of the theater in nullifying—or at least tempering—the effects of exile and provincialism was not lost on Saints or observers. "How [can I] suggest the indefinable something, the pleasure, the pain, the semi-solitude, the isolation?" recalled one veteran of the exodus.

How can I recall the humorous earnestness, the fine or roughness of fibre, the laughing or grim determination, the pathetic side of pioneer life? Yet it is all mixed up with my memories of the theatre. . . . It was erected by a people who had come over seas and plains and mountains; yes, people who had come through a country infested with savages, and into what had been formerly described as a region where the white man could not dwell, and this to establish a new commonwealth in the western wilderness. . . . The greater number of actors and actresses who belonged to the regular stock company had crossed the plains and mountains in ox or mule trains, more than one I believe, in a hand-cart company.[26]

Heber J. Grant later recalled a hostile General Lew Wallace, famed author of *Ben Hur* and governor of Arizona, who visited Salt Lake and was offered an introduction to Brigham Young by the theater manager. Wallace declined, believing the LDS leaders "a narrow, bigoted, sectarian lot." After touring a cooperative, a bank, and the Tabernacle, he finished up at the Salt Lake Theatre. Learning that Young was the force behind all four, he decided he wanted to meet the man after all, commenting on the breadth of mind of such a churchman.[27]

Theatrical entertainment may very well serve, in the form of spectacle or pageant, to convey in broad strokes a noble history or the rise and fall of ancient civilizations. And light dramatic fare was a staple of ward "road shows" for generations, providing clean fun and healthy competition. But Mormonism has not been conducive to the rise of the tragic genre itself, as Young's predilections foreshadowed. Some Mormon thinkers have recognized in this lack a cultural impoverishment. Philip Barlow, for instance, writes of passing a statue of a weeping man on the campus of the Episcopal Divinity School in Cambridge:

> I have considered the odds of such a troubled statue finding a home on Temple Square or on some other distinctly Mormon ground. The prospect seems unlikely. I do not mean a "look-how-much-the-pioneers-suffered-for-us" statue. We have that kind already and they are important tributes to valiant people. But I mean the art that reflects my stake in the universal plight of the race. It is hardly surprising that our public places house no such art, for Mormonism is an optimistic and proselyting faith, which desires—appropriately—to convey its optimism to others. Yet anguish is part of my reality, and Mormons are left largely without a profound public mechanism to convey and share that reality.[28]

One LDS critic likewise notes that Mormon writers "rarely employ tragedy in its classic form," but insists that "the aesthetic necessity of showing opposing forces, particularly in drama, is balanced in Mormon art by the value of showing how evil is overcome by forces of righteousness." This same critic finds a key to the Mormon aesthetic in the oft-cited Mormon scripture "Men are that they might have joy." Accordingly, he explains, "a spirit of buoyancy infuses Mormon expectations and finds expression in Mormon art. Emphasis on misery, degradation, and hopelessness are consistently absent."[29] At the theological level, this same tendency is manifest in the church's steadfast preference for the Christ of Gethsemane over the Christ of Calvary, air-brushed portraits of a serene Jesus rather than descents from the cross. When the Tabernacle Choir won a Grammy for "Battle Hymn of the Republic," it was no coincidence that it had changed the lyrics to one line in their recording: "let us *die* to make men free" became "let us *live* to make men free."

As Barlow intimates, a partial explanation is found in the Mormon missionary zeal that pervades the culture. "Every member a missionary," said the LDS prophet David O. McKay in 1961.[30] For almost a half-century, Mormons have had it drilled into their consciousness that they are under ceaseless obligation to teach the gospel and exemplify its positive fruits. Most are familiar with the Book of Mormon prophet Jacob's sobering words, "we did magnify our office unto the Lord, taking upon us the responsibility, answering the sins of the people upon our own heads if we did not teach them the word of God with all diligence" (Jacob 1:19). Mormon culture is clearly one of the most missionary-minded of contemporary Christian groups, having more full-time missionaries in the field at any given moment than the rest of a populous Protestantism combined. It is likely that, at the popular level, indulging a sense of the tragic would represent a kind of theological failure, a concession to the forces of evil and despair that engulf an apostate Christianity and a secular world.

The consequence for Mormon culture has been an affinity for art forms that celebrate life rather than those that investigate its tragic dimensions or probe its pathos. From Mormonism's earliest days, a kind of folk theology has emerged that virtually eliminates tragedy as the potent art form it could be. To begin with, Mormonism is thoroughly imbued with the conviction that major events of the restoration are providentially scripted. Even when events do not unfold according to plan, Mormons are convinced, as was C. S. Lewis, that "God can make good of all that happens." Or in the language of the Book of Mormon, "God . . . shall consecrate thine afflictions for thy gain," as Lehi promises his son Jacob (2 Nephi 2:2). And so it is that in Mormon history, even catastrophic events are ensconced in a narrative that turns the ostensibly tragic into triumph. Two prime examples are the fiasco of Zion's camp and the debacle of the Willie and Martin handcart companies.

In 1833, the Saints in Jackson County, Missouri, were driven from their homes in a nineteenth-century version of ethnic cleansing. Hearing of their sufferings, which included rape, pillage, property destruction, and death, Joseph responded by raising a paramilitary force of 200 men and marching to their relief. The group suffered persistent bickering and dissension along the way, lost more than a dozen to cholera, and disbanded upon arrival in Missouri, without effecting either the Saints' restoration to their forsaken lands or restitution for their loss.

In the cultural canon of Mormonism, however, Zion's camp fulfilled its purpose entirely—even if no one at the time knew what that purpose was. "When I returned from that mission to Kirtland," Young would later recount:

> a brother said to me, "Brother Brigham, what have you gained by this journey?" I replied, "Just what we went for; but I would not exchange the knowledge I have received this season for the whole of Geauga County; for property and mines of wealth are not to be compared to the worth of knowledge."

Similarly, Wilford Woodruff insisted:

> We gained an experience that we never could have gained in any other way. We had the privilege of beholding the face of the Prophet, and we had the privilege of traveling a thousand miles with him, and seeing the workings of the Spirit of God with him, and the revelations of Jesus Christ unto him and the fulfillment of those revelations. . . . Had I not gone up with Zion's Camp I should not have been here today, and I presume that would have been the case with many others in this Territory.[31]

As a modern leader summarizes, "out of this seeming 'furnace of affliction' came the refined cadre who, because of their experience, could call the cadence for future treks and who could pass through even sterner tests."[32]

The story of the heroic handcart companies is in some ways similar. Open handcarts six or seven feet in length, capable of holding 400–500 pounds of supplies, were cheaply and easily constructed, unlike the more capacious but expensive beast-driven wagons. In 1856, the church sponsored this innovative mode of travel, which had the great advantages of economy and simplicity appropriate to impoverished immigrants. The first groups arrived successfully in the fall of that year. But getting off to a late start, the last two companies of the season, commanded by James G. Willie and Edward Martin, were caught in deep Wyoming snows. Some 200 Saints eventually perished from cold and hunger before relief expeditions brought the suffering survivors into the valley.

It would seem natural to blame the church leadership for countenancing a 1,300-mile trek so late in the season, and a popular (but undocumented) LDS story recalls the response to one such example of assigning blame for the apparent tragedy. The incident is recounted in the tellingly titled *Best-Loved Stories of the LDS People* of how an aged man rose in a Sunday school class and addressed the fault finder:

> Mistake to send the Handcart Company out so late in the season? Yes. But I was in that company and my wife was in it and Sister Nellie Unthank whom you have cited was there, too. We suffered beyond anything you can imagine and many died of exposure and starvation, but did you ever hear a survivor of that company utter a word of criticism? Not one of that company ever apostatized [sic] or left the church, because everyone of us came through with the absolute knowledge that God lives for we became acquainted with him in our extremities. . . . Was I sorry that I chose to come by handcart? No. Neither then nor any minute of my life since. The price we paid to become acquainted with God was a privilege to pay, and I am thankful that I was privileged to come in the Martin Handcart Company.[33]

The compulsion to find providential design—or fortuitous consequence—in every catastrophe can obscure from Latter-day Saints the fact that, as Eugene England reminds them, "Mormon theology, revealed through Joseph Smith, claims that the universe is essentially, as well as existentially, paradoxical—and therefore is irreducibly tragic."[34] In the classic conception of tragedy first articulated by Hegel, tragedy is an irredeemable loss or renunciation necessitated by the collision of competing goods. In a teeming universe where many values with equal claim to legitimacy struggle for supremacy, it is inevitable that the good will often suffer at the hands of a greater or equivalent good. Hegel's prototypical example was the Theban heroine Antigone, caught between the incompatible demands of God and king, family and society, or the personal and the political. In LDS theology, a primal instance could be located in the irreconcilable tension between the dream of universal human happiness and the complicating gift of individual human agency. Latter-day Saints appear reluctant to plumb the implications of a theology that, ultimately, can afford no totalizing consolation. Yet any effort to gloss over the incalculable cost in human suffering entailed by human freedom ultimately can only be a misleading gesture, considering the fact that God himself, in the purported writings of Moses revealed by Joseph, is a weeping God:

> And it came to pass that the God of heaven looked upon the residue of the people, and he wept; and Enoch bore record of it, saying: How is it that the heavens weep, and shed forth their tears as the rain upon the mountains? And Enoch said unto the Lord: How is it that thou canst weep, seeing thou art holy, and from all eternity to all eternity? . . . and naught but peace, justice, and truth is the habitation of thy throne; and mercy shall go before thy face and have no end; how is it thou canst weep? The Lord said unto Enoch: Behold these thy brethren; they are the workmanship of mine own hands, and I gave unto them their knowledge, in the day I created them; and in the Garden of Eden, gave I unto man his agency; And unto thy brethren have I said, and also given commandment, that they should love one another, and that they should choose me, their Father; but behold, they are without affection, and they hate their own blood. (Moses 7:28–33, PGP)

It may be that historical distance from tragic circumstance is necessary before pain and sorrow become the object of aesthetic contemplation and creation. Or it may be that Mormonism has yet to find room in its buoyant optimism for the recognition of Lewis mentioned earlier: "God can make use of all that happens. But the loss is real." Yet this is a loss that is largely absent from Mormon consciousness. Perhaps crucially for its cultural mindset, Mormons sharply part company with fellow Christians at this critical juncture of the fall of man. "And now, behold," Nephi writes in the Book of Mormon:

> if Adam had not transgressed he would not have fallen, but he would have remained in the garden of Eden. And all things which were created must have remained in the same state in which they were after they were created; and they must have remained forever, and had no end. And they would have had no children; wherefore they would have remained in a state of innocence, having no joy, for they knew no misery; doing no good, for they knew no sin. But behold, all things have been done in the wisdom of him who knoweth all things. Adam fell that men might be; and men are, that they might have joy. (2 Nephi 2:22–25)

It may be difficult to overestimate the impact of a theology that begins its account of human history with foreordained triumph rather than universal catastrophe. Of course, even in a gospel where the fall is ultimately fortunate, the cost of that fall can be immense. But in the lexicon of nineteenth-century Mormon culture, the safety of certainties generally trumped the unsettling quest to fathom the depths of that price.

"NOVELS RATHER
THAN NOTHING"

Literature

It is not without significance that Mormonism, beginning with a book, had to make its appeal to a literate
following. The proselyte had to be able to read.

~ William Mulder

Joseph Smith was a poet, and poets are not like other
men; their gaze is deeper, and reaches the roots of the
soul; it is like that of the searching eyes of angels; they
catch the swift thought of God and reveal it to us.

~ Brigham Young

It is virtually taken as a truism today that great literature must be born of mental
anguish and existential disquiet, a mirror of the spirit's turmoil and the world's
fractured condition. That is, of course, a bias of the modern age, which is suspicious of absolutes and optimism. Dante's *Divine Comedy* is generally acclaimed
as the greatest literary production of the Middle Ages, but it reflects a religious
certainty such as few authors have claimed. His supreme self-confidence in his
religious vision imbues his poem with such magisterial authority that Harold
Bloom likens it to a third testament. Similarly, John Milton unabashedly proposes, in his epic *Paradise Lost*, to plumb the depths of heaven and hell, lay bare
the workings of the eternal mind, and "justify the ways of God to man." The
Trinity might be unfathomable even to a poet of Milton's stature, but God's
purposes and our place in the cosmos are not.

It may be the peculiar literary misfortune of Mormonism to have emerged on
the world stage at a time when certainty and spiritual self-assurance had fallen
into unambiguous disfavor. The optimism and confidence born of Christian
belief had long since fallen victim to Humean doubt and Enlightenment

rationalism. The smugness of Enlightenment rationalism, in its turn, was largely swept aside by Romanticism's infatuation with mystery, ineffability, and the great unknown. The idol of this new era was the sublime, and Immanuel Kant even propounded a philosophical basis for infatuation with this ineffable quality. It is prompted, he theorized, by the inability of the human imagination to represent to itself the concept of infinity evoked by nature. It is in the very structure of this mental failure, he asserts, that this sublime (which Edmund Burke calls the most powerful human emotion) is rooted. This failure, this imaginative incapacity in the face of the absolute, is the very ground of a kind of reverential awe with which we confront the universe.

No wonder that Mormonism from its very birth has found itself out of sync with the literary aesthetic that develops out of these Romantic agonies. For Mormonism is of all religions perhaps the most relentlessly incompatible with traditional conceptions of the holy, connected as those conceptions are to sublimity, incomprehensibility, immaterialism, and other guarantors of sacred distance. Renée Haynes has put the case most simply: "The more detailed pictures of life after death are, the less acceptable they seem to be."[1] But it is not just regarding the afterlife that Christians steer shy of specificity. As Emerson sums up his appraisal of the Christian mystic Emanuel Swedenborg's writings in general: "In his profuse and *accurate* imagery is no pleasure, for there is no beauty."[2] As William James so astutely observed, for some religious persons, "*richness* is the supreme imaginative requirement. When one's mind is of this type, [one's yearning is] for adjectives of mystery and splendor, derived in the last resort from the Godhead."[3]

Mormonism is in this regard a grand disappointment. A scholar of early Christianity, W. D. Davies, has noted the Mormon habit of taking "conventional modes of revelation found in the OT . . . so literally . . . as to give a facticity to what was intended as symbolic." After all, he writes, "the revelation to Moses as recorded in the OT can hardly be taken literally as an event in which the Divine handed over or dictated to Moses Ten Commandments."[4] But for Mormons, it *was* a literal handing over. Just as Moroni literally handed over to Joseph physical, tangible plates with heft and texture (heavy as lead, said Martin Harris; "beautifully engraved, not quite so thick as common tin," said Joseph and other witnesses). God has a body, Zion is a city, heaven is a real place (and so is the Book of Mormon city Zarahemla), and by the power of the Holy Ghost, "all things" may be known. Not much room for mystery, awe, or poetic yearning toward the ineffable in all of that, or so it would seem.

PLAIN AND PRECIOUS

Educator and Latter-day Saint Arthur Henry King finds in Joseph's expository prose describing his first visions a new and unexpected artistic treatment of the sacred. Joseph's description of a visit by God and his Son to a fourteen-year-old boy, King writes, is "an astonishingly matter-of-fact and cool account."[5]

Written in 1838, when Joseph was a man of thirty-three, the narrative canonized as the First Vision is, indeed, rhetorically sparse:

> After I had retired to the place where I had previously designed to go, having looked around me, and finding myself alone, I kneeled down and began to offer up the desires of my heart to God. . . . I saw a pillar of light exactly over my head, above the brightness of the sun, which descended gradually until it fell upon me. . . . When the light rested upon me I saw two Personages, whose brightness and glory defy all description, standing above me in the air. One of them spake unto me, calling me by name and said, pointing to the other—This is My Beloved Son. Hear Him!
>
> My object in going to inquire of the Lord was to know which of all the sects was right, that I might know which to join. No sooner, therefore, did I get possession of myself, so as to be able to speak, than I asked the Personages who stood above me in the light, which of all the sects was right (for at this time it had never entered into my heart that all were wrong)—and which I should join. I was answered that I must join none of them, for they were all wrong; and the Personage who addressed me said that all their creeds were an abomination in his sight; that those professors were all corrupt; that: "they draw near to me with their lips, but their hearts are far from me, they teach for doctrines the commandments of men, having a form of godliness, but they deny the power thereof." He again forbade me to join with any of them; and many other things did he say unto me, which I cannot write at this time. When I came to myself again, I found myself lying on my back, looking up into heaven. When the light had departed, I had no strength; but soon recovering in some degree, I went home. (Joseph Smith—History 1:15–20, PGP)

The account is most noteworthy for its understated, dispassionate tone. There is no effort to register in any degree either the emotional impact to the young boy, or the cosmic significance to an oblivious world. Not even a token gesture to convince or persuade an audience, even in the face of the naked implausibility of the God of heaven appearing in person to a boy in an upstate New York woods in 1820. One is reminded of the most unlikely of all Old Testament stories, the speaking of the ass to the prophet Balaam. Not that the miracle is itself any more incredible than parting seas or legions of angels and fiery chariots. It is that, spoken to by his suddenly articulate beast, Balaam responds without a hint of surprise—as if a talking ass were part of the fabric of every person's universe (Numbers 22). Not the bald supernaturalism, but Balaam's nonchalant reaction to such wildly incredible supernaturalism is what makes the account implausible.

Only in Joseph Smith's case, the stunned reaction is implicit in the account—it simply doesn't try to compete for prominence with the facts *conveyed* to Joseph through the miraculous encounter. After all, the boy—unlike Balaam—does need to "get possession of [him]self" before he can reply, and he requires some "recovering" when the episode is over. That he simply "went home" at the vision's conclusion marks a closure of both classic understatement—and ironic portent. For as we soon learn, he can of course never go back to a home or a world that is the same again.

Joseph's account of a subsequent visitation by the resurrected John the Baptist duplicates the eminently understated, matter-of-fact tone of his First Vision:

> [W]e on a certain day went into the woods to pray and inquire of the Lord respecting baptism for the remission of sins. . . . While we were thus employed, praying and calling upon the Lord, a messenger from heaven descended in a cloud of light, and having laid his hands upon us, ordained us. . . . [Then] he commanded us to go and be baptized, and gave us directions that I should baptize Oliver Cowdery and afterwards that he should baptize me. Accordingly we went and were baptized.[6]

Oliver Cowdery, Joseph's scribe, was a schoolteacher by profession and more given to conventional modes of rhetorical eloquence. His account of the same event is a powerful foil to the stark simplicity of Joseph's style:

> On a sudden, as from the midst of eternity, the voice of the Redeemer spake peace to us, while the veil was parted and the angel of God came down clothed with glory, and delivered the anxiously looked for message, and the keys of the Gospel of repentance. What joy! what wonder! what amazement! While the world was racked and distracted—while millions were groping as the blind for the wall, and while all men were resting upon uncertainty, as a general mass, our eyes beheld, our ears heard, as in the "blaze of day"; yes, more— above the glitter of the May sunbeam, which then shed its brilliancy over the face of nature! Then his voice, though mild, pierced to the center, and his words, "I am thy fellow-servant," dispelled every fear. We listened, we gazed,

we admired! 'Twas the voice of an angel from glory, 'twas a message from the Most High! And as we heard we rejoiced, while His love enkindled upon our souls, and we were wrapped in the vision of the Almighty! Where was room for doubt? Nowhere; uncertainty had fled, doubt had sunk no more to rise, while fiction and deception had fled forever![7]

Joseph's contrasting nonchalance in the face of the miraculous was perhaps best reprised a few years later, on the occasion of the extensive epiphany in which he described the various glories of the heavenly kingdoms as well as the fate of the damned. His associate Sidney Rigdon was privy to the same vision, while a dozen others witnessed the event at secondhand. One of them later remarked, "Joseph sat firmly and calmly all the time in the midst of a magnificent glory, but Sidney sat limp and pale, apparently as limber as a rag, observing which, Joseph remarked, smilingly, 'Sidney is not used to it as I am.' "[8]

But it would seem that more than habituation to the sacred is responsible for Joseph's assimilation of supernatural experience to naturalistic discourse, because to reject the language of transcendence is emphatically to assert a particular theological position. "It is no paradox," writes George Steiner, "to assert that in cardinal respects reality now begins outside verbal language."[9] He has in mind not just the improbabilities of the new quantum physics—but the historical impossibility of circumscribing sacred categories within normal human discourse. This history goes from the unspeakable tetragrammon (wherein JHVH represents the unsayable) through the *via negativa* of medieval theology (we can say what God is not but not what God is) to Steiner's own insistence:

> [A]t its furthest reach, where it borders on light, the language of men becomes inarticulate. . . . Those who would press language beyond its divinely ordained sphere, who would contract the Logos into the word, mistake both the genius of speech and the untranslatable immediacy of revelation. They thrust their hands into the fire instead of gathering light.[10]

But central to Joseph Smith's thought is the collapse of the sacred distance that consigns man and God to existentially and ontologically separate spheres. Consequently, Joseph's language must reflect that collapse.

At the same time, narrating sacred history and chronicling his interactions with the divine are not the same thing as giving voice to God's pronouncements themselves. For that reason, Joseph's prophetic voice, in which he assumes the position and authority of spokesman for God, *is* marked by distinctive diction and syntax, and with lasting effect on Mormon conceptions of sacred language.

Joseph's account of his First Vision did not come into general circulation in the church for many years. (Orson Pratt would first publish it to the world from Scotland in 1840, in *An Interesting Account of Several Remarkable Visions*.) But Joseph's literary style was widely disseminated through the many revelations he published in church newspapers from 1832 on and, beginning in 1835, in collected form. Like the Book of Mormon he translated, the revelations contained in the Book of Commandments (later expanded as the Doctrine and Covenants) were produced in the style of King James English.

As an intensely Bible-literate community, immersing itself in not just one, but four volumes of King Jamesian scripture, Latter-day Saint culture was, and continues to be, comfortably familiar with those speech patterns. The four works of scripture are exhaustively interrelated and interconnected, not only through an extensive footnote and cross-referencing apparatus, but through internal cross-citations. In the Book of Mormon, for instance, Christ quotes from the Book of John, and rehearses portions of the Sermon on the Mount, in many cases verbatim from the Authorized Version. Isaiah is profusely cited throughout the record, and in *The Pearl of Great Price*, the angel Moroni quotes other Old Testament prophets using diction, if not always wording, precisely like the King James version.

As a consequence of all this reinforcement, King James English is, in Mormonism, firmly identified with sacred language and absolutely immune to any modernizing reform in the realms of prayer, ordinances, or the scriptures themselves.

In addition to Joseph's scriptural production, a genre that would become a central mode for Mormon self-expression is the personal narrative, cast either as autobiography or as journal record. In stark contrast to the Old Testament, which begins as an impersonally narrated account of cosmic creation, the very first verse of the Book of Mormon introduces Nephi's work as the personal "record of [his] proceedings," thus forging a link between scripture and personal history that persists in Mormon culture. For the Puritans, journal keeping had been an important instrument of spiritual self-reflection and an occasion for discerning God's hand in both personal life and contemporary events. Puritan divines like John Cotton and Jonathan Edwards (as well as ministers' wives like Sarah Edwards), Puritan leaders like John Winthrop, Puritan merchants like Samuel Sewall, and Puritan women like Hety Shepard—all wrote to bear witness and to search their own souls. The titles they gave to their records, such as Simon Bradstreet's *Brief Record of Remarkable Providences and Accidents* and *Remembrances of the Greatest Changes in My Life* attest to their focus on the intersection of the personal and the providential.

Mormon record keepers drew upon these foundations, which were reinforced by an intense conviction of the historical uniqueness of their moment on the world stage. Bolstering this shift of historical consciousness from the private to the general was the divine command given on the day of the church's organization that "there shall be a record kept among you" (D&C 21:1) to chronicle the new dispensation. And once initiated, the Saints were convinced, nothing could slow the growing momentum of the divine juggernaut. "What power shall stay the heavens?" Joseph queried. "As well might man stretch forth his puny arm to stop the Missouri river in its decreed course" (D&C 121:33). In addition, the growing persecution they suffered as a movement, their fixation on persecution as a sign of chosen status, together with the specific injunction to chronicle those persecutions in detail, added a special emphasis to their record keeping. From his confinement in jail at Liberty, Missouri, Joseph urged upon his followers the "imperative duty that we owe, not only to our own wives and children, but to the widows and fatherless" to compile a record of "all the facts, and sufferings, and abuses put upon them" (D&C 123:9, 1).

Given this directive, and the fact that thousands of Latter-day Saints died directly or indirectly from persecution and exile in the church's first two decades, it is no surprise that many texts of great poignancy and sublimity emerge from those early years. Artemisia Sidnie Myers was a nine-year-old girl when she experienced the Haun's Mill massacre on the afternoon of October 30, 1838. She would later write of that night:

> About dark word came to us that the mobbers were coming, and that men, women and children had better hide in the woods as they intended to kill all they could find. . . . The men were told to hide by themselves. After the men were gone, the women took the children and went about a mile and a half to the woods, and after the children were got to sleep and lights put out, my mother put on a man's coat and stood guard until one or two o'clock when word was brought to us that they had had a battle at the mill and two of my brothers were wounded. . . . When we came to [my brother's] house, we went in and found him lying on the bed. When mother saw him she exclaimed, "O Lord have mercy on my boy." He replied, "Don't fret mother, I shall not die." He was very weak from loss of blood. I will here relate the manner of his escape in his own words as he told to us after he got better. Our guns were all in the blacksmith's shop when the mob came upon us unexpectedly. Orders were given to run to the shop. The mob formed a half circle on the north side of the shop extending partly across the east and west ends, so as to cover all retreat from the shop. They commenced firing before we could escape with our arms. . . . I made two or three jumps for the door when a bullet struck me a little below the right shoulder blade and lodged against the skin near the pit of

my stomach. I fell to the ground. Mother, if ever a boy prayed I did at this time. I thought it would not do to lie there, so I arose and ran for the mill dam and crossed over it, and ran up the hill; the bullets whistling by me all the time. When I came to the fence and was climbing over it a ball passed through my shirt collar. I walked as far as I could but soon became so weak from loss of blood, I had to get on my hands and knees and crawl the rest of the way home.... After mother had dressed George's wounds, we went to the mill, where we arrived just at break of day. I shall never forget the awful scene that met our eyes. When we got to Haun's house the first scene that presented itself in his dooryard was the remains of Father York and McBride and others covered with sheets. As we went down the hill to cross on the mill dam, there stood a boy over a pool of blood. He said to mother, "Mother Myers, this is the blood of my poor father." This, with the groans of the wounded, which we could distinctly hear, affected my mother so that she was unable to make any reply to the boy. We made our way to my brother Jacob's house.... From my brother's house we went to the blacksmith's shop where we beheld a most shocking sight. There lay the dead, the dying, and the wounded, weltering in their blood, where they fell. A young man, whose name was Simon Cox, who lived with my father lay there, four bullets having passed through his body above the kidneys. He was still alive. He said to mother, all he wanted was a bowl of sweet milk and a feather bed to lie on. He had just got a pair of new boots a few days before, and he told mother how they dragged him about the shop to get them off. He told us to be faithful, and said to me, "Be a good girl and obey your parents." He died in the afternoon about 24 hours after he was shot. After we went back to my brother's house, my father, David Evans, and Joseph Young, with one or two more came and gathered up the dead and carried them to my brother's place and put them into a well which he had been digging, but had not yet come to water. They brought them on a wide board and slid them off feet forward. Every time they brought one and slid him in I screamed and cried. It was such an awful sight to see them piled in the bottom in all shapes. After the dead were buried, (which was done in a great hurry,) father and the brethren went away and secreted themselves for fear the mobbers would come on them again.[11]

Myers's future husband, Warren Foote, was at the time of the massacre a twenty-one-year-old who had cast his lot with the Mormons, but whose interest and sympathy did not yet amount to conversion. In the area but alerted at the time of the massacre, he spent several nights hiding in the woods. An avid and literate diarist, he chronicled the persecutions, his own faith journey, and daily life in the exile he shared with thousands of others at this time. Of the days after Haun's Mill, he distilled the essence of ordinary life lived under extraordinary circumstances: "We had a great many spelling matches and parties in the neighborhood during the winter, and all enjoyed themselves, as well as they could under the circumstances. The mobbers did not allow the Saints to hold meetings but the young would have their amusements."[12]

Foote finally joined the church in 1842. Consequently, he experienced the events of August 1844 as something more than an interested observer:

> Elihu Allen and I were working in the harvest field cutting his wheat when about three o'clock P.M. my wife came and told us that word had just come that Joseph Smith and his brother Hiram [sic] was shot in Carthage Jail yesterday afternoon. I said at once, "that it cannot be so." Yet it so affected us that we dropped the cradle and rake and went home. We found that the word had come so straight that we could no longer doubt the truth of it. We all felt as though the powers of darkness had overcome, and that the Lord had forsaken His people. Our Prophet and Patriarch were gone! Who now is to lead the Saints? In fact, we mourned "as one mourneth for his only son." Yet after all the anguish of our hearts and the deep anguish of our souls a spirit seemed to whisper "All is well. Zion shall yet arise and spread abroad upon the earth, and the kingdoms of this world shall become the Kingdom of our God and His Christ." So we felt to trust in God.[13]

Probably the most eloquent of the first-generation chroniclers was Parley P. Pratt, though his rhetorical flourishes partake more of the Romantic age in which he lived than of the understated Puritan tradition of his forebears. In his account of Joseph's incarceration in Liberty jail, Pratt gives us perhaps the most striking instance of Joseph Smith hagiography. The scene unfolded mere days after the tragedy at Haun's Mill. Outnumbered and outgunned, the Saints in Far West, Missouri, capitulated to thousands of state militia men and mobbers. Betrayed under pretense of a parley, Joseph and several other leaders were arrested and sentenced to be shot. The order was not carried out, but instead the men were detained, tried, and later imprisoned in Liberty for several months. Detained briefly in Richmond, Missouri, Joseph and Pratt were subjected to a long night of abuse by their jailors:

> In one of those tedious nights we had lain as if in sleep till the hour of midnight had passed, and our ears and hearts had been pained, while we had listened for hours to the obscene jests, the horrid oaths, the dreadful blasphemies and filthy

language of our guards, Colonel Price at their head, as they recounted to each other their deeds of rapine, murder, robbery, etc., which they had committed among the "Mormons" while at Far West and vicinity. They even boasted of defiling by force wives, daughters, and virgins, and of shooting or dashing out the brains of men, women and children.

I had listened till I became so disgusted, shocked, horrified, and so filled with the spirit of indignant justice that I could scarcely refrain from rising upon my feet and rebuking the guards; but had said nothing to Joseph, or any one else, although I lay next to him and knew he was awake. On a sudden he arose to his feet, and spoke in a voice of thunder, or as the roaring lion, uttering, as near as I can recollect, the following words: "*SILENCE, ye fiends of the infernal pit. In the name of Jesus Christ I rebuke you, and command you to be still. I will not live another minute and hear such language. Cease such talk, or you or I die THIS INSTANT!*"

He ceased to speak. He stood erect in terrible majesty. Chained, and without a weapon; calm, unruffled and dignified as an angel, he looked upon the quailing guards; whose weapons were lowered or dropped to the ground, whose knees smote together, and who, shrinking into a corner, or crouching at his feet, begged his pardon, and remained quiet till a change of guards.

I have seen the ministers of justice, clothed in magisterial robes, and criminals arraigned before them, while life was suspended on a breath, in the courts of England; I have witnessed a Congress in solemn session to give laws to nations; I have tried to conceive of kings, of royal courts, of thrones and crowns; and of emperors assembled to decide the fate of kingdoms; but dignity and majesty have I seen but once, as it stood in chains, at midnight, in a dungeon in an obscure village of Missouri.[14]

POETRY

In the nineteenth century, poetry had few of the negative connotations of novels, and much to commend it as an expressive medium. "The breath and finer spirit of all knowledge," Wordsworth called poetry in 1798.[15] Even nonpoets knew that short lyric expression as found in the psalms was scripturally sanctioned. The text of sacred hymns was but poetry put to music. And while there would always be impassioned Petrarchs and even lurid Sapphos, the devotional and confessional aspects of poetry were generally paramount, and, as Francis Bacon had put the case with none to dissent, "Poesy was ever thought to have some participation of divineness." And, perhaps most important for its more general popularity, poetry was a form whose brevity and apparent simplicity could delude the dilettante into a feeling of cheerful competence in its execution (then as now).

And so it is not surprising that the first forays into creative writing by Mormons were in the field of poetry. It was, in fact, the rule rather than the exception for religious leaders themselves to dabble in poetic expression. Charles Wesley published extensively, and Joseph's contemporary Alexander Campbell, while insisting that "reformation is not a work of poetry, but of prose," still felt obliged to provide in his church paper "a little more poetry by way of relief," writing some verses himself.[16] Not to be left out, Joseph put his own hand (or at least his signature—the authorship is uncertain) to an extended poem, "The Vision." The title refers to his glimpse of the three kingdoms of glory, when

> I Joseph, the prophet, in spirit beheld,
>> And the eyes of the inner man truly did see
> Eternity sketch'd in a vision from God,
>> Of what was, and now is, and yet is to be.[17]

The poetry is mediocre, but the effort is notable as Joseph's only known foray into artistic expression of any kind. His particular support for the poetic enterprise was seconded by other LDS leaders. Franklin Richards, president of the European mission, in 1856 went so far as to urge, "[I]t is the duty and privilege of the Saints . . . to procure and study the poetical works of the Church, that their authors may be encouraged and the spirit of poetry [may be] cultivated in the bosoms of the readers."[18]

By the "works of the Church," Richards meant the poems of members like John Lyon, the "Scottish bard" of Mormonism. He was a convert whose poetry appeared regularly in the *Millennial Star*, the church's periodical published in Liverpool. In 1853, British church officials published an amazing 5,000-plus copies of a Lyon anthology, *The Harp of Zion*. Some 1,000 copies sold in the next two years in Britain, which was probably a disappointment. Given that five decades earlier, only half that number sold of William Wordsworth's brilliant inaugural collection in its first two years,[19] 1,000 copies was a more than respectable showing, especially considering that the British LDS audience was extremely small, largely destitute, and often husbanding their meager resources to emigrate to Utah.

Three years later, in 1856, the same European mission published Eliza R. Snow's *Poems: Religious, Political, Historical*. Already well-loved and -known among the American Saints, her work fared poorly in Britain, selling less than twenty copies. Snow's poetry still finds little readership now, though this plural wife of Joseph Smith almost single-handedly established the doctrine of a heavenly Mother through her poem composed upon Joseph's death, originally called "Invocation":

O my Father, thou that dwellest
In the high and glorious place,
When shall I regain thy presence
And again behold thy face?
In thy holy habitation,
Did my spirit once reside?
In my first primeval childhood,
Was I nurtured near thy side?

For a wise and glorious purpose
Thou hast placed me here on Earth
And withheld the recollection
Of my former friends and birth;
Yet ofttimes a secret something
Whispered, "You're a stranger here,"
And I felt that I had wandered
From a more exalted sphere.

I had learned to call thee Father,
Through thy Spirit from on high,
But, until the key of knowledge
Was restored, I knew not why.
In the heavens our parents single?
No, the thought makes reason stare!
Truth is reason; truth eternal
Tells me I've a mother there.

When I leave this frail existence,
When I lay this mortal by,
Father, Mother, may I meet you
In your royal court on high?
Then, at length, when I've completed
All you sent me for to do,
With your mutual approbation
Let me come and dwell with you.[20]

Not all of Snow's poetry was devotional—but even her playful vein is a bit ponderous by today's standards. In "Mental Gas," she employs mock-scientific language to reply to a student's query about nature and vacuums:

> ... That space of vacuum, sir, explain—
> When solid sense forsakes the brain,
>> Pray what supplies its place?
> O, sir, I think I see it now—
> When substance fails, you will allow
>> Air occupies the space.
> ... This gas, entire, may be obtain'd
> From skulls whence sense is mostly drain'd,
>> Or never had supplies:
> But were the noblest heads disclos'd,
> From acts and motives decompos'd,
>> This mental gas would rise.
> The parson's lecture, lawyer's plea,
> Devoted sums of charity,
>> The sage with book profound;
> The Muse's pen, the churchman's creed,
> The mill-boy on his pacing steed,
>> Are more or less compound.[21]

Both Lyon and Snow had been preempted in their ground-breaking poetry collections by the real pioneer of Mormon literature, however. Parley P. Pratt published a collection of his own poetry, consisting partly of hymn lyrics, as *The Millennium, a Poem: To Which Are Added Hymns and Songs*, in 1835, making it the first book of poetry published by a Mormon. Three of his compositions were published that same year in the first LDS hymnal, but he would eventually write more than fifty (including the Tabernacle Choir's signature "As the Dew from Heaven Distilling").

Pratt was both prolific and diverse. We saw that he published the first theological treatise of the new church, and in addition to writing the greatest autobiography of early Mormonism, Pratt wrote the first satire (*Demetrius the Silversmith*, published in England in 1840) and the first short story of Mormonism, the comic "Dialogue between Joseph Smith and the Devil," which was published in the *New York Herald* on the first day of 1844. Much of it is lighthearted fare that makes the gentlemanly Satan the corporate sponsor of orthodox Christianity ("I am fond of praying, singing, church-building, bell-ringing, going to meeting, preaching," etc., as long as churches steer clear of the "abominable doctrine . . . of direct communication with God, by new revelation"). The most striking idea Pratt introduces is what Satan describes as a shift in his strategy of undermining Joseph Smith. All prior representations of the Prophet as "a very ignorant, silly man" have by now, he explains, been given the lie by the manifest "torrent of intelligence" he has poured forth, and the "host of talented and thinking men around" him. Henceforth, he warns, he will embark on an opposite tack:

> I shall endeavor to magnify you and your success from this time forward and to make you appear as much larger than the reality as you have heretofore fallen short. If my former course has excited contempt and caused you to be despised and thus kept you out of notice, my future course will be to excite jealousy, fear and alarm, till all the world is ready to arise and crush you.[22]

Joseph coolly replies that he will "endeavor to go ahead to that degree that . . . all your representations of my greatness [shall] be a reality." Pratt was eerily prescient. Weeks later, Joseph decided to announce a campaign for the presidency of the United States, and martyrdom followed that summer, provoked in large measure by the fear and alarm his political aspirations generated.

Apart from Pratt's dialogue, precious little fiction was written by the early Saints. The assessment of Mormon historian Leonard Arrington has never been disputed: "the Latter-day Saints produced no imaginative literature for the national market. For all practical purposes, for the hundred years from the death of Joseph Smith to 1938, virtually no imaginative literature of our own creation went outside our own group." Arrington blames the usual culprits: fiction was a pastime that Saints in survival mode could ill afford, and they inherited the Puritan prejudice against an art form that trafficked in falsehood.[23]

True enough, nothing less than a revelation from God had commanded the Saints to "seek ye out of the best books words of wisdom" (D&C 88:118), but those best books were seldom taken to mean fiction. Indeed, creative exegesis often took those words to mean any books *but* the literary kind, and still does to an embarrassing degree. "Surely the best of the 'best books' are the scriptures," writes an LDS apostle, and LDS scriptural commentaries repeat that gloss (even though specific references enjoining scriptural study are abundant and unambiguous elsewhere).[24] "The two best books for a child are a good mother's face and life," opined a more original church editor.[25] Fearing lest liberality of interpretation countenance mere fiction, one mother writing to her children a few decades later explicitly declared that "Good books" implicitly excluded "foolish trash and novels."[26]

In part, Mormons were in this regard simply products of their time. Born in the age of sentimentalism and developed by the Romantics, the novel was originally characterized by excessive emotion or Gothic melodrama. No less a poet than William Wordsworth condemned the "frantic novels" of contemporary writers,[27] and even the master novelist Jane Austen defended them with ambiguous wit. Asked what she is reading, a feisty heroine replies sardonically, "Only a novel. Only some work in which the greatest powers of the mind are displayed, in which the most thorough knowledge of human nature, the happiest delineation of its varieties, the liveliest effusions of wit and humour, are conveyed to the world in the best-chosen language."[28] But that same character is about to find her mind as unbalanced by her habit as Don Quixote had been by the romances of earlier centuries.

To many nineteenth-century moralists, "the foolish novel reading of the present generation"[29] occupied the same place in American culture that TV viewing does today—reviled as a mindless addiction distracting young and old alike from more meaningful pursuits. To some extent, literary decadence was more associated with European trends, as when the church paper condemned "the new popular novels, the memoirs and the favorite melodramas of Paris, [which] beggar all description of their depravity."[30] But when it came to novels, the indictments generally knew no geographical exceptions. A church newspaper of 1835 warned of the "lying novel, that is calculated to lead the mind of lightness and lechery."[31] And in the words of a John Taylor editorial, novels were "as destitute of truth, true science and practical knowledge as Satan's promises were to Eve." Why, continued Taylor, "read the fancied brains of disappointed men and women, and then go the theatre; and ten to one, but you will be just like them."[32] It is also likely that, early in LDS history, the particular purposes American fiction was coming to serve added to the mutual antipathy of popular literature and Mormonism. By the early 1850s, as the first of over 100 novels lampooning and vilifying Mormons began to appear, the Saints could only be reinforced in their sense that novels were primarily the instruments of the devil, intrinsically hostile to God and godliness.

Joseph established in Nauvoo a library and literary institute, and while the records reveal a Mormon appetite for serious nonfiction, novels fared poorly. One scholar notes:

> Locke's *An Essay Concerning Human Understanding*, biographies of Napoleon, histories of England, France, and the United States were read frequently by the citizens of Nauvoo. Joseph Smith himself owned such works as Thomas Dick's *Philosophy of a Future State*, Mosheim's *Church History*, and the *Histoire de Charles*, to name only a few of the volumes in his Nauvoo library.[33]

Once arrived in Utah, the best endorsement Young could offer the novel was hardly praise: "If it would do any good, I would advise you to read books that are worth reading," but "I would rather that persons read novels than read nothing."[34] By the late nineteenth century, little had changed in what seemed to be a vendetta of the LDS against works of fiction. In 1888, an LDS editorialist even warned, "The mischief of voracious novel-reading is really much more like the mischief of dram-drinking than appears at first sight."[35]

Mormons were hardly alone in their exemption of the novel from the praise more generally accorded to other works of literary fiction. In the 1830s, few American authors had achieved international renown. In poetry, none had, and the novel was only beginning to enter its great age. James Fenimore Cooper, exploiting the historical novel pioneered only a few years earlier by Sir Walter Scott, began to apply European models to American contexts. Emerson's clarion call for an authentic American literature, which he issued to the Harvard Divinity School graduating class in 1837, thus gave impetus to a tendency already beginning to emerge. The golden age of American literature, called the American Renaissance, shortly followed, with Herman Melville, Walt Whitman, Nathaniel Hawthorne, Emerson himself, and Henry David Thoreau, along with a host of compatriots, creating a plethora of authentic American masterpieces.

At the time of Emerson's Phi Beta Kappa address, the Mormons were struggling for survival, dealing with internal dissension in Ohio and mobocrats in Missouri. As with American artists, it would take two generations and a period of relative stability before Mormon thoughts turned to aesthetic autonomy and independence from the cultural models that dominated their ancestors. Women's leaders like Emmeline B. Wells and Susa Young Gates had both been urging and modeling a resistance to gentile values and the production of a literature by and for Mormons, and a formal call was at last issued in 1888 by Orson Whitney, LDS apostle and man of letters. Just as Emerson had yearned for the time when America's "day of dependence," and "our long apprenticeship to the learning of other lands, draws to a close," and chided Americans for listening "too long to the courtly muses of Europe,"[36] so was Whitney's appeal both a chastisement and a challenge. With Victorian extravagance, he invoked the day

> when Zion, no longer the foot, but as the head, the glorious front of the world's civilization, would arise and shine "the joy of the whole earth," when, side by side with pure Religion, would flourish Art and Science, her fair daughters; when music, poetry, painting, sculpture, oratory and the drama, rays of light from the same central sun, ... would throw their white radiance full and direct upon the mirror-like glory of her towers.

Insisting that "culture is the duty of man" and that the particular burden of the Saints was to "do the works of Abraham," he transformed the church's long-standing ambivalence toward literature into unqualified endorsement. "What has all this to do with literature?" he asked. "It is by means of literature that much of this great work will have to be accomplished."

The literary tradition he hoped to foster he called a "home literature," and it was to follow the familiar cultural pattern of establishing both continuity and difference, of affirming Mormonism's credentials as a culturally literate community, even as it asserted its transcendent peculiarity:

> It is from the warp and woof of all learning, so far as we are able to master it and make it ours, that the fabric of our literature must be woven. . . . [But] above all things, we must be original. The Holy Ghost is the genius of "Mormon" literature. . . . No pouring of old wine into new bottles. No patterning after the dead forms of antiquity. Our literature must live and breathe for itself. Our mission is diverse from all others; our literature must also be. . . . In God's name and by his help we will build up a literature whose top shall touch heaven.[37]

Whitney's summons to greatness came not just in the midst of Mormon mediocrity, but during a literary low-water mark in American letters as well—at least as gauged by consumer appetite. The American market in the three previous decades had been dominated by the works of British and American masters. George Eliot, William Thackeray, Walt Whitman, Anthony Trollope, Charles Dickens, Emile Zola, Gustave Flaubert, and Robert Louis Stevenson had all been bestselling authors in the period from 1850 to the mid-1880s. The year of Whitney's address, the four bestselling authors were Hall Caine (*The Deemster*), Marie Corelli (*A Romance of Two Worlds*), A. C. Gunter (*Mr. Barnes of New York*), and Mrs. Humphry (Mary Augusta) Ward (*Robert Elsmere*).[38] Perhaps Whitney thought 1888 would be a propitious year for Mormon authors to shine in a rather undistinguished field.

Whitney's hope was that Mormon authors would produce a literature that explicitly espoused LDS values while achieving real aesthetic greatness. The project of combining faith and literary merit is certainly more difficult in a secular society than in the age of Milton or Dante, but clearly not impossible. Flannery O'Connor and Graham Greene, for instance, are unabashedly Catholic and undeniably great. But there is a difference between morally invested literature and moralistic literature. The response to Whitney's appeal, seconded by other leaders, was an outpouring of didactic literature, primarily through the medium of church-sponsored periodicals, but longer works of fiction appeared as well.

Whitney's summons to artistic excellence was the most prominent expression of the home literature movement, but the initiative had actually been under way for some time. In 1879, an editor remarked, "the exercises of writing essays, and publishing manuscript papers, have been quite generally adopted throughout the Territory, and have already resulted in the development of considerable literary talent among the members." To further this endeavor, the editor announced the inauguration of a church magazine called the *Contributor*, expressly designed to "foster and encourage the literary talent of their members . . . that it might say to every young man and every young lady among our people, having literary tastes and ability, *Write*."[39]

If they couldn't negate the encroachments of a worldly literary culture, they would surpass them with their own version, church leaders seemed to be saying. "If we can supplant in any degree the thrifty growth of worthless literature that has found root in all the towns and settlements of Utah, we shall congratulate ourselves on doing good service to the community." Even if, they added, "we do not claim high literary excellence" ourselves.[40] But the continuing barrage of mixed messages from the leadership stymied the effort if it didn't doom it to outright failure.

Dickens's *Hard Times* opens with the crusty Thomas Gradgrind announcing, "Now, what I want is Facts. Teach these boys and girls nothing but Facts. Facts alone are wanted in life. Plant nothing else, and root out everything else. You can only form the minds of reasoning animals upon Facts."[41] Literary satire became LDS counsel in the third issue of the *Contributor*, revealing a continuing LDS suspicion of fiction, and an equation of good literature with the factual, that would have put Gradgrind to shame:

> Only good books containing knowledge should be read by them. . . . The staff of intellectual life is *fact*, and only the healthful mind that so esteems it, is capable of justly weighing other reading matter, or deriving any benefit or real entertainment from it. Nothing conduces so much to reflection and the development of the mind as the simple statement of facts. . . . Make fact the basis of our reading—. . . . There is no more common result of the novel reading habit than the destruction of memory.[42]

Consequently, the *Contributor* was largely a miscellany of popular science, biography, travel, and sermonizing, with smatterings of poetry by Whitney, Emmeline B. Wells (frequently represented), and others thrown in. Not a short story or novella is to be found in those first issues. But Walter Scott, Felicia Hemans, and Robert Burns met with approbation. In November 1888, a recommended reading course for the youth of the church was outlined, comprising five works Only two gentile authors made the list: Charles Dickens, but for his *History of England*, not his novels. And Washington Irving, but for his essays on Christmas, not his fiction.[43] Thus, literature in these first years of the journal meant articles on "Oyster Raising" or "The Barber's Art."

But a momentous shift was already under way in Mormon attitudes and practice, propelled in part by a growing sense that Mormon culture was on the periphery of developments that would not allow them to ignore indefinitely the growing presence of fiction in American culture. B. H. Roberts, who saw the increasing centrality of the novel as the new dominant medium of intellectual exchange, embraced the challenge with both a reasoned analysis and an amateur's pen. "What in the main I wish to call attention to," wrote Roberts in the month after his own foray into fiction:

> is the fact that it is becoming generally recognized that the medium of fiction is the most effectual means of attracting the attention of the general public and instructing them. The dry facts of a theory respecting social reform must be made to live in persons and work out the results desired. The essayist is a character of the past, the novelist of a certain type is taking his place.[44]

Roberts went on to recognize a sea change in the scope of fiction. "It cannot be denied," he continued:

> that fiction has enlarged its field of late, until it has brought within its sphere all manner of subjects, social, political, religious and almost philosophical; as well as history—the affairs of the heart, "the trials of honest poverty," and the "struggle for ascendancy in fashionable circles." Indeed we may say, in common parlance, it has become quite the rage, now, if a new idea is to be presented to the world, or an old idea maintained, to write a novel, in which the aforesaid ideas are developed, either favorably or otherwise.[45]

Roberts had accurately perceived the dramatic significance that literature was coming to assume in American intellectual life. The great English critic Matthew Arnold had remarked ten years earlier that "whoever seriously occupies himself with literature will soon perceive its vital connections with other agencies."[46] As early as the 1830s, Thomas Carlyle had turned a largely frivolous medium to the treatment of serious themes, when he used his fiction to attack creeping secularism, cynicism, and unbounded capitalism (*Sartor Resartus*, 1833–1834). Harriet Beecher Stowe was one of a slew of abolitionist writers who made the novel a weapon of reform (*Uncle Tom's Cabin*, 1852), while Dickens had long been elevating the sentimental novel into a scorching instrument of social criticism, attacking child labor and neglect (*Oliver Twist*, 1837–1839), penal abuse (*Old Curiosity Shop*, 1840–1841), the legal profession (*Bleak House*, 1852–1853), education (*Hard Times*, 1854), and other subjects. Feminist thought was advanced through works of protest like Charlotte Bronte's *Shirley* (1849) and novels by George Eliot, who also broached subjects like the secret ballot and expanded suffrage in her work (*Felix Holt*, 1866). Charles Reade, a popular novelist of the day, tackled the abuses of lunatic asylums in *Hard Cash* (1863) and trade unionism in *Put Yourself in His Place* (1870). Closer to home, William Dean Howells, in 1880, had turned a genre long used against Catholicism to the censure of spiritualism (*The Undiscovered Country*), and the prolific Rebecca Harding Davis, in works like *A Law unto Herself* (1878) and *Natasqua* (1886), addressed almost every social issue of the day from a progressive standpoint. Indeed, by the time of Roberts's essay, a careful observer was justified in fearing that a people reluctant to take up the novelist's role would be locked out of all meaningful social debate.

The trends Roberts observed constitute what critics now refer to as the decades of American realism (1860–1890), a decisive shift toward earnest engagement with real issues of political, economic, and social moment. As one scholar has written, realism was essentially a "strategy for imagining and managing the threats of social change."[47] But at the same time, the subject of history, in particular, was reaching the masses through the new genre pioneered in England by Scott and in America by Cooper. "More people owe their knowledge of the history of Europe, and especially of England and Scotland, and of the social customs and manners under the Feudal system, to the novels of Sir Walter Scott, and the historical plays of Shakespeare, than to the works of Hallam, Smith, Hume or Macaulay," Roberts noted. He also admired in this regard Bulwer Lytton, William Thackeray, Robert Browning, George Eliot, and Victor Hugo.[48]

Mormons were fairly late in recognizing the urgency of adopting the new medium of novels. "Early in the century," records one literary historian:

religious educators like Mrs. Barbauld and Hannah More appropriated fiction to their purposes in something like the way in which early Christianity adopted pagan ceremonies. Thereby they established a climate for the novel as a moral force. Charlotte Elizabeth Tonna, editor of *The Christian Lady's Magazine*, turned reluctantly to the novel to spread her gospel. Their better successors, like Charlotte Yonge and Elizabeth Missing Sewell, moved readily into fiction from Sunday School teaching. Dinah Mulock, one of the most popular of mid-Victorian novelists, thought of herself as a lay minister . . . with a wider congregation and a greater command over them. "The essayist may write for his hundreds; the preacher preach to his thousands; but the novelist counts his audience by millions" she wrote in a critical article.[49]

Applying the lessons he had himself outlined, Roberts experimented with a Mormon version of historical fiction, beginning with "A Story of Zarahemla," a short story of some 5,500 words based on Book of Mormon characters.[50] "Careless of the unities, unmindful of character development, stilted in dialogue, and heavy-handed in its message," judges one of the few critics to have read it.[51] Roberts followed this up with a much longer—and more accomplished—work entitled "Corianton," which appeared serially over the next several issues of the *Contributor*, beginning in March 1889. From then on, short works of fiction by Latter-day Saints appeared with increasing frequency, written by Nephi Anderson, soon to achieve fame as a Mormon novelist, by the painter Alfred Lambourne, and others whose names have faded into oblivion.

Besides the *Contributor*, other journals served as popular forums for experiments with home literature, such as the *Woman's Exponent*, an independent magazine for women (founded in 1872 by Louisa Lula Greene). Leonard Arrington declared the journal "the first 'permanent' woman's magazine west of the Mississippi and second in the nation after the *Boston Woman's Journal*."[52] Founded as a semi-private venture, the magazine eventually became the official organ of the church's relief society and would run until 1914. Greene's friend Susa Young Gates would in 1888 correspond with Leo Tolstoy's daughter Tatyana. In one letter, she offered to send the young Russian woman copies of the journal as evidence, by virtue of both its production ("published and edited by women") and content (articles "having advocated Woman Suffrage for years"), that Mormon women were "very progressive in our views on the Women Question."[53]

The *Exponent* was certainly a powerful influence in the two ways Gates indicated. It demonstrated the viability of and institutional support for female initiative and independence, both in professional undertakings and in progressive politics—even if, to the consternation of their gentile sisters, Mormons used the pages of the journal to defend polygamy as well. However ironic it seemed, these twin commitments, to suffrage and polygamy, were stubbornly embodied in the journal's masthead: "The Rights of the Women of Zion and the Rights of the Women of All Nations." The journal also served as a vehicle for LDS women to contribute to theological debate and development. Eliza R. Snow published in 1873 an elaboration of Heber C. Kimball's theory of corporeal dualism (one part of the human body degrades and a purer part awaits resurrection). And the same journal provided space for women to retract their theological speculations when their prophet-husbands (in Eliza's case, Brigham Young) disagreed.[54] The ongoing tensions of creative speculation and orthodox constraint, individual initiative and priesthood intervention, could find few more poignant and painful illustrations than this picture of the prime instigator of a doctrine of a heavenly Mother continuing her searching forays to extend Mormon theology in new directions, only to be scolded into public retraction by the domineering Young.[55]

But surely one of the most important functions the journal served was to provide a powerful catalyst and forum for the encouragement of a woman's voice in literature and thus in the formation of Mormon cultural identity. In America at this time, journals devoted to women's writing were rare, even though in the field of fiction female authors had dominated the market since midcentury. ("America is now wholly given over to a damned mob of scribbling women," Hawthorne had famously groused in 1855.) In the pages of the *Exponent*, Mormon women found their voices through essays, autobiography, and poetry. Some contributors catered to the prevailing taste for sentimental fiction with its clichéd angel of the hearth, even as Emmeline B. Wells, Susa Young Gates, and kindred spirits developed and extended their feminist agenda. Gates would subsequently found the *Young Woman's Journal* in 1889. All told, in the fertile decades of the 1870s and 1880s, Mormon women would publish more than three dozen books of poetry, autobiography, and history, including the first Mormon novel, *John Stevens' Courtship*.[56] Then in 1915 the *Relief Society Magazine* premiered, and one of its departments for more than a half-century was "Art and Literature." Original fiction and poetry were published, and regular literature lessons trained readers in critical reading and appreciation.

The foundations were at last in place, and women's role in the Mormon literary tradition took firm root. With the coming of the next generation, Mormon authors at last began to produce works that deserved—and received—national attention. And it was no coincidence that when the literature of this "Lost Generation" of the thirties and forties appeared, female authors were in the vanguard.

"A Goodly Portion of Painters and Artists"

Visual Arts

If there is anything virtuous, lovely, or of good report,
or praiseworthy, we seek after these things.

~ Thirteenth Article of Faith

Those words could refer to the Red Cross as easily as to
a painting.

~ Richard Bushman[1]

Architecture is a science necessary to human habitation; music's place in religious tradition is beyond dispute; literature, at least in the form of diaries, epistles, and personal narratives, emerges independently of any considered commitment to artistic expression. But when we turn to the visual arts, we have entered the domain of the artist proper. Institutional and cultural attitudes toward art as art are therefore most manifest and most starkly contested in this realm. In Jacksonian America, the place of the artist was far from a comfortable one. Even before Emerson's famous summons for an authentic American culture, painters like Samuel F. B. Morse had been sounding the call for an American school of art—but found their compatriots unresponsive. Even the diehard nationalist Morse had to admit that England was a more congenial home for the practicing artist than was America, and pursued his training in London rather than at home. American painters Charles Wilson Peale and John Singleton Copley had succeeded in the revolutionary years, largely because their portraiture catered to the colonial aristocrats. Struggling to establish an authentically indigenous art, Morse prophesied a great future for American painting if artists could only manage to find "a taste in the country and a little more wealth."[2]

Part of the problem was implicit in Morse's formulation. Precisely because wealth is necessary to sponsor the arts, they are a luxury. And luxury, the inheritors of the Revolution well knew, was a sign of decadence, corruption, and impending tyranny. In a republic of virtue, luxury was not a simple distraction, but the principal enemy, "more baleful than pestilence or the sword."[3] Patriots like John Adams and Benjamin Rush, as a consequence, had actually argued that the fine arts were "a nefarious influence . . . and ought to be vigorously opposed."[4] It was not surprising, then, that the first American institution devoted to art, Charles Wilson Peale's Columbianum, an academy founded in Philadelphia in 1795, folded in less than a year. But another part of the problem—one facing art associations in particular—had to do with the fact that, unlike poets and dramatists and hymnists, professional artists frequently emerged out of academies modeled on a European system that tended toward elitism and heightened the distance of art from everyday citizens. Noah Webster firmly opposed such imitation: "It is perhaps always true," he argued, "that an old civilized nation cannot, with propriety, be the model for an infant nation, either in manners or fashions, in literature, or in government."[5] Or, presumably and especially, in art. As Morse struggled to establish a national academy, he was opposed by a widespread sentiment that artists teaching artists was a mistake. "I can conceive of nothing so directly calculated to degrade genius to the level of mediocrity," wrote C. Edwards Lester in the 1840s, "as the system of academies that has been the rage in Europe for two centuries."[6] Frances Trollope captured the precise source of such a pervasive public attitude when she criticized to an American she met "the frequency with which I had heard this phrase of *self-taught* used, not as an apology, but as positive praise. 'Well, madam, can there be a higher praise?'" he replied.[7]

In the era of Joseph Smith's youth, what historians have called a "village Enlightenment"[8] was under way, spurred by improved transportation and economic conditions, both of which tended toward more cosmopolitan attitudes and a consumerist appetite for unpretentious domestic arts, such as simple portraits, stenciled furniture, and both wall and floor painting. Rufus Porter was one itinerant artist who satisfied such a demand, even publishing in 1825 *A Select Collection of Valuable and Curious Arts . . . Which . . . May Be Prepared, Safely and at Little Expense*. It was essentially a layperson's guide to becoming enough of a country artisan to embellish one's own home. Perhaps from this or a similar guide, Lucy Mack Smith, mother of Joseph, acquired her own facility in just such a homespun art. "I had done considerable at painting oilcloth coverings for tables, stands, etc.," she would record:

> Therefore, I concluded to set up a business, and if prospered, I would try to supply the wants of the family. In this I succeeded so well that it was not long until we not only had an abundance of good and wholesome provision, but

I soon began to replenish my household furniture, a fine stock of which I had sacrificed entirely in moving.[9]

Joseph Smith's first exposure to art, therefore, would have been to a domestic craft practiced by his mother that was simple, practical, and remunerative. Nothing in his actions or writings suggest that he paid any notice to an effete art like painting, until he had the means and status, in September 1842, to have his portrait painted by one David Rogers of New York. Eerily, the only reference Joseph ever made to observing a painting was when, just days before his death, he noted that he had been "examining the painting, 'Death on the Pale Horse,' by Benjamin West, which has been exhibiting in my reading room for the last three days."[10]

Portraiture was in general exempt from Puritan-inspired suspicion of the visual arts, perhaps because in this case vanity trumped both religion and stinginess. One artist complained to the English visitor Frederick Marryat in 1837:

Americans in general do not estimate genius.... There is only one way to dispose of a painting in America, and that is, to raffle it; the Americans will then run the chance of getting it. If you do not like to part with your pictures in that way, you must paint portraits; people will purchase their own faces all over the world: the worst of it is, that in this country, they will purchase nothing else.[11]

Not surprisingly, portraiture was the first genre to appear among the Saints. Sutcliffe Maudsley (1809–1881), an English convert from Lancashire, painted unexceptional portraits of the Smith family in Nauvoo. Perhaps the first non-portrait rendered by a Mormon was the scene of Joseph's death, also executed by an English convert, William Warner Major, in late 1844 shortly after he arrived in Nauvoo. Relying upon verbal accounts or perhaps sketches of others, Major produced a painting of the Prophet's assassination and exhibited it in Nauvoo the next April. His migration to Utah with the main body of Saints guaranteed that at least one professional LDS artist would be on hand to chronicle the earliest scenes of Mormon settlement and its leaders. His landscapes have not survived, but many of his portraits have. His most famous work depicts the great colonizer Brigham Young as an English gentleman, in a monogamous family unit, surrounded by the fine trappings of aristocratic life. The setting probably owes much to the tradition of English country portraiture à la Gainsborough, but it is also consistent with Mormon attempts seen elsewhere to assert cultural refinement in spite of the crude realities of desert colonization.

Brigham Young may have been more pragmatic than Joseph—but his support of the arts extended to more than portrait sitting (as he did for Major). Much has been written of Young's emphasis, made even more urgent by their recent history, of establishing the Saints on an economically self-sufficient basis in the West. But it is clear that Young and other founding figures of Mormonism envisioned their enterprise as the founding of a community that was self-sufficient culturally as well as economically. As Erastus Snow asked his auditors only two decades after first settlement:

> How are we going to become self-sustaining unless we avail ourselves of the elements around us and provide ourselves and families with what we need to eat, drink and wear, and our implements of husbandry and other things of like nature? We need iron ware and machine shops. Our sons need teaching the various mechanical arts. Instead of raising them all to be farmers or mule drivers, we want a goodly portion of machinists, painters, artists, smiths, school teachers, and all other useful professions.[12]

Accordingly, the call went out to missionaries to target those with the skills and talents essential to building a society from the ground up. Apparently, the emphasis was fruitful. Contrary to early stereotypes, Mormon converts were drawn from a more skilled and socioeconomically advantaged pool than the typical working class. One study reveals that, of 410 converts from Victorian England, the highest single grouping, nearly one-third (31.2 percent), were artisans (carpenters, tailors, shoemakers, etc.).[13] Artists would have been included in this grouping, and evidence suggests that many such converts were appearing in Utah—at least enough to surprise the pioneer painter C. C. A. Christensen. After visiting the 1872 Utah Territorial Fair, he remarked, "I would never have believed so much talent could be found among us as a people who are nearly all gathered from among the most downtrodden classes of mankind."[14] Undoubtedly, converts from the British isles and Europe had more affinity toward, or at least less suspicion of, high culture than did their American counterparts. The difference may have been determinative in an LDS population constituted like the one in 1880 Utah. Sixty percent of the church's 145,000 members were at that time either foreign born or the children of foreign-born parents.[15]

Scandinavian Danquart Anthon Weggeland was one such convert. He studied both in Norway and at the Royal Academy of Fine Arts in Copenhagen. The fall of 1862 found him in Salt Lake City. Brigham Young commissioned him to do scenery and artwork in the Salt Lake Theatre; it wasn't the best use of his professional training, but it kept him from penury. Not that the Utah population couldn't muster enthusiasm for his beautifully rendered oil paintings—it was just that the economy could not yet sustain expensive luxuries like European-inspired artwork.

Popular interest in art was evident in the fact that Utah's yearly agricultural fairs, initiated in 1856, included a range of artworks. At the first event, both male and female artists exhibited two sculptures, pencil drawings, an India-ink portrait, and oil portraits. The very next year, participation was sufficient to offer prizes for "Best Bird's Eye View of Salt Lake City," "Best Landscape of Salt Lake City," and "Best Oil Painting."[16] Even so, the three major Utah artists of this early period were unanimous in their exasperation—even while their pathetic laments reveal an underlying current of popular interest producing a number of bartered deals. Weggeland mentions receiving as payment "a few home-knit sox or a basket of onions." Alfred Lambourne produced work that was "traded for a pair of boots ... framed and then sold for what the canvas cost ... [traded] for canary and cage ... sold at a ruinously low price ... raffled at $8.00, won by Briggy Young" (apparently Brigham Young, Jr.). And by 1872, George Ottinger, who had arrived in Utah a decade before, sold an impressive 223 paintings, but averaged only $15 each, and concluded, "I certainly must have no talent, no, nothing requisite to me that is needed for a successful painter."[17]

But Ottinger and fellow artists did have talent, and with the church's support and private commissions, they persevered and established both a Mormon artistic tradition and an important record of early Mormonism. Lacking the worship function of music, the instructional power of literature, and the practical utility of architecture, painting was nonetheless deemed important enough by the Utah church to be subsidized and encouraged. Apparently even Brigham Young was surprised at just how talented some of the Utah artists were. He commissioned a high-priced New York portraitist, Enoch Wood Perry, Jr., to paint his portrait in 1866 for $1,000. In 1872, the same job went to Ottinger, and Young remarked that the product was a better likeness than its expensive predecessor. But lacking thousand-dollar commissions, five years later, Ottinger would paint a striking portrait of himself in the uniform of his other profession—fire chief. Presented as standing apart from his volunteer crew, brass horn dangling idly at his side, eyes more listless than proud, the painting poignantly juxtaposes his evident artistic talent with the enforced burden of a profession that both paid the bills and usurped the time necessary to fully develop that talent. Still, he managed a considerable output, garnering some of his highest prices by catering to America's appetite for the genre of historical painting. His *Last of the Aztecs* fetched $300 and his *Washington at Trenton* $200.

Ottinger's primary influence would be felt in part through his instruction of Utah's second generation of artists, which began with his hiring as the first art instructor at the University of Deseret (the future University of Utah) in 1882. Also influential as a teacher was his fellow painter Weggeland. Called the "Father of Utah Art," Weggeland was a versatile painter and much beloved as an instructor, teaching drawing at Deseret from 1871. In 1863, Weggeland, Ottinger, and seven others had formed the Deseret Academy of Fine Arts—prematurely in light of its rapid demise. Still, the effort was a sign of the growing incorporation of the arts into the fabric of Salt Lake life. Portrait studios, photography galleries, itinerant painters, private academies, and press notices of acclaimed new works—all competed for buyers, students, and public notice throughout the sixties and beyond. Usually, the same few names dominated the prize lists and newspaper accounts, but sometimes painters new to the scene were added to the mix, like the Scot Nathaniel Spens, who brought a delightful, vigorous primitivism to his depictions of domestic life. Spens was by trade a farmer and wood carver, as well as a wood grainer and painter.

Still showing signs of its early attachment in America to the decorative arts generally, painting was frequently allied in this period with both older crafts and the newer art of photography. Charles Roscoe Savage arrived from New York City and established a photography studio in 1860, then soon entered into a partnership with Ottinger, offering, among other media, "photographs, plain and colored."[18] But it was landscapes of the dramatic desert, so alien to easterners and European converts alike, and portraits of prominent leaders and families that still dominated artistic subject matter. In the former category, Alfred Lambourne proved to be especially successful, executing extensive outdoor canvases to complement his acclaimed work on theater scenery.

In the late eighteenth century, a new art form, the panorama, was born, which fully came of age in the nineteenth century. In the panorama, the spectator becomes central rather than peripheral to the viewing experience, being surrounded by vast canvases of sweeping landscapes, exotic scenery, comprehensive vistas, and even special effects. Until it was displaced by the cinema, panoramas provided mass audiences with a visual experience that most nearly approximated immersion in the natural world. In the panorama's portable version (some were permanently housed), the presenter could roll up the prodigious length of canvas, transport it to another city, and reenact the experience for another mass audience.

So phenomenally popular was this form of art that it made the era's foremost practitioner, John Banvard, "the most famous living artist and the richest artist in history."[19] Even allowing for exaggeration, such plaudits suggest a suddenly discovered mass appeal previously unknown by the visual arts in America. His most celebrated work comprised 1,200-foot canvases of the Mississippi. As one scholar describes his practice:

[T]he huge canvases were wound on rolls at either side of the stage, like a giant papyrus. As the panorama was cranked from one roll to the other, it created an illusion that the audience was drifting downriver or steaming up it, depending on the show. Images of towns, bluffs, bandit-lairs, log cabins, flatboats and paddle-wheelers drifted by as the painter narrated the journey and added anecdotes about his adventures on the Mississippi.[20]

Lambourne teamed with another painter, Reuben Kirkham, to produce a more modest type of panorama, but one with its own brand of special effects. They called their work *Across the Continent; or, From the Atlantic to the Pacific*. One reviewer enthused:

[T]he pictures . . . are twelve feet, six inches long, and of proportionate height, save one, a view of Salt Lake City, which is twenty-five feet long. . . . The experience of the painters as scenic artists . . . enables them to execute the panoramic style, a leading quality necessary in which is boldness and dash . . . in which they have well succeeded in the present effort.[21]

The sixty-plus canvases were supplemented with moving-water effects and a fully rigged ship. The reaction in Salt Lake was enthusiastic enough to prompt a tour to major eastern cities. Philo Dibble was another artist who followed the same general form, presenting narrated panoramas in 1862.

The first generation of Mormon painters, then, offered fairly conventional portraits, landscapes that captured their immigrant fascination with western landscapes even as they fit into that era's obsession with wilderness themes, some genre paintings, and adaptations of the popular panoramas. Striking by its absence in early LDS artistic culture is the genre of religious painting. Occasionally, the odd instance appeared (Weggeland did *Crucifixion* in 1874), but little from the Old Testament, New Testament, or Book of Mormon scriptural tradition emerged with any regularity. Mormon visual art of this period was largely a vehicle for the individual artist to pursue his or her own vocation, often with new geographical settings feeding the creative mill, or with commissioned subjects prompting workmanlike portraits. Major painted Brigham Young, Native American chiefs, and desert landscapes. Weggeland did local scenes and local portraits, tinted photographs, painted signs, murals, and copies of old masters' paintings. Ottinger spent much of his life in pursuit of a genre or style that would make him a self-sustaining artist; he worked his way through portraits, chronicled the taming of the desert (with paintings of the mail stage and the Pony Express), and turned to a romanticized past with his *Last of the Aztecs* and *Marini*

Deriding the Mexican War God. He tried painting natural disasters, maritime disasters, sailing ships, scenes from mythology and history, an episode from the Book of Mormon (*Baptism of Limhi*), and more Aztec themes. William Prescott had published his *History of the Conquest of Mexico* in 1843, and prominent American painters like Emanuel Leutze had exploited the theme of Aztec defeat to great effect (as in *The Storming of the Teocalli by Cortez*, 1848). When Ottinger finally succeeded in placing a painting in a prominent exposition (the Philadelphia Centennial of 1876), it was his major work on this same theme: *Montezuma Receiving News of the Landing of Cortez* (1875).

When Alfred Lambourne wasn't employed on scenery for the theater, he was principally occupied with landscapes, many derived from his travels throughout southern Utah. Much of American art at this time was still steeped in the Romanticism that originated in continental and British landscape painting earlier in the century. Like Caspar David Friedrich in Germany or J. M. W. Turner in England, a number of American artists found the vast landscapes and dramatic vistas of the American wilderness perfect material for their highly subjective, at times mystical, engagement with a land they clearly saw as infused with divinity. Thomas Cole led the Hudson River School in celebrating the sublime grandeur of American forests and mountain peaks; phenomenally popular Albert Bierstadt found his material for an American Romanticism in the Rocky Mountains and Sierra Nevada. Not surprisingly, many of his paintings were set in the environs of Salt Lake City.

But the idealizing of nature is most easily accomplished by those whose engagement with it is casual rather than urgent. (Romanticism was born of aristocrats, not farmers.) Bierstadt's encounter with Utah, like Frederick Church's with the titanic waterfalls and canyons of South America, was that of a traveling artist with an eye for the beautiful and grandiose. But the first-generation Utah Mormons had crossed those mountains by wagon, by foot, and by handcart. (C. C. A. Christensen by the latter means; and Ottinger "walked every foot of the way from Florence [Nebraska], a distance of 1079 miles.")[22] The pioneer hands that held the paintbrush had also wielded the plow, planted the corn and poplars, and dug the irrigation canals that made the desert blossom. No wonder, then, that the landscapes of what one scholar calls this "Mormon period" of western settlement are characterized by "a fairly faithful representation" of reality.[23] They tend to emphasize the domestication of nature by the hand of man over the pristine beauty of a land unspoiled by the colonizer's spade. A generation later, Henry Culmer would wax visually rhapsodic in capturing the timelessness of the natural bridges of southern Utah (his work appeared in *National Geographic* in March 1907). But for now, Weggeland would chronicle the seeds of Mormon prosperity apparent in the tidy farms springing out of the desert, and others would record the growth of Salt Lake City itself. In this way, the rebirth of Zion in the midst of the barren desert to which they had fled, the juxtaposition of Eden and exile, emphasized not contradiction but triumph.

Ironically, when Mormon artists did romanticize the landscape, it was by returning east and finding, as the German Romantic Friedrich had, that landscape could be a vehicle for a particular kind of spirituality. In an era when Americans were beginning to memorialize and sacralize historical sites of special significance, Lambourne journeyed east, painting magnificent canvases of the New York hill where Joseph received the gold plates and the Missouri site that Joseph declared to be the original abode of Adam and Eve. With Romantic hues reminiscent of Turner, Lambourne, as one writer noted, "transformed the Hill Cumorah into an American Mount Sinai [and] embellished Adam-ondi-Ahman into a vision of Eden."[24] Befitting their status as representations of holy ground, these paintings were hung in the Salt Lake Temple.

The most conspicuously Mormon art, however, emerged as a modern counterpart to Renaissance persecution narratives by the masters. Ironically, Weggeland's best single work was perhaps not intended as Mormon art at all but was, perhaps appropriately, interpreted as such. This highly sentimentalized painting was accepted for display in the Philadelphia Centennial Exhibition of 1876 and carried the description "scene of a gypsy camp." At some point, *Gypsy Camp* acquired the title *Campsite on the Mormon Trail*.[25] It is likely that the travelers, with their wagon and pitched tents, dancing and playing music with cookfires and a western mountain peak in the background, all painted by a Latter-day Saint upon the heels of the pioneer period, enticed viewers to assume it was a scene from the Mormon migration. In any case, the painting is striking because while the trappings of the gypsy encampment bear apparent similarities to the Mormon pioneers, the painting's subtle thematic resonance is even more powerfully and poignantly evocative of the Mormon experience. In Weggeland's depiction, town dwellers with parasols and expensive suits visit a gypsy encampment, where a mixed-gender band plays music, a boy romps with a puppy, and others prepare food, all in bucolic splendor. But the scene is not deserted prairie or rugged desert; it is fertile farmland with fences and fashionable homes near to hand. It is, therefore, more like a scene of peasants making merry outside the gates of a rich man's feast than of the children of Israel fleeing Egypt for a promised land. The effect is a feeling of proximate exile, tenuous gaiety in the face of exclusion. And this striking juxtaposition powerfully foreshadows a theme that will emerge forcefully in Mormon art over the next generations: the nostalgia for community with a larger society, competing with pride in Zion's self-sufficiency. The ordered and festive gypsy camp, like the Mormon exodus generally, attests to a successful disengagement from the Babylon of the East. But the careful capturing of the affluent farmsteads in the background, with their neat fields and prosperous inhabitants, provides a clear and wistful indication of real loss.

The genre of Mormon historical painting received its most powerful impetus from the monumental canvases of C. C. A. Christensen, executed over two decades (1869–1890). Conversion in a foreign land, emigration to America, and a trek across the plains to Utah pulling a handcart were as authentic embodiments of the Mormon experience as one could hope to find. Christensen (1831–1912), a Danish convert, combined his training in the Royal Academy of Fine Art with his pioneer handcart experience and religious zeal to become the most effective and celebrated visual chronicler of early Mormon history. After stints at farming and scene painting, he began work on his *Mormon Panorama*, a series of twenty-three paintings that chronicled Mormon history from the First Vision of 1820 to the westward trek of 1847. The tempera paintings were a majestic six by ten feet each, and were stitched together in a scroll, which was unrolled in a traveling exhibition to the accompaniment of a lecture on Mormon history that Christensen delivered in scattered western communities. His paintings, in their homespun, quasi-primitive style, powerfully document the harrowing, the heroic, and the quotidian episodes of Mormonism's early history. Widely reproduced, they are the most influential face of early Mormon art and Mormon experience, and copies of them are omnipresent in Mormon chapels, office buildings, and homes.[26] Their hard-edged primitivism accentuates with a kind of earnest pathos the rugged theme of pioneer triumph over adversity in its many forms. His *Handcart Pioneers' First View of the Salt Lake Valley* (1890) is entirely typical in its perfect figuring of Mormon religiosity as gritty physical work. Family groupings surround two heavily laden handcarts, both pulled jointly. Proximate working hands are echoed by the entwined hands of children. Community—of family, pioneer companies, and the new Zion—is the dominant theme. Attaining the steep mountain summit, a triumphant couple raises hands in a jubilant gesture—but the blue sky at the apogee is no heavenly realm crowning their climb up Mount Purgatory. Zion and repose both wait upon their descent back down into earthy life and labor. It would be hard to more pointedly depict the collapse of yearning for transcendence and the heavenly city into the holiness of the prosaic.

By the 1880s, enough serious artists were on the Utah scene to form the Utah Art Association. With members like Ottinger, Weggeland, Lambourne, and Christensen, as well as John Tullidge, Lorus Pratt, and John Hafen, the group was able to host the first independent art exhibit in the territory. With something like a critical mass, this accumulation of artistic talent was sufficient to move beyond homespun renderings of local scenes and portraits. Restlessness in the cultural isolation of Utah, and a desire to reconnect with the larger artistic currents of Western art, with its center in Europe, would now lead to one of the most paradoxical missions in Mormon history. Having safely escaped the evils of a persecuting, hostile world, Mormon artists were now about to journey back across America and beyond in order to despoil the Egyptians.

1 *Lieutenant-General Joseph Smith in Uniform* (1842) by Sutcliffe Maudsley (gouache on paper). One of the very few portraits of the Prophet created from life. © Intellectual Reserve, Inc. Courtesy of the Museum of Church History and Art

2 *Brigham Young* (1872) by George Ottinger (oil on canvas). Young was reported to be pleasantly surprised to find Ottinger's likeness of himself better than a portrait earlier commissioned from a more-famous eastern artist. Courtesy of the Museum of Church History and Art

<u>3</u>

Orson Pratt. Called
Mormonism's "gauge of
philosophy," Pratt was the
outstanding intellectual of
the church's first generation.
Courtesy of the Church
Archives, Church of Jesus
Christ of Latter-day Saints

<u>4</u>

Parley P. Pratt. Orson's
brother Parley was enor-
mously influential as a
missionary, theologian,
pamphleteer, hymnodist,
historian, autobiographer,
poet, and satirist. Courtesy
of the Church Archives,
Church of Jesus Christ of
Latter-day Saints

5

Eliza R. Snow. Called
"Zion's poetess" by Joseph
Smith, Snow carved out
influential roles for pioneer
Mormon women in politics,
medicine, journalism, and
Utah's substantial home
production effort. Courtesy
of the Church Archives,
Church of Jesus Christ of
Latter-day Saints

6

Susa Young Gates. Prolific
and versatile, Gates was a
biographer, a novelist, and
the founder of two journals
and a department of music;
she participated locally
and internationally as a
women's advocate, in addition to pioneering genealogy
as an organized, profes-
sional endeavor. Courtesy
of the Church Archives,
Church of Jesus Christ of
Latter-day Saints

7

Emmeline B. Wells. Something of a paradox, writer and editor Wells was a fierce defender of women's rights, working with suffragists Susan B. Anthony and Elizabeth Cady Stanton, even as she defended plural marriage before congressional committees and three U.S. presidents. Courtesy of the Church Archives, Church of Jesus Christ of Latter-day Saints

8

B. H. Roberts. Roberts was a prolific writer and historian, a dominating orator, an impassioned defender of the faith, an influential church leader (a seventy and mission president), and a fiercely independent intellectual. Courtesy of the Church Archives, Church of Jesus Christ of Latter-day Saints

9 James E. Talmage. A brilliant scientist, university president, and apostle, Talmage's books on LDS Christology and doctrine, written at the request of the First Presidency, have quasi-canonical status in Mormonism. Courtesy of the Church Archives, Church of Jesus Christ of Latter-day Saints

10

Hugh Nibley. A prodigious linguist and scholar, Nibley was the church's most distinguished apologist and an outspoken critic of Mormon cultural foibles. Courtesy Hugh Nibley Family

11 Orson Pratt's Observatory. Pratt's observatory, built in the shadow of the rising temple in 1869, aptly captured the LDS effort to synthesize spiritual and secular learning. Courtesy of the Church Archives, Church of Jesus Christ of Latter-day Saints

12 Brigham Young Academy. Founded in 1875, the institution that would later become Brigham Young University dedicated its impressive Academy Building in 1892. It was designed to accommodate 1,000 students. Courtesy L. Tom Perry Special Collections, Harold B. Lee Library, Brigham Young University, Provo, Utah

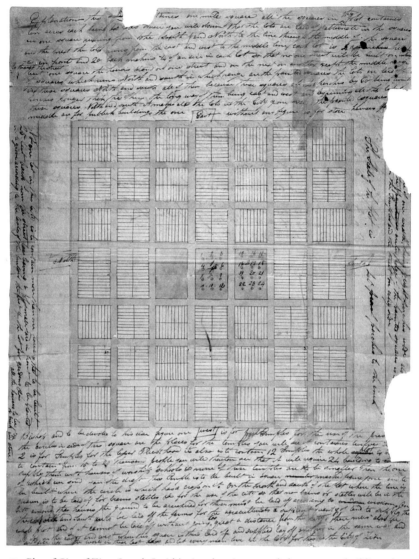

13 Plat of City of Zion. Joseph Smith's city planning extended to concrete building plans for the longed-for Zion of prophecy, which he located in Jackson County, Missouri. Courtesy of the Church Archives, Church of Jesus Christ of Latter-day Saints

14 Kirtland Temple (1833–1836). Brigham Young recalled how the temple, completed as inner turmoil and outside opposition wracked the church, was built by laborers "holding the sword in one hand to protect themselves from the mob, while they placed the stone and moved the trowel with the other." Courtesy of the Church Archives, Church of Jesus Christ of Latter-day Saints

15 Riverton Ward Meetinghouse (1898–1900). Mormons assimilated and innovated architectural styles freely in the late nineteenth and early twentieth centuries, as in this turn-of-the-century meetinghouse done in the Beaux Arts style. Used by permission, Utah State Historical Society, all rights reserved

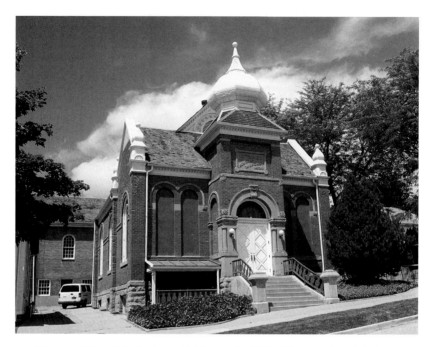

16 Nineteenth Ward Meetinghouse, Salt Lake City (1890). Though Salt Lake's "Oriental-ism in the extreme Occident" was a literary invention, this onion-domed chapel fit the stereotype. Courtesy Kenneth R. Mays

17 Provo Tabernacle (1883–1898). The first tabernacle outside Salt Lake was the Old Provo Tabernacle (1852–1867). This new Provo Tabernacle, minus its central tower, still stands.

18 Brigham City Tabernacle (1865–1881, 1889–1890, 1896). Twice reconstructed after fires, this High Gothic tabernacle has been named one of the five outstanding examples of Mormon architecture by the Utah Heritage Foundation.

19 Assembly Hall Ceiling (1880). In the early Utah period, murals and stained glass occasionally varied the usual interior austerity; the ornate ceiling of the Salt Lake Assembly Hall was even more atypical. Used by permission, Utah State Historical Society, all rights reserved

20 Nibley Park Ward, Salt Lake City (1926). By the 1920s, functionality was overwhelming aesthetics in meetinghouse design, as in this "colonel's twins" design wherein a vestibule connected a large cultural hall and a chapel. Used by permission, Utah State Historical Society, all rights reserved

<u>21</u> St. George Temple (1873–1877). First of the Utah temples to be completed, St. George with its massive towers and castellated walls suggests a nineteenth-century church that encompassed political as well as spiritual dominion. Courtesy of the Church Archives, Church of Jesus Christ of Latter-day Saints

22   Washington, D.C., Temple (1975). Consciously evoking the design of the Salt Lake Temple, and with its prominent location on the D.C. beltway, soaring spires, and resplendent white marble sheathing, the Washington Temple reflects the Mormons' triumphant return to the capital of the nation that once exiled them. Author photo

23 Mormon Tabernacle Choir (ca. 1900). From its successful appearance on the national stage at the 1893 World's Columbian Exposition to the present day, the choir has been the most-heard voice of Mormonism. Courtesy of the Church Archives, Church of Jesus Christ of Latter-day Saints

24 Girl Band. Brass bands were a popular but all-male domain among Mormons ever since the Nauvoo Brass Band. Disgruntled women petitioned for their own band at the church's Rick's Academy in 1909. Courtesy of Special Collections, David O. McKay Library, Brigham Young University, Idaho

25 Ballroom Dance. With their church called the "dancingest denomination in the country" by *Time* magazine, students from Brigham Young University began to win international competitions with this 1971 performance in London's Royal Albert Hall. Courtesy L. Tom Perry Special Collections, Harold B. Lee Library, Brigham Young University, Provo, Utah

26 Salt Lake Theatre (1861–1862). "Given a task of civilizing [a] people, I should straightway build a theatre," said Brigham Young. Work on this architectural gem was completed in 1862. It stood until 1928. Courtesy of the Church Archives, Church of Jesus Christ of Latter-day Saints

27 Salt Lake Theatre Interior (ca. 1900). Modeled conspicuously on Drury Lane, Salt Lake's theater attracted a host of nationally celebrated actors. Courtesy of the Church Archives, Church of Jesus Christ of Latter-day Saints

28 Hill Cumorah Pageant. In the field of drama, Mormonism's institutional efforts have become focused on popular outdoor spectacles, such as this mammoth annual production near Joseph Smith's boyhood home. Courtesy of the Church Archives, Church of Jesus Christ of Latter-day Saints

29 Road Show. These local amateur productions, prevalent in the church from the 1930s to the 1970s, could be said to have devolved from the more serious theatrical aspirations embodied in the Salt Lake Theatre and a smattering of "little theaters" throughout Utah. Courtesy of the Church Archives, Church of Jesus Christ of Latter-day Saints

30

Orson Whitney. In 1888, Whitney issued an influential challenge for Latter-day Saints to create a "home literature" of their own and led the way with mixed results. Courtesy of the Church Archives, Church of Jesus Christ of Latter-day Saints

31 (Left) Virginia Sorensen and (right) Maurine Whipple. In Mormon literature's Lost Generation of the 1940s, writers like Sorenson and Whipple created nationally recognized works that neither demonized nor sanitized the church, its past, or its larger-than-life founders. Used by permission, Utah State Historical Society, all rights reserved

32
Levi Peterson. Peterson typifies a brand of Mormons who write as insider/outsiders, deeply invested in Mormon culture while aloof from its theological commitments. Courtesy Levi Peterson

33 *Joseph Smith Addressing the Nauvoo Legion* (1845) by Robert Campbell (watercolor and ink on paper). One of the earliest paintings of an event in Latter-day Saint history, this work by the English immigrant Campbell depicts Smith's last public address before his martyrdom. © Intellectual Reserve, Inc. Courtesy of the Museum of Church History and Art

34 *Brigham and Mary Ann Angell Young and Their Children* (ca. 1845–1851) by William W. Major (oil on board). Polygamy and pioneer hardships wholly disappear in Major's portrait of genteel, monogamous refinement. Courtesy of the Museum of Church History and Art

35 *Gypsy Camp* (1875) by Danquart Anthon Weggeland (oil on canvas). Weggeland's depiction of a gypsy encampment echoes a perennial theme in Mormon culture: a celebration of elect status, tinged with a sense of alienation and exile. University of Utah Collection. From the Permanent Collection of the Utah Museum of Fine Arts

36 *Handcart Pioneers' First View of the Salt Lake Valley* (1890) by C. C. A. Christensen (oil on canvas). The Danish-born and -trained Christensen chronicled the Mormon pioneer experience, most notably in the monumental twenty-three canvases of the *Mormon Panorama*. Courtesy Springville Museum of Art, Springville, Utah

37 *Was I Nurtured Near Thy Side?* (1909) by John Hafen (oil on paper). Hafen's series of illustrations for the hymn "O My Father" blurs allegory and literal depictions alluding to
premortal life. Brigham Young University Museum of Art

38　*Farmington in Winter* (1926) by LeConte Stewart (oil on board). Stewart was the twentieth century's most prolific and accomplished painter of the Utah landscape. Courtesy Springville Museum of Art, Springville, Utah

39 *Dreaming of Zion* (1931) by Lee Greene Richards (oil on canvas). The first Utah artist honored by the Paris Salon (1904), Richards exhibited internationally and worked in a variety of genres in addition to portraiture, his specialty. Courtesy Springville Museum of Art, Springville, Utah

40 *Alma Baptizes in the Waters of Mormon* (ca. 1950) by Minerva Teichert (oil on masonite). A muralist trained at the Art Institute of Chicago, Teichert executed several national commissions, but her consuming passion was a series of over forty Book of Mormon paintings. Brigham Young University Museum of Art

41 *Lehi and His People Arrive in the Promised Land* (1952–1955) by Arnold Friberg (oil on canvas). Friberg's muscled Book of Mormon heroes and colorful settings were the first widely popular paintings that gave visual life to Mormonism's special scripture. © Intellectual Reserve, Inc. Courtesy of the Museum of Church History and Art

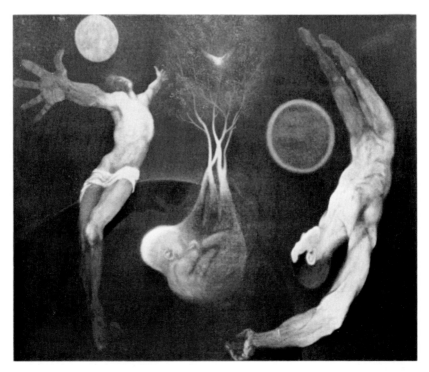

42 *Eternal Plan* (ca. 1966–1967) by Gary Smith (oil on canvas). In the Art and Belief movement, Smith and his fellow artists explored the possibilities of a uniquely Mormon art. Courtesy of Brigham Young University

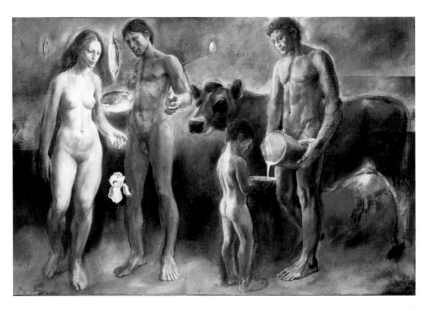

43 *Eden Farm* (1976) by Trevor Southey (oil on board). Southey pushed the boundaries of conventional religious art beyond where most Latter-day Saints felt comfortable. Courtesy Springville Museum of Art, Springville, Utah

44 *Alma Arise* (1999) by Walter Rane (oil on paper on board). Rane consciously evokes the style of the old masters in order to cast Book of Mormon themes and stories, like the conversion of Alma the Younger, as sublime religious art rather than as institutional illustration. © Intellectual Reserve, Inc. Courtesy of the Museum of Church History and Art

45 *Gethsemane* (1999) by James Christensen (oil on board). Mormons tend to shun both crosses and crucifixion scenes and to give theological emphasis to Christ's suffering in Gethsemane rather than his death on Calvary. © 1999 James C. Christensen, licensed by the Greenwich Workshop

46 *Exchange #8* (2004) by Ron Richmond (oil on canvas). In a church that employs art principally for didactic purposes, nonrepresentational art, like Richmond's meditation on the atonement, is rare. Brigham Young University Museum of Art

Tragedy at Winter Quarters
(1934) by Avard Fairbanks
(bronze). The most gifted and
prolific sculptor of Mormon
themes, Fairbanks fashioned in
this work a poignant symbol of
the heavy cost of the Mormon
exodus. Photograph by Avard
T. Fairbanks, courtesy of
Daniel J. Fairbanks

The Moment After (1980) by
Trevor Southey (bronze).
Southey's is a rare effort to
capture the personal and
evanescent, rather than the
historical and theological,
dimensions of Joseph's receipt
of the priesthood at the hands
of a resurrected Peter, James,
and John. © Intellectual
Reserve, Inc. Courtesy of
the Museum of Church
History and Art

PART III

THE VARIETIES OF MORMON CULTURAL EXPRESSION

A Movable Zion (1890–Present): Pioneer Nostalgia and Beyond the American Religion

No single year or event marked Utah's—or Mormonism's—acceptance as a fully American entity. With the driving of the golden spike at Promontory Point, Utah, in 1869, the geographical isolation of the Mormons came to a definitive end. As the turn of the century neared, the end of their political isolation was fast approaching as well. The church announced the cessation of plural marriage in 1890, and disbanded its statewide political party, the People's party, in 1891. Consequently, statehood was at last granted in 1896. With growing respect nationally, and an eye increasingly drawn to the outside world, the LDS church in the 1890s made significant strides toward cultural accommodation and integration as well. If 1890 marked the official end of the most prominent source of difference—the practice of plural marriage—then the year 1978 signaled the end of Mormonism's other most conspicuous marker of difference: its racially restrictive priesthood. Significantly, just as Spencer W. Kimball completed a process by which Mormon social and political values became compatible with American values, he gave new impetus to a missionary program through which Mormonism would become an aspiring global, rather than national, religion.

These successes in the arena of domestic public relations and assimilation came at a cost and presented Mormons with challenges of a new sort. With the eastern persecutions a distant memory, polygamy and its trials fading into the past, and the valiant colonization efforts soon to be the fodder of myth making, Utah

Saints now faced the daunting transition from reactive heroism to the terrors of complacency. One scholar has noted the parallel with second- and third-generation Puritans. Cotton Mather and his contemporaries "lament[ed] the declension of [their generation], who appear, page after page, in contrast to their mighty progenitors, about as profligate a lot as ever squandered a great inheritance." Accordingly, the later Puritans struggled with identity rather than with "the stones, storms, and Indians." "Similar lamentations," Reid Neilson writes, "'that all adventures are over, that no great days and no heroism lie ahead,' bleed through the diaries and letters of the second and third generation Mormons living in Utah in the late nineteenth century."[1]

The process of Americanization and accommodation profoundly altered the way Mormons defined—and represented—themselves to the dominant culture. Incorporation rather than isolation became the object, and that transformation inevitably had enormous implications for LDS cultural expression and activity. Without the burden—or the excuse—of environmental pressures on survival, attention to the arts accelerated, and they became an instrument for engaging the world rather than a simple diversion. Accordingly, while Mormon art did not necessarily have to mimic dominant modes of artistic expression, it could no longer unfold in relative obliviousness or indifference to that larger culture. Mormon art thus became at once more self-conscious and more inclined to cosmopolitanism.

Mormon theater, centered in the showpiece Salt Lake Theatre, had long been the cultural pride and joy of Utah Mormonism, giving the lie to charges of provincialism and barbarism. Almost every leading name in American theater headlined there in the early golden age of American drama. But few successful productions were of local authorship, and no Mormon author had produced anything of national note. In the waning years of the nineteenth century, an influential leader made a historic call for Mormons to produce a literature worthy of national attention, while embodying uniquely Mormon values—a "home literature." Ironically, this same decade saw art missionaries traveling abroad, imbibing European influences, and returning to infuse Utah art—and the temple—with new vitality and sophistication. At the same time, the Tabernacle Choir was fast becoming the new and highly visible face of a talented and patriotic Mormondom.

In America's bicentennial year, influential Mormon apostle Boyd K. Packer, an amateur painter and carver, revisited Orson Whitney's 1888 challenge to church members to produce their own "Miltons and Shakespeares." "Since that statement was made," he said, "those foundations have been raised up very slowly.... We move forward much slower than need be."[2] Essentially, it was

Whitney redux. Packer, like his predecessor, at once lamented the dearth of outstanding achievement, even as he shunned compromise as a solution. "Our most gifted members," he chided:

> are drawn to the world. They who are most capable to preserve our cultural heritage and to extend it, because of the enticements of the world, seek rather to replace it. . . . The greatest hymns and anthems have not been composed, nor have the greatest illustrations been set down, nor the poems written, nor the paintings finished. When they are produced, who will produce them? Will it be the most talented and the most highly trained among us? I rather think it will not. They will be produced by those who are the most inspired among us. Inspiration can come to those whose talents are barely adequate.[3]

The very next year, church president Spencer W. Kimball followed up Packer's remarks with a ringing endorsement, exuding similar disappointment but also buoyant optimism. Especially noteworthy was his openness to the full dimensions of the Mormon experience:

> For years I have been waiting for someone to do justice in recording in song and story and painting and sculpture the story of the Restoration, the reestablishment of the kingdom of God on earth, the struggles and frustrations; the apostasies and inner revolutions and counter-revolutions of those first decades; of the exodus; of the counter-reactions; of the transitions; of the persecution days; of the miracle man, Joseph Smith, of . . . the giant colonizer and builder, Brigham Young.[4]

But even as cultural expression received renewed vigor and diversity, intellectual life in the church suffered growing tensions that have yet to be resolved. As Mormon culture and Mormon history moved into the mainstream of academic study, the struggle to determine what Mormonism is, and how its story is told, took on greater urgency than ever before.

~ 11 ~

"FOMENTING THE POT"

The Life of the Mind

I want the liberty of thinking and believing as I please.
It feels so good not to be trammeled.

~ Joseph Smith

My experiences as a surgeon taught me the remarkable
potential for truth. It is a powerful sword—an instrument that can be wielded just like a surgeon's knife. It
can be guided well to bless. But it can also be crudely
applied to wound, to cripple, to damage, or even to
destroy!

~ Russell M. Nelson, LDS apostle

Shortly before his martyrdom, Joseph gathered together the Quorum of the
Twelve Apostles, in a mood made somber by presentiments of his death. He
spoke briefly of the need to execute one last action before his "work [would be]
done, and the foundation laid upon which the Kingdom of God is to be reared."
He then formally transferred his commission to them, saying, "I roll the burthen
and responsibility of leading this Church off from my shoulders on to yours.
Now, round up your shoulders and stand under it like men; for the Lord is going
to let me rest a while."[1] Parley P. Pratt recorded that, at this same time, Joseph
conferred on Brigham Young the keys of the sealing power, calling it, significantly, "the last key" and the "most sacred of all."[2]

With that gesture, Joseph did not exactly call the restoration complete. But
he had done more than just lay out foundations. The first generation of LDS
thinkers was faced with the task of systematizing, expounding, and propagating
the flood of revelations that Joseph Smith produced in the course of his brief
but eventful fourteen-year prophetic career. Like Joseph himself, those early
intellectuals and amateur theologians oscillated between emphasizing Christian

commonalities (as in Joseph's Thirteen Articles of Faith) and defending Mormonism's theological anomalies and idiosyncrasies (like plural marriage and the Book of Mormon). All of the major doctrinal developments had occurred by the time Joseph died in a hail of bullets at Carthage. Brigham Young would tentatively explore additional innovations, briefly teaching a peculiar concept of Adam as God. But lacking either full confidence and conviction in those ideas, or later determining that they lacked divine assent, he did not advocate them to the point of assigning them status as revelations he was prepared to formally present for canonization. Young and others of his generation also taught that murderers should have their blood spilled to atone for their crimes to achieve forgiveness in the next world. Quickly distorted and sensationalized, the doctrine of "blood atonement" loomed far larger in popular fiction than in Mormon theology.[3] Young, in other words, was far more effective as a colonizer of cities than as a revealer of new truth. He didn't like the term philosophy, and his successors were openly hostile to theology and its implications. Theology, after all, is what happens when revelation fails, in the Mormon view. John Taylor, Brigham Young's successor, considered theology "the greatest tomfoolery in the world."[4] And his successor, Wilford Woodruff, was a long way removed from the heady speculations and visions of Joseph Smith:

> I want to say this to all Israel: Cease troubling yourselves about who God is; who Adam is, who Christ is, who Jehovah is. For heaven's sake, let these things alone. Why trouble yourselves about these things? ... God is God. Christ is Christ. The Holy Ghost is the Holy Ghost. That should be enough for you and me to know. If we want to know any more, wait till we get where God is in person. I say this because we are troubled every little while with inquiries from elders anxious to know who God is, who Christ is, and who Adam is. I say to the elders of Israel, stop this.[5]

These shifting currents were in part a function of personality and in part a function of this moment in Mormon history. With the revocation of plural marriage in 1890, the greatest impetus to apologetics faded. And with the Book of Mormon little read even by faithful members in the nineteenth century,[6] another prod to the elaboration of a unique Mormon theology was lost. These shifting currents were also a function of this particular moment in Western history, when growing scientism and secularism seemed to confirm the Book of Mormon's prophetic warning about men who, beguiled by "the cunning plan of the evil one ... think they are wise" when they are merely learned (2 Nephi 9:28). The intellectual energies of Mormon leaders at this time would be focused on the latter conditions in particular.

SCIENCE AND RELIGION

In the same year that Joseph Smith incorporated a new church in upstate New York, John Murray, a friend and publisher of leading British radicals and revolutionaries (like the notorious Lord Byron), published a work that would shake the very foundations of organized religion. That was the year the first volume of Charles Lyell's *Principles of Geology* came off the press. It created major tremors that would anticipate—and amplify—the turbulent upheavals soon to follow in the wake of Charles Darwin's theory of natural selection as the force that drives evolution. But even before Darwin had compiled the notes for "species theory," the critic and erstwhile believer John Ruskin was insisting in 1851, "If only the Geologists would let me alone I could do very well, but those dreadful hammers! I hear the clink of them at the end of every cadence of the Bible verses!"[7] Lyell's contribution to orthodoxy's demise had been his compelling geologic evidence for an antiquity of the earth that far exceeded the mere six millennia suggested by Genesis. The overwhelming evidence for an earth age measured in millions of years meant that literal readings of the Bible were no longer tenable. "He did more than any other scientist," writes one scholar, "to disturb the religious faith of the 1830s and the century that followed."[8]

With the publication of Darwin's *Origin of Species* (1859), atheism was not the necessary consequence, but atheism was at least now becoming entirely intellectually respectable. It was not, however, the case that religion simply withered under the juggernaut of scientific progress. Moderate believers, like educated scientists, did not as a rule see the two paradigms as mutually hostile; even fifteen years after *Origin*, the vast majority of the leading fellows of England's Royal Society were members of the established churches, and 90 percent of them felt their traditional religious upbringings had no "deterrent effect . . . at all" on the freedom of their researches.[9] What changed in the closing years of the nineteenth century was the vehemence with which crusaders in both camps forced the issue to an either-or crisis. The 1860 debate between Thomas Huxley, "Darwin's bulldog," and the Anglican bishop Samuel Wilberforce in England, which presaged the prominent 1925 trial that opposed Clarence Darrow and William Jennings Bryan in America, typified the studied staging, rather than the natural unfolding, of confrontation and conflict between science and religion. Books written at the height of the Darwin controversy, with titles like *History of the Conflict between Religion and Science* (1874) and *History of the Warfare of Science with Theology* (1896), reaffirmed and exacerbated this perceived mutual hostility.[10]

It is commonly alleged that Mormonism tends toward fundamentalism in its literal reading of scripture, which would put the LDS church on the same collision course with modern science that evangelicals have faced. In fact, Mormonism is in this regard an inconsistent story, a mixture of both fundamentalism and radicalism, orthodox opinions and unexpected openness, as the case study of evolution illustrates. Traditional Christian belief regarding creation was rooted in three tenets: God created the earth out of nothingness (ex nihilo creation), the process lasted six literal days, and all of this transpired about 6,000 years ago. Mormonism did not align itself behind any of those three articles of faith.

Mormonism rejects ex nihilo creation outright. Joseph taught as early as 1833 that "the elements are eternal" (D&C 93:3). Elaborating years later, he insisted that creation (*baurau*) as employed in Genesis

> does not mean to create out of nothing; it means to organize; the same as a man would organize materials and build a ship. Hence we infer that God had materials to organize the world out of chaos—chaotic matter, which is element, and in which dwells all the glory. Element had an existence from the time He had. The pure principles of element are principles which can never be destroyed; they may be organized and re-organized, but not destroyed. They had no beginning and can have no end.[11]

How long those creative periods, or "days," lasted was not a matter of definitive official statement. The Book of Abraham, produced by Joseph in 1835, introduced indeterminate "times" into the creation story (4:5–31). And as for the dating of creation itself, Joseph's close associate W. W. Phelps recognized that Joseph's teachings in this regard conformed to, rather than conflicted with, the new science of geology. Writing to William Smith, he noted that Joseph had learned from his work on the papyri:

> [E]ternity, agreeably to the records found in the catacombs of Egypt, has been going on in this system, (not this world) almost two thousand five hundred and fifty five millions of years: and to know at the same time, that deists, geologists and others are trying to prove that matter must have existed hundreds of thousands of years;—it almost tempts the flesh to fly to God, or muster faith like Enoch to be translated.[12]

More than a decade after Darwin's *Origin*, Brigham Young could not restrain a touch of schadenfreude at the discomfiture of the fundamentalists in the face of geologic developments. "I am not astonished that infidelity prevails to a great extent among the inhabitants of the earth," he remarked, "for the religious teachers of the people advance many ideas and notions for truth which are in opposition to and contradict facts demonstrated by science, and which are generally understood."[13] Such liberal sentiments did not extend to an embrace of Darwin, but neither did the LDS church in the nineteenth century explicitly reject those developments. Brigham Young, in any case, did not. Darwin and his theories were seldom mentioned by name from the pulpit; when they were by Orson Pratt or Erastus Snow, it was with caution or mild dismissal.[14] Charles Penrose, who was not even an apostle in 1884, effected an unofficial compromise with which the church seemed happy. It was not rigorous science, but it evinced the attempt to accommodate scientific progress by surrendering whatever was seen to be expendable in the biblical creation story (namely, everything except fixity of species): "The doctrine of evolution, as it is called, is true in some respects—that is, that species can be improved, exalted, made better, but it remains of the same species."[15]

The reluctance to engage evolution—or scientism in general—in antagonistic debate was nothing new. From the beginning, Joseph's embrace of secular learning had established the compatibility of worldly with revealed truth. In the 1840s, explorations in Mesoamerica provided good reason to see archaeology as an ally of the Book of Mormon as literal history. Now, advances in geology, with its vast stretches of geologic time, seemed to corroborate Mormon rejection of ex nihilo creation and biblical fundamentalism. "Science confirms revelation," wrote Orson Whitney, "in declaring that not one particle of matter can either be created or destroyed. Creation is simply organization."[16]

At this same moment in their history, for the first time, Mormons were producing scientists of real stature. First among these was James E. Talmage (1862–1933), a geologist who had studied at Lehigh, Johns Hopkins, and Wesleyan (and was the first Mormon, in 1896, to receive a doctorate). He gained an international reputation, was made a fellow of several elite, learned societies (including the Royal Society of Edinburgh), comfortably embraced post-Darwinian science, led the University of Utah as president, and was ordained an apostle in 1911. His publication of two seminal works of LDS theology was therefore doubly important, first, because these two books were the only major theological works to be commissioned and approved by the LDS hierarchy. His *Articles of Faith* (1899) is therefore the only officially sanctioned treatise covering the virtual entirety of Mormon belief. A subsequent volume, *Jesus the Christ*, represents the church's definitive study of Christology (1915). Those volumes thus have quasi-canonical status in the LDS faith.

Second, additional significance derives from the fact that Mormonism's only commissioned works of theology, coming in the years between Huxley and Scopes, were produced by a prominent scientist. Talmage's scientific credentials sent a powerful message that secular learning was not only compatible with faith, but apparently a distinct advantage and qualification of Mormonism's most authoritative voice of the twentieth century.

About this time, two other scientists who would become apostles received their doctorates: John A. Widtsoe and Joseph F. Merrill. Widtsoe was a Norwegian immigrant who graduated summa cum laude in chemistry from Harvard and did advanced work in Göttingen. His work (he would publish thirty books in all) gives further emphasis to the shifting place of religion in the new intellectual landscape. Scientism, or the resolute faith in scientific progress and the necessity for all areas of human endeavor to conform to its paradigms, continued to sweep over the West in the second half of the nineteenth century. The assumptions that "for a subject to become a science is for it to go up in the world" or that "the acquisition of scientific status is always desirable"[17] became mania among scholars and laypersons alike. The term *scientist* wasn't even known until 1840. In the following years, every discipline wanted to produce its own. Parley P. Pratt had published his *Science of Theology* in 1855, in which he referred to the science of geography, the science of history, and prophetic science.[18] In 1858, Orson Hyde was teaching courses in the "science of the English language." By the next decade, political science departments at universities began to proliferate, along with an array of new "social sciences." Pratt, Heber C. Kimball, Orson Hyde, and Brigham Young were in these years referring to the "science of the Gospel of Christ," the "science of religion," the "science of salvation," and the "science of eternal life" and calling the gospel "this heavenly science" and the "science of life."[19] By 1879, even new denominations wanted in on the glorious aura of science (Christian Science).

It was out of such a milieu that the respected chemist, professor, and university president Widtsoe (1872–1952) produced his *Joseph Smith as Scientist* (1903–1904, 1908), *Science and the Gospel* (1908–1909), and *Rational Theology* (1915), among other writings. The first work was written to prove that "the teachings of Joseph Smith, the Mormon prophet, were in full harmony with the most advanced scientific thought, and that he anticipated the world of science in the statement of fundamental facts and theories of physics, chemistry, astronomy and biology."

Widtsoe maintained his argument that God is God by virtue of his mastery of natural law. Widtsoe's scheme is largely an extrapolation from Joseph Smith's metaphysical monism. "The philosophy of science," Widtsoe writes, "which is the basis of all rational philosophy, rests upon the doctrine of the indestructibility of matter." Joseph had posited the eternal nature of and subsuming of everything in matter. Therefore, what Coleridge referred to as the "heterogeneity of spirit and matter" collapses. Consequently, writes Widtsoe, the miraculous becomes the operating of higher law (the miracle is but "a law not understood"), and biological processes find spiritual counterparts. Therefore, though man's biological origin remains in doubt, what he called "moderate" evolution is but a shadow and type of the law of eternal progression manifest in Deity and mankind alike ("Joseph Smith taught the law of evolution as an eternal truth, twenty or more years before Darwin published his views"). Human progress in things intellectual as well as moral becomes an apprenticeship in what Peter called "the divine nature."[20]

This was not a work that in itself elaborated Mormon theology, but rather compared Joseph's thought with science to show their compatibility (in some cases missing the mark, as when he compared the light of Christ to the scientific "certainty" of the ether). It was the spirit, rather than the content, that was significant for this stage of Mormonism's intellectual history, an attempt to assure Mormons that not only is there no conflict, but "no difference between science and religion. The fundamental laws of the universe are foundations in both science and religion."[21] Or as Widtsoe would write elsewhere, "science . . . is the recognition by the mind through human senses of the realities of existence."[22]

The cumulative effect, however, of the writings of this early twentieth-century generation of scientist/theologians was to give emphatic utterance to a cosmological vision that one writer calls "philosophic realism," which entails several claims:

[First,] the existence of an objective reality apart from whether humans exist or not. Second, it asserts that humans can perceive this objective reality and that they can construct a clear understanding of it. Finally, it asserts what is real in terms of what is knowable. In this view, humans engage science as an enterprise that provides a real understanding of the world, of objective reality.[23]

In the case of B. H. Roberts, history as well as science was deemed capable of revealing an objective reality. Roberts (1857–1933) was far and away the most important Mormon historian of the era—and perhaps the most complete man of learning in church history. (He was ranked the leading intellectual of Mormonism in one unscientific poll.)[24] He edited the official *History of the Church* (1902–1932), drawn largely from the papers of Joseph Smith and his scribes, and authored a *Comprehensive History of the Church* (1930), which relied on contemporary historical documents and brought LDS history into the twentieth century. Roberts, who served as a mission president and in the First Council of Seventy, was orthodox in his history writing; in his theology, he could be the most independent-minded Mormon thinker since Orson Pratt; he was the scourge of anti-Mormons, but could be wearyingly strong-willed in contending against his own brethren.

Roberts was also the most accomplished Book of Mormon scholar of his generation, and he brought his confidence in the project of historical inquiry to that record. In practice, this meant that at the moment when scripture was increasingly being subjected to the scalpel of the demythologizers, Roberts was defending the Book of Mormon, whose historicity was similarly being called into question. Wilfred Cantwell Smith referred to the "relatively recent rise in Western consciousness, culminating in the nineteenth and early twentieth centuries, of the new sense of history, and the (consequent?) careful and rigorous distinction between history and myth." With this new paradigm, he argued, came the recognition that in biblical scripture, it is folly to believe "one is dealing here with historical time, rather than mythical time."[25]

From 1830 until the closing years of the century, Mormons were confident that Mesoamerican ruins provided satisfactory evidence of the advanced civilizations spoken of in the Book of Mormon. After John Lloyd Stephens published his 1841 account of his travels in Central America, describing stupendous temple complexes and palatial ruins, all of unknown origin, a church editorial enthused: "Even the most credulous cannot doubt. These wonderful ruins of *Palenque* are among the mighty works of the Nephites—and the mystery is solved."[26] The 1879 edition of the Book of Mormon evinced the impulse toward the synthesis of things earthly and heavenly, trends in biblical scholarship notwithstanding. Footnotes provided a thoroughgoing correlation of Book of Mormon place names with the geography of the Western hemisphere.

Roberts, the church's premier historian and dominant LDS intellectual of his era, felt as the new century dawned that nothing scientists or historians had advanced "conflicted with the claims of the Book of Mormon and . . . much of their work supported the story."[27] LDS confidence of that era that the Book of Mormon and archaeology, like science and religion, were natural allies led the church to sponsor an effort in 1900 to search along the banks of the Magdalena River in Colombia for the Nephite capital of Zarahemla. The ragtag expedition under Benjamin Cluff, the president of Brigham Young Academy who was trained in pedagogy and mathematics, ended in disappointment. Complications from Cluff's marriage to a plural (and post-manifesto) wife in Mexico, problems with discipline, and financial issues with border officials beset the group before it entered Mexico, and the church abruptly withdrew its endorsement. A small number pressed on, but the results fell far short of expectations—an early sign that the blithe belief in scientific avenues to gospel validation might be fraught with more dangers than benefits.[28]

Then, in 1921, James Talmage passed on to Roberts a letter that raised five concerns with Book of Mormon historicity.[29] Roberts found, in the course of addressing the questions, that they raised more difficulties than he had anticipated. After spending months on the issue, he requested of the First Presidency of the church permission to present his concerns to the assembled leadership. In two marathon sessions, on January 4–5, 1922, he did just that, presenting a 141-page report on "Book of Mormon Difficulties." His survey of the relevant scholarship left him much less sanguine about the future than he had felt in 1909:

> These questions are put by me . . . to bring to the consciousness of myself and my brethren that we face grave difficulties in all these matters. . . . I am sure that neither an appeal to the books written by men, nor even to the books of scripture now in our possession, will solve our present difficulties.[30]

Roberts found little sympathy for his concerns among the leadership, although Talmage had only recently, as head of the committee to reissue the Book of Mormon, urged the prudent gesture of removing all geographical cross-references in the new edition of the scripture. Roberts maintained his faith in the Book of Mormon, even as he privately worked on a series of manuscripts that investigated apparent anachronisms in the Book of Mormon, and assessed the case for its plagiarism.[31] It was his willingness to rigorously and honestly investigate naturalistic explanations for the Book of Mormon's creation that, as much as anything else, has made him a hero to contemporary Mormon intellectuals.

Roberts's failure to enlist LDS leadership in a more intellectual Book of Mormon engagement and apologetics would be followed by a greater disappointment. He published over thirty works, but his magnum opus was never published in his lifetime. *The Truth, the Way, the Life: An Elementary Treatise on Theology,* a masterwork on Mormon doctrine, was finished in 1928, but he was unwilling to make minor changes to accommodate a church committee that reviewed it.[32] The disputed passages were largely a consequence of the doctrinal speculations and conceptual bridges that he found necessary to achieve a perfect synthesis of the LDS scriptural corpus with the science—especially paleontology—of his day. Roberts had earlier shown a disposition to integrate Mormon theological positions with contemporary philosophers and psychologists. (He had drawn support from William James's speculation that "God himself may draw vital strength and increase of very being from our fidelity" for his point that it is no blasphemy to speak of "God's need of man.")[33] Now, in the scientific realm, he cited Herbert Spencer and Ernst Heinrich Haeckel to the effect that all matter in the universe is uncreated.[34] But more controversially for Latter-day Saints, he cited Lord Kelvin's theory of extraterrestrial origins for earth life as compatible with his view that Adam and Eve were translated beings brought here from another sphere (thereby preserving the scientific validity of evolution while exempting the human family).[35] He argued that the earth was constructed of "pre-existing world-stuff" (implicitly acknowledging the fossil record while making it irrelevant to the dating of creation).[36] He asserted that a cataclysm had annihilated earthly life before Eden (thus life and death preexisted Adam, but he was needed to "*replenish* the earth").[37] Accordingly, he made Adam head of a dispensation rather than the human race (thereby allowing for pre-Adamites, while making Adam the "first man" in that particular context).

The fact that his major work never saw the light of day was not the principal reason for Roberts's limited influence as a thinker. Increasingly, the role of theologizing and speculating LDS intellectuals like Roberts would be muted by the emergence of a church educational bureaucracy.

CHURCH EDUCATION

When it came to balancing the demands of faith with the advances of science, the stakes would understandably be considered highest where the vulnerable youth of the church were exposed most systematically to the tides of the new learning: the schoolroom. Education in Utah had begun as a nondenominational enterprise. Of course, liberal-mindedness in that regard was easier when there were virtually no non-Mormons in the valley. By 1870, as the influx of gentiles into Utah grew, Brigham Young had opened a series of LDS academies throughout the West. Salt Lake bishops had already agreed to counter the denominational academies suddenly proliferating after the Civil War by inaugurating Mormon Sabbath schools. Now, a church-supervised educational system would ensure, in the words of Joseph F. Smith, "that true religion undefiled before God the Father may be inculcated in the minds and hearts of our children ... in connection with the secular training that they receive in schools."[38] But in succeeding decades, as the public education system grew, LDS parents increasingly opted for the free schools, and the church reassessed its role in education. By 1925, the church was spending a quarter of its tithing income on educational support.[39] Consequently, the church began to withdraw from the private education sector, and redirect its efforts into part-time religious education through the seminary (classes offered during the high school years) and institute (classes offered for college students) programs.

The major exception to this shift was Brigham Young University (elevated from academy status in 1903). One rationale for its preservation was given by Joseph F. Merrill, a respected scholar, apostle, and church commissioner of education:

> We are living in a "scientific age," many are pleased to call it an age in which the methods of science have permeated to a greater or lesser extent into all the activities of the human mind. And do we not need in the church a group of scholars, learned in history, science and philosophy, scholars of standing and ability who can interpret for us and make plain to us the results of research and the reasoning of the human mind? When men find that we are learned in their science and philosophy they have respect for us, one that ignorance could never command.[40]

Increasingly, however, the intellectual culture of the institutional church would be reflected in the Church Educational System (CES), which was founded in the 1920s to supervise all of the educational programs of the church—full as well as part time.[41] In the first years of the CES, the intellectual liberalism and openness of the Widtsoe generation still pervaded all areas of the church. In the words of Armand Mauss, "the Church was still largely in the assimilationist mode, and its curriculum was more inclined to make use of non-Mormon scriptural and theological scholarship and to stress the articulation or the reconciliation of Mormon doctrine with the best in the 'wisdom of the world.' "[42]

Sidney Sperry was the first Mormon to obtain a degree in divinity studies, having enrolled at Chicago in 1925. Meanwhile, church education commissioner Adam S. Bennion was encouraging CES teachers to study cutting-edge historical and literary approaches to biblical scholarship. He organized a rigorous seminar for seminary teachers to "enrich and integrate the[ir] intellectual and theological thinking," and then, impressed with Sperry's training, he selected three teachers to follow in Sperry's path, even subsidizing their study.[43] Russel B. Swensen, George S. Tanner, and Daryl Chase were the first of several LDS teachers who pursued divinity studies at Chicago in that generation. They would be followed by T. Edgar Lyon, Carl J. Furr, Heber C. Snell, Vernon Larsen, Wesley P. Lloyd, Therald N. Jensen, and Anthony S. Cannon. At the same time, Merrill was bringing Edgar Goodspeed and other prominent biblical scholars to the

BYU campus to teach summer sessions of seminary teachers. Then suddenly, before the decade of the thirties was over, the flow of seminary teachers to the east halted. After a generation of intellectual eclecticism, the tide was changing.

Since 1890, the church had been in assimilationist mode, abandoning its cultural and political isolation, and achieving a fair measure of public respect. Intellectually, several leaders had demonstrated a capacity to excel in secular learning and to harmonize contemporary advances in science with Mormon theology, the best of eastern divinity training with church seminary education. Now the pendulum began to swing the other way, as new voices worried that such harmony was coming at the cost of moral and doctrinal purity and integrity. Roberts's controversial synthesis of Mormon theology had stalled in a committee of five apostles in 1930. One reason was Joseph Fielding Smith, a powerful voice who expressed a suspicion of "dangers lurking in modern thought."[44] Four months later, Smith publicly and forcefully "denounce[d] as absolutely false the opinions of some that this earth was peopled with a race before Adam" and condemned current efforts at a science/gospel synthesis.[45] His remarks would later be counterbalanced by a Talmage speech insisting on the harmony of true science and true gospel understanding, "The Earth and Man," which was, according to some sources, published by the church.[46] But the shift in the winds had begun. Then in 1933, both B. H. Roberts and James Talmage died. The same year, J. Reuben Clark was called to the First Presidency, a staunch conservative and defender of orthodoxy who, in Armand Mauss's opinion, "had a more profound impact on the Church than any other First Presidency appointment since Jedediah M. Grant's during the 'Reformation' in 1854."[47]

Until now, Mormonism had largely avoided the extremes of absolute scriptural literalism, on the one hand (prophets and temple ceremonies had long asserted the "figurative" nature of the creation story),[48] and the secular approach of higher criticism, on the other. With both the bureaucratic centralization of church education under the CES and the influence of doctrinally conservative leaders like Clark and several others in whose appointments he played a role— Mark E. Petersen, Harold B. Lee, Ezra Taft Benson, Bruce R. McConkie, and Joseph Fielding Smith—a line was soon drawn in the sand. Heber Snell had been one of those University of Chicago Divinity School graduates and now taught for the CES. His teaching and scholarship would become increasingly controversial. Typical of his modernist leanings was his criticism of Joseph Smith and other LDS figures for their tendency "to quote scripture and interpret it without regard to the historical milieu in which it arose."[49]

In the fading generation, the church's most erudite scholars had been called upon not just to expound LDS doctrine, but to produce numerous church teaching manuals. Talmage's *Great Apostasy* (1910) was originally designed as a manual for the young women's auxiliary, and his *Jesus the Christ* was the official Melchizedek priesthood manual in 1916. Roberts had produced a highly influential, five-volume *Seventies Course in Theology*, which was used in that quorum for the years 1907–1911; the Young Men's Mutual Improvement Association published a three-year manual based on his study of the Book of Mormon, *New Witness for God* (1903–1906). John Widtsoe's *Science and the Gospel* was the Young Men's Mutual Improvement Association manual of 1908–1909. His *Joseph Smith as Scientist* (1908) was adopted for that program in 1920–1921, and he also produced for that organization the tellingly titled manuals *How Science Contributes to Religion* (1927) and (the coauthored) *Heroes of Science* (1926–1927). Widtsoe's *Rational Theology* (1915) and *Priesthood and Church Government* (1936) were used as Melchizedek priesthood manuals. Clearly, the church intended to give these men of science a powerful role in shaping the attitudes of church members, and youth especially, toward science and the gospel.

Undoubtedly, the shifting fortunes of intellectual life in the church had much to do with the deaths of Roberts, Talmage, Widtsoe, and Merrill, and the rise of an influential generation of leaders less favorably inclined toward the scientific world view. The influence of an ultraconservative CES grew more pronounced, and it became increasingly rare to call men with scholarly backgrounds to leadership positions.[50] The church leadership had good reason to fear that secular détente was not working to the church's advantage. Some of the leaders may have been concerned about the faithfulness of church youth amid a rising tide of secularism, and now there was statistical evidence to verify a lack of faithfulness at the church's premier university. Surveys conducted in the mid-1930s of church youth, including BYU students and alumni in particular, revealed a number of worrisome facts: one study revealed that of rural Mormon youth, only half were regular churchgoers or tithed, and fully a third were not observing the Word of Wisdom (the LDS health code). BYU students and alumni reported only slightly higher levels of faithfulness. Among BYU students, 14 percent questioned whether the LDS church was more divine than other Christian churches, 20 percent doubted that church authorities received revelations or that God answered prayers through divine intervention, and nearly two-thirds doubted the church's teaching of an actual, embodied Satan. Perhaps more disturbing to LDS leaders, only 42 percent felt their faith in the church increased while at the church's university.[51]

Boyd K. Packer later expressed what apparently many leaders were deducing as a consequence of these numbers: the well-intentioned interchange with secular religious training had done more harm than good. "We wanted very much to grow in the eyes of the world, for in reaching for a standard of gospel scholarship we even looked outside of the church." While non-Mormon scholars "learned that we were decent folks, and we learned from them," Packer asserted, "there was a limit to what they could contribute.... They were without the priesthood and were therefore essentially uninspired."[52]

As a consequence, the church's educational system moved to draw sharp distinctions between the inspired gospel as restored by Joseph Smith and the teachings of the Christian world, between truth revealed from heaven and the theories and conjectures of men (especially scientists). As the size and stature of BYU grew, it assumed an increasingly important and conspicuous posture as the bellwether of LDS institutional attitudes toward the life of the mind. As early as 1911, three professors had resigned or been dismissed—for teaching evolution, according to most accounts. But in an era when church leaders differed on the subject and most advised caution, believing in evolution was not a cause for church sanction. In this case, it was a mixture of evolution, higher criticism, and intellectual self-assertiveness that created the problem. The professors were judged to be endorsing evolution "as a demonstrated law," treating the Bible "as a collection of myths," and in general undermining the faith of students.[53] Given a choice of conforming to church teachings or resigning, three professors left that year and one a few years thereafter.

Now, after a period of tolerance and flexibility, church leaders again moved to monitor the uneasy alliance at BYU of faith and intellectual independence. Faculty members were interviewed for their faithful incorporation of scholarship into their teaching, and a number left as a result of this oversight. In 1938, Clark gave an address to Mormon educators that was a manifesto of sorts, definitively reversing the intellectual liberalism of the preceding generation of leadership and laying down, with First Presidency approval, "the more outstanding and essential fundamentals underlying our Church school education." First, he declared:

> These students (to put the matter shortly) are prepared to understand and to believe that there is a natural world and there is a spiritual world; that the things of the natural world will not explain the things of the spiritual world; that the things of the spiritual world cannot be understood or comprehended by the things of the natural world; that you cannot rationalize the things of the spirit.

Further emphasizing a dichotomy between spirit and reason, church and world, he warned church educators:

[Y]ou are not to teach the philosophies of the world, ancient or modern, pagan or Christian, for this is the field of the public schools. Your sole field is the Gospel.... We pay taxes to support those state institutions whose function and work it is to teach the arts, the sciences, literature, history, the languages, and so on through the whole secular curriculum. These institutions are to do this work. But we use the tithes of the Church to carry on the Church school system, and these are impressed with a holy trust. The Church seminaries and institutes are to teach the Gospel.[54]

The strains of reconciling Zion and the world, spirit and matter, the sacred and the mundane, had proven too much.

Two years later, the increasingly influential Clark would direct Commissioner of Education Franklin West that teachers "should carefully refrain from saying anything that will raise doubt or question in the student's mind about the gospel.... Every fact, every argument, every reason that can be found must be used to support church doctrines—the gospel—not to question them."[55] In 1954, Joseph Fielding Smith's *Man: His Origin and Destiny* was published. Duane Jeffery has called it "a milestone. For the first time in Mormon history, and capping a full half-century of publication of Mormon books on science and religion, Mormonism had a book that was openly antagonistic to much of science."[56] The work was briefly employed as a CES training manual, but was quickly withdrawn. Because of its author, the book was widely viewed as authoritative nonetheless. Its dismissal of positions held by Talmage, Widtsoe, and respected LDS scientists like Henry Eyring left many Mormons confused and uncertain about the role of science and intellectualism in the church. The distance from Snell's liberal training to Smith's doctrinaire work revealed a growing sense of irreconcilable conflict.[57]

The next years witnessed a number of profound ironies regarding Mormonism and science. On the one hand, the highly influential Mormon apostle Bruce R. McConkie continued the polemics of his father-in-law, Joseph Fielding Smith, famously calling evolution one of the "Seven Deadly Heresies."[58] Apostles Ezra Taft Benson and Boyd K. Packer also criticized the theory. Meanwhile, evolutionary science was flourishing in dramatic fashion at the church's own university and environs. BYU is situated in one of the most geologically and paleontologically diverse regions on the planet. James Jensen of the BYU Geology Department was one of America's most prolific and famous dinosaur hunters. Known as "Dinosaur Jim," Jensen helped to generate a large dinosaur fossil collection at BYU that continues to be studied. William D. Tidwell, a BYU professor of botany, made BYU a leader in paleobotany through his extensive collection of plant fossils. And Utah is itself full of desert shrubs of the genus *Atriplex*, which, as documented through decades of research by BYU botany professor Howard C. Stutz, is undergoing what one plant geneticist calls "some of the most explosive evolution of any group, plant, or animal in the world."[59] And finally, Eldon J. Gardner, a devout Mormon and professor at two Utah universities, became one of the world's leading human geneticists of his day. Building in large measure on the foundations these scientists laid, BYU has had a long history of prominent evolutionary research and in recent years has been one of the world's leaders in molecular evolutionary biology.[60] And Duane Jeffery is nationally known for his work on science education with a focus on evolution. (He is currently on the board of directors of the National Center for Science Education, a leader in the opposition to the intelligent design movement.)

Clearly, Mormon scientists are finding support for efforts that not only incorporate evolutionary science, but break new ground in the field. What this reveals is that outspoken critics notwithstanding, the institutional church has aligned itself with the original spirit of Joseph Smith in this regard. Dallin Oaks was president of BYU in 1972, and he defended these scientific initiatives forcefully, arguing, "The bones are there and cannot really be ignored by a major university that is almost literally sitting on top of them." He advised giving "controlled but expanding support to research in Rocky Mountain paleontology and [to] pursue the private funding of a museum to exhibit findings. [In so doing] . . . we demonstrate that the church has nothing to fear from any legitimate research; in fact, the church university fosters it."[61]

Some trace this institutional stance to the reputation and persuasive skills of Henry Eyring (1901–1981). Perhaps the most internationally respected scientist the church has ever produced, Eyring taught at Princeton and served as president of the American Association for the Advancement of Science. He engaged Joseph Fielding Smith in civil debate on the subject of evolution, holding:

> [T]he church is committed to the truth whatever its source and each man is asked to seek it out honestly and prayerfully. It is, of course, another matter to teach as a doctrine of the church something which is manifestly contradictory and to urge it in and out of season. The author has never felt the least constraints in investigating any matter strictly on its merits.[62]

Good evidence suggests that Eyring was instrumental in provoking the church's official position of scientific openness and tolerance during a contentious era.[63] More recently, Duane Jeffery has worked to achieve satisfactory resolution of these issues as they impact Brigham Young University's curriculum.[64]

HISTORY AND FAITH

If science was the bugbear that challenged the limits of Joseph Smith's intellectual utopianism and ecumenicism in the second era of the church's existence, history was the fiery furnace of Mormonism's most recent generations. The office of church historian was decreed by revelation in the earliest days of the church's founding (D&C 69:3). As a consequence, whereas Mormon scientists and academics had long operated comfortably in the secular world, Mormon historians occupied with Mormon history had typically told their story to an audience of religious peers or a few curious outsiders, as an act of devotion and even defense. But in the years after World War II, Mormonism became a subject of interest to far more people than the Saints and their record keepers. Growing scrutiny from outside, and intellectual pressures from within, combined to focus much greater attention on the methods and aims of Mormon historiography.

The winds of intellectual change that came to the study of Mormon history in the 1940s precipitated storms that have yet to settle into calm. Challenges to Mormonism's telling of its history had long come from outsiders or angry defectors. But in 1945, a retelling of Mormonism's founding came from a source closer to home and harder to dismiss. That was the year Fawn Brodie published *No Man Knows My History: The Life of Joseph Smith*. It was not the first biography of Joseph Smith by a skeptic or dissenter from the faith—but it had the greatest impact. Brodie's was by no measure an attempt at objective history. In the author's own words, though raised a Latter-day Saint, she had become "convinced before I ever began writing that Joseph Smith was not a true Prophet." Confessing afterward to resentment at having been "conned" by the church, she set out to account for "the whole problem of [Joseph's] credibility."[65] In the resultant study, Brodie took enormous liberties through her psychobiographical approach, presenting a shrewd analysis of Joseph as a wily, deceiving, and self-deceiving character of real genius. But she was a gifted writer and historian, and unlike past exposés and critiques of the Prophet, Brodie's account acknowledged a high level of intellectual and creative capacity on the part of Joseph. Her extremely popular treatment was thus taken seriously by historians and general readers, and added a new dimension—a credible scholarly dimension—to attacks on the truthfulness and legitimacy of Mormonism's orthodox rendering of its own history. This was something the church had never confronted to any significant degree.

Then in 1950, Juanita Brooks published an account called *The Mountain Meadows Massacre*. Brooks, unlike Brodie, was a devout Mormon before and after her writing project. Meticulously researched, it pulled the curtain back on the darkest episode in Mormon history, the murder of a wagon train of immigrants in the midst of an emotionally volatile invasion of Utah by a federal army. Conventional accounts had downplayed Mormon involvement, attributing the orchestration and execution of the mass murder to local Native Americans. Brooks's book was not a hostile exposé, but the frankness and thoroughness with which she excavated the tragedy, and her unstinting assignment of blame to Mormon participants, was construed as disloyalty.[66] Her measured tone erupted occasionally into indignation, as when she took issue with a popular LDS history that asserts that the massacre was the crime of one person. "Yet in the collections of the historian's office of the Latter-day Saint Church," she writes, "records of which [Joseph Fielding Smith] is the custodian, there is ample evidence that this was definitely *not* the crime of a single individual, nor the responsibility of only one man. Even the most superficial research would show the utter ridiculousness of such a statement."[67] She also criticized church president David O. McKay and his counselor J. Reuben Clark for denying her access to certain primary documents.

While Brooks exonerated Brigham Young of ordering the massacre, she concluded that he and George A. Smith "did preach sermons and set up social conditions which made it possible," that though Young "would have prevented it if he could, Brigham Young was accessory after the fact," and that John D. Lee, the only Mormon executed for the crime, was a sacrificial scapegoat offered to the government by Young.[68] Such unflinching criticism from a devout believer marked another watershed in Mormon historiography. It could have been a watershed in institutional honesty as well—but the dangers seemed too great to countenance that degree of revelation. Brooks was not excommunicated (as was Brodie), but as she later mused, "this book branded me as an apostate."[69] Hindsight now confirms that by paving the way to a style of church history writing that was both honest and rancorless, she had indeed "done a wholesome thing and done the church I love a service."[70]

These books were followed by two more landmarks: Thomas O'Dea, a sociologist, produced a balanced and insightful study in 1957 (*The Mormons*), and the next year, LDS historian Leonard Arrington published his *Great Basin Kingdom: An Economic History of the Latter-day Saints, 1830–1900*. Each of those four contributions has been nominated by at least one scholar as the watershed book in Mormon historiography.[71]

Brodie and Brooks were but the earliest harbingers of a new trend that has only gained momentum since: the appropriation of Mormon historical investigation by professional academics. A pattern set in 1842 was at last in process of dramatic transformation. That was the year that Joseph sent his "Historical

Sketch" of the rise and progress of the church to John Wentworth for publication in a Chicago newspaper. In the same year, the disaffected and excommunicated John C. Bennett published his *History of the Saints: An Exposé of Joe Smith and Mormonism*. Faithful histories, missionary tracts, and conversion narratives would henceforth contend with exposés, character attacks, and captivity narratives in the war of words over Mormonism. Brodie and Brooks ushered in a new era of intellectually sophisticated appraisals of the Mormon past. Not that they were always, or perhaps ever, entirely objective in their treatments, but from the mid-twentieth century onward a new middle ground would increasingly emerge.

The LDS leadership was obviously unhappy with the impact such credible, secular scholarship was having on public perceptions. But developments within the faithful LDS historical community only blurred the black-and-white polarities of nineteenth-century historiography and compounded a now-growing dilemma. LDS historian Leonard Arrington recalled an episode in 1959 when, to his dismay, an article he wrote for the inaugural issue of the church-sponsored *BYU Studies* led to the journal's temporary suspension (it apparently dealt too frankly with Word of Wisdom observance—or lack thereof—in the nineteenth century).[72] Hoping to forge a middle ground between the cynical approach of dismissive historians, and the sanitized histories of LDS authors, Arrington and a number of similar-minded colleagues came together in 1965 to found the Mormon History Association (MHA), with the explicit goal of rendering the faithful study of Mormon history more professionalized.[73] What might have been a cause for unalloyed celebration was complicated in Mormon eyes by the group's decision to execute Mormon history in more "human or naturalistic terms."[74] Given the organization's concurrent goal "to include Reorganized LDS members, non-Mormons, [and] lapsed Mormons,"[75] the forum for uninhibited discussion and exploration of Mormonism outside the bounds of orthodox control would clearly be a potentially explosive experiment.

Initially, the surge of scholarly interest in the Mormon past ushered in a vibrant era of intellectual inquiry and productive work that received official praise and support. In fact, staunch conservative Joseph Fielding Smith, who in the 1960s was church historian as well as a senior apostle, was a prime mover in efforts to professionalize the office.[76] Membership in professional associations was urged on employees, trained archivists and librarians were hired, and upgraded facilities were planned. In 1966, the year after Arrington and his circle founded the Mormon History Association, the new trend of intellectual adventurism was accelerated with the launch of *Dialogue: A Journal of Mormon Thought*, edited by Stanford graduate student and poet Eugene England (along with G. Wesley Johnson) and supported by a group of young LDS intellectuals. Its inaugural issue did not sound the call to dissent or schism, but its invitation to test boundaries was implicit: the "independent national quarterly" aimed to "examine the relevance of religion to secular life," bring "faith into dialogue with human experience as a whole," and "encourage a variety of viewpoints."[77]

Some early supporters, such as LDS historian Richard Bushman, saw the initiative as a necessary broadening of Mormon intellectual horizons, to better equip twentieth-century members to confront a secular world that increasingly threatened to assimilate them:

> The new context of Harvard or Columbia or Africa requires a new definition [of Mormon identity]. I think that is one reason why we have lost many of our young people in eastern schools, or at the University of Utah for that matter. They are overpowered by a secular culture that dazzles them with its splendors and seemingly puts Mormon parochialism in the shade.[78]

By 1969, the changes in approach to the Mormon past taken by LDS scholars were marked enough that professor of history Moses Rischin concluded that developments constituted a "new Mormon history."[79] The foundations had actually been laid years earlier, with the pioneering historical studies of Eugene E. Campbell, praised for his efforts to "set the record straight," and Berkeley-trained S. George Ellsworth, who challenged traditional understandings of Mormonism's emergence.[80] But it was Arrington, encouraged in part by the scholarly apostle John A. Widtsoe, who brought his training in economic history to bear on Mormon history, proving that the enterprise could shed important new light and perspectives on both.

By 1971, even dissident Mormon Fawn Brodie described "a new climate of liberation" in Salt Lake City.[81] Then, in 1972, the historian's office was reorganized as the Church Historical Department, and, in a significant rupture with tradition, Arrington was appointed to the position of church historian—the first non-apostle and the first professionally trained historian so appointed. As soon-to-be-called assistant historian Davis Bitton described their mandate, the leadership wanted to generate scholarly production appropriate to scholarly journals, presses, and public forums, and also to produce historical material that would reach the LDS membership through more popular media like the church magazines. The hope, he believed, was for "a little judicious pump-priming that would yield positive long-range results—respect for the Church, its history, and leaders who were willing to support thorough scholarship."[82] The era of Camelot, as Arrington called the next years, would mark unprecedented access to church archives, and surging scholarly production of high quality and volume.

Outside official channels, developments were just as dramatic. By 1974, the Mormon History Association had almost a thousand members, with enough scholars, interested members of the public, and resources to launch the *Journal of Mormon History*. But it was a painfully short-lived Camelot. Also in 1974, Reed Durham, director of the LDS Institute of Religion at the University of Utah, delivered the MHA's presidential address, in which he explored Joseph Smith's links with Masonry and the occult, to the apparent consternation of church leaders. By this time, Mormon intellectual liberalism had ignited fires of controversy on other fronts as well.

Early issues of *Dialogue* had set out to establish the contours of Mormon artistic culture through introspection and assessment ("Mormonism and the Visual Arts," "Early Mormon Churches in Utah") and to affirm the compatibility of the intellectual and spiritual realms, with essays like "The Faith of a Psychologist" and "The Strength of the Mormon Position." But almost immediately, scholarship appeared with a harder edge, less sanguine about Mormon cultural orthodoxy. *Dialogue* was soon publishing a range of essays engaging controversies that continue to roil the church to the present day. Some of these were efforts to meet head-on major conundrums in Mormon canonical history, such as the very different accounts Joseph Smith provided of the First Vision, or to critique Mormon cultural foibles, such as "Anti-Intellectualism in Mormon History."[83] The frank and open self-examination was welcomed as a major development by most in the intellectual community. Readers praised "the intellectual evidences to the Mormon Doctrine," which "can't help but strengthen the Church." "*Dialogue* can become a source of intellectual satisfaction," wrote another, "that will complement and augment the spiritual satisfaction abundantly provided by the Church." "Some areas of fairly general consensus . . . could stand reexamination," cheered another. But others were less pleased: "he does not understand inspired leadership as an accepted doctrine of the Church," complained a reader of one scholar/author.[84]

Dialogue articles also addressed those aspects of Mormon thought and practice that were seen to intersect the political issues dominating headlines in the 1960s. In that decade, the church was still limiting the priesthood to males of non-African descent, and tended to be supportive of the Vietnam War.[85] *Dialogue* offered a rare forum for contesting and debating these and other hot-button issues of the 1960s. The journal published a roundtable discussion of the Vietnam War in its second year,[86] along with articles on "The Blasphemy of Indifference" (regarding race relations and modern warfare) and "A Voice against the War."[87] The journal tackled the racial question through a series of historical treatments and revisionist essays.[88] The civil rights movement, George

Romney's political visibility, and prominent Mormon intellectual Sterling Mc-Murrin's public criticisms had all focused attention on the controversial priesthood ban, and Mormon scholars began to investigate the doctrinal and historical foundations for the practice. Matters came to a head when Lester Bush prepared a comprehensive overview of the priesthood policy that, in his opinion, "virtually undermined the entire traditional case for the inspired origins of Mormon teachings" on the subject. He then submitted his manuscript to the apostle Boyd K. Packer for review.[89] Meeting personally with Packer, Bush would later insist that "there was no suggestion of don't publish it," and scholars in the church's Historical Department praised the manuscript. Nonetheless, when the article went to press as the centerpiece of a special *Dialogue* issue devoted to the race issue, repercussions followed.[90] Some of the records Bush had relied upon were recalled from public access in the BYU library, there was talk of the magazine having passed a "Rubicon" in the leadership's eyes, and rumors of angered general authorities and retaliatory actions swirled about. In fact, Bush himself wrote, a general authority assured him that in response to his article, "no ground swells" emerged and that the brethren were disappointed with but reconciled to its publication. The authority even went so far, years later, as to suggest it had "started to foment the pot" that would eventually lead the leadership to reconsider and then revoke the ban through a 1978 revelation.[91]

The incident may have been typical of a growing breach between leaders and independent scholars, insofar as the anxiety surrounding such conflicts, while it could veer toward paranoia and hysteria, also testified to the gradual erection of very real obstacles, emotional and practical, to historical research. One participant in these often-agonized debates was Eugene England, who would become increasingly vocal as a gifted essayist and provocative gadfly, offering candid critiques of the LDS racial policy and the church's ready accommodation to a conservative American political philosophy that was arguably hostile to church teachings in such areas as militarism, unfettered capitalism, and racial justice.[92]

England's was perhaps the most prominent voice attempting to bridge the growing divide between criticism and orthodoxy, intellectuals and loyalists, and to pioneer a path of faithful dissent. He was not sanguine about the prospects of success. In 1975, some graduate students at the University of California at Berkeley and the Graduate Theological Union there launched *Sunstone*, another independent LDS journal.[93] England, a principal founder of *Dialogue*, wrote a letter that appeared in *Sunstone*'s inaugural issue, admitting mild disappointment in his own journal's failure to succor "those who face special problems in developing their faith," and cautioning the new periodical's board to "put your loyalty to [the] work of saving souls above everything, above your own prestige and ambitions, your academic standards."[94] England's implicit foreboding was justified; the new journal continued and extended *Dialogue*'s edgy journalism—including thoughtful appraisals of Mormon art, culture, and history—but increasingly publishing unabashedly strident attacks on orthodoxy and defenses of dissident perspectives. Still, the very existence of forums in which to debate these issues was itself seen by many as a healthy sign of diversity and intellectual vigor.

Feminism was another area where the tension between wider, liberalizing trends and church orthodoxy, between the impulse toward individual autonomy and hierarchical control, was intensely focused in Mormon debate. By 1970, a dozen or so LDS women in the Boston area had formed a close-knit community which collaborated on a local guidebook and turned their thoughts to women's issues. Within months, they were offered an opportunity to guest edit a special issue of *Dialogue*. The "pink issue" appeared in the summer of 1971, marking a historic moment for Mormon feminists. A few years later, the group moved on to their next major journalistic enterprise. The *Woman's Exponent*, which one scholar calls "the first long-lived feminist periodical in the western United States," had been published by Mormon women from 1872 to 1914.[95] In 1974, the spirit of the original journal was resurrected as *Exponent II*, announcing itself as "poised on the dual platforms of Mormonism and Feminism." One of its founders, Claudia Bushman, saw the journal as an attempt to heal, rather than radicalize, divisions over the feminist issue.[96]

Still, divisions did of course persist, especially since in some ways Mormon feminism is an oxymoron. On the one hand, dimensions of Mormon history and theology alike have been empowering to women (the early Utah franchise, exaltation as a joint endeavor, a Mother in heaven). On the other, an all-male priesthood means that even when it comes to issues most directly touching women, policy and doctrine are dictated by men. Few women have objected to the church's opposition to abortion, but its public stand against the Equal Rights Amendment announced in 1976 was openly questioned in the pages of *Dialogue* in both articles and letters to the editor. The next year, at the Utah International Women's Year conference, controversy emerged over the question of whether the church was merely "encouraging them to be present and to reflect 'church standards' when appropriate" or actually instructing LDS delegates how to vote.[97] Organized activity supporting church positions was egregious enough that the role of the Relief Society, the church's women's auxiliary, elicited angry protests. The group's president acknowledged to the press afterward that "the Relief Society was used by the 'far right.' "[98] After outspoken feminist and critic of the church Sonia Johnson was excommunicated in 1979, *Dialogue* printed articles sympathetic to her and even let her air her views (and defense of the ERA) in a published interview.[99]

In 1981, Laurel Thatcher Ulrich, one of the moving forces behind the "pink issue" and *Exponent II*, assessed what she saw as the successes and failures of an LDS feminist movement, after its first decade:

> Considering IWY, the excommunication of Sonia Johnson and the resurgence of the radical right, it is not at all certain that the "ladies" have been heard or ever will be heard in high places. . . . As I think of the achievements of the past decade—the publication of *Mormon Sisters* and *Sister Saints*, the founding of *Exponent II*, the establishment of the BYU women's conferences, the securing of a feminist presence in *Dialogue* and *Sunstone* and in the Mormon History Association, the blossoming of women's fiction and poetry and especially the developing of an informal network of thinking Mormon women—I am warmed and enlivened.[100]

By 1981, the United States was out of Vietnam, the church had extended priesthood privileges to all worthy males, the ERA was dead, and Johnson was fading from public consciousness. Nonetheless, there was no stopping the intellectual momentum the Camelot era had heralded, most especially in the area of LDS history. In 1976, Historical Department researchers James B. Allen and Glen M. Leonard published their very successful *Story of the Latter-day Saints*. But their tendency to situate Mormon economic practices in a social and cultural context elicited criticism from Ezra Taft Benson, and the popular book was not reissued for a decade. Five years into his appointment, Arrington writes, the "conservative authorities" were expressing displeasure with "our galloping historical program," and G. Homer Durham was assigned to rein in the horses.[101] The experiment of a group of professional scholars working with relative autonomy under church auspices in the Historical Department was over. By 1982, Arrington had been released and he and his colleagues reassigned to disparate programs and locations. Arrington went to direct the newly formed Joseph Smith Institute for Church History at church-controlled Brigham Young University. While not having normal university department status, neither did the institute have either the prominent profile it had enjoyed at church headquarters, nor independence from church oversight. Its ambiguous status persisted until its quiet demise in 2005.

Apparently in response to the growth of the new Mormon history and related developments, apostle Boyd K. Packer at a 1981 Church Educational System Religious Educators' Symposium gave an address titled "The Mantle Is Far, Far

Greater than the Intellect." Two of his cautions stirred particular controversy. First, he advised, "There is no such thing as an accurate, objective history of the Church without consideration of the spiritual powers that attend this work."[102] This was clearly a rebuke of the new Mormon history which grew out of the Arrington-led initiative, with its emphasis on the cultural contexts of Mormonism's development and its incorporation, in Thomas Alexander's words, of "techniques derived from historical, humanistic, social-scientific, and religious perspectives."[103] From an orthodox perspective, Packer's concerns make perfect sense. For adherents, LDS history is not the story of a church founded and directed by some vague, mysterious workings of providence; it is a modern saga saturated with actual and repeated divine appearances, angelic visitations, Pentecostal episodes, heavenly interventions, and miraculously transmitted relics and scriptures. Such a history, shorn of the supernatural, is arguably a timorous evasion or unforgivable distortion of its essential nature.

The second Packer principle was to avoid the "temptation for the writer or the teacher of Church history to want to tell everything, whether it is worthy or faith promoting or not." Some LDS historians interpreted these remarks as a directive to produce only sanitized, hagiographic renderings of church founders and the pioneer past. Packer's argument, as Paul taught, was that some are not ready for meat before milk. One must be careful not to "destroy the faith of those not ready for 'advanced history.'" Whether average members would ever be ready to confront the most challenging aspects of Mormonism's past was and is an open question. But it was clear from the tenor of Packer's remarks that he felt some church scholars, under the sway of professional standards and norms, were producing history more conducive of doubt than faith in the minds of those who read it.

The address was fuel for the fire already raging, and brought about increasingly sharp lines of demarcation. Responses ranged from Sterling McMurrin's "reprehensible and odious" to D. Michael Quinn's more measured complaint that Packer wanted history "that would border on idolatry."[104] The public nature of the controversy led *Newsweek* to run a story entitled "Apostles vs. Historians" on February 15, 1982. BYU students were joining the fray as well. The newly founded *Seventh East Press* conducted an interview with outspoken Mormon dissenter McMurrin, who lobbed bombshells at Packer, the Book of Mormon, and Joseph Smith's credibility. ("You don't get books from angels and translate them by miracles; it is just that simple," he declared.)[105] When the interview appeared in 1983, BYU officials withdrew campus distribution privileges in consequence, and the paper folded. With Arrington's Historical Department disbanded, the *Seventh East Press* defunct, and the Mormon History Association flourishing, the energies and passions swirling around Mormon intellectual life were channeled into polarized camps. Publishing outlets for Mormon books were likewise increasingly categorized as orthodox (Foundation for Ancient Research and Mormon Studies, BYU studies) or liberal (Signature Books, Smith Research Associates). No wonder the religious historian Martin Marty could observe in 1983:

> Mormon thought is experiencing a crisis comparable to but more profound than that which Roman Catholicism recognized around the time of the Second Vatican Council (1962–5). Whatever other changes were occurring in the Catholic church, there was a dramatic, sometimes traumatic shift in ways of regarding the tradition. One of the conventional ways of speaking of this shift comes from the observation of philosopher Bernard Lonergan. He and others argued that Catholicism was moving from a "classic" view of dogma to a thoroughly "historical" view of faith. In the classic view Catholic teaching has come intact, as it were, protected from contingency, from a revealing God.[106]

In the case of Mormon studies, "ways of regarding the tradition" were and are certainly contested, but the church's leadership is hardly likely to respond with anything remotely parallel to the Vatican II of Catholicism.

THE MORMON INTELLECTUAL TODAY

One test of a religion's intellectual vitality is the capacity to tolerate dissent and difference while maintaining orthodoxy. By almost any standard, modern Galileos deserve their day in the court of public opinion. Even Joseph was of that mind:

> I [do] not like the old man being called up for erring in doctrine. It looks too much like the Methodists, and not like the Latter-day Saints. Methodists have creeds which a man must believe or be kicked out of their church. I want the liberty of thinking and believing as I please. It feels so good not to be trammeled. It does not prove that a man is not a good man because he errs in doctrine.[107]

At the same time, it is widely evident that the most thriving Christian religions of today are those that yield the least to secularism, modernism, and theological compromise. In the case of Mormonism, however, those forces are strongest within certain quarters of the LDS intellectual community itself. The sense of rupture within Mormonism was already apparent in 1967 to one reader of *Dialogue*, who lamented that the "one disturbing feature, and one which your efforts seem to have accentuated, is the breach which appears to be growing between the so-called faithful on one hand, and the so-called intellectual on the other."[108]

In theory, that is, in Mormon theology, no such breach need ever erupt. Joseph emphatically insisted on the harmony of all truth, that all things are spiritual, and that the glory of God is intelligence. Scientific laws of nature and the laws of God are one, affirmed Parley Pratt. Angels will effect the transformation of the earth through principles of chemistry, lectured Brigham Young, not through the waving of heavenly wands. So as one frustrated LDS academic asks, "why, with our extraordinary theological background in which all truth is meant to be circumscribed into one great whole, [do] we insist on fearfully dividing instead of fearlessly circumscribing?"[109]

Two factors in particular exacerbate the tensions, factors that a journal like *Dialogue* bring into focus. First is the lack of a well-theorized or systematic theology, which leaves a term like orthodoxy (or "faithful") fairly nebulous and contested. (This lack of theological precision would be one factor in the complaint of the American Association of University Professors that "the limitations discussed in the BYU statement on academic freedom strike us as very far from precise.")[110] To take but one example, Mormons have no creed, but do have Thirteen Articles of Faith, one of which asserts Mormon belief in the Bible "as the word of God, as far as it is translated correctly." But that expression doesn't really discriminate between positions that could range from liberal Protestant to fundamentalist. Consequently, institute teacher Heber Snell, one of the Latter-day Saint scholars trained at Chicago in the 1930s, could advocate a historical approach, according to which "[e]very biblical book is the product of some human mind, or minds, activated variously by the Divine Spirit and reacting to a certain environment."[111] His controversial 1948 book based on this modernist approach, *Ancient Israel*, elicited a firestorm of controversy in the church that led to a heresy hearing by the church's board of education (he was cleared). In an exchange with Joseph Fielding Smith, Snell identified the lack of terminological consensus in LDS theology as the real culprit:

I propose that we take up first the subject of revelation. I have made this concept central in my book, interpreting Ancient Israel as a revelation, a special revelation of God in the ancient world. I believe that you ... would probably think of revelation mostly as verbal communication from God. I think there may be an occasional revelation of this type, but that this use of the term by no means exhausts its meaning.[112]

Sterling McMurrin sees this general avoidance by LDS prophets of formal theology as having inescapable results: "the worst thing that could happen to any theology is now happening to the theology of the Mormons—by the default of the prophets it has been appropriated by the academics."[113]

Second, the role of history in LDS theology entails especially vexing dilemmas that even science does not provoke. The church could, in the same tumultuous years, approve funding for an earth science museum at BYU housing one of the world's largest dinosaur collections and foster a top-notch evolutionary biology program, because Mormonism does not stand or fall on the merits of evolutionary theory. But the case with history is different, because the church does stand or fall on the veracity of the official version of its early history. In the context of Mormon theology, history is not just one discipline among many. "History as theology is perilous," said Grant McMurray, past president of the Community of Christ (the former Reorganized Church of Jesus Christ of Latter Day Saints), a church that has moved ever further away from accepting Joseph Smith's visions and the scripture he produced as literally rooted in historical events.[114]

The debates over historicity could be circumvented, some argue, by a simple solution: sever the connection between history and theology. But the perils of history-based theology do not make that history any more expendable, in the minds of mainstream Mormons. On the contrary, the Latter-day Saint leadership appears steadfastly committed to the assertion of Schopenhauer. "Christianity, he wrote, "has this peculiar disadvantage of not being, like other religions, a pure doctrine, but is essentially and mainly a narrative or history, a series of events . . . ; and this very history constitutes the dogma, belief in which leads to salvation."[115] If this is true of Christianity in general, it is doubly true of Mormonism in particular. LDS doctrine as a whole is rooted inescapably in history; its claims to divine authority and restored truth are entirely dependent on the narratives of LDS origins. Without an uncompromising belief in Joseph Smith's literal visitation by God and heavenly angels, verbally communicating and physically transmitting to him ancient records and priesthood keys, and without verifiable evidence of a continuing conduit linking Joseph's successors to God—a God who personally directs the continuing work of the restoration—Mormonism would utterly lose its claim to be the unique institutional form of the one true gospel. What this means in practice is that challenges to orthodox accounts of the church's past strike at the very heart of the faith.

Not that any Mormon would dispute the fact that theology's reliance upon a particular history can make for peril. When in the 1980s Mark Hofmann forged a series of fabricated letters and documents that dramatically challenged orthodox versions of early Mormon history, critics celebrated and apologists scrambled to assimilate the difficult discoveries.[116] When the disputed documents were revealed as fraudulent, many Mormons breathed a collective sigh of relief. But the lesson is a powerful reminder of how inseparable Mormon faith is from a particular version of specific historical events, from the vision of the Father and Son to the appearance of Moroni to a host of heavenly manifestations and communications. Mormonism's self-conceiving is utterly dependent on the veracity of those accounts, since the historical reality of ancient Nephites and gold plates constitute the evidence of Joseph's prophetic calling, and the actual visitations of resurrected beings are the foundation of his priesthood authority. History, not theological plausibility, spiritual appeal, or even fruits of godliness, is the foundation of Mormonism.

Some portray the battle over Mormon history as between efforts at honest, full disclosure and paranoid, statist control of information. Others see it as a conflict between faith-inspired scholarship and a secular mania for debunking and humanizing the sacred. The struggle is largely over which institutional standards should prevail in the way truth—historical truth in particular—is pursued, packaged, and promulgated. On one side of the debate are those historians who emphasize that Mormon history is already mediated by fallible humans. As one points out, the LDS "'story' was never brought down from Mount Sinai or revealed in a sacred grove but was crafted by scribes and early historians, including Willard Richards, George A. Smith, Wilford Woodruff, Orson F. Whitney, and B. H. Roberts." He and his like-minded colleagues take it as self-evident that only history which aspires to be "rational," "objective," and "professional" is worthy of the name.[117] On the other side of the debate are faithful scholars who argue:

> [P]ositivism, objectivism, historicism, and environmentalism, with their interrelated vocabularies, cannot be used to establish the claim of secular histories to be "higher," "better," or "truer" than other histories. . . . Naturalistic explanation, locked in psychologism, introduces its own superstitions. The resulting histories do "violence" to the sacred language they seek to subsume, repressing its expression and silencing its claim.[118]

When intellectuals demand a less sanitized version of Mormon history, they are generally insisting on greater scrutiny into the details and cultural contexts surrounding certain key moments and pivotal events in the church's first seventy-five years. The opening epiphany of Mormonism, Joseph's First Vision, took different forms in several incarnations the Prophet gave it, and those discrepancies continue to elicit argument; circumstances surrounding the Mountain

Meadows massacre, wherein over 100 men and women perished when Mormons ambushed a wagon train, have been reexamined by a number of scholars inside and outside the church since the ground-breaking study by Juanita Brooks; details of Joseph's early involvement in plural marriages that challenged conventional treatments emerged; and research in the 1980s by D. Michael Quinn revealed the extent of plural marriages performed by church leaders after the 1890 public announcement of the practice's cessation.[119] In all of these and other cases, new research threatens to challenge the details, if not the essentials, of Mormonism's self-presentation.

ACADEMIC FREEDOM

In the decade after Quinn's disquieting revelations, intellectual frictions in the church moved to the volatile area of academic freedom. BYU has always claimed certain exemptions to secular standards of academic freedom because of the school's religious nature. However, while both the American Association of University Professors and the Northwest Association of Schools and Colleges acknowledge limitation clauses regarding academic freedom in religious institutions, they also require that the limitations be clearly stated and published. Until recent years, BYU had no written statement on academic freedom. Political pressures would force BYU into a more direct engagement with the contested claims of religious commitment and academic standards.

Brigham Young University, founded in 1875, is the largest private, church-sponsored university in the United States, with some 35,000 full-time students in almost 200 bachelor's, 68 master's, and 27 doctoral programs, who utilize what the Princeton Review called the number one "Great College Library" in the country.[120] It has nationally ranked programs across a spectrum of fields, and it ranks among the top twenty in National Merit scholars enrolled. Seventy-two percent of the student body speaks a second language, and most students take courses in one of 66 different languages offered at three times the national average.[121] Perhaps ironically, BYU leads the nation when it comes to integrating academic research and real-world applications, at least in the sciences. In the July 2002 edition of the *Chronicle of Higher Education*, BYU was recognized as the best in the nation at turning research dollars into inventions and new companies. (Technology from television to word processing was developed, in whole or in large measure, at BYU.) But when it comes to history, the meld between the church's interests and the academy's standards is a little more fractious. One consequence: its graduates are not eligible for the national honorary Phi

Beta Kappa, because of criticisms about academic freedom at the church-run school.

The competing imperatives of religion and the academy are bound to collide most violently in an institution that is both religious and academic, such as Brigham Young University. Given the fact that many—if not most—scholars of Mormon history have their professional home there, those faculty members were unavoidably caught in the eye of the gathering storm. A number of religious institutions have suffered the pains which some have called the de-Christianizing of American universities,[122] but BYU's are especially acute. In reaction mode, and responding to accelerating Mormon historical revisionism, the church in 1986 reversed the archival openness noted by Brodie in 1971. Patrons of the church's extensive historical collection were required to assign to the church the right to censor their findings. Under these and other pressures, Quinn in 1988 resigned his position as full professor, and Near Eastern languages professor David P. Wright was dismissed for his position in support of nineteenth-century origins to the Book of Mormon. But historians were not the only intellectuals creating dilemmas in the LDS community. In 1991 and 1992, feminist English professor Cecilia Konchar Farr spoke out and published in support of her prochoice position while employed at BYU. She was denied continuing status, in a decision process that criticized her violation of citizenship obligations and use of the classroom as a political forum.[123] While this case was unfolding, BYU formulated a statement on academic freedom which affirmed basic principles of intellectual inquiry while stipulating as a general exception "behavior or expression *seriously and adversely affecting* the university mission or the Church." Three examples were offered: public expression that "contradicts or opposes, rather than analyzes or discusses, fundamental church doctrine or policy; deliberately attacks or derides the church or its general leaders; or violates the Honor Code because the expression is dishonest, illegal, unchaste, profane, or unduly disrespectful of others."[124]

The timing of the document was no coincidence: academic freedom issues continued to erupt. The same year as Farr's case, anthropology professor David Knowlton presented a paper at the Sunstone Symposium explaining the rationale behind Latin American attacks on Mormon missionaries. Church leaders responded with a statement warning against presentations that "jeopardize the effectiveness or safety of our missionaries," leading to public rejoinders by Knowlton, and his dismissal. *Sunstone* was at this time acquiring fame as a haven for marginalized intellectuals and notoriety as a forum for those disaffected from and outspoken against the church. By 1983, the press reported, pressure had emerged from a Mormon apostle for stake presidents to interview church scholars who contributed to *Sunstone* and *Dialogue*.[125] Throughout the decade, the mutual suspicion between church leaders and intellectuals grew, culminating in apostle Dallin H. Oaks's reasoned defense of the church's concerns in a 1989 General Conference address. Noting that members were sometimes troubled by "alternate voices" and "confused about the Church's relationship to the alternate voices," he asserted the leadership's obligation to maintain "a spiritual quality control," and to "do all they can to avoid expressed or implied Church endorsement for teachings that are not orthodox." So while insisting that the church "does not attempt to isolate its members from alternate voices," he warned against lending tacit support to publications, conferences, or symposia that in addition to undoubtedly "good" content promoted that which is evil or destructive. He singled out for particular mention the public discussion and critique of sacred Mormon temple ceremonies—an occasional subject of the independent publications and symposia.[126] In 1991, the church issued a formal statement discouraging Latter-day Saints from participating in "independent symposiums on Mormonism," widely interpreted as referring to the Sunstone Symposium in particular.[127]

To some Mormons, the 1991 statement on symposia represented the latest step in a gradual repudiation of the intellectual openness of one of the last of the liberally inclined apostles, Hugh B. Brown. In 1969, he had told a BYU audience:

> [P]reserve, then, the freedom of your mind in education and in religion, and be unafraid to express your thoughts and to insist upon your right to examine every proposition. We are not so much concerned with whether your thoughts are orthodox or heterodox as we are that you shall have thoughts.[128]

But citing such a credo, church leaders would say, misses a crucial distinction between thoughts and public pronouncements.

In 1992, the church acknowledged that it had a committee charged with monitoring church dissidents and collecting their public pronouncements and publications. The *New York Times* reported leaders as explaining the committee was "designed to help them counsel with members who, however well-meaning, may hinder the progress of the church through public criticism."[129] Those public criticisms by a number of Mormons apparently crossed the line in 1993. That would go down in Mormon history as the year of the "September Six," a group of feminists and scholars disciplined by church councils. The church maintains a policy of strict confidentiality regarding proceedings, so it is not possible to discern all of the factors and details of such actions. But it appears that

D. Michael Quinn, who first caused consternation with his research into post-manifesto polygamy, was excommunicated for writings such as his 1987 study that saw Joseph Smith and the Book of Mormon largely as products of an early American hermetic and folk-magic culture. Lavina Fielding Anderson received the same sanction for her public campaign to chronicle and expose alleged ecclesiastical intimidation against Mormon intellectuals. Maxine Hanks and Lynne Kanavel Whitesides, both Mormon feminists, were disciplined for a combination of factors involving public criticism of church leaders and expressing what was considered extreme feminist theology, in some cases advocating prayer to a heavenly Mother. Paul Toscano, who had recently delivered a conference paper on "false teachings" of the church, suffered excommunication, as did Avraham Gileadi, an Isaiah scholar—who alone among the six maintained a low profile and soon rejoined the church. A few months later, David P. Wright was excommunicated, following his collaboration in a book that expressly disputed the authenticity of the Book of Mormon as ancient scripture.

Feminism would reemerge as a contested area in 1996, when BYU professor Gail Turley Houston and a small group of faculty asked the AAUP to investigate claims that her academic freedom was violated when she was denied continuing faculty status. Officials indicated that Houston engaged in a habit of "publicly contradicting fundamental Church doctrine and deliberately attacking the Church. For example, among other things, Professor Houston publicly endorsed the practice of praying to Heavenly Mother."[130] The AAUP censured BYU (through the rather disingenuous argument that Houston's public advocacy was not really public but "a description of personal vision") but subsequently the less-politicized and official accrediting body Northwest Association of Schools and Colleges found no cause for censure and specifically praised BYU's academic freedom statement. And the *Wall Street Journal* opined, "as for academic freedom, BYU is well within bounds. Religious colleges—particularly those sponsored directly by a church—have no legal duty to hire or grant tenure to professors who criticize the church or its policies."[131]

The real question of course, does not concern legalism, but the intellectual climate that has resulted from trends in Mormon historiography, feminist politics, and the perennial difficulties of balancing academic freedom with the mission of religiously affiliated universities. It was in these same decades that the Catholic church experienced similar tensions, most notably in the case of Charles Curran, a professor of moral theology at Catholic University of America, who offended the Vatican with his teachings on sexual morality. Upon losing his teaching privileges, he sued the university. He lost the suit, but the AAUP censured the institution in 1990 as it would BYU a few years later.

BOOK OF MORMON STUDIES

The search into Mormonism's history is even more contentious in the realm of a past that Joseph claimed to recover through a set of gold plates discovered in upstate New York. The challenge for intellectuals to take seriously the study of a record—allegedly inscribed on gold plates—that describes Israelite civilizations flourishing in ancient America and was delivered to a farm boy by an angel is daunting to say the least. B. H. Roberts had tried to interest church leaders in the merits of a scholarly Book of Mormon apologetics, but even a fellow intellectual like Talmage was uninterested. He dismissed Roberts's concerns about the scripture's credibility with a shrug: "many of the 'difficulties,' or objections as opposing critics would urge, are after all but negative in their nature. The Book of Mormon states that Lehi and his colony found horses upon this continent when they arrived; and therefore horses were here at that time."[132]

One reason Talmage and others could dismiss concerns was because the Book of Mormon was little read even in the church. By nonmembers, it was completely ignored or ridiculed as a prima facie absurdity. In the oft-quoted words of Thomas O'Dea: "The Book of Mormon has not been universally considered by its critics as one of those books that must be read in order to have an opinion of it."[133] On the other side, prevalent theories linking American Indians to the Lost Tribes of Israel; extensive, magnificent ruins of vanished civilizations suddenly coming to light in Mesoamerica; and the lack of sophisticated, archaeological tools with which to critique the record's contents combined to inspire early Mormons with the confidence that there was "sufficient evidence both circumstantial, and scriptural, to establish the authenticity of the Book of Mormon."[134] Not enough skeptics read the Book of Mormon to necessitate a serious apologetics, and not enough Mormon scholars were sufficiently interested or qualified to produce one.

This all changed in 1945. That year, the new president of Brigham Young University appointed M. Wells Jakeman, one of the first Mormons formally trained as an archaeologist, to a newly created chair of archaeology.[135] Soon, the new Department of Archaeology was sponsoring the first fieldwork in southeastern Mexico, which Mormon scholars would increasingly come to associate with Book of Mormon lands—thanks in good part to the work of John L. Sorenson in establishing plausible correlations between the Book of Mormon and Mesoamerican culture and geography.[136] Also in 1945, the dominant Mormon intellectual of the second half of the twentieth century, Hugh Nibley, attached himself to BYU. Nibley early showed himself to be a brilliant scholar and linguistic prodigy, publishing on a range of subjects in the best academic journals, ranging from *Revue de Qumran*, *Vigiliae Christianae*, and *Classical Journal*, to *Encyclopedia Judaica*, *Jewish Quarterly Review*, and *Church History*. Beginning in 1948, however, he began publishing a series on the Book of Mormon for the church's *Improvement Era*. Thereafter, he quickly became the most erudite and prolific LDS scholar to address Book of Mormon issues. He brought a formidable array of intellectual qualifications to the task and a more sophisticated approach than any of his predecessors. Shunning the quixotic quest for dramatic archaeological finds in the New World, for instance, he shifted attention from the Americas back to the Near Eastern context of the book, and asked questions about the totality of the world presented in the record:

> [D]oes it correctly reflect "the cultural horizon and religious and social ideas and practices of the time"? Does it have authentic historical and geographical background? Is the mise-en-scène mythical, highly imaginative, or extravagantly improbable? Is its local color correct, and are its proper names convincing? Until recent years men were asking the same questions of the book of Exodus, and scholars were stolidly turning thumbs down until evidence accumulating in its favor began to turn the scales. As one student described it, the problem "is rather to prove, by innumerable small coincidences, that which Ebers has so well called the 'Egypticity' of the Pentateuch, than to establish any particular historical point by external and monumental evidence." Just so the problem of 1 Nephi is to establish both its "Egypticity" and its "Arabicity" by like innumerable coincidences.[137]

Nibley's career is perhaps the premier instance of how a prodigious intellect melds his academic training with the particular supernaturalism of orthodox Mormonism. His fairly abrupt decision to change his audience, however, may illustrate either the limitations the secular world imposes upon such paradigm mixing, or Nibley's personal disillusionment with playing the role of true believer to an academic elite. In either case, as his work shifted increasingly to LDS-published apologetics, the church's best hope to engage other intellectuals in refereed forums about Mormon positions ceded the field and turned to address the choir.

Apologetics in the conventional sense has meant rhetorical and logical defense, but a defense directed toward a jury (as with Socrates) or an unbelieving emperor or public (as in Tertullian and other church fathers). As late as the nineteenth century, religious controversies still played themselves out in great public debates, pamphlet wars, and other public forums. In the twentieth century, religion moved increasingly to the private sphere, or became compartmentalized and domesticated in the academy. Attacks on particular faiths, as well as their defense, migrated largely to denominational presses, and increasingly religious writers directed their polemics to their own cobelievers, regardless of the object of discussion or the ostensible audience. Such was certainly the case with Hugh Nibley. His collected writings exceed fifteen substantial volumes; several argue the historical plausibility of the Book of Mormon by situating it in a Near Eastern world view and cultural milieu, or by using linguistics, textual criticism, or archaeology to document its Old World parallels. Other volumes situate Joseph's Abrahamic writings alongside recently recovered pseudepigraphal or apocryphal texts, while still others refute anti-Mormon arguments, document early Christianity's "apostasy," or celebrate Brigham Young's teachings and goad Mormons to better live up to their heritage.[138]

Nibley was probably the church's scholar who could present Mormon scripture and the Mormon interpretation of ecclesiastical history in the most intellectually compelling way. But in the 1950s, Nibley was writing less and less for his academic peers and more and more for an LDS readership. By 1960, he had turned his attention almost entirely to Mormon scripture and apologetics. With the momentous 1966 rediscovery of portions of the Joseph Smith papyri, he immersed himself in Egyptian and wrote a series of articles intended to defend *The Pearl of Great Price* against charges of Joseph's fraud or incompetence, again publishing in the church magazine. There is another indication that 1960 was the year that a trend in his scholarship became a decisive shift of direction. That was the year of Nibley's sabbatical at Berkeley, where he was offered a position. He declined.[139] It is hard to say what motivated Nibley's decision to forsake the secular academic audience for the Wasatch Front one, and a position at the premier university of the west for BYU. Perhaps he felt that strengthening members' convictions about their own scripture was more fruitful than engaging scholars about early Christian history. Perhaps it was an unavoidable development, given the peculiar challenge facing any Mormon apologist. Virtually alone among Christians, Mormons espouse belief in a set of scriptures of origin so implausible as to preclude serious engagement by most other Christian scholars. Nibley himself frequently expressed his exasperation that non-LDS critics would not take the step of actually reading the Book of Mormon, but acted like experts dismissing an alleged diamond found in a field without ever examining it.

Whatever the explanation, the decision of Mormonism's foremost intellect and scholar of early Christianity effectively to abrogate a dialogue with the secular academy may be construed as indicative of a kind of insularity in the church's intellectual engagement with the world at large. Ironically, as appreciated as Nibley's work is in many LDS circles, when he wrote a manual for church use, it only saw the light of day because the president of the church himself intervened to thwart its rejection in committee.[140] In earlier years, the church's leading intellectuals were prolific in their production of church manuals. The difficulties that Mormonism's leading intellectual of recent decades encountered in the path to publication, even with the president's personal and official support, suggests a major shift in attitudes. "Always think of yourself as addressing the tiredest farmer in Koosharem," Nibley reported one church leader as advising him.[141] Such catering to the lowest intellectual common denominator is a consequence of two factors in particular. First, as we saw, the Church Education System came to be dominated by men suspicious of intellectuals and concerned that secular educational ideals not triumph at the cost of spiritual strength. Second, under the presidency of David O. McKay (1951–1970), the church tripled in membership, from roughly 1 to 3 million. The need to centralize and standardize doctrine and instruction in such a large, growing, and disparate membership resulted in efforts to centrally control all church programs, efforts that would culminate in the priesthood program launched in 1961. Explaining the development, the First Presidency referred to "the need of a correlation between and among the courses of study put out by the General Priesthood Committee and by the responsible heads of other Committees of the General Authorities for the instruction of the Priesthood of the Church."[142] Standardization in a church now in excess of 12 million necessarily exerts pressure in the direction of simplicity, accessibility, and safety.

Correlation may have begun as an effort to coordinate and streamline church instruction. But the movement actually represented a drastic restructuring of church government, with far-reaching repercussions for the fragile balance between priesthood authority and individual autonomy, centralized mandates and local initiative. By the dawn of the twentieth century, as Greg Prince and William Wright write:

> [T]he lifeblood of the church, which gave it most of its identity, was a collection of auxiliary organizations that had all begun as grassroots initiatives addressing the needs of a growing and changing social and cultural body. The local success of these organizations subsequently catapulted them into churchwide adoption.[143]

The organizations—Primary for children, Mutual for young men and women, Relief Society for the women—and Sunday school had their own governing presidencies and boards that presided over their churchwide counterparts with relative autonomy and their own independent budgets, and did so with great success. In the view of one church leader, "the auxiliaries of the Church were far more effective and powerful in the members' idea and view than were the Priesthood quorums. . . . So I would say, to characterize the Church prior to Correlation, that the auxiliaries ran it and everything took second place to them."[144] In March 1960, the First Presidency directed the General Priesthood Committee of the church, chaired by senior apostle Harold B. Lee, to "make a study of the study courses of the Auxiliary Organizations with a view of having a well-correlated plan of study." It was soon evident, however, that in Prince and Wright's words, "curricular reform paled in significance to Lee's other goals of reining in the auxiliary organizations and placing day-to-day control of the church in the hands of the Twelve."[145] Unquestionably, correlation has produced a more efficient church organization, and a church that is virtually inoculated against doctrinal innovation or fragmentation. At the same time, many deplore the program, believing that the auxiliaries' loss of control over their own budgets, publications, and curricula portends and parallels a decline in spiritual and intellectual independence. An LDS civil service bureaucracy, responsible to the Quorum, has assumed the burden and power of approving all lesson content. Strictures on absolute conformity to uniform lesson manuals precludes most adaptation to local circumstance or audience, and stunts the intellectual initiative and spiritual self-reliance of the teacher. The result is instruction that is safe and unadventuresome. Another consequence, as a church seventy lamented, is that "correlation, like the Supreme Court, [is] becoming more and more the originator of thought, rather than the coordinator of thought."[146]

Nibley bristled at such conformity, and persisted in his outspokenness and intellectual independence but from a position of steadfast, even zealous faithfulness. His impact on the intellectual culture of Mormonism has been profound, and is still playing out with uncertain consequences. Following his lead, John Welch in 1979 founded the Foundation for Ancient Research and Mormon Studies (FARMS), an institute that coordinates and sponsors research linking the Book of Mormon to ancient origins by employing "literary, linguistic, historical, religious, political, military, legal, social, economic, and just basic textual" approaches in order to find if "aspects of the book reflect ancient culture, language, law and history."[147] Ironically, then, at the very moment when some Mormon scholars were working to bring LDS historiography in line with secular academic standards, another group of BYU-affiliated scholars were working to bring their critical skills to bear on Mormon scripture, but *assuming* rather than *bracketing* the supernatural dimensions of Mormon origins. Consequently, as Mormon history has been more fully incorporated into the mainstream, Mormon scriptural studies have become more distinctively Mormon. With the incorporation of the independent FARMS into BYU in 1997, the research is now even sponsored officially if indirectly by the church.[148]

Few critics can fault the sophistication of what Mormon scholars are doing to buttress claims to Book of Mormon historicity. For one thing, at the turn of the millennium, Mormon scholars were bringing unprecedented training to the task of Mormon scholarship. Those who have contributed to FARMS-related projects include Stephen E. Robinson, Duke Ph.D. in biblical studies (under W. D. Davies and James Charlesworth); S. Kent Brown, Brown Ph.D. working on the Nag Hammadi texts; Wilfred Griggs, Berkeley Ph.D. in ancient history (Egyptian Christianity); Kent P. Jackson, Michigan Ph.D. in Near Eastern studies (working under David Noel Freedman and Frank Moore Cross on the Ammonite language); Stephen D. Ricks, Berkeley and Graduate Theological Union Ph.D. in Near Eastern religions (under Jacob Milgrom); John Gee, Yale Ph.D. in Egyptology; Daniel Peterson, UCLA Ph.D. in Near Eastern languages and cultures; and Donald W. Parry, University of Jerusalem and University of Utah Ph.D. in Hebrew.

Neither are critics faulting the caliber of scholarship these academics are producing. In 1997, evangelical critics Carl Mosser and Paul Owen acknowledged the high quality of the scholarship they were endeavoring to refute. "[I]n recent years," they said, "the sophistication and erudition of LDS apologetics has risen considerably . . . [and] is clearly seen in their approach to the Book of Mormon." As difficult as it may be to accept the fact, they insisted, "LDS academicians are producing serious research which desperately needs to be critically examined."[149] With the death of Hugh Nibley in 2005, Mormonism lost its most erudite and distinctive voice. Yet in the early years of the new millennium, almost four dozen Latter-day Saints were enrolled in graduate schools of divinity, theology, and religious studies at Yale, Harvard, Chicago, and elsewhere.

Recent efforts to disprove the Book of Mormon through DNA analysis and spirited rebuttals are but the latest episode in an accelerating debate—engendered by both partisans and critics—that increasingly subjects the faith claims of Mormonism to the laboratories of science and the analysis of scholars.[150] As the professionalism and sophistication of the debaters and their tools increase, both sides exude growing confidence in breakthroughs.

The quality of their scholars and scholarship notwithstanding, Latter-day Saints may never find the holy grail of secular respect and serious academic engagement with their history, their theology, or their scriptures, thus making the Mormon intellectual qua Mormon intellectual a figure on the margins with no comfortable home. History has seen notable exceptions, with the widespread acclaim given Leonard Arrington and Richard Bushman, for instance. But in both cases, their areas of expertise and the source of their scholarly credibility came from their contributions to Western and early American history, respectively. In the case of theology, Mormon suspicion of the theological enterprise, the lack of a theologically trained leadership, the relative (until recently) paucity of Mormon scholars trained in formal theology, and especially, the doubtful existence of a Mormon theology in any systematic sense—all make progress in this area of intellectual give and take difficult. (One important development in this regard, however, was the organization of the Society for Mormon Philosophy and Theology in 2003. They have published a journal, *Element*, since 2005.) And finally, the Mormon scriptures themselves are hard to extricate from the historical circumstances of their initial presentation to the world. Joseph himself perennially emphasized their miraculous transmission and translation over their content, and their historical role was to ground Joseph's authority precisely by virtue of that supernaturalism. Academic study of the Bible is successful, in part, because believers and nonbelievers alike can at least agree on its antiquity and historical impact, its inherent literary complexities and beauties, and its demonstrable—if mixed—role as a moral force in much of the world's history. It is harder for scholars to invest in the study of a text that is generally assumed to be a modern fraud, is popularly reputed to be "chloroform in print" (in Mark Twain's witty dismissal), and has had negligible impact outside a (till now) relatively minor American denomination.

The bind in which this puts Mormon scriptural scholars is that, given the patent improbability of an authentically ancient provenance for the book, any research that probes its significance or status as an ancient text is seen, a priori, as inherently apologetic. A 2003 conference on Mormon theology and philosophy at Yale and a 2005 symposium at the Library of Congress on Joseph Smith were both marked by criticisms that Mormon scholars were engaging more in evangelizing than in legitimate academic exchange.[151] To some extent, this was true; Mormons, as one participant remarked, have a hard time passing up a good missionary opportunity. But it is also possible that presumptive labeling as apologetic of any inquiry into the Book of Mormon as an ancient text is equally wrongheaded. At least one impressive archaeological find substantiates Book of Mormon historicity,[152] and Methodist Old Testament scholar Margaret Barker found it possible to take the Book of Mormon's antiquity seriously, with impressive implications for her study of religious turmoil under King Josiah's reforms.[153]

One consequence of the professionalization and institutional growth of Mormon studies is that what it means to do Mormon studies, or to be a Mormon intellectual, is undergoing vigorous and sometimes contentious negotiation. Mormon studies, like women's studies or black studies, is a rubric fraught with high ideological stakes, confused by identity politics, and victimized by historical shifts and hopeless definitional ambiguity. For example, the pressures that FARMS scholars are creating to force the Book of Mormon to be taken more seriously are opposed by a class of Mormon intellectuals who themselves are embarrassed by association with angels, gold plates, and warring Nephites and Lamanites. While some of them have been excommunicated for their public attacks on the Book of Mormon's authenticity, they at the same time represent one version of a relatively recent phenomenon—the cultural Mormon. The best example (and one who maintained his LDS membership) is perhaps Sterling McMurrin, a distinguished philosopher and commissioner of education in the Kennedy administration (and the fourth most-distinguished Mormon intellectual, according to Arrington's informal poll). "I simply don't believe the Book of Mormon to be authentic," he said. "I think that all of the hassling over the authenticity of the Book of Mormon is just a waste of time."[154] McMurrin was not representative of a new class of Mormon intellectual—he embraced none of the core principles of Joseph's restoration theology and was not even a committed theist. His affiliation with Mormonism was little more than sentimental identification with the historical tradition out of which he came. He was more representative, perhaps, of the rough demarcations—however imperfectly or inconsistently drawn—between the individual's right to dissent and the institution's imperative to maintain orthodoxy.

As the Chicago Divinity School–educated Heber Snell found himself diverging more and more from Mormon orthodoxy, he bristled at criticisms of his heterodoxy. "There are some concepts relating to controversy on Church subjects," he said in a letter growing out of a fractious 1967 *Dialogue* roundtable on the Bible:

which, it seems to me, should be clarified. . . . One of these concepts may be stated as one's right (privilege, if you prefer the word) to disagree with Church teachings. Do we Mormons have this right without being "read out of the Church" by some brother who differs from us?

The answer, he insists, "is unmistakable: we do have this right."[155] How far that right extends is not always clear and precise, but McMurrin's view on the subject is helpful. "The problem," he said in an interview:

is that most people tend to confuse heresy with apostasy. In my language an apostate is one who turns against the Church. A heretic is simply a person who disbelieves in whole or in part the teachings of the Church. They sometimes, of course, go hand in hand, but not necessarily, and there is a difference. I readily admit to heresy, but I reject any charge that I am an apostate.[156]

The church affirmed this distinction in a statement issued after the excommunication of the September Six:

We have the responsibility to preserve the doctrinal purity of the Church.... Faithful members of the Church can distinguish between mere differences of opinion and those activities formally defined as apostasy. Apostasy refers to Church members who "(1) repeatedly act in clear, open, and deliberate public opposition to the Church or its leaders; or (2) persist in teaching as Church doctrine information that is not Church doctrine after being corrected by their bishops or higher authority; or (3) continue to follow the teachings of apostate cults (such as those that advocate plural marriage) after being corrected by their bishops or higher authority."[157]

Dissenters like McMurrin don't dispute these prerogatives:

I thought the church belonged to everyone, that it was as much the church of the unorthodox as the church of the orthodox; but I no longer think that. The church is an institution which is owned and operated by the people who pay the tithing and who do the believing; if they think dissidents like me don't belong in it, I wouldn't argue with them.[158]

Whether dissidents like McMurrin belong in the church, or are part of the Mormon intellectual tradition, appears unresolved. When he was performing his gadfly role in the 1950s, he met with two future LDS prophets: Harold B. Lee and Joseph Fielding Smith, then president of the Quorum of Twelve. In that meeting, he repudiated any belief in the divinity of Christ, Joseph Smith's visions, or the historicity of the Book of Mormon. Smith would subsequently encourage his excommunication, but President David O. McKay told McMurrin, "All I will say is that if they put you on trial for excommunication, I will be there as the first witness in your behalf.... You just think and believe as you please."[159] McKay was eloquent not just in defending intellectual freedom, but in being one of the last church leaders to dramatically exemplify it. "The Church of Jesus Christ of Latter-day Saints," he said, "makes an appeal to all men to seek the higher life, intellectual and spiritual, and to incite them to greater intelligence in striving for the abundant life."[160] Repaying irony with irony, the church not only tolerated McMurrin, its officials asked him to represent the church in giving a presentation on Mormonism at Ohio State and at a Utah lecture series in 1955 and 1957.[161] He outlived the excommunications of the September Six by three years, with his membership still intact.

It would be tempting to assume intellectual vitality and achievement must fall victim to such conflicts as Mormonism is and has been experiencing, between traditional canons of belief in a conservative church and the secular standards of the scientific and intellectual communities. Most arguments for success or failure rely upon subjective judgments. But in some statistical regards, the evidence bears out the church's strategies. At least, the Church Educational System seems to have accomplished its goal of shoring up the faith of its students considerably in the generations since the surveys that so alarmed church leaders in the thirties. A 1973 follow-up poll to the original, for example, found orthodoxy at BYU had increased by over 25 points overall.[162] The author of one of the most comprehensive studies to date of teenagers and religion writes, "Mormons generally have high expectations of their youth [and] invest a lot in educating them.... These investments pay off in producing Mormon teenagers who are, by sociological measures at least, more religiously serious and articulate than most other religious teenagers in the U.S." This increased religiosity does not seem to have come at a cost to Mormonism's commitment to a vigorous academic life. "Mormon teenagers fared best when it comes to avoiding risky behavior *and doing well in school*" the study concluded (emphasis added).[163]

Other evidence as well suggests that the institutional subordination of learning to faith that began in the 1930s and what could be interpreted as a creeping hostility to intellectual inquiry have not impaired the intellectual achievements of the members. On the contrary, census data for the same year of Clark's directive, 1940, indicated that Mormon-dominated Utah had the highest level of educational attainment of any state in America. Utah youth ranked highest for years of schooling: 11.7 while the national median was 10.3 years.[164] Much reported in Mormon circles were the results of studies conducted by E. L. Thorndike of Columbia University in that same decade. He found that Utah ranked number one as the birthplace of people listed in *American Men of Science*, number two as the state producing people listed in *Leaders in Education*, and the fourth most-prolific state in producing men and women listed in *Who's Who in America*.[165]

That the rising generation did not suffer adversely either was indicated by a study a generation later, analyzing the origins of American scientists and scholars. This 1974 report concluded:

The most productive state is Utah, which is first in productivity for all fields combined in all time periods. It is first in biological and social sciences, second in education, third in physical sciences, and sixth in arts and professions. Compared to other states in its region, it is defiantly productive. This result seems clearly to be due to the influence of Mormon values, because Mormon youth predominate in the colleges of the state, and because other variables, such as climate, geography, natural resources, and social class, do not appear to explain the exceptional record of this state.[166]

In one other regard, the Mormon case presents us with a significant sociological anomaly. Studies have found that, in general, educational attainment correlates negatively with religious belief. The better educated Christians become, the less committed to religious belief and practice they are. In the case of Latter-day Saints, however, "no evidence was found to indicate that college education is detrimental to the religiosity of Mormons." At the present time, Mormons in general obtain a higher level of education than other Americans, having higher rates of high school graduation, college graduation, and doctoral degrees.[167] Yet those "with post-bachelor's degrees are, on the average, more religious than those who never attended college. In short, college-educated Latter-day Saints . . . both as a group and by specific level of education, were, on the average, more religiously involved than noncollege-educated Latter-day Saints." In particular, "college-educated Mormons are *more* apt to attend church and to exhibit other manifestations of 'high' religiosity than are less-educated Mormons."[168] Alluding to the way in which LDS belief incorporates education into "the total religious milieu," the researcher concludes, "Latter-day Saint theology appears to negate the secularizing impact of education by sacralizing it."[169] Armand Mauss has warned against drawing "facile conclusions" from such studies, since the results are not consistent across college majors (philosophy and religion majors do not fare well in maintaining "high orthodoxy," for example).[170]

Still, the church's emphasis on education, the generally successful accommodation of the church's members to secular learning, and their intellectual aspirations manifest in doctrinal expression and historical fact attest to the insight of Thomas O'Dea. For the Mormons, he wrote, "the earthly sojourn [is] basically an educative process. Knowledge is necessary to . . . deification. . . . Education . . . advances [man] in his eternal progress."[171] Such a fundamental conception may prove to be an effective counterbalance to the normally stultifying influences of orthodoxy and hierarchical control. So we find in Mormon intellectual culture that the strictures of orthodox certainties coexist with the quest for eternal learning, and the security of nonnegotiable truths is tempered by commitment to open-ended process.

At the beginning of the twenty-first century, there are signs that the Mormon leadership believes they have weathered the worst of the storms, and are confident that even full disclosure cannot, ultimately, damage the foundations of Mormon belief. "Nothing can produce a more rapid deterioration of religious faith than the honest study of the history of religion," says Sterling McMurrin.[172] Clearly, LDS leaders do not agree. The Mormon church has published on seventy-four DVDs a collection of 400,000 images from its historical archives, making that trove of documents instantly available to the public. A second initiative, the Book of Mormon critical text project, began publication in 2001. The mammoth undertaking includes an analytical transcription of the printer's copies and extant original Book of Mormon manuscript, a comprehensive history of textual changes, and an analysis of every textual variant. And now the LDS church is in the process of expanding published accounts of Joseph Smith's papers from the two volumes available since 1989 to more than two dozen volumes comprising all contemporary documents relating to his life, currently in production with the endorsement of the National Archives Commission.

Such signs notwithstanding, at least two points of difference seem destined to preserve the tensions in Mormon intellectual culture. First is the question of whether certainty itself is possible or desirable. The Book of Mormon relates the story of the brother of Jared, whose faith led him to a visionary disclosure of a physically present Christ, which began with a glimpse of a single divine finger. That one glimpse, the scripture records, was the catalyst for the full epiphany that followed because, however inconsequential the object of his vision, it was contemplated with an absolute certainty. "And because of the knowledge of this man he could not be kept from beholding within the veil; and he saw the finger of Jesus, which, when he saw, he fell with fear; for he knew that it was the finger of the Lord; and he had faith no longer, for he knew, nothing doubting" (Ether 3:19).

On the other hand, many within the modern faith believe that uncertainty, even for Latter-day Saints, is an inescapable condition of the adult human condition. To those willing to listen to the "alternate voices" comprising the self-labeled intellectual community, Armand Mauss advises: "Abandon certainty all ye who enter herein! Never again will you enjoy the immunity to doubt and ambiguity that went with your previous life. But then the ability to live with perpetual ambiguity is also a trait that distinguishes adults from adolescents."[173]

A second point of differentiation has to do with the way in which truth is pursued. For one constituency, the route is simple. Truth must be pursued aggressively and courageously, whatever the costs. But in reality, the search for truth always takes place in the context of institutional imperatives and parameters; there are no standards for this quest that are not institutionally formulated and shaped. LDS apostle Russell M. Nelson is not alone in warning that even the truth, naked and recklessly wielded, can "cripple, damage, or destroy." Even journalists have a code of ethics with an entire section headed "Minimize Harm."[174] The breach that increasingly took shape in the 1970s, for example, was between those who favored a secular academic standard of unrestricted access to archival records and unfettered freedom to pursue any line of historical inquiry, on the one hand, and those guardians of a religious institution, on the other hand, who saw even truth as a surgeon's knife that could obliterate faith, given an incomplete context, a too-vulnerable audience, or insensitive treatment. These different institutions have different constituencies, priorities, and standards. This recognition is implicit in the dictum of apostle Neal Maxwell, who believes that true discipleship requires that one embrace the right set of standards and parameters: "The LDS scholar has his citizenship in the kingdom, but carries his passport into the professional world—not the other way around."[175] But even on such a journey, there is no guarantee that those scholars will be comfortable travelers.

"A Uniform Look
for the Church"

Architecture

> It was there, in the middle of the cemetery, that the
> alien building stood—an obvious mimic of old Mormon
> temple architecture, meaning it was a monstrosity of
> conflicting periods that somehow, perhaps through in-
> tense sincerity, managed to be beautiful anyway.
>
> ~ Orson Scott Card

Today, particular edifices like the neo-Gothic Salt Lake Temple or its adjacent turtleback Tabernacle are obvious icons of Mormonism. Architecture is,
of course, the most palpable and publicly visible evidence of cultural distinctive-
ness. But a single building, or even complex of buildings, does not a culture make.
What settlement in the West afforded was a canvas that spanned a good portion
of a continent. And the resultant patterns that emerged over the course of settlement and diffusion were so identifiable, so distinctive, and so uniform as to
elicit perhaps the earliest application to Mormonism of the designation "culture."
Before artists or novelists began to limn Mormon themes, and long before the
sheer bulk of Mormon converts prompted comparisons with ethnicity or cultural
categories, the visible textures of the Mormon diaspora took shape. "The earliest
geographical accounts," write Jeffrey S. Smith and Benjamin N. White, "recognize that the area dominated by Mormons is easily identifiable," and another
scholar calls that area "the most easily mapped and described" of all seven religious regions in the United States.[1] The contours of this "Mormon culture region" with its "visible imprint on the land" were first mapped by Donald Meinig
in 1965.[2]

Subsequent studies succeeded in articulating specific elements that made up
the essential ingredients in this Mormon landscape. Oliver Goldsmith famously
invented the town of Auburn to typify village conditions in early industrial

England ("The Deserted Village"). Richard Francaviglia was a bit more systematic in constructing the town of "Canaanville" as a composite of the Mormon settlements established in the second half of the nineteenth century throughout Utah, Idaho, and Arizona.[3] He notes that Mormon towns are generally strictly gridded along north-south and east-west axes, with uncommonly wide, straight streets. Small farms cluster together in orbit right up to the edge of a small, Main Street business district and a public square, which holds the LDS chapel and some older church building appropriate to gatherings, such as a Relief Society Hall. Dusty side streets are remarkably wide as well, but their most distinctive feature is the irrigation ditch that runs alongside of each, pervading the entire community, an alternately dry and fluid network that is a stark reminder of the community's precarious existence. The omnipresent irrigation gates, which grant access to a strictly regulated, limited supply to each property, signify as well the need for communal cooperation, fair dealing, and punctual compliance.

Architecturally, the dominant residential mode is what Francaviglia calls the central-hall plan house type, also known as "Nauvoo style houses," which are generally not found in non-Mormon western towns:

> Characterized by symmetrical plans and facades, one and a half to two stories in height, and, most importantly, with a chimney at each end, ... the home lends an Old World—almost English—appearance to the village, especially when its small peaked dormer gables interrupt the roof line. On some, the two doors seen on the façade often are called "polygamy doors."... Usually this type of house will have cornices of the Greek revival mode, which tend even more to create a heavy roof line and gable. This coupled with the fact that the central-hall type was often built in brick ... and stone, tends to make the house a very sturdy, almost fortress-like element in the landscape.[4]

Even more distinctive, perhaps, is the architecture of LDS chapels in this region. Large but low-lying, simple brick construction with few details and a simple steeple rising from an otherwise pedestrian structure signify a location that bears the label, but not the architecture, of sacred space. (Some lack even the steeple.) The result appears a casual compromise between pragmatism and functionalism, on the one hand, and spiritual and religious imperatives, on the other.

In total, Francaviglia identifies ten or so characteristics that appear almost uniquely in Mormon-colonized or Mormon-dominated communities. Most of these features seem random, rooted in no particular ideology or cultural values. They are just practices assimilated into a religious culture that individually are not significant or even noteworthy: "inside-out granaries," hay derricks, and a tendency toward brick construction in addition to the Nauvoo-style houses (which are not, popular mythology behind the two-door tendency notwithstanding, attributable to multiple wives). Other features are a lasting heritage of Joseph Smith's city planning: the wide streets, the regular appearance of farm parcels and structures inside town boundaries, and a central square. But the cumulative effect of all of these features, these deliberate innovations and accidents of history, these testaments to foresight and quirks of custom, is rightly called a distinctive Mormon landscape. And this distinctive quality both derives from, and serves to reinforce and extend, a sense of difference that transcends the merely visual.

In a telling experiment, Francaviglia showed two sets of comparable photographs—one from a Mormon community, and one from a non-Mormon community—to interviewees. The vast majority, almost four out of five, immediately recognized the Mormon example, usually on the professed basis of factors like "the Mormon house," the "Mormon fence," and the irrigation ditch.

At the turn of the nineteenth century, Mormon architecture, on the other hand, was becoming less, rather than more, distinctive. "No period of church architecture," writes one historian, "saw greater profusion and reaching out for new styles" than the generation beginning in 1890.[5] The Salt Lake Temple was dedicated at last in 1893, but by then, temples in St. George, Manti, and Logan had been used for years. The railroad had, since 1869, opened Utah to the world and vice versa, but American influences still affected Utah builders with a delayed reaction. The Gothic Revivalism evident in the temples had finally permeated meetinghouse design by 1880, and would persist through numerous permutations until the 1930s. Church architecture had always been largely an eclectic blend of inherited traditions, but by 1890 experimental approaches and blends were being combined with an exuberance that overcame even the restrained functionalism of simple meetinghouses. A Muscovite-looking creation in the Nineteenth Ward in Salt Lake (1890), a magnificently domed Beaux Arts–style meetinghouse in Riverton (1898–1890), and an Italianate/Spanish mission design in Payson (1906) exemplified this new cosmopolitanism. As Paul Anderson points out, the Mormons built "more than a thousand buildings during the first half of the twentieth century," incorporating "Renaissance domes, Gothic stained glass windows, scalloped Spanish Baroque gables, elaborate Romanesque archways and American Colonial steeples," as well as "the Prairie Style of Frank Lloyd Wright, the International Style of the European avant-garde, and the Art Deco and streamlined modernism of Jazz Age America."[6]

The staid Gothicism of the Salt Lake Temple was adorned with a Byzantine annex done in opulent Victorian style before the dedication even took place, thus tempering the stubborn conservatism with which the church belatedly accepted new gentile fashions into its valley. The tension between election and exile, autonomy and assimilation, was nowhere more visibly manifest, or more productive of aesthetically rich new forms, than in this era of church-building construction. As Anderson writes:

> Mormons asserted their respectability as upright American citizens and Christians by building churches that incorporated many of the elements of traditional American and Christian imagery. At the same time, they also tried to find ways to express their own distinctive place in Christianity, separate from the Catholic, Protestant, and Orthodox traditions. The process was at times a delicate balancing act, wanting to be different, but not different enough to be marginalized.[7]

Not only did the exteriors borrow boldly from prevalent styles—largely Gothic and Romanesque—but the interiors sported vaulted ceilings (Spring City, Utah, 1902–1910), ornamental pressed-tin panels (Nebo Stake Tabernacle, 1908), exposed trusses (Salt Lake Seventeenth Ward, 1907), even magnificent interior domes (Salt Lake Forest Dale Ward, 1902) with a daring utterly unlike the pioneer austerity or late twentieth-century blandness generally associated with Mormon architecture.[8] The exuberant burst of creativity lasted until the twenties, when the intransigent conservatism of church laity and leadership alike pressured a retreat into more-traditional forms—until the next wave of progressivism in the 1930s.

Other forces were at work shaping the course of church architecture in the early twentieth century. Demands for functionality increased as a number of roles once fulfilled by other structures were consolidated into meetinghouses. The omnipresent tithing office, an economic and ecclesiastical nucleus of Mormon society, disappeared with the cessation in 1908 of tithing in kind; modern bishops receive tithes and administer welfare from their meetinghouse offices. Ward recreation halls and relief society halls were likewise assimilated into new meetinghouse building plans. An integrated design had emerged by the 1920s, with the most popular versions being imitated or adapted for multiple sites. Instrumental in this regard was Don Carlos Young and his red brick "colonel's twins," which connected a large cultural hall and a chapel with a vestibule. Lacking even a steeple, the building's functionality by this point was clearly predominant. Some wards were building the recreation halls first, in order to use them as temporary chapels; others simply refitted those halls for use as chapels, in both cases demonstrating a premeditated porousness between the secular and sacred. Sometimes, however, even this basic template could result, with modifications, in buildings of uncommon beauty, like the Salt Lake Sugarhouse meetinghouse, finished in the Classical Revival style in 1935, complete with a triptych mural in the chapel by Torleif Knaphus.

The postwar years saw the development of a colonial style, popularized by prolific church architect Ted Pope. A critical development was the establishment, in 1946, of the Church Building Committee, which was charged with the centralized oversight of church construction projects. Explosive church growth (membership doubled from 1940 to 1960) mandated an approach that was more cost, time, and labor efficient. Standard plans were one consequence, as was the inevitable sacrifice of aesthetic concerns, regional flavor, and innovation, in a lamentable development that one writer has called "the cloning of Mormon architecture."[9] By the late 1970s, some sixty different plans were available, with minor modifications to façades and steeples possible upon petition and review.[10] At the peak of this growth, President David O. McKay initiated the building missionary program, calling hundreds of individuals not to proselytize, but to supervise or assist in the construction of chapels throughout the world. Such was the phenomenal pace of construction that, by 1964, more than 60 percent of all church buildings then in use had been built within the previous ten years.[11]

The standardized plans are eminently practical, and largely hostile to both aesthetic sense and the articulation of a sacred space. The general rule is for the sanctuary, or chapel, to merge seamlessly into a basketball court (or "cultural hall"), separated only by a movable curtain, with both surrounded by banks of classrooms and offices. Thus, two forces conspire to threaten the sacred experience. On the one hand, chapels are marked by a stark lack of signs of religiosity. As one non-Mormon architect complained, "I wouldn't have felt much different in the chapel had I had a basketball in my lap. . . . I had no sense that I had arrived any place. I wasn't in a gymnasium; it was definitely a ward house—I would have felt the same way, for example, if I had had a magazine in my lap. There was no religious connotation to the place."[12] With rare exceptions, Mormon chapels have no stained glass, religious art, icons, or paraphernalia and never any crosses, crucifixes, or altar.

On the other hand, what they *do* have, across the thin barrier of a curtain (which is not even present on overflow occasions), are basketball hoops. So the cultural signifiers that are present are secular, worldly, and boisterous. American LDS worship services are notorious for their lack of quietude and reverence. Most generally, this is attributed to the larger than normal proportion of toddlers and crying infants present in a typical meeting. But two facts about Mormon architectural culture are doubtless responsible as well. First are the environmental cues that betoken nonchalance about the parameters of the sacred. The eleven-year-old fidgeting during a stake conference can see on the carpet the mark he made playing broom hockey on the night previous. (And such carpeting and padded seats themselves emulate the familiarity of a living room, points out Ronald Molen, an LDS architect, whereas all of the building's austerity is misplaced in the classrooms.)[13] Second, temples are so radically demarcated as sacred spaces that children and many members do not even have exposure to the environment in which the holiest LDS rituals are performed. True reverence, for them, is something practiced behind opaque walls that even they cannot penetrate. And for templegoers, the contrast between temple reverence and meetinghouse familiarity and openness invites a corresponding bifurcation of conduct.

But it is not the areligious nature of meetinghouse architecture alone that disturbs architects. Limited modifications aside, their protest especially has been about the violation of a cardinal principle of architecture: the suitability of architectural design to the topographical, geographical, and cultural environment. "What we have now," lamented Molen in 1968, "is socialized architecture—we really do in every sense—bureaucratic, socialized architecture."[14]

In 2002, the trend was emphatically reinforced with the Worldwide Meetinghouse Standard Plan, which provided guidelines for urban, suburban, and rural areas. In the contest between aesthetics and economics, the outcome in a church as rapidly growing and fiscally prudent as the LDS was never in doubt. "If they look much the same," said an unapologetic President Gordon B. Hinckley of the cookie-cutter results, "it is because that is intended.... We save millions of dollars."[15] A church news release indicated yet another justification for aesthetic compromise: like the ubiquitous white shirts of missionaries, the standardized meetinghouse program "establishes a uniform look for the church."[16] While the release insisted that "an architect must take into account the culture [and] surroundings" of a particular area, the examples of variables and architectural discretion offered were not exactly cause for an orgy of aesthetic intervention: materials might vary locally, and the building might have "a natural or mechanical ventilation system."[17]

Temple architecture, meanwhile, has followed a tortuous path in the twentieth century. After dedicating the Salt Lake Temple in 1893, the church would wait more than a quarter-century before venturing outside Utah to build the Laie Hawaii Temple in 1919. The design was a conspicuous break with the architecture of the four Utah temples, which rupture some critics have seen as a repudiation of Utah Mormonism's founding principles and values, an effort to avoid any hint of the church as militant, defiant, or imperial (as the castellated temples might suggest).[18] But if the Utah temples evinced Mormon theology in their willingness to literalize the concept of a kingdom of God, prefiguring the millennial merger of church and state even as they enacted Brigham Young's earthly, theocratic version of it, the Hawaii Temple embodied different but equally vital aspects of Mormon religious culture. For the first time, the Book of Mormon, which had long inspired LDS music, literature, and painting, would register its impact on temple design.

Joseph Smith had initially associated the peoples and lands of the Book of Mormon with the mound builders of the Ohio and Mississippi valleys. But when he received in 1841 John Lloyd Stephens's freshly printed *Incidents of Travel in Central America, Chiapas, and Yucatan*, the detailed renderings of Mesoamerican ruins converted him to a new identification. "Their ruins speak of their greatness," he enthused. "The Book of Mormon unfolds their history."[19] One portion of the history recounted in the Book of Mormon concerns Hagoth, who disappeared after launching colonizing expeditions from a (presumably) Mesoamerican coast (Alma 63). In 1917, the president of the LDS mission in Hawaii, Samuel E. Woolley, gave voice to a popular Mormon folk tradition when he declared in a General Conference his belief "that the Hawaiian people were a part of that colony of Nephites that were migrating to the north, and the vessels became disabled and the natural current of the ocean carried them to Hawaii."[20]

The conjectures of Joseph Smith and S. E. Woolley converged in the design of the Hawaii Temple. Its architects, Hyrum Pope and Harold Burton, made actual use of Stephens's book on Mesoamerican ruins to design an edifice that would celebrate a Polynesian, rather than a Utah, Mormonism.[21] So though the temple was largely influenced by Frank Lloyd Wright's Unitarian church in Oak Park, Illinois, its situation on an elevated platform and its decorative friezes evoke the Yucatan ruins. As the first temple initiated since the death of Brigham Young, its construction provided a rare opportunity for the convergence of LDS artistic talent in the process. LeConte Stewart, who would emerge as the leading landscape artist of Utah, supervised the interior finishing and painted several of the murals, aided by A. B. Wright, J. Leo Fairbanks, and L. A. Ramsey. Fairbanks also designed most of the sculpture work, while Avard Fairbanks, who would emerge as the outstanding LDS sculptor of his generation, carved the oxen for the baptismal font and executed, with the help of Torleif Knaphus, the elaborate frieze.

The Hawaii Temple design actually grew out of a design for the Cardston, Alberta, Canada, temple, which was begun a few years earlier, but finished in 1923. The success of both designs, which the church insisted be done without costly towers of limited usefulness, demonstrated that initial efforts to improve functionality and thrift in church architecture could be done without compromising aesthetic quality. The other temple completed before the Second World War was another western temple, in Mesa, Arizona. It broke with the Wright influence and returned to a simple, restrained classicism. (Wright's Prairie-style architecture, however, would influence a generation of LDS meetinghouses over the next years.)

The next few decades would see the first temples in two more western states (Idaho, 1945; Los Angeles, 1956; Oakland, 1964), Europe (Switzerland, 1955), England (1958), and the South Pacific (New Zealand, 1958), before the church turned back to Utah for two more. Ogden and Provo received virtually identical temples in 1972, suggesting to some that mass production had now infiltrated temple building as well as chapel construction. Their futuristic design and mixed form drew more criticism than praise, the circular mass on a square base suggesting to some indecision and to others mercantilism.[22] The judgment may have been harsh, but the significance of the temple as one of the most prized manifestations of Mormon craftsmanship, sacrifice, and aesthetic import was giving place to new, irresistible forces that were the cost exacted by a church that was more successful in efficiently managing rapid growth than in sustaining an aesthetic commitment.

The Book of Mormon is the story not of one transoceanic migration, but of a successive array of flights into the wilderness, splinterings, and fleeing factions. Jaredites colonized the New World only to be succeeded by the families of Lehi and, virtually simultaneously, the people of Mulek. Within the Nephite saga, especially, the one great exodus is endlessly replicated and echoed: from Jerusalem to the wilderness outside Jerusalem, to the promised land of the New World, to a reoccupied Lehi-Nephi, to Alma's church in the wilderness, to the land of Zarahemla, to a poignant final image not of settlement, but of a homeless, wandering Moroni. "And I even remain alone to write the sad tale of the destruction of my people," he writes, "and whether they will slay me, I know not . . . and whither I go it mattereth not. . . . My father hath been slain in battle, and all my kinsfolk, and I have not friends nor whither to go" (Mormon 8:4). The Book of Mormon is in large part the story of the unending transmission of the gospel into new contexts, a chronicle of the volatility and fragility of lands of refuge, a testament of the portability and ceaseless transmutations of Zion.

In LDS church history, the pattern is similar. The young Joseph's family, seemingly positioning for his moment on the world stage, moved from Sharon, Vermont, to Tunbridge, and thence to Royalton, before crossing into Lebanon, New Hampshire, and finally to Palmyra, New York. With his initiation into the ministry, he fled to Harmony, Pennsylvania, then to Fayette, New York, before leading a fledgling church to Ohio, then to successive locations in Missouri, and finally to Nauvoo, Illinois. With the migration of the main church body to Utah in 1847, the years of wandering and exile seemed at an end; the durable, massive walls of the Salt Lake Temple bespeak a permanence no longer threatened.

But by 1900, the gathering was virtually over. And whereas the Mormon dominance of Utah and environs had produced visible, distinctive markers of difference, shifting church demographics meant that by 2000, this region was no longer home to most Mormons. Hence, it was the nucleus of an American Mormon culture, but could no longer lay claim to exemplifying an increasingly international church. A hundred years earlier, LDS leaders had found it desirable to yield the church's most culturally anomalous practices (polygamy and gathering) and urged cultural assimilation and accommodation as a path to statehood and greater respectability. Now, at the new millennium, openness to a variety of cultural norms and contexts became equally imperative. As the most institutionally directed of the arts, architecture provided the most immediate avenue for official recognition and accommodation of local aesthetic and cultural sensibilities. Architecture was also the area of the arts where such synthesis would seem to be most feasible and most urgent: feasible, because building several new chapels a week made design experimentation and innovation eminently possible on an ongoing basis; urgent, because the appropriation of public space in foreign cultures carries higher political stakes than the cloistered singing of Utah hymns or the coffeetable display of church magazines and books filled with distinctively American artwork and literature.

At the same time, however, the Mormon predilection for the practical and functional received added impetus from the enormous financial strains the church was undergoing as a higher and higher proportion of converts came from Latin American and African nations, reducing the median tithing base, while church growth and construction needs only increased. Finally, at this time, church president Spencer W. Kimball launched a building agenda of utterly unprecedented proportions, involving the most expensive of all LDS structures. Announcing a spate of proposed temples, he said, "[W]e will continue to build temples, and there will be hundreds, possibly thousands, of temples built to the Lord our God. We expect the Lord is just beginning."[23] From the fifteen temples operating when Kimball took office, the number tripled to more than forty-seven either operating or under way at the time of his death.

And the era of grand temple building on a heroic scale had one last gasp. The most spectacular temple built in the latter half of the twentieth century was undoubtedly the Washington, D.C., Temple, completed in 1974. The church's third-largest temple, the resplendent edifice is sheathed in 173,000 square feet of Alabama white marble, with gold-plated spires and an angel Moroni that soars to 288 feet. Initially, critical reaction was negative. The *U.S. News & World Report* called it "a striking monument," but many more were less impressed. Benjamin Forgey of the *Washington Star-News*, Wolf Von Eckhardt of the *Washington Post*, Paul Goldberger of the *New York Times*, and *Time* magazine joined a chorus of popular references to its Disneyland-like appearance ("release Dorothy" struck many motorists as apt nearby graffiti).[24] With time, however, the aesthetic qualities of the temple have proved to be more durable than the early reactions. Forgey even revisited his appraisal in 1984 and conceded that the "outstanding building" was an "almost bizarre combination of sophistication and sincerity, knowledgeability and naiveté. Above all it is memorable and likable."[25]

The symbolism was clear and highlights the tensions of integration and aloofness that have still not disappeared. The clear evocation of Salt Lake's six-spired structure, its monumentality and commanding presence on a prominence overlooking the capital's Beltway, is a clear statement of proud and permanent return to the heart of the nation from which Mormonism was formerly exiled. But the exuberant, almost audacious lines are broken not by windows but by fluting, emphasizing an impenetrability every bit as fixed as the massive granite walls of its western counterpart. Combined with its sleek futurism, the total effect is one of Mormon evolution and transformation without compromise.

Even as Kimball was dedicating this monument to Mormonism as a fully mature American religion, he was ushering in a new age of temple building. As we have seen, a persistent thread in Mormon culture has been the sometimes indiscriminate mingling of things heavenly and earthly. Almost as a reaction against the cognitive dissonance between the bifurcation incarnated in their architectural history, the jarring juxtaposition of cinderblock meetinghouses with gymnasiums, on the one hand, and ethereal temples, on the other, the 1980s saw the extremes converge in the mass building of standardized, modest, mini-temples. In 1960, it had been possible to lament, as one Mormon critic did:

> [W]e have been eclectic in our architecture to the point that we have churches in every conceivable style and combination thereof. Is there an architectural style somewhere in the past that belongs more completely to our theology, philosophy, religious orientation and practice? . . . It seems to me that we have floundered artistically and creatively.[26]

At the beginning of the 1980s, the extreme eclecticism and the artistic creativity would diminish, as the standardization that had been applied to worldwide meetinghouse construction was extended to temples, with the announcement of three standard plans to be used with a group of seven new, smaller temples. The economics of smaller temples was not only a prudent financial strategy—it marked a significant shift in Mormon religious culture. Previously, the temple had been to Mormons—especially Mormons outside Utah—a center of gathering or of pilgrimage. "It shall come to pass in the last days," wrote the much-quoted-by-Mormons Isaiah, "that the mountain of the Lord's house shall be established in the top of the mountains, and shall be exalted above the hills; and all nations shall flow unto it. And many people shall go and say, Come ye, and let us go up to the mountain of the Lord, to the house of the God of Jacob" (Isaiah 2:2–3). The imagery of coming from the four corners of the earth to build a temple, as in Kirtland and Nauvoo, or to find spiritual refuge there, as in Salt Lake, had long been literally enacted by the Saints, and the sacrifice of temple building and long-distance travel to worship there was a deeply engrained mythos. From the pioneer women who according to folklore crushed precious china for the Kirtland Temple glaze, to Samoan Saints who sold their all to make the pilgrimage to Hawaii (or even the nearer but still-distant New Zealand Temple) for sealing ordinances, the temple had been the shrine that drew the faithful to its altar.

Reversing the direction, the church under Kimball and his successors would increasingly be taken to the flock. Introducing a new concept into the vocabulary of temple worship, Kimball announced in 1980 anticipation of a day "when the sacred ordinances of the Church, performed in the temples, will be available to all members of the Church in *convenient* locations around the globe."[27] The seven temples announced at that time ranged in size from the 37,000-square-foot Atlanta Temple to a very modest 10,000 square feet in the case of the Tahitian version.

With the administration of Gordon B. Hinckley, the accelerated pace of the Kimball years became almost feverish. In 1997, he extended the pattern of economy and accessibility by announcing a series of "smaller-and-remote-area" temples, some of which would be less than 7,000 square feet. (At 6,800 square feet, the Colonia Juárez Chihuahua México Temple is the smallest in the church.) The results have transformed the role of temple worship in the Mormon faith and have doubtless strengthened a trend established in the 1970s. At that time, President Kimball announced "a great new adventure in taking the whole program of the Church out to the people of the whole world,"[28] through area conferences wherein the prophet and other general authorities would travel throughout the world to meet the Saints in their own lands in large convocations. In 1995, when Ezra Taft Benson died, forty-nine temples had been constructed. In just two years of his presidency (1999–2000), Hinckley oversaw the dedication of that exact same number, as many as all fourteen of his predecessors combined. Ten years into his ministry, the total number had almost tripled.

With the acceleration of temple building, the church followed the same policy embraced with the Hawaii Temple: incorporating some elements appropriate to the culture and locality of the temple region. The consequence is, with the exception of the almost ubiquitous angel Moroni, the lack of a recognizable common denominator in these most sacred edifices. After the Atlanta Temple, however, virtually every temple would at least share the common feature of the familiar scripture-bearing messenger atop a spire—even if that meant retrofitting older ones. So, through the flux of innovation, architectural eclecticism, and economizing standardization, the trumpeting Moroni betokens sacred practices and sacred space that began in Nauvoo and will persist, in Mormon belief, into the thousand years of millennial peace and a thousand years of bustling Mormon temple activity.

~ 13 ~

"NO TABERNACLE CHOIR
ON BROADWAY"

Music and Dance

I should only believe in a God that would know how
to dance.

~ Friedrich Nietzsche

No event was as richly symbolic of Mormonism's entry into a new era of public respectability as the performance of the Tabernacle Choir at the 1893 World's Columbian Exposition in Chicago, unless it was the fact that President Wilford Woodruff accompanied the group. Joseph Smith had died a martyr in Carthage, Illinois. Brigham Young had fled westward at the head of 15,000 exiles. John Taylor, his successor, died while hiding from federal authorities. Now, for the first time in almost fifty years, a president of the Mormon church walked among fellow Americans east of the Rocky Mountains.

The choir's performance was a moment of glory that overshadowed a simultaneous humiliation. In conjunction with the grandiose World's Columbian Exposition, organizers had planned a World's Parliament of Religion for September 11–22, 1893, in order to "promote and deepen the spirit of human brotherhood among religious men of diverse faiths." Ironically, however, the outreach was not sufficiently generous to embrace Mormonism within the compass of "diverse faiths." Latter-day Saint leaders were not extended an opportunity to address the parliament. As a consequence, the Mormon church lodged a protest, after which it was given a token invitation to read a paper in a small, out-of-the-way conference room. Denied the right, accorded all other faiths, to speak before the full conference, the LDS church declined the compromise.[1] It did, however, enter the choir in the choral competition.

So even while the church was denied a public voice in the parliament, its choir was singing its way to second place in both the formal competition and the audience's hearts. Many observers considered that, if not for the same prejudice manifest in the parliament, the choir would actually have won the gold. The road from Utah to Chicago had itself been a historic trip, as the choir successfully completed its first tour outside of Utah, initiating a still-ongoing tradition of serving as the most beloved public face of Mormonism.

Upon the choir's triumphant return to Utah, its New England Conservatory–trained director, Welshman Evan Stephens, parlayed the success into a much higher level of church support for the choir (as well as a salary for himself more befitting a professional musician). President Joseph F. Smith elevated the status of singers from part-time amateurs to artists performing a church "mission."[2] Just as the midcentury had witnessed an influx of celebrated gentile actors performing in the magnificent theater, so the newfound fame of the choir enticed many artists to perform with it in the Tabernacle, including Polish piano virtuoso Ignacy Jan Paderewski (1860–1941), whose first American tour provoked "Paddymania"; Ernestine Schumann-Heink (1861–1936), hailed as "the world's greatest contralto" in her prime years of 1898–1903; soprano star Dame Nellie Melba (1861–1931); and John Philip Sousa (1854–1932), who called the choir "the best trained of any in the United States."[3] The choir followed up its Chicago success with 1896 concerts in Oakland and San Francisco, and another trip to California in 1902.

Although the Chicago performance had been a coup, subsequent developments proved that Mormon hopes that they had at last achieved respectability were premature. Exactly ten years after the church's musical triumph, apostle Reed Smoot's election to the U.S. Senate prompted contentious hearings and a media frenzy that revealed the polygamy issue had not been laid to rest after all; plural marriages—even among church officials—had continued after the manifesto formally ending the practice, and church president Joseph F. Smith was himself still living with his plural wives. To the weapons of pulpit and popular fiction utilized in the nineteenth-century crusade against Mormons was now added the popular new technology of moving pictures. But notoriety is often the first part of a journey to recognition and even esteem. In these years, Temple Square with its Tabernacle Choir and its 12,000-pipe organ were promoted as tourist attractions. Negative publicity, frank curiosity, and genuine interest were combining by 1905 to bring 200,000 visitors to the square annually. Some came not just to hear the choir, but to hear famous Tabernacle organists. American icon Elbert Hubbard came shortly before his death to hear the playing of John McClellan, of whom he wrote:

If any man has the spirit of old Bach it is this man McClellan. He is a wizard of the keys. . . . I thought I had heard organ playing before, but the exquisite modulations, the tones and tints of sweet sounds that this man produces cannot be described. . . . What Paderewski is to the piano, McClellan is to the pipe-organ.[4]

With the coming of sound recordings, the choir was emerging as the best resource the church had to impress and inspire the American public far beyond the environs of the Tabernacle. In 1910, the choir recorded a dozen numbers for Columbia, and the wildly eclectic mix reflected the competing messages and purposes the choir was coming to embody. Distinctively Mormon hymns promulgated the doctrine of a living prophet and a heavenly Mother ("We Thank Thee O God for a Prophet" and "O My Father"), American anthems bore witness to the patriotic zeal of the choir and its church ("America" and "The Star-Spangled Banner"), and selections from Gounod, Rossini, and Verdi proclaimed a devotion to musical excellence devoid of political or religious motives. The next year, the choir embarked on an ambitious, twenty-three-city eastern tour and met with rave reviews but also boycotts and protests. It sang in Madison Square Garden, and before President and Mrs. William Howard Taft at the White House. Meanwhile, some churches complained in print that the tour was a Mormon strategy to "propitiate favor for Mormonism with the uninformed and thoughtless."[5] The first half of the claim was doubtless correct.

Then, in the twenties, radio came and transformed not just American popular culture, but Mormonism's place in it. The choir experimented with local broadcasts in 1927, and then in 1929 commenced a contract with NBC to broadcast from the Tabernacle on a weekly basis. That nationwide broadcast came on the eve of the Great Depression, and by the next year, America had greater worries than Mormon evangelizing. Arguably, over the next twelve months, Mormonism became more prominent as a symbol of mainstream values than of marginalized undesirables. In 1930, church president Heber J. Grant was featured on the cover of *Time*, and the Tabernacle broadcasts continued in a tradition that is still running strong at the present day.

Brigham Young's theater had succeeded, but at a cost: his dream of an art form freed from the violent themes and worldly lifestyles of the secular stage lost out to more pragmatic considerations. Giving the public what it wanted meant that the moral efficacy of the theater was diminished. With the Tabernacle Choir, a similar set of conflicts emerged. Mormon historian of music Michael Hicks sees in the LDS musical tradition "three points of tension" that echo the larger paradoxes we have seen throughout Mormon culture: "the will to progress versus the will to conserve, the need to borrow from outsiders versus the need for self-reliance, and the love of the aesthetic versus the love of utility."[6] Those competing imperatives were probably more self-consciously articulated and debated in the course of the choir's history than in any other aspect of Mormon culture. The drive to exploit the popularity of the choir meant artistic considerations could not be paramount. Giving the public what it wanted meant compromising artistic values. At least, that was the perception of J. Spencer Cornwall, who assumed the directorship of the choir in 1935. Fans, members, and leaders all had differing visions of what kind of music the choir should feature. "Bach or bunk" was one way the contest was framed. That CBS could call upon the choir to conduct a commemorative program upon the death of Franklin Roosevelt was a sign of how deeply secure its position had become as the musical voice of not just a church but a nation. But with such a position, the stakes were raised considerably, and exactly what face the choir would present to the world became more vigorously contested.

A few years later, after recording the choir's first record, Cornwall expressed his goals for the choir's next stage, and expressly made critical acclaim a higher priority than enhancing the church's image.[7] It was a direct confrontation with the age-old dilemma that divided the Campbellites from the Anglicans and countless factions before them: are high standards and artistic excellence the route to a higher form of worship, or a detour before the throne of a highly cultured Baal? The choir and its conductor would never resolve the question definitively, but their popularity kept growing as programming continued to be a focus of tension. In the postwar years, Mormon growth surged, and the choir began European tours in 1955. When Richard P. Condie succeeded Cornwall, he engineered a recording partnership with Eugene Ormandy and the Philadelphia Orchestra. Ironically, the Tabernacle Choir, established by a church in exile, achieved the summit of popular success upon releasing "The Battle Hymn of the Republic" in 1959 (selling 300,000 singles). Throughout the sixties and early seventies, popular tunes and ever-popular patriotic ballads and anthems permeated its repertoire. After a brief flirtation with serious contemporary music under Jay Welch, and an aborted Broadway tunes album ("I don't think the Tabernacle Choir belongs on Broadway," sniffed Joseph Fielding Smith),[8] the choir seems to have settled back comfortably into the mix of the classical, the popular, and the signature hymns of the church. As an ever-popular presidential inauguration presence (at least since Lyndon B. Johnson's) and international ambassador, the choir is the most visible portable emblem of Mormonism.

While the choir was presenting Mormon and American standards, some Latter-day Saints were at work creating the next great Mormon classic. One of the most ambitious of such compositions was by the choir's assistant conductor,

B. Cecil Gates. In 1916, he produced an oratorio called the *Restoration*, putting texts written by his mother, Susa Young Gates, to music of his own composing. He found the "old contrapuntal forms" apt to illustrate the dogmatism and contention of nineteenth-century religious upheavals, and "modern classical forms" appropriate for the truths of the restored gospel.[9] Highly praised by some contemporary critics, it nevertheless took six years before the church commissioned its own choir to perform the work. Even a public little versed in classical music is generally familiar with the oratorio as a musical form, since renditions of the *Messiah* are ubiquitous every Christmas season. Handel's *Messiah* is generally seen as the supreme musical profession and celebration of Christian faith (though in Mormon culture, Mendelssohn's oratorio *Elijah* has been almost as popular—presumably for reasons of special affinity to the prophet they associate with temple ordinances).[10] When Gates's oratorio was performed by the Tabernacle Choir in 1922, the response was so positive that he returned to that form the next year, producing, in the spirit of the popular *Elijah*, his *Salvation for the Dead*. Still, the next year, the influential B. H. Roberts was lamenting that "the great Oratorio of the New Dispensation remains to be written."[11]

The next year saw performances of a cantata by Evan Stephens called *The Vision*, and two more of his works, *Hosanna* and *The Martyrs*, were performed in that same decade. It was Leroy Robertson's work, however, that won the greatest acclaim and confidence of LDS church leaders. Trained at the New England Conservatory, Robertson won minor prizes for small compositions, and returned west to join the BYU faculty in 1925. Over the next few years, he would imbibe modernist tendencies from study with Ernest Bloch and, to a lesser extent, Arnold Schoenberg, producing works of international recognition. He had already won the New York Music Circle Award when he achieved even greater success with what may have been the largest prize ever given for a musical composition. In 1947, his *Trilogy* won the $25,000 Henry H. Reichhold Symphonic Award for best work in the Western Hemisphere. Church leaders believed they had in Robertson a composer of sufficient recognition and capacity to do justice to the Book of Mormon, and commissioned him to compose an oratorio.

Robertson completed his *Oratorio from the Book of Mormon* within a year of the 1947 commission, though it did not premiere until 1953 with Maurice Abravanel and the Utah Symphony. Response within the Mormon community was exuberant. Six sell-out performances followed rapidly, and a recording was made less than seven weeks after its premiere.[12] The oratorio did not achieve the critical acclaim of his prize-winning works, but it marked a significant milestone in Mormon music, and it may even be true that, as the church magazine enthused, LDS "musical history was made on February 18, 1953." The text of the oratorio, the item announced, had come from the Books of Helaman and 3 Nephi, and it cited the finale:

> The Lord hath made bare his holy arm
> In the eyes of all the nations.
> All the ends of the earth shall see the
> salvation of our God!
> Awake, awake, put on thy strength O Zion!
> Thy king cometh unto thee!
> Glory unto the Father, unto the Son and
> Holy Ghost.
> Worlds without end. Amen.[13]

The cited passages are a remarkable mélange of voices and sources that perfectly epitomize Mormonism's own work of synthesis and identity forging. The prophet Mormon was in the first four lines quoting Jesus, who is in the New World, quoting Isaiah to the Nephites (3 Nephi 20:35–36). The subsequent words derive from Zechariah (9:9) and are also quoted in Handel's *Messiah*. Finally, rather surprisingly, the section ends with the minor doxology ("Gloria Patri") with a minor modification (Joseph Smith's "worlds without end" [D&C 76:112] for the more-traditional "world without end"). So represented in this brief text are Isaiah, an American Jesus, Zechariah, Handel, an early Christian doxology, and Joseph Smith—all filtered through the voice of an ancient American prophet and record keeper.

In utilizing such a passage, Robertson was paying tribute to Mormonism's and Christianity's shared theological and cultural heritage by recognizing both the Messiah of biblical scripture and Handel's masterpiece of that name. Borrowing from a formula established in the fourth century and used in many Christian liturgies, Robertson found ready material from a time and tradition Mormons consider apostate (and which would shock most Mormons if they were apprised of the source). All this, while presenting the whole through a voice that was literally and figuratively Mormon. And indeed, the work as a whole bears the same relationship to Handel's *Messiah* as the Book of Mormon does to the Bible. The Old Testament prophecies of Christ's coming and the Old World scene of incarnation presented by Handel were supplemented in this case by an oratorio depicting American prophecies of his coming and a New World setting for his resurrected appearance. Whether or not the oratorio fulfilled the dream of Roberts, it did become, in one critic's words, the "only significant commercially recorded 'Mormon' composition of the Church's 137 years."[14] It continues in the present day, in whole and in part, to appear in Utah Symphony season reper- toires, but is little known outside the valley, in spite of recordings in 1961 (Vanguard) and 1978 (Columbia). Robertson's daughter wrote that a New York producer offered enthusiastic support for national promotion if he would change the title—but the composer declined.

The oratorio has continued as a sporadic form in Mormon music, popular with composers if not always audiences. Compositions on *The Psalm of Nephi*, the Book of Mormon character *Coriantumr, Apostasy and Restoration*, and *Visions of Eternity* mimic the efforts of Gates and Robertson—and even the 1979 excommunication of Sonia Johnson, feminist dissident, has been rendered or- atorically as the *Songs of Sonia*.[15] The most successful sequel to Robertson's achievement, however, has been Merrill Bradshaw's oratorio *The Restoration*, which premiered in 1974. Working to bridge the gap between high-brow music and Mormon culture, Bradshaw incorporated everything from jazz to familiar hymns to be sung by the audience, and avoided the more inaccessible elements of modernism. The eclecticism of Bradshaw's piece demonstrated just how far Mormon music could go in acceding to popular forms, while maintaining an authentically Mormon voice—at least in the opinion of the influential apostle Boyd K. Packer. His explicit endorsement of this work meant it had found acceptance as a "home-music" production faithful to Mormon values. But there were limits to such compromises, he declared. "We would be ill-advised to de- scribe [the First Vision] in company with rock music, even soft rock music, or to take equally sacred themes and set them to a modern beat. . . . I think it cannot be done."[16] The bicentennial of Joseph Smith's birth prompted a number of de- votional musical productions, most notable of which was an opera, *The Book of Gold*, which premiered at Brigham Young University with cast members of the Metropolitan Opera.

In any case, and by almost any measure, the audience for serious music like oratorios and opera is limited. It always has been. "The sweetest music is not in the oratorio, but in the human voice when it speaks from its instant life tones of tenderness, truth, or courage. The oratorio has already lost its relation to the morning, to the sun, and the earth," wrote Emerson over a century and a half ago.[17] And when Mormon musicians turn to more popular forms, the stakes shift accordingly. Mormons have not attempted their version of *Jesus Christ, Superstar*. But the very same year that Bradshaw premiered his oratorio, Lex de Azevedo stepped forward as Mormonism's answer to Andrew Lloyd Webber. In 1974, together with Doug Stewart, Azevedo invented the Mormon pop musical with *Saturday's Warrior*. The first major pop-cultural phenomenon to sweep

Mormonism, the musical was seen by over 1.5 million people in its first eight years alone,[18] making it by far the most successful commercial LDS production until then. Emphatically Mormon in its orientation, the story follows the saga of plighted lovers and a prodigal son through the stages of premortality, earth life, and the hereafter. Critics within the Mormon community, laboring for a morally and aesthetically serious art, were appalled. "Slick sophistication, misleading if not heretical theology, and stereotyping toward bigotry," blasted one influential voice.[19] Church leaders also criticized its trivialization of missionary work and sacred doctrines.

But Mormon youth especially felt they had found a way to celebrate their Mormon culture to the snappy beats and flattering lyrics of the Stewart-Azevedo duo (and the Osmonds had already barnstormed the entry of Mormon youth culture into pop music). It didn't hurt that the theme music touted the current generation of youth as the special spirits reserved for the Saturday evening of earth's history, now peopling the earth at the height of glorious spiritual warfare. Having discovered a hugely popular new medium, Azevedo and Stewart and a host of imitators spawned a series of sequels and clones that continued into the new millennium. In the years since, a genre of LDS pop has proliferated contemporaneously with the flowering of "Christian" music. One LDS Web site lists an impressive sixty-six individual Mormon recording artists in the "inspirational" category, in addition to some half-dozen groups with names that suggest the sometimes sentimental and tendentious, like Afterglow and NLightN. The singers freely incorporate Christian classics and original compositions, with a tendency to emphasize the more generic aspects of LDS belief.

There are also dozens of other LDS bands presumably not "inspirational" enough to make it onto the mainstream Web sites. Several of these (many are showcased on soundtracks to LDS comic films like *The RM* and *Singles Ward*) exhibit a delightful tongue-in-cheek attitude that mimics Robertson's syncretism with playful irony. Their repertoires include rock arrangements of several hymns, as well as a techno version of the Mormon children's song "Popcorn Popping on the Apricot Tree." Mormon boy bands are so ubiquitous that the phenomenon has led to one film parody, the mockumentary *Sons of Provo*. The uses these bands make of Mormon material suggest some awareness of the foibles and shortcomings of a culture that does not sufficiently discriminate between the sublime and the banal, the profoundly Christian and the (merely) culturally Mormon. Thus "I Hope They Call Me on a Mission" and "If You Could Hie to Kolob" are fair game for campy treatment, but "Abide with Me" and "Where Can I Turn for Peace" are not. It's as if the young rockers recognize distinctions that have eluded the culture as a whole.

It isn't just in their adolescence that Mormon youth are imbibing different musical influences than their parents. One interesting shift in Mormon hymnody has been the alternately growing then fading fortunes of the Book of Mormon in LDS hymnody. In 1889, the year after Orson Whitney's call for a home literature, the church published *The Latter Day Saints' Psalmody*. That publication represented the high-water mark of hymns featuring the Book of Mormon: thirteen. That compared with only five that mention or celebrate that scripture out of Emma Smith's original ninety hymns. In the two most recent editions of the LDS hymnals, 1950 and 1985, the number drops back down to five and six, respectively—but in a much larger field of hymns than Emma produced. Except for occasional examples of high art (such as oratorios), the Book of Mormon does not serve as material out of which a distinctive musical tradition is shaped, and the long-term trend is one of decline, not increase.[20] On the cultural radar of LDS children, on the other hand, the Book of Mormon registers very centrally. In one group, an informal poll revealed that four of the favorite ten children's songs are Book of Mormon–themed, and the figure is probably representative.[21] "Book of Mormon Stories" is music on the order of "Old Macdonald," but "We'll Bring the World His Truth" is a stirring anthem that ranks with the best hymns in the tradition. It seems reasonable to expect that the rising generation of Latter-day Saints, perhaps the first for whom the stories of Nephi and Captain Moroni are more familiar than Daniel and Noah, will be poised to expound a truly Mormon cultural grammar in the art and music to which they give voice. If so, the dilemma that has characterized Mormonism for so long, which is eloquently expressed by Michael Hicks, may no longer be relevant:

> This then may be the essential conundrum for the Saints and their music as they push forward toward the Millennium: how to reconcile their thirst for progress with their fear of contamination. While the Saints once wondered how they could sing the Lord's song in a strange land, they now wonder if they can sing a strange song in Zion.[22]

If the Mormon *Primary* is any indication, they will not have to.

There is no question that Mormons increasingly find themselves in strange lands and foreign cultures. Other denominations have found little difficulty in adapting everything from African drums to electric guitars into their worship services. LDS leaders have not shown that same eager eclecticism when it comes to sacred music. When Dallin H. Oaks warned that "the traditions or culture or way of life of a people inevitably include some practices that must be changed by those who wish to qualify for God's choicest blessings,"[23] he may or may not have had musical practices in mind. Even though he reassured foreign converts that "the present-day servants of the Lord do not attempt to make Filipinos or Asians or Africans into Americans,"[24] the process of winnowing expendable culture from essential spirituality is one that may end up working both ways, with results for music and the other arts that it is still too early to anticipate. A rare example of a personal initiative to find a culturally expansive view of music is offered by LDS convert Gladys Knight. She has formed her own "multicultural" choir, Saints Unified Voices. The group's Web site indicates, "it is the fulfillment of Sister Knight's desire to bring a new level of passion and cultural awareness to the traditionally reserved LDS hymns." This she does with the help of a synthesizer, electric guitar, and gospel-style vocals. "I look forward to the day when we can embrace music from other cultures without feeling uncomfortable," she says.[25] It is a striking sign of Mormon music's cultural evolution that in 2006, Knight's multicultural choir won the Grammy for best choir album—almost a half-century after the Mormon Tabernacle Choir won its first and only Grammy.[26] At the institutional level, the response to the challenge of multiculturalism has been to respect rather than incorporate cultural differences. After the 1985 edition of the LDS hymnal came out, for example, 100 of its hymns were chosen as the core music of the church, which form the basis for translation into foreign-language hymnals. The balance of the hymns are chosen—subject to church approval—on the basis of local preferences and contributions.

Cultural accommodation is sometimes easier to effect when it is contextualized as entertainment rather than worship. Dance, therefore, has provided one vehicle for Mormonism to celebrate a vibrant multiculturalism in nonthreatening ways. Dances of South Pacific cultures feature prominently in Hawaii's Polynesian Cultural Center, which the church opened in 1963. It is Hawaii's largest tourist attraction and one of the church's most successful forums for missionary work. Similar exposure has been achieved by the BYU folk dancers, who have performed throughout the world and at Olympics' opening ceremonies. While it is true that appreciation for cultural diversity is not the primary catalyst to these endeavors, it is also true that such multicultural expressions are a reflection of an LDS population that is unusually conversant in the language of multi—or at least bi—culturalism. BYU, for instance, has students from over 100 countries, and the overwhelming majority of its 35,000 students are conversant in at least one language besides English.

But there is another reason for the abiding popularity of dance in LDS culture, which is probably the result of a continuing sense in Mormonism that dance provides one of the safest avenues for channeling youthful sociability in controlled conditions. If a member complained to Joseph Smith that there was not visible "the least desire to glorify God in the dancing of the present day" in 1844, the same is true a fortiori of virtually any dance one could name in the contemporary Western world. One respected British convert to Mormonism complained that his newfound church countenanced dances as disparate as rock and the waltz, even though both ultimately conduce to "erotic intoxication."[27] If you can't beat them, supervise them, seems to be the Mormon response. A 1952 *New York Times Magazine* article reported that "Mormon liberalism" was shocking to other denominations because of their excessive indulgence in dancing, and in 1959, a *Time* article thought them "the dancingest denomination in the country."[28] At the current time, more than 12,000 Brigham Young University students enroll every year in a range of dance classes from ballroom to aerobic. Given that pool to draw upon, it is hardly surprising that BYU's Ballroom Dance Company has won numerous U.S. and British championships.

In the 1970s, what the expression "Mormon music" evoked depended on one's cultural proclivities: the sounds of the Mormon Tabernacle Choir or the Osmonds. In the years since, movement in the direction of a more recognizably Mormon music has been modest. The 1985 hymnal kept many Protestant classics, dropped some Mormon pieces, but added forty-four new LDS contributions. A few composers, like Janice Kapp Perry, produce a steady stream of new material used in church services and the children's *Primary*. And proliferating Mormon artists in the Christian music mold cater to a musically insatiable Mormon youth culture. Nothing as definitive as B. H. Roberts's devoutly desired great Mormon oratorio looms on the horizon. But it may be the perpetual negotiation between Christian precedents—be they Handel or Luther—and Mormon identity, and the unresolved tension between pop culture and distinctive LDS values, that continue, aptly, to typify Mormon culture.

"CINEMA AS SACRAMENT"

Theater and Film

> When a Jewish comic is making fun of Jews, I better
> not enter in, and when Mormons are making fun of
> Mormonism, I better not join in, because people who
> hardly know what's in their bones find it coming back
> and defending it. That's what I mean by saying it's a
> "peoplehood." ... What's interesting about the Mor-
> mons is that they are from a mixed ethnic stock not
> much different from the rest of the majority and yet
> they are a distinct people. A story makes a people.
>
> ~ Martin Marty

By 1911, one Utah editor was complaining:

> We have some interest in the old Salt Lake Theatre here, built by President
> Brigham Young to afford high-class amusement, intellectual, entertaining,
> interesting and instructive to those who desire such entertainment. It has been
> conducted along these lines for many years, but when we get a really high-class
> performance in that theatre, the benches are practically empty, while the
> vaudeville theatres, where are exhibitions of nakedness, of obscenity, of vul-
> garity and everything else that does not tend to elevate the thought and mind
> of man, will be packed from the pit to the dome.[1]

The theater lingered on for another decade and more, but in 1928 the aging
playhouse, at that time the third oldest in America,[2] was razed for an office
building. Yet the dramatic energies so embodied in and encouraged by Brigham
Young were already finding expression elsewhere with the development of a
variation on the "little theater"—called the "road show." One of the first versions
took place in early 1924, when the Granite, Utah, Stake organized a touring

variety show with short theatricals which they called a "Merry-go-Round." They performed dramatic monologues, musical numbers, "whistling solos," and dance acts, interspersed with offerings from the host wards. The elaborate undertaking involved 18 traveling troupes, 52 local acts, more than 250 participants, and 35 vehicles transporting them all. They performed in thirteen wards before an audience of 2,500, with prizes awarded to the best acts.[3] The idea quickly caught on. The very next month, the Utah Stake south of Salt Lake organized its own competition among some two dozen wards, with offerings ranging from a "Japanese Operetta" to the "King Tut Minstrel band" and a Hawaiian organ.[4] By 1928, the year the old theater was razed, the church's youth organization, the Mutual Improvement Association, had adopted the road show as a churchwide program, expressing the hope that the program would embody both "dignity and beauty" and serve as "a foundation for the expression of the artistic urges within."[5]

The next year, the church began publication of the MIA *Book of Plays*—an anthology of offerings largely obtained through national playhouses. The MIA's superintendent felt that such an annual publication "has created for itself a unique place in American art. It is perhaps the only one of its kind in the world, and deserves recognition in the development of drama in America." What he meant was that such a development, by facilitating the performance of quality drama on a churchwide basis, gave huge impetus to amateur drama on a large scale, effectively furthering what he called "the little theater movement of the church."[6]

Little theater had begun in Europe in the late nineteenth century, and migrated to Boston, New York, and Chicago as a self-conscious movement in the early years of the twentieth century. By 1917, there were over fifty little theaters in America. According to one historian of the movement, the name reflected a theater experience designed around "an intimate stage and auditorium" and a drama "established from love of drama, not love of gain."[7] It was thus distinct from commercialism, on the one hand, and from the purely frivolous private theatricals, on the other. Little theater aspired to genuine artistic endeavors on a small scale. One historian of drama considers the father of little theater to have been Brigham Young himself, and the adobe Social Hall in early Salt Lake to have been the first little theater in America.[8] The road show was but a different institutional version of the community theaters that radiated outward from Salt Lake, providing opportunities for exposure to significant drama, performed under modest circumstances. So important did little theater become as a cultural barometer that one critic observed he "could tell whether the art life of a city was an affectation or a reality by inquiring whether it supported a Little Theatre."[9]

The church could justify publishing its own annual anthology for in-house use, since by the late twenties Utah wards performed in one typical year 706 three-act and 918 one-act plays with some 23,000 persons participating. Soon, the annual road show competition, which increasingly featured ten- to fifteen-minute musicals or comedies, became a social—if not a cultural—high point in the Mormon cultural calendar. In 1932, the enthusiasm for and benefits of the new program were considered to be so great that the MIA general board initiated a churchwide road show competition, awarding cash prizes for the best entries, hoping thereby to foster productions worthy to be preserved for futurity.[10] For the rest of the century, the program thrived, peaking in the 1950s and 1960s with competitions that led all the way to Salt Lake City. Expectedly, such low-brow drama had its critics. "Must Mormon theater and drama eternally be apotheosized and cryogenically dwarfed at the glorified roadshow level?" asked one Mormon scholar. "Must a whole generation perish in theatrical unenlightenment?"[11]

Nevertheless, the summertime ritual was an integral part of church life for millions of Mormons for more than a half-century. One nostalgic journalist eulogized the end of an era:

> Many Mormons who have grown up in the LDS church have performed in a roadshow at least once in their lives. People who later grew up to be bankers, lawyers and professors, willingly—even happily—participated in that uniquely Mormon summertime ritual: the roadshow. However, in the past decade, roadshows have fallen prey to dwindling ward budgets, a lagging interest in the theatrical experience, and the predominance of passive entertainment such as TV, movies, and the Internet.[12]

After a decades-long decline in support for the program, road shows were effectively discontinued churchwide in 1999.

The Mormon love for theater found another impetus in the evangelizing potential of outdoor spectacle. B. H. Roberts delivered a speech on the occasion of the church's first centennial that evoked the sweep and pathos of Book of Mormon history so successfully that one journalist thought it "like some graphic panorama of the past," like a "Norse saga."[13] The church proceeded to acquire the hill and environs in upstate New York where the gold plates were recovered, and began to stage the spectacle Roberts had described, annually and on a grand scale beginning in 1937. Within a decade, yearly attendance at "America's Witness for Christ" would surpass 100,000.[14] The current incarnation features volcanoes, earthquakes, a seven-level stage, ten light towers, digitally recorded music, water curtains, a spectacular descent of Christ from heaven, and 640 other parts, including armored warriors, priests, court dancers, kings, and peasants. The script and musical score have passed through a number of revisions, with the current script penned by science fiction master Orson Scott Card. The pageant may not be great drama, but it is great spectacle, and as the country's largest and oldest outdoor drama is America's nearest equivalent to Germany's passion play at Oberammergau.

In 1947, to commemorate the Utah centennial, the church sponsored an elaborate pageant called *Promised Valley*, which one scholar has called "the most successful musical in the history of the church in terms of popular acclaim and financial gain."[15] It has played recurrently over the years, and features some of the best music of Mormon composition, a score by Crawford Gates (who also composed the outstanding Symphony No. 2 for the Hill Cumorah Pageant). Other major pageants include the *Mormon Miracle Pageant* in Manti, Utah, which attracts almost as many attendees as Cumorah; the *City of Joseph Pageant* in Nauvoo, Illinois; the *Castle Valley Pageant* in Castle Dale, Utah; and a host of lesser pageants at temples and historic sites.

Pageants are extremely popular with both Mormon and non-Mormon audiences because spectacle is an accessible, inclusive medium. (Even a lesser-known pageant like the Castle Valley production attracts over 25,000 viewers.)[16] In these cases, spectacles commemorate Mormon history and Mormon scripture, publicly and prominently displaying the twin messages of gospel and culture with unalloyed celebration and triumphalism. But the Mormon theatrical tradition, in spite of a remarkable history of church sponsorship, institutional support, and Salt Lake's own spectacular theater, has been late in fostering an indigenous drama.

In 1966, Clinton Larson became one of the first LDS writers of serious stature to publish a collection of dramas: *The Mantle of the Prophet and Other Plays*. The title play is a stately tragedy, more Attic than modern, replete with troubled, prophetic dreams, weeping women, somber speeches, and classical pathos. "I have come to this hour through the meadows of spring," Joseph intones at the commencement of the tragedy. The inevitability and ceremoniousness of his death endows the whole with the aura of sacred ritual: "the Greys in their hate lift us to Zion. / My conscience is the covenant of my being / before God and before all men."[17] It was a successful effort to elevate Joseph above the level of regional folk hero and into the pantheon of world-historic martyrs. Like a Tabernacle Choir record, Larson's other works in the collection alternated uniquely Mormon themes—Christ's visit to the Nephites, the brother of Jared's saga—with Christian standards, including the annunciation and the conversion of Saul.

Larson's work took Mormon drama to a new level, and he is arguably the father of modern Mormon drama. However, later critics would hold that writers like Larson were still constrained by miracle plays and hero stories as the only two operational genres in faithful Mormon literature. Martin Kelley pushed Mormon drama toward greater realism with his *And They Shall Be Gathered* (1969). We still have a story of conversion (an Armenian couple), faithfulness in the face of rejection, and exile from the homeland. But the dialogue is realistic, characters are multishaded, and we are confronted with a significant intrusion in the otherwise faith-affirming narrative: a nonmember child dies, in spite of missionary ministrations. It is as if Kelley approaches the miracle play format only to reject it, to make the case dramatically for a sublime without transcendence.

In 1971, Mormon drama returned to the promised-valley formula with another commercially successful Mormon musical. Carol Lynn Pearson, popular Mormon poet, wrote *The Order Is Love*, with lyrics by Lex de Azevedo. The story she retold focuses on a splendidly emblematic moment in the tragic encounter between Mormon isolation and self-sufficiency, on the one hand, and the allure of integration into a broader humanity with all its charms and dangers, on the other. In the twenty years from 1874 to 1893, more than 200 branches of the United Order were organized throughout the intermountain West.[18] Established as self-sufficient, communal enterprises, these communities, like the early Christians, put into practice the ideal of having "all things in common" (Acts 4:32). Orderville was one of the most successful and long lived of the experiments in Zion building. Pearson captures the moment when the dream splinters on the hard contours of materialism, selfishness, and individualism.

All of the conflicts are there in a style reminiscent of *Fiddler on the Roof*, Mormon style. Feisty, independent-spirited Catherine Ann protests the regimentation of communal life in a hierarchical society. "Do they sound the bugle if you're in the swings too long?" she asks Matthew. "No," he answers. "Only for gettin' up, going to prayer, eatin' breakfast, going to work, eatin' dinner, going to evenin' prayer, and going to bed."[19]

Certainty is shaken by exposure to a larger universe, and self-sufficiency is called into question as the inhabitants learn that cloistered contentment is forever fragile. "We don't need what's out in the world. We got everything that we need right here in Orderville," the boys insist to the peddler who has come to them as if from another realm. "Why, Son, you don't even know what's out in the world," he replies. And the merest glimpse he provides of that world outside Eden is enough to plant seeds of doubt.[20]

Temptations appear in forms as subtle as a rosebud and a piano; apparently, the survival of beauty and the artistic impulse themselves are threatened in a world so driven by Mormon pragmatism. Matthew is only half-joking when he responds to an exasperated Catherine Ann's query, "Oh, Matthew! Don't you ever think of anything unpractical?" "Try not to."[21]

Practicality can have inventive twists in this world that straddles the utopian and the oppressive. Town youth put a grindstone to ingenious use to circumvent the limitations that economic leveling imposes on their wardrobes. Finding that Matthew has gone outside the order to buy himself a fancy new pair of pants, the boys of Orderville take turns bending over a grindstone to accelerate the wear of their own. The incident, taken from history, is true enough. And such light-hearted rebellion adds to the play's ambiguity: is the demise of the United Order tragic failure or a necessary journey beyond Eden?

The success of this Mormon musical led directly to experiments in the genre by Orson Scott Card (*Stone Tables*, 1973, a play about Moses and Aaron) and the phenomenally successful *Saturday's Warrior* (1974) on which Lex de Azevedo collaborated with Doug Stewart. As we have seen, the production was driven more by its pop/rock music than by its script. In returning to Nephi Anderson's popular nineteenth-century novelized formula about the perseverance of premortal love (*Added Upon*), Stewart tapped the potential for Mormonism to provide a distinctive cultural variation on the star-crossed lovers theme that resonated with Mormon youth.

Saturday's Warrior relied for its dramatic force on the application of novel doctrines to the subject of popular romance. Such novelty was effectively a substitute for exploration of any kinds of subtlety in the characters, conflicts, or even those doctrines themselves. Of course, one defender was on target in protesting, "Directed as a farce, *Saturday's Warrior*'s weaknesses do not show up too glaringly."[22] The real complaint about the play is apparent in the lament of a reviewer who insisted in 1978, "*Saturday's Warrior* was not the only sold-out play in Utah. *Fires of the Mind, Huebener*, and Card's own *The Apostate* played to standing room only audiences at BYU, and none of them were musicals."[23] But the qualification in reference to venue was not a slight one. Just the year before, another theater critic had noted, "The scenery in Utah is littered with the corpses of dead theater companies. Val Johnson's three-year venture in Heber City; the short-lived McKay Ensemble; Orson Scott Card's abortive Utah Valley Repertory Theatre Company—and now?"[24]

So we are back to the universal problem of artistic quality versus commercial viability. Even Orson Scott Card lost dramatic collaborator Robert Stoddard, because he was "disturbed by what he saw as Card's growing concern with commercialism at the expense of art."[25] The best Mormon drama, however, does find appreciative audiences. Robert Elliot's *Fires of the Mind* was first produced in 1974, and has been considered "the best single play yet written about Mormon experience" ever since.[26] One of the first in a continuing line of missionary dramas, it tells the story of Elder Johnson, a missionary unable both to hear the voice of revelation and to live in a condition of uncertainty. Like Lagerkvist's Barabbas, Johnson hungers passionately for faith and yet, like his counterpart, cannot bring himself to realize the role of personal agency in that faith—that belief sooner or later becomes a freely chosen gesture of receptivity.

One of the most celebrated Mormon works is Thomas Rogers's *Huebener*. Written in 1976, it chronicles the true saga of Helmuth Huebener, a seventeen-year-old Latter-day Saint who was beheaded for his covert work to oppose the Nazi regime. The dilemma of opposing evil while "being subject to rulers" and "honoring, obeying, and sustaining the law" is not only as timeless as Antigone, but increasingly vexing for a church trying to gain political legitimacy and the freedom to proselytize in a number of undemocratic societies. *Huebener* is the most conflicted instance in Mormon history of an individual caught between the demands of conscience and faithfulness to the church, between legitimate institutional imperatives and the quest for personal integrity. That he was first excommunicated for his actions, then much later reinstated as a member, only serves to affirm the anguished nature of his predicament.

In other plays, Rogers continues to interrogate the rough edges of Mormon history and the unresolved dilemmas of discipleship. In *Fire in the Bones*, for example, he examines another deeply troubling episode in Mormonism's past: the Mountain Meadows massacre and subsequent scapegoating and execution of John D. Lee (also later reinstated as a member). By focusing on such collisions of conscience and church, Rogers does not resolve any tensions. On the contrary, he seems intent on reminding us that loyalty to a church and belief in legitimate authority, while principles he wishes to affirm, must never overwhelm individual agency. Those forces can only be kept in check by the deliberate counterweight of a most exacting and excruciating self-interrogation.

~

The invention of the motion picture spawned in 1905 the first of what would soon be thousands of nickelodeons where short films were screened to the accompaniment of an improvising pianist. In that first year of the new theaters, the American Mutoscope-Biograph Company produced a comic short entitled *A Trip to Salt Lake City*, which portrayed an overwhelmed polygamous husband faced with the daunting task of giving his numerous children piggyback rides while on a moving railway car. Humor soon turned to more virulent portrayals, however, with the 1911 Danish production of *A Victim of the Mormons*. Homegrown imitations of the genre followed that same year, including *The Mormon, Mountain*

Meadows Massacre, An Episode of Early Mormon Day Marriage or Death, and *The Danites*. The same themes that readers had relished in fiction were now vividly portrayed on the screen: church-sponsored massacres and the sexual exploitation of women. The barrage prompted the church to enter the field with its own (by contemporary standards) lavish production of *One Hundred Years of Mormonism* (1912). The effort involved a cast of over 1,000, an elaborate reconstruction of sections of Nauvoo, and four concurrently running cameras, resulting in a ninety-minute spectacle.[27]

LDS efforts to balance the record could not compete, however, with the lurid appeal of studio potboilers, and they were soon overwhelmed by a wave of harsh depictions, like the widely popular *A Mormon Maid* (1917), *Trapped by the Mormons* (1922), and others that carried the weight and appeal lent by the name of Zane Grey. Fox brought both his *Riders of the Purple Sage* and *The Rainbow Trail* to the screen in 1918.

As was the case with popular fiction, the new medium of motion pictures presented itself to Mormons primarily in the guise of a weapon wielded against the faith in modes both slanderous and derisive. So it is not surprising that in the formative years of those art forms, Mormons were slow to embrace them as canvases for their own creative expression. But as the popularity of film continued unabated, its usefulness as a medium of communication grew ever more obvious. (By the Depression era, motion pictures were the dominant mode of popular entertainment, with over 61 percent of Americans attending a weekly show.)[28] With the approach of the church centennial in 1930, B. H. Roberts hoped the church could again enter the field with its own production. He envisioned a major film based on the Book of Mormon,[29] but the project found no support among the church leadership. In the 1930s, the Production Code was adopted, which strictly prohibited the ridicule of religious denominations, their leaders, or adherents. As a consequence, Mormons seemed content to acquiesce in the kinder, gentler direction of Hollywood, typified by the star-studded Darryl Zanuck megaproduction *Brigham Young*.

Since the mid-twentieth century, a Mormon film culture has been developing, with several new trajectories. First is the church's sophisticated use of film as a public relations tool. Generations of LDS members could indulgently appreciate the sentimentalism of *The Mailbox* or the folksy chauvinism of *Johnny Lingo*, homegrown films intended for the edification of the church's youth. In 1972, the church initiated a long-running "Homefront" series on television, public service announcements that risked the maudlin, but were phenomenally successful due to their winsome humor and usually deft touch in portraying family themes. As the most-lauded public service campaign in history, the series solidified the LDS church's reputation as family-centered, while revealing the power of film to present a Mormon message effectively and nonthreateningly to a mass audience. Incorporating higher production values in films like *Legacy* (1990), a tribute to the Mormon pioneers; *The Testaments of One Fold and One Shepherd* (2000), a fictionalized treatment of Book of Mormon themes and culture; and *Joseph Smith, the Prophet of the Restoration* (2005), the church seems ready to invite public scrutiny through a medium with which it is clearly comfortable and proficient.

Meanwhile, independent Mormon filmmaking is coming into its own, characterized by tremendous variety, talent, and energy. The Association of Mormon Letters began awarding prizes for the best unpublished Mormon novel in 1998, and supporters of Mormon film have not been far behind. The first Young LDS Film Festival took place in Provo in 2001—and showcased more than seventy entries from around the world. Most popular at present is the genre of Mormon comedy. A popular series (*Singles Ward*, *The RM*, *The Home Teachers*) consists of snappy spoofs that good-naturedly satirize Mormon culture, but in ways that may be lost on non-Mormon audiences. They do show a healthy capacity for self-mockery, and manage succinctly to depict a huge variety of Mormon peculiarities. The cumulative effect, though at times rather heavy-handed, is to reveal an abundance of droll and distinctive LDS cultural markers (spare beds composed of freeze-dried stored food), cultural foibles (elaborate ice sculptures as centerpieces for thirty-minute lessons in the women's auxiliary), and cultural vocabulary ("you're not just an RM, you're an LDS RM who was trained at the MTC, who became a DL, a ZL, and then an AP, who was promised long ago by his bishop through a PPI after a BYC that someday he'd be the EQP. I smell GA!"). The coded language is a humorous yet striking sign of how fully evolved Mormonism has become as an autonomous culture not fully accessible by outsiders.

Almost a genre unto itself is the Mormon missionary film. Stage productions (and a video version) of *Saturday's Warrior* were enormously successful in the 1970s, relying in part upon a formula that combined thwarted romance (complicated, Mormon style, by birth's veil of forgetfulness), a comic version of missionary life, and unfiltered sentimentality. *The Best Two Years* reproduces this formula, mixing the humorous side of missionary culture with a sentimental depiction of one missionary's spiritual awakening, which is prompted by a nerdy but irrepressibly sincere companion. Comforting in its familiarity, sympathetic in its depiction of European missionary challenges, and ultimately faith affirming, the work is an uncomplicated film that strikes a resonant cord with Mormon audiences.

The popularity of these films would seem in part to derive from a people hungry for entertainment that validates their own cultural specificity. Like insiders to a private joke, Mormons can comfortably laugh at a genre that, by its focus on culturally distinctive eccentricities, promotes Mormon cohesion and reifies and confirms Mormon self-definition, even as it exploits a cultural grammar that is inherently exclusionary. For that reason, and because the films in this genre tend to rely excessively upon the subject rather than the medium for success, some in the Mormon community worry that the genre taps the potential for Mormon filmmaking in a painfully limited and limiting way.

In a more serious mode, some filmmakers have celebrated Mormon history and culture. *The Other Side of Heaven* (2001) portrays with light humor and spare sentimentality the true-life missionary experience of the young John Groberg, who spent three years in Tonga (1954–1957). Written and directed by Mitch Davis, the film was produced by Gerald Molen, who also produced the block-busters *Jurassic Park*, *Hook*, and *Schindler's List* (for which he won an Academy Award). Actual references to the Mormon faith which launched Groberg on this mission are conspicuously absent. It is not clear if such a decision was intended to universalize the message of Christian service and spiritual coming of age, or to avoid alienating a potential audience.

The Work and the Glory (2004) goes in the opposite direction, by explicitly addressing the message of Mormonism as both urgent and controversial. Tech-nically well done, the film, like the books on which it is based, focuses on the conflicts that both romance and religion introduce into the Steed family. Joseph Smith and Mormonism are thus presented as the context for a story whose dra-matic focus allows for an indirect account of the church's founder and early years. Though not produced by the church, it for all intents and purposes could have been. Building on the popularity of the bestselling (in Mormondom) series by Gerald Lund, the film is too overtly faith promoting and celebratory to penetrate a larger market.

One of the first makers of Mormon films to rise to the level of serious artist is the screenwriter/director/actor Richard Dutcher. With his work, we begin to see the first efforts in film to plumb the paradoxes and complexities of Mormon culture with a sophistication that literature has been manifesting since the forties. *God's Army* is a searingly accurate depiction of Mormon missionary work—and of the range of personalities that constitute a typical mission environment. With its drill-sergeant mission president, sophomoric missionary pranks, eccentric in-vestigators, and poignant spiritual experiences, the film is a starkly naturalistic depiction of themes sacred and familiar to Mormons.

The dramatic focus here is on the problem of doubt in Mormon life. It is hard enough to find space for doubt in a religious culture that asserts knowledge and certainty as a matter of course. It is virtually impossible in a missionary subculture where elders are sent forth not "to be taught, but to teach" (D&C 43:15). But in this particular missionary sextet, two elders are anything but certain. One character, Elder Kinegar, has been studying anti-Mormon literature. He openly discusses his doubts and findings, only to be met by the other missionaries' open hostility. As the chasm of doubt yawns wider, he is horror-struck by the possibility that he has been deceived. His wrenching exclamation—"what if they know it's all a big lie? . . . But they won't tell us! Damn them if it's not true! Damn them to hell!"—is an explosion pregnant with complex meaning. His terror and vehemence are proportional to the degree of certainty and the totality of the investment he has as a believing, i.e., knowing, Latter-day Saint. And that terror and vehemence betray the degree to which LDS testimonies are interdependent. My faith can never be a basis for your knowledge, because faith is by definition tenuous and personal, subjective. But my assertion of knowledge can be a legitimate basis for your faith, because as a declaration of certainty it makes a claim to objective truth. Mormons are admonished to "get their own testimonies," and not live by borrowed light. But immersion in a culture so saturated in the rhetoric of certainty inevitably produces the pressure to express, if not the reality to have, personal conviction; and it produces a socially reinforced confidence about those convictions. Perhaps this explains in part the proclivity of disaffected Mormons so frequently to react with bitterness and feelings of betrayal. It explains why people can leave the church but not leave it alone.

Elder Kinegar's travail ends at the bus station in an emotionally intense altercation. When the group's leader, "Pops" Dalton, tries to stop Kinegar from leaving, the elder-turned-apostate flings at the terminally ill Dalton a charge that is a projection of his own experience: "You are so afraid that you are just going to disappear!" That Dalton's only response is physical violence—they scuffle briefly—suggests that the charge may have struck close to home. More likely, the response simply typifies the difficulty in Mormon culture of addressing the doubting with cool rationality. And at a minimum, Dalton's reaction eradicates any moral high ground that he, as a believer, has vis-à-vis the other, as a doubter.

The spiritual odyssey of the protagonist, Elder Brandon Allen, threatens to duplicate the journey of the apostate. And given the banality of life in this missionary apartment and mission field, the sympathetic defection of the troubled elder, and the naturalism of the film, this would not be an unmotivated development. That is why when Allen's spiritual awakening and subsequent conversion unfold, they do so in a context that has been disarmingly shorn of sentimentality and advocacy. Dutcher thereby manages to center spiritual realities in a fallen world, where raucous roommates rather than the Tabernacle Choir provide the choral backdrop to sacred epiphanies. This may be the greatest accomplishment of the film: managing to naturalize the supernatural without stripping it of sublimity. Sometimes the disjunctions that get us there are dramatically intense, as when Allen ponders the meaning of having found his own path to the gospel via a pedophile stepfather. At other times, these juxtapositions take the form of lightly veiled self-irony, as when the missionaries hand out tracts to a soundtrack of jaunty fiddle music and Ryan Shupe's lyrics, "go to hell, go to hell, you're gonna go to hell, I hope you look good with horns and a tail," or when the film's pseudodocumentary "afterword" tells us that Carla, the former street hooker, is now the spiritual living teacher in her relief society. The result is a work that enacts filmically what Joseph's vision encompassed theologically: a successful integration of the quotidian and the celestial. But the film also suggests another theological pairing—intellectual openness and the quest for conviction, certainty and searching—that has a more uneasy alliance in Mormon culture. In Dutcher's vision, not all choices are validated, and his sympathies are clear. But they are sympathies that do not rely for their appeal upon sentimental manipulation.

Dutcher returned to a missionary setting with his 2005 *States of Grace*. It is lamentably ironic how grace can be edged out of Mormon theology, as a consequence of three pervasive paradoxes in particular: coexisting anxiously with deference for authority and hierarchy is an LDS emphasis on individual agency and accountability so profound as to invite the charge of Pelagianism, i.e., the heresy that salvation can be achieved independently of Christ through exertion of the will. In addition, the endless questing and eternal progression exemplified by Joseph is countered by a rhetoric and doctrine of epistemological certainty so impregnable that it can preempt faith and abject reliance upon the subtle workings of grace. Finally, compounding this tendency is the antipathy to mystery, the frequent eclipse in Mormonism of wonder and, occasioned by Joseph's collapse of sacred distance, an all-too-comfortable commingling of the heavenly and earthly. The result is a religious culture where the status of grace is uncertain, and its Author not always the thematic center of the stories Mormonism tells, in sermons or in art. Dutcher's project can be seen, in part, as a vigorous effort to recenter Christ and to rehabilitate grace in Mormon theology, as the title of his latest movie proclaims.

States of Grace is a no-holds-barred interrogation of a challenge endemic to organized religion, and Mormonism in particular: how to make room for grace to operate freely in an institution as regulated, rule governed, correlated, and orchestrated as the LDS church. Or as the film's Elder Lozano (Ignacio Serricchio) puts it more simply, "can we let obedience get in the way of righteousness?" Part of the film's beauty is in the way the humorless and strict Elder Farrell (Lucas Fleischer) unconsciously travels down the road that query marks, in tandem with Lozano's self-conscious odyssey. Lozano's decision leads him to take into the missionaries' apartment, in defiance of mission rules, a homeless street preacher in need of convalescence. Meanwhile, Farrell finds himself irresistibly drawn to befriend and fraternize with, also in breach of mission rules, the lonely (and lovely) hurting young woman Holly (Rachel Emmers).

Lozano's decision bears happy consequences, as Louis (Jo-sei Ikeda) escapes his alcoholism and finds his way to the pastorship of his own church (a conspicuously non-Mormon church at that). Farrell's decision bears agonizing fruit. In an excruciating sequence, we see him slip into sexual sin, experience devastating guilt, and attempt suicide. Non-Mormon viewers may respond to his reaction as does Holly—with incredulity that a moral slip is experienced as a private apocalypse. Dutcher is not, presumably, questioning the seriousness with which Latter-day Saints view this sin as "second only to murder" in their theology. The point is rather twofold. First, guilt that is inexpressibly intense must beckon forth a grace that is inexpressibly sublime. But second, guilt so extreme as to be virtually irredeemable must not be misconstrued in Mormonism as guilt that *is* irredeemable (as implied in the father's attitude, "better dead than unchaste"). That is Farrell's error. Holly's insistent gift of the crucifix necklace, which strikes the missionaries as naively inappropriate, becomes a symbol not of Christ's redemptive power, but of LDS awkwardness at knowing how to receive it in non-LDS packaging. Farrell's tragedy is contextualized by the third major plot of this movie mosaic, as gang-banger Carl finds his way to conversion and redemption with the assistance of Lozano, whose own gang-member past gives him special empathy.

If the film has a flaw, it is this: in Dutcher's zeal to celebrate the splendid and manifold intersections of grace, the film can become too conspicuous in its ecumenical utopianism—as in the scene where a Latino ex-gang-member missionary, a black Pentecostal preacher, a white porn actress, and a white-bread Utah missionary all cheerily toast Jesus on the balcony of a terrace apartment overlooking the ocean.

At the same time, if there is a moral in Dutcher's tale, it is neither facile nor unambiguous. For if we have been exposed to a redemption that is miraculous and moving in the person of Carl in particular, we have also been exposed to searing pain and unconsoled grief. Farrell's clasp of Holly's hand at the end may portend their happy resolution of sin, but Carl's conversion compounds rather than heals his pain, as the consequent murder of his young brother attests. And in an irony that may or may not be part of Dutcher's intent, we cannot help but realize, when all is said and done, that Farrell's fastidiousness, if it had not been checked by the more compassionate and spontaneous Lozano, would have been his spiritual preservation. Pharisaical attention to the rules (no taking in vagrants) would have precluded the chain of events that led inexorably to his personal tragedy. Maybe "obedience is better than sacrifice, and to hearken than the fat of rams" (1 Samuel 15:22). But the emphasis here is clearly on the incomparable beauty of redemption, not on the hand wringing of hindsight. That the redeemed is in this case the Mormon proselytizer is a powerful point. (Also left unaddressed is the question of exactly what it is that LDS missionaries have to offer the world that justifies their two-year sacrifice. The answer may be embedded in Lozano's early lament: "I was a better convert than missionary.")

The difficult moral here may be: for the spiritually superficial, the devastating taste of sin may be the precondition for true knowledge of Christ. Of course, that presents us with another dilemma before which even the apostle Paul could only recoil in inarticulate horror: "Shall we continue in sin, that grace may abound? God forbid" (Romans 6:1–2). But "God forbid" is not an answer. It merely confirms our frustrating incapacity to resolve rationally these troubling paradoxes.

In the face of such logical inadequacy, film can be articulate where speech cannot. That is one sense in which Dutcher's work is indeed "sacramental cinema."[30] In a cinematic juxtaposition influenced by *The Godfather*, which is troublingly beautiful (like all true sacraments), gang members walk almost ritualistically around the young boy they have just murdered. His eyes close in death at the same moment that his brother Carl's open, as Mormon elders finish baptizing and then confirming him, after which they ritualistically circle around him in a ring of newfound brotherhood.

In the film's closing scene, Elder Farrell watches a live manger scene. His final embrace of the Christ he has taught but never known is literally enacted as he asks to hold the Christ child and, weeping, finds hopeful catharsis. The entire cast is assimilated into what is now a *tableau vivant*. The scene comes perilously close to sentimental contrivance, but becomes instead a stylized allegory, demonstrating grace's universal reach and power to assimilate all, saints and sinners, converters and converts, Mormons and Methodists, into a story that began in Bethlehem.

Not all films in the new wave of LDS cinema blatantly embrace Mormon themes and characters. *Saints and Soldiers* (2004) is in this regard an effort to address more universal themes and experiences through the lens of an LDS sensibility. Winner of more than fifteen awards, this independent film, directed by Ryan Little with entirely professional production values, chronicles the odyssey of a small band of Allied soldiers fighting their way back to their own lines to deliver critical intelligence during the Battle of the Bulge. The title itself is a coy emblem of the film's double voice. To a general audience, the "saints" refer to those who valiantly struggle to maintain human integrity and virtue in the midst of the hell that is war. To those in the know, it is a clear reference to the third term of the acronym LDS.

The dramatic complication is twofold: on the verge of being shot by the Americans, a German soldier is recognized by the religiously devout Corporal Nathan "Deacon" Greer (Corbin Allred) as a man he baptized before the war, while a missionary in Germany. The dramatic and emotional revelation, which abruptly humanizes a nameless, faceless, and despised enemy, starkly reveals war as the ultimate perversion of human interactions and fellow-feeling. At the same time, the resilient humanity of Greer gradually wears down the misanthropy and encroaching nihilism of Brooklyn-born medic Alexander Polinsky (Alexander Niver). Almost the sole survivor of the band, Polinsky finds himself at story's end (or is it a beginning?) prompted to retrieve the pocket Bible from the dead Greer's pocket. Only, of course, LDS viewers will recognize in the unnamed scripture a pocket version of the Book of Mormon, which will, presumably, continue to do the miraculous work of conversion it has been doing since 1830.

With audiences still largely polarized by recognizably Mormon subjects, themes, or treatments, filmmakers can alienate or exclude the non-Mormons, or employ enough humor or subtlety to entice them into the audience. In this film, screenwriters Matt Whittaker and Geoffrey Pano choose instead to rely on a text coded in such a way that its meanings can be read in both particular and universal ways. This film is about a Mormon ex-missionary (and ex-deacon) whose proselytizing experiences allow him to save a convert's life as well as his soul, while planting the seeds (Book of Mormon) for yet another conversion even as his life ends. But it is also about a noble everyman, "Deacon" Greer, whose inherent goodness, in its capacity to transcend human evil, ignites the latent goodness of a fellow human being, ensuring the survival of that which is best in human nature and human civilization. Such strategies may prove to be one of the best ways to resolve the tension between celebrating Zion and lamenting lonely exile, affirming what is both culturally specific and what is culturally shared. Finding an artistic voice that exploits an authentic Mormon grammar, but also builds rather than burns bridges, is no easy feat.

In Richard Dutcher's second film, *Brigham City*, he addresses thematically what Little has addressed strategically: the uneasy demands of Zion building, on the one hand, and accommodation to life in Babylon, on the other. He asks some of the most urgent questions a Christian can ask in this regard, questions with special resonance for a people whose gathering was for generations literal. Can Eden survive if its borders are permeable? When does the quest for purity become a flight from responsible participation in the world we are called to serve? The sheriff (and bishop) of the small town of Brigham City is so determined to defeat the encroachments of worldliness into his life and community that he refuses even to countenance news broadcasts on his car radio. Because he is still profoundly stricken over the tragic death of his wife, his studied introversion is as credible a grief response as it is a plausible manifestation of saintliness. Whether such efforts to shield himself and his flock from the ugliness and sordidness of Babylon represent transcendence of the world or flight from the world is the vexing question his young deputy poses. In this film's unusually profound engagement with this central problematic of Mormon faith, we hear echoes of an older and more-traditional version of the dilemma. "Must we lose our innocence," one character asks, "in order to gain wisdom?" Nothing is so attractive to a serpent, another character presciently observes, as a little paradise. But the question here is not how long Eden can forestall the inroads of the devil. The question is, what is the price we pay, and is the cost too high, when we put a wall around Eden?

Ultimately, the sheltered community suffers the horrible ordeal of a string of serial murders. Initially, this would seem to be just another variation on an old theme, recapitulated time and again in Mormon history. The Saints build their refuge in Ohio, Missouri, Utah—only to find dissenters, mobbers, and the railroad entering the garden, bringing death, destruction, and sin in their wake. Except in this case, the sheriff finally confronts and kills the murderer—and it turns out to be his own deputy. The solution emerges only after the sheriff faces the terrible truth that the savage killings were possible only because of his own stubbornly trusting nature and insistent generosity of spirit. A little worldly savvy and skepticism would have precluded a gruesome string of tragedies. The same ingredients that constituted the city of Zion made possible the destruction of innocence.

The film's final scene is as emotionally wrenching as anything Hollywood has produced. The sheriff attends the Sunday service where he serves as the local bishop. Aware of his naïve complicity in and responsibility for the town's tragedy, he finds himself unable to partake of the emblems of the Eucharist (the "sacrament"). A shaken counselor (whose daughter was one of the murder victims) watches the bishop/sheriff in empathic discomfort, then likewise declines. So do the other communicants to whom the bread is next offered. We watch in pain and amazement as one by one, every single member of the congregation declines to participate in the most sacred ordinance of a Mormon's weekly devotional life. One reading of this shared gesture of self-punishment is that it represents a decision by the collective to share the burden that willful isolation from the world and its values entails. But—and here Dutcher is at his most provoking—to acknowledge the cost is not to repudiate the cost. The refusal to allow the sheriff to take upon himself the guilt of the group is an implicit re-affirmation even as it may be a recognition of the community's choices that precipitated the tragedy.

In the film's last moments, the young boy whose sister was the final victim of the sheriff's dogged blindness re-urges upon the bishop the sacred bread. Sobbing out of guilt, shared remorse, and shared forgiveness, he partakes. And then, gratefully and tearfully, his flock follows suit. For even in a Zion remote from the world, none are worthy without grace, and none are unworthy with it. That the FBI agent who has long struggled to comprehend this culturally impene-trable society chooses this moment to exit the sacrament service is an ambiguous finale. Either she finds illumination in the sequence just enacted and concludes her quest for understanding, or she realizes at that moment that she has tres-passed into a holy community which curious spectators have neither the right nor the ability, as the explorer Richard Burton learned, to enter. "There is in Mormondom, as in all other exclusive faiths," Burton wrote, "an inner life into which I cannot flatter myself or deceive the reader with the idea of my having penetrated."[31]

A film of brilliant quirkiness and deceptively serious intention is Greg Whitely's *New York Doll*. The premise of the film is so absurdly outrageous that the result is a documentary virtually indistinguishable from parody. Arthur "Killer" Kane was a founding member of the Dolls, a protopunk (also called glam-punk and mock-rock) band that was enormously influential in the New York club scene of the early 1970s (and upon subsequent generations of musicians across a broad spectrum). Sporting flamboyant makeup and drag, playing exuberant music in frenzied performances that reminded one fan of "Jagger and Richards on a bad-acid trip," the band flared briefly like a shooting star before dissolving in 1975. Kane sank into alcoholism, depression, and oblivion. Then, at the nadir of his life, he responded to a *Reader's Digest* ad, heard the missionary discussions, joined the LDS church, and became a volunteer at the Family History Library adjacent to the Los Angeles Temple (about as plausible a development, remarks one friend, "as Donny Osmond becoming a New York Doll"). The conversion is already a done deed when the film opens; even so, the film is a kind of conversion narrative—only it is ours, not Killer Kane's. The central, brilliant irony of the film is the complete nonchalance of the protagonist, his comfortable evolution into his new LDS life and role, and his obliviousness to the shock this transfor-mation engenders in anyone observing the radical disjunction between the be-fore and after photos. Like the ingenuous Peter Sellers in *Being There* (and with the same Christly overtones), or like the absurdly sanguine Balaam of the Old Testament (who responds earnestly and without a shudder to his miraculously talking ass), Killer Kane unblinkingly glides from one construction of reality into another. But as the film's real plot gets under way, Kane must enact an even more daunting transition: back to glam rocker, but this time without leaving behind his world view, his demeanor, his values, and all of his newly acquired Mormon cultural baggage, which seems at an infinite remove from the raucous Babylon he left behind. He is offered the opportunity to play a reunion concert with the two surviving Dolls in the London Royal Festival Hall.

Through this process, which is resurrection rather than conversion, Kane's gentle voice and tranquil speech betoken a steady calm at a swirling vortex of contradictions. There is something almost violently incessant about the director's montages and juxtapositions and substitutions, all conducing to the same purpose: the visual, auditory, and thematic dismantling of boundaries that keep the sacred and the profane safely demarcated and apart. We see Kane the church worker, with missionary attire and name tag, morph on the screen into a lip-sticked, fishnet-stockinged, flowing-maned punker, and back again. We hear church hymns interspersed with pulsing beats and screaming guitars; we hear Kane fondly described by a pair of kindly septuagenarian LDS coworkers in the Family History Library, who don't know what a bass guitar is, and by admirers from the Clash, Blondie, and the Pretenders. We see him in a dressing room casually and comfortably answering David Johansen (aka Buster Poindexter) as to what he would have to do to follow "John Smith and all those lovely Brigham Young people," likening tithing to "an agent's fee," and comparing personal revelation to "an LSD trip from the Lord," and we hear him give a prayer that sounds like an invocation to any Mormon meeting, only this is to assembled Dolls and colleagues as they prepare to dash onstage before 10,000 screaming fans. And we realize that the guitar he is playing was taken out of hock with funds that the church's home teacher provided "so he would have something to practice with."

The real message is articulated so quietly it is easy to miss. Sir Bob Geldof is lamenting the imminent return of Kane to Los Angeles, to obscurity, and to his pedestrian existence as a volunteer in a church library. "He looks at home . . . on the stage," he says. "He shouldn't go back to that library." As he mourns the music career that might have been, and still might be, Chrissie Hynde, lead singer of the Pretenders, softly mutters, "there is room for both." At the concert's finale, the band has carried it off brilliantly. The strobe lights are flashing, the thousands of fans are cheering, and the band members are an exuberant blur of delirious singing, and suddenly, almost imperceptibly, the music fades and the soundtrack—but only the soundtrack—is replaced by the poignant, sacred strains of a Tabernacle Choir hymn. Surprisingly, there is no discomfort, no discordance at all between the image and the music. And that seems to be the point: not merely a God or universe capacious enough to embrace diversity, but a universe in which the real and palpable possibilities of infinite transformation make all difference negligible.

Kane returns to Los Angeles and his library. Twenty-two days afterward, he is diagnosed with leukemia, and dies two hours later. It is hard to avoid the impression that a Deity scripted the prolongation of his life, just long enough for him to complete this morality tale. In our last view of him, he plays on the harmonica a simple Mormon hymn, the kind, he says, he would play for his friends at the center. Indeed, it would seem there *was* room for both.

All art forms have their high-brow and low-brow manifestations, but the temptation to sacrifice aesthetic standards for popular success is especially strong in a medium of mass appeal like film. Whitely, Little, and Dutcher have resisted those allures, and found at least a limited national success while engaging serious themes in serious ways. And with indie films becoming increasingly, and fashionably, popular, enterprising Mormon filmmakers are likely to find the resources and audiences to continue investigating and depicting Mormon culture in highly original ways, as in the work of Whitely. The critical praise accorded the work of these filmmakers and their successful reconciliation of serious moral purpose with real aesthetic merit are hopeful signs for all who lament the limitations of Hollywood-based cultural representations.

"TO THE FRINGES
OF FAITH"

Literature

> God, the best story-teller, has made a better story out of
> Joseph Smith and the Mormon wandering than fiction
> will ever equal.
>
> ~ Bernard DeVoto

The "home literature" movement spearheaded by Orson Whitney, with the
support and urging of Susa Young Gates, Emmeline B. Wells, and others, did
not immediately produce any lasting literary monuments, but it did set Mormonism on a course of studied engagement with literary expression that continues to the present. The most popular and enduring nineteenth-century work to
emerge from that effort was the novel *Added Upon* (1898) by Nephi Anderson,
which stayed in print almost a century (thirty-five editions through 1973). In the
author's own words, the story aimed to "give in brief an outline of 'the scheme of
things' as taught by the . . . Latter-day Saints."[1] This it did by fashioning a love
story with roots in the premortal world of spirits, following it through its earthly
phase in turn-of-the-century Dry Bench, Utah, beyond death into the spirit
world, and culminating with its characters resurrected and enjoying life in the
millennial kingdom of Christ. Along the way, characters enact or explain the
grand council and subsequent war in heaven, the plan of salvation, genealogy
and temple work, and eternal marriage. The dialogue is often wooden (" 'May
I come and talk with you again? It will give me much pleasure.' 'Which pleasure
will be mutual,' said she"). And Anderson expounds, rather than depicts, his
theology through blatant authorial intervention ("As there are gradations of
righteousness and intelligences in the spirit world, there must be a vast field of
usefulness for preaching the gospel, training the ignorant, and helping the
weak").[2] The phenomenal popularity of the novel is no doubt due to its success in
wedding the appeal of sentimental romance with a uniquely Mormon theological

time frame of more than epic length. The work, like others of that era, was an important step in embracing and experimenting with the possibilities of a distinctively Mormon literature. Its limitations were located by Edward Geary in its privileging of dogma over experience:

> It is one thing to ask the artist to put his religious duties before his literary vocation or to write from his deepest convictions. It is quite another to insist that he create from a base in dogma rather than a base in experience.... [Home literature] is not a powerful literature artistically, nor is it pure. In most cases its distinctive Mormon characteristics are only skin deep.[3]

Orson Whitney practiced what he preached by producing an epic poem on the subject of Mormonism, *Elias, an Epic of the Ages* (1904). It is a bit turgid, as one would expect of a religious verse-epic written at the twilight of Victorianism. But he successfully invokes at least the shadow of Milton in his ambition (twelve parts like Milton's twelve cantos), his scope (heavenly councils through terrestrial drama), and his neologisms (in this case, Mormonisms), complex syntax, and gravitas, as a few sample stanzas attest:

> In solemn council sat the Gods;
> From Kolob's height supreme,
> Celestial light blazed forth afar
> O'er countless kokaubeam;[4]
> And faintest tinge, the fiery fringe
> Of that resplendent day,
> 'Lumined the dark abysmal realm
> Where earth in chaos lay.
> Silence self-spelled; the hour was one
> When thought doth most avail;
> Of worlds unborn the destiny
> Hung trembling in the scale.
> Silence o'er all, and there arose,
> Those kings and priests among,
> A Power sublime, than whom appeared
> None nobler 'mid the throng.[5]

One product of this period did make it into the national spotlight, at least briefly. O. U. Bean adapted B. H. Roberts's short story "Corianton: A Nephite Story" into a play. After running successfully in the Salt Lake Theatre, it even appeared briefly on Broadway.[6] For the most part, however, the first decades of the twentieth century saw an efflorescence of short stories, but no flowering of work equal to the richness of Mormon theology or, more surprisingly perhaps, even approaching the sweep and grandeur of its founding history. All of this would change abruptly in the thirties.

In *The American Religion*, Harold Bloom prophesies that "a major American poet . . . some time in the future will write [the Mormon story] as the epic it was." And, he asserts, "nothing else in all of American history strikes me as *materia poetica* equal to the early Mormons, to Joseph Smith," and to his followers, and he calls for "strong poets, major novelists, [and] accomplished dramatists to tell [Joseph's] history."[7]

THE LOST GENERATION

Almost everyone who has assessed the field of LDS literature has cited the epic qualities of the Mormon story. Bernard DeVoto, much earlier than Bloom, recognized in these heroic dimensions an almost irresistible allure for the aspiring novelist but doubted any creative mind was adequate to the challenge. At least, he personally thought better of the attempt, after outlining a novel that began with Joseph Smith and culminated in the American West. It was, he famously declared, "the best book I am never going to write." For he was convinced that "God, the best story-teller, has made a better story out of Joseph Smith and the Mormon wandering than fiction will ever equal."[8] But even as he expressed his skepticism, the first serious attempts to capture the full sweep of the Mormon saga were under way. Most notable in these efforts were three works: *Children of God* (1939) by Vardis Fisher, *The Giant Joshua* (1941) by Maurine Whipple, and *A Little Lower than the Angels* (1942) by Virginia Sorensen.[9] With these three novels, writers proved capable of serious engagement with Mormonism as a literary theme and fostered a new era of public exposure of its history.

Children of God was an immense success, winning the Harper Prize as best novel of the year in 1939, becoming a bestseller, and forming the basis of Louis Bromfield's screenplay for Twentieth-Century Fox's *Brigham Young*. The book's popularity resulted in part from the fact that Fisher's treatment broke new ground in steering clear of either hagiography or indiscriminate demonization of his characters, while unfolding a tragic and triumphant American saga that spanned almost a century and most of a continent. A disaffected Mormon himself, Fisher had little reverence for Joseph and his colleagues. As a result, the Prophet and most of his followers are portrayed as a mix of the grotesque and the cartoonish. (Excusing himself from paying a call on a friend, Joseph explains, "I have to go deliver Jim Brewster to Satan now. He has been wicked.")[10] Martin Harris is a half-wit wife beater, Emma Smith is a coarse-tongued shrew, and the Kirtland Saints are a mix of simpletons and deranged prophets. Even while chronicling the dramatic rise of Mormonism, Fisher stops short of seriously inquiring after the reasons for its appeal or its resilience. Joseph is sexually charismatic, but without depth or complexity.

Young, on the other hand, Fisher clearly admires, depicting him as strong, pragmatic, and decisive ("'By damn,' said Brigham, 'I guess I'll get baptized'").[11] Pretending to no prophetic powers, Fisher's Young is the consummate organizer, motivator, and leader—a rougher version of George Washington in a frontier Valley Forge. It is in the collective, however, that Fisher's Saints command their great appeal. Harrowing scenes of rape, brutality, and murder by the Missouri mobbers are juxtaposed with the restraint and meekness of Mormon victims and their dogged persistence in holding to their ridiculed beliefs. Here Fisher is at his best, successfully portraying a people so welded together in adversity that onlookers want to join their ranks just to share in their steadfast solidarity. It is as if they are compelled to acknowledge that even the deluded and sinful are sanctified by that much suffering.

Polygamy is not the central thread in Fisher's narrative, but it comes close. It is integral to his story of the early church's internal dissensions, and of Joseph's fall and assassination. And it is integral to the second half of Fisher's novel, which tracks the course of the church during Utah's polygamous period, from 1847 to 1890. In fact, the book ends not in the glow of a prosperous Utah Mormon kingdom about to enter the American mainstream, but with a faithful band of exiles leaving the Salt Lake Valley so they can faithfully continue to live "the principle" in Canada or Mexico after the Salt Lake leaders have capitulated to federal pressure and ended the practice.

Building on the success of Fisher's novel, other works achieved national recognition as well, two of which explored the emotional and moral complexities of plural marriage in ways that Fisher had not. *The Giant Joshua* by Maurine Whipple is generally acclaimed as the greatest novel of Mormonism written by a faithful member. This is somewhat ironic, since in spite of its acclaim (it won the Houghton Mifflin Literary Prize, among other accolades), it never had popular approval from the Mormon people. Indeed, Whipple spoke of the "anguish and disillusionment" she felt in the wake of the book's chilly reception by LDS leaders.[12] The apostle John A. Widtsoe, who reviewed the book for the church's *Improvement Era*, found its portrayal of plural marriage "unfair."[13] In fact, it is frank without being lurid and unreservedly sympathetic to the painful emotional costs that the practice could sometimes exact from plural wives. The theme is not exploited, but it is certainly not celebrated or treated with reverence. As a consequence, Mormons showed little interest in purchasing reading copies—though Salt Lake City Public Library records indicate that guilty curiosity was sufficient to make it the most-borrowed book in the system.[14]

The novel's central character is Clorinda Agatha, a spirited young girl raised by her aunt and uncle: the dour, imposing Bathsheba and the dutiful, self-righteous Abijah. Immediately casting plural marriage in its most agonizing moral discordance, the book opens with Clory as the unhappy new bride of Abijah, making her a wife to an older man she still calls uncle, a competitor in affection with an unattractive but power-wielding matriarch, and the stepmother to a dashing young man with whom she shares a mutual—but now tragically thwarted—infatuation. Whipple avoids the facile caricature that Fisher made of polygamy (he has Joseph court one bride with the endearing logic that "the more wives I have, the sooner I'll be a god in the next life," and has him on another occasion offer to wrestle a competitor for an especially pretty candidate).[15] Whipple's men are as prone to carnality as any ("the light in Abijah's eyes was sometimes far from holy") but hers are the first male characters to bear their conjugal prerogatives with anything approaching grace and dignity. "If a man can't control himself he has no right to hold the priesthood," counsels the apostle Erastus Snow. "Just because marriage gives you the right to her bed, do not victimize your wife!"[16]

But the novelty and genius of Whipple's treatment is ultimately in presenting plural marriage as one more element in a marathon Abrahamic test that challenges the endurance of God's people. At her hands, it is revealed as no simple sexual aberration or indulgence, but an institution demanding the most profound emotional sacrifices and provoking the most trying spiritual struggles. Juxtaposed with the monumental task of colonizing the Dixie mission of southern Utah, plural marriage thus emerges as a domestic counterpart to the heroic physical exertions and suffering required to tame a parched, inhospitable desert. There are no victims and oppressors in Whipple's Mormon kingdom—only tragic heroes who must conquer both flesh and wilderness, and contend with the devastating floods of the Virgin River and the divisive power of possessive love.

No one has succeeded better than Whipple at capturing the recurrent Mormon paradox: the independence and loneliness of an exiled people. Not since the myth of the Pilgrims has the saga of a second Canaan been so compellingly told. In the fastness of Utah, Clory's alienation from American society is absolute. She will later recollect her "scared excitement over seeing a gentile, a real gentile, and her twinge of disappointment because he appeared, after all, so much like other men."[17] At her moment of death, Clory rehearses succinctly both the cost and the reward of such utter isolation:

> Life would go on.... She saw them, the whole heroic cavalcade, marching toward more deathless stars. And she knew with an ancient exultation ... that she would not have changed a moment of it. Tomahawk and war whoop, bran mush and lucerne greens, Virgin bloat, the Year of the Plagues, the Reign of Terror. She felt a detached pity for the generations yet to come who couldn't plan and build a world.[18]

Planning and building worlds, whether earthly Zions or celestial habitations, is an enduring feature of the LDS ethic. Even if the endeavor, like Enoch's Zion of old, is one that accentuates the rift, rather than the relation, with the earthly city of man. Of course, the initial exuberance of a people gathering in Missouri to build a literal Zion has gradually metamorphosed into the quieter contentment of a people satisfied with a Zion that is now figuratively rendered as the church itself. Still, Mormonism's immersion in a rhetoric of founding epiphanies, supernatural manifestations, dialogic revelation, and ongoing spiritual experiences sometimes collapses, in parallel fashion, the distance that separates gold plates from suburban testimony meetings. Thus Maurine Whipple's short story of pioneer faith ("They Did Go Forth") is entirely within the genre of pioneer hagiography, but it is also a bittersweet reminder of the distance Mormons have traveled since those not-so-distant days when burning bushes were not mere metaphors. In that early Mormon world of Old Testament literalism, it was entirely natural that the Lord should appear to Priddy Meeks "one day in the fields and counsel him to 'quit a-plowing and go to doctoring.' " Tildy Elizabeth is one of his patients. Temporarily abandoned by her missionary husband and nursing yet another dying child, she desperately awaits salvation at the hand of the legendary Three Nephites, ancient American disciples of Christ who never tasted of death but lingered on to minister eternally, like John the Beloved, to the earth's inhabitants. Reading the Book of Mormon account of those emissaries aloud, "Tildy Elizabeth did not hear the door open. Only when she sensed the presence of another person in the room, did she look up." The immortal Nephite not only saves the child, but succors her far-distant, suffering husband as well, leaving a telltale linen napkin that survives to the present day as a heritable trace of a family history that intersected with the miraculous. The story is told without irony, without smugness or cynicism. The narrative voice affirms with its matter-of-factness the utter plausibility of angelic visitants and miraculous healings. Still, the fact remains that the linen napkin, "yellowed and frayed," is now an inert artifact, an emblem whose faded hue and tattered edges only emphasize the remoteness of its original, living context.[19]

Whipple incorporates in her work the array of those tensions that constitute the Mormon identity—making it perhaps the fullest cultural expression of the Mormon experience. Whipple compels us, as does Fisher, to admire the "certain magnificence"[20] of the Mormon people, in part by focusing, again like Fisher, on the deeds, not the beliefs, of the pioneers. Her protagonist in *The Giant Joshua* shares this orientation, but it puts her out of sync with the Saints, for whom the reverse seems to be true. As an excommunicated but virtuous man complains, "Though a man be guilty of ever so heinous a crime, if he can stand up and say that he believes the same as you do, you will hold to him and keep him in fellowship." But lacking "the testimony that Mormonism is true," the individual is cast out.[21] For Clory, the lack of her own personal conviction is a torment greater than her struggles with polygamy, because it impugns her status as a real Mormon:

> [Clory] wondered about this thing called a testimony; this divine fire for which men would give up family and kindred rather than renounce. All about her tongues faltered, in an effort to express this gratitude of the heart. The old phrases glib upon the tongue: *I know Joseph Smith to be a prophet of God!* But how, *how* did one come to know it? And you couldn't say it if you didn't know it. . . . Clory wondered again if this dreadful lack in her soul would some day fester upon the surface for all men to see; she was like a person born with a hand missing, or an eye.[22]

Only on her deathbed does Clory come to appreciate that her path to glory has been a blessedness that was not self-aware:

> And now there is no more time. Already the radiance is trembling on the horizon, the flushed light leans down from the west, the Great Smile beckons. And suddenly, with a shock of a thousand exploding light-balls, she recognizes the Great Smile at last. That which she had searched for all her life had been right there in her heart all the time. She, Clorinda McIntyre, had a testimony![23]

The tragic loss in this case is that the cultural pressures of Mormon certainty had transformed Clory's life of faith into a life of concealed shame and torment.

Another problem with a religion of certitude and pragmatism, many Mormons have learned to their chagrin, is that the verities of eternal truth are no substitute for awe in the face of mystery; the familiarization of the divine and its attendant collapse of sacred distance can leave one with a sense of loss. One wants, whether by cultural training or by psychological disposition, to stand with trepidation in the face of the "mysterium tremendum," or, in the phrase of William James, to have objects to which we can attach "adjectives of mystery and splendor." The religion of Brigham Young, however, is one in which a pause to reflect on the sacred imponderables can appear to be a self-indulgent distraction from practical religion. "I would say to you always," he counsels Brother Mac, "pay your debts, keep your bowels open, walk uprightly before God and you will never have a care."[24] Or as another Mormon explains to a gentile, "We believe that everything a man does is a form of worship—pitching hay and scrubbing floors! That God was never meant to belong to one day only out of seven."[25]

But if the sublime is whatever transports us beyond the quotidian or arrests our soul in the course of its customary rounds, then how to find it in a world where every day is a sabbath—and worship just so much gritty labor? This dilemma is especially vexing for Mercy, the heroine of Virginia Sorensen's *A Little Lower than the Angels*. Published in 1942, this work lacks the epic sweep of Whipple's book, but outshines it in its lyricism and depth of expression. Like Whipple, Sorensen tells her chapter of Mormon history (in this case, the settlement of and expulsion from Nauvoo) through the eyes of a female protagonist (Mercy), whose spiritual struggle with plural marriage is an only slightly muted counterpart to the harrowing hardship, persecution, and brutality around her. There is just no getting around the fact that the public's fascination with Mormonism has been predominantly a prurient obsession with this strange institution. And though Sorensen, like Whipple, addresses this consumer passion as readily as any author of an anti-Mormon bodice-ripper, at least she is more attuned to the emotional anguish than to the sexual dynamics of plural marriage. And few have plumbed those emotional depths with her subtlety or understated pathos. "The one Simon," Mercy calls her beloved husband, with ironic foreboding.[26] And in her guileless meditation on the beauty of monogamous love, we see into the heart of plurality's awful cost: "And it was something that belonged to you alone, knowing so much of one man and saying to yourself at meeting or during a polka or anywhere, looking at him: 'He is mine and I know him as nobody else knows him.'"[27] The consequent agony that the sacred betrayal of such oneness entails is almost too great to be borne by the first wife alone. The sense of spillover is captured when the young Jarvie is an accidental witness to an intimate encounter between his father and his father's secret plural wife. "It was horrible, horrible, it was unbearable, more than a human being could bear in his ears or in his eyes or in his brain or in this world, hearing her laugh and talk like that to Father."[28]

Polygamy was a principle officially practiced for less than a quarter of the church's past. Its manifestations were largely regional and historically delimited. Sorensen's portrayal of the Mormon experience encompasses principles equally vexing, while more universal and timeless, that continue to foster cultural tensions in the faith today. One of these is the yearning for transcendence that collides with a religion of pragmatism and materialism. As great as Mercy's felt need for monogamous love, readers soon learn, is her hunger for manifestations of the sacred in a world saturated in the religious. "Put your religion in everything," the Prophet counsels one of his supporters, "put it in every hour of the day. There is no place where religion does not belong."[29] Such language evokes the outlook of Romanticism, with its glorification of the commonplace, William Blake's "world in a grain of sand and heaven in a wildflower." But, as we have seen, by collapsing the sacred and the profane, we may illuminate the world with divine light, but we also run the risk of contaminating heaven with earthly shadows. Time and again, trying to particularize the ineffable can turn the transcendent into the banal:

> Mercy had heard many problems about heaven discussed weightily as though being of great immediate importance. If one man will rule over all his posterity, as God rules over us, what posterity will his sons have to rule over? . . . If a woman's children belong to the first husband, . . . what of the second husband who is loved with another and superior love and is flesh-father to those children? It was fascinating to consider eternity a practical problem—it had endless possibilities.[30]

But such intrusions of worldly paradigms and problems into the domain of the sacred may be a flirtation with blasphemy. As Eliza asks Mercy, "did—did you ever try to imagine God was so close you could touch Him with your hands?" And Mercy replies, "Yes. I think I did. Sometimes I've thought I had Him right in my arms and He was Simon and Simon was Him. There wasn't any difference."[31] Such misplaced adoration was not what the pious Eliza had in mind. Perhaps, we are left to infer, only burning bushes can tolerate such proximity to unmasked glory without becoming consumed, on the one hand, or too familiar, on the other.

And indeed, Mercy initially convinces herself that a romanticized, natural religion is the solution to a Mormon spirituality that can veer toward the pedestrian. "She would always be listening for Pan while she prayed to the angels."[32] So it is that even as she complies with the ritual of baptism, she watches a mother comfort her baby and wonders, "if the mother came, as Mercy had, to receive the badge of belief, what was it that could add an iota of divinity to her as she stood here comforting her child in the wind?"[33] Still, she can't help but scan the heavens hopefully as she is confirmed upon the bank after emerging from the water. But "when she looked up, she saw how mottled the sky was, unchanged, full of disgruntled wind. But there was not a white dove—not even a pigeon— not a bird of any kind in the sky."[34]

The insistent hunger for transcendence, mystery, and ineffability takes allegorical form in this novel with the tale of the Darling Lady. This mysterious figure is known to the community only as an unembodied voice making nighttime visitations to comfort fretsome infants and sick children. Like a soft-spoken paraclete, her ministry becomes the sacred mystery that animates and enlivens the neighborhood, even as it unifies it in a bond of shared wonder. "It had been a pretty legend," Mercy notes, "and a service of love to fill lonely nights with."[35] It is not that mystification obscures a truth too terrible to confront, Sorensen seems to imply. It is rather that some hint of otherworldliness is essential as a promise of self-transcendence, growth, and beauty beyond the narrow circle of present experience. "Lift not the painted veil," the poet Shelley warned, which provides "a splendour among shadows, a bright blot upon this gloomy scene."[36]

Mercy's sister-wife, the shrewish and unimaginative Charlot, an embodiment of mirthless pioneer pragmatism and Mormon monism, doesn't hesitate to lift painted veils. She unmasks the hapless angel of mercy, and sends her packing: "You go on home and mind your own business! The idea, coming around like that this time of night yelling in folks' windows!" So much for mystery and transcendence. But Mercy counts the cost: "Because it was here, only a little while ago, the legend had been destroyed and the fairy godmother stripped of her mystery." And now she "kept thinking of the boy who lost the fairies because he went a-peeping. There is a penalty for curiosity—loss of the legend, loss of the fairies themselves."[37] That night, Melissa Vermazon, the Darling Lady, tumbles over a cliff to her death. Mormonism too teeters at the precipice, flirting with banality in its humanization of God and its sacralizing of the commonplace.

The satisfactions of certainty, Mormonism seems to suggest, can adequately substitute for the thrilling abyss of mystery. But that makes the pressures all the more intense for those who lack the certitudes of testimony. Like Cory, Mercy never feels the fires of faith in her own heart; she nourishes her private doubts and feels spiritually alienated from her own people—and her own husband— as a result. "The[se] people are too flat and patient," she says by way of self-justification, "taking things the way they do and believing them."[38] Still, her inability to believe is a source of both pain and shame. When her child lies dying of fever, the Prophet comes and blesses him. Then he advises Mercy as to the appropriate remedy to be used "when faith is lacking." While she spends a frantic night in the woods procuring the right tree bark, her son rises from his bed, healed and sound. When she collapses, weeping in fatigue, it is unclear if her tears are of relief or disgrace.

Incredulous at her father's capacity for belief, Mercy had asked enviously as a child, " 'But you believe it, Father, you really do?' 'I believe all I can, Mercy girl, all I can. Everywhere I go I'm looking for more good things to believe. Even if it's the be-all and the end-all here, then we'd better keep busy believing good things. Hadn't we?' "[39] Still, it is clear that such steady certainty, or sanguine acquiescence to the unknown, precludes a kind of restless yearning, anxious struggle, and animating curiosity that exists across the divide from the orthodox Mormon personality. " 'Who then lacked faith?,' Mercy asks herself. . . . *Mercy Baker, she was always one to wonder.* One of the neighbors had even told that to Simon just before he married her. *Mercy Baker has always been one to wonder.*"[40]

Mercy's doubts nourished in secret, her resistance to polygamy, and her yearning for sublimity—all mark her as independent, different, alienated from her own people. And in yet another gesture toward Mormon paradox, Sorensen makes such alienation a general, rather than individual, consequence of LDS history and theology. The irony is that a gospel of universal brotherhood, rooted in a commission to proselytize the world, is so marked on every hand by borders, boundaries, and radical difference. Mercy notes this existential isolation and reacts with a powerful nostalgia for connectedness, in an early passage of remarkable poignancy:

> [A]s it rose higher, it paled, and presently was the moon she knew. There, that was better. After all, the moon had no right to be different anywhere. Even if a woman came west with her family, looking for home, and everything else changed, the land and the people and the talk even, and living grew to be an intense and difficult thing, she should still be able to look up and see the moon the same.[41]

Like the heroine whose life she chronicles, Sorensen's work maintains a fragile dialectic, trying to skirt the perils of complacency toward one's own culture, on the one hand, and repudiation of a larger social and cultural identity, on the other, fully at home in neither realm. Though acclaimed by critics like Clifton Fadiman and Bernard DeVoto and praised in the *New York Times*, the *Nation*, and elsewhere, *A Little Lower than the Angels* was condemned by LDS leaders for precisely the same attributes that the press lauded. "Poignantly human," opined *Newsweek*'s critic; Joseph and the other characters were portrayed as too "ordinary," complained LDS apostle John A. Widtsoe in a church editorial.[42] Without official commendation, Utah sales lagged. And the larger public was not yet ready to accord Mormon writers more than short-lived attention and passing glimpses into the peculiar past and present they offered.

Critically acclaimed treatments of Mormonism by these celebrated authors should have come as a welcome development to the Latter-day Saints. After Twain's scattered barbs about Mormon women and chloroform scripture, Conan Doyle's depictions of murderous "avenging angels," and Zane Grey's "harems of the elders," not to mention scores of more brutal caricatures at the hands of hack writers, these serious novels were an aesthetic and public relations leap forward. But from the perspective of the Mormon faithful and their leaders, these depictions, however skillful or even sympathetic, still exploited the public's fascination with the religion's peculiarities at a time when the church was fully prepared to enter the mainstream as bona fide American. It is questionable whether Whipple, Fisher, Sorensen, and others of what has come to be called Mormon literature's Lost Generation[43] would have achieved even their passing popularity if they had not grounded so much dramatic tension on the harrowing and demeaning dimensions of polygamy and the controversial career of Joseph Smith himself.

Of course, Lost Generation writers could find the humor in Mormon culture as well. Samuel Taylor published in 1948 *Heaven Knows Why*, written in the familiar Hollywood mode of the angel who is allowed to return to earth to encourage a rascally descendant to change his ways. One way for Mormons to treat of angels and other anomalies in their art is with a touch of the facetious. Taylor's gentle self-mockery is in part preemptive—best to domesticate the miraculous by just acknowledging its absurdity. After all, Mormons never said the story of resurrected prophet/warriors giving magical "interpreters" and gold plates to young farm boys isn't outlandish—just that it's true. In addition, humor allows Taylor to address the conspicuous decline of public revelation in the Brigham Young years and beyond—something seldom done. In explaining his skepticism about Clarence-the-angel types, a Utah bishop explains: "After Joseph passed on, Brigham Young got up and told people there'd been too many visitations and he figured he could get along a spell on what was stored up."[44]

But in a church whose entire raison d'être is the reality and continued presence of those phenomena, the bishop's flight from the marvelous is just wishful thinking. As the young Jackson insists, to explain a spate of epiphanies, "Maybe we're running short again." The problem that the bishop correctly foresaw, of course, is that in a church that still insists on dialogic revelation and angelic visitations, and that claims perfect continuity with the miraculous dispensation

Joseph ushered in, the line between the sacred and the banal can so easily disappear entirely. Historical distance and scarcity guarantee at least the veneer of decorum. But in the good bishop's ward:

> Take Sister Ormand. . . . Hear her tell it, God Almighty don't have nothing more to do, nothing else on His mind, than to supply her with messengers from heaven to tell her she'd better wear her rubbers because it's going to rain, or to show her where she put down her glasses, or to give her a new block design for a quilt. Just last Fast Sunday she got up and told how the Lord had prompted her to straighten up the front room, and how it wasn't five minutes later that the ward teachers arrived.[45]

Some Latter-day Saints reading this would be waiting for the punch line.

In retrospect, the literature of the Lost Generation was clearly a transitional body of work, in which Mormon writers of real stature first introduced Mormon subject matter into serious literature that deserved—and received—national attention. Perhaps unfortunately, it appeared in a decade marked in Mormonism by a sense of Fawn Brodie's colossal disloyalty in publishing her psychobiography of Joseph Smith (*No Man Knows My History*, 1945), and Utah audiences were more than usually suspicious of attempts to naturalize or humanize the pioneer past. So just as the home literature movement was impeded by obsessive concern with didacticism, the generation of Whipple and Fisher and Sorensen was, at least in the eyes of their Mormon critics, too compliant with the voices of criticism and cynicism to produce an art fully worthy of its subject.

A generation later, the call for a Mormon literature would be renewed, as if to redirect the considerable talent that had emerged in the previous decades and merge it with a more orthodox sensibility, resulting in what LDS critic Eugene England calls the era of "faithful realism." By 1974, Richard Cracroft and Neal Lambert were ready to publish their anthology of Mormon literature, *A Believing People*. The collection attempts to make "a beginning in identifying [the Mormon] cultural heritage"[46] that evolved from the production of new scripture like the Book of Mormon, and from subsequent literary works of human rather than heavenly inspiration and origin. Their project brought within two covers a rich array of journal writing, biography, and history, as well as samples of LDS poetry and fiction—and represented a compelling case for an amorphous but distinctive tradition that ranged, in their words, from Panglossian simple-mindedness to the dignified and profound, but all "strikingly at odds with the humanistic existentialism of modern literary fashion."[47] It was an important step that moved significantly forward the question: is there a Mormon (literary) art?

The anthology emerged at a time when Mormon literature was experiencing a burst of productive energy. The following year, the same authors found that instead of combining works in a dozen genres written over a century and a half to produce a respectable sampling, they were able to produce another volume comprising only the best fiction to appear in the previous dozen years (*Twenty-two Young Mormon Writers*). And the year after that, 1976, influential apostle Boyd K. Packer delivered a stirring charge to pick up the baton that Orson Whitney's generation had carried forth three-quarters of a century earlier. Packer's address was at the same time a lament over past mediocrity, a warning against worldly compromise, and a summons to greatness. First delivered to the BYU community, his remarks were reprinted, widely discussed, and influential.[48] When the church reprinted a similarly themed talk by beloved church prophet Spencer W. Kimball the next year, it was clear that the leadership was lending both support and urgency to Mormon aesthetic achievement with an intensity not before seen by the generation then living.

"It was following the historic addresses of Packer and Kimball," noted the astute literary scholar and Mormon critic Eugene England, that there occurred "the first major blossoming of a mature Mormon literature."[49] Other events confirmed his judgment. In 1976, in the months between the appeals by Packer and Kimball, a group of scholars created the Association for Mormon Letters, which promotes the reading and writing of Mormon literature. (Today, it is a thriving organization with over 350 members.) *Dialogue: A Journal of Mormon Thought* had been publishing, in addition to free-thinking essays and revisionist historical research, original fiction and poetry since 1966 (as had the similarly toned *Sunstone* beginning in 1974). Over the next two decades, a rich outpouring of work was sampled in two more anthologies of Mormon fiction, *Greening Wheat: Fifteen Mormon Short Stories* (Levi Peterson, ed., 1983) and *Bright Angels and Familiars: Mormon Short Stories* (Eugene England, ed., 1992), and one of poetry (*Harvest: Contemporary Mormon Poems*, ed. Eugene England and Dennis Clark, 1989).

POETRY

While Virginia Sorensen and Maurine Whipple were producing fiction of national notice, May Swenson was making her mark as the most prominent poet to emerge in Mormonism. "One of our few unquestionably major poets," American poet and critic John Hollander calls her.[50] She would eventually publish eleven volumes of poetry, win a MacArthur fellowship, and serve as chancellor for the

Academy of American Poets. Still, she suffered much the same fate as the Lost Generation writers, being more appreciated outside her culture than within. "May Swenson is better known in New York and Paris than she is in Utah," remarks one literary scholar.[51] Raised a Mormon, she abandoned the faith of her parents, but remained to some extent immersed in its cultural vocabulary, and her self-exile from the church could at times ironically mirror the Mormon ambiguity about belonging and alienation. "As a Mormon poet in exile," writes one critic, "Swenson both laments the loss of home and celebrates freedom from it."[52]

In "My Name Was Called," Swenson addresses the divide between her youthful religion with its "redundant prayer" and her pinnacle of worldly fame with its attendant honors. Strikingly, the disjunction is bridged by a common thread: the nervousness attendant upon her reception of an honorary degree and the childlike fear she recalls as an eight-year-old about to enter baptismal waters. The covenantal significance of the latter is swallowed up in girlish preoccupation with "suggestively wet" clothes and "deafening bubbles." In the former instance, "greatest honor" succumbs to the "freshest horror" of self-awareness, as her "spotted hand" and "old pouched lashless eyes" loom large onscreen. Tempting as it is to read the poem as a leveling of the sacred into the banal, finding only self-conscious anxiety as the common denominator in sacred ritual and receipt of worldly laurels, other hints suggest that both moments actually foreshadow a third and greater meaning: "I didn't know what would be / done, in the white dress or in the black, / when my name was called," the poem ends. Its rootedness in religious imagery, the signs of extreme age, a last fleeting allusion to "the truth of my future face,"[53] the dichotomous colors of baptismal white and institutional black amplify the intuitive significance of the title as referring to the soul's ultimate disposition when one's name is called.

Swenson's fame and talent notwithstanding, Mormons had to look elsewhere if they were to pursue a program of faithful realism in poetry. They found a role model in Clinton F. Larson. The year 1967 saw the publication of the first collection of poetry by Larson, who is coming to be recognized as the founder of a genuine Mormon poetic tradition, skirting both overt evangelizing and modern cynicism. "It does not show art filling a religious purpose, but shows . . . religion succeeding in an esthetic way," one critic writes.[54] An example is his understated paean to gentle mercy, "Granddaughter":

> Next to tears for the supposed naughtiness
> Of tipping oatmeal from her pastel bowl
> And spilling milk under our haughtiness,
> She displays the repentance of her soul

Over there. Her gaze is tenuous with sorrow
As she looks at the world, hoping for the best,
Arms folded to gather herself for the harrow
Of scolding. "Amen," she says in a tentative test
Of our love, grace over, but willing to pray.
I saw that the lip of her tray had tipped her bowl,
She not knowing why her oatmeal in disarray
Was so, but feeling the sackcloth of her role.
And there stand I as well with her as anywhere,
Marveling how to keep some order at hand,
Displaying my hope glossily to keep fair
Days of charity flowing like hourglass sand.[55]

While much of Larson's poetry is not self-consciously, or readily identifiable as, Mormon, much of it is. Like the regional painters of 1930s and 1940s Utah, Larson and his contemporaries often use their creative vision to capture their sense of place rather than belief—or they find that geography, in some fundamental sense, *is* identity.

He captures both the sanctity of suffering and an unabashedly heroic sense of self-exile in his poignant "A Letter from Israel Whiton, 1851." After the death of his wife, a casualty of the exodus, the pioneer Whiton commits an undeliverable missive to the wind:

But Eliza is still as I write, and I must only
Listen. I, Israel Whiton of the Salt Lake Valley,
Write this letter to you, Mother, from the canyons
And the butte above my land; it is a leaf
From the spring before we came, as both you and Eliza
Know, unanswerable except in the signs that come,
That I cannot seek. So I give it to the wind
From the tips of piñons or the butte, and it lifts
Away, and I try to see it as it diminishes
Away, then vanishing though I know it is there,
As you know better than I, Mother . . . And it will rise
Beyond the golden seal and tough the white hand
In the cirri pluming the Oquirrh crest west
Over the sunset, and it is as if I take a veil
Full in my hand as I write, as if to let it yield
To the days consecrated to the journey west

That holds me aloof from all I have ever known,
The East and the cities of my common being,
As I am here, in Zion, wondering about you
Who cannot respond except in the barest hints
Of being that lift over me and show me the way
To yield and rise into the Kingdom, the sky
And the land like the white silver spirit
That we know but is fathomless before us
And indefinite as the planes of God rising
Into the sun.[56]

Following Larson's lead in the sixties and seventies were BYU colleagues Edward L. Hart, Marden J. Clark, and John S. Harris. Most popular of that generation was Carol Lynn Pearson, and one of the most talented, Emma Lou Thayne. The most widely read LDS poet in the late twentieth century, Carol Lynn Pearson's appeal is largely a result of her populist style (over a quarter-million copies of her poetry books are in print). "Poetry should clarify, not obscure life,"[57] she has said, and her poetry reflects in simple, concise terms the essential hallmarks of LDS belief and sensibility, as in "The Eleventh Hour":

Had I been born
To other centuries—
How pleasant
To stretch
In the sun
And choose from
All life's
Possibilities
This one,
Or that.
To prove the
Earth is round,
Or tame the ocean,
To write a dictionary
Or expound
On Shakespeare's
Subtle irony.
But these are
Daytime jobs

> And,
> As I was born
> To time's
> Saturday night
> My ordained task
> Is to kindle
> The Sabbath light.[58]

Like Emily Dickinson, who is so clearly her inspiration, Pearson's conciseness is itself one of her hallmarks, as in this succinct stanza:

> Think:
> Worlds from now
> What might we be?—
> We,
> Who are seed
> Of Deity.[59]

Dale Fletcher, an appreciative Mormon critic, predicted early on:

Mormons will love this poetry and the reason it is different from the poetry of the world and the reason it is Mormon Art and the reason it is desperately cogent for our world right now—because the key of knowledge is not just a truth, nor just another truth, but the critical truth for us and the answer to the philosophical, political, social, and personal dilemma of our times.[60]

Fortunately, the aggressive certainty that pervades such an appraisal does not pervade the poetry itself. Fletcher is correct that Pearson's poetry, like most Mormon poetry, answers questions rather than explores problems. But Pearson gets away with it, because her Dickinsonian wit undermines smugness, her brevity precludes ponderous ostentation, and her style is much more Mormon pop than probing theology (her poems have appeared in such popular venues as *Chicken Soup for the Soul* and Ann Landers's columns).

One poet who has been likened to May Swenson is Emma Lou Thayne. Perhaps the greatest of the living poets writing firmly within (but not solely within) an LDS framework, Thayne takes the traditional tension between certitude and searching, the angst of the closet doubter and divided Mormon self to a higher level of resolution than may have been possible in the still-early days of mid-twentieth-century Mormonism. Like a number of Saints who are unwilling or unable to bring the burden of angels and other anomalies into the intellectual arenas of the twenty-first century, Thayne suggests that wholeness and healing may be found in cultural solidarity, rather than doctrinal conformity, in heritage rather than precepts. In "Sunday School Picture," for example, she finds hints even in her childhood that duplicate photographs of her seven-year-old self "went on becoming two people," the rupture flashing again into dangerous potentiality when she resists

> reciting
> a two-and-a-half minute ordeal
> that my mother knew I knew on Why I Want
> To Be Baptized,
>   which I didn't.

Only now, upon sober reflection, does she discern that the coherence of her life and identity derive from a history in a community. And the tranquil gathering into herself is the culmination of a chain of recollections that ties her to that community, with threads as ineffable but as certain as the pervasive, penetrating tones of a church organ:

> Sometimes I look
> at that thousand-peopled picture when I'm sorting
> things and marvel a lot, and even otherwise, I find
> myself saying, Highland Park Ward, my roller skates
> still rattle down your dented driveway, and
> my absent waiting is sometimes done against
> the brown banisters below the Garden of Gethsemane
> in your raised entry,
>   and mostly, your organ
> churns under its outside loft across the filled
> fields where our short-cuts are long buried
> in old foundations,
>   and like the green-grained oak
> of your chapel doors, it closes with gentle right
> my separateness and gathers my wandering
> double selves together.[61]

Thayne can also be far more direct in her treatment of the tension between searching and certitude, as in the brief "Heretic":

Indulge
    my searching
    my unsteady voice:
You share
    the blame;
    it's You
        who gave me
        choice.[62]

This theme runs persistently through so many of her works that it constitutes a leitmotif of vacillation between the wonder of faith and the loneliness of doubt. "Often exiled in doubts / inflamed by dogma's small discipleship," she poignantly laments.[63] But elsewhere she marvels at a faith that invades her almost like irresistible grace, bringing more tension than resolution. "I don't know why I know," she writes:

believing goes so often skittering
From those who need and grasp the most;
Then what incredible (as always) Grace
Makes me its doubtful, easy host?[64]

Bruce W. Jorgensen finds in the ballad form an apt vehicle for rendering sacred epiphany as old-time religion, collapsing the sacred into the comfortable and familiar like an African-American spiritual in "The Light Come Down":

Just a dusty country boy
Praying in the trees,
Knocked out flat and speechless,
Again up on his knees
    And the light come down,
    Lord, the light come down.

Sharper than suns he sweated in,
It slapped that April mud,
It withered the one that threatened him
And stunned him where he stood.
    Yes the light come down,
    Lord, it did come down.

And he was just fourteen
Mixed up, and read your book
And took you at your word
And asked—and Lord,
  You let the light come down,
  O Lord, a comin down.

Old Adam had a farmer's son
And Abraham did too—
All made of mud but you made em good
And brought em home to you,
  For the light come down,
  It always did come down.

So Lord look down on country boys
That stink and puzzle and pray,
And strike the light to blind their sight
And make their night your day.
  O let the light come down,
  Yes, bring the light on down.

And bless you, Lord, for country boys,
Each hungry mother's son
Treading the furrow his father plowed
Just like your single son
  When you and him come down,
  When you the light come down.[65]

In more recent years, a newer generation of LDS poets is taking the contemporary equivalent of home literature in fruitful contemporary directions. Lance Larsen manages a wonderful blend of allegory, Old Testament resonances, and suggestive parallels with young boys as purveyors of light. The most striking feature of this poem is the playfulness with which the disjunction between the era of bloodied lintels and the world of door-to-door salesmen is made to disappear; a modern boy as bringer of illumination becomes, suddenly, near description rather than remote allegory, as once again the Mormon mythos is shorn of sacred distance:

Light

A boy comes selling light,
no badges or letters of introduction,

just a paper sack of no-name bulbs
and a story about wanting to visit
his grandfather in Escondido. All this
on a morning so yellow that apricot buds,
tight as fists, threaten to unsmile.
But I believe him—for two dollars
I get a variable wattage and a sweepstake
chance at a telescope. And safety.
I wrap my bulb in cashmere and lock it away.
For now I'll use G.E. bulbs.
But later, on a night when the moon
wears its blood in a smile
and the angels of light have been coffined
and the earth reels through the air
on the back of a drunken mule,
I'll replace the bulb on the porch.
Then from my front room, I'll watch,
like any patient child of the covenant,
for the destroying angel to pass me by.[66]

Susan Howe continues the tradition of pioneer anthems, this time sung from an airliner:

Caught here, in an arc
Between the sea coast where your ocean
Voyage left you, and the mountains
Where you walked to make your home.[67]

The speed and ease highlight the hardships of laborious treks, but also diminish the present world, with its pat technologies and characters whose esteem for past heroes always threatens to reveal itself as nostalgia for the self-definition of hardship, exile, and difference.

Howe's "Things in the Night Sky" is like myriad other poems that transform a view of the heavens into a rhapsody of yearning, introspection, and perspectival realignment. Only Howe's musings are grounded in a theology that here glides easily into poetry:

We are surrounded by ancient light
We can't see, come millions of years

Through space we can't recite.
When things in the night sky
Impose themselves on us, imprint
Their being into our slim hearts,
We might approach our work of becoming.
Sight will exceed density,
And we'll rise beyond Earth,
Beyond our own names,
Receiving infinite differences,
Dark centers of bright stars.[68]

SHORT FICTION

In the second half of the twentieth century, short fiction has been the most fertile ground plowed by Mormon writers. In this realm, Donald Marshall, Douglas Thayer, and Levi Peterson probe the foibles and ironies of Mormon culture with deft characterizations and abundant wit. A far cry from the home literature meant to inspire and edify, but also largely avoiding focus on the historical peculiarities of nineteenth-century Mormonism, these writers demonstrate the seriousness of intent of the Lost Generation, but rely mostly upon humor and irony to interrogate affectionately their own culture's paradoxes.

Foremost among this group is Levi S. Peterson, whom England calls the Mormon Flannery O'Connor and who is one of the first Mormon short story writers to win national recognition. In his "Christianizing of Coburn Heights," Peterson tackles the familiar problem of Mormon do-goodism, which can too easily turn the call to human compassion—and the human subject in particular—into a "project," one that eclipses the humanity of the Samaritan and the wounded traveler alike. The outrageously disruptive Rendella Kranpitz is an embarrassment to the affluent Coburn Heights Stake, and a blot on its record of a uniformly staid, respectable Mormon lifestyle. The church musters its forces: stake and ward leaders together with local members plan, correlate their efforts, and deploy their forces, but to no avail. Fiercely independent, nonconformist, and perversely contrary, Rendella successfully resists their combined efforts to make her respectable. Her response to their collective investment in her spiritual well-being is a mound of human excrement served up on a saucer and left on the doorstep of the president, in a dark parody of the phantom doorstep gifts of baked goods so common in Mormon culture. The conclusion leaves the reader perfectly poised between exasperation with her crude recalcitrance and guilty admiration for her resistance to the Mormon mold. It is the classic LDS dilemma: how to salvage individualism and authenticity in a culture supersaturated with norms, programs, commandments, and expectations. Rendella epitomizes the dilemma but hardly incarnates a comfortable solution.

The principle of eternal progression, with its culture of perfectionism, its emphasis on personal agency, and its celebration of choice and accountability, does not preclude a theology of grace. After all, "[i]t is by grace that we are saved," wrote Nephi, "after all we can do" (2 Nephi 25:23). But in between the spiritual certainties of testimony, and personal responsibility for working out one's salvation, grace does not always know where to fit in. The resulting tensions can pit artless spontaneity against programmed, systematic progress; wholesale submission of self against absolute self-sufficiency. Ironically, then, individuality can be threatened or even subsumed by those very structures elaborated to foster and celebrate personal potential.

While Mormons are not full-blown Pelagians, grace has a hard time finding a place in a system where the sense of orderly, systematic, checklist progress pervades all aspects of Mormon life. Sanctification, or the process of becoming saved and partaking of the "divine nature," is doctrinally predicated on Christ's atonement, which makes remission of sins—and thus any kind of progress at all—possible to begin with. But nothing could be further than Mormonism from the Protestant experience of salvation as a finite moment of transformation. Mormon religious culture is characterized by a pervasively systematic monitoring of and reification of progress. Scouting is the official young men's program of the church—meaning that planned progress through ranks is interwoven with religious training. Boys "progress" through the priesthood offices from deacon to priest. Young women had a "pursuit of excellence" program, later transformed into a "personal progress" program. Home and visiting teaching responsibilities are tracked and recorded, temple admission interviews cover a checklist of questions, and the consequent temple recommendation gives tangible evidence of renewable worthiness. Although priesthood callings are not ranks, a hierarchy that proceeds from local bishop to stake president to area authority to seventy to apostle to the office of prophet and president, staffed almost entirely by lay members, can create a sense that all men progress through church offices as well. Mormon theology reinforces belief in an ordered heaven, divided into three tiers, progress through which is depicted in Mormon temple rituals. The ultimate consummation of a life of such strenuous effort is the devoutly anticipated "calling and election made sure," wherein the individual's salvation is explicitly assured. Even then, the deeply entrenched doctrine of eternal progression suggests that dynamic growth and development are never ending.

Douglas Thayer's powerful story "Under the Cottonwoods" depicts the burden of, and then the transcendence of, such acculturation in the case of a young man named Paul. As a boy, his fixation on timely progress is little removed from neurosis:

> He had a calendar in his room, a clock, wore a watch, became aware of seconds, minutes, hours, days, weeks, months. . . . There was so much to do, so little time to do it in. . . . He had to be able to look back on a day and see what he had done with twenty-four hours, how he had used them. . . . And he had a time chart on his wall, put little checks in the squares, made a new chart each month, saved the old charts in a pile because they showed what he had done, were another way of measuring time.[69]

A problem emerges as he realizes, as a young man:

> [H]e couldn't remember being a boy. He had graduated from Provo High School, filled a mission for the church, been in the army, gotten married, graduated from B.Y.U. and then dental school, finished an orthodontics residency and been in practice one year. He would build a house, a clinic of his own, . . . have three or four more children, and he would probably move up from second counselor to bishop in the Palo Alto Ward, be in the high council, maybe be stake president in ten years. He had done and would do all of those things he was expected to, but his whole life seemed so ordered, predetermined, rushed, tense. At times he felt like a robot, had little sense of controlling his own life, being individual.[70]

For outsiders, Mormon talk about humans becoming deities sounds foolish or presumptuous. "The Mormons: Just ordinary people trying to become Gods," jokes one Mormon wag. The jest is actually a salutary bridge between the pretentiousness of the aspiration and the realism of most Mormons: few take themselves so seriously as to make deification a daily goal. Still, the burdens of such actual, however muted, potential can weigh heavily. The weight of his father's hand on Paul's shoulder is but a metaphor for the onerous task that oppresses him: "He wanted to do all and be all of those things his parents wanted of him, wanted the perfection, Godhood, his mother talked about, would sacrifice anything for her belief in that, even himself."[71]

Under the cottonwoods, in a beloved swimming hole, he spends an evening cavorting in the water with his father. Raucous splashing alternates with stretches of silence, and the father's memories of youthful fun only heighten the boy's

sense of his own boyhood freedom—never fully realized or felt. He returns to
the hole often, to fish and to swim. Now a married adult, he returns home, and
plans a day of fishing with his father and brother. But this time, he envisions a
crucial difference in the coming sport—one that heralds either transcendence or
its unrealized dream:

> Mark and his father would kill the trout that they caught, clean them, leave
> the entrails on the shore for the patrolling gulls the next morning. But he
> wouldn't. After he had fought a trout, felt the movement and pull, the heavy
> pulse coming up through the line and rod into his hand and arm, seen it in
> front of him in the water, he would free it. He would hold the rainbow in the
> net to see it shining rose-silver, pull the hook from the lip, then release it, see
> the trout hover then flash back into the deep water, vanish.[72]

That Thayer would have Paul plan, rather than enact, this vicarious celebration
of a freedom he never knew, typifies one difference of Thayer's generation from
the Lost Generation. Thayer and his peers are uncertain rather than triumphant
about Mormonism's potential to resolve the paradoxes that lie at its heart.

In a spirit similar to Thayer's, Kevin Cassity writes in "The Age-Old Problem of Who" of a well-intentioned youth whose gospel knowledge is rooted in
"church books and quote books," and whose systematic endeavors toward righteousness include shunning television and proselytizing coworkers. As a product of an LDS culture that correlates, packages, and standardizes the Imitatio
Christi, he finds himself utterly unequipped to fathom the world of a gentle-
souled boy who encountered Jesus outside institutionalized religion, who follows
the voice of a Spirit that "bloweth where it listeth." (No small irony, this, that a
vague echo of Joseph Smith's character is too alien to assimilate into Peter's LDS
universe.) Peter is "caught off guard" by a spirituality that so challenges the
regimentation of his own, but the "slowly shifting earth beneath his feet" is not a
simple dig at Mormon provincialism. In Peter's openness to new possibilities,
Cassity may be chiding as hindrance rather than as insuperable blindness the
consequences of Mormon certainty and corporate-mindedness. In this story of
crisis and awakening, Peter begins to know that sanctification is not a twelve-
step program, that the operations of the Spirit confine themselves to no manual. Even amid the cultural weight of lock-step programming, he suggests, the
maverick spirituality and initiative embodied by Joseph Smith may yet be re-
discovered.[73]

Of course, any culture that develops in remote isolation and in opposition to a
dominant secular world is, almost by definition, prey to a quaint provincialism.

This cultural rather than religious shelteredness is gently probed in Donald Marshall's "The Week-End." At last untethered from a life of filial servitude by her mother's death, Thalia is still reluctant to defy the literal meaning of the dying woman's last injunction: "You've always been good, Thalia. Stay—."[74] Uncertain whether the command was to remain faithful or remain in the small Mormon town of Ephraim, Thalia's gesture of independence can extend no further than a self-indulgent—but brief—escape to southern California. Her fantasy weekend in a Carmel-by-the-Sea house is only slightly tainted by learning that the street name is Lincoln rather than "Monte Verde, Camino Real, Casanova." Splurging meager funds on a jar of marinated artichoke hearts, "she was disappointed that she did not particularly like them but contented herself with the knowledge that there were people back in Ephraim who did not even know whether they liked them or not."[75] Thalia's limited self-discovery, like the journey of Mormonism itself to establish an autonomous culture in blithe indifference to, as much as in studied defiance of, mainstream Babylon, oscillates uncertainly between the merely pathetic and the quietly heroic.

The Lost Generation literature frequently explored—often from a woman's point of view—the agonies and tensions of plural marriage. Polygamy is a historical relic for Latter-day Saints, but patriarchy is not. In recent generations, the enduring dilemma of gender roles that must accommodate both this entrenched patriarchy and women's dignity and equality is a defining feature of Mormon modernity. In "Sayso or Sense," Eileen Kump chooses the fertile and resonant subject of a woman whose dream house is being constructed jointly by her husband and father-in-law. Bit by bit, day by day, every carefully conceived and devoutly desired embodiment of feminine domesticity is systematically and brutally expunged from the ongoing construction by the tyrannical, unyielding decrees of male authority. At the point of frustrated breakdown, Amy has a dream that proves her salvation:

> God was conducting priesthood meeting and Grandpa and Israel and the carpenter were on the front row, hanging on every word. God said when they came to earth, men could have the choice—sayso or sense—but they couldn't have both because that wouldn't be fair to the women. He called a vote, and Grandpa's hand shot up for sayso before God had finished speaking. Amy awoke, sure the choice had been unanimous.[76]

The humor is, of course, doubly subversive. Not only do women find consolation in the knowledge of their superior good sense; this knowledge itself comes to them as a direct revelation that occurs outside the (male) priesthood channels through which God generally bestows authoritative knowledge upon his Saints. But there is pathos behind the humor, as we are left with a heroine who laments her lost innocence and will forever pine for "that trust that made obedience beautiful."[77]

The problems of religious certainty are only compounded in a modern age that has infinitely more respect for "the spirit which is not too sure that it is right" than for the believer who is. "It is true, isn't it? You know it's true, don't you?" asks a spiritually tortured teenager of her youth advisor in Karen Rosenbaum's "Hit the Frolicking, Rippling Brooks." "I look at her. I can't give her what she wants. 'It works for me,' I say."[78] An honest but miserably inadequate response in the Mormon culture of certainty.

The advisor is married to the perfect Mormon man. He makes casseroles, writes to troubled youth consoling "everythingwillworkoutforthebest" letters, and will probably die in his Sunday-go-to-meeting shoes, because he is generally to be found wearing them to his every-other-day-of-the-week meetings, which he faithfully and uncomplainingly attends. The only dissonance in their lives is suggested when she replies to an admiring friend's comments that she is her husband's night and day by correcting her: "more like his mid-afternoon."

Collapsing into bed, exhausted from the grueling schedule of that day ironically called the Mormon day of rest, an epiphany threatens to invade her numb life of faithful but soulless routine:

Something is rattling around in the room. A moth I think. I look up. Tiny lights flashing wildly across the ceiling. It last[s] forever, maybe three minutes. In a Flannery O'Connor short story it would be a symbol of the Holy Ghost. In a Mickey-like [wife] it might be a terrifying suggestion of a heavenly visitation. I yawn. The firefly is gone. I roll over, nuzzle into Ben's back, and call it a Sunday.[79]

A yawn in the face of transcendent possibilities is a defeat of sorts, a bitter resignation. Modern Christians have had two millennia to accustom themselves to the exile of the miraculous. Mormons have had less than two centuries. Hence the guilt and the uneasy accommodation to a world—or a religion—in which miracle is merely metaphor. "Earth is crammed with heaven," wrote Elizabeth Barrett Browning, "and every common bush afire with God. But only he who sees, takes off his shoes; the rest sit round it and pluck blackberries."[80] The poet's appeal to find wonder in the universe is poignant and a sublime resignation to the fact that Moses's burning bush is no more—but it is resignation nonetheless.

Most religions accommodate the sad truth that the days of Pentecost are past. But in a religious culture like the Mormons', where buoyant optimism, living prophets, and the discourse of private revelations, testimony, and spiritual experiences dominate, the pressures to continually reenact the founding epiphanies of the first Prophet make for a culture that is spiritually vibrant but also, at times, quietly polarizing. The social polarities operate on two distinct levels. The young women's advisor who must mask her honest doubt in a culture of certainty typifies a significant rupture at the heart of Mormon life. One need only turn to LDS intellectual culture to see a population vigorously working to carve out a niche for themselves in a church they find increasingly inhospitable to closet doubters and zealous revisionists alike. Liberal journals like *Sunstone* and *Dialogue* reflect even as they exacerbate this cultural divide, by forcing into the open what has hitherto lain dormant and unexposed—except in fiction. The Lost Generation, as we saw, frequently celebrated characters isolated from their peers by nagging doubts. Mormons imbibe and exude the certainty celebrated in their scriptures, one of which stipulates that "to know" the certitudes of the gospel is a gift of the Spirit. They generally neglect to register the subsequent verse, which informs that to some, merely "believing on [the] words" of those who know is itself a heavenly dispensation (D&C 46:13–14).

But writers have belabored a second polarization as well, and that is the isolation of those who know, or are supposed to know, from a larger culture that appears, by contrast, benighted and inferior. The character Paul, in Thayer's "Under the Cottonwoods," feels the cost of chosenness as such a burden. "He became lonely. It was easier not to have too many friends, easier to believe in his own perfection that way."[81]

THE CONTEMPORARY NOVEL

The standard for the contemporary Mormon novel was set by Levi Peterson's *The Backslider* in 1986. Peterson manages to touch on most every facet and foible of Mormon culture, from testimonies tied to Tabernacle acoustics to Three Nephite mythologies that proliferate like fungi. Like so many of Peterson's other characters, Frank Windham is a man consumed by guilt and self-loathing. Angry at God's failure to prevent his girlfriend's engagement to another man, he decides to rebel against his Mormon faith and principles. He is caught up short when his brother unexpectedly plunges into madness and castrates himself. Thinking the tragedy foreshadows God's vengeance on himself, Frank embarks on a course of strict self-reformation. A simple, carnal creature of the flesh, he

equates physical appetites with sin, and asceticism and discipline with righteousness. Frank quickly descends into a perverse parody of the Mormon calculus of
salvation, living out the fallacy of spirituality as self-perfection. Registering good
deeds and ill in a notebook, "it frightened him to see how the marks were
accumulating because he didn't know how to undo them. They were lining up
like pickets in the fences of hell." When he "adds up the good deeds he had
performed during the past week" and compares them to his tally of shortcomings, "his book wouldn't balance."[82]

Frank is a hapless victim to cultural Mormonism's own special version of the
either-or fallacy: faith or works? grace or personal accountability? a sanctified
spirit or a body steeped in satisfactions of the flesh? the sacred or the profane?

When Frank's young Protestant wife prays for him, it is, tellingly and poignantly, to say, "Sweet Jesus, please don't be like Frank thinks you are."[83] And
when Frank finally finds his healing epiphany, it takes the form of collapsing
dualisms so shocking as to flirt with blasphemy:

> The urinal faded from his sight and he saw a stand of scrubby junipers....
> [There] emerged a shiny roan mounted by a rider. The cowboy had a beard
> and he wore boots, ancient chaps, a denim shirt, a creased, sweat-stained
> Stetson. Touching spurs lightly to his mount, he reined toward Frank. Coming
> close, he halted and lifted a hand. It was Jesus, his face as kind as an August
> dawn.
>
> "You're lost," he said.
>
> Ashamed, Frank cast his eyes downward. "I expect I am."
>
> "You are feeling awful bad."
>
> "It's not much of anything."
>
> "It isn't any bother. Hearing your griefs is my business. Go ahead and
> tell me."
>
> The rider pushed back his Stetson and cocked a leg over the saddlehorn....
>
> "My grandmother lost four babies and went crazy in the sandhills," Frank
> said.
>
> "I'm sorry about that."
>
> "My little sister Elizabeth died and my mother can't get over it."
>
> "I know," Jesus said. "Your family is a sad one."
>
> "My dad died when I was ten."
>
> "That's tough," Jesus agreed.
>
> "Also, my brother cut himself off. He took a hunting knife and laid waste
> to his privates. Now he thinks he's a little girl named Alice. This afternoon he

dug himself a pit and sat in it. He said he was waiting for the ladder of Lazarus. He's pure as an angel. He can't sin, no matter what."

"The poor crazy devil."

"The thing I feel worst about is I can't live righteously," Frank said. "I've got a wife I can't leave alone. I make love to her all the time. I'm cunning and devilish about thinking up new ways to do it too. I hate healthy, decent food. I love ham and broiled steaks and pie and ice cream. I wish I had my shiny blue pickup back and my gelding Booger and my boots and jeans and pearlbuttoned shirts. I wish I had my deer rifle back so I could go deer hunting. I wish I would take my wife trout fishing."

Jesus had pulled a sack of Bull Durham from his shirt pocket and was rolling a cigarette. . . .

"I love the world," Frank said. "I love my wife and my little kid that hasn't been born yet and I love a big truck under me and sunrise out over the Escalante breaks and I love the sound of diesels running the pumps in the middle of the night. That's what I love. I hate God."

"Well, I'm sorry to hear that. Myself, I love God."[84]

That Frank loves what he should love, but hates himself for doing so, is testament to his inherent goodness and to the painful and even tragic confusions that paradox can so often inflict on the unreflective. But what is indicated by this vision of a smoking cowboy Jesus is not a simple projection of a desire for cheap grace, embodied in a comfortable God of our own fashioning. When Jesus calls smoking his "little habit," and counsels Frank to "enjoy [his wife] like a husband would who has some good sense," we hear echoes of Joseph Smith's God, the physically embodied God of celestial marriage and dancing in the temple, who insisted that "all things which come of the earth" are given "to please the eye and to gladden the heart; Yea, for food and for raiment, for taste and for smell, to strengthen the body and to enliven the soul" (D&C 59:18–19). The dramatic irony of Frank's misguided guilt is emphatically predicated on the powerful resonance of a vision, not a moral conduct, that needs reconstituting. Significantly, this saving epiphany comes minutes after his wife, who first knew the cowboy Jesus in her own daydreams and taught Frank of his grace, is herself baptized into Frank's faith. As in Dutcher's films, the message here seems to be that the journey to resolve Mormonism's paradoxes may require a detour through traditions that are not so removed from Mormon theology as Mormons have thought. The funniest line of Peterson's novel may have been written therefore more in earnest than in jest: Frank's Lutheran father-in-law is asked at

Marianne's baptism, "'And are you taking the missionary lessons too?' 'No ma'am,' Wesley replied. 'My wife and I consider ourselves sufficiently papered Christians already. Our home is a feeding lot or a breeding farm, if you will, for fine Christian children, which we produce for a variety of churches.'"[85]

A genre unto itself is the Mormon missionary novel. The bildungsroman, the coming-of-age novel or novel of moral awakening, is one of the oldest forms of the novel. In the Mormon faith, the two-year mission is a rite of passage that frames that development in a focused and culturally distinctive way. So it is no surprise that much of contemporary Mormon fiction, like Mormon film, revolves around the missionary experiences of young LDS men. The mission is an inviting focus of dramatic interest because that period represents an intensification of tensions that are common but more diffused in Mormon culture generally. For at the tender age of nineteen, the most emotionally volatile, hormonally charged, and intellectually adventuresome stage of life, young men (and, less frequently, women at twenty-one) are called to be self-assured, inflexible beacons of certainty and conviction. A conversion account, forced by the press of circumstance and cultural pressure is one common outcome. But more interesting are the works that focus not on the pat resolution of spiritual uncertainty, but on the painful working through of the cultural disharmony between a world of black and white and a world of grays, between fixed formulas of mission life and the bewildering abyss of freedom afterward.

Michael Fillerup's *Beyond the River*, one of the best Mormon novels since the mid-1990s, is a poignant masterpiece about a good Mormon boy whose complacency, faith, and self-understanding are shattered by his relationship with Nancy Von Kleinsmid, an eccentric, artsy, intellectual maverick. It is not his beliefs that she assaults, but the mechanization of belief. Hamlet-like, Jon Reeves finds himself paralyzed by the dilemma of affirming individualism in a universe—and a religion—that has all of his parts scripted. "That you believe in your church so deeply," she insists, "I could respect.... But you're just plain afraid not to.... You thought you couldn't fly solo after all."[86] Art is the only pure self-expression, she preaches, and the truest form of moral courage, precisely because it is a solitary leap into the unknown. Jon must find his salvation in art or merge it with his faith:

> If I believed all you claim to believe, I'd be drooling to write about it.... Think of the possibilities! All those beautiful concepts that have become fossilized by centuries of abuse and overuse that now exist only as provender for scheming preachers—why, you could breathe life into those words! You could give them flesh and blood, bodies, souls. You could resurrect them. Don't you see? We're the real godmakers.[87]

After Jon's return from a mission, he is struck by the "opulent stink of California"—a culture disturbingly, comfortably inclusive of an affluent Mormon culture. He finds that his aged father wears makeup and hair color, the bishop is a "pompadoured young obstetrician," and "everyone in the ward had money." During a sacrament service, he finds, "I tried to think about the atonement and the Savior's spiritual convulsions in Gethsemane on my behalf. But I was distracted by the plastic cups, the lipstick stains the women left on the rims, and the clink-clink-clink as they dropped into the metal trays, the inimitable sound of money."[88] What he discovers is that his spiritual quest begins with his mission release, it does not end with it. Coming home turns out to be exile, and he must endure his own "spiritual convulsions" before, as the book so pointedly ends, he can *"begin* the long descent home."

Mostly, however, this is a novel about the terrible cost of freedom and compassion, and their inescapable revelation of a tragic dimension to the universe that neither certainty nor salvation can entirely efface. One childhood memory in particular becomes a haunting leitmotif: as a tender child, Jon attempts to euthanize an injured kitten, with gruesome, wrenching consequences. Even his later chastity injures Nancy's self-esteem, to the point of the book's most heartbreaking tragedy. Fillerup is not an author who revels in the tragic or indeterminate, but his book is a call for Mormonism to explore more fully the sometimes catastrophic cost even of doing good. As he asks the reader as well as himself:

> Am I playing Penelope, unweaving as I weave? Or does it take an eternity to smooth out the rough edges? Then help me tell the real story, the deep truth which too often has to sneak in like a Greek bearing illumination but not always good tidings of great joy. Which is the whole point, the irony, the freedom, and the beauty of it.[89]

Successful Catholic writers like Graham Greene and Flannery O'Connor succeed in reaching a wider audience through mastering their medium, but it helps that Greene's lustful whiskey priests and O'Connor's deranged preachers and grotesque human menageries are hardly the stuff of artful propaganda. Writers of the caliber of Fillerup deserve wider exposure, but Mormon fiction at this stage of development, to the extent that it exhibits faithful realism, may be seen as too overtly faithful and not sufficiently realistic by today's critical standards. By avoiding the simple conversion-narrative formula, Fillerup avoids the worst excesses of that genre. Another writer who has successfully rendered the Mormon missionary experience in novel form is Alan Mitchell, with his *Angel of the Danube* (2000).[90] Mitchell's work focuses almost entirely on the humorous and heartfelt struggles of a missionary coming to terms with his own lack of success. No crisis of faith, no spiritual illumination, and no tendentious sense of a potential convert reading over the shoulder, *Angel of the Danube* shows the cultural maturity of a writer who neither condescends nor evangelizes. "There's a lot to get depressed about on a mission if you let it," the narrator informs us, "especially in Austria."[91]

Just before his release, Barry is fired with the thought that he has only days left to forge his legacy, and he decides to go out like Noah, Paul, and Joseph Smith wrapped in one. The scenes that ensue, taking him on a frenetic romp through bus terminals, visiting a drunken *Fasching* (Carnival) celebration, and ending in a courthouse, are as zany as a Dom Delillo novel. But the humor can also veil criticism of Mormon culture and recognition of the same dilemmas Fillerup addressed. One missionary is more converted by the institution than the gospel it teaches: "The Lord had devised the best social organization, the most encompassing insurance policy, the best health and fitness program, the best welfare system, and the most spiritual program ever devised, and He had wrapped it into one gigantic success-machine." Returning home, this Stepford-wived missionary "sat down and cried—it hurt so bad to be released as a salesman for the best product in the world." He can only find emotional consolation when he finds that he can substitute selling encyclopedias door to door instead of salvation.[92]

Like Fillerup's Jon Reeves, Barry discovers it is harder to adjust to life after the mission than during. He wants to meet Linda Ronstadt after a concert, because he thinks he has the answers to the questions posed in one of her soulful songs, and he struggles to decide if God now wants him "to get on back to school, enter motocross races, or preach at the beach."[93] That the novel ends with him meeting his pretty Austrian convert at the airport makes for a nice romantic resolution. But it also makes for a deeper ambiguity about the difficulty of re-forging a connection with a larger community outside the narrow channels of Mormon culture, and the narrower ones of mission life.

And finally, while Taylor finds humor in the Mormon concept of a church full of prophets, Margaret Blair Young explores the darker side of the principle. A winner of several awards, *Salvador* was called in 1992 "the finest Mormon novel in today's market."[94] Certainly one of the most mature and lyrical voices in Mormon writing, Young fashions an utterly convincing narrative about the seductive appeal of some of Mormonism's headiest ideals: Zion building, spiritual autonomy, priesthood power, and the prophetic calling. But madmen and prophets both hear voices, and in a church where all are called to be revelators and priests, authority is often a fragile hedge against the excesses of spiritual initiative and independence. Young's narrative is so powerful in part because she enacts rather than describes these very dangers, which are also Mormonism's greatest virtues, catching the reader in the snares of charismatic appeal, lofty idealism, and utopian projects.

Deftly and with great subtlety, Young also intimates the dangers of a Mormon propensity to be bestowers rather than recipients of grace. This tendency is implicit in the notion we have seen time and again of salvation as a project, as a Faustian striving toward apotheosis, which can overwhelm the opposing gesture of acquiescence to the divine, submersion of the self and will. Reenacting on a smaller scale the empire-building, saint-making enterprise of Brigham Young or the Dixie mission colonizers, Julie hopes to recuperate from a failed marriage by assisting in the commune-like community of Zarahemla—a Salvadoran plantation run by the charming and visionary Johnny, who aspires to recreate the Book of Mormon's legendary "center of peace . . . , a sort of Zion."[95] "I loved the bigness of my work," Julie frankly concedes. "I was significant, competent, adored. A white saint, a savior with a sunburned nose, re-creating a world, making sense and shelter where there weren't any."[96] Julie's innocent flirtation with a sense of mission does not take the sinister turn it might have, because her missionary zeal and sense of certainty are tempered by a capacity for doubt that saves her in the end, in an ambiguous anti-apotheosis. "All my doubts—the precious secrets and wonderings I had pushed to the fringes of my faith—were orbiting me as I drifted. They popped, like the snaps of a cap gun, reminding me that they had been there forever."[97]

Set in the lush jungles of El Salvador, the novel is also noteworthy because of how successfully it escapes the tired confines of the Mormon cultural region, and it develops a Mormon sense of sacred space based on scripture, on Mormon mythology, and on the church's international character. A Mormon version of *Heart of Darkness*, the novel achieves what the great Mormon novel has to: moral complexity, an unflinching gaze into the universe's tragic dimension, and a celebration of life that is stripped of sentimentality but not sentiment.

SCIENCE FICTION

Orson Scott Card has been called the Mormon "who to this point best—and most radically—fulfills the great prophetic hopes for a world-class as well as genuinely Mormon literature."[98] One of the most prolific and arguably the best science fiction writer alive, Card is best known for his Ender's saga, the first volume of which won an unprecedented doubleheader, scoring both the Nebula and the Hugo awards, as did its sequel, in a feat still unequaled (*Ender's Game*, 1986;

Speaker for the Dead, 1987). Some of his corpus is recognizably Mormon in fairly conspicuous ways. *Saints* and *Folk of the Fringe*, for instance, represent direct engagement, the former historical and the latter futuristic, with Mormonism itself. His *Tales of Alvin Maker* series (six volumes and counting) is a thinly veiled version of Joseph Smith's life, cast as fantasy that reconceptualizes American history. Earlier, he published a five-volume science fiction series clearly based on the Book of Mormon (*Homecoming*, 1992–1996).

Science fiction (or the more-encompassing "speculative fiction"), though still struggling for respect as serious art, is the literary form best suited to the exposition and exploration of ideas at the margins of conventional thinking, whether in technology, ethics, politics, or religion. And indeed, some Mormon doctrine is so unsettling in its transgression of established ways of conceiving reality that it may be more at home in the imagined universes of Card than in journals of theology. This may explain the demonstrable affinity between the genre and the faith. As one Web site notes:

> In a literary survey of novels which have won the highest awards in science fiction, the Hugo or Nebula award, twenty-five percent (25%) had Latter-day Saint characters or Utah/Latter-day Saint references. These include books by Heinlein, Philip K. Dick, Orson Scott Card, Arthur C. Clarke and Greg Bear.[99]

Another site opines, "It may be the culture. It may be religion or the landscape. Maybe it's something in the water. Whatever the reason, Utah has some of the nation's most prolific producers and ravenous readers of science fiction and fantasy, known in the book world as 'speculative fiction.' "[100]

Most universities produce a literary magazine. BYU produces a science fiction magazine: the *Leading Edge*. Theology is certainly one explanation behind this phenomenon. God, claim the Mormons, revealed as long ago as 1830 that "worlds without number have I created; and I also created them for mine own purpose;... And the first man of all men have I called Adam, which is many" (Moses 1:33–34, PGP). The reality of multiple inhabited worlds is not the only doctrine that invites creative speculation of an LDS bent. As Card says, by way of explaining the wide Mormon participation as producers and consumers of the genre, "We have no qualms about the idea of life on other planets, faster-than-light travel, ancient 'lost' civilizations, supernatural events with natural explanations."[101] Another example, appearing in Card's own work, is the Mormon theme of apotheosis, or man becoming God, which is generally seen as beyond the pale theologically and is treated in most literature as criminal pathology deserving the retribution that usually follows (as with *The Man Who Would Be King* or Joseph Conrad's Kurtz). But in Card's *Hot Sleep*, Jason Worthing founds a new world, presides over a human race, benevolently rejoices in "the best part of being God, you know—when you create someone who surpasses you," and imitates the weeping God motif found in Joseph Smith's Enoch text, when he grieves over his burden of godhood.[102]

In this regard and others, science fiction is operating in one of its standard modes: to naturalize the supernatural, to bridge the distance that separates the proximate and quotidian from the distant and (nearly) inconceivable, and to vastly enlarge the scope of the paradigm which encompasses normality—not by circumventing reality, but by extrapolating it. Science fiction is, in this regard, as Card has called it, "radical realism." It should be apparent that the cultural work that this genre performs is aptly suited to a religion in which the sacred and the banal intermingle so indiscriminately. For Mormonism is, as Card again says, "every bit as radically realistic as science fiction; if Joseph Smith and the rest of us in our subsequent theological collective evolution have done anything, we have explained godhood in a completely rationalistic way."[103]

At times, Card seems to be arguing in his fiction fairly explicitly against the same dichotomizing that C. S. Lewis lamented, and that Mormonism shuns, which consigns the rational and predictable to the natural order, and the divine and ineffable to the religious. The *Alvin Maker* series is conspicuous for its transparent adaptation of Mormon historical material. But it also reenacts the core ideological tension that puts Mormonism at odds with its host community—a particular brand of supernaturalism that is not readily domesticated by prevailing secular or religious models. Card's dour, orthodox Reverend Thrower repudiates the supernaturalism of the Makers and their community, insisting that the two categories of "science and Christianity" are sufficient to explain all phenomena. But his "science" is sorely limited and crude—typified by the phrenology so popular in Joseph's day. And his "Christianity" is narrow-minded and superstitious in its own way—denying the miraculous but fearful of "devilspawn."

Finally, Card fictively enacts another of the core tensions of Mormonism, that between Eden and exile, community and isolation. It is a tension he feels personally, declaring, "those of us who grew up in Mormon society and remain intensely involved are only nominally members of the American community. We can fake it, but we're always speaking a foreign language."[104] Like many science fiction writers, Card deals extensively with themes of migration and colonization. And almost all post-Romantic heroes revel in a kind of existential solitude. Still, Card thematizes the tension between the impulse toward community and disconnection from larger society in especially pointed ways, at times signified by the works' titles (as in *Folk of the Fringe*).

One of the major works produced by Horace Bushnell, a leading nineteenth-century theologian, was *Nature and the Supernatural* (1858). A major purpose of this book, written in an age of growing skepticism, was to establish intellectual bases for supernaturalism. The best speculative fiction attempts to do the same thing. As does Mormonism. Perhaps that's why it is proving to be such a fruitful alliance.

THE ESSAY

As the most intellectually self-conscious mode of literary expression, the essay has deep Mormon roots in nineteenth-century missionary tracts, religious pamphlets, and polemical writings defending an array of contested Mormon doctrines. In the twentieth century, the form has largely been appropriated by writers at the margins. Church magazines, once a principal forum for budding writers and provocative essayists, have become entirely vehicles for the official declaration of church doctrines and sermonizing. That leaves the unofficial magazines as the primary outlet for writing that probes the complexities, ambiguities, or perceived dissonances in the faith and in the culture. Like Montaigne, who pioneered the genre, Mormon essayists may write on virtually any subject from "monstrous children" to "defects in our government." It is in exploring the meaning of Mormon community itself, however, that Mormon intellectuals and writers especially attuned to life at the peripheries can be particularly provocative and poignant.

Eugene England was one of the most beloved and respected essayists of the mid- to late twentieth century, in large measure due to his efforts to create bridges between an alienated intellectual community and a church and leadership to which he was uncompromisingly if ambiguously committed. Essays with provocative titles like "Why Utah Mormons Should Become Democrats" were effective precisely because they were deviations from the party line offered from within the church. In his influential "Why the Church Is as True as the Gospel," England attacked a cliché cherished by many: that foibles and fallacies in church government and doctrine could be overlooked by remembering that "the gospel is true and perfect, but the church isn't." Urging a novel appreciation for the redemptive efficacy of community, England argued:

> [T]he Church is as true—as effective—as the gospel because it involves us directly in proving contraries, working constructively with the oppositions

within ourselves and especially between people, struggling with paradoxes and polarities at an experiential level that can redeem us. The Church is true because it is concrete, not theoretical; in all its contradictions and problems, it is at least as productive of good as is the gospel.[105]

From further outside the parameters of orthodox belief, Elbert Peck, for many years the editor of *Sunstone*, offered a similar evaluation of the Mormon community. "After running an errand to BYU," he wrote, "I took an introspective journey around the campus, recollecting my simpler, believing college days." Contemplating the intellectual odyssey that removed him far from those times of spiritual certainty, he

> began to weep, sensing how far I had journeyed from this pure religion of interconnected love and life which I had known most of my life. My nugatory answerless doubts paled compared to the complete emotional, social, and spiritual depths I had experienced then. Sobbing and gesturing to the vacant, yet crowded theatre, I recited the last lines of the Frost poem, this time the theatrics were gone. I was bitterly and joyfully acknowledging a re-revealed truth: "Here are your waters and your watering place. / Drink and be whole again beyond confusion." As I navigated my blurry-eyed way to the visitor's parking lot, there began distilling in me a deep, calm commitment to return and drink of living waters from my watering place—my Mormon community.[106]

And the gifted Mormon writer and self-professed doubter Levi Peterson conveys both the transcendent power of Mormon cultural connectedness and the blind spots that cultural conformity and certitudes can nurture. "I am like Rappaccini's daughter in Hawthorne's famous story," he writes. "She could not associate with ordinary mortals because her very breath would kill them. As I say, I find in Hawthorne's story an apt figure for my relationship with those faithful Mormons who hold me in greatest affection. At times I feel my mere presence is a poison." The painful barriers he experiences are occasioned, he admits, by his "own provocative and ribald behavior." Also factors, doubtless, are the general LDS discomfort with those who self-identify as Mormons without embracing the doctrines of the faith and the common LDS incapacity to empathize with Mormon doubters. His most powerful insight, however, is that lack of doubt can breed a lack of holy wonder:

> If Christ has indeed purchased eternal life for humanity, I for one will awaken to the reality of his gift with an immeasurable gratitude. In the meantime,

I make it the center of my Christian worship to anticipate that gratitude when I partake of the sacrament. I do not belittle the communion of my fellow Mormons. It is not an unworthy way of celebrating the Lord's Last Supper to measure one's successes and failures in keeping the commandments and to renew one's covenants to live righteously. Yet in a sense it seems a pity to take one's immortality for granted, to expect it and count on it. It seems a pity to be so sheltered from the terror of death that one's gratitude for the resurrection is merely dutiful and perfunctory. Perhaps truly there are religious advantages to doubt. Perhaps only a doubter can appreciate the miracle of life without end.[107]

All artistic production embodies values and ideals. But literature is the most culturally impregnated with ideas, themes, meanings, and anxieties. And that is why Mormon writers have been most effective in shaping, from the center and margins alike, a tapestry of Mormon identity with so many identifiable threads. One observer of Mormonism has cited the "remarkable and impressive flowering of Mormon literature" as evidence not just of a gifted generation of writers, but as evidence for the creation of "a clear cultural identity" that is "thriving." She continues, "[T]he groundedness of the short stories, the novels, even the essays persuade the reader that obituaries for Mormon ethnicity are decidedly premature."[108]

~ 16 ~

"PAINTING THE
MORMON STORY"

Visual Arts

I overheard a lot of earnest discussion among the students and also among the faculty [at BYU] about being an artist and being a Mormon. The general tone of it was the underlying question whether the two could co-exist morally. That kind of talk is absent in New York, at least it's absent from my circle of acquaintance[s]. The New York version of that dialogue has nothing to do with right and wrong; instead, we talk about money: Can I be an artist and pay the rent?

~ Glen Nelson, Mormon Artists Group[1]

The success of the Tabernacle Choir at the 1893 Chicago World's Fair was both a milestone and a portent of shifting winds. Not only did it mark a growing respectability of the LDS church outside the confines of the Wasatch Mountains, but it marked a turn of the church toward cultural, as well as political, integration into the larger world. A similarly momentous, if largely symbolic, event had occurred months earlier. The Salt Lake Temple, after four decades of construction, was at last ready to be dedicated. The Salt Lake Theatre, until then the most visible monument of Mormon cultural achievement, was about to be definitively and permanently displaced as the architectural showpiece of the city. On April 5, 1893, the inner precincts of the completed sacred edifice would be opened to the eyes of a curious, non-Mormon public. The inner adornments would serve to inspire and edify generations of the faithful, but on this day, they would bear the scrutiny of a gentile gaze. What visitors saw on this occasion, among the ornate furnishings and exquisite craftsmanship, was a series of magnificent murals, whose origins were to be found in one of the LDS church's most unique missionary assignments.

In 1888, Utahns Harriet Richards, James T. Harwood, Cyrus Dallin, and John W. Clawson traveled to Paris to study art. Two years later, in 1890, young artists John Hafen, John B. Fairbanks, and Lorus Pratt, supported by their instructors Dan Weggeland and George Ottinger, approached George Q. Cannon of the First Presidency with a proposal. If the church would provide financial support for the students to study in France, they would use their training upon their return to adorn the interior walls of the new temple. The presidency approved the plan, and the first wave of "art missionaries"—eventually to include Edwin Evans and Herman Haag as well—soon enrolled as students in the Julian Academy in Paris, then considered to be the premier art school in the world. So even as Mormon choirs prepared to display their talents in Chicago— not to reveal to an amused public the ethnologically interesting tunes of an isolated cultural curiosity, but to compete successfully on equal terms with America's finest choirs—Mormon leaders were preparing to assimilate into the decor of their most sacred edifice the cutting-edge influences of the European art establishment. Into the world and into the temple—henceforth, Mormon culture and the secular cultural mainstream would flow more freely into each other. A dozen more Latter-day Saint artists would make the pilgrimage to Paris in the next few decades—many with church sponsorship and some independently.

Paris in 1890 was a time of rich ferment and overlapping, intersecting movements, both literary and visual, and flocks of American artists made their pilgrimages there (and to Munich) to imbibe the latest trends. Art nouveau, with its curving sensuous lines, was under way. The symbolist manifesto had just appeared in 1886, emphasizing the subjective, the ambiguous, and the mysterious as opposed to the realistic (no "plain meanings, . . . false sentimentality and matter-of-fact description").[2] Decadence was a closely allied trend, exploiting narcissistically the morbid and the erotic. Impressionism had peaked a few years earlier, and the postimpressionists were in the ascendant, headed by artists like Henri de Toulouse-Lautrec, Paul Gauguin, and Paul Cezanne. Meanwhile, Georges Seurat and Paul Signac were at work pioneering pointillism. All of these fresh currents constituted fertile soil for artistic innovation, but hardly the stuff out of which temple murals are born. Nevertheless, the Mormon artists immersed themselves in the core curriculum of the Paris academies. There, they focused their formal education on academic figure drawing, sketching the male and female nude. Most of the LDS students found themselves gradually migrating from the confines of the academies to plein-air painting. They imbibed the influences of impressionism, which had by then peaked, but were most taken by the Barbizon School of landscape realism, which they absorbed from Albert-Gabriel Rigolot (1862–1932), their principal teacher in landscape. The use of church funds for artists to practice drawing nude models in fin-de-siècle Paris in preparation for adorning the sacred inner precincts of a Mormon temple is surely one of the great ironies of Mormon religious history. Michelangelo's *ignudi* were at home in the Sistine Chapel, for the Roman church had long ago taken secular art into its bosom. The accommodation has been more difficult to resolve in LDS culture, where the church school currently bans nude models.

With the return in 1892 of the Paris art missionaries, Utah had a talent pool with the formal European training to inaugurate a new era of artistic accomplishment. Their degree of professionalism had little equal in frontier America. According to their agreement, four art missionaries set to work on the Salt Lake Temple murals. Some of their finest work also would adorn the walls of chapels throughout Utah and other states. One testament to both their individual talent and to the church's earlier aesthetic devotion is the Salt Lake Highland Park chapel. Built in the English Tudor style, with a large vaulted chapel ceiling and at one time a hand-carved oak seat for the bishop, the building houses several murals as well. A large sacred grove mural by Lee Greene Richards is at the front of the chapel behind the podium (he followed the art missionaries to Paris in 1901). In the corners are four smaller murals by Richards. Two large murals by John B. Fairbanks grace the foyer.

With their obligations to the church fulfilled, the Paris missionaries then went on to establish their careers as artists and teachers. Fairbanks met with modest success, as did Pratt. Hafen, probably the most talented of the group, is today better appreciated for his impressionist palette than he was at the time; he constantly struggled with poverty, and eventually left Utah for more lucrative markets. Evans was perhaps the most successful, producing an extensive corpus and winning honors at the Columbian Exposition of 1893.

With its emphasis on the drama of natural light and rural settings, impressionism was easily and successfully assimilated into the art of Mormon Utah. Sagebrush was at times substituted for wheat sheaves, and the Wasatch Mountains intruded as a conspicuous backdrop to golden, light-drenched fields, making the Mormon landscape a popular subject. The entire episode of the art mission was probably more significant for what it said about the church's relationship to the wider culture than for any particular influence those experiences had on the shaping of a unique Mormon artistic tradition. Coming at the apogee of Utah's campaign to purge itself of polygamy and a church-sponsored political party, the church's integration of its musicians and artists into the larger secular culture was both a denial of its cultural provincialism and a recognition that while the religion of the Egyptians was corrupt, their gold might be worth appropriating.

With the coming of the thirties, there developed a native American style known as "American wave," "American scene," or regionalism. American regionalism emphasized midwestern farms and towns, agrarian values, and small-town life. Fortuitously, the movement coincided with the most productive period of Utah's foremost regionalist, LeConte Stewart (1891–1990). Today one of Utah's most-collectible artists, he thoroughly dominated Utah landscape painting for a half-century. Side by side with landscapes and a developing Utah regionalism, portraiture continued to be ably executed by Hafen, Clawson, and subsequently by Lee Greene Richards, with Clawson especially working in an impressionist mode reminiscent of John Singer Sargent.

Not surprisingly, Mormon women were as apt to pursue the artist's vocation as were their gentile counterparts. The top art prizes of the first two Utah agricultural fairs, in 1856 and '57, had both been won by Sarah Ann Burbage Long. And before the church saw fit to subsidize the Paris art mission, Harriet Richards and Marie Gorlinski, followed by Lara Rawlins, Maye Jennings, and the most promising student of the group, Mary Teasdel, had already taken the initiative to study there on their own accord. Teasdel, the closest thing Mormonism has had to a Mary Cassatt, spent three years in Paris and exhibited in the French Salon before returning to Salt Lake to teach and paint.

Not all Mormon artists found their training in Paris. Minerva Teichert (1888–1976) studied at the Art Institute in Chicago and the New York Art Students League. Like the art missionaries before her, she received official church support for her studies: she was set apart as a missionary so she could accompany other Latter-day Saints going to the Midwest. Her most prominent teacher was Robert Henri, but Teichert borrowed little from his style or that of the associated Ashcan School. Mormon to the core, Teichert longed to express her faith and culture through her art. Henri encouraged her in this regard, telling her to "go home and paint the Mormon story." Consequently, she would become the most Mormon-themed painter of significance since Christensen. But like Christensen, her major contributions were not fully recognized during her lifetime.

At the Chicago Institute, Teichert fell under the spell of proponents of the mural as a powerful educational medium (such as Edwin H. Blashfield, 1848–1936), and soon came to regard mural painting as the highest form of art. In the decade of the thirties in particular, the profusion of public murals reflected a desire to translate art into a mass medium that celebrated American values and the farmers and laborers of the nation for a general audience. In that decade,

Teichert did over sixty murals, and she eventually completed projects from Ellis Island to the Manti Temple in Utah.

It was inevitable, then, that she would find the heroic proportions of such a celebratory, public medium apt to chronicle the two sagas of her faith: the colonization of the West by the Mormons and the history of Nephite civilization related in the Book of Mormon. She painted a number of canvases on western and pioneer themes, but the Book of Mormon mural project became her consummate passion. She eventually executed a series of over forty murals in the same thirty-six-inch by forty-eight-inch format. In *Ammon before King Limhi* and *An Angel Appears to Alma and the Sons of Mosiah*, she employs exaggerated flamboyance and variety of costume, Mesoamerican design motifs, and tropical flora in order to constitute a sense of cultural otherness, distinctness, and authenticity, evoking a fully realized world that thrusts the Book of Mormon and its characters into vivid, lived reality—though the unrealized faces and features give a hazy effect to it all. She thus anticipated the project only recently initiated by Mormon scholars and church media personnel of transforming the Book of Mormon from its oblique position as a scriptural artifact, largely unread and unexamined, into a prominent place, not just in Mormon consciousness and worship but in actual historical time and geographical situatedness.

Teichert was not the first artist of renown to make the Book of Mormon her subject; that role fell to Arnold Friberg (b. 1913), called by one art historian "a transitional figure who helped break the taboo in Utah of painting religious art."[3] Although he was Utah's most important western genre artist, he first came to prominence as a result of his work for Cecil B. DeMille when the latter was producing *The Ten Commandments*. The children's auxiliary of the LDS church had commissioned Friberg to produce a series illustrating the Book of Mormon in 1952, and DeMille had seen some of those paintings. In 1957–1958, Friberg's fifteen monumental paintings for the Charlton Heston film toured the world, at the end of which he was made a lifetime member of the Royal Society of Arts, London. He went on to do numerous Canadian Mounties pictures, a much-reproduced *Prayer at Valley Forge*, and notable western art. But most Latter-day Saints know him as the first and foremost illustrator of Book of Mormon scenes that feature prominently in millions of copies of that scripture.

Teichert's series may have been earlier, but until it was given to BYU in 1969, it received little public exposure even in Mormon circles. Friberg's work, by contrast, was used to illustrate copies of the Book of Mormon distributed throughout the world during the second half of the twentieth century. His hulking, overmuscled Nephites and Lamanites, his romanticized visions of their wars and heroes and villains, all done within the general parameters of a realist style, have vastly more appeal to the general public than the idiosyncratic treatments of Teichert. Tempting as it is to consider him a mere illustrator, his work as portraitist to the British royal family (both Elizabeth II and Prince Philip), his treatments of western themes, and his enormously popular religious paintings bear witness to a major talent.

The church was willing to train and commission its own to adorn the walls of its temples, but it relied on a non-Mormon sculptor, Utahn Cyrus Dallin, to produce the most conspicuous artistic emblem of Mormonism—the angel Moroni atop the Salt Lake Temple. At the same time, a sculptor whose international reputation would surpass even Dallin's was making a name for himself. Though not as devotedly Mormon as his name would suggest ("Mahonri" is a Book of Mormon character, "Young" is from his grandfather Brigham), Mahonri Young (1877–1957) would become the church's most celebrated sculptor, and today his works are in over fifty museums, including the Metropolitan. He fought tenaciously to secure church commissions for work that commemorated the pioneer past, thus foreshadowing a type of cultural Mormon, who evinces powerful identification with the church even though spiritually disaffected or alienated.

A firm realist, Young painted and etched, but made his greatest contributions in the area of traditional monument. The statues of Joseph and Hyrum Smith now displayed on Temple Square were two of his first church commissions. His *Seagull Monument* for Temple Square was dedicated in 1913. Perhaps America's most famous monument to a bird, the sculpture celebrates a miracle as potent in Mormon mythology as the manna in the wilderness was for the Hebrews. The year after the Saints entered the valley, the ripening grain was being devoured by swarms of crickets. After all efforts to save the crop and forestall starvation had failed, flocks of seagulls descended on the fields, consumed the crickets, flew away to disgorge, and returned to repeat the saving process. Some years later, Young completed work on what he considered his magnum opus, the *This Is the Place Monument* in 1947. The huge structure measures sixty feet tall and eighty-six feet long. The sculpture groups and bas reliefs include Spanish missionaries and explorers, trappers, the Donner party, and Mormon pioneers, including Brigham Young, Heber C. Kimball, and Wilford Woodruff, whose figures stand atop the monument. And lastly, though Brigham Young was caught countless times on canvas and in bronze, it was Mahonri Young's oversized rendition in white Carrara marble that was Utah's choice to represent the state in the Statuary Hall of the U.S. Capitol in Washington, D.C.

Although the church had turned to a non-Mormon to adorn the spire of the Salt Lake Temple, from 1969 to 1973 the commission for the Washington

Temple Moroni would go to one of its own. Avard Fairbanks (1897–1987), son of painter John B. Fairbanks, made his mark early. Reputed to be the youngest person ever admitted to the French Salon (at seventeen), he excelled as a youth in sculpting animals before he expanded his range and mastery of the human figure. His exquisite *Nursing Mother* (1928) in white marble, says Vern Swanson, Utah art historian, may have helped to crack the Mormon taboo against the nude, with its portrayal of a beautiful young woman, in Eve-like innocence and naked splendor, nursing her baby.[4] Fairbanks would come to be recognized far outside Utah's borders: he was knighted by King Paul of Greece for his *Lycurgus the Lawgiver*. But he devoted much of his energy to producing work that captured poignantly and powerfully the essence of the Mormon faith. In 1936, the church dedicated Winter Quarters Pioneer Cemetery near Omaha, Nebraska, where some 600 Mormons are buried, most victims of the disease and exposure incident to the Illinois expulsion of 1846. Fairbanks prepared for the dedication his masterpiece, a grieving mother and father huddled over the open grave of their infant. His *Restoration of the Aaronic Priesthood* (depicting John the Baptist ordaining Joseph Smith and Oliver Cowdery), the sculpture group *The Three Witnesses*, and his reverent portrayal of a young Joseph receiving the First Vision are among his other great works.

By midcentury, the great age of temple mural painting was coming to a close. Temple murals had provided the pretext, if not actual motive, for the original art missions. And many LDS painters of the first half-century had received church commissions to contribute to the Utah temples and to adorn meeting-houses. Now, the encroachments of modernism were displacing traditionalism even among the Latter-day Saint community of artists. Instrumental in this regard were University of Utah–affiliated artists George Dibble and Alvin Gittins (who would leave the church) and the imported Angelo Caravaglia, while Avard Fairbanks, dominating Utah sculpture, continued to fight for the traditional figurative agenda. BYU soon drifted toward more contemporary trends as well, making it yet more challenging for Mormon artists to forge religious art along traditional lines. In addition, any institution with the LDS church's sense of mission, theological certainty, and impulse toward centralized administration and doctrinal standardization is bound to prefer orthodox illustration to creative expression in the art it commissions. The ironic consequence is that when the church needed religious art for institutional purposes, it turned primarily in the next years to the nineteenth-century religious Danish master Carl Bloch or to three contemporary non-Mormons. Harry Anderson, Tom Lovell, and Kenneth Riley have created most of the images that recent generations of Latter-day Saints associate with Mormon iconography. Few Mormons seem to have noticed, however, that all of Anderson's many LDS-commissioned pieces are limited to biblical scenes. A committed Seventh-day Adventist, Anderson was unwilling to use his talent to portray Book of Mormon or restorationist themes.[5] For those subjects, the church most frequently turned to Lovell, a friend of Anderson who earned his early reputation as a magazine illustrator. A nationally renowned illustrator/artist of this period, Kenneth Riley also completed a number of LDS paintings featuring Joseph Smith and seminal moments in the church's history. The works of these three artists have achieved pervasive exposure through their appearance in church magazines and their prominent display in LDS meeting-houses around the world. So in the experience of the LDS membership, religious art is essentially didactic or illustrative and, even in the case of LDS-themed art, created by nonmembers. Because of the omnipresence of these church-commissioned works, the church's zeal for standardization and central correla-tion, and the paramount consideration it gives to the message of the restoration, artistic expression and exploration themselves have had little chance of flour-ishing under official auspices. Speaking of the effective monopoly of that trio and the earlier Friberg, one Salt Lake City gallery owner laments, "They set such a tone there is no room for the new guys."[6]

Church commissions for established traditional LDS artists whose careers were thriving, such as Arnold Friberg, LeConte Stewart, and Avard Fairbanks, de-clined or altogether ceased during this period. As the decade of the 1960s pro-gressed, a number of Latter-day Saints would decide it was time to reassess the synthesis of artistic vision and religious belief and to forge an authentic Mormon art of their own.

There was a time, not so very long ago, when Western art *was* religious art. To speak of the tradition of great Christian art, for instance, is to conjure up im-ages of Leonardo's Madonnas, Titian's *Depositions*, or Bosch's *Garden of Earthly Delights*. In America, religious art never achieved a foothold. Puritans and co-lonials, like virtuous republicans generally, were suspicious from the beginning of the arts and little inclined to patronize, let alone subsidize, paintings and sculptures of religious themes. The fortunes of religious art further declined in the West once Romanticism substituted a natural sublime for a divine one. In the twentieth century, a long tradition of benign cultural neglect turned into some-thing more like profound incompatibility. Beginning in architecture, but soon spreading to the visual arts and beyond, came the movements that drew heavily upon consumer culture and philosophical cynicism and that celebrated fragmen-tation, difference, anxiety, alienation, and the ubiquity of the superficial. These movements emphatically resisted any effort to privilege history, venerate human-ity, or express religiosity.

By this time in history, LDS institutional support, training, and patronage of the arts were largely centered in the Art Department of the church's Brigham Young University. By 1965, tentative efforts were under way to forge an aesthetic that would incorporate LDS religiosity into studio art. One early result was an exhibition in Salt Lake City entitled Art and Belief, which took place in the winter of 1966–1967. Dale T. Fletcher, Trevor Southey, Gary E. Smith, Dennis Smith, and Larry Prestwich were prime exhibitors. Fletcher saw the exhibit as the first alternative to the bleakness of abstract expressionism, minimalism, and pop art, with their "open surrender to the predicament—[evident] in the black square, the soup can, the raw portrayal of sexual confusion, the twiddling of the optic nerve."[7] The question, of course, was what would constitute the alternative. In the first generation of the church, Mormon artists had emphasized portraiture, landscape, and some historical themes. From the turn of the century on, art practiced by Mormons self-conscious of their religion tended toward a kind of regional rather than theological Mormonism—further developing a tradition of Mormon landscape. With the Art and Belief movement, accomplished artists would experiment with themes more explicitly identifiable with Mormon theology and culture. But others in the movement were not sure that a common idiom would—or should—emerge. Trevor Southey wanted to emphasize an art accessible to all, which could build faith. Dennis Smith wanted to focus on individual expression. Fletcher felt that the underlying tone must be the distinctive hallmark. "The critical fact of Mormonism," he said:

> is that it is *authentic*. This places the person with a testimony in a different metaphysical orientation from our brethren outside the Church. The remedy is back. The foundation is under us again, so that to paint after the glory of reality is no longer escapism as it must seem in the world. The destiny of the Kingdom is secure.[8]

But it is really an epistemology rather than a metaphysics that he is describing. As ever, it is the Mormon culture of *certainty* that words like "testimony," "foundation," "reality," and "secur[ity]" evoke.

Unlike their peers in BYU's commercial art division, many of these artists did succeed in filling their canvases with art of affirmation and celebration, without falling into the pat, the smug, or the two-dimensional. Not an easy task, of course, as intimated in Tolstoy's opening line of *Anna Karenina*: "Happy families are all alike; every unhappy family is unhappy in its own way." It has been a long time since artists or audiences have expended aesthetic attention on harmonious marriages, contented families, utopian congregational communities, or other ideals of Mormon cultural life. Angst, not complacency, is the hallmark of modern artistic sensibility.

The Art and Belief exhibit was followed months later by Spencer W. Kimball's clarion call for members to embrace "The Gospel Vision of the Arts."[9] Continuing momentum led BYU organizers by 1969 to initiate the Mormon Arts Festival as a showplace for some of their best religious art. Much of the work produced by these artists was daring in its effort to incorporate progressive styles with religious subject matter. Southey and Gary Smith especially produced fresh allegorical and surrealist-tinged canvases. In 1972, Lorin F. Wheelwright was sufficiently optimistic about developments to launch his sumptuous coffeetable book entitled *Mormon Arts*, with the hopeful subtitle "Volume I" (the implicit expectation of subsequent volumes was disappointed). "We are on a threshold of artistic development within the Mormon culture and . . . this festival is expanding our awareness of the spiritual power of our religion to inspire artistic endeavor," he wrote, while acknowledging that, "at the moment, Mormon art reflects an image that is somewhat blurred because its distinctive characteristics are diffused rather than focused in a unique style."[10]

Such optimism soon proved to be premature. Whereas the art missionaries rarely showed their nudes, their Art and Belief successors brought them into prominent display, to mixed reception and occasional controversy. Even the BYU art museum routinely displays nudity in art, but Southey's nude murals in the Salt Lake airport drew heat from antipornography activists. And Mormons were largely unprepared for nontraditional renderings of religious themes, however reverently or earnestly portrayed. Dennis Smith, best known for his eleven statues done in a conservative, realistic style, which constitute the bulk of the *Relief Society Monument to Women* at Nauvoo, Illinois, would later conclude, "This overtly Mormon period became a turning point for all of us. We soon discovered that creating 'Mormon Art' was a dead end." He considered the main obstacle to be "an institution seemingly interested only in illustration of 'official' interpretation."[11]

Dialogue was an important vehicle for innovative Mormon art, and it has continued to promote Mormon artists in its pages and on its covers, though its reputation among the leadership may predispose conservative reader/viewers to suspect art displayed in such a progressive forum. In 1976, Boyd K. Packer expressed disappointment from this other side of the great divide: "The reason we have not yet produced a greater heritage in art and literature and music and drama is not, I am very certain, because we have not had talented people. . . . Some have reached great heights in their chosen fields. But few have captured the spirit of the gospel of Jesus Christ and the restoration." He concluded,

"[T]here are many who struggle and climb and finally reach the top of the ladder, only to find that it is leaning against the wrong wall."[12]

Members of the Art and Belief movement would probably insist that they *were* aspiring to a synthesis of the beautiful and the sacred. But this is one case where the conflict between authority and freedom, the sacred and the secular, certainty and searching, finds no happy resolution. Southey moved to San Francisco, Fletcher turned to pursue other interests, and the effort dissipated. A measure of the movement's failure is evident in the decision, in 1985, to excise the word "Mormon" from the name of the group's festival. Ironically, this happened in the year following the church's dedication on Temple Square of the Museum of Church History and Art. Together, these two events suggested that the past of Mormon art looked brighter than its future.

As the Art and Belief movement lost steam, BYU—the church's best hope for fostering Mormon art—continued in the direction of other university art departments, toward nonobjective, nonfigurative art, "soft postmodernism" in Vern Swanson's words.[13] Swanson is director of the Springville Art Museum, which houses the largest collection of Utah art, and therefore of work by LDS artists, in the state. In his opinion, BYU forsook its birthright—and its responsibility— to foster a distinctively Mormon art and to collect and display the results. The best hope for a world-class Mormon art, believes Swanson, is in a return to figure drawing as an artistic foundation. The modest Springville Academy is intended to provide just that. With the role of nudes in figure drawing and in traditional modes of representational art an ever-present dilemma for LDS standard-bearers, BYU has good reason to keep to the safe road of nonrepresentational art. As recently as 1997, the university administration removed four nudes by Rodin from a visiting exhibit. The resultant outcry from the community and from many in the student body demonstrated that even in a conservative Mormon community, there is no consensus on how to reconcile aesthetic freedom and an austere sexual morality.

Part of the challenge that today's Mormon artists face is the long hiatus since a centuries-long tradition of sacred art; part is the lack of emphasis today on academic figure drawing; and part is a strong church preference for noncontroversial art. The LDS artists today who are most reproduced for religious purposes have a tendency to veer toward the sentimental. Grey Olsen and Liz Lemon have successfully rendered Mormon themes in that vein. Some LDS artists, such as William Whitaker, Bruce Hixon Smith, and Peter Meyer, have found success and national recognition in a traditional approach. Others, like Southey and his colleagues, circumvented the problem by avoiding traditional forms. One recent artist, Walter Rane, has invoked the style of the masters to create a corpus of

Mormon art that transcends mere illustration. He has produced a gamut of religious art, but his series on the Book of Mormon is an especially rare effort to make Mormon scripture a major source of artistic expression. An artist in recent years who has found success both in the Mormon and in the larger community is James C. Christensen, who has achieved international popularity for his work of striking visual intensity that celebrates the whimsical and the fantastical. Most of his religious forays—such as illustrations of the parables of Jesus—stop short of the particular features of an LDS faith perspective or Mormon subjects, thus maintaining a more universal appeal to his work. Ron Richmond, on the other hand, is one of several Mormon artists taking modern, nonnarrative approaches to religious themes.

In 1980, BYU Press published a collection of essays that aimed to address the difficult synthesis of creativity and faith that had received renewed emphasis in the previous two decades, *Arts and Inspiration*. The dean of BYU's Fine Arts Department had in 1961 voiced the question that still finds no consensus among Latter-day Saints:

> [W]e are a peculiar people in possession of the fullness of the Gospel and the keys of the Last Dispensation. As such, what is our responsibility as artists, musicians, and writers? . . . Our religion is not Catholic in the Greek or Roman sense. It is not Protestant in the Lutheran, Episcopal, or Presbyterian sense. Should our architecture, music, painting, and writing be mainly a continuity of the traditional standards and styles from these cultures?[14]

Apostle Boyd K. Packer's summons to disregard the world's values and canon and to celebrate Mormon achievements, even while reaching for greater excellence, served in the collection to epitomize the institutional demands of Mormonism that art be morally edifying and that LDS artists produce LDS art. Meanwhile, some were wondering what all the angst and self-reproach were about. Hugh Nibley thought the very preoccupation misguided. Who are we, he queried, to presume to produce a Shakespeare or Beethoven in 150 years, when Western civilization sees their like only a few times a millennium? Karl Keller, in reviewing the *Arts and Inspiration* volume, concurred that Mormons are inventing a problem, "and since Mormons like to think of themselves as problem-solvers, then there must be a solution somewhere." The arts, he continues, "are always in and of and by and about and for this world," and to emphasize the hostility of the world to the church is to create a paranoid cosmic drama.[15]

But such a criticism fails to address an inescapable dilemma in Mormonism. For clearly any church, and a fortiori any restoration church, exists precisely because it offers values, ideals, and priorities at odds with the prevailing culture. Surely to expect a Mormon aesthetic to reflect these countercultural elements is not illogical or unreasonable. In the eyes of some, it is finding room for Mormon art, not its particular contours, that is the paramount obstacle. Karen Lynn's diagnosis is not hopeful: "The arts cannot be central to Mormon life no matter how many times we may claim otherwise." At least one reason for this, in Lynn's opinion, has to do with the culture of certainty, or what she calls "the Disallowing of Perplexity," which is at heart antithetical to artistic exploration.[16] It is also a question of enduring religious perspectives that see the beautiful as secondary to the true, that hold art to be mere adornment rather than illumination or vision. No wonder, as Southey noted despondently, a survey of responses to the first Mormon Arts Festival revealed that "more than one-third of all patrons believed that art was basically irrelevant to the church."[17]

Even granting myriad reasons for the peripheral significance of art in Mormon culture, the church and the individual artists are still left to resolve the question of whether they have a special role to play, and whether arts should be distinctive when practiced by a Latter-day Saint. Mormons' propensity to invoke the Thirteenth Article of Faith about the pursuit of things lovely and praiseworthy, and to cite Lehi's declaration that man's central purpose is to have joy (2 Nephi 2:25), both in an effort to ground theologically an essential role for the aesthetic, are indications of a persisting disposition to incorporate the beautiful into Mormon theology. But a determinative factor in the fortunes of Mormon art would seem to be the church's hypercentralization, with its priesthood correlation program, All-Church Coordinating Council, Presiding Bishopric, and kindred elements and structures that ensure the standardization of everything from church magazines and lesson manuals to meetinghouse art. The church's Curriculum Department even provides a "Gospel Art Picture Kit" with 104 approved illustrations, which have been distributed by the tens of thousands to church units and individuals. And it is, of course, the church's employment of art in predominantly illustrative ways, rather than expressive or creative ways, that allows little room for the development of a truly religious art.

The story of Mormon art has, until now, been largely a history of Utah Mormon art. A few decades after the decline of the Art and Belief movement, a new center of activity coalesced in New York City. There, the Mormon Artists Group has grown from a small number of photographers in 1999 to a collective of fifty or so creative artists from across the spectrum of arts. They mount exhibitions and engage in collaborative projects with each other and with Mormon artists elsewhere, and in other ways work to foster an array of creative activity.[18] With the church possessing a membership that has since the mid-1990s shifted to a predominantly non-American one, Utah landscapes and even pioneer history will have less resonance to Mormon ears and eyes, and the center of gravity will continue to shift further afield. Even renditions of scriptural characters and motifs will necessarily be rethought and reworked, to lose their American coloration and cultural naïveté, as had to happen to the blue-eyed Jesus of the Victorians. As one Latin American leader in the church protested, when the subject of Arnold Friberg's paintings came up (the ones that still illustrate the Book of Mormon), "These paintings are not paintings we can show to an educated Mexican. They're well done, but they show such an enormous ignorance of culture that they are offensive." "Imperialism in art," he called them.[19]

Since 1991, the church has moved to address these issues, in part through hosting an international art exhibit at the Museum of Church History and Art every three years. In 2003, 171 exhibits from artists representing thirty different nations were featured. With a church music committee in charge of music, hymnals that incorporate new material only every generation or two, and major musical compositions needing institutional support, music has a number of disadvantages in the way of becoming the medium of choice of an international Mormon culture. Literature and drama encounter the language barrier, and architecture requires resources that put it beyond the scope of individualistic expression. As response to the international art exhibit shows, however, art holds forth the promise of giving the most immediate, vibrant, and creative expression to the diversity of an international Mormon culture.

Acclaimed artists already include LDS immigrants Wulf Barsh (b. 1943) from Germany and Soren Edsberg (b. 1945) from Denmark. (The latter is a winner of the Prix de Rome.) Johan Bentin (b. 1936), also from Denmark, and two Italians, Giovanna Lacerti (b. 1935) and Pino Drago (b. 1947), have made successful careers in Europe. Latin Americans Jorge Cocco (b. 1936) of Mexico and Antonio Madrid (b. 1949) of Panama, along with Haitian-born Henri-Robert Bresil (b. 1952), have incorporated Mormon themes into their careers. With successful precedent to rely upon, and continuing institutional encouragement from Salt Lake, it is likely that in another generation, "Mormon art" will be the focus of the church's most creative energy and a potent element in shaping a rapidly transforming Mormon culture.

CONCLUSION

"Through the Particular to the Universal"

Literary experience heals the wound, without undermining the privilege, of individuality.

~ C. S. Lewis

Brigham Young's dream for Zion entailed an isolation—if not a celestial transcendence—every bit as complete as the ascension that swept up Enoch's entire
city. "We do not intend to have any trade or commerce with the gentile world,"
Young said with a defiance that must have seemed both deluded and dangerous,
as he stood in the utter barrenness of an unsettled Utah desert:

> [F]or so long as we buy of them we are in a degree dependent upon them. The
> Kingdom of God cannot rise independent of the gentile nations until we
> produce, manufacture, and make every article of use, convenience, or necessity
> among our people. . . . I am determined to cut every thread of this kind and
> live free and independent, untrammeled by any of their detestable customs and
> practices.[1]

Economic independence turned out to be the easy part, relatively speaking, of
the challenge. It has been the task of this book to assess the success—and the
meaning—of the "customs and practices" part of the equation. John Sorenson
noted in 1973 that "the literature of the social sciences seems to suggest that when
Mormons are viewed in terms of their overt behavior, as the sociologists . . . tend
to view them, they appear quite thoroughly American." But when it comes to
"Mormon artistic and humanistic life," he wrote, observers "have often felt that a
distinctive Mormon essence does exist, or at least ought to."[2]

It is this "ought to" that has dominated Mormon self-conceiving to a striking
degree. "It seems almost unbelievable that after all these years of the development

of Mormon thought we still have no genuine Mormon aesthetic theory," wrote Mormon composer Merrill Bradshaw in 1981.[3] "Though there is a 'solid, undeniably Mormon' way of life," responded Mormon musicologist Michael Hicks, "there is little such Mormon philosophy on which to erect a scaffolding of aesthetics." Besides, he insisted, that would be a constraining orthodoxy in any case.[4]

In John the apostle's apocalyptic vision, a confusion of things past and yet to come, the revelator describes a woman who gives birth to a manchild, while a dragon stands nearby ready to devour him. "And the woman fled into the wilderness," John writes, "where she hath a place prepared of God, that they should feed her there a thousand two hundred and threescore days" (Revelation 12:6).[5] Joseph Smith declared the woman to be "the kingdom of our God and his Christ," and this imagery of revelation has long been interpreted by Mormons as foreshadowing the great apostasy, the banishment of Christ's true church into the wilderness of spiritual death. Mormon discussions of apostasy generally proceed along the premise that truth and authority were completely taken from the earth or so corrupted as to be effectually absent. Yet the scripture which Joseph glosses refers to an entity that is fed and nourished for a prolonged period, even while inhabiting a religious wilderness. Certainly it seems reasonable in the LDS theological context to assume that poets have spoken when prophets haven't, and that the good, the true, and the beautiful have persisted through inspired artistic expression, as beacons in the midst of darkness, succoring the good and honest in heart. Mormon love for (and frequent performance of) Handel's *Messiah*, common and even prophetic invocations of Shakespeare as the standard to which LDS writers aspire, pride of place given in LDS visitor centers (in Salt Lake City and Washington, D.C.) to Bertel Thorvaldsen's magnificent *Christus* statue, and the reverential celebration and employment of these and other artistic treasures that preceded the restoration suggest a holy regard for an artistic tradition whose inspiration did not falter even through times of religious apostasy. These examples of inspiration that survives apostasy, transcends denominations, and connects past peoples and contemporary Mormons to that inspiration's source betoken an emphatic, edifying, perhaps salvational universalism associated with artistic excellence.

William Mulder and others have often referred to a Mormon idea, unique among Christians, that gives special value and motive force to the universal human attraction to and appreciation for aesthetic achievement:

If souls have a pre-existence, then artist and audience have a slumbering memory of the good, the true, and the beautiful, requiring only to be awakened, with works of literature and art (including the performing arts) the means of that awakening. Art indeed is less cognition than recognition. We have a "double witness," says Robert Rees, "when our awareness of things either terrestrial or celestial is quickened by the aesthetic as well as by the spiritual imagination." Given this concept the creative process is more discovery or disclosure than invention, and when the artist feels the work is "right," he will, says Merrill Bradshaw, have a sense of a "celestial kiss," which I take to be a sensory experience of artistic grace not unlike Jonathan Edwards's "sense of the heart," palpable, to use Edwards's own figure, as the taste of honey on the tongue.[6]

Mormon belief in human preexistence provides just one possible avenue to the elaboration of a specifically Mormon theory of the beautiful, reminiscent of Platonic forms, eternal absolutes that hover at the far boundaries of recollection. When mortals cross over the veil of death, Brigham Young taught, they will see "that they had formerly lived there for ages, that they had previously been acquainted with every nook and corner, with the palaces, walks, and gardens."[7] That would comport well with the human response to earthly beauty, a beauty expressly designed, say LDS scriptures, to "please the eye and gladden the heart, ... for taste and for smell ... and to enliven the soul" (D&C 59:18–19). An aesthetics predicated upon intimations of celestial backgrounds points toward a universal, though not universally acknowledged, dimension of human existence.

Hicks believes that the more esoteric theology explored by Brigham Young, the Pratt brothers, and B. H. Roberts holds the promise of an aesthetic sensibility even more deeply rooted than premortal intimations of the celestial. Either as eternally self-existent consciousness or upon the immensely distant "dawning of conscious life," individual spirits are possessed of the "power of deliberation." And, Hicks reasons, "the ability to appreciate seems inextricably bound up with the abilities to perceive and judge." The recognition and love of beauty, in other words, may be a fundamental and timeless ingredient of the eternal human soul.[8]

Reliance upon such spiritual anthropologies nudges Mormon aesthetics in the direction of what is universally human rather than culturally particular. And indeed, the apostle John's vision of a lasting spiritual darkness tempered by persistent gleams of spiritual light is seconded by Joseph Smith's wide-ranging intellectual eclecticism and openness. And so it too offers the promise of an aesthetic that is outward looking rather than narrowly provincial. But at the same time, these possibilities indicate a kind of universalism that Mormonism has always found simultaneously enticing and threatening. "Enticing" because to invoke universally accessible absolutes is to appeal to that which is self-evidently, necessarily true and to therefore find the same relationship to those timeless beauties and verities as a common humanity. In such common recognition, there is community and belonging. Art, in these terms, can call Latter-day Saints to affirm values that are a human rather than Latter-day Saint inheritance. But "threatening" because Mormonism is so historically and theologically invested in difference as that which defines and gives meaning to their past travails, their present faith, and their missionary mandate. Some of the most beautiful creations by Mormon artists do achieve sublimity precisely because they have stripped away from human experience all that is contingent, parochial, and culturally specific—leaving a kind of pristine sparseness that makes no special pleading, and is utterly unself-conscious. Such a work is the lyrically perfect poem "To a Dying Girl" by Clinton Larson:

> How quickly must she go?
> She calls dark swans from mirrors everywhere:
> From halls and porticos, from pools of air.
> How quickly must she know?
> They wander through the fathoms of her eye,
> Waning southerly until their cry
> Is gone where she must go.
> How quickly does the cloudfire streak the sky,
> Tremble on the peaks, then cool and die?
> She moves like evening into night,
> Forgetful as the swans forget their flight
> Or spring the fragile snow,
> So quickly must she go.[9]

At the same time, of course, human beings cannot escape their situatedness in time and place, they cannot elude their past that shadows them and the cultural and conceptual vocabularies they inhabit like a second skin. And so Philip White's voice is no strained claim to exceptionalism or myth making when he writes:

> I was born in the desert
> Brigham made bloom.
> I was reared among the dry grass.
> Measured water

came each two weeks,

and even God

could not make it reach

to the far fence corners.[10]

Negotiating this balance between the universal and the particular is one of the central challenges of any culture. It is not easy to define the self in relationship to the other, without distorting both in the process. The tendency toward shallow triumphalism, on the one hand, and facile demonizing, on the other, has plagued more than one people in the process of self-definition. These tendencies may be one explanation for what Eugene England calls Mormonism's "parochial anti-parochialism," by which he means a disdainful repudiation of Mormon peculiarism that is an exaggerated and insecure response to superficial expressions of Mormon peculiarity. But shame is not an effective catalyst to some ideal cosmopolitanism outside the Wasatch Valley, and local culture is not some temporary condition to be transcended. Mormonism conditions a Latter-day Saint's lived experience of the world in ways that deserve to be both interrogated and affirmed, even as Mormonism's spiritual, intellectual, and aesthetic eclecticism make an overlap of Mormon and non-Mormon culture both more inevitable and more abundant than many Saints realize (like the doxology that appears in a restoration oratorio). Ultimately, Eugene England is right about the necessity of giving each set of imperatives its due:

The only way to the universal is through the particular. The only honesty, ultimately, is honesty to that which we know in our own bones and blood and spirit, our own land and faith, our own doubts and battles and victories and defeats. Mormonism cannot be separated from these things because, unlike religions such as Lutheranism or Christian Science, it makes a large number of rather absolute claims about the nature of the universe and God and human beings, about specific historical events, past and future, about language and form and content—and because it is grounded in a sufficiently unusual and cohesive and extended historical and cultural experience growing directly from those claims that it has become like a nation, an ethnic culture as well as a religion.[11]

As an ethnic culture, Mormonism may still be in its adolescence. But Joseph Smith appears to have provided that culture with sufficient tensions and paradoxes to generate vigorous artistic and intellectual expression for another 200 years. The competing centrifugal and centripetal forces that characterize Mormonism show no sign—fortunately—of imminent resolution. The safety and comfort of centralized authority, the rhetoric and promise of theological certainty, the collapse of the sacred into the familiar, and the retreat into chosen isolation—all find their opposite and salutary temptation in the allure of radical individualism, the boundlessness of eternal progress and learning, the exploration of new modes of representing the sublime, and the imperative to search out, proselytize, and bind together in truth and beauty the entire human family, living and dead.

NOTES

~ INTRODUCTION

1. Joseph Smith, Jr., *History of the Church of Jesus Christ of Latter-day Saints*, 7 vols., ed. James Mulholland, Robert B. Thompson, William W. Phelps, Willard Richards, George A. Smith, and, later, B. H. Roberts (Salt Lake City: Deseret News Press, 1902–1912; 2nd rev. ed., Salt Lake City: Deseret Book, 1951), 7:235.

2. William Smith, Letter to Brigham Young, 27 August 1844, quoted in D. Michael Quinn, "The Mormon Succession Crisis of 1844," *BYU Studies* 16.2 (Winter 1976): 202. William Smith soon reconsidered and made his own bid for the leadership position.

3. Oliver Cowdery, John Taylor, Brigham Young, and Joseph F. Smith contributed one each (134, 135, 136, 138). Wilford Woodruff and Spencer W. Kimball produced an appendixed "official declaration" each.

4. Harold Bloom, *The American Religion: The Emergence of the Post-Christian Nation* (New York: Simon and Schuster, 1992), 96.

5. These three meanings are enumerated by Raymond Williams, *Culture and Society* (London: Chatto and Windus, 1958), in addition to his fourth, which encompasses the "whole way of life, material, intellectual, and spiritual." His definition, along with Herder's views, are addressed in Frederick Barnard's excellent survey of "Culture and Civilization in Modern Times," in *Dictionary of the History of Ideas*, ed. Philip P. Wiener (New York: Scribner's, 1973), 1:613–21.

6. Graydon F. Snyder, *Ante Pacem: Archaeological Evidence of Church Life before Constantine* (Macon, Ga.: Mercer University Press, 1985), cited in Rodney Stark, *The Rise of Christianity* (Princeton, N.J.: Princeton University Press, 1996), 8–9.

7. Thomas O'Dea's claim is paraphrased in Dean L. May, "Mormons," in *Harvard Encyclopedia of American Ethnic Groups*, ed. Stephan Thernstrom (Cambridge, Mass.: Harvard University Press, 1980), 720. As early as 1954, O'Dea referred to the Mormons as a "near nation," an "incipient nationality," a "subculture with its own peculiar conceptions and values," and "a people." See his "Mormonism and the Avoidance of Sectarian Stagnation: A Study of Church, Sect, and Incipient Nationality," *American Journal of Sociology* 60.3 (November 1954): 285–93. Later, he would say, "the Mormon group *came closer* to evolving an ethnic identity on this continent than did any other comparable group" (my emphasis). O'Dea, *The Mormons* (Chicago: University of Chicago Press, 1957), 116.

8. Barnard, "Culture," 618.

9. Gilbert K. Chesterton, *Orthodoxy* (New York: John Lane, 1908), 50.

∼ CHAPTER 1

In the prophet Lehi's vision in the Book of Mormon, a rod of iron alongside a straight and narrow path leads directly to the tree of life. Subsequent to the vision, Lehi finds a liahona, a kind of compass that gives the possessors orientation in the wilderness "according to the[ir] faith and diligence" (1 Nephi 8:19–20; 16:10, 28).

1. As one of the four LDS compilations of scripture (in addition to the Bible and the Book of Mormon), Doctrine and Covenants will be cited parenthetically hereafter as D&C.

2. Adam Clarke, *The Holy Bible Containing the Old and New Testaments with a Commentary and Critical Notes*, 3 vols. (Nashville, Tenn.: Abingdon, n.d.), 6:1008; J. R. Dummelow, *One Volume Bible Commentary* (1908; rpt., New York: Macmillan, 1975), 1082.

3. Abraham 3:22–23, in *The Pearl of Great Price* (Salt Lake City: Church of Jesus Christ of Latter-day Saints, 1981). The fourth of the LDS scripture compilations, this will be hereafter cited parenthetically as *PGP*.

4. B. H. Roberts denied that God fashioned or begat "intelligence" into individual spirits, basing his interpretation solely on a reputed indefinite article: transcribers of Joseph's King Follett sermon have him saying, "intelligence is . . . *a* spirit from age to age" (Joseph Fielding Smith, ed., *Teachings of the Prophet Joseph Smith* [Salt Lake City: Deseret, 1973], 354n). Also supporting this view is the fact that from the age of Shakespeare through Milton and into the nineteenth century, "intelligence" had the meaning of an incorporeal or spirit being. Mormon theologian James Talmage, on the other hand, disagreed, calling the human spirit "an organized intelligence" (James E. Talmage, *The Vitality of Mormonism* [Boston: Gorham, 1919], 241).

5. See the extensive treatment by Daniel C. Peterson, " 'Ye Are Gods': Psalm 82 and John 10 as Witnesses to the Divine Nature of Mankind," in *The Disciple as Scholar: Essays on Scripture and the Ancient World in Honor of Richard Lloyd Anderson*, ed. Stephen D. Ricks, Donald W. Parry, and Andrew H. Hedges (Provo, Utah: Foundation for Ancient Research and Mormon Studies, 2000).

6. This is how Bruce Kuklick summarizes Edwards's argument in his *History of Philosophy in America* (Oxford: Oxford University Press, 2001), 22.

7. William Godwin, "Enquiry Concerning Political Justice," in *English Romantic Poetry and Prose*, ed. Russell Noyes (New York: Oxford University Press, 1956), 179–80.

8. George M. Marsden, *Jonathan Edwards: A Life* (New Haven, Conn.: Yale University Press, 2003), 177.

9. Marsden, *Edwards*, 439.

10. Jacob Arminius, *The Works of Arminius*, 3 vols., trans. James Nichols and William Nichols (Grand Rapids, Mich.: Baker Book House, 1991), 3:192.

11. Ralph Waldo Emerson, *The Complete Works of Ralph Waldo Emerson* (Boston: Houghton Mifflin, 1903), 1:113.

12. Richard Bushman, *Rough Stone Rolling* (New York: Knopf, 2005), 458.

13. Hugh W. Nibley, "Before Adam," in *Old Testament and Related Studies*, in *The Collected Works of Hugh Nibley*, ed. John W. Welch et al. (Salt Lake City and Provo, Utah: Deseret Book and Foundation for Ancient Research and Mormon Studies, 1986), 1:71.

14. Marsden, *Edwards*, 444.

15. Marsden, *Edwards*, 453.

16. "Whether Man Has Free Will: Objection 3 and Response to Objection 3," in Aquinas, *Summa Theologica*, 7 vols. (New York: Benziger Brothers, 1947), 1:418. (Aquinas is quoting Aristotle's *Metaphysics* i, 2.)

17. Aquinas escapes the quagmire by simply asserting in his response that "it does not of necessity belong to liberty that what is free should be the first cause of itself" (Aquinas, *Summa*, 1:418).

18. John Taggart Ellis McTaggart, *Some Dogmas of Religion* (London: Edward Arnold, 1906), 165.

19. The reported word was coequal. I am in agreement with the note of B. H. Roberts on this word choice: "Undoubtedly the proper word here would be 'co-eternal,' not 'co-equal.' This illustrates the imperfection of the report made of the sermon. For surely [in Joseph Smith's opinion] the mind of man is not co-equal with God except in the matter of its co-eternity." Smith, *Teachings*, 353n.

20. Stan Larson, "The King Follett Discourse: A Newly Amalgamated Text," *BYU Studies* 18.2 (Winter 1978): 203–4.

21. "There are three independent principles—the spirit of God, the spirit of man, and the spirit of the devil. All men have power to resist the devil." Joseph Smith, *The Words of Joseph Smith: The Contemporary Accounts of the Nauvoo Discourses of the Prophet Joseph*, ed. Andrew F. Ehat and Lyndon W. Cook (Provo, Utah: BYU Religious Studies Center, 1980), 74.

22. *Journal of Discourses*, 26 vols., reported by G. D. Watt et al. (Liverpool, England: Richards et al., 1851–1886; rpt., Salt Lake City: n.p., 1974), 3:316.

23. *Journal of Discourses* 10:57–58; Joseph Smith, Jr., *History of the Church of Jesus Christ of Latter-day Saints*, 7 vols., ed. James Mulholland, Robert B. Thompson, William W. Phelps, Willard Richards, George A. Smith, and, later, B. H. Roberts (Salt Lake City: Deseret News Press, 1902–1912; 2nd rev. ed., Salt Lake City: Deseret Book, 1951), 2:6–7.

24. See the important study on the subject by Nathan Hatch, *The Democratization of American Christianity* (New Haven, Conn.: Yale University Press, 1991). Thomas O'Dea was one of the first scholars to find the Mormon tension between authority and individualism a "source of strain." See his brief discussion in *The Mormons* (Chicago: University of Chicago Press, 1957), 242–43.

25. Joseph Smith, *Lectures on Faith: Delivered to the School of the Prophets in Kirtland, Ohio, 1834–35* (Salt Lake City: Deseret, 1985), Lecture Third, 2–4. Joseph's actual authorship of the *Lectures* has become increasingly doubtful; what is not doubtful is that they were, at the least, authorized by him and a reflection of his theological views.

26. Smith, *History*, 5:387–88, 403.

27. Brigham Young said, "We have not, neither can we receive here, the ordinance and the keys of the resurrection. They will be given to those who have passed off this stage of action and have received their bodies again." Brigham Young, *Discourses of Brigham Young*, ed. John A. Widtsoe (Salt Lake City: Deseret, 1954), 397.

28. Smith, *History*, 3:385–86.

29. William Cathcart, ed., *The Baptist Encyclopedia* (Philadelphia: Everts, 1881), 1253; Williams's awaiting of new apostles was characterized as such by his contemporary John Cotton, in James Ernst, *Roger Williams: New England Firebrand* (New York: Macmillan, 1932), 479.

30. African Americans, as reputed members of the cursed lineage of Cain and Ham, were banned from the priesthood by Brigham Young; the ban was removed in 1978.

31. Marsden, *Edwards*, 350–51.

32. The nine formal charges against Cowdery and his letter of response are in B. H. Roberts, *Comprehensive History of the Church of Jesus Christ of Latter-day Saints* (Provo, Utah: Church of Jesus Christ of Latter-day Saints, 1957), 1:431–34.

33. Cowdery's reply to the charges was largely confined to the one issue of the limits of ecclesiastical authority. As a result, he was excommunicated for those charges to which he had not deigned to respond, including legal harassment of church leaders and dishonesty. See Roberts, *Comprehensive History*, 1:432.

34. E. E. Ericksen suggested a tension tangential to the one I am discussing when he noted a fundamental paradox in Joseph Smith himself that became

> deeply embedded in the institutions of the church and in the mind[s] of his people. The tension between these two principles (the prophetic and the priestly), the dynamic and the conservative, the inspiration toward the new and the stabilizing and the authoritative power of the old, constitutes the problem of twentieth century Mormonism.

Ephraim E. Ericksen, "Priesthood and Philosophy," *Utah Academy of Sciences, Arts, and Letters: Proceedings* 34 (1957): 14–15.

35. Hugh Nibley, "Educating the Saints: A Brigham Young Mosaic," *BYU Studies* 11.1 (Autumn 1970): 63.

36. In Keith E. Yandell, ed., *Myth and Narrative* (New York: Oxford University Press, 2001), 85.

37. William J. Abraham, *Divine Revelation and the Limits of Historical Criticism* (New York: Oxford University Press, 1982), 24.

38. The account was apparently first shared with Snow's granddaughter Allie Young Pond and was published in *Improvement Era* (September 1933): 677.

39. Dennis L. Lythgoe, "Lengthening Our Stride: The Remarkable Administration of Spencer W. Kimball," *BYU Studies* 25.4 (Fall 1985): 12.

40. *LDS Church News*, 21 December 1991.

41. *Newsweek* (1 September 1980): 68.

42. *Improvement Era* 48.6 (June 1945): 354.

43. "Pope John Paul II: Life and Papacy on World Stage," *Washington Post* (3 April 2005).

44. "Catholics are as likely as women in the general population to have an abortion. . . . Catholic women of childbearing age are 29% more likely than their Protestant counterparts to have abortions. The rate is even higher—33%—if Hispanics are factored in." Stanley K. Henshaw and Kathryn Kost, "Abortion Patients in 1994–1995: Characteristics and Contraceptive Use," *Family Planning Perspectives* 28.4 (July–August 1996): 140. Among 15- to 19-year-old women, the abortion rate in 1999 was 8 per thousand in Utah, 52 per thousand in New York, and 120 per thousand in Washington, D.C. "Abortion and Pregnancy Rates by State," Guttmacher Institute, www.agi-usa.org/pubs/state_facts99.html.

45. "Over seventy percent of married American women with children are in the labor force, compared to only forty-nine percent of Mormon women." Bruce A. Chadwick and H. Dean Garrett, "Choose Ye This Day Whom Ye Will Serve," in *Mormon Identities in Transition*, ed. Douglas Davies (London: Cassell, 1996), 173.

46. Results of the National Study of Youth and Religion were summarized in "Study Finds Mormon Teens Fare Best," www.news14.com, downloaded 12 March 2005. The study, the most comprehensive to date, was published in Christian Smith and Melinda Lundquist Denton, *Soul Searching: The Religious and Spiritual Lives of American Teenagers* (New York: Oxford University Press, 2005). Several other studies find additional examples of high correlation between LDS teaching and cultural practice. See several of the studies gathered and summarized in James T. Duke, ed., *Latter-day Saint Social Life: Social Research on the LDS Church and Its Members* (Provo, Utah: Religious Studies Center, 1998).

47. Armand L. Mauss, "Assimilation and Ambivalence: The Mormon Reaction to Americanization," *Dialogue: A Journal of Mormon Thought* 22.1 (Spring 1989): 50.

48. "MX Opposition Soars since LDS Statement," *Deseret News* (25 May 1981): B2. Quoted in Edwin Brown Firmage, "A Church Cannot Stand Silent in the Midst of Moral Decay," *Sunstone* 6.4 (July 1981): 42.

49. Henry D. Moyle in *Conference Report of the Church of Jesus Christ of Latter-day Saints* (October 1947): 46.

50. Boyd K. Packer, "The Mantle Is Far, Far Greater than the Intellect," Annual Church Educational Systems Religious Educators' Symposium, 22 August 1981, Brigham Young University, Provo, Utah, published in *BYU Studies* 21.3 (Summer 1981): 259–78.

51. Richard Poll, "What the Church Means to People Like Me," *Dialogue: A Journal of Mormon Thought* 2.4 (Winter 1967): 107–17.

52. Joseph Smith, *The Personal Writings of Joseph Smith*, ed. Dean C. Jessee (Salt Lake City: Deseret, 1984), 396.

53. *Journal of Discourses* 8:185.

54. *Journal of Discourses* 3:45.

55. *Journal of Discourses* 9:150.

56. J. Golden Kimball in *Conference Report of the Church of Jesus Christ of Latter-day Saints* (April 1904): 97.

57. Letter of President George Albert Smith to Dr. J. Raymond Cope, 7 December 1945. Cited in "A 1945 Perspective," *Dialogue: A Journal of Mormon Thought* 19.1 (Spring 1986): 38.

58. Henry D. Taylor in *Conference Report of the Church of Jesus Christ of Latter-day Saints* (April 1966): 82.

59. *Journal of Discourses* 4:297–98.

60. *Journal of Discourses* 22:366.

61. Dallin H. Oaks, "Weightier Matters," *Ensign* 32.1 (January 2001): 18.

∼ CHAPTER 2

1. Joseph Smith, Jr., *History of the Church of Jesus Christ of Latter-day Saints*, 7 vols., ed. James Mulholland, Robert B. Thompson, William W. Phelps, Willard Richards, George A. Smith, and, later, B. H. Roberts (Salt Lake City: Deseret News Press, 1902–1912; 2nd rev. ed., Salt Lake City: Deseret Book, 1951), 5:340.

2. Joseph Smith, *Lectures on Faith: Delivered to the School of the Prophets in Kirtland, Ohio, 1834–35* (Salt Lake City: Deseret, 1985), Lecture Second, 56.

3. Joseph Smith, *The Words of Joseph Smith: The Contemporary Accounts of the Nauvoo Discourses of the Prophet Joseph*, ed. Andrew F. Ehat and Lyndon W. Cook (Provo, Utah: BYU Religious Studies Center, 1980), 12.

4. Joseph Smith, *The Personal Writings of Joseph Smith*, ed. Dean C. Jessee (Salt Lake City: Deseret, 1984), 408.

5. Smith, *History*, 6:305.

6. Smith, *History*, 3:381.

7. Eve LaPlante, *American Jezebel: The Uncommon Life of Anne Hutchinson, the Woman Who Defied the Puritans* (New York: HarperCollins, 2004), 118.

8. LaPlante, *American Jezebel*, 124–25.

9. Alexander Campbell, *The Christian System*, 10, cited in Hyrum L. Andrus, "The Second American Revolution: Era of Preparation," *BYU Studies* 1.2 (Autumn 1959): 80.

10. Alexander Campbell, "Delusions: An Analysis of the Book of Mormon," *Millennial Harbinger* 2 (7 February 1831): 85–96. Reprinted in part in Francis W. Kirkham, *A New Witness for Christ in America*, 2 vols. (Independence, Mo.: Zion's, 1951), 2:101–9.

11. Luke Tyerman, *The Oxford Methodists* (London, 1873), 64. Quoted in Roy Hattersley, *The Life of John Wesley: A Brand from the Burning* (Garden City, N.Y.: Doubleday, 2003), 101; in one instance, deliberating a marriage proposal, he marked lots "Marry," "Think Not This Year," and "Think of It No More." The young lady lost out. Hattersley, *Life of John Wesley*, 120; see also 128.

12. Gilbert Wardlaw, *The Testimony of Scripture to the Obligations and Efficacy of Prayer* (Boston: Peirce and Williams, 1830), 8, 59, 97n.

13. Spencer W. Kimball's "official declaration" extending the priesthood to all worthy males was received and canonized in 1978. Joseph F. Smith's vision of the spirit world was canonized in 1976 (D&C 138), but received in 1918. Similarly, Joseph

Smith's revelation on the salvation of children was canonized in 1976 (D&C 137) but received in 1836.

14. As both David Knowlton and Armand Mauss have pointed out, these testimonies, formerly steeped in firsthand experiences, miraculous healings, and spiritual encounters with the divine, have attained a highly formulaic and ritualized dimension, prime evidence of which is the frequent participation of little children reciting the formulas they have imbibed. (In an effort to curb this last trend, at least, the First Presidency issued a statement discouraging that practice in 2002.) See David Knowlton, "Belief, Metaphor, and Rhetoric: The Mormon Practice of Bearing Testimonies," *Sunstone* 15.1 (April 1991): 20–27; Armand L. Mauss, *The Angel and the Beehive: The Mormon Struggle with Assimilation* (Urbana: University of Illinois Press, 1994), 28–30; Letter of the First Presidency, 2 May 2002. Author's files.

15. Smith, *History*, 1:6.

16. Jessee, *Personal Writings*, 6.

17. Smith, *History*, 1:6.

18. Eliza R. Snow Smith, *Biography and Family Record of Lorenzo Snow* (Salt Lake City: Deseret News, 1884), 7–8.

19. Thomas O'Dea, *The Mormons* (Chicago: University of Chicago Press, 1957), 151–52. O'Dea attributes the phrase "vigorous exercise of the will" to an unnamed "Mormon thinker."

20. William Blake, "Marriage of Heaven and Hell," in *Blake: The Complete Poems*, ed. W. H. Stevenson (London: Longman, 1989), 105.

21. Smith, *History*, 5:401.

22. Smith, *History*, 6:428.

23. Smith, *History*, 5:215.

24. Jessee, *Personal Writings*, 420.

25. Hyrum L. Andrus and Helen Mae Andrus, *They Knew the Prophet: Personal Accounts from over 100 People Who Knew Joseph Smith* (Salt Lake City: Bookcraft, 1974), 140.

26. Virginia Woolf, *A Room of One's Own* (New York: Harcourt Brace Jovanovich, 1989), 3–4.

27. Hattersley, *Life of John Wesley*, 130.

28. Johann Wolfgang von Goethe, *Faust*, trans. Walter Arndt (New York: Norton, 2001), 46.

29. *Journal of Discourses*, 26 vols., reported by G. D. Watt et al. (Liverpool, England: Richards et al., 1851–1886; rpt., Salt Lake City: n.p., 1974), 9:242.

30. Smith, *History*, 6:306–7.

31. *Journal of Discourses* 7:3.

32. Hattersley, *Life of John Wesley*, 132–33.

33. *Journal of Discourses* 10:269.

34. Smith elaborates the doctrine of the second comforter" or the "calling and election made sure," as a revelation of one's own salvation. However, even in this case, the recipient of the assurance has the *promise* of eternal life, not the condition.

35. *Journal of Discourses* 3:47.

36. Irving Dilliard, ed., *The Spirit of Liberty: Papers and Addresses of Learned Hand* (Chicago: University of Chicago Press, 1977), 190.

37. Louis Ginzberg, *Legends of the Bible* (New York: Simon and Schuster, 1956), 601.

38. Succeeding Pope John Paul II, Pope Benedict XVI quickly moved to disavow the concept of limbo.

39. C. S. Lewis, *Perelandra* (New York: Scribner's, 1996), 152.

40. *Deseret News Weekly*, 7 November 1896. Cited in Alma P. Burton, ed., *Discourses of the Prophet Joseph Smith* (Salt Lake City: Deseret, 1977), 268.

~ CHAPTER 3

1. Jonathan Edwards, *Heaven Is a World of Love*, cited in George M. Marsden, *Jonathan Edwards: A Life* (New Haven, Conn.: Yale University Press, 2003), 191.

2. Lord Byron, "Cain," in *Byron*, ed. Jerome J. McGann (Oxford: Oxford University Press, 1986), 902.

3. William Wordsworth, "The Excursion," in *Poetical Works*, ed. Thomas Hutchinson and Ernest de Selincourt (Oxford: Oxford University Press, 1989), 627.

4. [François René de] Chateaubriand, *The Genius of Christianity* (New York: Howard Fertig, 1976), 51–52.

5. Robert Browning, "Two in the Campagna," in *The Poetical Works of Robert Browning* (Boston: Houghton Mifflin, 1974), 189.

6. Stan Larson, "The King Follett Discourse: A Newly Amalgamated Text," *BYU Studies* 18.2 (Winter 1978): 201. The discourse was so called because at its commencement, Joseph offered words of consolation to the family of the recently deceased Follett.

7. "Hold whatever interpretation of the psalm [82] you please. It has been shown that they were considered worthy to become gods." Justin Martyr, *Dialogue with Trypho*, trans. Thomas B. Falls (Washington, D.C.: Catholic University of America Press, 2003), 187. "Yea, I say, the Word of God became a man so that you might learn from a man how to become a god" (St. Clement of Alexandria); "The Word was made flesh in order that we might be enabled to be made gods," "He became man that we might be made divine" (Athanasius); "But he himself that justifies also deifies, for by justifying he makes sons of God. 'For he has given them power to become the sons of God' [John 1:12]. If then we have been made sons of God, we have also been made gods" (Augustine). The Clement, Athanasius, and Augustine citations are in Stephen Robinson, *Are Mormons Christian?* (Salt Lake City: Bookcraft, 1991), 61. "Finite beings (with free wills) [may progress] into—well, Gods." C. S. Lewis, Letter to Mrs. Edward A. Allen (1 Nov. 1954), in *Letters of C. S. Lewis*, ed. Walter Hooper (New York: Harcourt Brace, 1993), 440. "There are no ordinary people. We live in a society of possible gods and goddesses." C. S. Lewis, *The Weight of Glory* (London: Society for Promoting Christian Knowledge, 1942), 22.

8. Larson, "King Follett," 204.

9. Truman Madsen, "Are Christians Mormon?" *BYU Studies* 15.1 (Autumn 1974): 89.

10. Bruce Hafen, *The Broken Heart* (Salt Lake City: Deseret, 1989), 149.

11. Joseph Smith, Jr., *History of the Church of Jesus Christ of Latter-day Saints*, 7 vols., ed. James Mulholland, Robert B. Thompson, William W. Phelps, Willard Richards, George A. Smith, and, later, B. H. Roberts (Salt Lake City: Deseret News Press, 1902–1912; 2nd rev. ed., Salt Lake City: Deseret Book, 1951), 4:588.

12. Smith, *History*, 2:11–12.

13. Plato, *Timaeus*, in *Plato in Twelve Volumes*, trans. R. G. Bury (Cambridge, Mass.: Harvard University Press, 1929), 55.

14. Augustine, *Confessions*, trans. F. J. Sheed (Indianapolis, Ind.: Hackett, 1993), bk. IV:xv, 63.

15. Dante Alighieri, *Paradiso*, trans. Allen Mandelbaum (New York: Bantam, 1984), canto VII, ll. 97–101.

16. Dante, *Paradiso*, 335.

17. Marsden, *Edwards*, 112.

18. Eliza R. Snow Smith, *Biography and Family Record of Lorenzo Snow* (Salt Lake City: Deseret News, 1884), 46.

19. Parley P. Pratt, *Key to the Science of Theology* (Liverpool, England: Richards, 1855), 33, 36.

20. Samuel T. Coleridge, "Notebooks," in *Samuel Taylor Coleridge*, ed. H. J. Jackson (Oxford: Oxford University Press, 1985), 555.

21. Roger Finke and Rodney Stark, *The Churching of America, 1776–1990: Winners and Losers in Our Religious Economy* (New Brunswick, N.J.: Rutgers University Press, 1993), 237–75.

22. J. F. C. Harrison, *The Second Coming: Popular Millenarianism, 1780–1850* (New Brunswick, N.J.: Rutgers University Press, 1979), 191. Cited in Gordon S. Wood, "Evangelical America and Early Mormonism," *New York History* 61 (October 1980): 380.

23. Larson, "King Follett," 200.

24. Ogden Kraut, in *Jesus Was Married* (n.p., 1969), documents a number of early LDS leaders who taught that Christ was married, including Orson Hyde, Orson Pratt, and Orson Spencer. In 1912, the First Presidency declared, "[T]he Church has no authoritative declaration on the subject." *Improvement Era* 15.11 (1912): 1042.

25. John Milton, *Paradise Lost*, bk. VIII, ll. 615–27, in *Milton's Complete Poetical Works* (Boston: Houghton Mifflin, 1899), 193.

26. Emanuel Swedenborg, *Marital Love: Its Wise Delights*, trans. William Frederic Wunsch (New York: Swedenborg Publishing Association, 1938), 73–74.

27. Alfred Kazin, ed., *The Portable Blake* (New York: Viking, 1946), 40.

28. Sigmund Freud is one of several writers who attribute the phrase to Augustine. See *Civilization and Its Discontents* (New York: Norton, 1989), 43. It may originate much later, with Bernard of Clairvaux.

29. William Blake, "Marriage of Heaven and Hell," in *Blake: The Complete Poems*, ed. W. H. Stevenson (London: Longman, 1989), 109.

30. Thomas O'Dea, *The Mormons* (Chicago: University of Chicago Press, 1957), 150.

31. *Journal of Discourses*, 26 vols., reported by G. D. Watt et al. (Liverpool, England: Richards et al., 1851–1886; rpt., Salt Lake City: n.p., 1974), 7:138.

32. *Journal of Discourses* 8:128–29.

33. Rex Skidmore, "Mormon Recreation in Theory and Practice: A Study in Social Change" (Ph.D. diss., University of Pennsylvania, 1941), 5. Cited in O'Dea, *Mormons*, 147.

34. *Journal of Discourses* 7:271.

35. *Journal of Discourses* 15:127.

36. *Journal of Discourses* 7:157.

37. *Journal of Discourses* 9:167.

38. Josiah Quincy, *Figures of the Past from the Leaves of Old Journals* (Boston: Little, Brown, 1926), 326.

39. Dean D. McBrien, "The Economic Content of Early Mormon Doctrine," *Southwestern Political and Social Science Quarterly* 6 (1925): 180. Cited in Leonard J. Arrington, "Religion and Economics in Mormon History," *BYU Studies* 3.3–4 (Spring 1960–Summer 1961): 16.

40. Jan Shipps, *Mormonism: A New Religious Tradition* (Urbana: University of Illinois Press, 1985), 125.

41. Armand L. Mauss, "Assimilation and Ambivalence: The Mormon Reaction to Americanization," *Dialogue* 22.1 (Spring 1989): 30–31. See his book on the subject, *The Angel and the Beehive: The Mormon Struggle with Assimilation* (Urbana: University of Illinois Press, 1994).

42. Rudolf Otto, *The Idea of the Holy*, 2nd ed., trans. J. W. Harvey (Oxford: Oxford University Press, 1950), 27n.

43. Ezra Booth to Reverend I. Eddy, *Ohio Star* 24 (October 1831); J. M. Peck, *A Gazetteer of Illinois* (Jacksonville, Ill.: Goudy, 1834), 53–54; Charles Dickens, "In the Name of the Prophet—Smith!" *Household Words* 3 (19 July 1851): 385.

44. Friedrich Nietzsche, *The Genealogy of Morals*, trans. Walter Kaufmann and R. J. Hollingdale, in *The Genealogy of Morals and Ecce Homo* (New York: Vintage, 1989), 157.

45. Otto, *Idea of the Holy*, 146.

46. Emil Brunner, *Our Faith* (New York: Scribner's, 1954), 11–12.

47. Elizabeth A. Johnson, *She Who Is: The Mystery of God in Feminist Theological Discourse* (New York: Crossroad, 1992), 7. Her citations are Augustine, *Sermo* 52, c. 6, n. 16 (PL 38.360); Anselm, *Proslogium* chaps. 2–3, in *Saint Anselm: Basic Writings*, trans. S. N. Deane (LaSalle, Ill.: Open Court, 1974); Hildegaard of Bingen, *Scivias*, trans. Mother Columba Hart and Jane Bishop (New York: Paulist, 1990), bk. 1, vision 1, *ST* I, q. 3, preface; Luther, theses 19 and 20, "The Heidelberg Disputation," in *Luther: Early Theological Works*, trans. and ed. James Atkinson (Philadelphia: Westminster, 1962); Simone Weil, *Waiting for God*, trans. Emma Craufurd (New York: Harper and Row, 1973), 32; and Sallie McFague, *Models of God: Theology for an Ecological, Nuclear Age* (Philadelphia: Fortress, 1987), 35 and passim.

48. His actual words were, "the Son of God was crucified: . . . it is immediately credible—because it is silly [*ineptum*]. He was buried, and rose again: it is certain—because it is impossible [*certum est quia impossibile est*]." Ernest Evans, trans., *Tertullian: De Carne Christi* (London: SPCK, 1956), 19.

49. George Steiner, *Real Presences* (Chicago: University of Chicago Press, 1989), 91–92.

50. Edmund Burke, *A Philosophical Inquiry into the Origin of Our Ideas of the Sublime and Beautiful*, in *The Works of the Right Honorable Edmund Burke*, 12 vols. (Boston: Little, Brown, 1869), 1:133–37.

51. Chateaubriand, *Genius of Christianity*, 51–52.

52. William James, *Varieties of Religious Experience* (Cambridge, Mass.: Harvard University Press, 1985), 362.

53. C. S. Lewis, *Perelandra* (New York: Macmillan, 1965), 11.

54. Mary Shelley, *Frankenstein; or, The Modern Prometheus* (New York: Signet, 1963), 39.

55. Shelley, *Frankenstein*, 56.

56. Shelley, *Frankenstein*, 56.

57. George Steiner, *Martin Heidegger* (New York: Viking, 1978), 54. The wording is Steiner's paraphrase.

58. Albert Einstein, *The World as I See It* (New York: Philosophical Library, 1949), 5.

～ CHAPTER 4

1. Bruce Kuklick, *History of Philosophy in America* (Oxford: Oxford University Press, 2001), 26.

2. George M. Marsden, *Jonathan Edwards: A Life* (New Haven, Conn.: Yale University Press, 2003), 349.

3. Ronald D. Dennis, "The Reverend W. R. Davies vs. Captain Dan Jones," *BYU Studies* 27.2 (Spring 1987): 57.

4. The expression "the catholic and only true Church" was used at least as early as Eusebius of Caesarea in his *Ecclesiastical History* (325 A.D.). The pope of Vatican I, Pius IX, reaffirmed on 9 December 1854 "that outside the Apostolic Roman Church, no one can be saved." Cited in Henry Denzinger, *The Sources of Catholic Dogma*, trans. Roy J. Deferrari (St. Louis, Mo.: Herder, 1955), 416. The stance has softened since Vatican II, but the claim is still to be found frequently in Catholic publications.

5. Armand L. Mauss discusses some of these movements and their secular counterparts in "In Search of Ephraim: Traditional Mormon Conceptions of Lineage and Race," *Journal of Mormon History* 25.1 (Spring 1999): 136ff.

6. Mauss, "In Search," 143. See also his *All Abraham's Children: Changing Mormon Conceptions of Race and Lineage* (Urbana: University of Illinois Press, 2003), especially chapter 2.

7. Mauss, "In Search," 149.

8. From a document produced in Clay County, Missouri, June 1836, in Joseph Smith, Jr., *History of the Church of Jesus Christ of Latter-day Saints*, 7 vols., ed. James Mulholland, Robert B. Thompson, William W. Phelps, Willard Richards, George A. Smith, and, later, B. H. Roberts (Salt Lake City: Deseret News Press, 1902–1912; 2nd rev. ed., Salt Lake City: Deseret Book, 1951), 2:450.

9. *Journal of Discourses*, 26 vols., reported by G. D. Watt et al. (Liverpool, England: Richards et al., 1851–1886; rpt., Salt Lake City: n.p., 1974), 12:272.

10. Smith, *History*, 6:300.

11. The "scientific" report cited a description by U.S. Army Assistant Surgeon Roberts Bartholow: "This condition is shown by ... the large proportion of albuminous and gelatinous types of constitution, and by the striking uniformity in facial expression and in physical conformation of the younger portion of the community.... The yellow, sunken, cadaverous visage; the greenish-colored eyes; the thick, protuberant lips; the low forehead; the light, yellowish hair, and the lank, angular person, constitute an appearance so characteristic of the new race, the production of polygamy, as to distinguish them at a glance." Surgeon General's Office, *Statistical Report on the Sicknes[s] and Mortality in the Army of the United States ... from January, 1855 to January, 1860* (Washington, D.C.: Bowman, 1860), 301–2.

12. Woodruff said that God told him that persistence in polygamy would eventuate in "the confiscation and loss of all the Temples, and the stopping of all the ordinances therein," "the imprisonment of the First Presidency and Twelve," and a condition where "confusion would reign throughout Israel." From an address given in Logan, Utah, 1 November 1891, appended to D&C, Official Declaration, 1.

13. For a study of this ethnic construction interpreted as a response to the threat suggested by a "viper on the hearth," see the work of that title: Terryl Givens, *Viper on the Hearth* (New York: Oxford University Press, 1997).

14. Not only biblical, but LDS scriptures are emphatic on the point of God's universalism. See Arnold H. Green's examples and a survey of the larger tension they indicate with LDS notions of lineage and election in "Gathering and Election: Israelite Descent and Universalism in Mormon Discourse," *Journal of Mormon History* 25.1 (April 1999): 195–228.

15. *Times and Seasons* 5.15 (15 August 1844): 625.

16. "Striving for Acceptance," *Washington Post*, 9 February 2002, p. B9; "United Methodists Claim LDS Not Really Christian," *Idaho Statesman*, 11 May 2000, p. A2.

17. Stephen E. Robinson, *Are Mormons Christian?* (Salt Lake City: Bookcraft, 1991); Truman Madsen, "Are Christians Mormon?" *BYU Studies* 15.1 (Autumn 1974): 73–94.

18. Jan Shipps, *Mormonism: The Story of a New Religious Tradition* (Urbana: University of Illinois Press, 1985), 46.

19. Obviously, Mormons will always be Christian in the sense of considering Christ the author and finisher of their salvation. But the debate is really about Mormonism's conformity with a historically evolved agglomeration of faith groups defined by assent to normative creeds.

20. Spencer W. Kimball, "The Role of Righteous Women," *Ensign* 10 (November 1979): 104.

21. *60 Minutes* program on the LDS church, broadcast on CBS, 7 April 1996. Transcript available at http://www.lds-mormon.com/60min.shtml.

22. Armand Mauss has written extensively on this theme. "The past few decades have witnessed an increasing reaction of the Mormons against their own successful assimilation," he wrote in 1994, "as though trying to recover some of the cultural

tension and special identity associated with their earlier 'sect-like' history." Tracing the consequent realignments and transformations is the burden of his *The Angel and the Beehive: The Mormon Struggle with Assimilation* (Urbana: University of Illinois Press, 1994).

23. Tolstoy reportedly remarked to Andrew D. White, then president of Cornell University, that "the Mormon people teach the American religion." *Improvement Era* 32.2 (February 1939). Bloom remarks on "how American both [Joseph Smith] and his religion have proved to be." Harold Bloom, *The American Religion: The Emergence of the Post-Christian Nation* (New York: Simon and Schuster, 1992), 127.

24. *Chicago Times*, 7 August 1875, in Lyndon W. Cook, ed., *David Whitmer Interviews: A Restoration Witness* (Orem, Utah: Grandin, 1991), 7.

25. For a discussion of the role of this verse and the Book of Mormon in establishing the LDS understanding of an American Zion, see Grant Underwood, *The Millenarian World of Early Mormonism* (Urbana: University of Illinois Press, 1999), 77–79.

26. Richard Edwards, "Buddhist Imagery," *BYU Studies* 12.1 (Autumn 1971): 75.

27. Dallin H. Oaks, "Repentance and Change," *Ensign* 33.11 (November 2003): 38.

28. *Journal of Discourses* 13:335.

~ PART II

1. Cited in "The Historians Corner," *BYU Studies* 17.3 (Spring 1977): 351.

2. "To His Excellency, Daniel Dunklin," *Evening and the Morning Star* 2.15 (December 1833): 114.

3. *Contributor* 1.1 (October 1879): 13.

~ CHAPTER 5

1. Charles Dickens, "In the Name of the Prophet—Smith!" *Household Words* 8 (19 July 1851): 340.

2. *Elders Journal* 1.4 (August 1838): 54.

3. Adophe E. Meyer, *An Educational History of the American People* (New York: McGraw-Hill, 1957), 150.

4. This figure is given for the early nineteenth century, before the commencement of the Erie Canal, by Peter L. Bernstein, *Wedding of the Waters* (New York: Norton, 2005), 23.

5. Joseph Smith, Jr., *History of the Church of Jesus Christ of Latter-day Saints*, 7 vols., ed. James Mulholland, Robert B. Thompson, William W. Phelps, Willard Richards, George A. Smith, and, later, B. H. Roberts (Salt Lake City: Deseret News Press, 1902–1912; 2nd rev. ed., Salt Lake City: Deseret Book, 1951), 1:7.

6. William Mulder, "Mormonism and Literature," *Western Humanities Review* 9 (Winter 1954–1955), 85.

7. Lucy Mack Smith, *History of Joseph Smith by His Mother* (Salt Lake City: Stevens and Wallis, 1945), 82.

8. Francis J. Bremer, *John Winthrop: America's Forgotten Founding Father* (New York: Oxford University Press, 2003), 310.

9. Samuel Eliot Morison, *The Oxford History of the American People* (New York: Oxford University Press, 1965), 71.

10. Towns of 50 or more households were required to employ a reading and writing instructor; 100 or more and a grammar school was mandated. Bremer, *Winthrop*, 311.

11. W. W. Sweet, *Religion on the American Frontier* (Chicago: University of Chicago Press, 1936), 2:249–50. Cited in T. Scott Miyakawa, *Protestants and Pioneers: Individualism and Conformity on the American Frontier* (Chicago: University of Chicago Press, 1964), 86.

12. Roy Hattersley, *The Life of John Wesley: A Brand from the Burning* (Garden City, N.Y.: Doubleday, 2003), 306.

13. Hattersley, *Life of John Wesley*, 261, 264.

14. Nathan Bangs, *A History of the Methodist Episcopal Church*, 3rd ed., 4 vols. (New York: Lane and Sandford, 1840–1853), 3:45, 47.

15. A. D. Gillette, ed., *Minutes of the Philadelphia Baptist Association* (Minneapolis, Minn.: James, 1851), 50–51.

16. Miyakawa, *Protestants*, 88. He is citing the *Baptist Almanac* of 1853.

17. B. H. Carroll, Jr., *The Genesis of American Anti-Missionism* (Louisville, Ky.: Baptist Book Concern, 1902), 131–34. Cited in Miyakawa, *Protestants*, 89.

18. Marvin Hill, "The Shaping of the Mormon Mind in New England and New York," *BYU Studies* 9.3 (Spring 1969): 353.

19. J. M. Peck, *A Gazetteer of Illinois* (Jacksonville, Ill.: Goudy, 1834), 92.

20. Lucy Mack Smith, *History*, 90.

21. Harold Bloom, *The American Religion: The Emergence of the Post-Christian Nation* (New York: Simon and Schuster, 1992), 123.

22. Thomas O'Dea, *The Mormons* (Chicago: University of Chicago Press, 1957), 147–48.

23. Stan Larson, "The King Follett Discourse: A Newly Amalgamated Text," *BYU Studies* 18.2 (Winter 1978): 201.

24. The letter is reproduced in Dean C. Jessee, "New Documents and Mormon Beginnings," *BYU Studies* 24.4 (Fall 1984): 403. The story of the forgery, one of several perpetrated by Mark Hofmann, is told in Linda Sillitoe and Allen Roberts, *Salamander: The Mormon Forgery Murders* (Salt Lake City: Signature, 1988). An account more sympathetic to the LDS church is Richard E. Turley, *Victims: The LDS Church and the Mark Hofmann Case* (Urbana: University of Illinois Press, 1992).

25. D. Michael Quinn, *Early Mormonism and the Magic World View* (Salt Lake City: Signature, 1986).

26. John L. Brooke, *The Refiner's Fire: The Making of Mormon Cosmology, 1644–1844* (Cambridge: Cambridge University Press, 1994), xiii.

27. Bloom, *American Religion*, 101.

28. Bloom, *American Religion*, 99, 105. An overview of these developments is found in Lance S. Owens, "Joseph Smith and the Kabbalah: The Occult Connection," *Dialogue: A Journal of Mormon Thought* 27.3 (Fall 1994): 117–94.

29. Brooke, *Refiner's Fire*, xiv.

30. Even the terribly important temple endowment, in which members are given special words and signs preparatory to eventual exaltation, must be seen in light of (1) the larger, all-consuming project of knowledge acquisition as an eternal endeavor, and (2) its highly ritualistic and expressly symbolic nature.

31. Richard Dawkins, "Is Science a Religion?" *Humanist* (January–February 1997), 26–29.

32. *Journal of Discourses*, 26 vols., reported by G. D. Watt et al. (Liverpool, England: Richards et al., 1851–1886; rpt., Salt Lake City: n.p., 1974), 14:115–17.

33. John Taylor, *The Gospel Kingdom: Selections from the Writings and Discourses of John Taylor*, ed. G. Homer Durham (Salt Lake City: Improvement Era, 1941), 93.

34. Smith, *History*, 1:196. Smith here refers to a log house. Other reports clarified that it was a schoolhouse. See Daniel H. Ludlow, *Encyclopedia of Mormonism*, 4 vols. (New York: Macmillan, 1992), 4:1653.

35. Smith, *History*, 1:238.

36. Sidney Rigdon gave 2 July 1833 as the date of the work's completion. See *Times and Seasons* 6.2 (4 February 1845): 803. But Smith's wife Emma and Brigham Young both referred to Smith's unfulfilled intention to return to the work and complete it. See Terryl L. Givens, *The Latter-day Saint Experience in America* (Westport, Conn.: Greenwood, 2004), 164.

37. Henry Barnard, "The American Lyceum," *American Journal of Education* 14 (1865): 525, cited in Cecil B. Hayes, "The American Lyceum: Its History and Contribution to Education," *Office of Education Bulletin* 12 (1932): vii.

38. James B. Allen and Glen M. Leonard, *The Story of the Latter-day Saints*, 2nd ed. (Salt Lake City: Deseret, 1992), 107.

39. Smith, *History*, 2:318. Seixas arrived in January 1836 and instructed for a seven-week term. See Louis C. Zucker, "Joseph Smith as a Student of Hebrew," *Dialogue: A Journal of Mormon Thought* 3.2 (1968): 44.

40. Smith, *History*, 2:344.

41. Smith, *History*, 2:396.

42. "The Journal and Record of Heber Chase Kimball," quoted in Dean C. Jessee, "The Kirtland Diary of Wilford Woodruff," *BYU Studies* 12.4 (Summer 1972): 373–74.

43. John W. Hess, "Recollections of the Prophet Joseph Smith," *Juvenile Instructor* 27 (1892).

44. John Corrill, cited in "By No Means Men of Weak Minds," in *Among the Mormons: Historic Accounts by Contemporary Observers*, ed. William Mulder and Russell Mortensen (Lincoln: University of Nebraska Press, 1958), 87.

45. See Milton V. Backman, Jr., *The Heavens Resound: A History of the Latter-day Saints in Ohio 1830–1838* (Salt Lake City: Deseret, 1983), 272.

46. James H. Eells to Br. Leavitt, Kirtland, Ohio (1 April 1835), in Mulder and Mortensen, *Among the Mormons*, 88.

47. *Improvement Era* 53.12 (December 1950).

48. "History of Orson Hyde," *Millennial Star* 26 (1864): 744, 760.

49. Orson F. Whitney, *History of Utah*, 4 vols. (Salt Lake City: Cannon, 1904), 4:29.

50. Thomas Alexander, *Things in Heaven and Earth: The Life and Times of Wilford Woodruff, a Mormon Prophet* (Salt Lake City: Signature, 1993), 13.

51. Alexander, *Things in Heaven*, 41, 47.

52. Eliza R. Snow Smith, *Biography and Family Record of Lorenzo Snow* (Salt Lake City: Deseret News, 1884), 3.

53. "Autobiography of Caroline Barnes Crosby, 1836," cited in Backman, *Heavens*, 272.

54. Pearl Wilcox, *Latter Day Saints on the Missouri Frontier* (Independence, Mo.: n.p., 1972), 102.

55. For a fuller discussion of the subject, see George W. Givens, *In Old Nauvoo: Everyday Life in the City of Joseph* (Salt Lake City: Deseret, 1990), 227–36.

56. Thomas Woody, *A History of Women's Education in the United States*, 2 vols. (New York: Science Press, 1929), 2:229.

57. Miyakawa, *Protestants*, 107.

58. Miyakawa, *Protestants*, 104–5.

59. Meyer, *Educational History*, 190.

60. Erastus Snow, "A Journal or Sketch of the Life of Erastus Snow," 26, typescript, Special Collections, Harold B. Lee Library, Brigham Young University, Provo, Utah.

61. "Memoirs of Geo. A. Smith," cited in Dean C. Jessee, "The Kirtland Diary of Wilford Woodruff," *BYU Studies* 12.4 (Summer 1972): 400, 385.

62. Orsamus Turner, *History of the Pioneer Settlement of Phelps and Gorham's Purchase, and Morris' Reserve* (Rochester, N.Y., 1852), 214, cited in Richard Lloyd Anderson, "Circumstantial Confirmation of the First Vision through Reminiscences," *BYU Studies* 9.3 (Spring 1969): 378–79.

63. Smith, *History*, 2:317.

64. Smith, *History*, 2:330.

65. Smith, *History*, 2:317–18. Smith was still urging moderation when he spoke in Nauvoo years later. On one such occasion, Mercy R. Thompson "heard him reprove the brethren for giving way to too much excitement and warmth in debate." Joseph Smith, *The Words of Joseph Smith: The Contemporary Accounts of the Nauvoo Discourses of the Prophet Joseph*, ed. Andrew F. Ehat and Lyndon W. Cook (Provo, Utah: BYU Religious Studies Center, 1980), xix–xx.

66. Smith, *History*, 2:334.

67. Smith, *History*, 4:513–14.

68. Smith, *History*, 2:318.

69. Smith, *History*, 4:235–36, 249.

70. "History of Orson Hyde," 791.

71. *Times and Seasons* 4.23 (15 October 1843): 358.

72. Givens, *In Old Nauvoo*, 237, 242.

73. Allen and Leonard, *Story of the Latter-day Saints*, 158.

74. *Autobiography of Warren Foote*, 3 vols. (Mesa, Ariz.: Dale Arnold Foote, 1997), 1:52. Pagination follows the originals, which are in the LDS Historical Department, Salt Lake City, Utah.

75. Givens, *In Old Nauvoo*, 242.

76. H. Dean Garrett, ed., *Regional Studies in Latter-day Saint History: Illinois* (Provo, Utah: Department of Church History and Doctrine, 1995), 341.

77. Smith, *History*, 4:243.

78. Meyer, *Educational History*, 193.

79. F. C. Holliday, *Indiana Methodism* (Cincinnati, Ohio: Hitchcock and Walden, 1873), 317–29. Cited in Miyakawa, *Protestants*, 108.

80. Andrew Delbanco, "Colleges: An Endangered Species," *New York Review of Books* 52.4 (10 March 2005): section 2, 19.

81. Smith, *History*, 4:269.

82. Smith, *History*, 4:293.

83. *Times and Seasons* 5.24 (1 January 1844): 761.

84. Smith, *History*, 4:338.

85. The Seventy was a quorum of "traveling ministers" functioning under the direction of the Twelve Apostles, organized in 1835. The Seventies Hall, completed in 1844, was used for various priesthood meetings and missionary classes and housed a modest library and museum.

86. *Times and Seasons* 3.2 (15 November 1841): 606.

87. "Rising in the World," *New York Herald*, 13 August 1842.

88. Donald Q. Cannon cites evidence that Orson Pratt taught classes for the university from 1841 to 1843. See Breck England, *The Life and Thought of Orson Pratt* (Salt Lake City: University of Utah Press, 1985), 72, 84. Cannon provides an overview of the university's history in "Joseph Smith and the University of Nauvoo," in *Joseph Smith: The Prophet, the Man*, ed. Susan Easton Black and Charles D. Tate, Jr. (Provo, Utah: Religious Studies Center/Brigham Young University Press, 1993), 285–300.

89. "Highly Important from the Mormon Empire," *New York Herald*, 17 June 1842.

90. Joseph Smith, Letter to John M. Bernhisel, 16 November 1841, in *The Personal Writings of Joseph Smith*, ed. Dean C. Jessee (Salt Lake City: Deseret, 1984), 502.

91. *Times and Seasons* 4.13 (15 May 1843): 201. Little progress in the collection occurred during Joseph's lifetime.

92. "Seventies' Library," *Times and Seasons* 5.24 (1 January 1844): 763. Kirjath Sepher, mentioned in Joshua 15:15, was a city in the hill country of Judah. The name "seems to indicate that it was the 'city of the roll,' *i.e.*, for enrolment or enlisting purposes; but the second element, 'sepher,' may possibly be the name of a deity. To explain it as 'Library-city' appears to be assuming too much." Isidore Singer et al., eds., *The Jewish Encyclopedia*, 12 vols. (New York: Funk and Wagnalls, 1916), 7:509.

93. Kenneth W. Godfrey, "A Note on the Nauvoo Library and Literary Institute," *BYU Studies* 14 (Spring 1974): 386–89.

94. Frank L. Mott, *American Journalism*, 3rd ed. (New York: Macmillan, 1962), 216. Cited in David J. Whittaker, *Early Mormon Pamphleteering* (Provo, Utah: BYU Studies/Joseph Fielding Smith Institute for Latter-day Saint History, 2003), 1–2. Whittaker provides a brief but useful overview of the rise of the religious press in antebellum America.

95. George M. Stephenson, *The Puritan Heritage* (New York: Macmillan, 1952), 157. Cited in Whittaker, *Early Mormon*, 3.

96. Whittaker, *Early Mormon*, 10.

97. *Evening and the Morning Star* 1.1 (June 1832): 6.

98. The subscription numbers and crowd incident are drawn from the work of Heather Hardy, who has made a study of Woodruff's 1835–1836 mission to Tennessee and Kentucky, based on his journal, daybook, and membership record book, all housed in the LDS archives. Personal correspondence, 21 October 2005.

99. "To the Elders of the Church of Latter-day Saints" appeared in three parts in the *Messenger and Advocate* for September, November, and December 1835.

100. The Articles of Faith were included in a letter to John Wentworth, and included an overview of the church's rise and development and an outline of its beliefs. Known as the Wentworth letter, it was signed by Joseph Smith but may have been drafted by William W. Phelps, who was Joseph's political writer during this period.

101. Whittaker, *Early Mormon*, 18.

102. Parley P. Pratt, *A Voice of Warning and Instruction to All People* (New York: Sanford, 1837), 69–71.

103. Pratt, *Voice*, 126, 132–33.

104. Winfred Ernest Garrison and Alfred T. DeGroot, *The Disciples of Christ: A History* (St. Louis, Mo.: Bethany, 1958), 188.

105. "Education," *Times and Seasons* 6.20 (1 January 1846): 1078–79.

106. James R. Clark, comp., *Messages of the First Presidency of the Church of Jesus Christ of Latter-day Saints*, 6 vols. (Salt Lake City: Bookcraft, 1965–1975), 1:323.

107. Jan Shipps, *Mormonism: A New Religious Tradition* (Urbana: University of Illinois Press, 1985), 125.

108. Maureen Ursenbach, "Three Women and the Life of the Mind," *Utah Historical Quarterly* 43 (Winter 1975): 40.

109. *Times and Seasons* 2.9 (1 March 1841): 337.

110. Details of territorial and other libraries from an address of Leonard H. Kirkpatrick, 2 October 1961, in *BYU Speeches of the Year* (Provo, Utah: Brigham Young University Press, 1961), 5.

111. *Journal of Discourses* 6:373.

112. David J. Whittaker, "Joseph B. Keeler, Print Culture, and the Modernization of Mormonism, 1885–1918," in *Religion and the Culture of Print in Modern America*, ed. James P. Danky (Madison: University of Wisconsin Press, forthcoming).

113. Ursenbach, "Three Women," 26–40. The society reorganized at a much later date.

114. *Journal of Discourses* 9:369.

115. T. Edgar Lyon, Jr., *John Lyon: The Life of a Pioneer Poet* (Provo, Utah: BYU Religious Studies Center, 1989), 225.

116. Cited in Ronald Walker, "Growing Up in Early Utah: The Wasatch Literary Association, 1874–1878," *Sunstone* 6.6 (November 1981): 45.

117. Gary James Bergera, ed., *Autobiography of B. H. Roberts* (Salt Lake City: Signature, 1990), 54.

118. The prominent leaders of the Godbeite movement were excommunicated in 1869. For an excellent overview of the movement, see Ronald W. Walker, *Wayward Saints: The Godbeites and Brigham Young* (Urbana: University of Illinois Press, 1998).

119. Orson Pratt, "Prospectus of 'The Seer,'" *Seer* 1.1 (January 1853): 1.

120. Samuel T. Coleridge, "Notebooks," in *Samuel Taylor Coleridge*, ed. H. J. Jackson (Oxford: Oxford University Press, 1985), 555.

121. Pratt, "The Pre-Existence of Man," *Seer* 1.2 (February 1853), 23–24.

122. T. Edgar Lyon, "Orson Pratt: Early Mormon Leader" (M.A. thesis, University of Chicago, 1932), 125.

123. Peter Crawley, "Parley P. Pratt: Father of Mormon Pamphleteering," *Dialogue: A Journal of Mormon Thought* 15.3 (Autumn 1982): 17–18.

124. Parley P. Pratt, *Key to the Science of Theology* (Liverpool, England: Richards, 1855), 33, 149.

125. Pratt, *Key to the Science*, 126, 128.

126. Pratt, *Key to the Science*, 156–57.

127. *Journal of Discourses* 7:285.

128. *Millennial Star* 17 (1855): 297–98.

129. Gary James Bergera, "The Orson Pratt–Brigham Young Controversies: Conflict within the Quorums, 1853–1868," *Dialogue: A Journal of Mormon Thought* 13.2 (Summer 1980): 19. For a fuller treatment, see his *Conflict in the Quorum: Orson Pratt, Brigham Young, Joseph Smith* (Salt Lake City: Signature, 2002).

130. Bergera, "Orson Pratt," 23.

131. Bergera, "Orson Pratt," 20.

132. General epistle issued from Salt Lake City by the First Presidency in the spring of 1849, in Roberts, *Comprehensive History*, 6:507.

133. Ronald E. Thrift, "Two Paths to Utopia: An Investigation of Robert Owen in New Lanark and Brigham Young in Salt Lake City" (Ph.D. diss., University of New Mexico, 1976), 120, 127.

134. Leonard J. Arrington and Davis Bitton, *The Mormon Experience* (New York: Random House, 1979), 337.

135. "Projecting Bachelor Degree Recipients by Gender," *Postsecondary Opportunity* 102 (December 2000), http://www.postsecondary.org/archives/previous/1021200 GENDER.pdf; Mabel Newcomer, *A Century of Higher Education for American Women* (New York: Harper, 1959), 46.

136. Cited in Vicky Burgess-Olson, *Sister Saints* (Provo, Utah: Brigham Young University Press, 1978), viii.

137. Jill Mulvay Derr, Janath Russell Cannon, and Maureen Ursenbach Beecher, *Women of Covenant: The Story of Relief Society* (Salt Lake City: Deseret, 1992), 107.

138. Claudia L. Bushman, *Mormon Sisters: Women in Early Utah* (Logan: Utah State University Press, 1997), 58–59.

139. *Contributor* 10.8 (June 1889): 301–2.

140. Statistics quoted by Charles Ellis, a non-Mormon, in *Scrapbook of Mormon Literature* (n.p.: Ben Rich, n.d.) 2:151–52; ranking from *Contributor* 4.5 (February 1883): 183.

~ CHAPTER 6

1. Roy Hattersley, *The Life of John Wesley: A Brand from the Burning* (Garden City, N.Y.: Doubleday, 2003), 217.

2. Joseph Smith, Jr., *History of the Church of Jesus Christ of Latter-day Saints*, 7 vols., ed. James Mulholland, Robert B. Thompson, William W. Phelps, Willard Richards, George A. Smith, and, later, B. H. Roberts (Salt Lake City: Deseret News Press, 1902–1912; 2nd rev. ed., Salt Lake City: Deseret Book, 1951), 4:610.

3. Smith, *History*, 4:610.

4. Alexander Campbell, *Delusions: An Analysis of the Book of Mormon* (Boston: Greene, 1832), 12.

5. "The spread of the Christian religion" among the "Gentiles" was how a prominent commentator glossed the passage referring to the gathering of the elect in Matthew 24. Adam Clarke, *The Holy Bible Containing the Old and New Testaments with a Commentary and Critical Notes*, 3 vols. (Nashville, Tenn.: Abingdon, n.d.), 1:232.

6. Smith, *History*, 2:254–55.

7. "The Elders Stationed in Zion to the Churches Abroad, in Love, Greeting," *Evening and the Morning Star* 2.14 (July 1833): 110.

8. Eve LaPlante, *American Jezebel: The Uncommon Life of Anne Hutchinson, the Woman who Defied the Puritans* (New York: HarperCollins, 2004), 85.

9. C. Mark Hamilton, *Nineteenth Century Mormon Architecture and City Planning* (New York: Oxford University Press, 1995), 14.

10. Smith, *History*, 1:357.

11. Lucy Mack Smith, *The Revised and Enhanced History of Joseph Smith by His Mother*, ed. Scot Facer Proctor and Maurine Jensen Proctor (Salt Lake City: Bookcraft, 1996), 111–12.

12. "History of Parley P. Pratt," *Deseret News*, 19 May 1858. Quoted in Richard Lloyd Anderson, "The Impact of the First Preaching in Ohio," *BYU Studies* 11.4 (Summer 1971): 475.

13. Meetinghouses were planned, and perhaps constructed, in New Portage, Ohio (in 1834), and Norway, Illinois (in 1844). See Smith, *History*, 2:25; 7:312.

14. They were the Baptists and Reformed Baptists. See Milton V. Backman, Jr., *The Heavens Resound: A History of the Latter-day Saints in Ohio 1830–1838* (Salt Lake City: Deseret, 1983), 38.

15. Truman O. Angell, "Journal," quoted in Elwin C. Robison, *The First Mormon Temple: Design, Construction, and Historic Context of the Kirtland Temple* (Provo, Utah: Brigham Young University Press, 1997), 8.

16. Russel Blaine Nye, *The Cultural Life of the New Nation* (New York: Harper and Row, 1960), 274.

17. *Times and Seasons* 6.7 (15 April 1845): 867–68.

18. As his son Joseph Millet recorded, "the secret was given him by revelation. Many have tried to solve the problem but have failed." "J. Millet on C[ape] B[reton] Island 1927," microfilm of holograph, in LDS church archives. Cited in Elwin C. Robison, *The First Mormon Temple* (Provo, Utah: Brigham Young University Press, 1997), 81.

19. The dispute was with William Weeks over circular as opposed to semicircular windows. Smith's heaven-endorsed circular windows won out. Smith, *History*, 6:196–97.

20. E. Cecil McGavin, *Nauvoo the Beautiful* (Salt Lake City: Stevens and Wallis, 1946), 43.

21. Glen M. Leonard and T. Edgar Lyon, "The Nauvoo Years," *Ensign* 9.9 (September 1979): 11; John Greenleaf Whittier, "A Mormon Conventicle," in *Among the Mormons: Historic Accounts by Contemporary Observers*, ed. William Mulder and A. Russell Mortensen (Lincoln: University of Nebraska Press, 1958), 159.

22. J. Earl Arrington, "William Weeks, Architect of the Nauvoo Temple," *BYU Studies* 19.3 (Spring 1979): 340.

23. Smith, *History*, 4:608.

24. Smith, *History*, 6:319.

25. Kimball's role in the removal is related secondhand in a number of sources, but may be no more than oral folklore. In a similar, earlier gesture (at least by 1948), the LDS hymnbook reflected the decision, in the paean to Joseph Smith "Praise to the Man," to have his blood "plead unto heaven" rather than "stain Illinois."

26. David S. Andrew and Laurel N. Blank, "The Four Mormon Temples in Utah," *Journal of the Society of Architectural Historians* 30.1 (March 1971): 51.

27. President Heber J. Grant in *Conference Report of the Church of Jesus Christ of Latter-day Saints* (April 1921): 211–12.

28. A modest, two-story Endowment House in Salt Lake City was used for ritualistic purposes from 1855 to 1889.

29. Laurel B. Andrew, *The Early Temples of the Mormons: The Architecture of the Millennial Kingdom in the American West* (Albany: State University of New York Press, 1978), 177.

30. Andrew, *Early Temples*, 188.

31. *Deseret News*, 4 September 1867. Cited in Hamilton, *Mormon Architecture*, 60.

32. Ray Luce, "Building the Kingdom of God: Mormon Architecture before 1847," *BYU Studies* 30.2 (Spring 1990): 43. The tabernacle is not entirely an extinct form; witness the large Interstake Center built in Oakland, California, in 1959.

33. Allen D. Roberts, "Religious Architecture of the LDS Church: Influences and Changes since 1847," *Utah Historical Quarterly* 43.3 (1975): 307.

34. Hamilton, *Mormon Architecture*, 82–85.

35. Daniel H. Ludlow, *A Companion to Your Study of the New Testament: The Four Gospels* (Salt Lake City: Deseret, 1982), 56.

36. From Richard Parker's *Scholastical Discourse against Symbolizing with AntiChrist in Ceremonies: Especially in the Signe of the Crosse*, quoted in Adam Nicolson, *God's Secretaries: The Making of the King James Bible* (New York: HarperCollins, 2003), 36.

37. Robert Paul, "Joseph Smith and the Manchester Library," *BYU Studies* 22.3 (Summer 1982): 344.

38. John Fox, *Book of Martyrs* (Middletown, N.Y.: Edwin Hunt, 1833), iv.

39. "Today [the crucifix] is more the symbol of the apostate churches of Christendom." George Reynolds and Janne M. Sjodahl, *Commentary on the Book of Mormon*, ed. Philip C. Reynolds, 7 vols. (Salt Lake City: Deseret, 1955–1961), 6:230–31. "Crucifixes [are] inharmonious with . . . a true Christian's remembrance of the Lord's suffering and death." Bruce R. McConkie, *Mormon Doctrine* (Salt Lake City: Bookcraft, 1989), 172–73.

40. Josh Probert, "Remembering Brother Joseph: Iconography of Joseph Smith in Mormon Worship Spaces," paper given at the Mormon History Association, Killington, Vermont, 28 May 2005.

41. The expression is from Charles Heber Clark [Max Adeler, pseud.], *The Tragedy of Thompson Dunbar: A Tale of Salt Lake City* (Philadelphia: Stoddart, 1879), 11.

42. *Contributor* 11.3 (January 1890): 119.

~ CHAPTER 7

1. Letter of C. F. W. Walther, 23 January 1883. Available at http://www.angelfire .com/ny4/djw/lutherantheology.walthermethodist.html. Ironically, on a current Web page linked to the Evangelical Lutheran Synod, LDS hymns are downloadable, with the notation that "some [LDS hymns] are used by us and are quite good." http:// www.elhmidi.freeservers.com/links.htm.

2. B. H. Roberts, *A Comprehensive History of the Church of Jesus Christ of Latter-day Saints*, 6 vols. (Salt Lake City: Deseret News Press, 1930), 1:84.

3. *The Bay Psalm Book: The Whole Booke of Psalmes Faithfully Translated into English Meter, Whereunto Is Prefixed a Discourse Declaring Not Only the Lawfullness, but Also the Necessity of the Heavenly Ordinance of Singing Scripture Psalmes in the Churches of God* (Cambridge, Mass.: Stephen Day, 1640).

4. John R. Weinlick, *Count Zinzendorf* (New York: Abingdon, 1961), 98.

5. George Smith, Leslie Stephen, and Sidney Lee, eds., *Dictionary of National Biography* (Oxford: Oxford University Press, 1917–), 20:979–80.

6. "The American Education Society estimated in 1830 that of the nation's leading denominations, there were 2,743,453 Calvinist Baptists, 2,600,000 Methodists, 1,800,000 Presbyterians, 1,260,000 Congregationalists, & 1,260,000 Episcopalians." Egal Feldman, *Dual Destinies: The Jewish Encounter with Protestant America* (Urbana: University of Illinois Press, 1990), 49. Those numbers are probably too high. Estimates of American Methodists in 1850, for example, range from 1,324,000 (Frank S. Mead, *Handbook of Denominations in the United States*, 10th ed. [Nashville, Tenn.: Abingdon, 1995], 157) to 2,700,000 (Roger Finke and Rodney Stark, *The Churching of America, 1776–1990* [New Brunswick, N.J.: Rutgers University Press, 1997], 113).

7. Jay Leon Slaughter, "The Role of Music in the Mormon Church, School, and Life" (Ph.D. diss., Indiana University, 1964), 49.

8. Michael Hicks, *Mormonism and Music: A History* (Urbana: University of Illinois Press, 1989), 10–11.

9. "New Hymns," *Evening and the Morning Star* 1.9 (February 1833): 72.

10. "Songs of Zion," *Evening and the Morning Star* 1.12 (May 1833): 97.

11. Emma Smith, *A Collection of Sacred Hymns, for the Church of the Latter Day Saints* (Kirtland, Ohio: F. G. Williams, 1835), iv.

12. Hicks, *Mormonism and Music*, 21.

13. First published in the *Messenger and Advocate* 1:3 (December 1834): 34.

14. Hicks, *Mormonism and Music*, 39.

15. *Evening and the Morning Star* 2.16 (January 1834): 128. Hicks gives this and other examples of tongue singing in *Mormonism and Music*, 35–37.

16. Benjamin; Abraham; Bethel; Daniel; Eden; Goshen; Jacob City; Jericho; Jericho Junction; Jerusalem; Jordan; Jordanelle; Moab; Mt. Carmel; Ephraim; Zion vs. Bountiful; Lehi; Deseret; Moroni; Nephi.

17. *The Psalmody Reformer* (Halifax, Nova Scotia: n.p., 1853), 5.

18. Thomas Walter, *The Ground and Rules of Musick Explained* (Boston, 1721), 3–4, 6.

19. Joseph Smith, Jr., *History of the Church of Jesus Christ of Latter-day Saints*, 7 vols., ed. James Mulholland, Robert B. Thompson, William W. Phelps, Willard Richards, George A. Smith, and, later, B. H. Roberts (Salt Lake City, Utah: Deseret News Press, 1902–1912; 2nd rev. ed., Salt Lake City, Utah: Deseret Books, 1951), 2:274.

20. Smith, *History*, 2:188.

21. "Musical Lyceum," *Times and Seasons* 3.6 (15 January 1842): 666.

22. *Times and Seasons* 3.5 (1 January 1842): 653.

23. Helen Mar Whitney, *A Woman's View: Helen Mar Whitney's Reminiscences of Early Church History* (Provo, Utah: BYU Religious Studies Center, 1999), 129.

24. *Contributor* 1.6 (March 1880): 135.

25. George W. Givens, *In Old Nauvoo: Everyday Life in the City of Joseph* (Salt Lake City: Deseret, 1990), 177.

26. From "A Book Containing the Minutes of Joseph's City Band," quoted in *Contributor* 1.9 (June 1880): 196.

27. Quoting Robert C. Bowden, conductor of the Mormon Symphony and Mormon Youth Chorus, "Praise the Lord with Singing, Music," *LDS Church News* (13 September 1997).

28. Givens, *In Old Nauvoo*, 178.

29. Smith, *History*, 7:363.

30. Givens, *In Old Nauvoo*, 177.

31. Whitney, *A Woman's View*, 225.

32. *Contributor* 1.9 (June 1880): 196.

33. Hicks, *Mormonism and Music*, 60.

34. *Contributor* 1.9 (June 1880): 197.

35. Quoted in Daniel Tyler, *A Concise History of the Mormon Battalion in the Mexican War, 1846–47* (Salt Lake City: n.p., 1881), 82–83.

36. Leona Holbrook, "Dancing as an Aspect of Early Mormon and Utah Culture," *BYU Studies* 16.1 (Autumn 1975): 119. The Shakers could be considered another exception, although the only dance they countenanced was a highly ritualized form that constituted part of their worship services.

37. T. Scott Miyakawa, *Protestants and Pioneers: Individualism and Conformity on the American Frontier* (Chicago: University of Chicago Press, 1964), 112.

38. Miyakawa, *Protestants*, 111, quoting W. W. Sweet, *Circuit Rider Days along the Ohio* (New York: Methodist Book Concern, 1923), 200.

39. John Donne, "Holy Sonnet VI," in *Poems of John Donne*, ed. E. K. Chambers (London: Lawrence and Bullen, 1896), 1:160.

40. William Blake, *The Marriage of Heaven and Hell* (Oxford: Oxford University Press, 1975), 4.

41. G. Smith, ed., *History of the Methodist Church in Great Britain* (London: Longman, 1862), 4:649.

42. H. D. Lehman and Paul A. Witty, *Psychology of Play Activities* (New York: Barnes, 1927), 1–2. Cited in Holbrook, "Dancing," 119.

43. R. Lawrence Moore, "Learning to Play: The Mormon Way and the Way of Other Americans," *Journal of Mormon History* 16 (1990): 91.

44. William Law, *A Serious Call to a Devout and Holy Life* (New York: Paulist, 1978), 108.

45. Quoted in John Brewer, *The Pleasures of the Imagination: English Culture in the Eighteenth Century* (Chicago: University of Chicago Press, 1997), 402.

46. *Journal of Discourses*, 26 vols., reported by G. D. Watt et al. (Liverpool, England: Richards et al., 1851–1886; rpt., Salt Lake City: n.p., 1974), 9:243–44.

47. Smith, *History*, 5:517.

48. *Journal of Discourses* 6:149.

49. "Nauvoo Conference Minutes," *Millennial Star* 5.8 (January 1845): 123.

50. Smith, *History*, 2:519.

51. Holbrook, "Dancing," 123.

52. *Contributor* 1.6 (March 1880): 136.

53. *Times and Seasons* 5.5 (1 March 1844): 460.

54. *Times and Seasons* 5.20 (2 November 1844): 694.

55. Quoted in Tyler, *Concise History*, 82–83.

56. William A. Chandless, *A Visit to Salt Lake: Being a Journey across the Plains, and a Residence in the Mormon Settlements at Utah* (New York: AMS, 1971), 238.

57. John Hyde, *Mormonism: Its Leaders and Designs* (New York: Fetridge, 1857), 118–19.

58. George Reynold quoted Young's views in *Woman's Exponent* 4 (1 January 1876): 117; Rachel Grant Taylor, "When Brigham Young Watched a Waltz," *Improvement Era* 44.11(November 1941): 678; *Deseret News*, 20 September 1877. All cited in Davis Bitton, "'These Licentious Days': Dancing among the Mormons," in Bitton, *The Ritualization of Mormon History and Other Essays* (Urbana: University of Illinois Press, 1994), 103–5.

59. Paul E. Dahl, "'All Is Well . . .': The Story of 'the Hymn That Went around the World,'" *BYU Studies* 21.4 (Fall 1981): 523.

60. *Autobiography of Warren Foote*, 3 vols. (Mesa, Ariz.: Dale Arnold Foote, 1997), 1:97. Originals are in the LDS Historical Department, Salt Lake City, Utah.

61. *Contributor* 1.2 (November 1879): 31.

62. From the 1941 John Ford movie *How Green Was My Valley*, based on the Richard Llewellyn novel of that name (London: Michael Joseph, 1939).

63. Hicks, *Mormonism and Music*, 49.

64. Hicks, *Mormonism and Music*, 95.

65. Smith, *History*, 1:269.

66. *Deseret News*, 15 July 1863.

67. This is one point made in Leonard Arrington's "An Economic Interpretation of the 'Word of Wisdom,'" *BYU Studies* 1.1 (Winter 1959): 37–48.

68. "Singing in Sunday Schools," *Utah Musical Times* 2 (1 May 1877): 25. Cited in Hicks, *Mormonism and Music*, 109.

~ CHAPTER 8

1. Quoted in Robert D. Richardson, Jr., *Emerson: The Mind on Fire* (Berkeley: University of California Press, 1995), 42.

2. Joseph J. Ellis, *After the Revolution: Profiles of Early American Culture* (New York: Norton, 1979), 129.

3. William Dunlap, *History of the American Theatre* (London, 1833), 1:130; cited in Ellis, *After the Revolution*, 154.

4. Ellis, *After the Revolution*, 140.

5. Frances Trollope, *Domestic Manners of the Americans* (New York: Knopf, 1949), 209.

6. Allen Wiley, "Methodism in Southeastern Indiana," *Indiana Magazine of History* 23 (June 1927): 181, cited in T. Scott Miyakawa, *Protestants and Pioneers: Individualism and Conformity on the American Frontier* (Chicago: University of Chicago Press, 1964), 112–13.

7. R. Lawrence Moore, "Learning to Play: The Mormon Way and the Way of Other Americans," *Journal of Mormon History* 16 (1990): 90.

8. *Journal of Discourses*, 26 vols., reported by G. D. Watt et al. (Liverpool, England: Richards et al., 1851–1886; rpt., Salt Lake City: n.p., 1974), 2:94.

9. *Journal of Discourses* 9:243–44.

10. *Autobiography of Warren Foote*, 3 vols. (Mesa, Ariz.: Dale Arnold Foote, 1997), 1:43.

11. George W. Givens, *In Old Nauvoo: Everyday Life in the City of Joseph* (Salt Lake City: Deseret, 1990), 173.

12. John S. Lindsay, *The Mormons and the Theatre* (Salt Lake City: n.p., 1905), 6–7.

13. Rex A. Skidmore, "Mormon Recreation in Theory and Practice: A Study of Social Change" (Ph.D. diss., University of Pennsylvania, 1941), 47.

14. Clarissa Young Spencer, *Brigham Young at Home* (Salt Lake City: Deseret, 1961), 140–41.

15. David Carlyon, *Dan Rice: The Most Famous Man You've Never Heard Of* (New York: Public Affairs, 2001), 57.

16. Spencer, *Brigham Young*, 142.

17. Spencer, *Brigham Young*, 144.

18. "The Story of the Salt Lake Theatre," *Improvement Era* 18.7 (May 1915): 580.

19. Samuel Bowles, *Across the Continent* (1866), cited in B. H. Roberts, *A Comprehensive History of the Church of Jesus Christ of Latter-day Saints*, 6 vols. (Salt Lake City: Deseret News Press, 1930), 5:146.

20. Alfred Lambourne, "Reminiscences of the Salt Lake Theatre," *Improvement Era* 15.8 (June 1912): 696.

21. Lindsay, *Mormons*, 25.

22. Oscar G. Brockett, *History of the Theatre* (Boston: Allyn and Bacon, 1968), 485.

23. "The Story of the Salt Lake Theatre," *Improvement Era* 18.7 (May 1915): 585.

24. Horace Whitney, "A Word to Dramatic Clubs," *Improvement Era* 13.6 (April 1910): 559.

25. Lambourne, "Reminiscences" (June 1912): 698.

26. Lambourne, "Reminiscences" (June 1912): 697.

27. Alfred Lambourne, "Reminiscences of the Salt Lake Theatre," *Improvement Era* 15.6 (April 1912).

28. Philip L. Barlow, "The Uniquely True Church," in *A Thoughtful Faith: Essays on Belief by Mormon Scholars*, ed. Philip L. Barlow (Centerville, Utah: Canon, 1986), 237–38.

29. Lorin F. Wheelwright, ed., *Mormon Arts: Volume One* (Provo, Utah: Brigham Young University Press, 1972), 2.

30. Though President McKay certainly popularized the slogan and is credited with first formulating it, the phrase was in use two decades earlier. See the address by Thomas E. McKay in *Conference Report of the Church of Jesus Christ of Latter-day Saints* (April 1944): 62.

31. *Journal of Discourses* 2:10; 13:158.

32. Neal A. Maxwell, *All These Things Shall Give Thee Experience* (Salt Lake City: Deseret, 1979), 117.

33. *Relief Society Magazine* (January 1948): 8. Cited in Jack M. Lyon, Linda Ririe Gundry, and Jay A. Parry, eds., *Best-Loved Stories of the LDS People* (Salt Lake City: Deseret, 1997), 114.

34. Eugene England, "Joseph Smith and the Tragic Quest," in his *Dialogues with Myself: Personal Essays on Mormon Experience* (Salt Lake City: Signature, 1984), 16.

~ CHAPTER 9

1. Quoted in Colleen McDannell and Bernhard Lang, *Heaven: A History* (New Haven, Conn.: Yale University Press, 1988), 322.

2. Ralph Waldo Emerson, "Swedenborg; or, The Mystic," in *Complete Writings of Ralph Waldo Emerson* (New York: Wise, 1929), 370.

3. William James, *Varieties of Religious Experience* (Cambridge, Mass.: Harvard University Press, 1985), 362.

4. W. D. Davies, "Reflections on the Mormon 'Canon,'" *Harvard Theological Review* 79 (January 1986): 64n.

5. Arthur Henry King, *The Abundance of the Heart* (Salt Lake City: Bookcraft, 1986), 200–201.

6. Joseph Smith, Jr., *History of the Church of Jesus Christ of Latter-day Saints*, 7 vols., ed. James Mulholland, Robert B. Thompson, William W. Phelps, Willard Richards, George A. Smith, and, later, B. H. Roberts (Salt Lake City: Deseret News Press, 1902–1912; 2nd rev. ed., Salt Lake City: Deseret Book, 1951), 1:39.

7. *Messenger and Advocate* 1.1 (October 1834): 16.

8. Philo Dibble, "Recollections of the Prophet Joseph Smith," *Juvenile Instructor* 27 (May 1892): 304.

9. George Steiner, *Language and Silence* (New York: Atheneum, 1967), 17.

10. Steiner, *Language*, 41.

11. Artemisia Foote, "Artemisia Sidnie Myers Foote's Experiences in the Persecuting of the Latter-day Saints in Missouri" (typescript, LDS Historical Department, Salt Lake City, Utah).

12. *Autobiography of Warren Foote*, 3 vols. (Mesa, Ariz.: Dale Arnold Foote, 1997), 1:33.

13. *Autobiography of Warren Foote*, 1:73.

14. Parley P. Pratt, *Autobiography of Parley P. Pratt* (Salt Lake City: Deseret, 1985), 179–80.

15. William Wordsworth, "Preface to Lyrical Ballads," in *Poetical Works*, ed. Thomas Hutchinson and Ernest de Selincourt (Oxford: Oxford University Press, 1989), 734.

16. "Poetry," *Millennial Harbinger* 3.8 (August 1846): 469.

17. *Millennial Star* 4.3 (July 1843): 51.

18. *Millennial Star* 18 (16 February 1856): 106. Cited in Thomas E. Lyon, "Publishing a Book of Mormon Poetry: The Harp of Zion," *BYU Studies* 27.1 (Winter 1987): 85.

19. Wordsworth's *Lyrical Ballads* sold some 500 copies between its publication in 1798 and 1800.

20. *Times and Seasons* 6.17 (15 November 1845): 1039.

21. Eliza R. Snow, *Poems, Religious, Historical, and Political*, 2 vols. (Salt Lake City: Latter-day Saints' Printing and Publishing, 1877), 1:49–50.

22. Parley P. Pratt, "Dialogue between Joseph Smith and the Devil," *New York Herald* (1 January 1844).

23. Leonard J. Arrington, "Mormonism: Views from Without and Within," *BYU Studies* 14.2 (Winter 1974): 149.

24. Jeffrey R. Holland, "Daddy, Donna, and Nephi," *Ensign* 7 (September 1976): 7; Daniel H. Ludlow, *A Companion to Your Study of the Doctrine and Covenants*, 2 vols. (Salt Lake City: Deseret, 1978), 1:557–58.

25. *Contributor* 6.3 (December 1884): 87.

26. Sarah DeArmon Pea Rich, "Autobiography," in Milton V. Backman, Jr., and Keith W. Perkins, eds., *Writings of Early Latter-day Saints and Their Contemporaries: A Database Collection*, 2nd ed. (Provo, Utah: BYU Religious Studies Center, 1996), electronic edition, 21.

27. Wordsworth, "Preface," 735.

28. Jane Austen, *Northanger Abbey* (Bonn: Koneman, 1999), 29–30.

29. *Times and Seasons* 6.8 (1 May 1845): 892.

30. *Evening and the Morning Star* 2.13 (June 1833): 103.

31. *Messenger and Advocate* 2:14 (November 1835): 223.

32. *Times and Seasons* 5.20 (November 1844): 697.

33. Kenneth W. Godfrey, "Some Thoughts Regarding an Unwritten History of Nauvoo," *BYU Studies* 15.4 (Summer 1975): 421.

34. *Journal of Discourses*, 26 vols., reported by G. D. Watt et al. (Liverpool, England: Richards et al., 1851–1886; rpt., Salt Lake City: n.p., 1974), 9:173.

35. *Contributor* 10.1 (November 1888): 18.

36. Ralph Waldo Emerson, "The American Scholar," in *Complete Writings of Ralph Waldo Emerson* (New York: Wise, 1929), 25, 36.

37. Orson Whitney, "Home Literature," *Contributor* 9.8 (June 1888): 296–300.

38. Frank Luther Mott, *Golden Multitudes: The Story of Best Sellers in the United States* (New York: Macmillan, 1947), 310–11.

39. *Contributor* 1.1 (October 1879): 12.

40. *Contributor* 1.1 (October 1879): 12.

41. Charles Dickens, *Hard Times* (New York: Norton, 1966), 1.

42. *Contributor* 1.3 (December 1879): 61.

43. *Contributor* 10.1 (November 1888): 35.

44. *Contributor* 10.4 (February 1889): 135.

45. *Contributor* 10.4 (February 1889): 134–35.

46. The citation from *Mixed Essays* (1879) is quoted in Peter Keating, *A Social History of the English Novel 1875–1914* (London: Secker and Warburg, 1989), vii.

47. Amy Kaplan, *Social Construction of American Realism* (Chicago: University of Chicago Press, 1992), ix.

48. *Contributor* 10.4 (February 1889): 134–35.

49. Robert Alan Colby, *Fiction with a Purpose: Major and Minor Nineteenth-Century Novels* (Bloomington: Indiana University Press, 1967), 10.

50. *Contributor* 10.3 (January 1889).

51. Richard H. Cracroft, "The Didactic Heresy as Orthodox Tool: B. H. Roberts as Writer of Home Literature," in *Tending the Garden: Essays on Mormon Literature*, ed. Eugene England and Lavina Fielding Anderson (Salt Lake City: Signature, 1996), 125.

52. Leonard Arrington, "Blessed Damozels: Women in Mormon History," *Dialogue: A Journal of Mormon Thought* 6.2 (Summer 1971): 26.

53. Letter to Tatyana Tolstoy, 18 October 1888, quoted in Leland A. Fetzer, "Tolstoy and Mormonism," *Dialogue: A Journal of Mormon Thought* 6.1 (Spring 1971): 20.

54. See Maureen Ursenbach Beecher, "The Eliza Enigma," *Dialogue: A Journal of Mormon Thought* 11.1 (Spring 1978): 38.

55. She published her retraction in the *Deseret News*, 5 April 1876. See Beecher, "Eliza Enigma," 38.

56. Arrington, "Blessed Damozels," 27. Gates's novel was initially serialized in the *Young Woman's Journal*, then published as *John Stevens' Courtship: A Story of the Echo Canyon War* (Salt Lake City: Deseret News, 1909).

~ CHAPTER 10

1. Richard L. Bushman, "Would Joseph Smith Attend the New York State Arts Festival?" *Dialogue: A Journal of Mormon Thought* 35.3 (Fall 2002): 212.

2. Frances K. Pohl, *Framing America: A Social History of American Art* (New York: Thames and Hudson, 2002), 113.

3. Christopher Crotchet, "The Salad, No. 5," *Port Folio* 5 (May 1811): 407. Cited in Neil Harris, *The Artist in American Society: The Formative Years 1790–1860* (Chicago:

University of Chicago Press, 1982), 31. Harris documents a vast array of similar expressions of warning and concern about luxury in the early republic.

4. Joseph J. Ellis, *After the Revolution: Profiles of Early American Culture* (New York: Norton, 1979), 61.

5. Ellis, *After the Revolution*, 195.

6. Harris, *The Artist in American Society*, 99.

7. Frances Trollope, *Domestic Manners of the Americans* (New York: Knopf, 1949), 394.

8. See, for example, David Jaffee, *People of the Wachusett: Greater New England in History and Memory, 1630–1860* (Ithaca, N.Y.: Cornell University Press, 1999), 218–27.

9. Lucy Mack Smith, *The Revised and Enhanced History of Joseph Smith by His Mother*, ed. Scot Facer Proctor and Maurine Jensen Proctor (Salt Lake City: Bookcraft, 1996), 86.

10. Joseph Smith, Jr., *History of the Church of Jesus Christ of Latter-day Saints*, 7 vols., ed. James Mulholland, Robert B. Thompson, William W. Phelps, Willard Richards, George A. Smith, and, later, B. H. Roberts (Salt Lake City: Deseret News Press, 1902–1912; 2nd rev. ed., Salt Lake City: Deseret Book, 1951), 6:471–72.

11. Captain [Frederick] Marryat, *A Diary in America, with Remarks on Its Institutions* (Philadelphia, 1839), cited in Allan Nevins, *American Social History as Recorded by British Travellers* (New York: Holt, 1934), 235.

12. *Journal of Discourses*, 26 vols., reported by G. D. Watt et al. (Liverpool, England: Richards et al., 1851–1886; rpt., Salt Lake City: n.p., 1974), 12:179.

13. James B. Allen, Ronald K. Esplin, and David J. Whittaker, *Men with a Mission, 1837–1841: The Quorum of the Twelve Apostles in the British Isles* (Salt Lake City: Deseret, 1992), 337–38.

14. William Mulder, *Homeward to Zion* (Minneapolis: University of Minnesota Press, 1957), 113. Cited in John L. Haseltine, "Mormonism and the Visual Arts," *Dialogue: A Journal of Mormon Thought* 1.2 (Summer 1966): 17.

15. Douglas Tobler, "Europe, the Church in," in *Encyclopedia of Mormonism*, 4 vols., ed. Daniel Ludlow (New York: Macmillan, 1992), 2:470.

16. Vern G. Swanson, Robert S. Olpin, and William C. Seifrit, *Utah Painting and Sculpture* (Salt Lake City: Gibbs-Smith, 1997), 15.

17. All quotations are from Haseltine, "Mormonism and the Visual Arts," 17.

18. Swanson et al., *Utah Painting*, 18.

19. Paul Collins, *Banvard's Folly* (New York: Picador, 2001), 15. Cited in Joe Essid, "The Artist as Adventurer: The Stories about Banvard," unpublished manuscript, 1. Author's files.

20. Essid, "Artist," 1.

21. Swanson et al., *Utah Painting*, 25.

22. Swanson et al., *Utah Painting*, 16.

23. Richard V. Francaviglia, *The Mormon Landscape: Existence, Creation, and Perception of a Unique Image in the American West* (New York: AMS, 1978), 127. Quoting D. M. Smedley, "An Investigation of Influences on Representative Mormon Art" (M.A. thesis, University of Southern California, 1939), 39.

24. Paul L. Anderson, "Heroic Nostalgia: Enshrining the Mormon Past," *Sunstone* 5.4 (July 1980): 50.

25. Painted in 1874–1875, the painting is referred to in an authoritative study of Utah art as *Gypsy Camp*, based presumably on the description that accompanied the original canvas when application was made for the exhibition. See Swanson et al., *Utah Painting*, 22. The University of Utah Museum of Fine Arts, where the painting is housed, has it listed as *Campsite on the Mormon Trail*.

26. Mostly housed in the BYU Museum of Art, these paintings have been published (*Art in America* 58 [May–June 1970]: 52–65) and exhibited in the Whitney Museum of American Art, also in 1970.

~ PART III

1. Neilson is quoting Perry Miller's *Errand into the Wilderness* (Cambridge, Mass.: Harvard University Press, 1956), 14–15. His discussion is in "Strangers in a Strange Land: The Rise and Demise of the Early LDS Japan Mission, 1901–24" (Ph.D. diss., University of North Carolina, Chapel Hill, 2006), 99–100.

2. Boyd K. Packer, "The Arts and the Spirit of the Lord," *BYU Studies* 16.4 (Summer 1976), 577 (first delivered as an address at Brigham Young University, 1 February 1976).

3. Packer, "The Arts," 577.

4. Spencer W. Kimball, "The Gospel Vision of the Arts," *Ensign* 7.7 (July 1977): 5. This speech had been delivered at Brigham Young University in 1967, but publication in the church magazine gave it wider distribution and prominence.

~ CHAPTER 11

1. From a detailed account in the Brigham Young Papers, cited by Ronald K. Esplin, "Joseph, Brigham and the Twelve: A Succession of Continuity," *BYU Studies* 21.3 (Summer 1981): 320.

2. "Proclamation of Parley P. Pratt, 1 January 1845," *Millennial Star* 5 (March 1845): 151.

3. In 1891, President Wilford Woodruff responded to inflamed reports of the doctrine:

> It is part of our faith that the only atonement a murdered [*sic*] can make for his "sin unto death" is the shedding of his own blood [through capital punishment as practiced by the state and not the church] according to the fiat of the Almighty after the flood: "Whoso sheddeth man's blood by man shall his blood be shed." But the law must be executed by the lawfully appointed officer. This is "blood atonement" so much perverted by maligners of our faith. We believe also in the atonement wrought by the shedding of Christ's blood on Calvary; that it is efficacious for all the race of Adam for the sin committed by Adam, and for the individual sins of all who believe, repent, are baptized by one having authority, and who receive the Holy Ghost by the laying on of authorized hands. Capital crime committed by such an enlightened person cannot be condoned by the Redeemer's blood. For him there

is "no more sacrifice for sin"; his life is forfeit, and he can only pay the penalty. There is no other blood atonement taught, practiced or made part of the creed of the Latter-day Saints.

Wilford Woodruff, Letter to the Editor, *Illustrated American* (9 January 1891), cited in Martin R. Gardner, "Mormonism and Capital Punishment: A Doctrinal Perspective, Past and Present," *Dialogue: A Journal of Mormon Thought* 12.1 (Spring 1979): 12.

4. *Journal of Discourses*, 26 vols., reported by G. D. Watt et al. (Liverpool, England: Richards et al., 1851–1886; rpt., Salt Lake City: n.p., 1974), 5:240.

5. G. Homer Durham, ed., *The Discourses of Wilford Woodruff* (Salt Lake City: Bookcraft, 1946), 235–36.

6. See the persuasive evidence of this fact in Noel B. Reynolds, "The Coming Forth of the Book of Mormon in the Twentieth Century," *BYU Studies* 38.2 (1999): 6–47.

7. Letter to Henry Acland, 24 May 1851, in John Ruskin, *Works*, 39 vols., ed. E. T. Cook and Alexander Wedderburn (London: George Allen, 1903–1912), 36:115.

8. A. N. Wilson, *God's Funeral* (New York: Norton, 1999), 178–79.

9. Wilson, *God's Funeral*, 189.

10. John W. Draper, *History of the Conflict between Religion and Science* (New York: Appleton, 1874); Andrew D. White, *History of the Warfare of Science with Theology in Christendom* (New York: Appleton, 1896).

11. Joseph Smith, Jr., *History of the Church of Jesus Christ of Latter-day Saints*, 7 vols., ed. James Mulholland, Robert B. Thompson, William W. Phelps, Willard Richards, George A. Smith, and, later, B. H. Roberts (Salt Lake City: Deseret News Press, 1902–1912; 2nd rev. ed., Salt Lake City: Deseret Book, 1951), 6:308–9.

12. Cited in *Times and Seasons* 5.24 (1 January 1845): 758.

13. *Journal of Discourses* 14:115.

14. Pratt would preach, "We have the general characteristics of the human form, and we do not look like the original of man according to Darwin's idea; we do not look like the monkey or baboon, from which Darwin says man originated" (*Journal of Discourses* 17:32–33). Erastus Snow in 1878 opined:

There is a theory put forth by Mr. Darwin, and others, that is the school of modern philosophers, which is termed in late years, the theory of Evolution . . . in short, that our great-grandfathers were apes and monkeys. . . . But we find nothing on the earth, or in the earth, nor under the earth, that indicates that any of these monkeys or apes, or any other orders of creation below man have ever accomplished any great exploits; . . . nor any other scientists have ever been able . . . to indicate that there was any such vitality in them, as to develop in their future progress, the present order of beings we call man.

He added that "they fail to demonstrate their theories, simply because they are not demonstrateable" (*Journal of Discourses* 19:271, 325–26). The same year, Orson Pratt referred to "the evolution theory; in other words, that which you learn from books, [is] the creation of man's folly and foolishness" (*Journal of Discourses* 20:76).

15. *Journal of Discourses* 26:21.

16. Orson F. Whitney, "Latter-Day Saint Ideals and Institutions," *Improvement Era* 30.10 (August 1927): 854.

17. Tom Sorell, *Scientism: Philosophy and the Infatuation with Science* (New York: Routledge, 1991), 1.

18. Parley P. Pratt, *Key to the Science of Theology/A Voice of Warning* (Salt Lake City: Deseret, 1978), 100–101.

19. *Journal of Discourses* 1:8–9, 336; 4:15; 6:374; 8:70, 328; 9:107.

20. John A. Widtsoe, *Joseph Smith as Scientist: A Contribution to Mormon Philosophy* (Salt Lake City: Bookcraft, 1964), 11, 139, 34, 146.

21. Widtsoe, *Joseph Smith*, preface.

22. John A. Widtsoe, *In Search of Truth* (Salt Lake City: Deseret, 1930), 36–37.

23. Erich Robert Paul, *Science, Religion, and Mormon Cosmology* (Urbana and Chicago: University of Illinois Press, 1992), 26.

24. Leonard Arrington, "The Intellectual Tradition of the Latter-day Saints," *Dialogue: A Journal of Mormon Thought* 4.1 (Spring 1969): 23.

25. Wilfred Cantwell Smith, "The Study of Religion and the Study of the Bible," in *Rethinking Scripture: Essays from a Comparative Perspective*, ed. Miriam Levering (Albany: State University of New York Press, 1989), 26.

26. *Times and Seasons* 3.21 (1 September 1842): 914–15.

27. B. H. Roberts, *New Witnesses for God* (Salt Lake City: Deseret News, 1909), 2:356–70, 415–16.

28. A favorable overview of the expedition is found in Ernest L. Wilkinson and W. Cleon Skousen, *Brigham Young University: A School of Destiny* (Provo, Utah: Brigham Young University Press, 1976), 151–62. Another appraisal, much harsher than theirs (and Cluff's), is that the venture "ended in embarrassment for all involved, [and] affected the school's academic advancement over the next three decades." Gary James Bergera and Ronald Priddis, *Brigham Young University: A House of Faith* (Salt Lake City: Signature, 1985), 10. Journals from several expedition members and several photographs are housed in Special Collections, Harold B. Lee Library, Brigham Young University, Provo, Utah.

29. The questions had been posed by one Mr. Couch and sent to Talmage by an intermediary:

1. How to explain the immense diversity of Indian languages, if all are supposed to be relatively recent descendents [*sic*] of Lamanite origin?
2. How can the Book of Mormon mention the horse, if it was not introduced until the time of the Conquest?
3. How can Nephi mention having a bow of steel before such metal was known to the Jews?
4. How can the Book of Mormon mention "cimiters" before the rise of Mohammedan power?
5. How could the Nephites possess "silk," if it was unknown to America at that time?

W. E. Riter to James E. Talmage, 22 August 1921, cited in B. H. Roberts, *Studies of the Book of Mormon*, ed. Brigham D. Madsen (Salt Lake City: Signature, 1992), 35–36.

30. B. H. Roberts, "Book of Mormon Difficulties," in *Studies of the Book of Mormon*, 115.

31. Roberts investigated in particular the parallels between the Book of Mormon and Ethan Smith's 1823 *View of the Hebrews*. See his "A Book of Mormon Study," in *Studies of the Book of Mormon*, 149–319.

32. An account of this episode is given by Richard Sherlock, "'We Can See No Advantage to a Continuation of the Discussion': The Roberts/Smith/Talmage Affair," *Dialogue: A Journal of Mormon Thought* 13.3 (Fall 1980): 63–76.

33. William James, *The Will to Believe* (New York: Dover, 1956), 61; B. H. Roberts, "God's Need of Man," *Improvement Era* 24 (August 1921): 907–11. Both sources are cited in Truman Madsen, "Philosophy," in B. H. Roberts, *The Truth, the Way, the Life*, ed. John W. Welch (Provo, Utah: BYU Studies, 1994), lxxviii.

34. Roberts, *The Truth*, 43.

35. Roberts, *The Truth*, 238. Brigham Young had so speculated earlier. See *Journal of Discourses* 7:285.

36. "Worlds and world systems," he wrote, fulfill their purpose, pass away, and are "reformed into more desirable worlds or world systems" (Roberts, *The Truth*, 232). Other writers had so argued in order to reconcile fossils with a biblical 6,000 years of creation. Not being a literalist, Roberts accepted geologic time and didn't need this avenue of escape, but it would implicitly appease those Mormons who did.

37. "Some cataclysm . . . emptied the earth of all its forms of life—including the human or near human." Roberts, *The Truth*, 324.

38. *Conference Report of the Church of Jesus Christ of Latter-day Saints* (October 1915): 4.

39. Richard O. Cowan, *The Church in the Twentieth Century* (Salt Lake City: Bookcraft, 1985), 109.

40. Cowan, *The Church*, 110.

41. An overview of the LDS seminary program and the CES is in Armand L. Mauss, *The Angel and the Beehive: The Mormon Struggle with Assimilation* (Urbana: University of Illinois Press, 1994), 26–28, 71–72, 95–99, 136–39.

42. Armand L. Mauss, "Assimilation and Ambivalence: The Mormon Reaction to Americanization," *Dialogue: A Journal of Mormon Thought* 22.1 (Spring 1989): 48–49. Mauss would expand this argument into an impressive study that examines post-1950 "retrenchment" in the LDS church as a reaction against its too-successful assimilation since the turn of the nineteenth century. He thus focuses on the most historically concentrated example of what I am calling the tension between election and exile. See his *Angel and the Beehive*.

43. Russel B. Swensen, "Mormons at the University of Chicago Divinity School: A Personal Reminiscence," *Dialogue: A Journal of Mormon Thought* 7.2 (Summer 1972): 39–40.

44. From a meeting of the Twelve, 7 January 1930. Cited in James B. Allen, "The Story of *The Truth, the Way, the Life*," in Roberts, *The Truth*, clxxviii.

45. *Deseret News*, 5 April 1930, 8. Cited in Allen, "The Story," clxxix.

46. "I can state positively that it was not published by the Church, nor by the approval of the Authorities of the Church," wrote Joseph Fielding Smith. Cited in

Steven H. Heath, "The Reconciliation of Faith and Science: Henry Eyring's Achievement," *Dialogue: A Journal of Mormon Thought* 15.3 (Autumn 1982): 93.

47. Mauss, "Assimilation," 43.

48. Spencer W. Kimball is one of the more recent leaders to explicitly call Eve's creation "figurative." See his *Woman* (Salt Lake City: Deseret, 1979), 80. Brigham Young repeatedly did so. See *Journal of Discourses* 1:50; 3:319; 7:285.

49. Heber C. Snell, "The Bible in the Church," *Dialogue: A Journal of Mormon Thought* 2 (Spring 1967): 60. For an account of the controversy Snell's scholarship generated among church leaders, see Richard Sherlock, "The Snell Controversy," *Dialogue: A Journal of Mormon Thought* 12.1 (Spring 1979): 27–38.

50. Mauss noted in 1994 that, "among the thirty or so apostles appointed since President Clark's arrival, those with backgrounds in business or law have been favored to the near exclusion of any with training in scholarly pursuits." See his numbers for lower-echelon leadership as well, and a fuller discussion of "the emergence of a new leadership orientation," in *Angel and the Beehive*, 81–85.

51. Harold T. Christensen and Kenneth L. Cannon, "The Fundamentalist Emphasis at Brigham Young University: 1935–1973," *Journal for the Scientific Study of Religion* 17.1 (March 1978): 55.

52. Boyd K. Packer, *That All May Be Edified* (Salt Lake City: Bookcraft, 1982), 43; cited in Bergera and Priddis, *Brigham Young University*, 53–54.

53. The charges were outlined in a report by church superintendent of education Horace Cummings, recorded in the manuscript "History of Brigham Young University," compiled by J. Marinus Jensen, N. I. Butt, Elsie Carroll, and Bertha Roberts, on file at the Harold B. Lee Library, Brigham Young University, Provo, Utah. Cited in Richard Sherlock, "Campus in Crisis," *Sunstone* 10.5 (May 1985): 32.

54. J. Reuben Clark, "The Charted Course of the Church in Education," *Improvement Era* 41.9 (September 1938): 573.

55. First Presidency to Franklin L. West, 29 February 1940, Harris Papers; cited in Bergera and Priddis, *Brigham Young University*, 62.

56. Duane E. Jeffery, "Seers, Savants and Evolution: The Uncomfortable Interface," *Dialogue: A Journal of Mormon Thought* 8.3–4 (Autumn–Winter 1973): 66. Jeffery's is perhaps the best history of the evolution controversy in the LDS church. See also D. E. Jeffery and W. E. Evanson, *Mormonism and Evolution: The Authoritative LDS Statements* (Salt Lake City: Kofford, 2006).

57. The controversy over Joseph Fielding Smith's book is treated in several studies of the larger faith-science debate of that era. See, for example, Heath, "The Reconciliation of Faith and Science," 87–98.

58. BYU Devotional Address, 1 June 1980. Printed in *BYU Speeches of the Year* (Provo, Utah: Brigham Young University Press, 1980), 74–80.

59. Dr. Daniel Fairbanks, personal correspondence with the author, 10 September 2005.

60. Keith Crandall, Michael Whiting, and Jack Sites are the best known for molecular evolution. All three are major players in the National Science Foundation's Tree of Life project. Crandall is an authority on HIV evolution, with multiple articles in *Nature* and *Science*. Whiting is best known for his work on the evolution

of insect wings and has been featured on *Nature*'s cover. A specialist on lizard evolution, Sites is one of a select group of scientists to be elected as a fellow of the American Association for the Advancement of Science.

61. Bergera and Priddis, *Brigham Young University*, 163.

62. Henry Eyring, "A Tribute to President Joseph Fielding Smith," *Dialogue: A Journal of Mormon Thought* 7.1 (Spring 1972): 15–16.

63. See especially Heath, "The Reconciliation of Faith and Science," 87–98. A more complete account of Eyring's professional and religious life is in S. H. Heath, "Henry Eyring: Mormon Scientist" (master's thesis, University of Utah, June 1980).

64. See Bergera and Priddis, *Brigham Young University*, 161–71.

65. "Biography of Fawn McKay Brodie." Interview with Shirley E. Stephenson, 30 November 1975, Oral History Collection, Fullerton State University, Fullerton, California. Cited in Newell G. Bringhurst, "Fawn Brodie and Her Quest for Independence," *Dialogue: A Journal of Mormon Thought* 22.2 (Summer 1986): 79.

66. The fullest account of the repercussions of her scholarship on her affiliation with Mormonism is in Levi Peterson, *Juanita Brooks: Mormon Woman Historian* (Salt Lake City: University of Utah Press, 1988), 209–43.

67. Juanita Brooks, *The Mountain Meadows Massacre* (Norman: University of Oklahoma Press, 1950), 217.

68. Brooks, *Mountain Meadows*, 219.

69. Davis Bitton and Maureen Ursenbach, "Riding Herd: A Conversation with Juanita Brooks," *Dialogue: A Journal of Mormon Thought* 9.1 (Spring 1974): 29.

70. Juanita Brooks to Albert R. Lyman, cited in Peterson, *Juanita Brooks*, 210.

71. Robert Flanders considered Brodie's book a "landmark" which influenced all subsequent history; James B. Allen cited Brooks's study as a "symbolic turning point"; Moses Rischin believed Thomas O'Dea's work set a new pattern; and Thomas G. Alexander considered Arrington's history "probably the single most significant bellwether of the new Mormon history." Robert Bruce Flanders, "Some Reflections on the New Mormon History," *Dialogue: A Journal of Mormon Thought* 9 (Spring 1974): 35; James B. Allen, "Since 1950: Creators and Creations of Mormon History," in *New Views of Mormon History: A Collection of Essays in Honor of Leonard J. Arrington*, ed. Davis Bitton and Maureen Ursenbach Beecher (Salt Lake City: University of Utah Press, 1987), 411; Moses Rischin, "The New Mormon History," *American West* 6 (April 1969): 49; Thomas G. Alexander, "Toward the New Mormon History: An Examination of the Literature on the Latter day Saints in the Far West," in *Historians and the American West*, ed. Michael P. Malone (Lincoln: University of Nebraska Press, 1983), 354. All cited in Clara V. Dobay, "Intellect and Faith: The Controversy over Revisionist Mormon History," *Dialogue: A Journal of Mormon Thought* 27.1 (Spring 1994): 92.

72. Leonard J. Arrington, *Adventures of a Church Historian* (Urbana: University of Illinois Press, 1998), 58.

73. Arrington gives his account of the founding and early years of the MHA in *Adventures*, 58–61.

74. Leonard J. Arrington, "Scholarly Studies of Mormonism in the Twentieth Century," *Dialogue: A Journal of Mormon Thought* 1.1 (Spring 1966): 28.

75. Arrington, *Adventures*, 59.

76. In the 1960s, Smith directed his assistant's involvement in professional organizations and oversaw the hiring of employees with professional credentials, the implementation of more professional cataloging practices, and the planning of new facilities. See Arrington, *Adventures*, 69.

77. *Dialogue: A Journal of Mormon Thought* 1.1 (Spring 1966): 1.

78. Letter to the Editor, *Dialogue: A Journal of Mormon Thought* 1.1 (Spring 1966): 12.

79. Moses Rischin, "The New Mormon History," *American West* 6 (March 1969): 49, cited in Ronald W. Walker, David J. Whittaker, and James B. Allen, *Mormon History* (Urbana: University of Illinois Press, 2001), 60. This chapter is the best overview of the new Mormon history; chapter 2 provides an authoritative account of LDS historiography from 1900 to 1950.

80. Walker et al., *Mormon History*, 61–62.

81. Fawn Brodie, *No Man Knows My History: The Life of Joseph Smith*, 2nd ed. (New York: Knopf, 1971), xii.

82. Davis Bitton, "Ten Years in Camelot: A Personal Memoir," *Dialogue: A Journal of Mormon Thought* 16.3 (Autumn 1983): 10. Leonard Arrington covers the period more extensively in *Adventures*, 74–174.

83. James B. Allen, "The Significance of Joseph Smith's 'First Vision' in Mormon Thought," *Dialogue: A Journal of Mormon Thought* 1.3 (Autumn 1966): 29–45; Davis Bitton, "Anti-Intellectualism in Mormon History," *Dialogue: A Journal of Mormon Thought* 1.3 (Autumn 1966): 111–34.

84. *Dialogue: A Journal of Mormon Thought* 1.4 (Winter 1966): 13; 2.1 (Spring 1967): 2; 2.2 (Summer 1967): 5; 2.1 (Spring 1967): 6.

85. One poll at BYU found almost 86.4 percent of students supportive of or indifferent to American involvement in the war. Knud S. Larsen and Gary Schwendiman, "The Vietnam War through the Eyes of a Mormon Subculture," *Dialogue: A Journal of Mormon Thought* 3.3 (Autumn 1968): 154.

86. Ray C. Hillam, Eugene England, and John L. Sorenson, "Roundtable: Vietnam," *Dialogue: A Journal of Mormon Thought* 2.4 (Winter 1967): 64–100.

87. Knud S. Larsen, "A Voice against the War," *Dialogue: A Journal of Mormon Thought* 2.3 (Autumn 1967): 163–66; M. Neff Smart, "The Blasphemy of Indifference," *Dialogue: A Journal of Mormon Thought* 2.2 (Summer 1967): 155–59.

88. Armand L. Mauss gave a provocative overview and critique in "Mormonism and the Negro: Faith, Folklore, and Civil Rights," *Dialogue: A Journal of Mormon Thought* 2.4 (Winter 1967): 19–40. The topic was raised frequently in subsequent articles like Royal Shipp, "Black Images and White Images: The Combustibility of Common Misconceptions," *Dialogue: A Journal of Mormon Thought* 3.4 (Winter 1968): 87–91, and in numerous letters and other articles.

89. Lester Bush, "Writing 'Mormonism's Negro Doctrine: An Historical Overview' (1973): Context and Reflections, 1998," *Journal of Mormon History* 25.1 (Spring 1999): 249. Bush had shown the manuscript to Janath Cannon, who passed it on to Packer on her own initiative but with Bush's approval. Bush, "Writing," 247.

90. Bush, "Writing," 252. His research was published as "Mormonism's Negro Doctrine: An Historical Overview," *Dialogue: A Journal of Mormon Thought* 8.1 (Spring 1973).

91. Bush, "Writing," 260–66.

92. See, for example, England's "Tragedy of Vietnam and the Responsibility of Mormons," *Dialogue: A Journal of Mormon Thought* 2.4 (Winter 1967): 71–91; "The Mormon Cross," *Dialogue: A Journal of Mormon Thought* 8.1 (Spring 1973): 78–85.

93. For an account of *Sunstone*'s early years, see Elbert Peck, "The Origin and Evolution of the Sunstone Species: Twenty-Five Years of Creative Adaptation," *Sunstone* 22.3–4 (December 1999): 5–14.

94. Eugene England, "Letter to the Editor," *Sunstone* 1.1 (Winter 1975): 5.

95. Claudia L. Bushman, "A Wider Sisterhood," *Dialogue: A Journal of Mormon Thought* 11.1 (Spring 1978): 96.

96. "Exponent II encourages this unity in a wider sisterhood, believing that fighting is bootless." Bushman, "Wider," 98.

97. Dixie Snow Huefner, "Church and Politics at the Utah IWY Conference," *Dialogue: A Journal of Mormon Thought* 11.1 (Spring 1978): 58.

98. Barbara Smith, as quoted in the *Salt Lake Tribune* (14 August 1977). Cited in Huefner, "Church and Politics," 67.

99. As an example of sympathetic coverage, see Mary L. Bradford, "The Odyssey of Sonia Johnson," *Dialogue: A Journal of Mormon Thought* 14.2 (Summer 1981): 14–26. The interview was in the same issue, 27–47.

100. Laurel Thatcher Ulrich, "The Pink Dialogue and Beyond," *Dialogue: A Journal of Mormon Thought* 14.4 (Winter 1981): 30. Two treatments of the church's involvement in the IWY and ERA are Martha Sonntag Bradley, "The Mormon Relief Society and the International Women's Year," *Journal of Mormon History* 21.1 (Spring 1995): 105–67; and D. Michael Quinn, "The LDS Church's Campaign against the Equal Rights Amendment," *Journal of Mormon History* 20.2 (Fall 1994): 85–155.

101. Arrington, *Adventures*, 160.

102. Boyd K. Packer, "The Mantle Is Far, Far Greater than the Intellect," Annual Church Educational System Religious Educators' Symposium, 22 August 1981, Brigham Young University, Provo, Utah, published in *BYU Studies* 21.3 (Summer 1981): 259–78.

103. Thomas G. Alexander, "Toward the New Mormon History: An Examination of the Literature on the Latter-day Saints in the Far West," in *Historians and the American West*, ed. Michael P. Malone (Lincoln: University of Nebraska Press, 1983), 344.

104. Blake Ostler, "An Interview with Sterling McMurrin," *Dialogue: A Journal of Mormon Thought* 17.1 (Spring 1984): 20. Originally published in *Seventh East Press* (11 January 1983): 5–7, 10–11; "Mormon Media Image," *Sunstone Review* 2.2 (March 1982): 10.

105. Ostler, "Interview with Sterling McMurrin," 25.

106. Martin E. Marty, "Two Integrities: An Address to the Crisis in Mormon Historiography," *Journal of Mormon History* 10 (1983): 3.

107. "History of Joseph Smith," *Millennial Star* 20 (1858): 774.

108. "Letters," *Dialogue: A Journal of Mormon Thought* 2.2 (Summer 1967): 15.

109. Scott Abbott, "One Lord, One Faith, Two Universities: Tensions between 'Religion' and 'Thought' at BYU," *Sunstone* 16.3 (September 1992): 15.

110. AAUP, Letter to Professor Houston, 15 August 1996, cited in BYU chapter of AAUP, Letter to President Merrill J. Bateman, 24 September 1996, available on-line at http://www.lds-mormon.com/aaupchapbat4.shtml?FACTNet.

111. Heber C. Snell, "The Bible in the Church," *Dialogue: A Journal of Mormon Thought* 2.1 (Spring 1967): 63.

112. Heber Snell to Joseph Fielding Smith, 5 June 1950. Quoted in Richard Sherlock, "Faith and History: The Snell Controversy," *Dialogue: A Journal of Mormon Thought* 12.1 (Spring 1979): 35.

113. Sterling McMurrin, "On Mormon Theology," *Dialogue: A Journal of Mormon Thought* 1.2 (Summer 1966): 141.

114. Grant McMurray made this statement in his keynote address at the Mormon History Association annual meeting, Kirtland, Ohio, 22 May 2003.

115. Arthur Schopenhauer, *Parerga and Paralipomena: Short Philosophical Essays*, trans. E. F. J. Payne (Oxford: Clarendon, 1974), 2:369.

116. Hofmann's forgeries spurred a series of major revisionist histories whose influence persists, even though the main catalyst—a letter signed by Martin Harris in which he quotes Joseph Smith describing a salamander that transformed into an angel—was revealed as fraudulent. Two studies of the Hofmann episode are Richard E. Turley, *Victims: The LDS Church and the Mark Hofmann Case* (Urbana: University of Illinois Press, 1992); and Linda Sillitoe and Allen Roberts, *Salamander: The Story of the Mormon Forgery Murders* (Salt Lake City: Signature, 1990).

117. George D. Smith, *Faithful History: Essays on Writing Mormon History* (Salt Lake City: Signature, 1992), 269.

118. David Bohn, "The Larger Issue," *Sunstone* 16.8 (February 1994): 45.

119. Anti-Mormon polemical works routinely cite the various First Vision accounts as a discrediting factor. LDS treatments include Allen, "Significance of Joseph Smith's 'First Vision' "; and Dean C. Jessee, "Early Accounts of Joseph Smith's First Vision," *BYU Studies* 9.3 (Spring 1969): 275–98. Juanita Brooks wrote the first thorough treatment of the event, *Mountain Meadows*. Will Bagley produced a scathing indictment of Mormon culpability in *Blood of the Prophets: Brigham Young and the Massacre at Mountain Meadows* (Norman: University of Oklahoma Press, 2002). A rebuttal/ critique of Bagley is Robert D. Crockett, "A Trial Lawyer Reviews Will Bagley's *Blood of the Prophets*," *FARMS Review* 15.2 (2003): 199–254. For post-manifesto polygamy, see D. Michael Quinn, "LDS Church Authority and New Plural Marriages, 1890–1904," *Dialogue: A Journal of Mormon Thought* 18.1 (Spring 1985): 9–104.

120. "Y Tops List in Seven Areas," *Deseret Morning News* (17 August 2004): B-1.

121. Most of these statistics are available on the BYU Web site: www.byu.edu.

122. In recent years, Baylor, Furman, Mercer, Wake Forest, and the University of Richmond are just some of the Baptist schools to have joined a long list of other colleges and universities that have severed connections with their founding religious institutions.

123. Catherine R. Stimpson, "The Farr Case: The Next Chapter in the History of Academic Freedom," http://www.findarticles.com/p/articles/mi_m1254/is_n5_v25/ai_14265753.

124. Statement on Academic Freedom at BYU, 14 September 1992, available at the BYU Web site, www.byu.edu.

125. Apprised of the apostle's actions, the First Presidency directed that he desist. See more details from one of those summoned in Mauss, *Angel and the Beehive*, 182–83.

126. Dallin H. Oaks, "Alternate Voices," *Ensign* (May 1989): 27–30. For examples of temple ceremony treatments, see David John Buerger, "The Development of the Temple Endowment Ceremony," *Dialogue* 20.4 (Winter 1987): 33–76; Margaret Toscano and Paul Toscano, "The Mormon Endowment," in *Strangers in Paradox: Explorations of Mormon Theology*, ed. Toscano and Toscano (Salt Lake City: Signature, 1990), 278–91.

127. "There are times," the statement concludes:

when it is better to have the Church without representation than to have implications of Church participation used to promote a program that contains some (though admittedly not all) presentations that result in ridiculing sacred things or injuring The Church of Jesus Christ, detracting from its mission, or jeopardizing the well-being of its members.

The church issued the statement on 23 August 1991. It was reprinted in *Sunstone* 15.4 (October 1991): 58.

128. Bergera and Priddis, *Brigham Young University*, 71.

129. "Secret Files," *New York Times* (22 August 1992).

130. "The Issue of Academic Freedom: An Interview with Jim Gordon," *Brigham Young Magazine* 51.4 (Winter 1997): 30.

131. Naomi Schaefer, "Brigham Young in Boston: Can a Liberal State Tolerate Mormon Religious Beliefs?" *Opinion Journal from the Wall Street Journal Editorial Page* (1 November 2002), http://www.opinionjournal.com/taste/?id=110002562.

132. James E. Talmage, Journal, January 1922, cited in Brigham D. Madsen's introduction to Roberts, *Studies of the Book of Mormon*, 22.

133. Thomas O'Dea, *The Mormons* (Chicago: University of Chicago Press, 1957), 26.

134. Benjamin Winchester, "The Claims of the Book of Mormon Established," *Gospel Reflector* 1.5 (1 March 1841): 105.

135. The first professional archaeologist and Mesoamerican scholar in the LDS church was apparently Paul Henning, a German convert born in 1872. He participated in the Cluff expedition and later encouraged Book of Mormon–related studies, but never published his many papers on the subject. See Robert F. Fullmer, "Paul Henning: The First Mormon Archaeologist," *Journal of Book of Mormon Studies* 9.1 (2000): 64–65.

136. Sorenson was building on the efforts of his predecessors, but his work was by far the most extensive and meticulous. See his *An Ancient American Setting for the Book of Mormon* (Salt Lake City and Provo, Utah: Deseret Book and FARMS, 1996).

137. Hugh W. Nibley, "Lehi in the Desert," in *The Collected Works of Hugh Nibley*, ed. John W. Welch, Darrell L. Matthews, and Stephen R. Callister (Provo, Utah: Deseret and FARMS, 1988), 5:4.

138. Fifteen volumes of *The Collected Works of Hugh Nibley* have been published since 1986, with at least one more expected.

139. According to Nibley's biographer, the offer was probably oral. In addition to Nibley's personal account of the offer, circumstantial evidence includes a written reply from church apostle Joseph Fielding Smith in response to Nibley's apparent query as to whether he should consider the relocation. Personal correspondence with Boyd Peterson, 12 January 2006. For Smith's reply, see Peterson, *Hugh Nibley: A Consecrated Life* (Salt Lake City: Kofford, 2002), 292.

140. The president was the sympathetic David O. McKay. See Boyd J. Peterson, *"Something to Move Mountains": The Book of Mormon in Hugh Nibley's Correspondence* (Provo, Utah: FARMS, 1997), 1–25. In addition to the controversial manual, two of his serials on the Book of Mormon did appear in the church's *Improvement Era*. "Lehi in the Desert" (1950) and "World of the Jaredites" (1951–1952) were published jointly as a book in 1952.

141. Hugh W. Nibley, *Brother Brigham Challenges the Saints* (Salt Lake City: Deseret Book and FARMS, 1994), 394.

142. Harold B. Lee in *Conference Report of the Church of Jesus Christ of Latter-day Saints* (April 1963): 82.

143. Gregory A. Prince and William Robert Wright, *David O. McKay and the Rise of Modern Mormonism* (Salt Lake City: University of Utah Press, 2005), 141. Prince and Wright's chapter on "Correlation and Church Administration" is the most detailed and authoritative account of this topic.

144. A. Theodore Tuttle interview, 11 October 1977. Quoted in Prince and Wright, *McKay*, 143.

145. First Presidency, Letter to the General Priesthood Committee, 24 March 1960. Cited in Prince and Wright, *McKay*, 145–46, 155.

146. Paul H. Dunn interview, 6 October 1995, in Prince and Wright, *McKay*, 158.

147. Interview with John Welch in "Church News," *Ogden Standard-Examiner*, 1 December 1984, 12; Bell, "Taking the Stand," *This People* (February–March 1987): 63.

148. FARMS was subsequently incorporated into BYU's Institute for the Study and Preservation of Ancient Religious Texts (ISPART), which in 2006 was rechristened the Neal A. Maxwell Institute for Religious Scholarship.

149. Carl Mosser and Paul Owen, "Mormon Apologetic[s], Scholarship and Evangelical Neglect: Losing the Battle and Not Knowing It?" *Trinity Journal* 19 (Fall 1998): 181, 185, 189.

150. The most extensive DNA-based critique of Book of Mormon historicity is Simon G. Southerton, *Losing a Lost Tribe: Native Americans, DNA, and the Mormon Church* (Salt Lake City: Signature, 2004). Mormon apologists insist the critique is both a straw-man attack (since the relationship between Book of Mormon Lamanites and Native Americans is not clear-cut in that record) and based on faulty science. See the extensive rebuttals by Ryan Parr, "Missing the Boat to Ancient America . . . Just

Plain Missing the Boat," *FARMS Review* 17.1 (2005): 84–106; and John L. Sorenson et al., "The Book of Mormon at the Bar of DNA 'Evidence,'" *Journal of Book of Mormon Studies* 12.1 (2003): 4–51.

151. In addition to off-the-record criticisms by participants at Yale and the Library of Congress, an exasperated Douglas Davies chided in public remarks that LDS participants needed to decide if they were having an academic conference or evangelizing, at the conclusion of the Joseph Smith Bicentennial Symposium, New South Wales Parliament, Sydney, Australia, 21 May 2005.

152. In the early 1990s, a German archaeology team discovered a carved altar a few dozen miles east of modern San'a inscribed with a reference to the tribe of NHM, and another with a like inscription has since been located in the same area. Found in the very area where Nephi's record locates Nahom (1 Nephi 16), these altars are the most impressive concrete evidence to date of the Book of Mormon's historicity. See Terryl L. Givens, *By the Hand of Mormon: The American Scripture That Launched a New World Religion* (New York: Oxford University Press, 2003), 120.

153. Margaret Barker, "Joseph Smith and Preexilic Israelite Religion," in *The Worlds of Joseph Smith: A Bicentennial Conference at the Library of Congress*, ed. John Welch (Provo, Utah: Brigham Young University Press, 2006), 69–82.

154. Ostler, "Interview with Sterling McMurrin," 25.

155. Heber C. Snell, Letter, *Dialogue: A Journal of Mormon Thought* 2.3 (Autumn 1967): 17.

156. Ostler, "Interview with Sterling McMurrin," 27.

157. Statement by the First Presidency and the Quorum of the Twelve, 17 October 1993. The definition of *apostasy* is from *General Handbook of Instructions* (Salt Lake City: Church of Jesus Christ of Latter-day Saints, 1989), 10–13.

158. Sterling M. McMurrin and L. Jackson Newell, *Matters of Conscience: Conversations with Sterling M. McMurrin on Philosophy, Education, and Religion* (Salt Lake City: Signature, 1996), 203.

159. McMurrin and Newell, *Matters of Conscience*, 199–200.

160. Prince and Wright, *McKay*, 40.

161. The lectures were published as *The Philosophical Foundations of Mormon Theology* (Salt Lake City: University of Utah Press, 1959).

162. Christensen and Cannon, "The Fundamentalist Emphasis," 55.

163. "Study Finds Mormon Teens Fare Best," AP Internet story, 14 March 2005, www.news14.com. The results are published in Christian Smith and Melinda Lundquist Denton, *Soul Searching: The Religious and Spiritual Lives of American Teenagers* (New York: Oxford University Press, 2005).

164. Cowan, *The Church*, 122–23.

165. E. L. Thorndike, "The Origin of Superior Men," *Scientific Monthly* 56 (1943): 426.

166. Kenneth R. Hardy, "Social Origins of American Scientists and Scholars," *Science* 185 (1974): 500.

167. James T. Duke, "Cultural Continuity and Tension," in *Latter-day Saint Social Life: Social Research on the LDS Church and Its Members*, ed. James T. Duke (Provo, Utah: Religious Studies Center, 1998), 83.

168. Howard M. Bahr and Renata Tonks Forste, "Toward a Social Science of Contemporary Mormondom," in Duke, *Latter-day Saint Social Life*, 157.

169. Gerald Stott, "Effects of College Education on the Religious Involvement of Latter-day Saints," *BYU Studies* 24.1 (Winter 1984): 52.

170. Mauss, *Angel and the Beehive*, 68–70. As Mauss argues, geography may also prove to be an important factor.

171. O'Dea, *Mormons*, 147–48.

172. Ostler, "Interview," 20.

173. Armand Mauss, "Alternate Voices: The Calling and Its Implications," *Sunstone* 14.2 (April 1990): 9.

174. Society of Professional Journalists, "Code of Ethics," http://www.spj.org/ethics_code.asp.

175. Neal A. Maxwell, "Some Thoughts on the Gospel and the Behavioral Sciences," *BYU Studies* 16.4 (Summer 1976): 589.

～ CHAPTER 12

1. Jeffrey S. Smith and Benjamin N. White, "Detached from Their Homeland: The Latter-day Saints of Chihuahua, Mexico," *Journal of Cultural Geography* 21.2 (Summer 2004): 61; and Wilbur Zelinski, "An Approach to the Religious Geography of the United States: Patterns of Church Membership in 1952," *Annals of the Association of American Geographers* 51.2 (1961): 164, cited in Smith and White, "Detached," 61.

2. D. W. Meinig, "The Mormon Culture Region: Strategies and Patterns in the Geography of the American West, 1847–1964," *Annals of the Association of American Geographers* 55 (1965): 191–220.

3. Richard V. Francaviglia, *The Mormon Landscape: Existence, Creation, and Perception of a Unique Image in the American West* (New York: AMS, 1978).

4. Francaviglia, *Mormon Landscape*, 18.

5. Allen D. Roberts, "Religious Architecture of the LDS Church: Influences and Changes since 1847," *Utah Historical Quarterly* 43.3 (1975): 321.

6. Paul Lawrence Anderson, "Mormon Moderne: New Directions in Latter-day Saint Architecture, 1890–1955" (unpublished manuscript), 1. Author's files.

7. Anderson, "Mormon Moderne," 1.

8. For these and other examples, see the illustrations collected in Anderson, "Mormon Moderne," 13–18.

9. Martha Sonntag Bradley, "The Cloning of Mormon Architecture," *Dialogue: A Journal of Mormon Thought* 14.1 (Spring 1981): 20–31.

10. Bradley, "Cloning," 26–27.

11. Richard O. Cowan, *The Church in the Twentieth Century* (Salt Lake City: Bookcraft, 1985), 297–98.

12. Donald Bergsma et al., "The Lamps of Mormon Architecture," *Dialogue: A Journal of Mormon Thought* 3.1 (Spring 1968): 19. Comment by Bergsma.

13. Bergsma, "The Lamps," 19.

14. Quoted in Bergsma, "The Lamps," 19.

15. *Ensign* (November 2004): 4.

16. Nicole Seymour, "Standardized Meetinghouses Worldwide Give More Members a Place to Worship," http://www.lds.org/library/display/0,44,40–1–3324–4,00 .html.

17. Seymour, "Standardized Meetinghouses."

18. David S. Andrew and Laurel N. Blank, "The Four Mormon Temples in Utah," *Journal of the Society of Architectural Historians* 30.1 (March 1971): 65.

19. "American Antiquities," *Times and Seasons* 3.18 (15 July 1842): 860.

20. Samuel E. Woolley in *Conference Report of the Church of Jesus Christ of Latter-day Saints* (October 1917), 79.

21. Paul L. Anderson, "A Jewel in the Gardens of Paradise: The Art and Architecture of the Hawaii Temple," *BYU Studies* 39.4 (2000): 170.

22. "It would have been nice had they made up their minds whether they wanted it square or round," groused Hugh Nibley in "The Circle and the Square," in *Temple and Cosmos: Beyond This Ignorant Present*, ed. Don E. Norton (Salt Lake City and Provo, Utah: Deseret and FARMS, 1992), 149; Donald J. Bergsma referred to the "mercantilistic quality of the design" in "The Temple as Symbol," *Dialogue: A Journal of Mormon Thought* 3.1 (Spring 1968): 27.

23. Dennis L. Lythgoe, "Lengthening Our Stride: The Remarkable Administration of Spencer W. Kimball," *BYU Studies* 25.4 (Fall 1985): 10.

24. These critical comments are all cited by Stephen W. Stathis and Dennis L. Lythgoe, "Mormonism in the Nineteen-Seventies: The Popular Perception," *Dialogue: A Journal of Mormon Thought* 10.3 (Spring 1977): 104.

25. *Washington Post* (17 November 1984), quoted in "News and Reviews," *Sunstone* 10.3 (March 1985): 56.

26. Conan E. Mathews, "Art and the Church," *BYU Studies* 3.1 (Autumn 1960): 6.

27. *Ensign* 10.5 (May 1980): 99.

28. *Church News*, 12 July 1975.

～ CHAPTER 13

1. See B. H. Roberts, *Comprehensive History of the Church of Jesus Christ of Latter-day Saints*, 6 vols. (Provo, Utah: Church of Jesus Christ of Latter-day Saints, 1957), 6:236–41.

2. Michael Hicks, *Mormonism and Music: A History* (Chicago: University of Chicago Press, 1989), 153.

3. Joan H. Iverson, "The Tabernacle Choir," *Improvement Era* 58.8 (August 1955): 591.

4. Quoted by Richard R. Lyman in *Conference Report of the Church of Jesus Christ of Latter-day Saints* (October 1925), 123.

5. *Richmond News Leader*, 15 November 1911, quoted in Hicks, *Mormonism and Music*, 156.

6. Hicks, *Mormonism and Music*, x.

7. Hicks, *Mormonism and Music*, 162.

8. Hicks, *Mormonism and Music*, 164.

9. Hicks, *Mormonism and Music*, 174.

10. Mormons find additional significance in the fact that Mendelssohn reportedly conceived the idea for his oratorio on Elijah mere months after he appeared in the Kirtland Temple to Joseph Smith and Oliver Cowdery on 3 April 1836.

11. Roberts, *Comprehensive History*, 6:245.

12. See the reminiscences of the composer's daughter, Marian Robertson Wilson, "Leroy Robertson and the Oratorio from the Book of Mormon," *Journal of Book of Mormon Studies* 8.2 (1999): 4–13.

13. "New Music for the World," *Improvement Era* 56.4 (April 1953): 210–211.

14. Lowell M. Durham, "A Mormon Record," *Dialogue: A Journal of Mormon Thought* 2.3 (Autumn 1967): 149.

15. Kenneth Hicken's *The Psalm of Nephi*, oratorio in German, is mentioned in "Church News," *Deseret News and Salt Lake Telegram* (19 January 1957): 13; *Coriantumr* by Rowan Taylor premiered in East Los Angeles in 1960 (manuscript copy, L. Tom Perry Special Collections, Harold B. Lee Library, Brigham Young University); *Apostasy and Restoration* by David Sargent, 1974, is discussed in Hicks, *Mormonism and Music*, 183; for *Songs of Sonia*, see Anne Worthington Prescott, *Journal of Women and Religion* 1 (Winter 1984): 51–57; Crawford Gates's *Visions of Eternity* premiered at Ricks College, Idaho, in 1993.

16. Boyd K. Packer, "The Arts and the Spirit of the Lord," *BYU Studies* 16.4 (Summer 1976): 580.

17. Alfred R. Ferguson and Jean Ferguson Carr, eds., *The Collected Works of Ralph Waldo Emerson*, 6 vols. (Cambridge, Mass.: Harvard University Press, 1979), 2:216.

18. "Since the early 1970s, as many as 1.5 million people, mostly Mormons, have seen the show." D. J. Burton, "Saturday's Warrior: A Battlefield Casualty?" *Sunstone Review* 2.9 (September 1982): 14.

19. Eugene England, "The Dawning of a Brighter Day: Mormon Literature after 150 Years," *BYU Studies* 22.1 (Fall 1982): 17.

20. The figures come from Karen Lynn Davidson, "The Book of Mormon in Latter-day Saint Hymnody," *Journal of Book of Mormon Studies* 9.1 (2000): 14.

21. Karen Lynn Davison, "The Book of Mormon in Latter-day Saint Hymnody," *Journal of Book of Mormon Studies* 9.1 (2000): 15.

22. Hicks, *Mormonism and Music*, 229.

23. Dallin H. Oaks, "Repentance and Change," *Ensign* 33 (November 2003): 38.

24. Oaks, "Repentance," 39.

25. From the SUV Choir Web site: http://www.suvchoir.org/about.html.

26. The Tabernacle Choir won the Grammy for best performance by a vocal group or chorus for "Battle Hymn of the Republic" in 1960.

27. Arthur Henry King, *The Abundance of the Heart* (Salt Lake City: Bookcraft, 1986), 10.

28. Cited in Dennis L. Lythgoe, "The Changing Image of Mormonism," *Dialogue: A Journal of Mormon Thought* 3.4 (Winter 1968): 48.

~ CHAPTER 14

1. "Editor's Table," *Improvement Era* 14.7 (May 1911): 639.

2. Harold H. Jenson, "Joseph Smith at Nauvoo," *Improvement Era* 32.11 (September 1929).

3. "Mutual Work," *Improvement Era* 27.7 (May 1924).

4. "Mutual Work," *Improvement Era* 27.7 (May 1924).

5. "Mutual Work," *Improvement Era* 31.5 (March 1928).

6. Joseph J. Cannon, "The Little Theater Movement of the Church," *Improvement Era* 46.10 (October 1943).

7. Constance D'Arcy Mackay, *The Little Theatre in the United States* (New York: Holt, 1917), 1–3.

8. Kenneth Macgowan, *Footlights across America* (New York: Harcourt, Brace, 1929), 43–44.

9. Mackay, *Little Theatre*, 23.

10. "Mutual Messages," *Improvement Era* 35.11 (September 1932).

11. Stanley B. Kimball, "Prometheus Hobbled: The Intellectual in Mormondom," *Dialogue* 18.1 (Spring 1985): 112–13.

12. Peggy Fletcher Stack, "Mormon Roadshows Sent Packing," *Salt Lake Tribune* (31 July 1999): L2.

13. B. H. Roberts, *Comprehensive History of the Church of Jesus Christ of Latter-day Saints* (Provo, Utah: Church of Jesus Christ of Latter-day Saints, 1957), 6: 524–26.

14. Richard O. Cowan, *The Church in the Twentieth Century* (Salt Lake City, Utah: Bookcraft, 1985), 168.

15. A. Laurence Lyon, "Lyrics and Love in Orderville," *Dialogue: A Journal of Mormon Thought* 6 (1971): 122.

16. "Pageant in Castle Valley Is All about 'Crying, Laughing, Feeling,'" *LDS Church News* (16 August 1997).

17. Clinton Larson, *The Mantle of the Prophet and Other Plays* (Salt Lake City: Deseret, 1966), 3, 4.

18. Dwight Israelsen, "An Economic Analysis of the United Order," *BYU Studies* 18.4 (Summer 1978): 538.

19. Carol Lynn Pearson, *The Order Is Love*, lyrics by Lex de Azevedo (Provo, Utah: Trilogy Arts, 1971), 44.

20. Pearson, *Order*, 67.

21. Pearson, *Order*, 41.

22. Frederick Bliss and P. Q. Gump, "Mormon Shakespeares: A Study of Contemporary Mormon Theatre," *Sunstone* 1.2 (Spring 1976): 60.

23. Clayne Robison, "Review," *Sunstone* 3.3 (March 1978): 32.

24. Frederick Bliss and P. Q. Gump, "Not Just Another Theatre?" *Sunstone* 2.2 (Summer 1977): 43.

25. Bliss and Gump, "Mormon," 60.

26. Eugene England, "Book Reviews," *BYU Studies* 26.3 (Summer 1986): 112.

27. Richard Alan Nelson, "From Antagonism to Acceptance: Mormons and the Silver Screen," *Dialogue: A Journal of Mormon Thought* 10.3 (Spring 1977): 63.

28. James V. D'Arc, "Darryl F. Zanuck's 'Brigham Young': A Film in Context," *BYU Studies* 29.1 (Winter 1989): 6.

29. Truman G. Madsen, "B. H. Roberts and the Book of Mormon," *BYU Studies* 19.4 (Summer 1979): 436.

30. I find Gideon Burton's application of that term to Dutcher's films especially apt. See his paper, "Sacramental Mormon Cinema," LDS Film Forum, 5th Annual LDS Film Festival, Orem, Utah, 26 January 2006. He credits the term to Peter Fraser, *Images of the Passion: The Sacramental Mode in Film* (Westport, Conn.: Praeger, 1998); and notes Sarah Beckwith's reference to "sacramental theater" in her *Signifying God: Social Relation and Symbolic Act in the York Corpus Christi Plays* (Chicago: University of Chicago Press, 2001).

31. Richard Burton, *City of the Saints* (1861; rpt., ed. Fawn M. Brodie, New York: Knopf, 1963), 224.

～ CHAPTER 15

1. Nephi Anderson, *Added Upon: A Story* (1898; rpt., Salt Lake: Bookcraft, 1967), preface to third edition.

2. Anderson, *Added Upon*, 17, 143.

3. Edward Geary, "The Poetics of Provincialism: Mormon Regional Fiction," *Dialogue: A Journal of Mormon Thought* 11 (Summer 1978): 15.

4. According to an ancient text revealed by Joseph Smith, "kokaubeam" signifies stars, and "Kolob" is a star near the abode of God. See Abraham 3, PGP.

5. Orson Ferguson Whitney, *Elias: An Epic of the Ages* (New York: Knickerbocker Press, 1904), 30.

6. Noel B. Reynolds, ed., *Book of Mormon Authorship: New Light on Ancient Origins* (Provo, Utah: BYU Religious Studies Center, 1982), 17–18. The work originally appeared as "Corianton: A Nephite Story," *Contributor* 10 (March–July 1889): 171, 206, 245, 286, 324. Later, it was published as *Corianton: A Nephite Story* (Salt Lake City: Deseret News Press, 1902).

7. Harold Bloom, *The American Religion: The Emergence of the Post-Christian Nation* (New York: Simon and Schuster, 1992), 82, 127.

8. Bernard DeVoto, "Vacation," *Harper's* 177 (1938): 560.

9. Vardis Fisher, *Children of God* (New York: Harper, 1939); Maurine Whipple, *The Giant Joshua* (Boston: Houghton Mifflin, 1941); Virginia Sorensen, *A Little Lower than the Angels* (New York: Knopf, 1942; rpt., Salt Lake City: Signature, 1997).

10. Fisher, *Children*, 113.

11. Fisher, *Children*, 121.

12. Maurine Whipple to Tom Spies (n.d.), cited in Katherine Ashton, "Whatever Happened to Maurine Whipple," *Sunstone* 14.2 (April 1990): 36.

13. John Widtsoe, "On the Book Rack," *Improvement Era* 44.2 (February 1941): 93.

14. Curtis Taylor, "The Giant Joshua and Latter-day Fiction," *LDS Booksellers Association Newsletter* (February 1989): 6–7, cited in Ashton, "Whatever Happened," 36.

15. Whipple, *Giant Joshua*, 246, 259.

16. Whipple, *Giant Joshua*, 5, 101.

17. Whipple, *Giant Joshua*, 73.

18. Whipple, *Giant Joshua*, 632.

19. Maurine Whipple, "They Did Go Forth," *Dialogue: A Journal of Mormon Thought* 24.4 (Winter 1991): 165–72.

20. The expression is from an admiring *New York Times* review, cited in *Monthly Bulletin of the Doubleday One Dollar Book Club* 12.4 (n.d.): 3.

21. Whipple, *Giant Joshua*, 132–33.

22. Whipple, *Giant Joshua*, 282–83.

23. Whipple, *Giant Joshua*, 633.

24. Whipple, *Giant Joshua*, 261.

25. Whipple, *Giant Joshua*, 365.

26. Sorensen, *A Little Lower*, 5.

27. Sorensen, *A Little Lower*, 114.

28. Sorensen, *A Little Lower*, 306.

29. Sorensen, *A Little Lower*, 43.

30. Sorensen, *A Little Lower*, 344.

31. Sorensen, *A Little Lower*, 107.

32. Sorensen, *A Little Lower*, 352.

33. Sorensen, *A Little Lower*, 57.

34. Sorensen, *A Little Lower*, 60.

35. Sorensen, *A Little Lower*, 345.

36. Percy Bysshe Shelley, "Lift Not the Painted Veil," in *Complete Poetical Works*, ed. George Edward Woodberry (Boston: Houghton Mifflin, 1901), 363–64.

37. Sorensen, *A Little Lower*, 345–46.

38. Sorensen, *A Little Lower*, 315.

39. Sorensen, *A Little Lower*, 55.

40. Sorensen, *A Little Lower*, 22.

41. Sorensen, *A Little Lower*, 4.

42. John Widtsoe, "On the Book Rack," *Improvement Era* 45.6 (June 1942): 380. Quoted by Mary Lythgoe Bradford, preface to Sorensen, *A Little Lower*, x–xi.

43. The term was first applied by Edward A. Geary in his insightful survey, "Mormonism's Lost Generation: The Novelists of the 1940s," *BYU Studies* 18.1 (Fall 1977): 89–98.

44. Samuel Taylor, *Heaven Knows Why* (New York: Wyn, 1948), 39.

45. Taylor, *Heaven Knows Why*, 39–40.

46. Richard H. Cracroft and Neal E. Lambert, eds., *A Believing People* (Provo, Utah: Brigham Young University Press, 1974).

47. Cracroft and Lambert, *Believing People*, 5.

48. Boyd K. Packer, "The Arts and the Spirit of the Lord," *BYU Studies* 16.4 (Summer 1976): 577 (first delivered as an address at Brigham Young University, 1 February 1976).

49. Eugene England, "Mormon Literature: Progress and Prospects," in *Mormon Americana*, ed. David Whittaker (Provo, Utah: BYU Studies, 1995), 456.

50. Cited by Laraine Wilkins, "A Figure in the Tapestry: The Poet's Feeling Runs Ahead of Her Imagination," paper presented at the Salt Lake Sunstone Symposium, 13 August 2004.

51. Ken Brewer, quoted in Rhett James, "Discovering May Swenson: The Most Distinguished American Poet of Mormon Heritage," *Mormon Heritage Magazine* 1.6 (March–April 1995): 20.

52. Laraine Wilkins, "The Mormon Poet in Exile: Poetry, Identity, and the Case of May Swenson," paper presented at the Rocky Mountain Modern Language Association Conference, 20–22 October 2005.

53. May Swenson, "My Name Was Called," *The New Yorker*, 13 June 1988.

54. Karl Keller, "A Pilgrimage of Awe," *Dialogue: A Journal of Mormon Thought* 3.1 (Spring 1968): 112.

55. Clinton Larson, "Granddaughter," in Cracroft and Lambert, *Believing People*, 295.

56. Clinton Larson, "A Letter from Israel Whiton, 1851," *Dialogue: A Journal of Mormon Thought* 4.3 (Autumn 1969): 95–99.

57. Dale Fletcher, "God, Man, and Art," *Dialogue: A Journal of Mormon Thought* 2.4 (Winter 1967): 124.

58. Carol Lynn Pearson, "The Eleventh Hour," in her *Beginnings* (Provo, Utah: Trilogy Arts, 1967), 11.

59. Carol Lynn Pearson, "Beginnings," in Pearson, *Beginnings*, 7.

60. Fletcher, "God, Man, and Art," 126.

61. Emma Lou Thayne, "Sunday School Picture," in her *Until Another Day for Butterflies* (n.p.: Parliament, 1973), 60–63.

62. Thayne, "Heretic," in her *Spaces in the Sage* (n.p.: Parliament, 1971), 39.

63. Thayne, "Conversion," in Thayne, *Until Another Day*, 50.

64. Thayne, "Affirmation," in Thayne, *Spaces in the Sage*, 9.

65. Bruce Jorgensen, "The Light Come Down," *Sunstone* 4.3 (May 1979): 16.

66. Lance Larsen, "Light," in *Harvest: Contemporary Mormon Poems*, ed. Eugene England and Dennis Clark (Salt Lake City: Signature, 1989), 233.

67. Susan Howe, "To My Great-great Grandmother, Written on a Flight to Salt Lake City," in England and Clark, *Harvest*, 194.

68. Susan Howe, "Things in the Night Sky," in England and Clark, *Harvest*, 195.

69. Douglas H. Thayer, "Under the Cottonwoods," in Thayer, *Under the Cottonwoods and Other Mormon Stories* (Provo, Utah: Frankson, 1977), 165.

70. Thayer, "Cottonwoods," 158.

71. Thayer, "Cottonwoods," 168.

72. Thayer, "Cottonwoods," 172.

73. Kevin Cassity, "The Age-Old Problem of Who," in *Greening Wheat: Fifteen Mormon Short Stories*, ed. Levi S. Peterson (Midvale, Utah: Signature, 1983), 7–15.

74. Donald R. Marshall, "The Week-End," in Marshall, *The Rummage Sale: Collections and Recollections* (1972; rpt., Salt Lake City: Tabernacle Books, 1999), 3.

75. Marshall, "The Week-End," 16.

76. Eileen Gibbons Kump, "Sayso or Sense," *BYU Studies* 14.2 (Winter 1974): 267.

77. Kump, "Sayso," 268.

78. Karen Rosenbaum, "Hit the Frolicking, Rippling Brooks," *Dialogue: A Journal of Mormon Thought* 11.3 (Autumn 1978): 70.

79. Rosenbaum, "Hit the Frolicking," 71.

80. Elizabeth Barrett Browning, *Aurora Leigh* (Athens: Ohio University Press, 1992), 487.

81. Thayer, "Cottonwoods," 168.

82. Levi S. Peterson, *The Backslider* (Salt Lake City: Signature, 1986), 276–77.

83. Peterson, *The Backslider*, 285.

84. Peterson, *The Backslider*, 353–55.

85. Peterson, *The Backslider*, 357.

86. Michael Fillerup, *Beyond the River* (Salt Lake City: Signature, 1995), 233.

87. Fillerup, *Beyond the River*, 235.

88. Fillerup, *Beyond the River*, 91–92.

89. Fillerup, *Beyond the River*, 250.

90. Alan Mitchell, *Angel of the Danube* (Springville, Utah: Bonneville, 2000).

91. Mitchell, *Angel*, 5.

92. Mitchell, *Angel*, 155–56.

93. Mitchell, *Angel*, 170–73.

94. Sally Taylor, from jacket blurb of Margaret Blair Young, *Salvador* (Salt Lake City: Aspen, 1992).

95. Young, *Salvador*, 5.

96. Young, *Salvador*, 72.

97. Young, *Salvador*, 190.

98. Eugene England, "Pastwatch: The Redemption of Orson Scott Card," paper presented at Life, the Universe, and Everything XV: An Annual Symposium on the Impact of Science Fiction and Fantasy, Provo, Utah, 28 February 1997.

99. "Sampling of Latter-day Saint/Utah Demographics and Social Statistics from National Sources," http://www.adherents.com/largecom/lds_dem.html.

100. "Utahns Devour and Write a Galaxy of Science Fiction," *Rednova Space News*, downloaded 25 August 2003, http://www.rednova.com/news/space/17639/utahns_devour_and_write_a_galaxy_of_fantasy_fiction.

101. E-mail message, quoted in *Rednova Space News*, 25 August 2003.

102. Orson Scott Card, *Hot Sleep: The Worthing Chronicle* (London: Futura, 1980), 404–5. Norman Beswick cites these and several other instances of LDS influence on Card's writing in his perceptive "Amblick and After: Aspects of Orson Scott Card," *Foundation* 45 (Spring 1989): 49–62. The weeping God is found in Moses 7, PGP.

103. Orson Scott Card, "Letter," *Dialogue: A Journal of Mormon Thought* 18.2 (Summer 1985): 13.

104. Orson Scott Card, "Author's Note: On Sycamore Hill," in his *The Folk of the Fringe* (New York: Orb, 1989), 253.

105. Eugene England, "Why the Church Is as True as the Gospel," *Sunstone* 10.10 (April 1986): 32.

106. Elbert Peck, "Weeping by the Waters of Zion," *Sunstone* 14.6 (December 1990): 9–10.

107. Levi S. Peterson, "A Christian by Yearning," *Sunstone* 12.5 (September 1988): 19, 22.

108. Patricia Nelson Limerick, "Peace Initiative: Using the Mormons to Rethink Culture and Ethnicity in American History," in *The Mormon History Association's Tanner Lectures: The First Twenty Years*, ed. Dean L. May and Reid Neilson (Chicago: University of Chicago Press, 2006), 199.

~ CHAPTER 16

1. Personal correspondence with the author, 2 March 2006.

2. "Le Symbolisme," *Le Figaro*, 18 September 1886.

3. Vern Swanson, Robert S. Olpin, and William C. Seifrit, *Utah Painting and Sculpture* (Salt Lake City: Gibbs-Smith, 1997), 189.

4. Personal interview, 8 June 2004.

5. Jay Todd, managing editor of the *Ensign*, remarked that "as long as the Church commissioned biblical work, something that [Anderson] deeply believed in, he accepted the commissions." Quoted in Robert T. Barrett and Susan Easton Black, "Setting a Standard in LDS Art: Four Illustrators of the Mid-Twentieth Century," *BYU Studies* 44.2 (2005): 49.

6. David Erickson to Susan Easton Black, cited in "Setting a Standard," 68.

7. Dale T. Fletcher, "Art and Belief: A Group Exhibition," *Dialogue: A Journal of Mormon Thought* 2.1 (Spring 1967): 51.

8. Fletcher, "Art and Belief," 51.

9. Spencer W. Kimball, "The Gospel Vision of the Arts," *Ensign* 7 (July 1977): 5. First delivered as an address at Brigham Young University in 1967.

10. Lorin F. Wheelwright, *Mormon Arts: Volume I* (Provo, Utah: Brigham Young University Press, 1972), 1.

11. Dennis Smith, "Drawing on Personal Myths," *Dialogue: A Journal of Mormon Thought* 20.3 (Fall 1987): 109.

12. Boyd K. Packer, "The Arts and the Spirit of the Lord," *BYU Studies* 16.4 (Summer 1976): 581.

13. Personal interview, 8 June 2004.

14. Conan E. Mathews, "Art and the Church," *BYU Studies* 2.3 (Winter 1961): 5–6.

15. Karl Keller, "Mormon Arts: A Contradiction," *Dialogue: A Journal of Mormon Thought* 14.2 (Summer 1981): 134.

16. Karen Lynn, "The Mormon Sacred and the Mormon Profane," in *Arts and Inspiration*, ed. Steven Sondrup (Provo, Utah: Brigham Young University Press, 1980), 48.

17. Gary James Bergera and Ronald Priddis, *Brigham Young University: A House of Faith* (Salt Lake City: Signature, 1985), 310.

18. The group maintains a Web site at www.mormonartistsgroup.com/mag/index .html.

19. LaMond Tullis, "The Church Moves Outside the United States: Some Observations from Latin America," *Dialogue: A Journal of Mormon Thought* 13.1 (Spring 1980): 67.

~ CONCLUSION

1. "Norton Jacobs Record," 28 July 1847, cited in Eugene England, "Brigham's Gospel Kingdom," *BYU Studies* 18.3 (Spring 1978): 338.

2. John Sorenson, "Mormon World View and American Culture," *Dialogue: A Journal of Mormon Thought* 8.2 (Summer 1973): 19.

3. Merrill Bradshaw, "Toward a Mormon Aesthetic," *BYU Studies* 21.1 (Winter 1981): 91.

4. Michael Hicks, "Eternity, Capacity, and Will: Three Puzzles for a Mormon Aesthetics," *Sunstone* 8.1–2 (January 1983): 12.

5. This discussion owes much to Fiona Givens's sensitive reading of this passage.

6. William Mulder, "Telling It Slant: Aiming for Truth in Contemporary Mormon Literature," *Dialogue: A Journal of Mormon Thought* 26.2 (Summer 1993): 169.

7. *Journal of Discourses*, 26 vols., reported by G. D. Watt et al. (Liverpool, England: Richards et al., 1851–1886; rpt., Salt Lake City: n.p., 1974), 4:216, 268.

8. Hicks, "Eternity," 9–11.

9. Clinton Larson, "To a Dying Girl," in *Harvest: Contemporary Mormon Poems*, ed. Eugene England and Dennis Clark (Salt Lake City: Signature, 1989), 30.

10. Philip White, "Seed," in England and Clark, *Harvest*, 239.

11. Eugene England, "The Dawning of a Brighter Day: Mormon Literature after 150 Years," *BYU Studies* 22.1 (Fall 1982): 17.

INDEX